EXPLORING MICROSOFT® WORD 2000

EXPLORING MICROSOFT® WORD 2000

Robert T. Grauer / Maryann Barber

University of Miami

Prentice Hall, Upper Saddle River, New Jersey 07458

Executive Editor: Alex von Rosenberg
Managing Editor: Susan Rifkin
Editorial Assistant: Jennifer Surich
Director of Strategic Marketing: Nancy Evans
Production Manager: Gail Steier
Production Editor: Greg Hubit
Project Manager: Lynne Breitfeller
Senior Manufacturing Supervisor: Paul Smolenski
Manufacturing Coordinator: Dawn-Marie Reisner
Manufacturing Manager: Vincent Scelta
Design Manager: Patricia Smythe
Cover Design: Marjory Dressler
Composition: GTS Graphics, Inc.

ISBN 0-13-020489-7

Prentice-Hall International (UK) Limited, London
Prentice-Hall of Australia Pty. Limited, Sydney
Prentice-Hall Canada Inc., Toronto
Prentice-Hall Hispanoamericana, S.A., Mexico
Prentice-Hall of India Private Limited, New Delhi
Prentice-Hall of Japan, Inc., Tokyo
Editora Prentice-Hall do Brasil, Ltda., Rio de Janeiro

Printed in the United States of America

10 9 8 7 6 5 4 3 2

To Marion—my wife, my lover, and my best friend
—Robert Grauer

To my Mother and Father—for all their love and support
these many years
—Maryann Barber

CONTENTS

3

ENHANCING A DOCUMENT: THE WEB AND OTHER RESOURCES   109

4

ADVANCED FEATURES: OUTLINES, TABLES, STYLES, AND SECTIONS   155

5

DESKTOP PUBLISHING: CREATING A NEWSLETTER   209

6

CREATING A HOME PAGE: INTRODUCTION TO HTML   255

7

THE EXPERT USER: WORKGROUPS, FORMS, MASTER DOCUMENTS, AND MACROS   291

APPENDIX A: MAIL MERGE   345

APPENDIX B: OBJECT LINKING AND EMBEDDING   361

APPENDIX C: TOOLBARS   379

PREREQUISITES: ESSENTIALS OF WINDOWS 95/98   1

INDEX

PREFACE

We are proud to announce the fourth edition of the *Exploring Windows* series in conjunction with Microsoft® Office 2000. The series has expanded in two important ways—recognition by the ***Microsoft Office User Specialist (MOUS)*** program, and a significantly expanded Web site at ***www.prenhall.com/grauer***. The Web site provides password-protected solutions for instructors and online study guides (Companion Web sites) for students. Practice files and PowerPoint lectures are available for both student and instructor. The site also contains information about Microsoft Certification, CD-based tutorials for use with the series, and SkillCheck® assessment software.

The organization of the series is essentially unchanged. There are separate titles for each application—*Word 2000, Excel 2000, Access 2000,* and *PowerPoint 2000,* a book on *Windows® 98,* and eventually, *Windows® 2000.* There are also four combined texts—*Exploring Microsoft Office Professional, Volumes I* and *II, Exploring Microsoft Office Proficient Certification Edition,* and *Brief Office. Volume I* is a unique combination of applications and concepts for the introductory computer course. It covers all four Office applications and includes supporting material on Windows 95/98, Internet Explorer, and Essential Computing Concepts. The modules for Word and Excel satisfy the requirements for proficient certification. The *Proficient Certification Edition* extends the coverage of Access and PowerPoint from *Volume I* to meet the certification requirements, but (because of length) deletes the units on Internet Explorer and Essential Computing Concepts that are found in *Volume I. Volume II* includes the advanced features in all four applications and extends certification to the expert level. *Brief Office* is intended to get the reader "up and running," without concern for certification requirements.

The Internet and World Wide Web are integrated throughout the series. Students learn Office applications as before, and in addition are sent to the Web as appropriate for supplementary exercises. The sections on Object Linking and Embedding, for example, not only draw on resources within Microsoft Office, but on the Web as well. Students are directed to search the Web for information, and then download resources for inclusion in Office documents. The icon at the left of this paragraph appears throughout the text whenever there is a Web reference.

The *Exploring Windows* series is part of the Prentice Hall custom-binding (*Right PHit*) program, enabling instructors to create their own texts by selecting modules from *Volume I, Volume II,* the *Proficient Certification Edition,* and/or *Brief Office* to suit the needs of a specific course. An instructor could, for example, create a custom text consisting of the proficient modules in Word and Excel, coupled with the brief modules for Access and PowerPoint. Instructors can also take advantage of our *ValuePack program* to shrink-wrap multiple books together at a substantial saving for the student. A ValuePack is ideal in courses that require complete coverage of multiple applications.

Instructors will want to obtain the *Instructor's Resource CD* from their Prentice Hall representative. The CD contains the student data disks, solutions to all exercises in machine-readable format, PowerPoint lectures, and the Instructor Manuals themselves in Word format. The CD also has a Windows-based test generator. Please visit us on the Web at ***www.prenhall.com/grauer*** for additional information.

FEATURES AND BENEFITS

Exploring Microsoft® Word 2000 is written for the computer novice and assumes no previous knowledge about Microsoft® Windows. A Prerequisites section introduces the reader to the operating system and emphasizes the file operations he or she will need to create Office documents.

A total of 26 in-depth tutorials (hands-on exercises) guide the reader at the computer. Each tutorial is illustrated with large, full-color screen captures that are clear and easy to read. This example is taken from Chapter 3, which describes how to download resources from the Web for inclusion in a Word document.

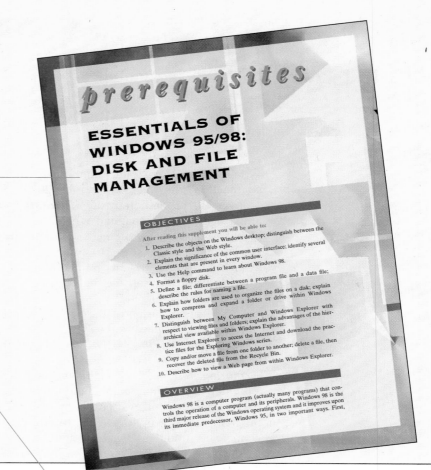

prerequisites

ESSENTIALS OF WINDOWS 95/98: DISK AND FILE MANAGEMENT

OBJECTIVES

After reading this supplement you will be able to:

1. Describe the objects on the Windows desktop; distinguish between the Classic style and the Web style.
2. Explain the significance of the common user interface; identify several elements that are present in every window.
3. Use the Help command to learn about Windows 98.
4. Format a floppy disk.
5. Define a file; differentiate between a program file and a data file; describe the rules for naming a file.
6. Explain how folders are used to organize the files on a disk; explain how to compress and expand a folder or drive within Windows Explorer.
7. Distinguish between My Computer and Windows Explorer with respect to viewing files and folders; explain the advantages of the hierarchical view available within Windows Explorer.
8. Use Internet Explorer to access the Internet and download the practice files for the Exploring Windows series.
9. Copy and/or move a file from one folder to another; delete a file, then recover the deleted file from the Recycle Bin.
10. Describe how to view a Web page from within Windows Explorer.

OVERVIEW

Windows 98 is a computer program (actually many programs) that controls the operation of a computer and its peripherals. Windows 98 is the third major release of the Windows operating system and it improves upon its immediate predecessor, Windows 95, in two important ways. First,

---

HANDS-ON EXERCISE 2

Word 2000 and the Web

Objective: To download a picture from the Internet for use in a Word document; to insert a hyperlink into a Word document; to save a Word document as a Web page. The exercise requires an Internet connection.

STEP 1: Search the Web

➤ Start **Internet Explorer**. Click the **Maximize button** so that Internet Explorer takes the entire screen.

➤ Click the **Search button** on the Internet Explorer toolbar to open the Explorer bar. The option button to find a Web page is selected by default. Enter **John Kennedy** in the text box, then click the **Search button.**

➤ The results of the search are displayed in the left pane. You can follow any of the links returned by your search engine, or you can attempt to duplicate our results using **Yahoo.** Click the **down arrow** on the **Next button,** then select **Yahoo** as the search engine.

➤ The list of hits is displayed at the bottom of the left pane as shown in Figure 3.9a. (Your list may be different from ours.) Click any link and the associated page is displayed in the right pane. We chose the first category. The links for that category are displayed in the right pane, where we chose the link to **Photo History of JFK.**

➤ Close the left pane to give yourself more room to browse through the site containing the Kennedy photographs. (You can click the **Search button** at any time to reopen the Explorer bar to choose a different site.)

Click to close Explorer bar

Click drop-down arrow on Next button

Search text

Click category

Click link to Photo History of JFK

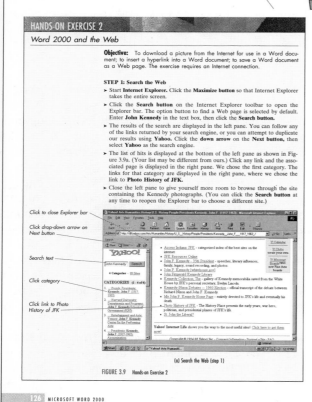

(a) Search the Web (step 1)

FIGURE 3.9   Hands-on Exercise 2

STEP 2: Save the Picture

➤ Point to the picture of President Kennedy you want to use in your document. Click the **right mouse button** to display a shortcut menu, then click the **Save Picture As command** to display the Save As dialog box in Figure 3.9b.

• Click the **drop-down arrow** in the Save in list box to specify the drive and folder in which you want to save the graphic.

• Internet Explorer supplies the file name and file type for you. You may change the name, but you cannot change the file type.

• Click the **Save button** to download the image. Remember the file name and location, as you will need to access the file in the next step.

➤ The Save As dialog box will close automatically after the picture has been downloaded. Click the **Minimize button** in the Internet Explorer window, since you are temporarily finished using the browser.

Point to picture and click right mouse button to display shortcut menu

Click to select desired drive and/or folder

Enter filename

Do not change file type

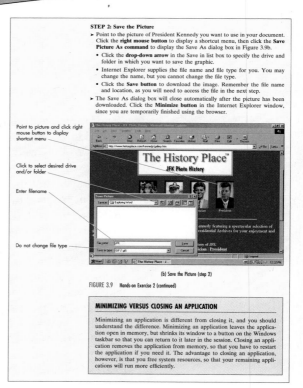

(b) Save the Picture (step 2)

FIGURE 3.9   Hands-on Exercise 2 (continued)

MINIMIZING VERSUS CLOSING AN APPLICATION

Minimizing an application is different from closing it, and you should understand the difference. Minimizing an application leaves the application open in memory, but shrinks its window to a button on the Windows taskbar so that you can return to it later in the session. Closing an application removes the application from memory, so that you have to restart the application if you need it. The advantage to closing an application, however, is that you free system resources, so that your remaining applications will run more efficiently.

UM Jazz Band
Plays Dixieland

Where: Gusman Hall

When: Wednesday
November 10

Time: 8:00 PM

(a)

CIS 120 Study Sessions

For those who don't know a bit from a byte
Come to Stanford College this Tuesday night
We'll study the concepts that aren't always clear
And memorize terms that hackers hold dear

We'll hit the books from 7 to 10
And then Thursday night, we'll do it again
It can't hurt to try us - so come on by
And give the CIS tutors that old college try!

(b)

FIGURE 5.10   The Flyer (Exercise 2)

---

3. The Masthead: Figure 5.11 displays three additional mastheads suitable for the newsletter that was developed in the chapter. Each masthead was created as follows:
   a. A two-by-two table was used in Figure 5.11a in order to right justify the date of the newsletter.
   b. Microsoft WordArt was used to create the masthead in Figure 5.11c.
   c. A different font was used for the masthead in Figure 5.11b.
   Choose the masthead you like best, then modify the newsletter as it existed at the end of the second hands-on exercise to include the new masthead. Submit the modified newsletter to your instructor.

Creating a Newsletter
Volume 1, Number 1   Spring 1999

Creating a Newsletter

Creating a Newsletter

FIGURE 5.11   The Masthead (Exercise 3)

4. A Guide to Smart Shopping: This problem is more challenging than the previous exercises in that you are asked to consider content as well as design. The objective is to develop a one- (or two-) page document with helpful tips to the novice on buying a computer. We have, however, written the copy for you and put the file on the data disk.
   a. Open and print the *Chapter 5 Practice 4* document on the data disk, which takes approximately a page and a half as presently formatted. Read our text and determine the tips you want to retain and those you want to delete. Add other tips as you see fit.
   b. Examine the available clip art through the Insert Picture command or through the Microsoft Clip Gallery. There is no requirement, however, to include a graphic; that is, use clip art only if you think it will enhance the document.
   c. Consult a current computer magazine (or another source) to determine actual prices for one or more configurations, then include this information prominently in your document.
   d. Create the masthead for the document, then develop with pencil and paper a rough sketch of the completed document showing the masthead, the placement of the text, clip art, and the special of the month (the configuration in part c).
   e. Print the completed document for your instructor.

Every chapter includes multiple assignments to avoid repetition from one semester to the next. The exercises progress in scope and difficulty and encourage the student to create a variety of documents. These examples are taken from Chapter 5 on desktop publishing.

Every chapter also contains a number of less-structured case studies to further challenge the student. The Web icon appears throughout the text whenever the student is directed to the World Wide Web as a source of additional material.

CASE STUDIES

Companion Web Sites

A Companion Web site (or online study guide) accompanies each book in the *Exploring Microsoft Office 2000* series. Go to the Exploring Windows home page at www.prenhall.com/grauer, click the book to Office 2000, and click the Companion Web site tab at the top of the screen. Choose the appropriate text (Exploring Word 2000) and the chapter within the text (e.g., Chapter 1). Each chapter contains a series of short-answer exercises (multiple-choice, true/false, and matching) to review the material in the chapter. You can take practice quizzes by yourself and/or e-mail the results to your instructor. You can try the essay questions for additional practice and engage in online chat sessions. We hope you will find the online guide to be a valuable resource.

It's a Mess

Newcomers to word processing quickly learn the concept of word wrap and the distinction between hard and soft returns. This lesson was lost, however, on your friend who created the *Please Help Me* document on the data disk. The first several sentences were entered without any hard returns at all, whereas the opposite problem exists toward the end of the document. This is a good friend, and her paper is due in one hour. Please help.

Planning for Disaster

Do you have a backup strategy? Do you even know what a backup strategy is? You should learn, because sooner or later you will wish you had one. You will erase a file, be unable to read from a floppy disk, or worse yet suffer a hardware failure in which you are unable to access the hard drive. The problem always seems to occur the night before an assignment is due. The ultimate disaster is the disappearance of your computer, by theft or natural disaster (e.g., Hurricane Andrew). Describe in 250 words or less the backup strategy you plan to implement in conjunction with your work in this class.

A Letter Home

You really like this course and want very much to have your own computer, but you're strapped for cash and have decided to ask your parents for help. Write a one-page letter describing the advantages of having your own system and how it will help you in school. Tell your parents what the system will cost, and that you can save money by buying through the mail. Describe the configuration you intend to buy (don't forget to include the price of software) and then provide prices from at least three different companies. Cut out the advertisements and include them in your letter. Bring your material to class and compare your research with that of your classmates.

Computer Magazines

A subscription to a computer magazine should be given serious consideration if you intend to stay abreast in a rapidly changing field. The reviews on new products are especially helpful and you will appreciate the advertisements should you

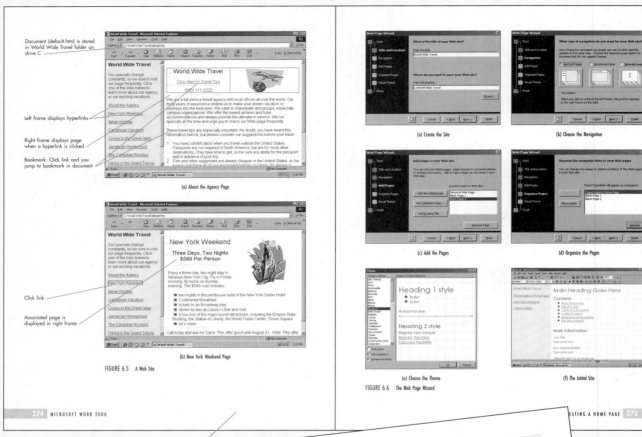

Document (default.htm) is stored in World Wide Travel folder on drive C

Left frame displays hyperlinks

Right frame displays page when a hyperlink is clicked

Bookmark: Click link and you jump to bookmark in document

(a) About the Agency Page

Click link

Associated page is displayed in right frame

(b) New York Weekend Page

FIGURE 6.5 A Web Site

(a) Create the Site

(b) Choose the Navigation

(c) Add the Pages

(d) Organize the Pages

(e) Choose the Theme

(f) The Initial Site

FIGURE 6.6 The Web Page Wizard

Chapter 6 describes how to create HTML documents using the tools that are built into Word 2000. The chapter also introduces the Web Page Wizard that enables the reader to create a Web site consisting of several pages, as opposed to a simple home page.

Object linking and embedding (OLE) is stressed throughout the series, as students use multiple applications to create documents. This example from Chapter 3 asks the reader to download the iCOMP index from the Intel Web site, and then to incorporate that chart into a Word document.

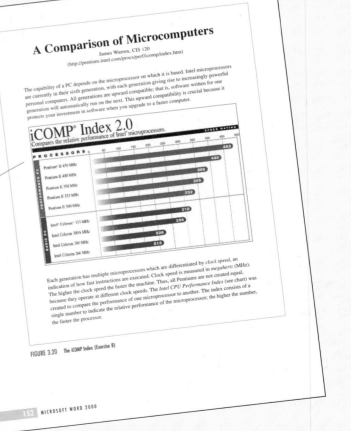

A Comparison of Microcomputers

James Warren, CIS 120

(http://pentium.intel.com/procs/perf/icomp/index.htm)

The capability of a PC depends on the microprocessor on which it is based. Intel microprocessors are currently in their sixth generation, with each generation giving rise to increasingly powerful personal computers. All generations are upward compatible; that is, software written for one generation will automatically run on the next. This upward compatibility is crucial because it protects your investment in software when you upgrade to a faster computer.

Each generation has multiple microprocessors which are differentiated by *clock speed*, an indication of how fast instructions are executed. Clock speed is measured in *megahertz* (MHz). The higher the clock speed the faster the machine. Thus, all Pentiums are not created equal, because they operate at different clock speeds. The *Intel CPU Performance Index* (see chart) was created to compare the performance of one microprocessor to another. The index consists of a single number to indicate the relative performance of the microprocessor; the higher the number, the faster the processor.

FIGURE 3.20   The iCOMP Index (Exercise 8)

Chapter 7 focuses on the advanced topics that are required for certification at the expert level in the Microsoft Office User Specialist program. The student learns about workgroups, forms, master documents, and macros, as he or she becomes a true expert in Microsoft Word 2000.

Chapter 5 presents the basics of desktop publishing. Students not only learn the mechanics of Word but are also taught the basics of graphic design. This unique combination of concepts and keystrokes is one of the distinguishing features of the *Exploring Windows* series.

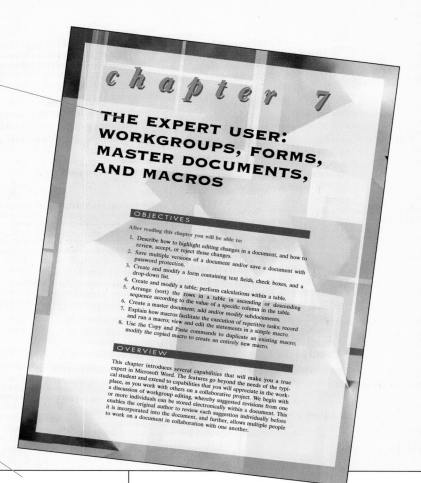

chapter 7

THE EXPERT USER: WORKGROUPS, FORMS, MASTER DOCUMENTS, AND MACROS

OBJECTIVES

After reading this chapter you will be able to:

1. Describe how to highlight editing changes in a document, and how to review, accept, or reject those changes.
2. Save multiple versions of a document and/or save a document with password protection.
3. Create and modify a form containing text fields, check boxes, and a drop-down list.
4. Create and modify a table; perform calculations within a table.
5. Arrange (sort) the rows in a table in ascending or descending sequence according to the value of a specific column in the table.
6. Create a master document; add and/or modify subdocuments.
7. Explain how macros facilitate the execution of repetitive tasks; record and run a macro; view and edit the statements in a simple macro.
8. Use the Copy and Paste commands to duplicate an existing macro; modify the copied macro to create an entirely new macro.

OVERVIEW

This chapter introduces several capabilities that will make you a true expert in Microsoft Word. The features go beyond the needs of the typical student and extend to capabilities that you will appreciate in the workplace, as you work with others on a collaborative project. We begin with a discussion of workgroup editing, whereby suggested revisions from one or more individuals can be stored electronically within a document. This enables the original author to review each suggestion individually before it is incorporated into the document, and further, allows multiple people to work on a document in collaboration with one another.

The essence of **desktop publishing** is the merger of text with graphics to produce a professional-looking document without reliance on external services. Desktop publishing will save you time and money because you are doing the work yourself rather than sending it out as you did in traditional publishing. That is the good news. The bad news is that desktop publishing is not as easy as it sounds, precisely because you are doing work that was done previously by skilled professionals. Nevertheless, with a little practice, and a basic knowledge of graphic design, you will be able to create effective and attractive documents.

Our chapter begins with the development of a simple newsletter in which we create a multicolumn document, import clip art and other objects, and position those objects within a document. The newsletter also reviews material from earlier chapters on bullets and lists, borders and shading, and section formatting. The second half of the chapter presents additional tools that you can use to enhance your documents. We describe the Drawing toolbar and explain how it is used to add objects to a Word document. We also introduce Microsoft Graph, an application that creates (and modifies) a graph based on numerical data that you enter or import from another application.

THE NEWSLETTER

The newsletter in Figure 5.1 demonstrates the basics of desktop publishing and provides an overview of the chapter. The material is presented conceptually, after which you implement the design in two hands-on exercises. We provide the text and you do the formatting. The first exercise creates a simple newsletter from copy that we provide. The second exercise uses more sophisticated formatting as described by the various techniques mentioned within the newsletter. Many of the terms are new, and we define them briefly in the next few paragraphs.

A **reverse** (light text on a dark background) is a favorite technique of desktop publishers to emphasize a specific element. It is used in the **masthead** (the identifying information) at the top of the newsletter and provides a distinctive look to the publication. The number of the newsletter and the date of publication also appear in the masthead in smaller letters.

A **pull quote** is a phrase or sentence taken from an article to emphasize a key point. It is typically set in larger type, often in a different typeface and/or italics, and may be offset with parallel lines at the top and bottom.

A **dropped-capital letter** is a large capital letter at the beginning of a paragraph. It, too, catches the reader's eye and calls attention to the associated text.

Clip art, used in moderation, will catch the reader's eye and enhance almost any newsletter. It is available from a variety of sources including the **Microsoft Clip Gallery,** which is included in Office 2000. Clip art can also be downloaded from the Web, but be sure you are allowed to reprint the image. The banner at the bottom of the newsletter is not a clip art image per se, but was created using various tools on the **Drawing toolbar.**

Borders and shading are effective individually, or in combination with one another, to emphasize important stories within the newsletter. Simple vertical and/or horizontal lines are also effective. The techniques are especially useful in the absence of clip art or other graphics and are a favorite of desktop publishers.

Lists, whether bulleted or numbered, help to organize information by emphasizing important topics. A **bulleted list** emphasizes (and separates) the items. A **numbered list** sequences (and prioritizes) the items and is automatically updated to accommodate additions or deletions.

All of these techniques can be implemented with commands you already know, as you will see in the hands-on exercise, which follows shortly.

Creating a Newsletter

Volume 1, Number 2   Spring 1999

Desktop publishing is easy, but there are several points to remember. This chapter will take you through the steps in creating a newsletter. The first hands-on exercise creates a simple newsletter with a masthead and three-column design. The second exercise creates a more attractive document by exploring different ways to emphasize the text.

Clip Art and Other Objects

Clip art is available from a variety of sources. You can also use other types of objects such as maps, charts, or organization charts, which are created by other applications, then brought into a document through the Insert Object command. A single dominant graphic is usually more appealing than multiple smaller graphics.

Techniques to Consider

Our finished newsletter contains one or more examples of each of the following desktop publishing techniques. Can you find where each technique is used, and further, explain, how to implement that technique in Microsoft Word?

1. Pull Quotes
2. Reverse
3. Drop Caps
4. Tables
5. Styles
6. Bullets and Numbering
7. Borders and Shading
8. The Drawing Toolbar

Newspaper-Style Columns

The essence of a newsletter is the implementation of columns in which text flows continuously from the bottom of one column to the top of the next. You specify the number of columns, and optionally, the space between columns. Microsoft Word does the rest. It will compute the width of each column based on the number of columns and the margins.

Beginners often specify margins that are too large and implement too much space between the columns. Another way to achieve a more sophisticated look is to avoid the standard two-column design. You can implement columns of varying width and/or insert vertical lines between the columns.

The number of columns will vary in different parts of a document. The masthead is typically a single column, but the body of the newsletter will have two or three. Remember, too, that columns are implemented at the section level and hence, section breaks are required throughout a document.

Typography

Typography is the process of selecting typefaces, type styles, and type sizes, and is a critical element in the success of any document. Type should reinforce the message and should be consistent with the information you want to convey. More is not better, especially in the case of too many typefaces and styles, which produce cluttered documents that impress no one. Try to limit yourself to a maximum of two typefaces per document, but choose multiple sizes and/or styles within those typefaces. Use boldface or italics for emphasis, but do so in moderation, because if you use too many different elements, the effect is lost.

A pull quote adds interest to a document while simultaneously emphasizing a key point. It is implemented by increasing the point size, changing to italics, centering the text, and displaying a top and bottom border on the paragraph.

Use Styles as Appropriate

Styles were covered in the previous chapter, but that does not mean you cannot use them in conjunction with a newsletter. A style stores character and/or paragraph formatting and can be applied to multiple occurrences of the same element within a document. Change the style and you automatically change all text defined by that style. You can also use styles from one edition of your newsletter to the next to insure consistency.

Borders and Shading

Borders and shading are effective individually or in combination with one another. Use a thin rule (one point or less) and light shading (five or ten percent) for best results. The techniques are especially useful in the absence of clip art or other graphics and are a favorite of desktop publishers.

All the News that Fits

FIGURE 5.1   The Newsletter

Acknowledgments

We want to thank the many individuals who have helped to bring this project to fruition. We are especially grateful to Nancy Evans and PJ Boardman, who continue to offer inspiration and guidance. Alex von Rosenberg, executive editor at Prentice Hall, has provided new leadership in extending the series to Office 2000. Nancy Welcher did an absolutely incredible job on our Web site. Susan Rifkin coordinated the myriad details of production and the certification process. Greg Christofferson was instrumental in the acquisition of supporting software. Lynne Breitfeller was the project manager. Paul Smolenski was senior manufacturing supervisor. Greg Hubit has been masterful as the external production editor for every book in the series. Cecil Yarbrough did an outstanding job in checking the manuscript for technical accuracy. Jennifer Surich was the editorial assistant. Leanne Nieglos was the supplements editor. Cindy Stevens, Karen Vignare, and Michael Olmstead wrote the Instructor Manuals. Patricia Smythe developed the innovative and attractive design. We also want to acknowledge our reviewers who, through their comments and constructive criticism, greatly improved the series.

Lynne Band, Middlesex Community College
Don Belle, Central Piedmont Community College
Stuart P. Brian, Holy Family College
Carl M. Briggs, Indiana University School of Business
Kimberly Chambers, Scottsdale Community College
Alok Charturvedi, Purdue University
Jerry Chin, Southwest Missouri State University
Dean Combellick, Scottsdale Community College
Cody Copeland, Johnson County Community College
Larry S. Corman, Fort Lewis College
Janis Cox, Tri-County Technical College
Martin Crossland, Southwest Missouri State University
Paul E. Daurelle, Western Piedmont Community College
David Douglas, University of Arkansas
Carlotta Eaton, Radford University
Judith M. Fitspatrick, Gulf Coast Community College
Raymond Frost, Central Connecticut State University
Midge Gerber, Southwestern Oklahoma State University
James Gips, Boston College
Vernon Griffin, Austin Community College
Michael Hassett, Fort Hays State University
Wanda D. Heller, Seminole Community College
Bonnie Homan, San Francisco State University
Ernie Ivey, Polk Community College
Mike Kelly, Community College of Rhode Island
Jane King, Everett Community College
Rose M. Laird, Northern Virginia Community College
John Lesson, University of Central Florida
David B. Meinert, Southwest Missouri State University
Bill Morse, DeVry Institute of Technology
Alan Moltz, Naugatuck Valley Technical Community College
Kim Montney, Kellogg Community College
Kevin Pauli, University of Nebraska
Mary McKenry Percival, University of Miami
Delores Pusins, Hillsborough Community College
Gale E. Rand, College Misericordia
Judith Rice, Santa Fe Community College
David Rinehard, Lansing Community College
Marilyn Salas, Scottsdale Community College
John Shepherd, Duquesne University
Barbara Sherman, Buffalo State College
Robert Spear, Prince George's Community College
Michael Stewardson, San Jacinto College—North
Helen Stoloff, Hudson Valley Community College
Margaret Thomas, Ohio University
Mike Thomas, Indiana University School of Business
Suzanne Tomlinson, Iowa State University
Karen Tracey, Central Connecticut State University
Sally Visci, Lorain County Community College
David Weiner, University of San Francisco
Connie Wells, Georgia State University
Wallace John Whistance-Smith, Ryerson Polytechnic University
Jack Zeller, Kirkwood Community College

A final word of thanks to the unnamed students at the University of Miami, who make it all worthwhile. Most of all, thanks to you, our readers, for choosing this book. Please feel free to contact us with any comments and suggestions.

Robert T. Grauer
rgrauer@sba.miami.edu
www.bus.miami.edu/~rgrauer
www.prenhall.com/grauer

Maryann Barber
mbarber@sba.miami.edu
www.bus.miami.edu/~mbarber

chapter 1

MICROSOFT® WORD 2000: WHAT WILL WORD PROCESSING DO FOR ME?

OBJECTIVES

After reading this chapter you will be able to:

1. Define word wrap; differentiate between a hard and a soft return.
2. Distinguish between the insert and overtype modes.
3. Describe the elements on the Microsoft Word screen.
4. Create, save, retrieve, edit, and print a simple document.
5. Check a document for spelling; describe the function of the custom dictionary.
6. Describe the AutoCorrect and AutoText features; explain how either feature can be used to create a personal shorthand.
7. Use the thesaurus to look up synonyms and antonyms.
8. Explain the objectives and limitations of the grammar check; customize the grammar check for business or casual writing.
9. Differentiate between the Save and Save As commands; describe various backup options that can be selected.

OVERVIEW

Have you ever produced what you thought was the perfect term paper only to discover that you omitted a sentence or misspelled a word, or that the paper was three pages too short or one page too long? Wouldn't it be nice to make the necessary changes, and then be able to reprint the entire paper with the touch of a key? Welcome to the world of word processing, where you are no longer stuck with having to retype anything. Instead, you retrieve your work from disk, display it on the monitor and revise it as necessary, then print it at any time, in draft or final form.

This chapter provides a broad-based introduction to word processing in general and Microsoft Word in particular. We begin by presenting (or perhaps reviewing) the essential concepts of a word processor, then show you how these concepts are implemented in Word. We show you how to create a document, how to save it on disk, then retrieve the document you just created. We introduce you to the spell check and thesaurus, two essential tools in any word processor. We also present the grammar check as a convenient way of finding a variety of errors but remind you there is no substitute for carefully proofreading the final document.

THE BASICS OF WORD PROCESSING

All word processors adhere to certain basic concepts that must be understood if you are to use the programs effectively. The next several pages introduce ideas that are applicable to any word processor (and which you may already know). We follow the conceptual material with a hands-on exercise that enables you to apply what you have learned.

The Insertion Point

The *insertion point* is a flashing vertical line that marks the place where text will be entered. The insertion point is always at the beginning of a new document, but it can be moved anywhere within an existing document. If, for example, you wanted to add text to the end of a document, you would move the insertion point to the end of the document, then begin typing.

Word Wrap

A newcomer to word processing has one major transition to make from a typewriter, and it is an absolutely critical adjustment. Whereas a typist returns the carriage at the end of every line, just the opposite is true of a word processor. One types continually *without* pressing the enter key at the end of a line because the word processor automatically wraps text from one line to the next. This concept is known as *word wrap* and is illustrated in Figure 1.1.

The word *primitive* does not fit on the current line in Figure 1.1a, and is automatically shifted to the next line, *without* the user having to press the enter key. The user continues to enter the document, with additional words being wrapped to subsequent lines as necessary. The only time you use the enter key is at the end of a paragraph, or when you want the insertion point to move to the next line and the end of the current line doesn't reach the right margin.

Word wrap is closely associated with another concept, that of hard and soft returns. A *hard return* is created by the user when he or she presses the enter key at the end of a paragraph; a *soft return* is created by the word processor as it wraps text from one line to the next. The locations of the soft returns change automatically as a document is edited (e.g., as text is inserted or deleted, or as margins or fonts are changed). The locations of the hard returns can be changed only by the user, who must intentionally insert or delete each hard return.

There are two hard returns in Figure 1.1b, one at the end of each paragraph. There are also six soft returns in the first paragraph (one at the end of every line except the last) and three soft returns in the second paragraph. Now suppose the margins in the document are made smaller (that is, the line is made longer) as shown in Figure 1.1c. The number of soft returns drops to four and two (in the first and second paragraphs, respectively) as more text fits on a line and fewer lines are needed. The revised document still contains the two original hard returns, one at the end of each paragraph.

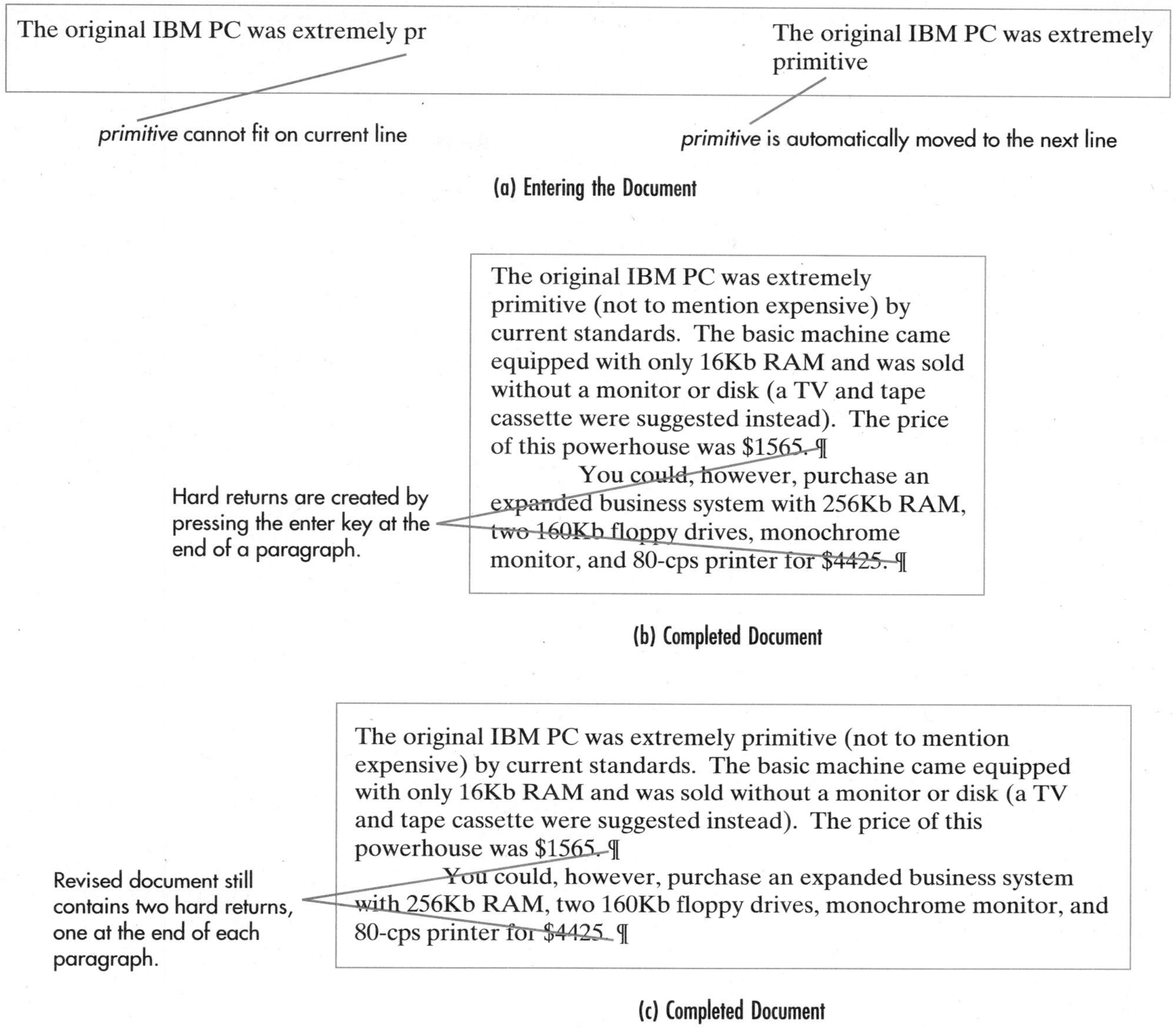

The original IBM PC was extremely pr

primitive cannot fit on current line

The original IBM PC was extremely primitive

primitive is automatically moved to the next line

(a) Entering the Document

The original IBM PC was extremely primitive (not to mention expensive) by current standards. The basic machine came equipped with only 16Kb RAM and was sold without a monitor or disk (a TV and tape cassette were suggested instead). The price of this powerhouse was $1565. ¶
    You could, however, purchase an expanded business system with 256Kb RAM, two 160Kb floppy drives, monochrome monitor, and 80-cps printer for $4425. ¶

Hard returns are created by pressing the enter key at the end of a paragraph.

(b) Completed Document

The original IBM PC was extremely primitive (not to mention expensive) by current standards. The basic machine came equipped with only 16Kb RAM and was sold without a monitor or disk (a TV and tape cassette were suggested instead). The price of this powerhouse was $1565. ¶
    You could, however, purchase an expanded business system with 256Kb RAM, two 160Kb floppy drives, monochrome monitor, and 80-cps printer for $4425. ¶

Revised document still contains two hard returns, one at the end of each paragraph.

(c) Completed Document

FIGURE 1.1   Word Wrap

Toggle Switches

Suppose you sat down at the keyboard and typed an entire sentence without pressing the Shift key; the sentence would be in all lowercase letters. Then you pressed the Caps Lock key and retyped the sentence, again without pressing the Shift key. This time the sentence would be in all uppercase letters. You could repeat the process as often as you like. Each time you pressed the Caps Lock key, the sentence would switch from lowercase to uppercase and vice versa.

The point of this exercise is to introduce the concept of a ***toggle switch,*** a device that causes the computer to alternate between two states. The Caps Lock key is an example of a toggle switch. Each time you press it, newly typed text will change from uppercase to lowercase and back again. We will see several other examples of toggle switches as we proceed in our discussion of word processing.

Insert versus Overtype

Microsoft Word is always in one of two modes, **insert** or **overtype**, and uses a toggle switch (the Ins key) to alternate between the two. Press the Ins key once and you switch from insert to overtype. Press the Ins key a second time and you go from overtype back to insert. Text that is entered into a document during the insert mode moves existing text to the right to accommodate the characters being added. Text entered from the overtype mode replaces (overtypes) existing text. Regardless of which mode you are in, text is always entered or replaced immediately to the right of the insertion point.

The insert mode is best when you enter text for the first time, but either mode can be used to make corrections. The insert mode is the better choice when the correction requires you to add new text; the overtype mode is easier when you are substituting one or more character(s) for another. The difference is illustrated in Figure 1.2.

Figure 1.2a displays the text as it was originally entered, with two misspellings. The letters *se* have been omitted from the word *insert,* and an *x* has been erroneously typed instead of an *r* in the word *overtype.* The insert mode is used in Figure 1.2b to add the missing letters, which in turn moves the rest of the line to the right. The overtype mode is used in Figure 1.2c to replace the *x* with an *r.*

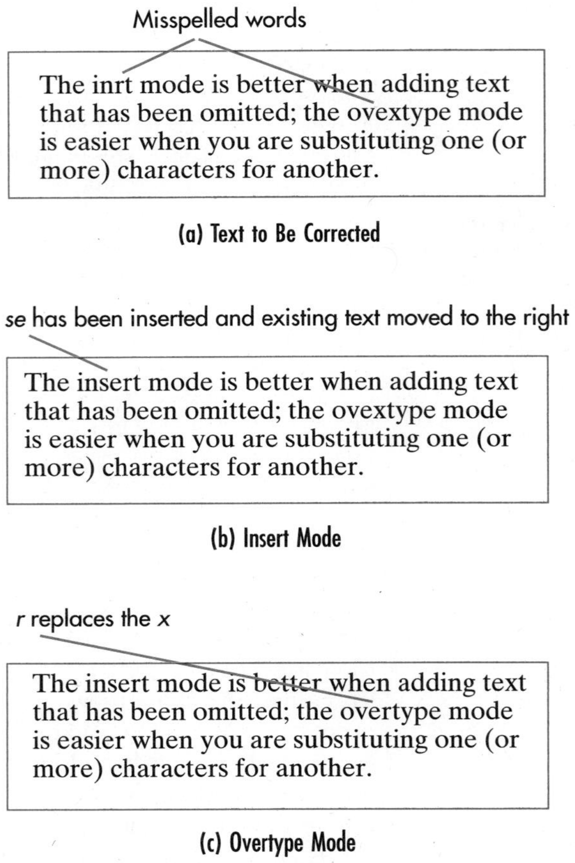

Misspelled words

The inrt mode is better when adding text
that has been omitted; the ovextype mode
is easier when you are substituting one (or
more) characters for another.

(a) Text to Be Corrected

se has been inserted and existing text moved to the right

The insert mode is better when adding text
that has been omitted; the ovextype mode
is easier when you are substituting one (or
more) characters for another.

(b) Insert Mode

r replaces the *x*

The insert mode is better when adding text
that has been omitted; the overtype mode
is easier when you are substituting one (or
more) characters for another.

(c) Overtype Mode

FIGURE 1.2   Insert and Overtype Modes

Deleting Text

The backspace and Del keys delete one character immediately to the left or right of the insertion point, respectively. The choice between them depends on when you need to erase a character(s). The backspace key is easier if you want to delete a character immediately after typing it. The Del key is preferable during subsequent editing.

You can delete several characters at one time by selecting (dragging the mouse over) the characters to be deleted, then pressing the Del key. And finally, you can delete and replace text in one operation by selecting the text to be replaced and then typing the new text in its place.

LEARN TO TYPE

The ultimate limitation of any word processor is the speed at which you enter data; hence the ability to type quickly is invaluable. Learning how to type is easy, especially with the availability of computer-based typing programs. As little as a half hour a day for a couple of weeks will have you up to speed, and if you do any significant amount of writing at all, the investment will pay off many times.

INTRODUCTION TO MICROSOFT WORD

We used Microsoft Word to write this book, as can be inferred from the screen in Figure 1.3. Your screen will be different from ours in many ways. You will not have the same document nor is it likely that you will customize Word in exactly the same way. You should, however, be able to recognize the basic elements that are found in the Microsoft Word window that is open on the desktop.

There are actually two open windows in Figure 1.3—an application window for Microsoft Word and a document window for the specific document on which you are working. The application window has its own Minimize, Maximize (or Restore) and Close buttons. The document window has only a Close button. There is, however, only one title bar that appears at the top of the application window and it reflects the application (Microsoft Word) as well as the document name (Word Chapter 1). A menu bar appears immediately below the title bar. Vertical and horizontal scroll bars appear at the right and bottom of the document window. The Windows taskbar appears at the bottom of the screen and shows the open applications.

Microsoft Word is also part of the Microsoft Office suite of applications, and thus shares additional features with Excel, Access, and PowerPoint, that are also part of the Office suite. *Toolbars* provide immediate access to common commands and appear immediately below the menu bar. The toolbars can be displayed or hidden using the Toolbars command in the View menu.

The *Standard toolbar* contains buttons corresponding to the most basic commands in Word—for example, opening a file or printing a document. The icon on the button is intended to be indicative of its function (e.g., a printer to indicate the Print command). You can also point to the button to display a *ScreenTip* showing the name of the button. The *Formatting toolbar* appears under the Standard toolbar and provides access to common formatting operations such as boldface, italics, or underlining.

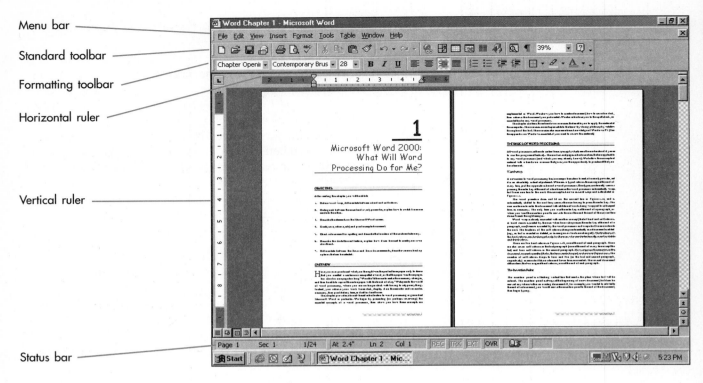

Menu bar

Standard toolbar

Formatting toolbar

Horizontal ruler

Vertical ruler

Status bar

FIGURE 1.3 Microsoft Word

The toolbars may appear overwhelming at first, but there is absolutely no need to memorize what the individual buttons do. That will come with time. We suggest, however, that you will have a better appreciation for the various buttons if you consider them in groups, according to their general function, as shown in Figure 1.4a. Note, too, that many of the commands in the pull-down menus are displayed with an image that corresponds to a button on a toolbar.

The *horizontal ruler* is displayed underneath the toolbars and enables you to change margins, tabs, and/or indents for all or part of a document. A *vertical ruler* shows the vertical position of text on the page and can be used to change the top or bottom margins.

The *status bar* at the bottom of the document window displays the location of the insertion point (or information about the command being executed.) The status bar also shows the status (settings) of various indicators—for example, OVR to show that Word is in the overtype, as opposed to the insert, mode.

CHANGES IN OFFICE 2000

Office 2000 implements one very significant change over previous versions in that it displays a series of short menus that contain only basic commands. The bottom of each menu has a double arrow that you can click to display the additional commands. Each time you execute a command it is added to the menu, and conversely, Word will remove commands from a menu if they are not used after a period of time. You can, however, display the full menus through the Customize command in the Tools menu by clearing the check boxes associated with personalized menus and toolbars.

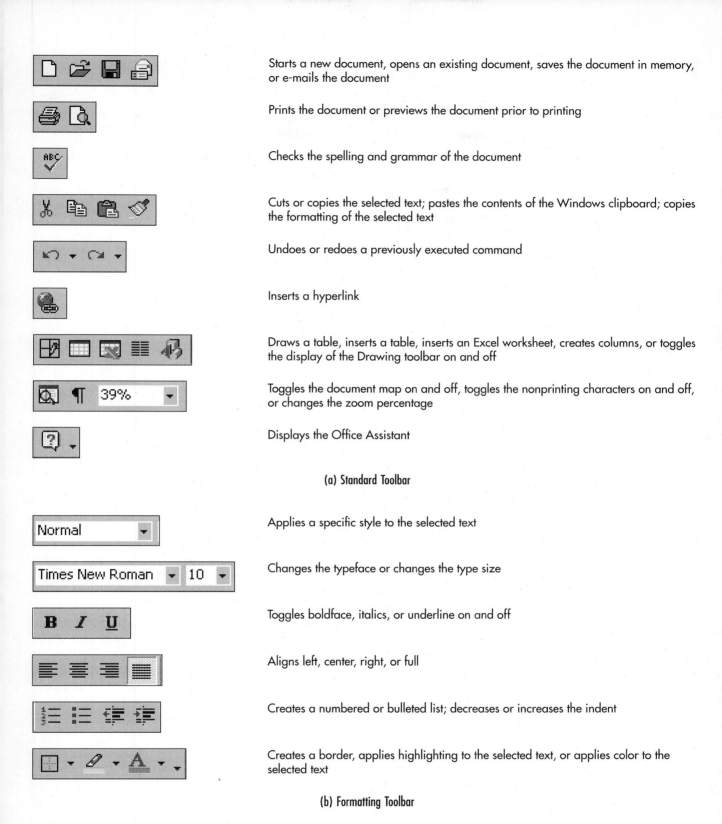

Starts a new document, opens an existing document, saves the document in memory, or e-mails the document

Prints the document or previews the document prior to printing

Checks the spelling and grammar of the document

Cuts or copies the selected text; pastes the contents of the Windows clipboard; copies the formatting of the selected text

Undoes or redoes a previously executed command

Inserts a hyperlink

Draws a table, inserts a table, inserts an Excel worksheet, creates columns, or toggles the display of the Drawing toolbar on and off

Toggles the document map on and off, toggles the nonprinting characters on and off, or changes the zoom percentage

Displays the Office Assistant

(a) Standard Toolbar

Applies a specific style to the selected text

Changes the typeface or changes the type size

Toggles boldface, italics, or underline on and off

Aligns left, center, right, or full

Creates a numbered or bulleted list; decreases or increases the indent

Creates a border, applies highlighting to the selected text, or applies color to the selected text

(b) Formatting Toolbar

FIGURE 1.4   Toolbars

The *File Menu* is a critically important menu in virtually every Windows application. It contains the Save and Open commands to save a document on disk, then subsequently retrieve (open) that document at a later time. The File Menu also contains the *Print command* to print a document, the *Close command* to close the current document but continue working in the application, and the *Exit command* to quit the application altogether.

The *Save command* copies the document that you are working on (i.e., the document that is currently in memory) to disk. The command functions differently the first time it is executed for a new document, in that it displays the Save As dialog box as shown in Figure 1.5a. The dialog box requires you to specify the name of the document, the drive (and an optional folder) in which the document is stored, and its file type. All subsequent executions of the command will save the document under the assigned name, each time replacing the previously saved version with the new version.

The *file name* (e.g., My First Document) can contain up to 255 characters including spaces, commas, and/or periods. (Periods are discouraged, however, since they are too easily confused with DOS extensions.) The Save In list box is used to select the drive (which is not visible in Figure 1.5a) and the optional folder (e.g., Exploring Word). The *Places Bar* provides a shortcut to any of its folders without having to search through the Save In list box. Click the Desktop icon, for example, and the file is saved automatically on the Windows desktop. The *file type* defaults to a Word 2000 document. You can, however, choose a different format such as Word 95 to maintain compatibility with earlier versions of Microsoft Word. You can also save any Word document as a Web page (or HTML document).

The *Open command* is the opposite of the Save command as it brings a copy of an existing document into memory, enabling you to work with that document. The Open command displays the Open dialog box in which you specify the file name, the drive (and optionally the folder) that contains the file, and the file type. Microsoft Word will then list all files of that type on the designated drive (and folder), enabling you to open the file you want. The Save and Open commands work in conjunction with one another. The Save As dialog box in Figure 1.5a, for example, saves the file My First Document in the Exploring Word folder. The Open dialog box in Figure 1.5b loads that file into memory so that you can work with the file, after which you can save the revised file for use at a later time.

The toolbars in the Save As and Open dialog boxes have several buttons in common that facilitate the execution of either command. The Views button lets you display the files in either dialog box in one of four different views. The Details view (in Figure 1.5a) shows the file size as well as the date and time a file was last modified. The Preview view (in Figure 1.5b) shows the beginning of a document, without having to open the document. The List view displays only the file names, and thus lets you see more files at one time. The Properties view shows information about the document including the date of creation and number of revisions.

SORT BY NAME, DATE, OR FILE SIZE

The files in the Save As and Open dialog boxes can be displayed in ascending or descending sequence by name, date modified, or size. Change to the Details view, then click the heading of the desired column; e.g., click the Modified column to list the files according to the date they were last changed. Click the column heading a second time to reverse the sequence.

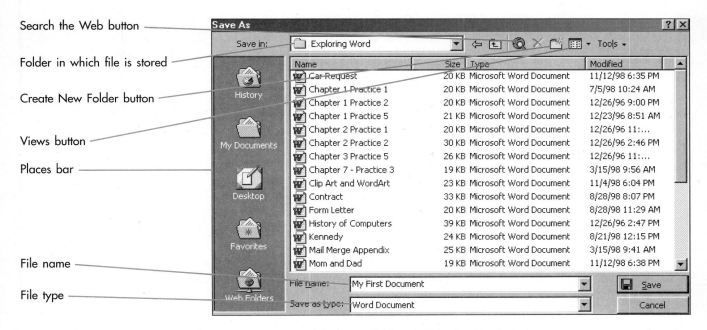

Search the Web button
Folder in which file is stored
Create New Folder button
Views button
Places bar
File name
File type

(a) Save As Dialog Box (details view)

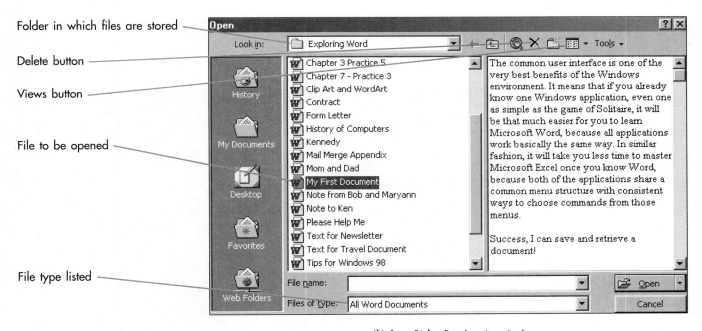

Folder in which files are stored
Delete button
Views button
File to be opened
File type listed

(b) Open Dialog Box (preview view)

FIGURE 1.5   The Save and Open Commands

LEARNING BY DOING

Every chapter contains a series of hands-on exercises that enable you to apply what you learn at the computer. The exercises in this chapter are linked to one another in that you create a simple document in exercise one, then open and edit that document in exercise two. The ability to save and open a document is critical, and you do not want to spend an inordinate amount of time entering text unless you are confident in your ability to retrieve it later.

My First Document

Objective: To start Microsoft Word in order to create, save, and print a simple document; to execute commands via the toolbar or from pull-down menus. Use Figure 1.6 as a guide in doing the exercise.

STEP 1: The Windows Desktop

➤ Turn on the computer and all of its peripherals. The floppy drive should be empty prior to starting your machine. This ensures that the system starts from the hard disk, which contains the Windows files, as opposed to a floppy disk, which does not.

➤ Your system will take a minute or so to get started, after which you should see the Windows desktop in Figure 1.6a. Do not be concerned if the appearance of your desktop is different from ours.

➤ You may see additional objects on the desktop in Windows 95 and/or the active desktop content in Windows 98. It doesn't matter which operating system you are using because Office 2000 runs equally well under both Windows 95 and Windows 98 (as well as Windows NT).

➤ You may see a Welcome to Windows 95/Windows 98 dialog box with command buttons to take a tour of the operating system. If so, click the appropriate button(s) or close the dialog box.

Start button

(a) The Windows Desktop (step 1)

FIGURE 1.6   Hands-on Exercise 1

STEP 2: Obtain the Practice Files

➤ We have created a series of practice files (also called a "data disk") for you to use throughout the text. Your instructor will make these files available to you in a variety of ways:

- The files may be on a network drive, in which case you use Windows Explorer to copy the files from the network to a floppy disk.

- There may be an actual "data disk" that you are to check out from the lab in order to use the Copy Disk command to duplicate the disk.

➤ You can also download the files from our Web site provided you have an Internet connection. Start Internet Explorer, then go to the Exploring Windows home page at **www.prenhall.com/grauer.**

- Click the book for **Office 2000,** which takes you to the Office 2000 home page. Click the **Student Resources tab** (at the top of the window) to go to the Student Resources page as shown in Figure 1.6b.

- Click the link to **Student Data Disk** (in the left frame), then scroll down the page until you can select Word 2000. Click the link to download the student data disk.

- You will see the File Download dialog box asking what you want to do. The option button to save this program to disk is selected. Click **OK.** The Save As dialog box appears.

- Click the down arrow in the Save In list box to enter the drive and folder where you want to save the file. It's best to save the file to the Windows desktop or to a temporary folder on drive C.

- Double click the file after it has been downloaded to your PC, then follow the onscreen instructions.

➤ Check with your instructor for additional information.

Click tab to go to Student Resources page

Click here for student data disk

Click here for Companion Web site (see problem 8 at the end of the chapter)

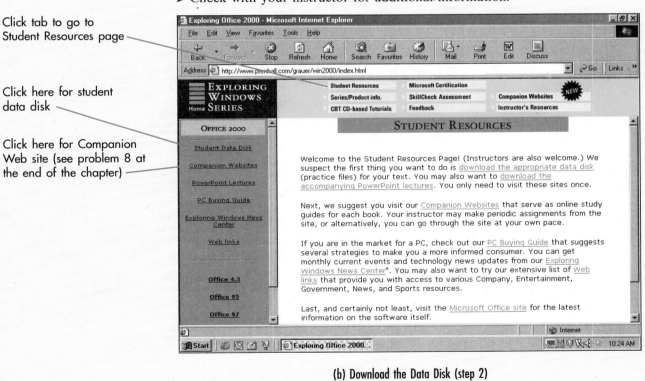

(b) Download the Data Disk (step 2)

FIGURE 1.6   Hands-on Exercise 1 (continued)

STEP 3: Start Microsoft Word

➤ Click the **Start button** to display the Start menu. Click (or point to) the **Programs menu,** then click **Microsoft Word 2000** to start the program.

➤ Click and drag the Office Assistant out of the way. (The Office Assistant is illustrated in step 6 of this exercise.)

➤ If necessary, click the **Maximize button** in the application window so that Word takes the entire desktop as shown in Figure 1.6c.

➤ Do not be concerned if your screen is different from ours as we include a troubleshooting section immediately following this exercise.

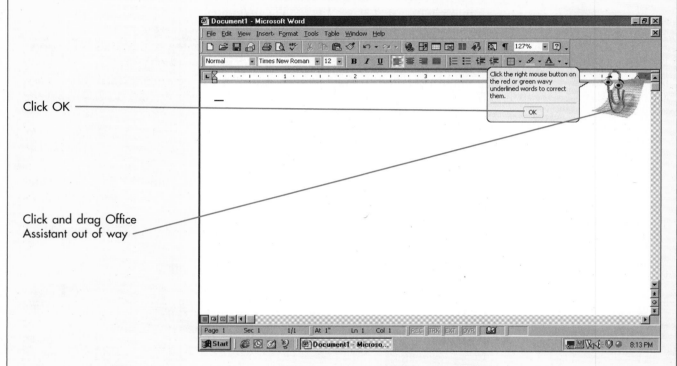

Click OK

Click and drag Office Assistant out of way

(c) Start Microsoft Word (step 3)

FIGURE 1.6   Hands-on Exercise 1 (continued)

ABOUT THE ASSISTANT

The Assistant is very powerful and hence you want to experiment with various ways to use it. To ask a question, click the Assistant's icon to toggle its balloon on or off. To change the way in which the Assistant works, click the Options tab within this balloon and experiment with the various check boxes to see their effects. If you find the Assistant distracting, click and drag the character out of the way or hide it altogether by pulling down the Help menu and clicking the Hide Office Assistant command. Pull down the Help menu and click the Show Office Assistant command to return the Assistant to the desktop.

STEP 4: Create the Document

➤ Create the document in Figure 1.6d. Type just as you would on a typewriter with one exception; do *not* press the enter key at the end of a line because Word will automatically wrap text from one line to the next.

➤ Press the **enter key** at the end of the paragraph.

➤ You may see a red or green wavy line to indicate spelling or grammatical errors respectively. Both features are discussed later in the chapter.

➤ Point to the red wavy line (if any), click the **right mouse button** to display a list of suggested corrections, then click (select) the appropriate substitution.

➤ Ignore the green wavy line (if any).

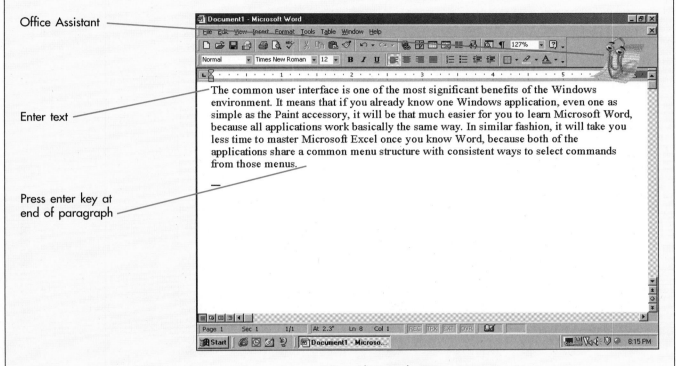

Office Assistant

Enter text

Press enter key at end of paragraph

(d) Create the Document (step 4)

SEPARATE THE TOOLBARS

Office 2000 displays the Standard and Formatting toolbars on the same row to save space within the application window. The result is that only a limited number of buttons are visible on each toolbar, and hence you may need to click the double arrow (More Buttons) tool at the end of the toolbar to view additional buttons. You can, however, separate the toolbars. Pull down the Tools menu, click the Customize command, click the Options tab, then clear the check box that has the toolbars share one row.

STEP 5: Save the Document

➤ Pull down the **File menu** and click **Save** (or click the **Save button** on the Standard toolbar). You should see the Save As dialog box in Figure 1.6e.

➤ If necessary, click the **drop-down arrow** on the View button and select the **Details View,** so that the display on your monitor matches our figure.

➤ To save the file:

- Click the **drop-down arrow** on the Save In list box.
- Click the appropriate drive, e.g., drive C or drive A, depending on whether or not you installed the data disk on your hard drive.
- Double click the **Exploring Word folder,** to make it the active folder (the folder in which you will save the document).
- Click and drag over the default entry in the File name text box. Type **My First Document** as the name of your document. (A DOC extension will be added automatically when the file is saved to indicate that this is a Word document.)
- Click **Save** or press the **enter key.** The title bar changes to reflect the document name.

➤ Add your name at the end of the document, then click the **Save button** on the Standard toolbar to save the document with the revision. This time the Save As dialog box does not appear, since Word already knows the name of the document.

Save button

Click to select drive and/or folder

Views button

Enter file name

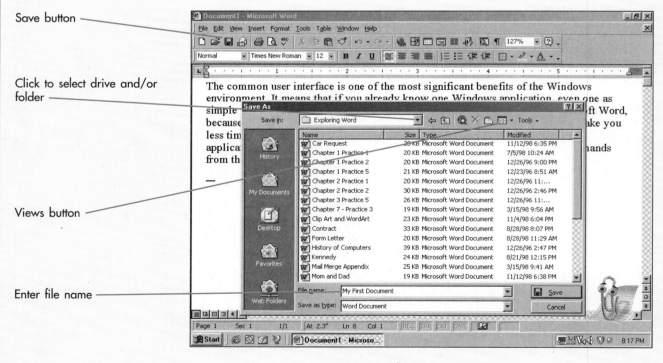

(e) Save the Document (step 5)

FIGURE 1.6   Hands-on Exercise 1 (continued)

STEP 6: The Office Assistant

➤ If necessary, pull down the **Help menu** and click the command to **Show the Office Assistant.** You may see a different character than the one we have selected.

➤ Click the Assistant, enter the question, **How do I print?** as shown in Figure 1.6f, then click the **Search button** to look for the answer. The size of the Assistant's balloon expands as the Assistant suggests several topics that may be appropriate.

➤ Click the topic, **Print a document** which in turn displays a Help window that contains links to various topics, each with detailed information. Click the Office Assistant to hide the balloon (or drag the Assistant out of the way).

➤ Click any of the links in the Help window to read the information. You can print the contents of any topic by clicking the **Print button** in the Help window. Close the Help window when you are finished.

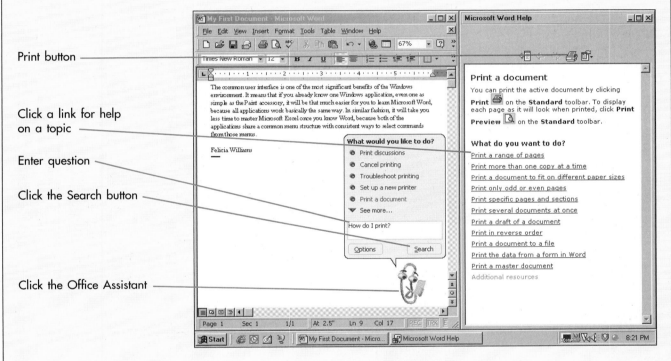

Print button

Click a link for help on a topic

Enter question

Click the Search button

Click the Office Assistant

(f) The Office Assistant (step 6)

FIGURE 1.6   Hands-on Exercise 1 (continued)

TIP OF THE DAY

You can set the Office Assistant to greet you with a "tip of the day" each time you start Word. Click the Microsoft Word Help button (or press the F1 key) to display the Assistant, then click the Options button to display the Office Assistant dialog box. Click the Options tab, then check the Show the Tip of the Day at Startup box and click OK. The next time you start Microsoft Word, you will be greeted by the Assistant, who will offer you the tip of the day.

STEP 7: Print the Document

➤ You can print the document in one of two ways:

* Pull down the **File menu.** Click **Print** to display the dialog box of Figure 1.6g. Click the **OK command button** to print the document.
* Click the **Print button** on the Standard toolbar to print the document immediately without displaying the Print dialog box.

Print button

Click OK to print the file

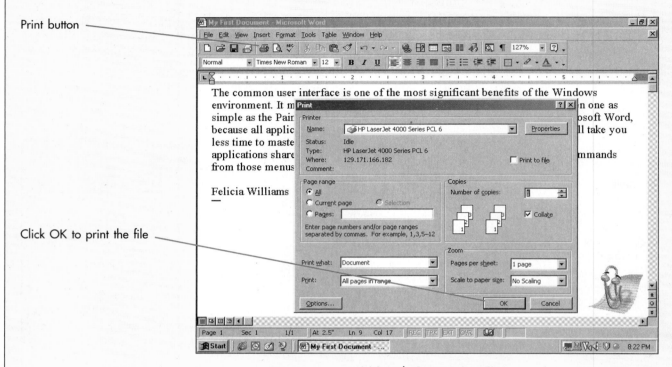

(g) Print the Document (step 7)

FIGURE 1.6   Hands-on Exercise 1 (continued)

ABOUT MICROSOFT WORD

Pull down the Help menu and click About Microsoft Word to display the specific release number and other licensing information, including the product ID. This help screen also contains two very useful command buttons, System Information and Technical Support. The first button displays information about the hardware installed on your system, including the amount of memory and available space on the hard drive. The Technical Support button provides telephone numbers for technical assistance.

STEP 8: Close the Document

➤ Pull down the **File menu.** Click **Close** to close this document but remain in Word. If you don't see the Close command, click the double arrow at the bottom of the menu. Click **Yes** if prompted to save the document.

➤ Pull down the **File menu** a second time. Click **Exit** to close Word if you do not want to continue with the next exercise at this time.

TROUBLESHOOTING

We trust that you completed the hands-on exercise without difficulty, and that you were able to create, save, and print the document in the exercise. There is, however, considerable flexibility in the way you do the exercise in that you can display different toolbars and menus, and/or execute commands in a variety of ways. This section describes various ways in which you can customize Microsoft Word, and in so doing, will help you to troubleshoot future exercises.

Figure 1.7 displays two different views of the same document. Your screen may not match either figure, and indeed, there is no requirement that it should. You should, however, be aware of different options so that you can develop preferences of your own. Consider:

- Figure 1.7a uses the default settings of short menus (note the double arrow at the bottom of the menu to display additional commands) and a shared row for the Standard and Formatting toolbars. Figure 1.7b displays the full menu and displays the toolbars on separate rows. We prefer the latter settings, which are set through the Customize command in the Tools menu.

- Figure 1.7a shows the Office Assistant (but drags it out of the way) whereas Figure 1.7b hides it. We find the Assistant distracting, and display it only when necessary by pressing the F1 key. You can also use the appropriate option in the Help menu to hide or show the Assistant and/or you can right click the Assistant to hide it.

- Figure 1.7a displays the document in the *Normal view* whereas Figure 1.7b uses the *Print Layout view.* The Normal view is simpler, but the Print Layout view more closely resembles the printed page as it displays top and bottom margins, headers and footers, graphic elements in their exact position, a vertical ruler, and other elements not seen in the Normal view. We alternate between the two. Note, too, that you can change the magnification in either view to make the text larger or smaller.

- Figure 1.7a displays the ¶ and other nonprinting symbols whereas they are hidden in Figure 1.7b. We prefer the cleaner screen without the symbols, but on occasion display the symbols if there is a problem in formatting a document. The *Show/Hide ¶ button* toggles the symbols on or off.

- Figure 1.7b displays an additional toolbar, the Drawing toolbar, at the bottom of the screen. Microsoft Word has more than 20 toolbars that are suppressed or displayed through the Toolbars command in the View menu. Note, too, that you can change the position of any visible toolbar by dragging its move handle (the parallel lines) at the left of the toolbar.

THE MOUSE VERSUS THE KEYBOARD

Almost every command in Office can be executed in different ways, using either the mouse or the keyboard. Most people start with the mouse and add keyboard shortcuts as they become more proficient. There is no right or wrong technique, just different techniques, and the one you choose depends entirely on personal preference in a specific situation. If, for example, your hands are already on the keyboard, it is faster to use the keyboard equivalent. Other times, your hand will be on the mouse and that will be the fastest way.

Click ⩗ to display additional commands

Nonprinting characters

Office Assistant is displayed

Normal View button

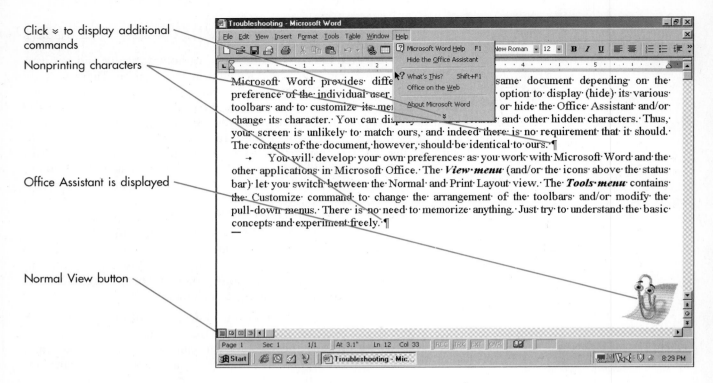

(a) Normal View

Show/Hide button

Page margins are displayed

Vertical ruler

Print Layout View button

Drawing toolbar

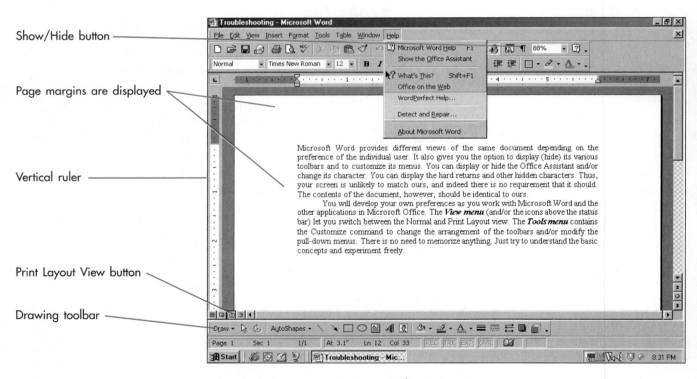

(b) Print Layout View

FIGURE 1.7   Troubleshooting

HANDS-ON EXERCISE 2

Modifying an Existing Document

Objective: To open an existing document, revise it, and save the revision; to use the Undo and Help commands. Use Figure 1.8 as a guide in doing the exercise.

STEP 1: Open an Existing Document

➤ Start Microsoft Word. Click and drag the Assistant out of the way if it appears.

➤ Pull down the **File menu** and click **Open** (or click the **Open button** on the Standard toolbar). You should see a dialog box similar to the one in Figure 1.8a.

➤ To open a file:

- If necessary, click the **drop-down arrow** on the View button and change to the **Details view.** Click and drag the vertical border between columns to increase (or decrease) the size of a column.

- Click the drop-down arrow on the Look In list box.

- Click the appropriate drive; for example, drive C or drive A.

- Double click the **Exploring Word folder** to make it the active folder (the folder from which you will open the document).

- Click the **down arrow** on the vertical scroll bar in the Name list box, then scroll until you can select the **My First Document** from the first exercise. Click the **Open command button** to open the file.

➤ Your document should appear on the screen.

Click to select drive/folder

View button

Select file

Click to scroll through filenames

Drag Office Assistant out of way

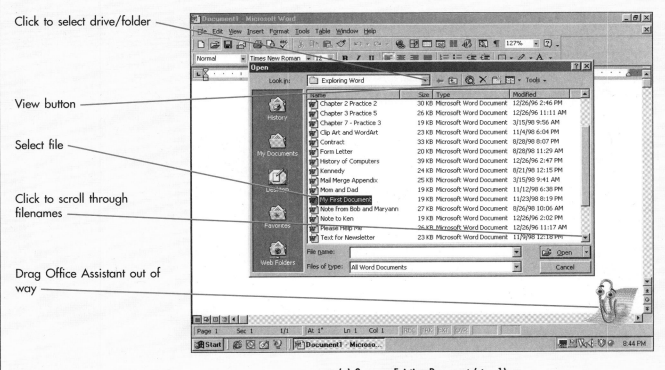

(a) Open an Existing Document (step 1)

FIGURE 1.8 Hands-on Exercise 2

STEP 2: Troubleshooting

➤ Modify the settings within Word so that the document on your screen matches Figure 1.8b.

- To separate the Standard and Formatting toolbars, pull down the **Tools menu,** click **Customize,** click the **Options tab,** then clear the check box that indicates the Standard and Formatting toolbars should share the same row.

- To display the complete menus, pull down the **Tools menu,** click **Customize,** click the **Options tab,** then clear the **Menus show recently used commands** check box.

- To change to the Normal view, pull down the **View menu** and click **Normal** (or click the **Normal View** button at the bottom of the window).

- To change the amount of text that is visible on the screen, click the drop-down arrow on the **Zoom box** on the Standard toolbar and select **Page Width.**

- To display (hide) the ruler, pull down the **View menu** and toggle the **Ruler command** on or off. End with the ruler on. (If you don't see the Ruler command, click the double arrow at the bottom of the menu, or use the Options command in the Tools menu to display the complete menus.)

➤ Click the **Show/Hide ¶ button** to display or hide the hard returns as you see fit. The button functions as a toggle switch.

➤ There may still be subtle differences between your screen and ours, depending on the resolution of your monitor. These variations, if any, need not concern you as long as you are able to complete the exercise.

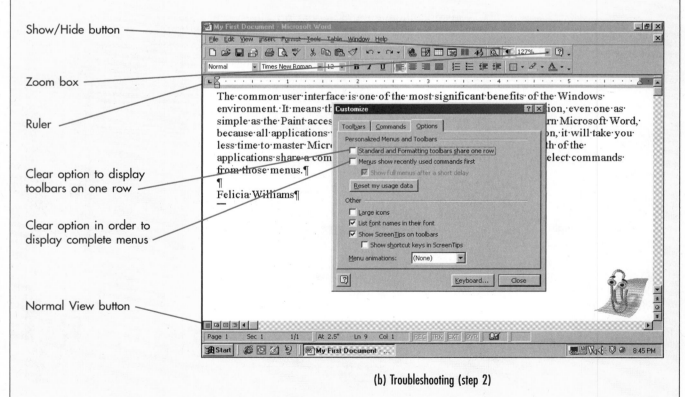

Show/Hide button

Zoom box

Ruler

Clear option to display
toolbars on one row

Clear option in order to
display complete menus

Normal View button

(b) Troubleshooting (step 2)

FIGURE 1.8   Hands-on Exercise 2 (continued)

STEP 3: Modify the Document

➤ Press **Ctrl+End** to move to the end of the document. Press the **up arrow key** once or twice until the insertion point is on a blank line above your name. If necessary, press the **enter key** once (or twice) to add additional blank line(s).

➤ Add the sentence, **Success, I can save and retrieve a document!,** as shown in Figure 1.8c.

➤ Make the following additional modifications to practice editing:

   • Change the phrase *most significant* to **very best.**

   • Change *Paint accessory* to **game of Solitaire.**

   • Change the word *select* to **choose.**

➤ Use the **Ins key** to switch between insert and overtype modes as necessary. (You can also double click the **OVR indicator** on the status bar to toggle between the insert and overtype modes.)

➤ Pull down the **File menu** and click **Save,** or click the **Save button.**

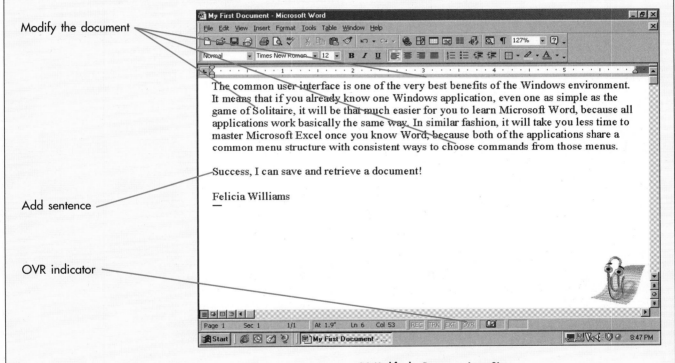

(c) Modify the Document (step 3)

FIGURE 1.8   Hands-on Exercise 2 (continued)

MOVING WITHIN A DOCUMENT

Press Ctrl+Home and Ctrl+End to move to the beginning and end of a document, respectively. You can also press the Home or End key to move to the beginning or end of a line. These shortcuts work not just in Word, but in any Office application, and are worth remembering as they allow your hands to remain on the keyboard as you type.

STEP 4: Deleting Text

➤ Press and hold the left mouse button as you drag the mouse over the phrase, **even one as simple as the game of Solitaire,** as shown in Figure 1.8d.

➤ Press the **Del** key to delete the selected text from the document. Pull down the **Edit menu** and click the **Undo command** (or click the **Undo button** on the Standard toolbar) to reverse (undo) the last command. The deleted text should be returned to your document.

➤ Pull down the **Edit menu** a second time and click the **Redo command** (or click the **Redo button**) to repeat the Delete command.

➤ Click the **Save button** on the Standard toolbar to save the revised document a final time.

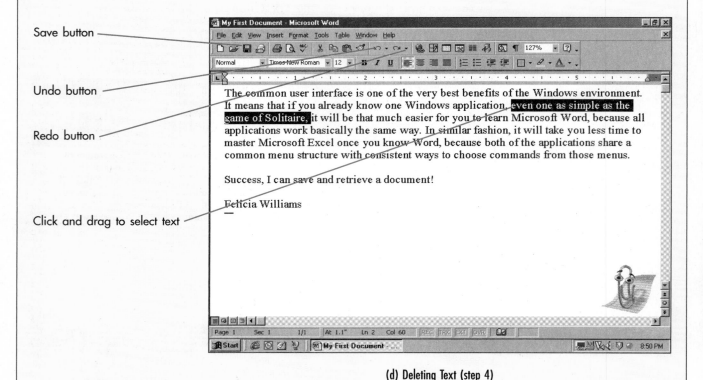

Save button

Undo button

Redo button

Click and drag to select text

(d) Deleting Text (step 4)

FIGURE 1.8   Hands-on Exercise 2 (continued)

THE UNDO AND REDO COMMANDS

Click the drop-down arrow next to the Undo button to display a list of your previous actions, then click the action you want to undo which also undoes all of the preceding commands. Undoing the fifth command in the list, for example, will also undo the preceding four commands. The Redo command works in reverse and cancels the last Undo command.

STEP 5: The Office Assistant

➤ Click the **Office Assistant** to display the balloon. Enter a question such as **How do I get help,** then click the **Search button.** The Assistant returns a list of topics that it considers potential answers. Click any topic you think is appropriate (we chose **How to get started with Word 2000**) to open the Help window as shown in Figure 1.8e.

➤ Click the link to **printed and online resources that are available.** Read the information, then click the **Print button** in the Help window to print this topic.

➤ Use the **Contents, Answer Wizard,** and/or **Index tabs** to search through the available help. Close the Help window when you have finished.

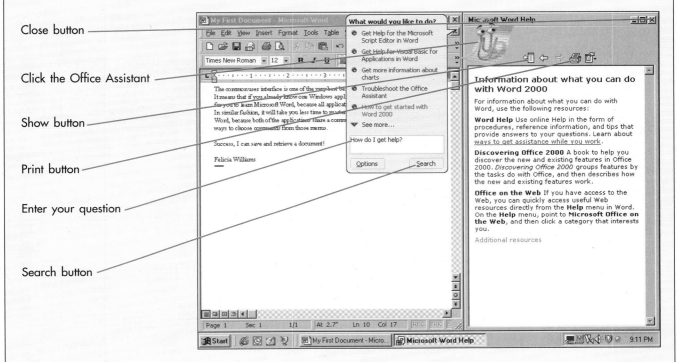

(e) The Office Assistant (step 5)

FIGURE 1.8   Hands-on Exercise 2 (continued)

CHOOSE YOUR OWN ASSISTANT

You can choose your own personal assistant from one of several available candidates. If necessary, press the F1 key to display the Assistant, click the Options button to display the Office Assistant dialog box, then click the Gallery tab where you choose your character. (The Office 2000 CD is required in order to select some of the other characters.) Some assistants are more animated (distracting) than others. The Office logo is the most passive, while Rocky is quite animated. Experiment with the various check boxes on the Options tab to see the effects on the Assistant.

STEP 6: E-mail Your Document

➤ You should check with your professor before attempting this step.

➤ Click the **E-mail button** on the Standard toolbar to display a screen similar to Figure 1.8f. The text of your document is entered automatically into the body of the e-mail message.

➤ Enter your professor's e-mail address in the To text box. The document title is automatically entered in the Subject line. Press the **Tab key** to move to the body of the message. Type a short note above the inserted document to your professor, then click the **Send a Copy button** to mail the message.

➤ The e-mail window closes and you are back in Microsoft Word. The introductory text has been added to the document. Pull down the **File menu.** Click **Close** to close the document (there is no need to save the document).

➤ Pull down the **File menu.** Click **Exit** if you do not want to continue with the next exercise at this time.

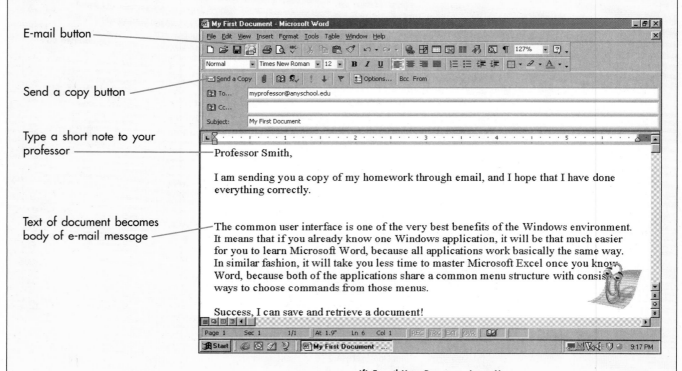

E-mail button

Send a copy button

Type a short note to your professor

Text of document becomes body of e-mail message

(f) E-mail Your Document (step 6)

FIGURE 1.8   Hands-on Exercise 2 (continued)

DOCUMENT PROPERTIES

Prove to your instructor how hard you've worked by printing various statistics about your document including the number of revisions and the total editing time. Pull down the File menu, click the Print command to display the Print dialog box, click the drop-down arrow in the Print What list box, select Document properties, then click OK. You can view the information (without printing) by pulling down the File menu, clicking the Properties command, then selecting the Statistics tab.

There is simply no excuse to misspell a word, since the ***spell check*** is an integral part of Microsoft Word. (The spell check is also available for every other application in the Microsoft Office.) Spelling errors make your work look sloppy and discourage the reader before he or she has read what you had to say. They can cost you a job, a grade, a lucrative contract, or an award you deserve.

The spell check can be set to automatically check a document as text is entered, or it can be called explicitly by clicking the Spelling and Grammar button on the Standard toolbar. The spell check compares each word in a document to the entries in a built-in dictionary, then flags any word that is in the document, but not in the built-in dictionary, as an error.

The dictionary included with Microsoft Office is limited to standard English and does not include many proper names, acronyms, abbreviations, or specialized terms, and hence, the use of any such item is considered a misspelling. You can, however, add such words to a ***custom dictionary*** so that they will not be flagged in the future. The spell check will inform you of repeated words and irregular capitalization. It cannot, however, flag properly spelled words that are used improperly, and thus cannot tell you that *Two bee or knot too be* is not the answer.

The capabilities of the spell check are illustrated in conjunction with Figure 1.9a. Microsoft Word will indicate the errors as you type by underlining them in red. Alternatively, you can click the Spelling and Grammar button on the Standard toolbar at any time to move through the entire document. The spell check will then go through the document and return the errors one at a time, offering several options for each mistake. You can change the misspelled word to one of the alternatives suggested by Word, leave the word as is, or add the word to a custom dictionary.

The first error is the word *embarassing,* with Word's suggestion(s) for correction displayed in the list box in Figure 1.9b. To accept the highlighted suggestion, click the Change command button and the substitution will be made automatically in the document. To accept an alternative suggestion, click the desired word, then click the Change command button. Alternatively, you can click the AutoCorrect button to correct the mistake in the current document, and, in addition, automatically correct the same mistake in any future document.

The spell check detects both irregular capitalization and duplicated words, as shown in Figures 1.9c and 1.9d, respectively. The last error, *Grauer,* is not a misspelling per se, but a proper noun not found in the standard dictionary. No correction is required and the appropriate action is to ignore the word (taking no further action)—or better yet, add it to the custom dictionary so that it will not be flagged in future sessions.

A spell check will catch embarassing mistakes, iRregular capitalization, and duplicate words words. It will also flag proper nouns, for example Robert Grauer, but you can add these terms to a custom dictionary. It will not notice properly spelled words that are used incorrectly; for example, too bee or knot to be are not the answer.

(a) The Text

FIGURE 1.9   The Spell Check

Word not found in dictionary ———

Suggestion ———

Change button ———

AutoCorrect button ———

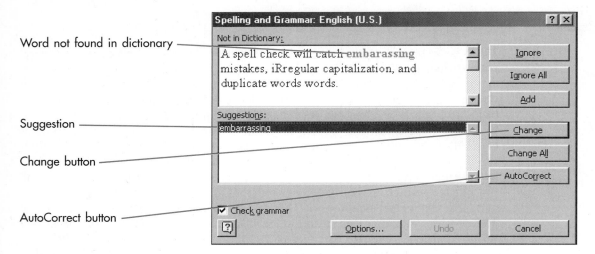

(b) Ordinary Misspelling

Irregular capitalization
is flagged ———

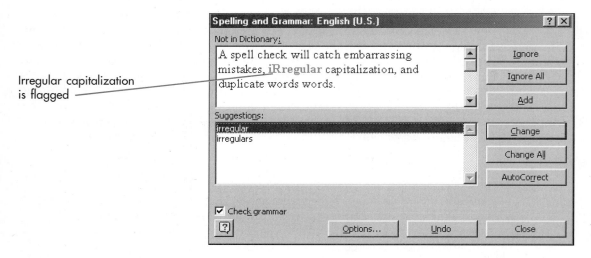

(c) Irregular Capitalization

Duplicated words are flagged ———

Click to delete duplicated word ———

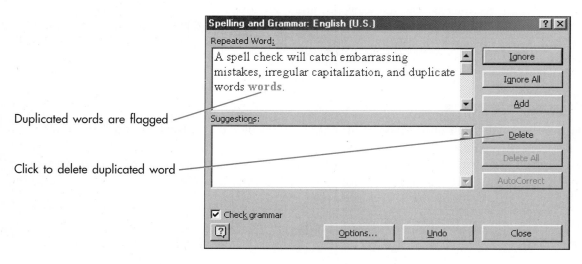

(d) Duplicated Word

FIGURE 1.9   The Spell Check (continued)

AutoCorrect and AutoText

The **AutoCorrect** feature corrects mistakes as they are made without any effort on your part. It makes you a better typist. If, for example, you typed *teh* instead of *the,* Word would change the spelling without even telling you. Word will also change *adn* to *and, i* to *I,* and occur*e*nce to occu*rr*ence. All of this is accomplished through a predefined table of common mistakes that Word uses to make substitutions whenever it encounters an entry in the table. You can add additional items to the table to include the frequent errors you make. You can also use the feature to define your own shorthand—for example, cis for Computer Information Systems as shown in Figure 1.10a.

The AutoCorrect feature will also correct mistakes in capitalization; for example, it will capitalize the first letter in a sentence, recognize that MIami should be Miami, and capitalize the days of the week. It's even smart enough to correct the accidental use of the Caps Lock key, and it will toggle the key off!

The **AutoText** feature is similar in concept to AutoCorrect in that both substitute a predefined item for a specific character string. The difference is that the substitution occurs automatically with the AutoCorrect entry, whereas you have to take deliberate action for the AutoText substitution to take place. AutoText entries can also include significantly more text, formatting, and even clip art.

Microsoft Word includes a host of predefined AutoText entries. And as with the AutoCorrect feature, you can define additional entries of your own. (You may, however, not be able to do this in a computer lab environment.) The entry in Figure 1.10b is named "signature" and once created, it is available to all Word documents. To insert an AutoText entry into a new document, just type the first several letters in the AutoText name (signature in our example), then press the enter key when Word displays a ScreenTip containing the text of the entry.

Other automatic corrections

Enter addition to table of common mistakes

Table of common mistakes

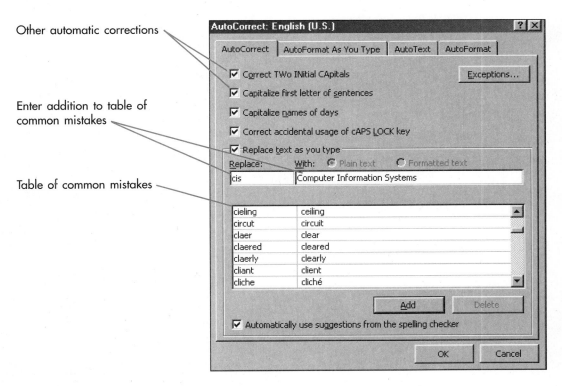

(a) AutoCorrect

FIGURE 1.10   AutoCorrect and AutoText

Name of AutoText entry

Predefined AutoText entries

Text of AutoText entry

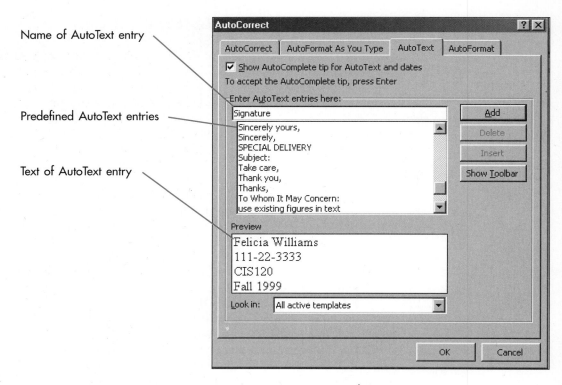

(b) AutoText

FIGURE 1.10   AutoCorrect and AutoText (continued)

THESAURUS

The *thesaurus* helps you to avoid repetition and polish your writing. The thesaurus is called from the Language command in the Tools menu. You position the cursor at the appropriate word within the document, then invoke the thesaurus and follow your instincts. The thesaurus recognizes multiple meanings and forms of a word (for example, adjective, noun, and verb) as in Figure 1.11a. Click a meaning, then double click a synonym to produce additional choices as in Figure 1.11b. You can explore further alternatives by selecting a synonym or antonym and clicking the Look Up button. We show antonyms in Figure 1.11c.

Meanings of selected word

Selected meaning

Synonyms for selected meaning; double click to look up meanings

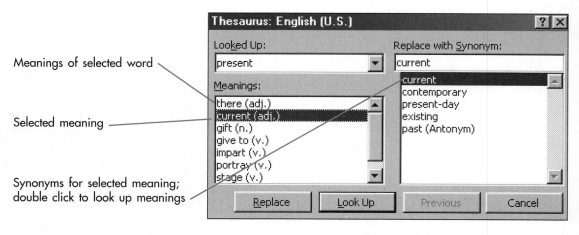

(a) Initial Word

FIGURE 1.11   The Thesaurus

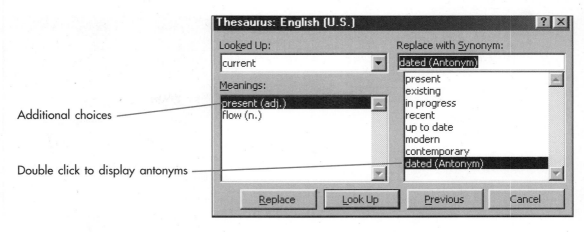

Additional choices

Double click to display antonyms

(b) Additional Choices

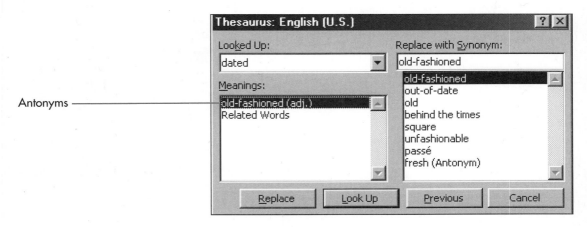

Antonyms

(c) Antonyms

FIGURE 1.11   The Thesaurus (continued)

GRAMMAR CHECK

The ***grammar check*** attempts to catch mistakes in punctuation, writing style, and word usage by comparing strings of text within a document to a series of predefined rules. As with the spell check, errors are brought to the screen where you can accept the suggested correction and make the replacement automatically, or more often, edit the selected text and make your own changes.

You can also ask the grammar check to explain the rule it is attempting to enforce. Unlike the spell check, the grammar check is subjective, and what seems appropriate to you may be objectionable to someone else. Indeed, the grammar check is quite flexible, and can be set to check for different writing styles; that is, you can implement one set of rules to check a business letter and a different set of rules for casual writing. Many times, however, you will find that the English language is just too complex for the grammar check to detect every error, although it will find many errors.

The grammar check caught the inconsistency between subject and verb in Figure 1.12a and suggested the appropriate correction (am instead of are). In Figure 1.12b, it suggested the elimination of the superfluous comma. These examples show the grammar check at its best, but it is often more subjective and less capable. It detected the error in Figure 1.12c, for example, but suggested an inappropriate correction, "to complicate" as opposed to "too complicated". Suffice it to say, that there is no substitute for carefully proofreading every document.

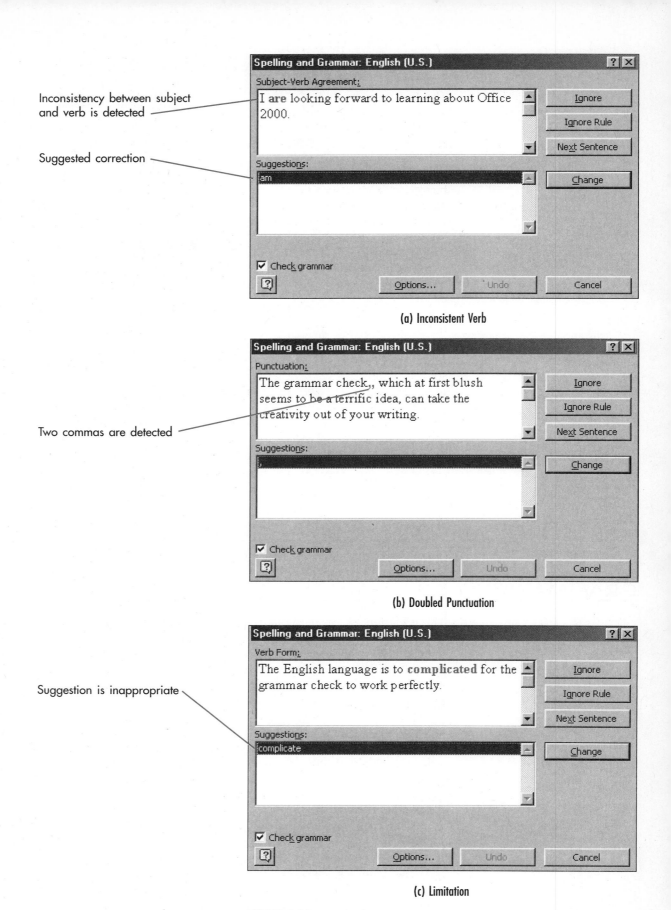

Inconsistency between subject and verb is detected

Suggested correction

(a) Inconsistent Verb

Two commas are detected

(b) Doubled Punctuation

Suggestion is inappropriate

(c) Limitation

FIGURE 1.12   The Grammar Check

The Save command was used in the first two exercises. The Save As command will be introduced in the next exercise as a very useful alternative. We also introduce you to different backup options. We believe that now, when you are first starting to learn about word processing, is the time to develop good working habits.

You already know that the Save command copies the document currently being edited (the document in memory) to disk. The initial execution of the command requires you to assign a file name and to specify the drive and folder in which the file is to be stored. All subsequent executions of the Save command save the document under the original name, replacing the previously saved version with the new one.

The **Save As command** saves another copy of a document under a different name (and/or a different file type), and is useful when you want to retain a copy of the original document. The Save As command provides you with two copies of a document. The original document is kept on disk under its original name. A copy of the document is saved on disk under a new name and remains in memory. All subsequent editing is done on the new document.

We cannot overemphasize the importance of periodically saving a document, so that if something does go wrong, you won't lose all of your work. Nothing is more frustrating than to lose two hours of effort, due to an unexpected program crash or to a temporary loss of power. Save your work frequently, at least once every 15 minutes. Pull down the File menu and click Save, or click the Save button on the Standard toolbar. Do it!

QUIT WITHOUT SAVING

There will be times when you do not want to save the changes to a document, such as when you have edited it beyond recognition and wish you had never started. Pull down the File menu and click the Close command, then click No in response to the message asking whether you want to save the changes to the document. Pull down the File menu and reopen the file (it should be the first file in the list of most recently edited documents), then start over from the beginning.

Backup Options

Microsoft Word offers several different **backup** options. We believe the two most important options are to create a backup copy in conjunction with every save command, and to periodically (and automatically) save a document. Both options are implemented in step 3 in the next hands-on exercise.

Figure 1.13 illustrates the option to create a backup copy of the document every time a Save command is executed. Assume, for example, that you have created the simple document, *The fox jumped over the fence* and saved it under the name "Fox". Assume further that you edit the document to read, *The quick brown fox jumped over the fence,* and that you saved it a second time. The second save command changes the name of the original document from "Fox" to "Backup of Fox", then saves the current contents of memory as "Fox". In other words, the disk now contains two versions of the document: the current version "Fox" and the most recent previous version "Backup of Fox".

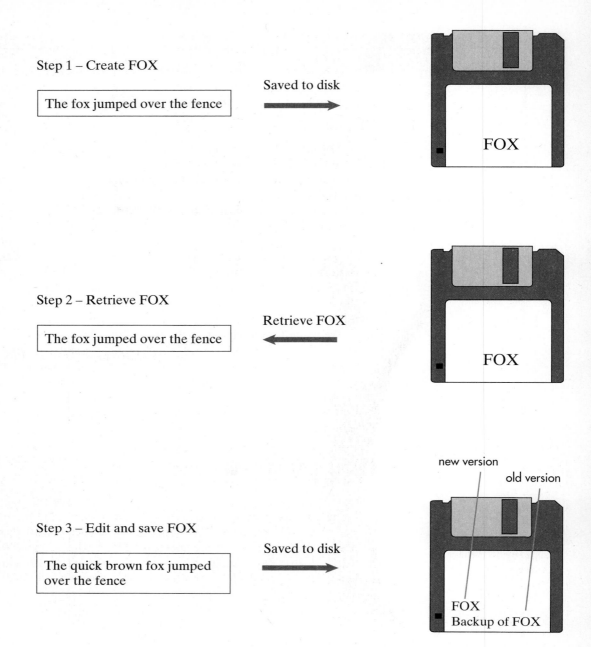

Step 1 – Create FOX

The fox jumped over the fence

Saved to disk

FOX

Step 2 – Retrieve FOX

The fox jumped over the fence

Retrieve FOX

FOX

Step 3 – Edit and save FOX

The quick brown fox jumped over the fence

Saved to disk

new version

old version

FOX
Backup of FOX

FIGURE 1.13   Backup Procedures

The cycle goes on indefinitely, with "Fox" always containing the current version, and "Backup of Fox" the most recent previous version. Thus if you revise and save the document a third time, "Fox" will contain the latest revision while "Backup of Fox" would contain the previous version alluding to the quick brown fox. The original (first) version of the document disappears entirely since only two versions are kept.

The contents of "Fox" and "Backup of Fox" are different, but the existence of the latter enables you to retrieve the previous version if you inadvertently edit beyond repair or accidentally erase the current "Fox" version. Should this occur (and it will), you can always retrieve its predecessor and at least salvage your work prior to the last save operation.

The Spell Check

Objective: To open an existing document, check it for spelling, then use the Save As command to save the document under a different file name. Use Figure 1.14 as a guide in the exercise.

STEP 1: Preview a Document

➤ Start Microsoft Word. Pull down the **Help menu.** Click the command to **Hide** the **Office Assistant.**

➤ Pull down the **File menu** and click **Open** (or click the **Open button** on the Standard toolbar). You should see a dialog box similar to the one in Figure 1.14a.

➤ Select the appropriate drive, drive C or drive A, depending on the location of your data. Double click the **Exploring Word folder** to make it the active folder (the folder from which you will open the document).

➤ Scroll in the Name list box until you can select (click) the **Try the Spell Check** document. Click the **drop-down arrow** on the **Views button** and click **Preview** to preview the document as shown in Figure 1.14a.

➤ Click the **Open command button** to open the file. Your document should appear on the screen.

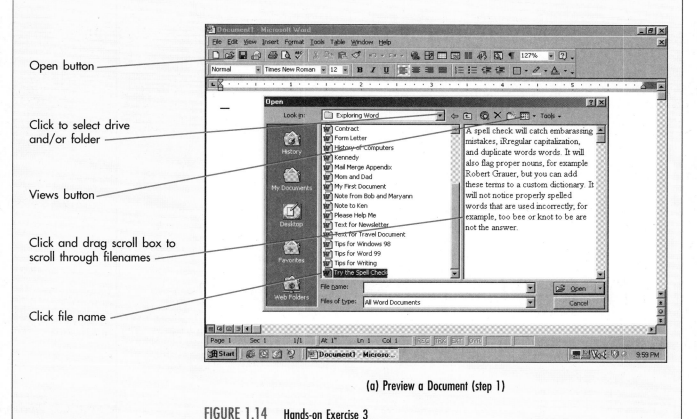

(a) Preview a Document (step 1)

FIGURE 1.14 Hands-on Exercise 3

STEP 2: The Save As Command

➤ Pull down the **File menu.** Click **Save As** to produce the dialog box in Figure 1.14b.

➤ Enter **Modified Spell Check** as the name of the new document. (A file name may contain up to 255 characters, and blanks are permitted.) Click the **Save command button.**

➤ There are now two identical copies of the file on disk: Try the Spell Check, which we supplied, and Modified Spell Check, which you just created. The title bar shows the latter name as it is the document in memory.

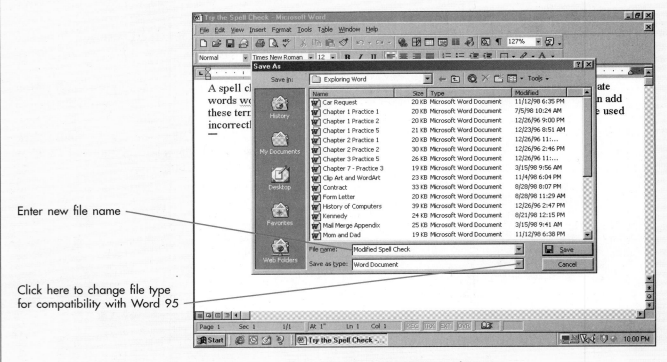

Enter new file name

Click here to change file type for compatibility with Word 95

(b) The Save As Command (step 2)

FIGURE 1.14   Hands-on Exercise 3 (continued)

DIFFERENT FILE TYPES

The file format for Word 2000 is compatible with Word 97, but incompatible with earlier versions such as Word 95. The newer releases can open a document that was created using the older program (Word 95), but the reverse is not true; that is, you cannot open a document that was created in Word 2000 in Word 95 unless you change the file type. Pull down the File menu, click the Save As command, then specify the earlier (Word 6.0/Word 95) file type. You will be able to read the file in Word 95, but will lose any formatting that is unique to the newer release.

STEP 3: Create a Backup Copy

➤ Pull down the **Tools menu.** Click **Options.** Click the **Save tab** to display the dialog box of Figure 1.14c.

➤ Click the first check box to choose **Always create backup copy.**

➤ Set the other options as you see fit; for example, you can specify that the document be saved automatically every 10–15 minutes. Click **OK.**

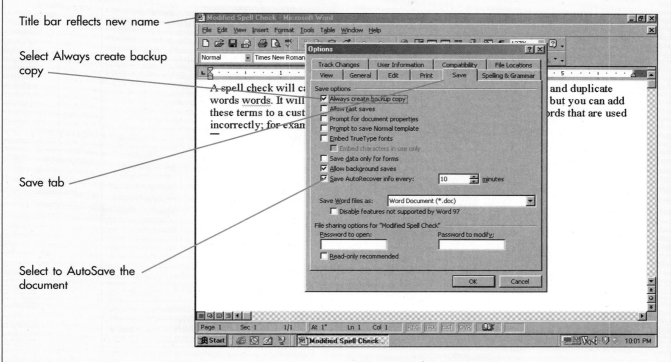

Title bar reflects new name

Select Always create backup copy

Save tab

Select to AutoSave the document

(c) Create a Backup Copy (step 3)

FIGURE 1.14   Hands-on Exercise 3 (continued)

STEP 4: The Spell Check

➤ If necessary, press **Ctrl+Home** to move to the beginning of the document. Click the **Spelling and Grammar button** on the Standard toolbar to check the document.

➤ "Embarassing" is flagged as the first misspelling as shown in Figure 1.14d. Click the **Change button** to accept the suggested spelling.

➤ "iRregular" is flagged as an example of irregular capitalization. Click the **Change button** to accept the suggested correction.

➤ Continue checking the document, which displays misspellings and other irregularities one at a time. Click the appropriate command button as each mistake is found.

• Click the **Delete button** to remove the duplicated word.

• Click the **Ignore button** to accept Grauer (or click the **Add button** to add Grauer to the custom dictionary).

➤ The last sentence is flagged because of a grammatical error and is discussed in the next step.

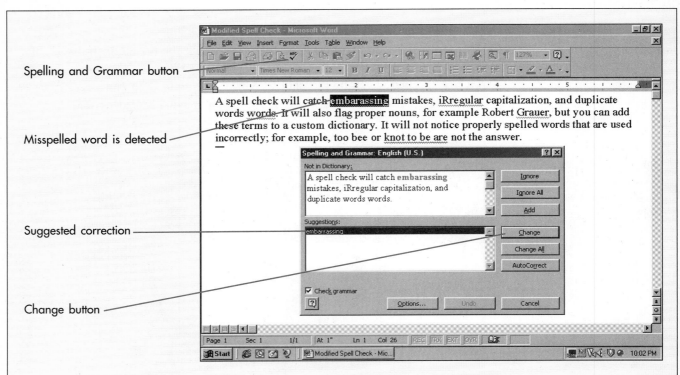

Spelling and Grammar button

Misspelled word is detected

Suggested correction

Change button

(d) The Spell Check (step 4)

FIGURE 1.14   Hands-on Exercise 3 (continued)

AUTOMATIC SPELLING AND GRAMMAR CHECKING

Red and green wavy lines may appear throughout a document to indicate spelling and grammatical errors, respectively. Point to any underlined word, then click the right mouse button to display a context-sensitive help menu with suggested corrections. To enable (disable) these options, pull down the Tools menu, click the Options command, click the Spelling and Grammar tab, and check (clear) the options to check spelling (or grammar) as you type.

STEP 5: The Grammar Check

➤ The last sentence, "Two bee or knot to be is not the answer", should be flagged as an error, as shown in Figure 1.14e. If this is not the case:

• Pull down the **Tools menu,** click **Options,** then click the **Spelling and Grammar tab.**

• Check the box to **Check Grammar with Spelling,** then click the button to **Recheck document.** Click **Yes** when told that the spelling and grammar check will be reset, then click **OK** to close the Options dialog box.

• Press **Ctrl+Home** to return to the beginning of the document, then click the **Spelling and Grammar button** to recheck the document.

➤ Click the **Office Assistant button** in the Spelling and Grammar dialog box.

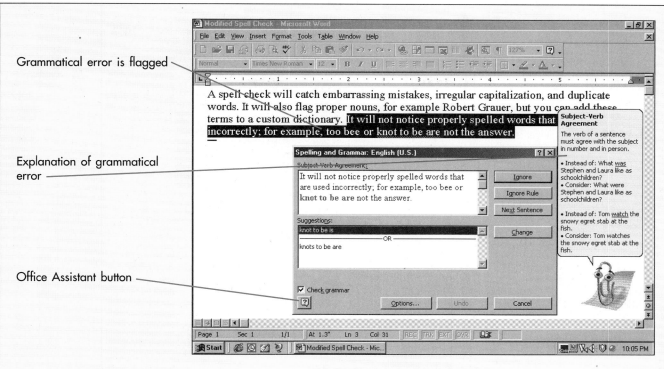

Grammatical error is flagged

Explanation of grammatical error

Office Assistant button

(e) The Grammar Check (step 5)

FIGURE 1.14   Hands-on Exercise 3 (continued)

➤ The Office Assistant will appear, indicating that there needs to be number agreement between subject and verb. Hide the Office Assistant after you have read the explanation.

➤ Click **Ignore** to reject the suggestion. Click **OK** when you see the dialog box, indicating the spelling and grammar check is complete.

CHECK SPELLING ONLY

The grammar check is invoked by default in conjunction with the spell check. You can, however, check the spelling of a document without checking its grammar. Pull down the Tools menu, click Options to display the Options dialog box, then click the Spelling and Grammar tab. Clear the box to check grammar with spelling, then click OK to accept the change and close the dialog box.

STEP 6: The Thesaurus

➤ Select (click) the word *incorrectly,* which appears on the last line of your document as shown in Figure 1.14f.

➤ Pull down the **Tools menu,** click **Language,** then click **Thesaurus** to display synonyms for the word you selected.

➤ Select (click) *inaccurately,* the synonym you will use in place of the original word. Click the **Replace button** to make the change automatically.

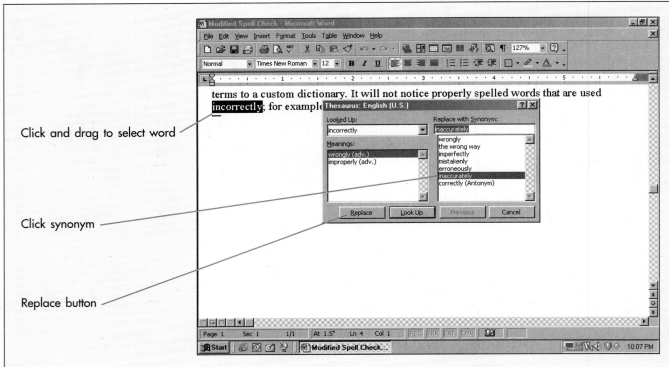

Click and drag to select word

Click synonym

Replace button

FIGURE 1.14   Hands-on Exercise 3 (continued)

STEP 7: AutoCorrect

➤ Press **Ctrl+Home** to move to the beginning of the document.

➤ Type the *misspelled* phrase **Teh Spell Check was used to check this document.** Try to look at the monitor as you type to see the AutoCorrect feature in action; Word will correct the misspelling and change *Teh* to *The*.

➤ If you did not see the correction being made, click the arrow next to the Undo command on the Standard toolbar and undo the last several actions. Click the arrow next to the Redo command and redo the corrections.

➤ Pull down the **Tools menu** and click the **AutoCorrect command** to display the AutoCorrect dialog box. If necessary, click the AutoCorrect tab to view the list of predefined corrections.

➤ The first several entries in the list pertain to symbols. Type (c), for example, and you see the © symbol. Type :) or :(and you see a happy and sad face, respectively. Click **Cancel** to close the dialog box.

CREATE YOUR OWN SHORTHAND

Use AutoCorrect to expand abbreviations such as "usa" for United States of America. Pull down the Tools menu, click AutoCorrect, type the abbreviation in the Replace text box and the expanded entry in the With text box. Click the Add command button, then click OK to exit the dialog box and return to the document. The next time you type usa in a document, it will automatically be expanded to United States of America.

STEP 8: Create an AutoText Entry

➤ Press **Ctrl+End** to move to the end of the document. Press the **enter key** twice. Enter your name, social security number, and class.

➤ Click and drag to select the information you just entered. Pull down the **Insert menu,** select the **AutoText command,** then select **AutoText** to display the AutoCorrect dialog box in Figure 1.14g.

➤ Your name (Felicia Williams in our example) is suggested automatically as the name of the AutoText entry. Click the **Add button.**

➤ To test the entry, you can delete your name and other information, then use the AutoText feature. Your name and other information should still be highlighted. Press the **Del key** to delete the information.

➤ Type the first few letters of your name and watch the screen as you do. You should see a ScreenTip containing your name and other information. Press the **enter key** or the **F3 key** when you see the ScreenTip.

➤ Save the document. Print the document for your instructor. Exit Word.

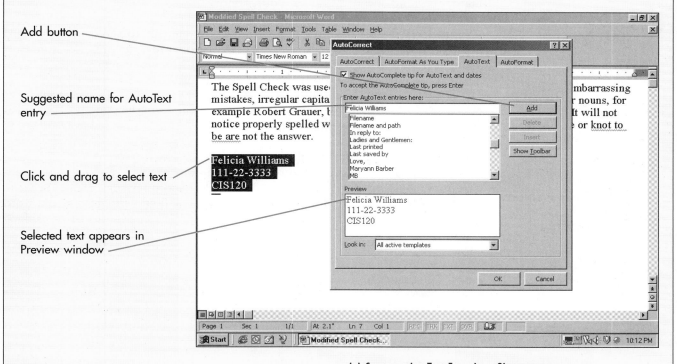

Add button

Suggested name for AutoText entry

Click and drag to select text

Selected text appears in Preview window

(g) Create an AutoText Entry (step 8)

FIGURE 1.14   Hands-on Exercise 3 (continued)

THE AUTOTEXT TOOLBAR

Point to any visible toolbar, click the right mouse button to display a context-sensitive menu, then click AutoText to display the AutoText toolbar. The AutoText toolbar groups the various AutoText entries into categories, making it easier to select the proper entry. Click the down arrow on the All Entries button to display the various categories, click a category, then select the entry you want to insert into the document.

The chapter provided a broad-based introduction to word processing in general and to Microsoft Word in particular. Help is available from many sources. You can use the Help menu or the Office Assistant as you can in any Office application. You can also go to the Microsoft Web site to obtain more recent, and often more detailed, information.

Microsoft Word is always in one of two modes, insert or overtype; the choice between the two depends on the desired editing. The insertion point marks the place within a document where text is added or replaced.

The enter key is pressed at the end of a paragraph, but not at the end of a line because Word automatically wraps text from one line to the next. A hard return is created by the user when he or she presses the enter key; a soft return is created by Word as it wraps text and begins a new line.

The Save and Open commands work in conjunction with one another. The Save command copies the document in memory to disk under its existing name. The Open command retrieves a previously saved document. The Save As command saves the document under a different name and is useful when you want to retain a copy of the current document prior to all changes.

A spell check compares the words in a document to those in a standard and/or custom dictionary and offers suggestions to correct the mistakes it finds. It will detect misspellings, duplicated phrases, and/or irregular capitalization, but will not flag properly spelled words that are used incorrectly.

The AutoCorrect feature corrects predefined spelling errors and/or mistakes in capitalization, automatically, as the words are entered. The AutoText feature is similar in concept except that it can contain longer entries that include formatting and clip art. Either feature can be used to create a personal shorthand to expand abbreviations as they are typed.

The thesaurus suggests synonyms and/or antonyms. It can also recognize multiple forms of a word (noun, verb, and adjective) and offer suggestions for each. The grammar check searches for mistakes in punctuation, writing style, and word usage by comparing strings of text within a document to a series of predefined rules.

KEY WORDS AND CONCEPTS

AutoCorrect	Insert mode	Soft return
AutoText	Insertion point	Spell check
Backup	Normal view	Standard toolbar
Close command	Office Assistant	Status bar
Custom dictionary	Open command	Text box
Exit command	Overtype mode	Thesaurus
File menu	Places Bar	Toggle switch
File name	Print command	Toolbar
File type	Print Layout view	Undo command
Formatting toolbar	Save As command	Vertical ruler
Grammar check	Save command	View menu
Hard return	ScreenTip	Word wrap
Horizontal ruler	Show/Hide ¶ button	

MULTIPLE CHOICE

1. When entering text within a document, the enter key is normally pressed at the end of every:
   (a) Line
   (b) Sentence
   (c) Paragraph
   (d) All of the above

2. Which menu contains the commands to save the current document, or to open a previously saved document?
   (a) The Tools menu
   (b) The File menu
   (c) The View menu
   (d) The Edit menu

3. How do you execute the Print command?
   (a) Click the Print button on the standard toolbar
   (b) Pull down the File menu, then click the Print command
   (c) Use the appropriate keyboard shortcut
   (d) All of the above

4. The Open command:
   (a) Brings a document from disk into memory
   (b) Brings a document from disk into memory, then erases the document on disk
   (c) Stores the document in memory on disk
   (d) Stores the document in memory on disk, then erases the document from memory

5. The Save command:
   (a) Brings a document from disk into memory
   (b) Brings a document from disk into memory, then erases the document on disk
   (c) Stores the document in memory on disk
   (d) Stores the document in memory on disk, then erases the document from memory

6. What is the easiest way to change the phrase, *revenues, profits, gross margin*, to read *revenues, profits, and gross margin?*
   (a) Use the insert mode, position the cursor before the *g* in *gross*, then type the word *and* followed by a space
   (b) Use the insert mode, position the cursor after the *g* in *gross*, then type the word *and* followed by a space
   (c) Use the overtype mode, position the cursor before the *g* in *gross*, then type the word *and* followed by a space
   (d) Use the overtype mode, position the cursor after the *g* in *gross*, then type the word *and* followed by a space

7. A document has been entered into Word with a given set of margins, which are subsequently changed. What can you say about the number of hard and soft returns before and after the change in margins?
   (a) The number of hard returns is the same, but the number and/or position of the soft returns is different
   (b) The number of soft returns is the same, but the number and/or position of the hard returns is different
   (c) The number and position of both hard and soft returns is unchanged
   (d) The number and position of both hard and soft returns is different

8. Which of the following will be detected by the spell check?
   (a) Duplicate words
   (b) Irregular capitalization
   (c) Both (a) and (b)
   (d) Neither (a) nor (b)

9. Which of the following is likely to be found in a custom dictionary?
   (a) Proper names
   (b) Words related to the user's particular application
   (c) Acronyms created by the user for his or her application
   (d) All of the above

10. Ted and Sally both use Word but on different computers. Both have written a letter to Dr. Joel Stutz and have run a spell check on their respective documents. Ted's program flags *Stutz* as a misspelling, whereas Sally's accepts it as written. Why?
    (a) The situation is impossible; that is, if they use identical word processing programs they should get identical results
    (b) Ted has added *Stutz* to his custom dictionary
    (c) Sally has added *Stutz* to her custom dictionary
    (d) All of the above reasons are equally likely as a cause of the problem

11. The spell check will do all of the following *except:*
    (a) Flag properly spelled words used incorrectly
    (b) Identify misspelled words
    (c) Accept (as correctly spelled) words found in the custom dictionary
    (d) Suggest alternatives to misspellings it identifies

12. The AutoCorrect feature will:
    (a) Correct errors in capitalization as they occur during typing
    (b) Expand user-defined abbreviations as the entries are typed
    (c) Both (a) and (b)
    (d) Neither (a) nor (b)

13. When does the Save As dialog box appear?
    (a) The first time a file is saved using either the Save or Save As commands
    (b) Every time a file is saved by clicking the Save button on the Standard toolbar
    (c) Both (a) and (b)
    (d) Neither (a) nor (b)

14. Which of the following is true about the thesaurus?

    (a) It recognizes different forms of a word; for example, a noun and a verb

    (b) It provides antonyms as well as synonyms

    (c) Both (a) and (b)

    (d) Neither (a) nor (b)

15. The grammar check:

    (a) Implements different rules for casual and business writing

    (b) Will detect all subtleties in the English language

    (c) Is always run in conjunction with a spell check

    (d) All of the above

ANSWERS

1. c	**6.** a	**11.** a
2. b	**7.** a	**12.** c
3. d	**8.** c	**13.** a
4. a	**9.** d	**14.** c
5. c	**10.** c	**15.** a

PRACTICE WITH MICROSOFT WORD

1. Retrieve the *Chapter1 Practice 1* document shown in Figure 1.15 from the Exploring Word folder, then make the following changes:

    a. Select the text *Your name* and replace it with your name.

    b. Replace *May 31, 1999* with the current date.

    c. Insert the phrase *one or* in line 2 so that the text reads . . . *one or more characters than currently exist.*

    d. Delete the word *And* from sentence four in line 5, then change the w in *when* to a capital letter to begin the sentence.

    e. Change the phrase *most efficient* to *best.*

    f. Place the insertion point at the end of sentence 2, make sure you are in the insert mode, then add the following sentence: *The insert mode adds characters at the insertion point while moving existing text to the right in order to make room for the new text.*

    g. Place the insertion point at the end of the last sentence, press the enter key twice in a row, then enter the following text: *There are several keys that function as toggle switches of which you should be aware. The Caps Lock key toggles between upper- and lowercase letters, and the Num Lock key alternates between typing numbers and using the arrow keys.*

    h. Save the revised document, then print it and submit it to your instructor.

2. Select-Then-Do: Formatting is not covered until Chapter 2, but we think you are ready to try your hand at basic formatting now. Most formatting operations are done in the context of select-then-do as described in the document in Figure 1.16. You select the text you want to format, then you execute the appropriate formatting command, most easily by clicking the appropriate button on the Formatting toolbar. The function of each button should be apparent from its icon, but you can simply point to a button to display a ScreenTip that is indicative of the button's function.

To: Your name

From: Robert Grauer and Maryann Barber

Subject: Microsoft® Word 2000

Date: May 31, 1999

This is just a short note to help you get acquainted with the insertion and replacement modes in Word for Windows. When the editing to be done results in more characters than currently exist, you want to be in the insertion mode when making the change. On the other hand, when the editing to be done contains the same or fewer characters, the replacement mode is best. And when replacing characters, it is most efficient to use the mouse to select the characters to be deleted and then just type the new characters; the selected characters are automatically deleted and the new characters typed take their place.

FIGURE 1.15   Editing Text (Exercise 1)

An unformatted version of the document in Figure 1.16 exists on the data disk as *Chapter1 Practice 2.* Open the document, then format it to match the completed version in Figure 1.16. Just select the text to format, then click the appropriate button. We changed type size in the original document to 24 points for the title and 12 points for text in the document itself. Be sure to add your name and date as shown in the figure, then submit the completed document to your instructor.

3. Your Background: Write a short description of your computer background similar to the document in Figure 1.17. The document should be in the form of a note from student to instructor that describes your background and should mention any previous knowledge of computers you have, prior computer courses you have taken, your objectives for this course, and so on. Indicate whether you own a PC, whether you have access to one at work, and/or whether you are considering purchase. Include any other information about yourself and/or your computer-related background.

Place your name somewhere in the document in boldface italics. We would also like you to use boldface and italics to emphasize the components of any computer system you describe. Use any font or point size you like. Note, too, the last paragraph, which asks you to print the summary statistics for the document when you submit the assignment to your instructor. (Use the tip on Document Properties on page 25 to print the total editing time and other information about your document.)

4. The Cover Page: Create a cover page that you can use for your assignments this semester. Your cover page should be similar to the one in Figure 1.18 with respect to content and should include the title of the assignment, your name, course information, and date. The formatting is up to you. Print the completed cover page and submit it to your instructor for inclusion in a class contest to judge the most innovative design.

Select-Then-Do

Many operations in Word are executed as select-then-do operations. You first select a block of text, and then you issue a command that will affect the selected text. You may select the text in many different ways, the most basic of which is to click and drag over the desired characters. You may also take one of many shortcuts, which include double clicking on a word, pressing Ctrl as you click a sentence, and triple clicking on a paragraph.

Once text is selected, you may then delete it, **boldface** or *italicize* it, or even change its color. You may move it or copy it to another location in the same or a different document. You can highlight it, underline, or even check its spelling. Then, depending on whether or not you like what you have done, you may undo it, redo it, and/or repeat it on subsequently selected text.

Jessica Kinzer
March 1, 1999

FIGURE 1.16   Select-Then-Do (Exercise 2)

The Computer and Me

My name is Jessica Kinzer and I am a complete novice when it comes to computers. I did not take a computer course in high school and this is my first semester at the University of Miami. My family does not own a computer, nor have I had the opportunity to use one at work. So when it comes to beginners, I am a beginner's beginner. I am looking forward to taking this course, as I have heard that it will truly make me computer literate. I know that I desperately need computer skills not only when I enter the job market, to but to survive my four years here as well. I am looking forward to learning Word, Excel, and PowerPoint and I hope that I can pick up some Internet skills as well.

I did not buy a computer before I came to school as I wanted to see what type of system I would be using for my classes. After my first few weeks in class, I think that I would like to buy a 400 *MZ Pentium II* machine with *64MB RAM* and a *10 GB hard drive*. I would like a *DVD CD-ROM* and a *sound card* (with *speakers*, of course). I also would like to get a high-speed *modem* and a *laser printer*. Now, if only I had the money.

This document did not take long at all to create as you can see by the summary statistics that are printed on the next page. I think that I will really enjoy this class.

Jessica Kinzer
March 2, 1999

FIGURE 1.17   Your Computer Background (Exercise 3)

Exploring Word Assignment

Jessica Kinzer
CIS 120
March 2, 1999

FIGURE 1.18   The Cover Page (Exercise 4)

5. Proofing a Document: Figure 1.19 contains the draft version of the *Chapter 1 Practice 5* document contained on the data disk.

   a. Proofread the document and circle any mistakes in spelling, grammar, capitalization, or punctuation.

   b. Open the document in Word and run the spell check. Did Word catch any mistakes you missed? Did you find any errors that were missed by the program?

   c. Use the thesaurus to come up with alternative words for *document,* which appears entirely too often within the paragraph.

   d. Run the grammar check on the revised document. Did the program catch any grammatical errors you missed? Did you find any mistakes that were missed by the program?

   e. Add a short paragraph with your opinion of the spelling and grammar check.

   f. Add your name to the revised document, save it, print it, and submit the completed document to your instructor.

6. Webster Online: Figure 1.20 shows our favorite online dictionary. We have erased the address, however, or else the problem would be too easy. Thus, you have to search the Web to look for our dictionary or its equivalent. Once you locate a dictionary, enter the word you want to look up (*oxymoron,* for example), then press the Look Up Word button to display the definition in Figure 1.21. This is truly an interactive dictionary because most words in it are created as hyperlinks, which in turn will lead you to other definitions. Use the dictionary to look up the meaning of the word *palindrome.* How many examples of oxymorons and palindromes can you think of?

The Grammar Check

All documents should be thoroughly proofed before they be printed and distributed. This means that documents, at a minimum should be spell cheked, grammar cheked,, and proof read by the author. A documents that has spelling errors and/or grammatical errors makes the Author look unprofessional and illiterate and their is nothing worse than allowing a first impression too be won that makes you appear slopy and disinterested, and a document full or of misteakes will do exactly that. Alot of people do not realize how damaging a bad first impression could be, and documents full of misteakes has cost people opportunities that they trained and prepared many years for.

Microsoft Word includes an automated grammar check that will detect many, but certainly not all, errors as the previous paragraph demonstrates. Unlike the spell check, the grammar check is subjective, and what seems appropriate to you may be objectionable to someone else. The English language is just to complicated for the grammar check to detect every error, or even most errors. Hence, there is no substitute for carefully proof reading a document your self. Hence there is no substitute for carefully proof reading a document your self.

FIGURE 1.19   Proofing a Document (Exercise 5)

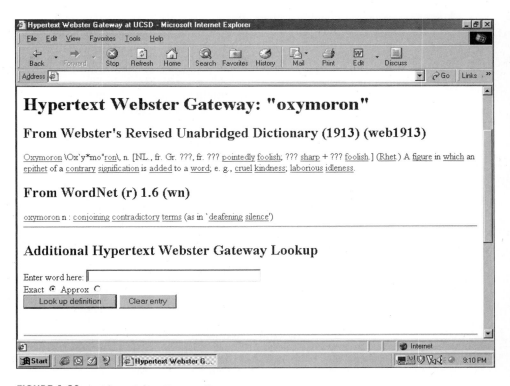

FIGURE 1.20   Webster Online (Exercise 6)

CASE STUDIES

Companion Web Sites

A Companion Web site (or online study guide) accompanies each book in the *Exploring Microsoft Office 2000* series. Go to the Exploring Windows home page at www.prenhall.com/grauer, click the book to Office 2000, and click the Companion Web site tab at the top of the screen. Choose the appropriate text (Exploring Word 2000) and the chapter within the text (e.g., Chapter 1).

Each chapter contains a series of short-answer exercises (multiple-choice, true/false, and matching) to review the material in the chapter. You can take practice quizzes by yourself and/or e-mail the results to your instructor. You can try the essay questions for additional practice and engage in online chat sessions. We hope you will find the online guide to be a valuable resource.

It's a Mess

Newcomers to word processing quickly learn the concept of word wrap and the distinction between hard and soft returns. This lesson was lost, however, on your friend who created the *Please Help Me* document on the data disk. The first several sentences were entered without any hard returns at all, whereas the opposite problem exists toward the end of the document. This is a good friend, and her paper is due in one hour. Please help.

Planning for Disaster

Do you have a backup strategy? Do you even know what a backup strategy is? You should learn, because sooner or later you will wish you had one. You will erase a file, be unable to read from a floppy disk, or worse yet suffer a hardware failure in which you are unable to access the hard drive. The problem always seems to occur the night before an assignment is due. The ultimate disaster is the disappearance of your computer, by theft or natural disaster (e.g., Hurricane Andrew). Describe in 250 words or less the backup strategy you plan to implement in conjunction with your work in this class.

A Letter Home

You really like this course and want very much to have your own computer, but you're strapped for cash and have decided to ask your parents for help. Write a one-page letter describing the advantages of having your own system and how it will help you in school. Tell your parents what the system will cost, and that you can save money by buying through the mail. Describe the configuration you intend to buy (don't forget to include the price of software) and then provide prices from at least three different companies. Cut out the advertisements and include them in your letter. Bring your material to class and compare your research with that of your classmates.

Computer Magazines

A subscription to a computer magazine should be given serious consideration if you intend to stay abreast in a rapidly changing field. The reviews on new products are especially helpful and you will appreciate the advertisements should you need to buy. Go to the library or a newsstand and obtain a magazine that appeals to you, then write a brief review of the magazine for class. Devote at least one paragraph to an article or other item you found useful.

A Junior Year Abroad

How lucky can you get? You are spending the second half of your junior year in Paris. The problem is you will have to submit your work in French, and the English version of Microsoft Word won't do. Is there a foreign-language version available? What about the dictionary and thesaurus? How do you enter the accented characters, which occur so frequently? You are leaving in two months, so you'd better get busy. What are your options? *Bon voyage!*

The Writer's Reference

The chapter discussed the use of a spell check, thesaurus, and grammar check, but many other resources are available. The Web contains a host of sites with additional resources that are invaluable to the writer. You can find Shakespeare online, as well as Bartlett's quotations. You can also find Webster's dictionary as well as a dictionary of acronyms. One way to find these resources is to click the Search button in Internet Explorer, then scroll down the page to the Writer's Reference section. You can also go to the address directly (home.microsoft.com/access. allinone.asp). Explore one or more of these resources, then write a short note to your instructor to summarize your findings.

Microsoft Online

Help for Microsoft Word is available from a variety of sources. You can consult the Office Assistant, or you can pull down the Help menu to display the Help Contents and Index. Both techniques were illustrated in the chapter. In addition, you can go to the Microsoft Web site to obtain more recent, and often more detailed, information. You will find the answers to the most frequently asked questions and you can access the same knowledge base used by Microsoft support engineers. Experiment with various sources of help, then submit a summary of your findings to your instructor. Try to differentiate among the various techniques and suggest the most appropriate use for each.

Changing Menus and Toolbars

Office 2000 implements one very significant change over previous versions of Office in that it displays a series of short menus that contain only basic commands. The additional commands are made visible by clicking the double arrow that appears at the bottom of the menu. New commands are added to the menu as they are used, and conversely, other commands are removed if they are not used. A similar strategy is followed for the Standard and Formatting toolbars that are displayed on a single row, and thus do not show all of the buttons at one time. The intent is to simplify Office 2000 for the new user by limiting the number of commands that are visible. The consequence, however, is that the individual is not exposed to new commands, and hence may not use Office to its full potential. Which set of menus do you prefer? How do you switch from one set to the other?

chapter 2

GAINING PROFICIENCY: EDITING AND FORMATTING

After reading this chapter you will be able to:

1. Define the select-then-do methodology; describe several shortcuts with the mouse and/or the keyboard to select text.
2. Move and copy text within a document; distinguish between the Windows clipboard and the Office clipboard.
3. Use the Find, Replace, and Go To commands to substitute one character string for another.
4. Define scrolling; scroll to the beginning and end of a document.
5. Distinguish between the Normal and Print Layout views; state how to change the view and/or magnification of a document.
6. Define typography; distinguish between a serif and a sans serif typeface; use the Format Font command to change the font and/or type size.
7. Use the Format Paragraph command to change line spacing, alignment, tabs, and indents, and to control pagination.
8. Use the Borders and Shading command to box and shade text.
9. Describe the Undo and Redo commands and how they are related to one another.
10. Use the Page Setup command to change the margins and/or orientation; differentiate between a soft and a hard page break.
11. Enter and edit text in columns; change the column structure of a document through section formatting.

The previous chapter taught you the basics of Microsoft Word and enabled you to create and print a simple document. The present chapter significantly extends your capabilities, by presenting a variety of commands to change the contents and appearance of a document. These operations are known as editing and formatting, respectively.

You will learn how to move and copy text within a document and how to find and replace one character string with another. You will also learn the basics of typography and be able to switch between the different fonts included within Windows. You will be able to change alignment, indentation, line spacing, margins, and page orientation. All of these commands are used in three hands-on exercises, which require your participation at the computer, and which are the very essence of the chapter.

As you read the chapter, realize that there are many different ways to accomplish the same task and that it would be impossible to cover them all. Our approach is to present the overall concepts and suggest the ways we think are most appropriate at the time we introduce the material. We also offer numerous shortcuts in the form of boxed tips that appear throughout the chapter and urge you to explore further on your own. It is not necessary for you to memorize anything as online help is always available. Be flexible and willing to experiment.

WRITE NOW, EDIT LATER

You write a sentence, then change it, and change it again, and one hour later you've produced a single paragraph. It happens to every writer—you stare at a blank screen and flashing cursor and are unable to write. The best solution is to brainstorm and write down anything that pops into your head, and to keep on writing. Don't worry about typos or spelling errors because you can fix them later. Above all, resist the temptation to continually edit the few words you've written because overediting will drain the life out of what you are writing. The important thing is to get your ideas on paper.

SELECT-THEN-DO

Many operations in Word take place within the context of a *select-then-do* methodology; that is, you select a block of text, then you execute the command to operate on that text. The most basic way to select text is by dragging the mouse; that is, click at the beginning of the selection, press and hold the left mouse button as you move to the end of the selection, then release the mouse.

There are, however, a variety of shortcuts to facilitate the process; for example, double click anywhere within a word to select the word, or press the Ctrl key and click the mouse anywhere within a sentence to select the sentence. Additional shortcuts are presented in each of the hands-on exercises, at which point you will have many opportunities to practice selecting text.

Selected text is affected by any subsequent operation; for example, clicking the Bold or Italic button changes the selected text to boldface or italics, respectively. You can also drag the selected text to a new location, press the Del key to erase the selected text, or execute any other editing or formatting command. The text continues to be selected until you click elsewhere in the document.

INSERT THE DATE AND TIME

Most documents include the date and time they were created. Pull down the Insert menu, select the Date and Time command to display the Date and Time dialog box, then choose a format. Check the box to update the date automatically if you want your document to reflect the date on which it is opened or clear the box to retain the date on which the document was created. See exercise seven at the end of the chapter.

MOVING AND COPYING TEXT

The ability to move and/or copy text is essential in order to develop any degree of proficiency in editing. A move operation removes the text from its current location and places it elsewhere in the same (or even a different) document; a copy operation retains the text in its present location and places a duplicate elsewhere. Either operation can be accomplished using the Windows clipboard and a combination of the *Cut, Copy,* and *Paste commands.*

The *Windows clipboard* is a temporary storage area available to any Windows application. Selected text is cut or copied from a document and placed onto the clipboard from where it can be pasted to a new location(s). A move requires that you select the text and execute a Cut command to remove the text from the document and place it on the clipboard. You then move the insertion point to the new location and paste the text from the clipboard into that location. A copy operation necessitates the same steps except that a Copy command is executed rather than a cut, leaving the selected text in its original location as well as placing a copy on the clipboard.

The Cut, Copy, and Paste commands are found in the Edit menu, or alternatively, can be executed by clicking the appropriate buttons on the Standard toolbar. The contents of the Windows clipboard are replaced by each subsequent Cut or Copy command, but are unaffected by the Paste command. The contents of the clipboard can be pasted into multiple locations in the same or different documents.

Office 2000 introduces its own clipboard that enables you to collect and paste multiple items. The *Office clipboard* differs from the Windows clipboard in that the contents of each successive Copy command are added to the clipboard. Thus, you could copy the first paragraph of a document to the Office clipboard, then copy (add) a bulleted list in the middle of the document to the Office clipboard, and finally copy (add) the last paragraph (three items in all) to the Office clipboard. You could then go to another place in the document or to a different document altogether, and paste the contents of the Office clipboard (three separate items) with a single command.

Selected text is copied automatically to the Office clipboard regardless of whether you use the Copy command in the Edit menu, the Copy button on the Standard toolbar, or the Ctrl+C shortcut. You must, however, use the Clipboard toolbar to paste items from the Office clipboard into a document.

UNDO, REDO, AND REPEAT COMMANDS

The *Undo command* was introduced in Chapter 1, but it is repeated here because it is so valuable. The command is executed from the Edit menu or by clicking the Undo button on the Standard toolbar. Word enables you to undo multiple changes to a document. You just click the down arrow next to the Undo button on the Standard toolbar to display a reverse-order list of your previous commands, then you click the command you want to undo, which also undoes all of the preceding commands. Undoing the fifth command in the list, for example, will also undo the preceding four commands.

The *Redo command* redoes (reverses) the last command that was undone. As with the Undo command, the Redo command redoes all of the previous commands prior to the command you select. Redoing the fifth command in the list, for example, will also redo the preceding four commands. The Undo and Redo commands work in conjunction with one another; that is, every time a command is undone it can be redone at a later time. The *Repeat command* does what its name implies and repeats the last action or command. It is executed from the Edit menu.

FIND, REPLACE, AND GO TO COMMANDS

The Find, Replace, and Go To commands share a common dialog box with different tabs for each command as shown in Figure 2.1. The **Find command** locates one or more occurrences of specific text (e.g., a word or phrase). The **Replace command** goes one step further in that it locates the text, and then enables you to optionally replace (one or more occurrences of) that text with different text. The **Go To command** goes directly to a specific place (e.g., a specific page) in the document.

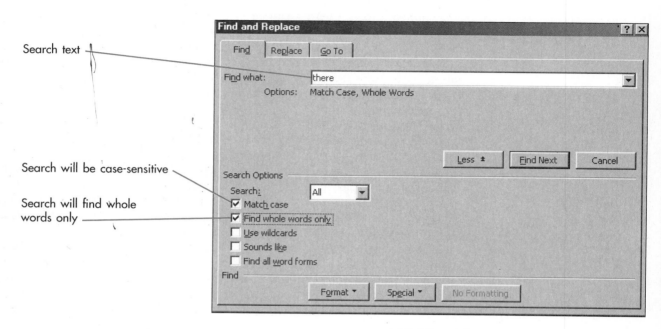

(a) Find Command

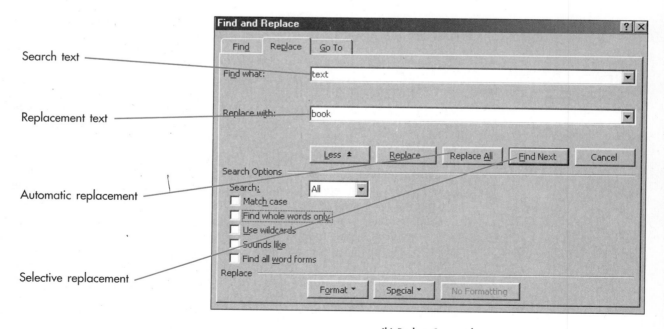

(b) Replace Command

FIGURE 2.1   The Find, Replace, Go To Commands

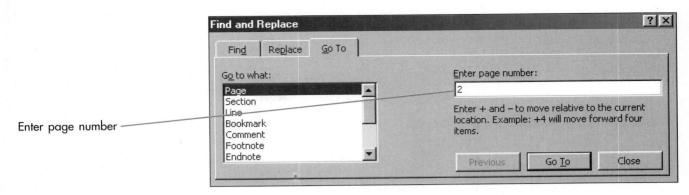

Enter page number

(c) Go To Command

FIGURE 2.1   The Find, Replace, and Go To Commands (continued)

The search in both the Find and Replace commands is case-sensitive or case-insensitive. A ***case-sensitive search*** (where Match Case is selected as in Figure 2.1a) matches not only the text, but also the use of upper- and lowercase letters. Thus, *There* is different from *there,* and a search on one will not identify the other. A ***case-insensitive search*** (where Match Case is *not* as selected in Figure 2.1b) is just the opposite and finds both *There* and *there.* A search may also specify ***whole words only*** to identify *there,* but not *therefore* or *thereby.* And finally, the search and replacement text can also specify different numbers of characters; for example, you could replace *16* with *sixteen.*

The Replace command in Figure 2.1b implements either ***selective replacement,*** which lets you examine each occurrence of the character string in context and decide whether to replace it, or ***automatic replacement,*** where the substitution is made automatically. Selective replacement is implemented by clicking the Find Next command button, then clicking (or not clicking) the Replace button to make the substitution. Automatic replacement (through the entire document) is implemented by clicking the Replace All button. This often produces unintended consequences and is not recommended; for example, if you substitute the word *text* for *book,* the phrase *text book* would become *text text,* which is not what you had in mind.

The Find and Replace commands can include formatting and/or special characters. You can, for example, change all italicized text to boldface, or you can change five consecutive spaces to a tab character. You can also use special characters in the character string such as the "any character" (consisting of ^?). For example, to find all four-letter words that begin with "f" and end with "l" (such as *fall, fill,* or *fail*), search for f^?^?l. (The question mark stands for any character, just like a wild card in a card game.) You can also search for all forms of a word; for example, if you specify *am,* it will also find *is* and *are.* You can even search for a word based on how it sounds. When searching for *Marion,* for example, check the Sounds Like check box, and the search will find both *Marion* and *Marian.*

SCROLLING

Scrolling occurs when a document is too large to be seen in its entirety. Figure 2.2a displays a large printed document, only part of which is visible on the screen as illustrated in Figure 2.2b. In order to see a different portion of the document, you need to scroll, whereby new lines will be brought into view as the old lines disappear.

To: Our Students
From: Robert Grauer and Maryann Barber

Welcome to the wonderful world of word processing and desktop publishing. Over the next several chapters we will build a foundation in the basics of Microsoft Word, then teach you to format specialized documents, create professional looking tables and charts, publish well-designed newsletters, and create Web pages. Before you know it, you will be a word processing and desktop publishing wizard!

The first chapter presented the basics of word processing and showed you how to create a simple document. You learned how to insert, replace, and/or delete text. This chapter will teach you about fonts and special effects (such as **boldfacing** and *italicizing*) and how to use them effectively — how too little is better than too much.

You will go on to experiment with margins, tab stops, line spacing, and justification, learning first to format simple documents and then going on to longer, more complex ones. It is with the latter that we explore headers and footers, page numbering, widows and orphans (yes, we really did mean widows and orphans). It is here that we bring in graphics, working with newspaper-type columns, and the elements of a good page design. And without question, we will introduce the tools that make life so much easier (and your writing so much more impressive) — the Spell Check, Grammar Check, Thesaurus, and Styles.

If you are wondering what all these things are, read on in the text and proceed with the hands-on exercises. We will show you how to create a simple newsletter, and then improve it by adding graphics, fonts, and WordArt. You will create a simple calendar using the Tables feature, and then create more intricate forms that will rival anything you have seen. You will learn how to create a résumé with your beginner's skills, and then make it look like so much more with your intermediate (even advanced) skills. You will learn how to download resources from the Internet and how to create your own Web page. Last, but not least, run a mail merge to produce the cover letters that will accompany your resume as it is mailed to companies across the United States (and even the world).

It is up to you to practice for it is only through working at the computer, that you will learn what you need to know. Experiment and don't be afraid to make mistakes. Practice and practice some more.

Our goal is for you to learn and to enjoy what you are learning. We have great confidence in you, and in our ability to help you discover what you can do. Visit the home page for the Exploring Windows series. You can also send us e-mail. Bob's address is rgrauer@sba.miam.edu. Maryann's address is mbarber@sba.miami.edu. As you read the last sentence, notice that Word 2000 is Web-enabled and that the Internet and e-mail references appear as hyperlinks in this document. Thus, you can click the address of our home page from within Word, then view the page immediately, provided you have an Internet connection. You can also click the e-mail address to open your mail program, provided it has been configured correctly.

We look forward to hearing from you and hope that you will like our textbook. You are about to embark on a wonderful journey toward computer literacy. Be patient and inquisitive.

(a) Printed Document

FIGURE 2.2   Scrolling

Click to scroll up in document ————

Scroll box indicates you are
viewing middle portion of
document ————

Hyperlink ————

Click e-mail address to send a
message ————

Click to scroll down in document ————

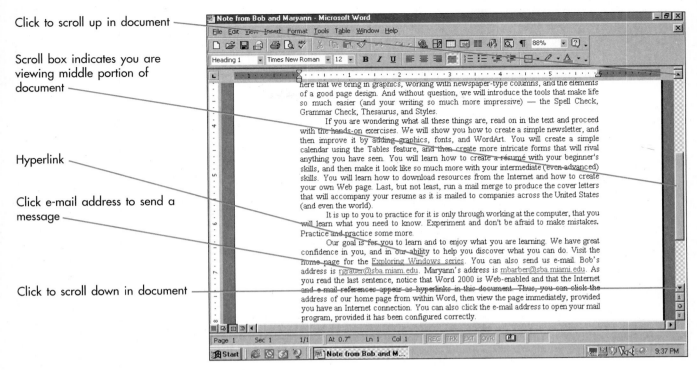

(b) Screen Display

FIGURE 2.2   Scrolling (continued)

Scrolling comes about automatically as you reach the bottom of the screen. Entering a new line of text, clicking on the down arrow within the scroll bar, or pressing the down arrow key brings a new line into view at the bottom of the screen and simultaneously removes a line at the top. (The process is reversed at the top of the screen.)

Scrolling can be done with either the mouse or the keyboard. Scrolling with the mouse (e.g., clicking the down arrow in the scroll bar) changes what is displayed on the screen, but does not move the insertion point, so that you must click the mouse after scrolling prior to entering the text at the new location. Scrolling with the keyboard, however (e.g., pressing Ctrl+Home or Ctrl+End to move to the beginning or end of a document, respectively), changes what is displayed on the screen as well as the location of the insertion point, and you can begin typing immediately.

Scrolling occurs most often in a vertical direction as shown in Figure 2.2. It can also occur horizontally, when the length of a line in a document exceeds the number of characters that can be displayed horizontally on the screen.

IT'S WEB-ENABLED

Every document in Office 2000 is Web-enabled, which means that Internet and e-mail references appear as hyperlinks within a document. Thus you can click the address of any Web page from within Word to display the page, provided you have an Internet connection. You can also click the e-mail address to open your mail program, provided it has been configured correctly.

The ***View menu*** provides different views of a document. Each view can be displayed at different magnifications, which in turn determine the amount of scrolling necessary to see remote parts of a document.

The ***Normal view*** is the default view and it provides the fastest way to enter text. The ***Print Layout*** view more closely resembles the printed document and displays the top and bottom margins, headers and footers, page numbers, graphics, and other features that do not appear in the Normal view. The Normal view tends to be faster because Word spends less time formatting the display.

The ***Zoom command*** displays the document on the screen at different magnifications; for example, 75%, 100%, or 200%. (The Zoom command does not affect the size of the text on the printed page.) A Zoom percentage (magnification) of 100% displays the document in the approximate size of the text on the printed page. You can increase the percentage to 200% to make the characters appear larger. You can also decrease the magnification to 75% to see more of the document at one time.

Word will automatically determine the magnification if you select one of four additional Zoom options—Page Width, Text Width, Whole Page, or Many Pages (Whole Page and Many Pages are available only in the Print Layout view). Figure 2.3a, for example, displays a two-page document in Print Layout view. Figure 2.3b shows the corresponding settings in the Zoom command. (The 37% magnification is determined automatically once you specify the number of pages as shown in the figure.)

Zoom button

Two pages are displayed

Print Layout View button

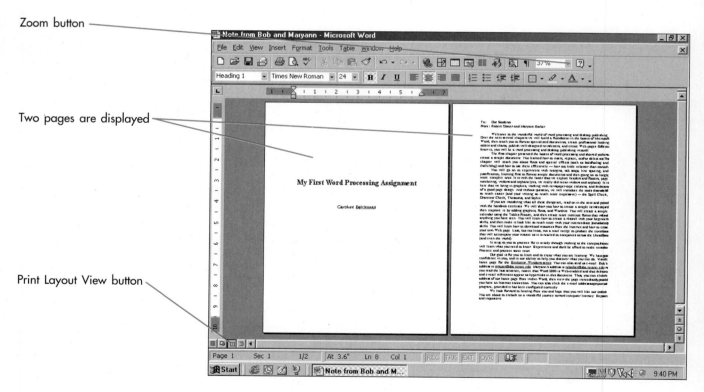

(a) Page Layout View

FIGURE 2.3   View Menu and Zoom Command

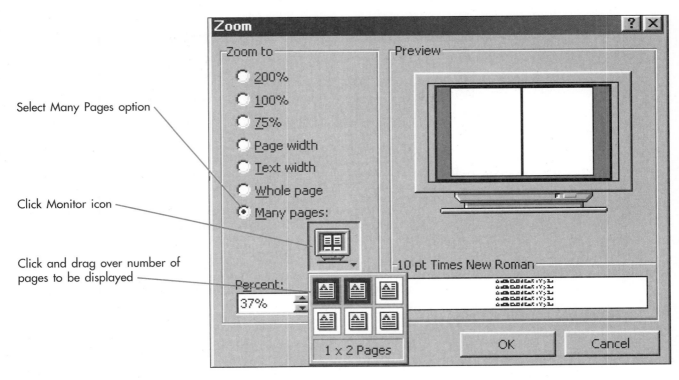

Select Many Pages option

Click Monitor icon

Click and drag over number of pages to be displayed

(b) Zoom Command

FIGURE 2.3   View Menu and Zoom Command (continued)

HANDS-ON EXERCISE 1

Editing a Document

Objective: To edit an existing document; to change the view and magnification of a document; to scroll through a document. To use the Find and Replace commands; to move and copy text using the clipboard and the drag-and-drop facility. Use Figure 2.4 as a guide in the exercise.

STEP 1: The View Menu

➤ Start Word as described in the hands-on exercises from Chapter 1. Pull down the **File menu** and click **Open** (or click the **Open button** on the toolbar).

- Click the **drop-down arrow** on the Look In list box. Click the appropriate drive, drive C or drive A, depending on the location of your data.

- Double click the **Exploring Word folder** to make it the active folder (the folder in which you will save the document).

- Scroll in the Name list box (if necessary) until you can click the **Note from Bob and Maryann** to select this document. Double click the **document icon** or click the **Open command button** to open the file.

➤ The document should appear on the screen as shown in Figure 2.4a.

➤ Change to the Print Layout view at Page Width magnification:

- Pull down the **View menu** and click **Print Layout** (or click the **Print Layout View button** above the status bar) as shown in Figure 2.4a.

- Click the **down arrow** in the Zoom box to change to **Page Width.**

Zoom box

Print Layout View button

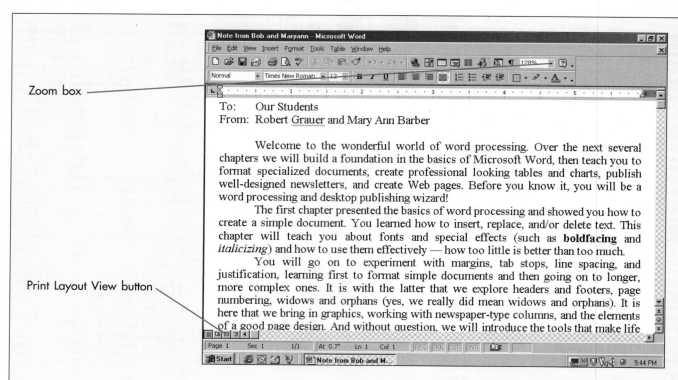

To: Our Students
From: Robert Grauer and Mary Ann Barber

Welcome to the wonderful world of word processing. Over the next several chapters we will build a foundation in the basics of Microsoft Word, then teach you to format specialized documents, create professional looking tables and charts, publish well-designed newsletters, and create Web pages. Before you know it, you will be a word processing and desktop publishing wizard!

The first chapter presented the basics of word processing and showed you how to create a simple document. You learned how to insert, replace, and/or delete text. This chapter will teach you about fonts and special effects (such as **boldfacing** and *italicizing*) and how to use them effectively — how too little is better than too much.

You will go on to experiment with margins, tab stops, line spacing, and justification, learning first to format simple documents and then going on to longer, more complex ones. It is with the latter that we explore headers and footers, page numbering, widows and orphans (yes, we really did mean widows and orphans). It is here that we bring in graphics, working with newspaper-type columns, and the elements of a good page design. And without question, we will introduce the tools that make life

(a) The View Menu (step 1)

FIGURE 2.4   Hands-on Exercise 1

➤ Click and drag the mouse to select the phrase **Our Students,** which appears at the beginning of the document. Type your name to replace the selected text.

➤ Pull down the **File menu,** click the **Save As** command, then save the document as **Modified Note.** (This creates a second copy of the document.)

CREATE A BACKUP COPY

Microsoft Word enables you to automatically create a backup copy of a document in conjunction with the Save command. Pull down the Tools menu, click the Options button, click the Save tab, then check the box to always create a backup copy. The next time you save the file, the previously saved version is renamed "Backup of document" after which the document in memory is saved as the current version. In other words, the disk will contain the two most recent versions of the document.

STEP 2: Scrolling

➤ Click and drag the **scroll box** within the vertical scroll bar to scroll to the end of the document as shown in Figure 2.4b. Click immediately before the period at the end of the last sentence.

➤ Type a **comma** and a space, then insert the phrase **but most of all, enjoy.**

➤ Drag the **scroll box** to the top of the scroll bar to get back to the beginning of the document. Click immediately before the period ending the first sentence, press the **space bar,** then add the phrase **and desktop publishing.**

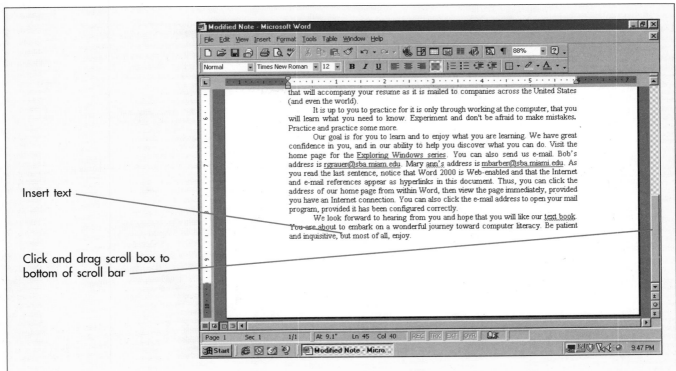

Insert text

Click and drag scroll box to bottom of scroll bar

(b) Scrolling (step 2)

FIGURE 2.4   Hands-on Exercise 1 (continued)

THE MOUSE AND THE SCROLL BAR

Scroll quickly through a document by clicking above or below the scroll box to scroll up or down an entire screen. Move to the top, bottom, or an approximate position within a document by dragging the scroll box to the corresponding position in the scroll bar; for example, dragging the scroll box to the middle of the bar moves the mouse pointer to the middle of the document. Scrolling with the mouse does not change the location of the insertion point, however, and thus you must click the mouse at the new location prior to entering text at that location.

STEP 3: The Replace Command

➤ Press **Ctrl+Home** to move to the beginning of the document. Pull down the **Edit menu.** Click **Replace** to produce the dialog box of Figure 2.4c. Click the **More button** to display the available options.

  • Type **text** in the Find what text box.

  • Press the **Tab key.** Type **book** in the Replace with text box.

➤ Click the **Find Next button** to find the first occurrence of the word *text*. The dialog box remains on the screen and the first occurrence of *text* is selected. This is *not* an appropriate substitution; that is, you should not substitute *book* for *text* at this point.

➤ Click the **Find Next button** to move to the next occurrence without making the replacement. This time the substitution is appropriate.

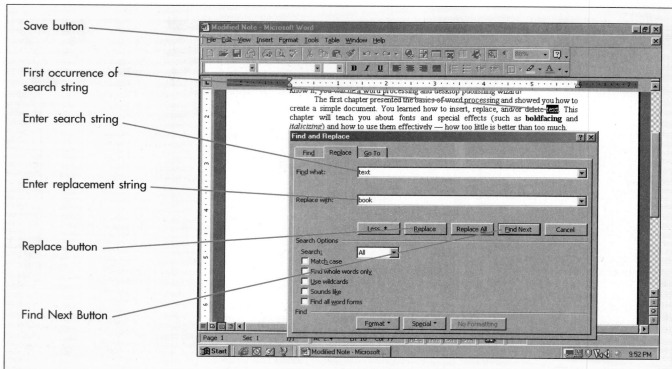

Save button

First occurrence of
search string

Enter search string

Enter replacement string

Replace button

Find Next Button

(c) The Replace Command (step 3)

FIGURE 2.4   Hands-on Exercise 1 (continued)

➤ Click **Replace** to make the change and automatically move to the next occurrence where the substitution is again inappropriate. Click **Find Next** a final time. Word will indicate that it has finished searching the document. Click **OK.**

➤ Change the Find and Replace strings to **Mary Ann** and **Maryann,** respectively. Click the **Replace All** button to make the substitution globally without confirmation. Word will indicate that it has finished searching and that two replacements were made. Click **OK.**

➤ Click the **Close command button** to close the dialog box. Click the **Save button** to save the document. Scroll through the document to review your changes.

SCROLLING WITH THE KEYBOARD

Press Ctrl+Home and Ctrl+End to move to the beginning and end of a document, respectively. Press Home and End to move to the beginning and end of a line. Press PgUp or PgDn to scroll one screen in the indicated direction. The advantage of scrolling via the keyboard (instead of the mouse) is that the location of the insertion point changes automatically and you can begin typing immediately.

STEP 4: The Windows Clipboard

➤ Press **PgDn** to scroll toward the end of the document until you come to the paragraph beginning **It is up to you.** Select the sentence **Practice and practice some more** by dragging the mouse over the sentence. (Be sure to include the period.) The sentence will be selected as shown in Figure 2.4d.

➤ Pull down the **Edit menu** and click the **Copy command** or click the **Copy button** on the Standard toolbar.

➤ Press **Ctrl+End** to scroll to the end of the document. Press the **space bar.** Pull down the **Edit menu** and click the **Paste command** (or click the **Paste button** on the Standard toolbar).

➤ Move the insertion point to the end of the first paragraph (following the exclamation point after the word *wizard*). Press the **space bar.** Click the **Paste button** on the Standard toolbar to paste the sentence a second time.

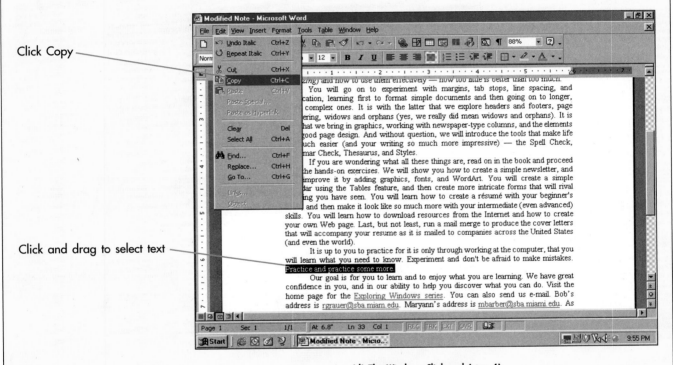

(d) The Windows Clipboard (step 4)

FIGURE 2.4   Hands-on Exercise 1 (continued)

CUT, COPY, AND PASTE

Ctrl+X, Ctrl+C, and Ctrl+V are keyboard shortcuts to cut, copy, and paste, respectively. (The shortcuts are easier to remember when you realize that the operative letters X, C, and V are next to each other at the bottom left side of the keyboard.) You can also use the Cut, Copy, and Paste buttons on the Standard toolbar.

STEP 5: The Office Clipboard

➤ Pull down the **View menu,** click (or point to) the **Toolbars command,** then click **Clipboard** to display the Clipboard toolbar as shown in Figure 2.4e.

➤ Scroll down in the document until you can click and drag to select the two sentences that indicate you can send us e-mail, and that contain our e-mail addresses. Click the **Copy button** to copy these sentences to the Office clipboard, which now contains the icons for two Word documents.

➤ Press **Ctrl+End** to move to the end of the document, press **enter** to begin a new paragraph, and press the **Tab key** to indent the paragraph. Click the **Paste All button** on the Office clipboard to paste both items at the end of the document. (You may have to add a space between the two sentences.)

➤ Close the Clipboard toolbar.

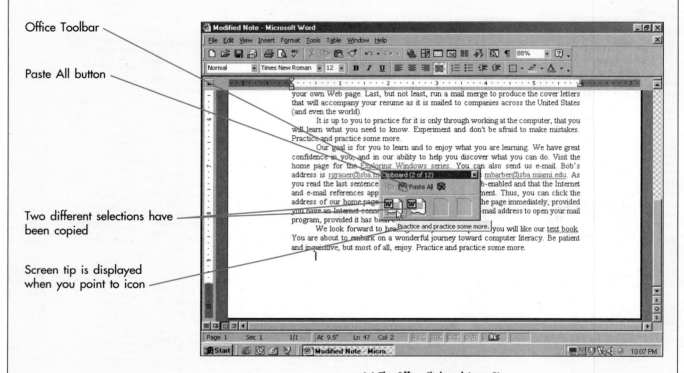

(e) The Office Clipboard (step 5)

FIGURE 2.4   Hands-on Exercise 1 (continued)

TWO DIFFERENT CLIPBOARDS

The Office clipboard is different from the Windows clipboard. Each successive copy operation adds an object to the Office clipboard (up to a maximum of 12 objects), whereas it replaces the contents of the Windows clipboard. Execution of the Paste command (via the Edit menu, Paste button, or Ctrl+V shortcut) pastes the contents of the Windows clipboard or the last item on the Office clipboard. The Office clipboard, however, lets you paste multiple objects. Note, too, that clearing the Office clipboard also clears the Windows clipboard.

STEP 6: Undo and Redo Commands

➤ Click the **drop-down arrow** next to the Undo button to display the previously executed actions as in Figure 2.4f. The list of actions corresponds to the editing commands you have issued since the start of the exercise. (Your list will be different from ours if you deviated from any instructions in the hands-on exercise.)

➤ Click **Paste** (the first command on the list) to undo the last editing command; the sentence asking you to send us e-mail disappears from the last paragraph.

➤ Click the **Undo** button a second time and the sentence, Practice and practice some more, disappears from the end of the first paragraph.

➤ Click the remaining steps on the undo list to retrace your steps through the exercise one command at a time. Alternatively, you can scroll to the bottom of the list and click the last command, which automatically undoes all of the preceding commands.

➤ Either way, when the undo list is empty, you will have the document as it existed at the start of the exercise.

➤ Click the **drop-down arrow** for the Redo command to display the list of commands you have undone.

➤ Click each command in sequence (or click the command at the bottom of the list) and you will restore the document.

➤ Save the document.

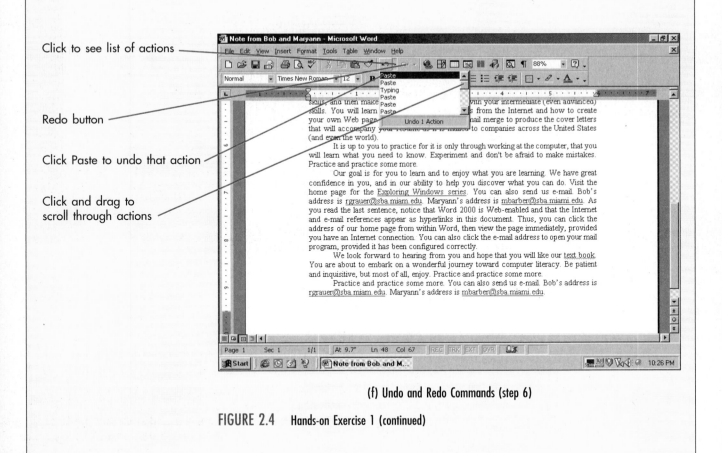

(f) Undo and Redo Commands (step 6)

FIGURE 2.4   Hands-on Exercise 1 (continued)

STEP 7: Drag and Drop

➤ Click and drag to select the phrase **format specialized documents** (including the comma and space) as shown in Figure 2.4g, then drag the phrase to its new location immediately before the word *and*. (A dotted vertical bar appears as you drag the text, to indicate its new location.)

➤ Release the mouse button to complete the move.

➤ Click the **drop-down arrow** for the Undo command; click **Move** to undo the move.

➤ To copy the selected text to the same location (instead of moving it), press and hold the **Ctrl key** as you drag the text to its new location. (A plus sign appears as you drag the text, to indicate it is being copied rather than moved.)

➤ Practice the drag-and-drop procedure several times until you are confident you can move and copy with precision.

➤ Click anywhere in the document to deselect the text. Save the document.

Print Preview button

Click and drag to select text

Drag to new location

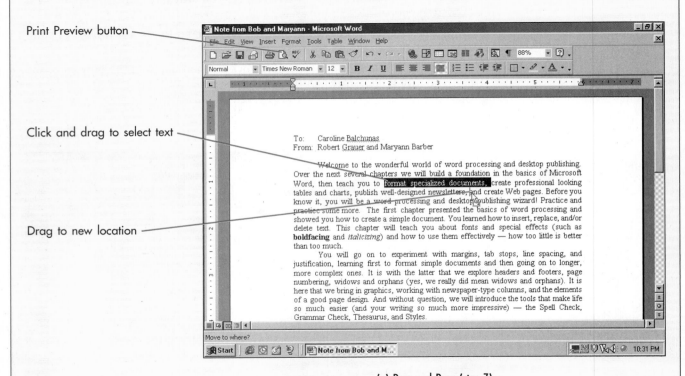

(g) Drag and Drop (step 7)

FIGURE 2.4   Hands-on Exercise 1 (continued)

STEP 8: The Print Preview Command

➤ Pull down the **File menu** and click **Print Preview** (or click the **Print Preview button** on the Standard toolbar). You should see your entire document as shown in Figure 2.4h.

➤ Check that the entire document fits on one page—that is, check that you can see all three lines in the last paragraph. If not, click the **Shrink to Fit button** on the toolbar to automatically change the font size in the document to force it on one page.

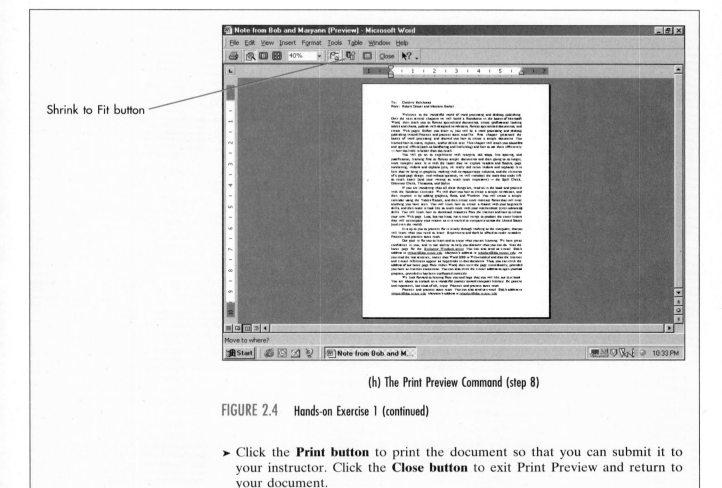

Shrink to Fit button

(h) The Print Preview Command (step 8)

FIGURE 2.4   Hands-on Exercise 1 (continued)

➤ Click the **Print button** to print the document so that you can submit it to your instructor. Click the **Close button** to exit Print Preview and return to your document.

➤ Close the document. Exit Word if you do not want to continue with the next exercise at this time.

TYPOGRAPHY

Typography is the process of selecting typefaces, type styles, and type sizes. The importance of these decisions is obvious, for the ultimate success of any document depends greatly on its appearance. Type should reinforce the message without calling attention to itself and should be consistent with the information you want to convey.

Typeface

A ***typeface*** or ***font*** is a complete set of characters (upper- and lowercase letters, numbers, punctuation marks, and special symbols). Figure 2.5 illustrates three typefaces—***Times New Roman, Arial,*** and ***Courier New***—that are supplied with Windows, and which in turn are accessible from any Windows application.

A definitive characteristic of any typeface is the presence or absence of tiny cross lines that end the main strokes of each letter. A ***serif*** typeface has these lines. A ***sans serif*** typeface (*sans* from the French for *without*) does not. Times New Roman and Courier New are examples of a serif typeface. Arial is a sans serif typeface.

Typography is the process of selecting typefaces, type styles, and type sizes. A serif typeface has tiny cross strokes that end the main strokes of each letter. A sans serif typeface does not have these strokes. Serif typefaces are typically used with large amounts of text. Sans serif typefaces are used for headings and limited amounts of text. A proportional typeface allocates space in accordance with the width of each character and is what you are used to seeing. A monospaced typeface uses the same amount of space for every character. A well-designed document will limit the number of typefaces so as not to overwhelm the reader.

(a) Times New Roman (serif and proportional)

Typography is the process of selecting typefaces, type styles, and type sizes. A serif typeface has tiny cross strokes that end the main strokes of each letter. A sans serif typeface does not have these strokes. Serif typefaces are typically used with large amounts of text. Sans serif typefaces are used for headings and limited amounts of text. A proportional typeface allocates space in accordance with the width of each character and is what you are used to seeing. A monospaced typeface uses the same amount of space for every character. A well-designed document will limit the number of typefaces so as not to overwhelm the reader.

(b) Arial (sans serif and proportional)

```
Typography is the process of selecting typefaces, type styles,
and type sizes. A serif typeface has tiny cross strokes that end
the main strokes of each letter. A sans serif typeface does not
have these strokes. Serif typefaces are typically used with large
amounts of text. Sans serif typefaces are used for headings and
limited amounts of text. A proportional typeface allocates space
in accordance with the width of each character and is what you
are used to seeing. A monospaced typeface uses the same amount of
space for every character. A well-designed document will limit
the number of typefaces so as not to overwhelm the reader.
```

(c) Courier New (serif and monospaced)

FIGURE 2.5   Typefaces

Serifs help the eye to connect one letter with the next and are generally used with large amounts of text. This book, for example, is set in a serif typeface. A sans serif typeface is more effective with smaller amounts of text and appears in headlines, corporate logos, airport signs, and so on.

A second characteristic of a typeface is whether it is monospaced or proportional. A *monospaced typeface* (e.g., Courier New) uses the same amount of space for every character regardless of its width. A *proportional typeface* (e.g., Times New Roman or Arial) allocates space according to the width of the character. Monospaced fonts are used in tables and financial projections where text must be precisely lined up, one character underneath the other. Proportional typefaces create a more professional appearance and are appropriate for most documents. Any typeface can be set in different *type styles* (such as regular, **bold,** or *italic*).

TYPOGRAPHY TIP—USE RESTRAINT

More is not better, especially in the case of too many typefaces and styles, which produce cluttered documents that impress no one. Try to limit yourself to a maximum of two typefaces per document, but choose multiple sizes and/or styles within those typefaces. Use boldface or italics for emphasis; but do so in moderation, because if you emphasize too many elements, the effect is lost.

Type Size

Type size is a vertical measurement and is specified in points. One *point* is equal to $1/72$ of an inch; that is, there are 72 points to the inch. The measurement is made from the top of the tallest letter in a character set (for example, an uppercase T) to the bottom of the lowest letter (for example, a lowercase y). Most documents are set in 10 or 12 point type. Newspaper columns may be set as small as 8 point type, but that is the smallest type size you should consider. Conversely, type sizes of 14 points or higher are ineffective for large amounts of text.

Figure 2.6 shows the same phrase set in varying type sizes. Some typefaces appear larger (smaller) than others even though they may be set in the same point size. The type in Figure 2.6a, for example, looks smaller than the corresponding type in Figure 2.6b even though both are set in the same point size. Note, too, that you can vary the type size of a specific font within a document for emphasis. The eye needs at least two points to distinguish between different type sizes.

Format Font Command

The *Format Font command* gives you complete control over the typeface, size, and style of the text in a document. Executing the command before entering text will set the format of the text you type from that point on. You can also use the command to change the font of existing text by selecting the text, then executing the command. Either way, you will see the dialog box in Figure 2.7, in which you specify the font (typeface), style, and point size.

You can choose any of the special effects (e.g., ~~strikethrough~~ or SMALL CAPS) and/or change the underline options (whether or not spaces are to be underlined). You can even change the color of the text on the monitor, but you need a color printer for the printed document. (The Character Spacing and Text Effects tabs produce different sets of options in which you control the spacing and appearance of the characters and are beyond the scope of our discussion.)

This is Arial 8 point type

This is Arial 10 point type

This is Arial 12 point type

This is Arial 18 point type

This is Arial 24 point type

This is Arial 30 point type

(a) Sans Serif Typeface

This is Times New Roman 8 point type

This is Times New Roman 10 point type

This is Times New Roman 12 point type

This is Times New Roman 18 point type

This is Times New Roman 24 point type

This is Times New Roman 30 point

(b) Serif Typeface

FIGURE 2.6   Type Size

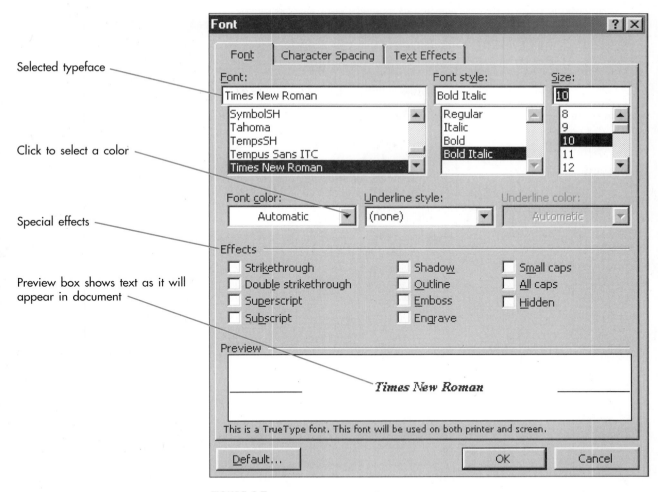

Selected typeface

Click to select a color

Special effects

Preview box shows text as it will appear in document

FIGURE 2.7   Format Font Command

The Preview box shows the text as it will appear in the document. The message at the bottom of the dialog box indicates that Times New Roman is a TrueType font and that the same font will be used on both the screen and the monitor. TrueType fonts ensure that your document is truly WYSIWYG (What You See Is What You Get) because the fonts you see on the monitor will be identical to those in the printed document.

PAGE SETUP COMMAND

The *Page Setup command* in the File menu lets you change margins, paper size, orientation, paper source, and/or layout. All parameters are accessed from the dialog box in Figure 2.8 by clicking the appropriate tab within the dialog box.

The default margins are indicated in Figure 2.8a and are one inch on the top and bottom of the page, and one and a quarter inches on the left and right. You can change any (or all) of these settings by entering a new value in the appropriate text box, either by typing it explicitly or clicking the up/down arrow. All of the settings in the Page Setup command apply to the whole document regardless of the position of the insertion point. (Different settings for any option in the Page Setup dialog box can be established for different parts of a document by creating sections. Sections also affect column formatting, as discussed later in the chapter.)

Margin tab ——————

Enter new value to
change setting ——————

Click to change setting ——————

Preview box ——————

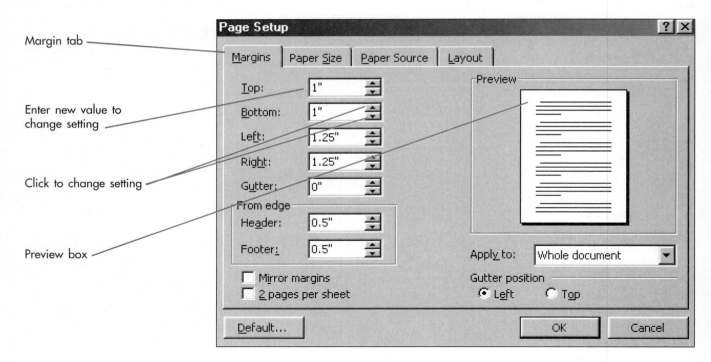

(a) Margins

Paper Size tab ——————

Preview box ——————

Click to select orientation ——————

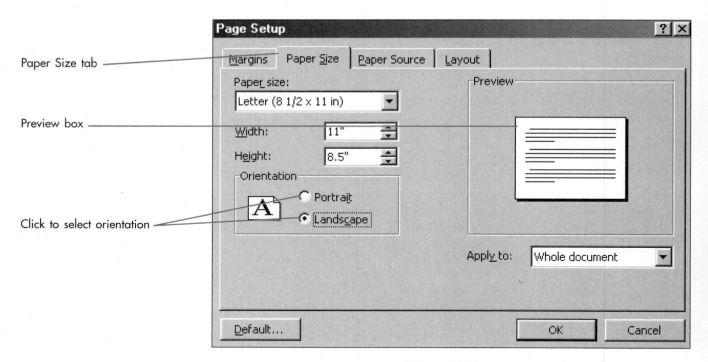

(b) Size and Orientation

FIGURE 2.8   Page Setup Command

The Paper Size tab within the Page Setup command enables you to change the orientation of a page as shown in Figure 2.8b. **Portrait orientation** is the default. **Landscape orientation** flips the page 90 degrees so that its dimensions are 11 × 8½ rather than the other way around. Note, too, the Preview area in both Figures 2.8a and 2.8b, which shows how the document will appear with the selected parameters.

The Paper Source tab is used to specify which tray should be used on printers with multiple trays, and is helpful when you want to load different types of paper simultaneously. The Layout tab is used to specify options for headers and footers (text that appears at the top or bottom of each page in a document), and/or to change the vertical alignment of text on the page.

Page Breaks

One of the first concepts you learned was that of word wrap, whereby Word inserts a soft return at the end of a line in order to begin a new line. The number and/or location of the soft returns change automatically as you add or delete text within a document. Soft returns are very different from the hard returns inserted by the user, whose number and location remain constant.

In much the same way, Word creates a **soft page break** to go to the top of a new page when text no longer fits on the current page. And just as you can insert a hard return to start a new paragraph, you can insert a **hard page break** to force any part of a document to begin on a new page. A hard page break is inserted into a document using the Break command in the Insert menu or more easily through the Ctrl+enter keyboard shortcut. (You can prevent the occurrence of awkward page breaks through the Format Paragraph command as described later in the chapter.)

AN EXERCISE IN DESIGN

The following exercise has you retrieve an existing document from the set of practice files, then experiment with various typefaces, type styles, and point sizes. The original document uses a monospaced (typewriter style) font, without boldface or italics, and you are asked to improve its appearance. The first step directs you to save the document under a new name so that you can always return to the original if necessary.

There is no right and wrong with respect to design, and you are free to choose any combination of fonts that appeals to you. The exercise takes you through various formatting options but lets you make the final decision. It does, however, ask you to print the final document and submit it to your instructor. Experiment freely and print multiple versions with different designs.

IMPOSE A TIME LIMIT

A word processor is supposed to save time and make you more productive. It will do exactly that, provided you use the word processor for its primary purpose—writing and editing. It is all too easy, however, to lose sight of that objective and spend too much time formatting the document. Concentrate on the content of your document rather than its appearance. Impose a time limit on the amount of time you will spend on formatting. End the session when the limit is reached.

Objective: To experiment with character formatting; to change fonts and to use boldface and italics; to copy formatting with the format painter; to insert a page break and see different views of a document. Use Figure 2.9 as a guide in the exercise.

STEP 1: Open the Existing Document

➤ Start Word. Pull down the **File menu** and click **Open** (or click the **Open button** on the toolbar). To open a file:

- Click the **drop-down arrow** on the Look In list box. Click the appropriate drive, drive C or drive A, depending on the location of your data.
- Double click the **Exploring Word folder** to make it the active folder (the folder in which you will open and save the document).
- Scroll in the **Open list box** (if necessary) until you can click **Tips for Writing** to select this document.

➤ Double click the **document icon** or click the **Open command button** to open the file.

➤ Pull down the **File menu.** Click the **Save As command** to save the document as **Modified Tips.**

➤ Pull down the **View menu** and click **Normal** (or click the **Normal View button** above the status bar).

➤ Set the magnification (zoom) to **Page Width.**

SELECTING TEXT

The selection bar, a blank column at the far left of the document window, makes it easy to select a line, paragraph, or the entire document. To select a line, move the mouse pointer to the selection bar, point to the line and click the left mouse button. To select a paragraph, move the mouse pointer to the selection bar, point to any line in the paragraph, and double click the mouse. To select the entire document, move the mouse pointer to the selection bar and press the Ctrl key while you click the mouse.

STEP 2: The Right Mouse Button

➤ Select the first tip as shown in Figure 2.9a. Point to the selected text and click the **right mouse button** to display a context-sensitive or shortcut menu.

➤ Click outside the menu to close the menu without executing a command.

➤ Press the **Ctrl key** as you click the selection bar to select the entire document, then click the **right mouse button** to display the shortcut menu.

➤ Click **Font** to execute the Format Font command.

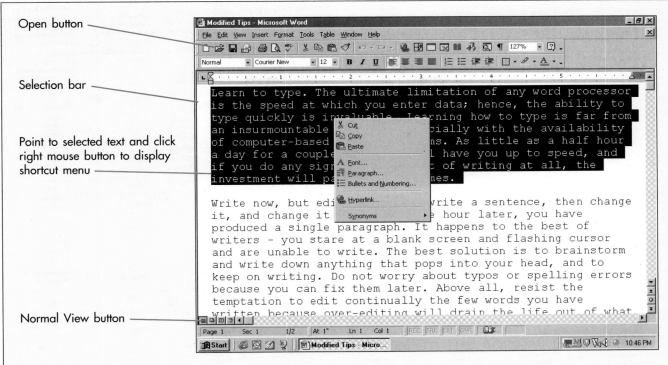

Open button

Selection bar

Point to selected text and click right mouse button to display shortcut menu

Normal View button

(a) The Right Mouse Button (step 2)

FIGURE 2.9   Hands-on Exercise 2

STEP 3: The Format Font Command

➤ Click the **down arrow** on the Font list box of Figure 2.9b to scroll through the available fonts. Select a different font, such as Times New Roman.

➤ Click the **down arrow** in the Font Size list box to choose a point size.

➤ Click **OK** to change the font and point size for the selected text.

➤ Pull down the **Edit menu** and click **Undo** (or click the **Undo button** on the Standard toolbar) to return to the original font.

➤ Experiment with different fonts and/or different point sizes until you are satisfied with the selection. We chose 12 point Times New Roman.

FIND AND REPLACE FORMATTING

The Replace command enables you to replace formatting as well as text. To replace any text set in bold with the same text in italics, pull down the Edit menu, and click the Replace command. Click the Find what text box, but do *not* enter any text. Click the More button to expand the dialog box. Click the Format command button, click Font, click Bold in the Font Style list, and click OK. Click the Replace with text box and again do *not* enter any text. Click the Format command button, click Font, click Italic in the Font Style list, and click OK. Click the Find Next or Replace All command button to do selective or automatic replacement. Use a similar technique to replace one font with another.

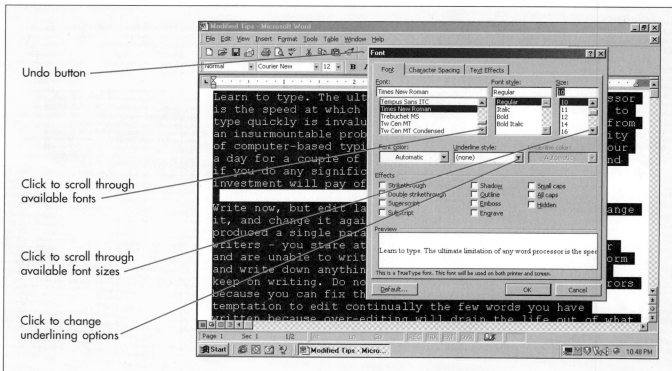

Undo button

Click to scroll through available fonts

Click to scroll through available font sizes

Click to change underlining options

(b) The Format Command (step 3)

FIGURE 2.9   Hands-on Exercise 2 (continued)

STEP 4: Boldface and Italics

➤ Select the sentence **Learn to type** at the beginning of the document.

➤ Click the **Italic button** on the Formatting toolbar to italicize the selected phrase, which will remain selected after the italics take effect.

➤ Click the **Bold button** to boldface the selected text. The text is now in bold italic.

➤ Experiment with different styles (bold, italics, underlining, or bold italic) until you are satisfied. The Italic, Bold, and Underline buttons function as toggle switches; that is, clicking the Italic button when text is already italicized returns the text to normal.

➤ Save the document

UNDERLINING TEXT

Underlining is less popular than it was, but Word provides a complete range of underlining options. Select the text to underline, pull down the Format menu, click Font to display the Font dialog box, and click the Font tab if necessary. Click the down arrow on the Underline Style list box to choose the type of underlining you want. You can choose whether to underline the words only (i.e., the underline does not appear in the space between words). You can also choose the type of line you want—solid, dashed, thick, or thin.

STEP 5: The Format Painter

➤ Click anywhere within the sentence Learn to Type. **Double click** the **Format Painter button** on the Standard toolbar. The mouse pointer changes to a paintbrush as shown in Figure 2.9c.

➤ Drag the mouse pointer over the next title, **Write now, but edit later,** and release the mouse. The formatting from the original sentence (bold italic as shown in Figure 2.9c) has been applied to this sentence as well.

➤ Drag the mouse pointer (in the shape of a paintbrush) over the remaining titles (the first sentence in each paragraph) to copy the formatting.

➤ Click the **Format Painter button** after you have painted the title of the last tip to turn the feature off.

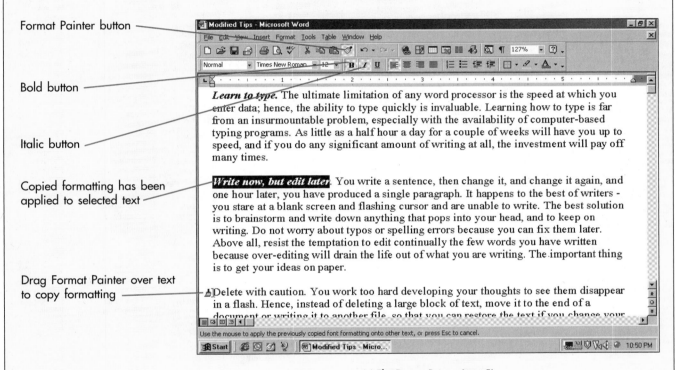

(c) The Format Painter (step 5)

FIGURE 2.9 Hands-on Exercise 2 (continued)

THE FORMAT PAINTER

The Format Painter copies the formatting of the selected text to other places in a document. Select the text with the formatting you want to copy, then click or double click the Format Painter button on the Standard toolbar. Clicking the button will paint only one selection. Double clicking the button will paint multiple selections until the feature is turned off by again clicking the Format Painter button. Either way, the mouse pointer changes to a paintbrush, which you can drag over text to give it the identical formatting characteristics as the original selection.

STEP 6: Change Margins

➤ Press **Ctrl+End** to move to the end of the document as shown in Figure 2.9d. You will see a dotted line indicating a soft page break. (If you do not see the page break, it means that your document fits on one page because you used a different font and/or a smaller point size. We used 12 point Times New Roman.)

➤ Pull down the **File menu.** Click **Page Setup.** Click the **Margins tab** if necessary. Change the bottom margin to **.75** inch. Check that these settings apply to the **Whole Document.** Click **OK.**

➤ The page break disappears because more text fits on the page.

Soft page break

Click Margins tab

Change bottom margin to .75"

Settings apply to Whole Document

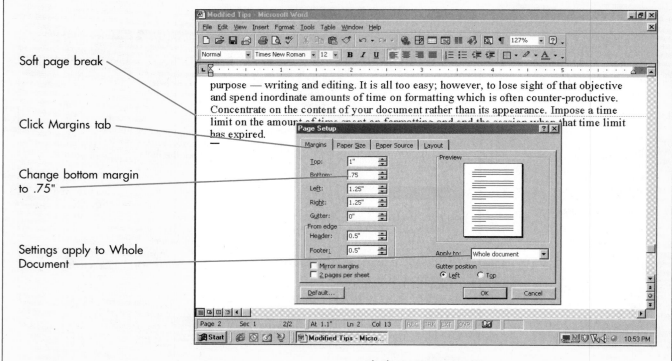

(d) Change Margins (step 6)

FIGURE 2.9   Hands-on Exercise 2 (continued)

DIALOG BOX SHORTCUTS

You can use keyboard shortcuts to select options in a dialog box. Press Tab (Shift+Tab) to move forward (backward) from one field or command button to the next. Press Alt plus the underlined letter to move directly to a field or command button. Press enter to activate the selected command button. Press Esc to exit the dialog box without taking action. Press the space bar to toggle check boxes on or off. Press the down arrow to open a drop-down list box once the list has been accessed, then press the up or down arrow to move between options in a list box.

STEP 7: Create the Title Page

➤ Press **Ctrl+Home** to move to the beginning of the document. Press **enter** three or four times to add a few blank lines.

➤ Press **Ctrl+enter** to insert a hard page break. You will see the words "Page Break" in the middle of a dotted line as shown in Figure 2.9e.

➤ Press the **up arrow key** three times. Enter the title **Tips for Writing.** Select the title, and format it in a larger point size, such as 24 points.

➤ Enter your name on the next line and format it in a different point size, such as 14 points. Select both the title and your name as shown in the figure. Click the **Center button** on the Formatting toolbar. Save the document.

Center button

Font Size box

Click and drag to select

Press Ctrl+Enter to create a hard page break

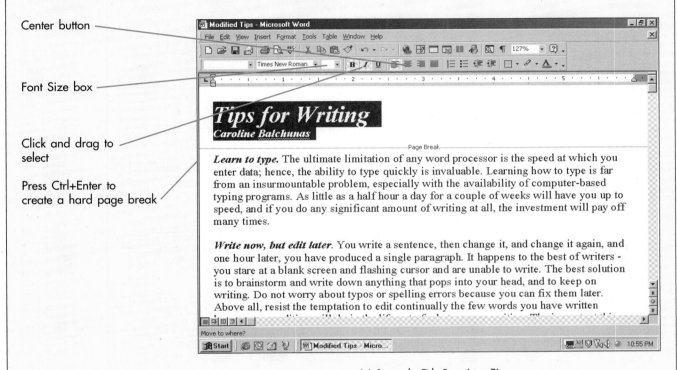

(e) Create the Title Page (step 7)

FIGURE 2.9   Hands-on Exercise 2 (continued)

DOUBLE CLICK AND TYPE

Creating a title page is a breeze if you take advantage of the (double) click and type feature in Word 2000. Pull down the View menu and change to the Print Layout view, then look closely at the mouse pointer and notice the horizontal lines that surround the I-beam shape. Double click anywhere on the page and you can begin typing immediately at that location, without having to type several blank lines, or set tabs. The feature does not work in the Normal view or in a document that has columns. To enable (disable) the feature, pull down the Tools menu, click the Options command, click the Edit tab, then check (clear) the Enable Click and Type check box.

STEP 8: The Completed Document

➤ Pull down the **View menu** and click **Print Layout** (or click the **Print Layout button** above the status bar).

➤ Click the **Zoom Control arrow** on the Standard toolbar and select **Two Pages.** Release the mouse to view the completed document in Figure 2.9f. You may want to add additional blank lines at the top of the title page to move the title further down on the page.

➤ Save the document a final time. Exit Word if you do not want to continue with the next exercise at this time.

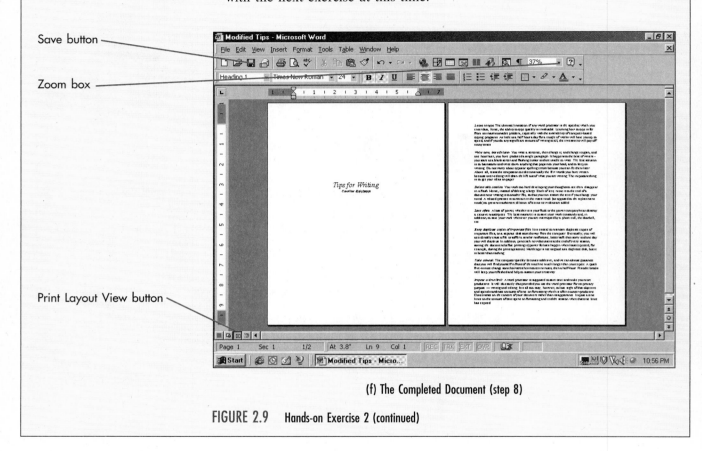

Save button

Zoom box

Print Layout View button

(f) The Completed Document (step 8)

FIGURE 2.9   Hands-on Exercise 2 (continued)

PARAGRAPH FORMATTING

A change in typography is only one way to alter the appearance of a document. You can also change the alignment, indentation, tab stops, or line spacing for any paragraph(s) within the document. You can control the pagination and prevent the occurrence of awkward page breaks by specifying that an entire paragraph has to appear on the same page, or that a one-line paragraph (e.g., a heading) should appear on the same page as the next paragraph. You can include borders or shading for added emphasis around selected paragraphs.

All of these features are implemented at the paragraph level and affect all selected paragraphs. If no paragraphs are selected, the commands affect the entire current paragraph (the paragraph containing the insertion point), regardless of the position of the insertion point when the command is executed.

Alignment

Text can be aligned in four different ways as shown in Figure 2.10. It may be justified (flush left/flush right), left aligned (flush left with a ragged right margin), right aligned (flush right with a ragged left margin), or centered within the margins (ragged left and right).

Left aligned text is perhaps the easiest to read. The first letters of each line align with each other, helping the eye to find the beginning of each line. The lines themselves are of irregular length. There is uniform spacing between words, and the ragged margin on the right adds white space to the text, giving it a lighter and more informal look.

Justified text produces lines of equal length, with the spacing between words adjusted to align at the margins. It may be more difficult to read than text that is left aligned because of the uneven (sometimes excessive) word spacing and/or the greater number of hyphenated words needed to justify the lines.

Type that is centered or right aligned is restricted to limited amounts of text where the effect is more important than the ease of reading. Centered text, for example, appears frequently on wedding invitations, poems, or formal announcements. Right aligned text is used with figure captions and short headlines.

Indents

Individual paragraphs can be indented so that they appear to have different margins from the rest of a document. Indentation is established at the paragraph level; thus different indentation can be in effect for different paragraphs. One paragraph may be indented from the left margin only, another from the right margin only, and a third from both the left and right margins. The first line of any paragraph may be indented differently from the rest of the paragraph. And finally, a paragraph may be set with no indentation at all, so that it aligns on the left and right margins.

The indentation of a paragraph is determined by three settings: the *left indent,* the *right indent,* and a *special indent* (if any). There are two types of special indentation, first line and hanging, as will be explained shortly. The left and right indents are set to zero by default, as is the special indent, and produce a paragraph with no indentation at all as shown in Figure 2.11a. Positive values for the left and right indents offset the paragraph from both margins as shown in Figure 2.11b.

The *first line indent* (Figure 2.11c) affects only the first line in the paragraph and is implemented by pressing the Tab key at the beginning of the paragraph. A *hanging indent* (Figure 2.11d) sets the first line of a paragraph at the left indent and indents the remaining lines according to the amount specified. Hanging indents are often used with bulleted or numbered lists.

INDENTS VERSUS MARGINS

Indents measure the distance between the text and the margins. Margins mark the distance from the text to the edge of the page. Indents are determined at the paragraph level, whereas margins are established at the section (document) level. The left and right margins are set (by default) to 1.25 inches each; the left and right indents default to zero. The first line indent is measured from the setting of the left indent.

We, the people of the United States, in order to form a more perfect Union, establish justice, insure domestic tranquillity, provide for the common defense, promote the general welfare, and secure the blessings of liberty to ourselves and our posterity, do ordain and establish this Constitution for the United States of America.

(a) Justified (flush left/flush right)

We, the people of the United States, in order to form a more perfect Union, establish justice, insure domestic tranquillity, provide for the common defense, promote the general welfare, and secure the blessings of liberty to ourselves and our posterity, do ordain and establish this Constitution for the United States of America.

(b) Left Aligned (flush left/ragged right)

We, the people of the United States, in order to form a more perfect Union, establish justice, insure domestic tranquillity, provide for the common defense, promote the general welfare, and secure the blessings of liberty to ourselves and our posterity, do ordain and establish this Constitution for the United States of America.

(c) Right Aligned (ragged left/flush right)

We, the people of the United States, in order to form a more perfect Union, establish justice, insure domestic tranquillity, provide for the common defense, promote the general welfare, and secure the blessings of liberty to ourselves and our posterity, do ordain and establish this Constitution for the United States of America.

(d) Centered (ragged left/ragged right)

FIGURE 2.10   Alignment

The left and right indents are defined as the distance between the text and the left and right margins, respectively. Both parameters are set to zero in this paragraph and so the text aligns on both margins. Different indentation can be applied to different paragraphs in the same document.

(a) No Indents

Positive values for the left and right indents offset a paragraph from the rest of a document and are often used for long quotations. This paragraph has left and right indents of one-half inch each. Different indentation can be applied to different paragraphs in the same document.

(b) Left and Right Indents

A first line indent affects only the first line in the paragraph and is implemented by pressing the Tab key at the beginning of the paragraph. The remainder of the paragraph is aligned at the left margin (or the left indent if it differs from the left margin) as can be seen from this example. Different indentation can be applied to different paragraphs in the same document.

(c) First Line Indent

A hanging indent sets the first line of a paragraph at the left indent and indents the remaining lines according to the amount specified. Hanging indents are often used with bulleted or numbered lists. Different indentation can be applied to different paragraphs in the same document.

(d) Hanging (Special) Indent

FIGURE 2.11   Indents

Tabs

Anyone who has used a typewriter is familiar with the function of the Tab key; that is, press Tab and the insertion point moves to the next *tab stop* (a measured position to align text at a specific place). The Tab key is much more powerful in Word as you can choose from four different types of tab stops (left, center, right, and decimal). You can also specify a *leader character,* typically dots or hyphens, to draw the reader's eye across the page. Tabs are often used to create columns of text within a document.

The default tab stops are set every ½ inch and are left aligned, but you can change the alignment and/or position with the Format Tabs command. Figure 2.12 illustrates a dot leader in combination with a right tab to produce a Table of Contents. The default tab stops have been cleared in Figure 2.12a, in favor of a single right tab at 5.5 inches. The option button for a dot leader has also been checked. The resulting document is shown in Figure 2.12b.

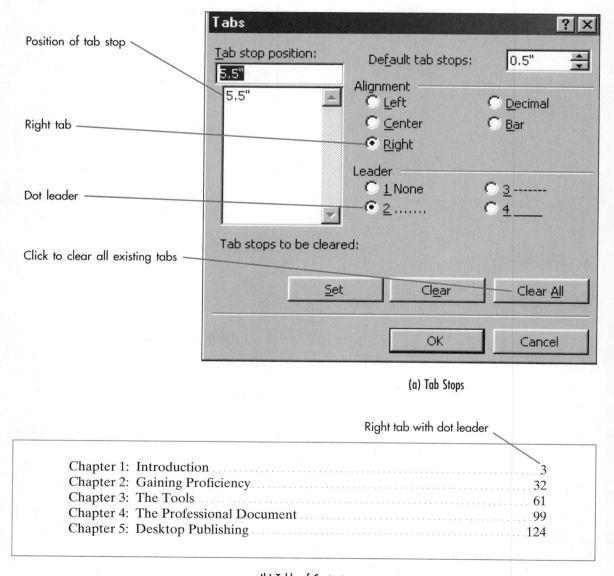

(a) Tab Stops

(b) Table of Contents

FIGURE 2.12   Tabs

Hyphenation

Hyphenation gives a document a more professional look by eliminating excessive gaps of white space. It is especially useful in narrow columns and/or justified text. Hyphenation is implemented through the Language command in the Tools menu. You can choose to hyphenate a document automatically, in which case the hyphens are inserted as the document is created. (Microsoft Word will automatically rehyphenate the document to adjust for subsequent changes in editing.)

You can also hyphenate a document manually, to have Word prompt you prior to inserting each hyphen. Manual hyphenation does not, however, adjust for changes that affect the line breaks, and so it should be done only after the document is complete. And finally, you can fine-tune the use of hyphenation by preventing a hyphenated word from breaking if it falls at the end of a line. This is done by inserting a *nonbreaking hyphen* (press Ctrl+Shift+Hyphen) when the word is typed initially.

Line Spacing

Line spacing determines the space between the lines in a paragraph. Word provides complete flexibility and enables you to select any multiple of line spacing (single, double, line and a half, and so on). You can also specify line spacing in terms of points (there are 72 points per inch).

Line spacing is set at the paragraph level through the Format Paragraph command, which sets the spacing within a paragraph. The command also enables you to add extra spacing before the first line in a paragraph or after the last line. (Either technique is preferable to the common practice of single spacing the paragraphs within a document, then adding a blank line between paragraphs.)

FORMAT PARAGRAPH COMMAND

The *Format Paragraph command* is used to specify the alignment, indentation, line spacing, and pagination for the selected paragraph(s). As indicated, all of these features are implemented at the paragraph level and affect all selected paragraphs. If no paragraphs are selected, the command affects the entire current paragraph (the paragraph containing the insertion point).

The Format Paragraph command is illustrated in Figure 2.13. The Indents and Spacing tab in Figure 2.13a calls for a hanging indent, line spacing of 1.5 lines, and justified alignment. The preview area within the dialog box enables you to see how the paragraph will appear within the document.

The Line and Page Breaks tab in Figure 2.13b illustrates an entirely different set of parameters in which you control the pagination within a document. The check boxes in Figure 2.13b enable you to prevent the occurrence of awkward soft page breaks that detract from the appearance of a document.

You might, for example, want to prevent widows and orphans, terms used to describe isolated lines that seem out of place. A *widow* refers to the last line of a paragraph appearing by itself at the top of a page. An *orphan* is the first line of a paragraph appearing by itself at the bottom of a page.

You can also impose additional controls by clicking one or more check boxes. Use the Keep Lines Together option to prevent a soft page break from occurring within a paragraph and ensure that the entire paragraph appears on the same page. (The paragraph is moved to the top of the next page if it doesn't fit on the bottom of the current page.) Use the Keep with Next option to prevent a soft page break between the two paragraphs. This option is typically used to keep a heading (a one-line paragraph) with its associated text in the next paragraph.

Indents and Spacing tab ———

Full justification ———

Hanging indent ———

Preview of paragraph formatting selected ———

1½ line spacing ———

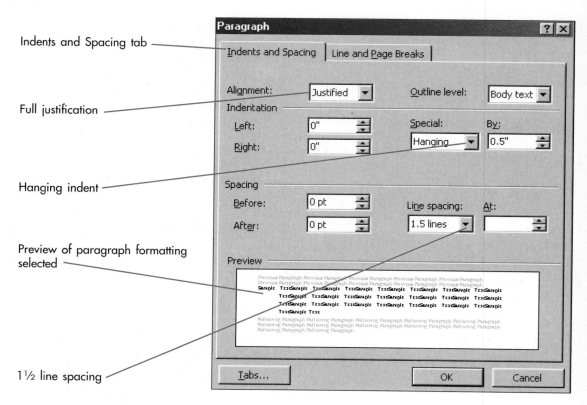

(a) Indents and Spacing

Line and Page Breaks tab ———

Options to control soft page breaks ———

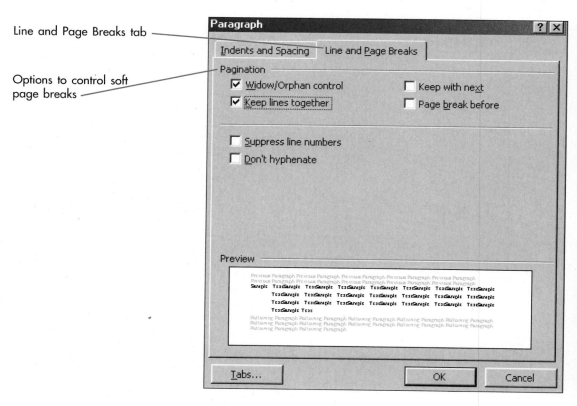

(b) Line and Page Breaks

FIGURE 2.13   Format Paragraph Command

Borders and Shading

The **Borders and Shading command** puts the finishing touches on a document and is illustrated in Figure 2.14. The command is applied to selected text within a paragraph or to the entire paragraph if no text is selected. Thus, you can create boxed and/or shaded text as well as place horizontal or vertical lines around a paragraph. You can choose from several different line styles in any color (assuming you have a color printer). You can place a uniform border around a paragraph (choose Box), or you can choose a shadow effect with thicker lines at the right and bottom. You can also apply lines to selected sides of a paragraph(s) by selecting a line style, then clicking the desired sides as appropriate.

Shading is implemented independently of the border. Clear (no shading) is the default. Solid (100%) shading creates a solid box where the text is turned white so you can read it. Shading of 10 or 20 percent is generally most effective to add emphasis to the selected paragraph. The Borders and Shading command is implemented on the paragraph level and affects the entire paragraph—either the current or selected paragraph(s).

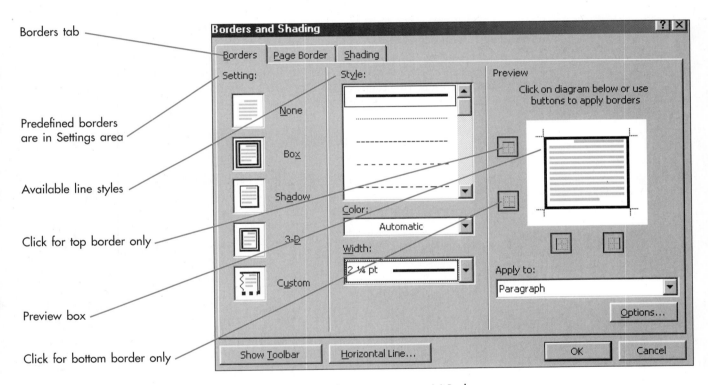

(a) Borders

FIGURE 2.14   Paragraph Borders and Shading

FORMATTING AND THE PARAGRAPH MARK

The paragraph mark ¶ at the end of a paragraph does more than just indicate the presence of a hard return. It also stores all of the formatting in effect for the paragraph. Hence in order to preserve the formatting when you move or copy a paragraph, you must include the paragraph mark in the selected text. Click the Show/Hide ¶ button on the toolbar to display the paragraph mark and make sure it has been selected.

Columns add interest to a document and are implemented through the ***Columns command*** in the Format menu as shown in Figure 2.15. You specify the number of columns and, optionally, the space between columns. Microsoft Word does the rest, calculating the width of each column according to the left and right margins on the page and the specified (default) space between columns.

The dialog box in Figure 2.15 implements a design of three equal columns. The 2-inch width of each column is computed automatically based on left and right page margins of 1 inch each and the ¼-inch spacing between columns. The width of each column is determined by subtracting the sum of the margins and the space between the columns (a total of 2½ inches in this example) from the page width of 8½ inches. The result of the subtraction is 6 inches, which is divided by 3, resulting in a column width of 2 inches.

There is, however, one subtlety associated with column formatting, and that is the introduction of the ***section,*** which controls elements such as the orientation of a page (landscape or portrait), margins, page numbers, and/or the number of columns. All of the documents in the text thus far have consisted of a single section, and therefore section formatting was not an issue. It becomes important only when you want to vary an element that is formatted at the section level. You could, for example, use section formatting to create a document that has one column on its title page and two columns on the remaining pages. This requires you to divide the document two sections through insertion of a ***section break.*** You then format each section independently and specify the number of columns in each section.

Preset design

Column width is calculated automatically

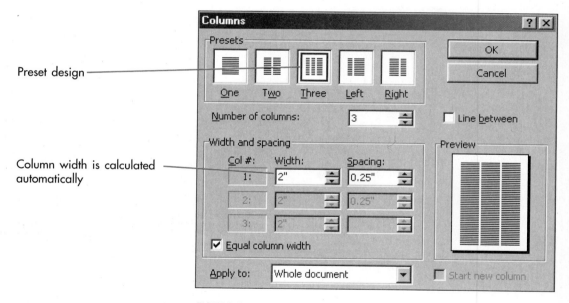

FIGURE 2.15   The Format Columns Command

THE SECTION VERSUS THE PARAGRAPH

Line spacing, alignment, tabs, and indents are implemented at the paragraph level. Change any of these parameters anywhere within the current (or selected) paragraph(s) and you change *only* those paragraph(s). Margins, page numbering, orientation, and columns are implemented at the section level. Change these parameters anywhere within a section and you change the characteristics of every page within that section.

Paragraph Formatting

Objective: To implement line spacing, alignment, and indents; to implement widow and orphan protection; to box and shade a selected paragraph.

STEP 1: Select-Then-Do

➤ Open the **Modified Tips** document from the previous exercise. If necessary, change to the Print Layout view. Click the **Zoom drop-down arrow** and click **Two Pages** to match the view in Figure 2.16a.

➤ Select the entire second page as shown in the figure. Point to the selected text and click the **right mouse button** to produce the shortcut menu. Click **Paragraph.**

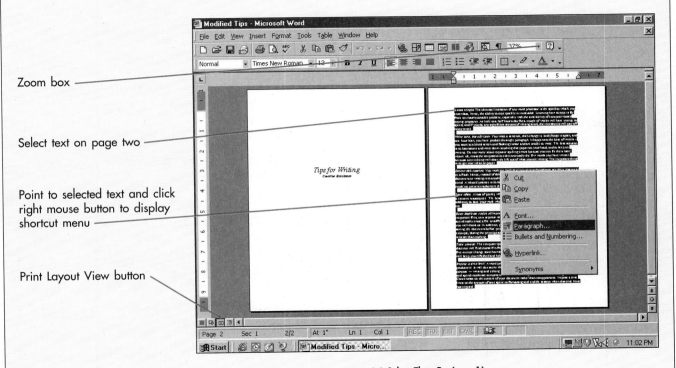

Zoom box

Select text on page two

Point to selected text and click right mouse button to display shortcut menu

Print Layout View button

(a) Select-Then-Do (step 1)

FIGURE 2.16 Hands-on Exercise 3

SELECT TEXT WITH THE F8 EXTEND KEY

Move to the beginning of the text you want to select, then press the F8 (extend) key. The letters EXT will appear in the status bar. Use the arrow keys to extend the selection in the indicated direction; for example, press the down arrow key to select the line. You can also press any character— for example, a letter, space, or period—to extend the selection to the first occurrence of that character. Press Esc to cancel the selection mode.

STEP 2: Line Spacing, Justification, and Pagination

➤ If necessary, click the **Indents and Spacing tab** to view the options in Figure 2.16b.

- Click the **down arrow** on the list box for Line Spacing and select **1.5 Lines.**
- Click the **down arrow** on the Alignment list box and select **Justified** as shown in Figure 2.16b.
- The Preview area shows the effect of these settings.

➤ Click the tab for **Line and Page Breaks.**

- Check the box for **Keep Lines Together.** If necessary, check the box for **Widow/Orphan Control.**

➤ Click **OK** to accept all of the settings in the dialog box.

➤ Click anywhere in the document to deselect the text and see the effects of the formatting changes:

- The document is fully justified and the line spacing has increased.
- The document now extends to three pages, with the fifth, sixth, and seventh paragraphs appearing on the last page.
- There is a large bottom margin on the second page as a consequence of keeping the lines together in paragraph five.

➤ Save the document.

Click Indents and Spacing tab

Click to select alignment

Click to select line spacing

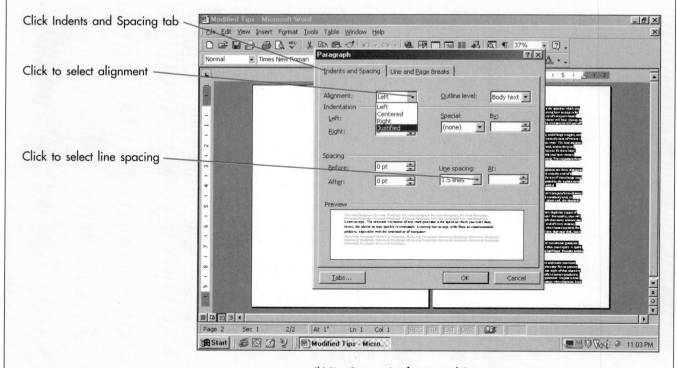

(b) Line Spacing, Justification, and Pagination (step 2)

FIGURE 2.16   Hands-on Exercise 3 (continued)

STEP 3: Indents

➤ Select the second paragraph as shown in Figure 2.16c. (The second paragraph will not yet be indented.)

➤ Pull down the **Format menu** and click **Paragraph** (or press the **right mouse button** to produce the shortcut menu and click **Paragraph**).

➤ If necessary, click the **Indents and Spacing tab** in the Paragraph dialog box. Click the **up arrow** on the Left Indentation text box to set the **Left Indent** to **.5** inch. Set the **Right indent** to **.5** inch. Click **OK.** Your document should match Figure 2.16c.

➤ Save the document.

Click and drag to set right indent

Click and drag to set left indent and first line indent at same time

Select paragraph two

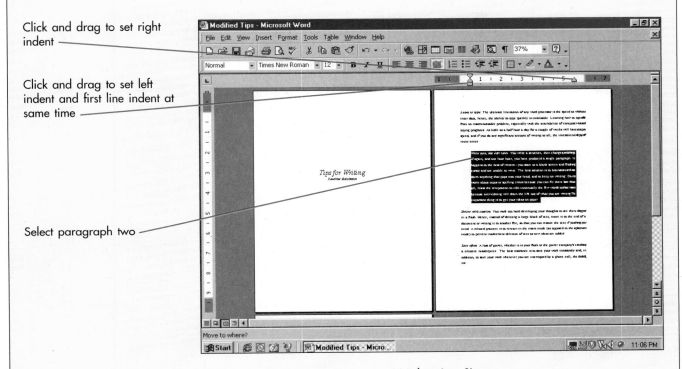

(c) Indents (step 3)

FIGURE 2.16   Hands-on Exercise 3 (continued)

INDENTS AND THE RULER

Use the ruler to change the special, left, and/or right indents. Select the paragraph (or paragraphs) in which you want to change indents, then drag the appropriate indent markers to the new location(s). If you get a hanging indent when you wanted to change the left indent, it means you dragged the bottom triangle instead of the box. Click the Undo button and try again. (You can always use the Format Paragraph command rather than the ruler if you continue to have difficulty.)

STEP 4: Borders and Shading

➤ Pull down the **Format menu.** Click **Borders and Shading** to produce the dialog box in Figure 2.16d.

➤ If necessary, click the **Borders tab.** Select a style and width for the line around the box. Click the rectangle labeled **Box** under Setting.

➤ Click the **Shading Tab.** Click the **down arrow** on the Style list box. Click **10%.**

➤ Click **OK** to accept the settings for both Borders and Shading. Click outside the paragraph.

➤ Save the document.

Click Borders tab

Select a line style

Click Box style

Select a line width

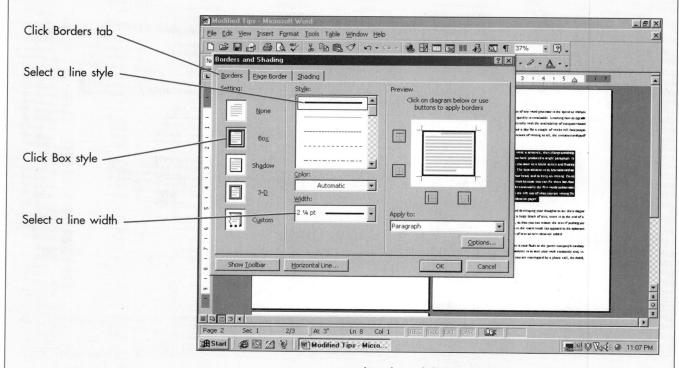

(d) Borders and Shading (step 4)

FIGURE 2.16 Hands-on Exercise 3 (continued)

THE PAGE BORDER COMMAND

You can apply a border to the title page of your document, to every page except the title page, or to every page including the title page. Pull down the Format menu, click Borders and Shading, and click the Page Borders tab. First design the border by selecting a style, color, width, and art (if any). Then choose the page(s) to which you want to apply the border by clicking the drop-down arrow in the Apply to list box. Close the Borders and Shading dialog box. See practice exercise 5 at the end of the chapter.

STEP 5: Help with Formatting

➤ Pull down the **Help menu** and click the **What's This command** (or press **Shift+F1**). The mouse pointer changes to an arrow with a question mark.

➤ Click anywhere inside the boxed paragraph to display the formatting information shown in Figure 2.16e.

➤ Click in a different paragraph to see its formatting. Press the **Esc key** to return the pointer to normal.

DISPLAY THE HARD RETURNS

Many formattting commands are implemented at the paragraph level, and thus it helps to know where a paragraph ends. Click the Show/Hide ¶ button on the Standard toolbar to display the hard returns (paragraph marks) and other nonprinting characters (such as tab characters or blank spaces) contained within a document. The Show/Hide ¶ functions as a toggle switch; the first time you click it the hard returns are displayed, the second time you press it the returns are hidden, and so on.

STEP 6: The Zoom Command

➤ Pull down the **View menu.** Click **Zoom** to produce the dialog box in Figure 2.16f. Click the **Many Pages** option button.

➤ Click the **monitor icon** to display a sample selection box, then click and drag to display three pages across. Release the mouse. Click **OK.**

STEP 7: Help for Word 2000

➤ Display the Office Assistant if it is not already visible on your screen. Pull down the **Help menu** and click the command to **Show the Office Assistant.**

➤ Ask the Assistant a question, then press the **Search button** in the Assistant's balloon to look for the answer. Select (click) the appropriate topic from the list of suggested topics provided by the Assistant.

➤ Click the **Show button** in the Help window that is displayed by the Assistant, then use either the **Contents** or **Index tab** to search for additional information. Close the Help window.

➤ If you have an Internet connection, pull down the **Help menu** and click **Microsoft on the Web** to connect to the Microsoft Web site for additional information. Explore the site, then close the browser and return to your document.

ADVICE FROM THE OFFICE ASSISTANT

The Office Assistant indicates it has a suggestion by displaying a lightbulb. Click the lightbulb to display the tip, then click the OK button to close the balloon and continue working. The Assistant will not, however, repeat a tip from an earlier session unless you reset it at the start of a new session. This is especially important in a laboratory situation where you are sharing a computer with many students. To reset the tips, click the Assistant to display a balloon asking what you want to do, click the Options button in the balloon, click the Options tab, then click the button to Reset my Tips.

Paragraph formatting in effect

Click to display formatting specifications

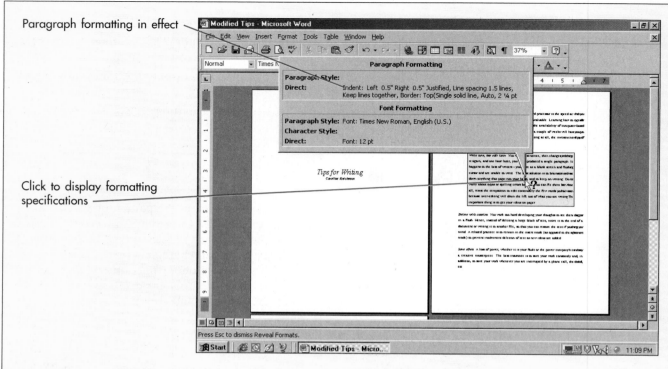

(e) Help with Formatting (step 5)

Many Pages option button

Monitor icon

Click and drag over three pages in same row of grid

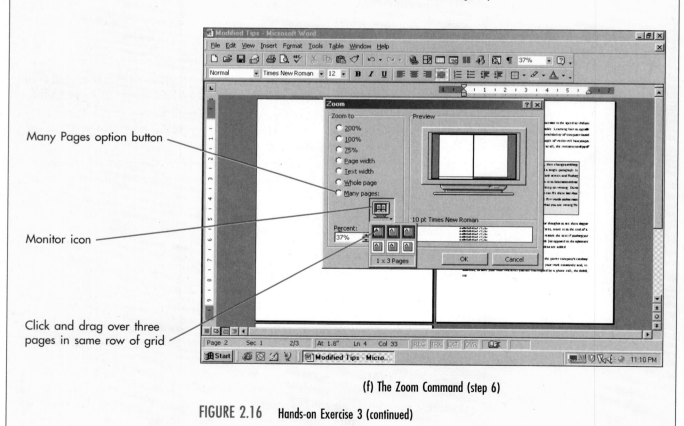

(f) The Zoom Command (step 6)

FIGURE 2.16   Hands-on Exercise 3 (continued)

STEP 8: The Completed Document

➤ Your screen should match the one in Figure 2.16g, which displays all three pages of the document.

➤ The Print Layout view displays both a vertical and a horizontal ruler. The boxed and indented paragraph is clearly shown in the second page.

➤ The soft page break between pages two and three occurs between tips rather than within a tip; that is, the text of each tip is kept together on the same page.

➤ Save the document a final time. Print the completed document and submit it to your instructor.

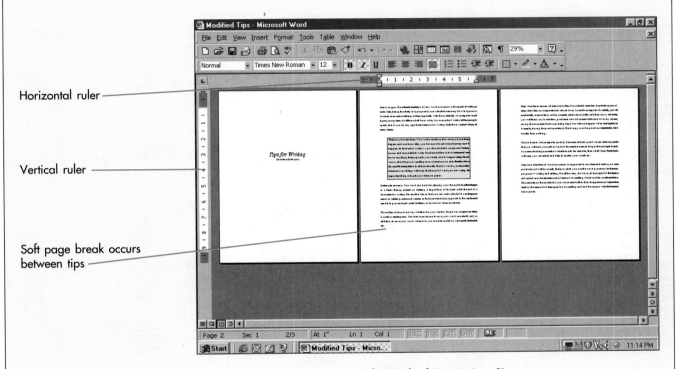

(g) The Completed Docment (step 8)

FIGURE 2.16   Hands-on Exercise 3 (continued)

PRINT SELECTED PAGES

Why print an entire document if you want only a few pages? Pull down the File menu and click Print as you usually do to initiate the printing process. Click the Pages option button, then enter the page numbers and/or page ranges you want; for example, 3, 6–8 will print page three and pages six through eight. You can also print multiple copies by entering the appropriate number in the Number of copies list box.

STEP 9: Change the Column Structure

➤ Click the **down arrow** on the Zoom list box and return to **Page Width.** Press the **PgDn key** to scroll until the second page comes into view.

➤ Pull down the **File menu** and click the **Page Setup command** to display the Page Setup dialog box. Click the **Margins tab,** then change the Left and Right margins to 1″ each. Click **OK** to accept the settings and close the dialog box.

➤ Click anywhere in the paragraph, "Write Now but Edit Later". Pull down the **Format menu,** click the **Paragraph command,** click the Indents and Spacing tab if necessary, then change the left and right indents to 0.

➤ All paragraphs in the document should have the same indentation as shown in Figure 2.16h. Pull down the **Format menu** and click the **Columns command** to display the Columns dialog box.

➤ Click the icon for **three columns.** The default spacing between columns is .5″, which leads to a column width of 1.83″. Click in the Spacing list box and change the spacing to **.25″,** which automatically changes the column width to 2″.

➤ Check the box for the **Line Between** columns. Click **OK.**

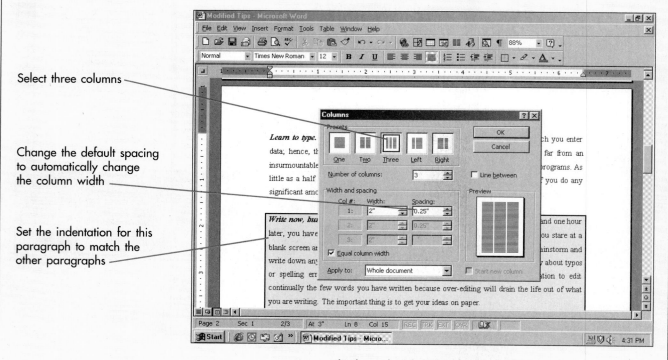

Select three columns

Change the default spacing to automatically change the column width

Set the indentation for this paragraph to match the other paragraphs

(h) Change the Column Structure (step 9)

FIGURE 2.16   Hands-on Exercise 3 (continued)

USE THE RULER TO CHANGE COLUMN WIDTH

Click anywhere within the column whose width you want to change, then point to the ruler and click and drag the right margin (the mouse pointer changes to a double arrow) to change the column width. Changing the width of one column in a document with equal-sized columns changes the width of all other columns so that they remain equal. Changing the width in a document with unequal columns changes only that column.

STEP 10: Insert a Section Break

➤ Pull down the **View menu,** click the **Zoom command,** then click the **Many Pages** option button. The document has switched to column formatting.

➤ Click at the beginning of the second page, immediately to the left of the first paragraph. Pull down the **Insert menu** and click **Break** to display the dialog box in Figure 2.16i.

➤ Click the **Continuous option button,** then click **OK** to accept the settings and close the dialog box.

➤ Click anywhere on the title page (before the section break you just inserted). Click the **Columns button,** then click the first column.

➤ The formatting for the first section of the document (the title page) should change to one column; the title of the document and your name are centered across the entire page.

➤ Print the document in this format for your instructor. Decide in which format you want to save the document—i.e., as it exists now, or as it existed at the end of step 8. Exit Word.

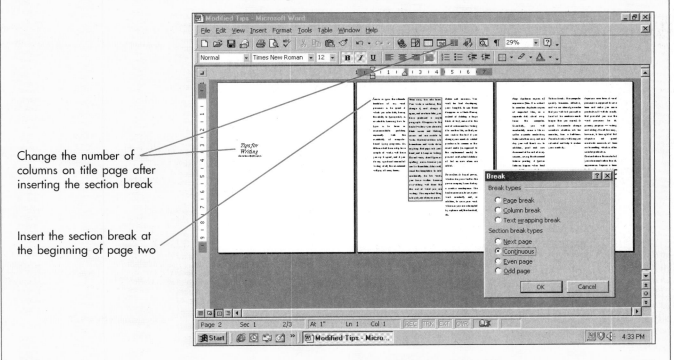

Change the number of columns on title page after inserting the section break

Insert the section break at the beginning of page two

(i) Insert a Section Break (step 10)

FIGURE 2.16 Hands-on Exercise 3 (continued)

THE COLUMNS BUTTON

The Columns button on the Standard toolbar is the fastest way to create columns in a document. Click the button, drag the mouse to choose the number of columns, then release the mouse to create the columns. The toolbar lets you change the number of columns, but not the spacing between columns. The toolbar is also limited, in that you cannot create columns of different widths or select a line between the columns.

Many operations in Word are done within the context of select-then-do; that is, select the text, then execute the necessary command. Text may be selected by dragging the mouse, by using the selection bar to the left of the document, or by using the keyboard. Text is deselected by clicking anywhere within the document.

The Find and Replace commands locate a designated character string and optionally replace one or more occurrences of that string with a different character string. The search may be case-sensitive and/or restricted to whole words as necessary.

Text is moved or copied through a combination of the Cut, Copy, and Paste commands and/or the drag-and-drop facility. The contents of the Windows clipboard are modified by any subsequent Cut or Copy command, but are unaffected by the Paste command; that is, the same text can be pasted into multiple locations.

The Undo command reverses the effect of previous commands. The Undo and Redo commands work in conjunction with one another; that is, every command that is undone can be redone at a later time.

Scrolling occurs when a document is too large to be seen in its entirety. Scrolling with the mouse changes what is displayed on the screen, but does not move the insertion point; that is, you must click the mouse to move the insertion point. Scrolling via the keyboard (for example, PgUp and PgDn) changes what is seen on the screen as well as the location of the insertion point.

The Print Layout view displays top and bottom margins, headers and footers, and other elements not seen in the Normal view. The Normal view is faster because Word spends less time formatting the display. Both views can be seen at different magnifications.

TrueType fonts are scaleable and accessible from any Windows application. The Format Font command enables you to choose the typeface (e.g., Times New Roman or Arial), style (e.g., bold or italic), point size, and color of text.

The Format Paragraph command determines the line spacing, alignment, indents, and text flow, all of which are set at the paragraph level. Borders and shading are also set at the paragraph level. Margins, page size, and orientation, are set in the Page Setup command and affect the entire document (or section).

KEY WORDS AND CONCEPTS

Alignment	Find command	Line spacing
Arial	First line indent	Margins
Automatic replacement	Font	Monospaced typeface
Borders and Shading command	Format Font command	Nonbreaking hyphen
Case-insensitive replacement	Format Painter	Normal view
Case-sensitive replacement	Format Paragraph command	Office clipboard
Clipboard toolbar	Go To command	Page break
Columns command	Hanging indent	Page Setup command
Copy command	Hard page break	Paste command
Courier New	Hyphenation	Point size
Cut command	Indents	Portrait orientation
Drag and drop	Landscape orientation	Print Layout view
	Leader character	Proportional typeface
	Left indent	Redo command
		Repeat command

Replace command	Serif typeface	Typography
Right indent	Shortcut menu	Underlining
Sans serif typeface	Soft page break	Undo command
Scrolling	Special indent	View menu
Section	Tab stop	Whole word replacement
Section break	Times New Roman	Widows and orphans
Select-Then-Do	Typeface	Wild card
Selection bar	Type size	Windows clipboard
Selective replacement	Type style	Zoom command

MULTIPLE CHOICE

1. Which of the following commands does *not* place data onto the clipboard?
   (a) Cut
   (b) Copy
   (c) Paste
   (d) All of the above

2. What happens if you select a block of text, copy it, move to the beginning of the document, paste it, move to the end of the document, and paste the text again?
   (a) The selected text will appear in three places: at the original location, and at the beginning and end of the document
   (b) The selected text will appear in two places: at the beginning and end of the document
   (c) The selected text will appear in just the original location
   (d) The situation is not possible; that is, you cannot paste twice in a row without an intervening cut or copy operation

3. What happens if you select a block of text, cut it, move to the beginning of the document, paste it, move to the end of the document, and paste the text again?
   (a) The selected text will appear in three places: at the original location and at the beginning and end of the document
   (b) The selected text will appear in two places: at the beginning and end of the document
   (c) The selected text will appear in just the original location
   (d) The situation is not possible; that is, you cannot paste twice in a row without an intervening cut or copy operation

4. Which of the following are set at the paragraph level?
   (a) Alignment
   (b) Tabs and indents
   (c) Line spacing
   (d) All of the above

5. How do you change the font for *existing* text within a document?
   (a) Select the text, then choose the new font
   (b) Choose the new font, then select the text
   (c) Either (a) or (b)
   (d) Neither (a) nor (b)

6. The Page Setup command can be used to change:
   (a) The margins in a document
   (b) The orientation of a document
   (c) Both (a) and (b)
   (d) Neither (a) nor (b)

7. Which of the following is a true statement regarding indents?
   (a) Indents are measured from the edge of the page rather than from the margin
   (b) The left, right, and first line indents must be set to the same value
   (c) The insertion point can be anywhere in the paragraph when indents are set
   (d) Indents must be set with the Format Paragraph command

8. The spacing in an existing multipage document is changed from single spacing to double spacing throughout the document. What can you say about the number of hard and soft page breaks before and after the formatting change?
   (a) The number of soft page breaks is the same, but the number and/or position of the hard page breaks is different
   (b) The number of hard page breaks is the same, but the number and/or position of the soft page breaks is different
   (c) The number and position of both hard and soft page breaks is the same
   (d) The number and position of both hard and soft page breaks is different

9. The default tab stops are set to:
   (a) Left indents every ½ inch
   (b) Left indents every ¼ inch
   (c) Right indents every ½ inch
   (d) Right indents every ¼ inch

10. Which of the following describes the Arial and Times New Roman fonts?
    (a) Arial is a sans serif font, Times New Roman is a serif font
    (b) Arial is a serif font, Times New Roman is a sans serif font
    (c) Both are serif fonts
    (d) Both are sans serif fonts

11. The find and replacement strings must be
    (a) The same length
    (b) The same case, either upper or lower
    (c) The same length and the same case
    (d) None of the above

12. Assume that you are in the middle of a multipage document. How do you scroll to the beginning of the document and simultaneously change the insertion point?
    (a) Press Ctrl+Home
    (b) Drag the scroll bar to the top of the scroll box
    (c) Both (a) and (b)
    (d) Neither (a) nor (b)

13. Which of the following substitutions can be accomplished by the Find and Replace command?

(a) All occurrences of the words "Times New Roman" can be replaced with the word "Arial"

(b) All text set in the Times New Roman font can be replaced by the Arial font

(c) Both (a) and (b)

(d) Neither (a) nor (b)

14. Which of the following deselects a selected block of text?

(a) Clicking anywhere outside the selected text

(b) Clicking any alignment button on the toolbar

(c) Clicking the Bold, Italic, or Underline button

(d) All of the above

15. Which view, and which magnification, lets you see the whole page, including top and bottom margins?

(a) Print Layout view at 100% magnification

(b) Print Layout view at Whole Page magnification

(c) Normal view at 100% magnification

(d) Normal view at Whole Page magnification

Answers

1. c	**6.** c	**11.** d
2. a	**7.** c	**12.** a
3. b	**8.** b	**13.** c
4. d	**9.** a	**14.** a
5. a	**10.** a	**15.** b

PRACTICE WITH MICROSOFT WORD

1. Formatting a Document: Open the *Chapter 2 Practice 1* document that is displayed in Figure 2.17 and make the following changes.

a. Copy the sentence *Discretion is the better part of valor* to the beginning of the first paragraph.

b. Move the second paragraph to the end of the document.

c. Change the typeface of the entire document to 12 point Arial.

d. Change all whole word occurrences of *feel* to *think*.

e. Change the spacing of the entire document from single spacing to 1.5. Change the alignment of the entire document to justified.

f. Set the phrases *Format Font command* and *Format Paragraph command* in italics.

g. Indent the second paragraph .25 inch on both the left and right.

h. Box and shade the last paragraph.

i. Create a title page that precedes the document. Set the title, *Discretion in Design,* in 24 point Arial bold and center it approximately two inches from the top of the page. Right align your name toward the bottom of the title page in 12 point Arial regular.

j. Print the revised document and submit it to your instructor.

It is not difficult, especially with practice, to learn to format a document. It is not long before the mouse goes automatically to the Format Font command to change the selected text to a sans-serif font, to increase the font size, or to apply a boldface or italic style. Nor is it long before you go directly to the Format Paragraph command to change the alignment or line spacing for selected paragraphs.

What is not easy, however, is to teach discretion in applying formats. Too many different formats on one page can be distracting, and in almost all cases, less is better. Be conservative and never feel that you have to demonstrate everything you know how to do in each and every document that you create. Discretion is the better part of valor. No more than two different typefaces should be used in a single document, although each can be used in a variety of different styles and sizes.

It is always a good idea to stay on the lookout for what you feel are good designs and then determine exactly what you like and don't like about each. In that way, you are constantly building ideas for your own future designs.

FIGURE 2.17 Formatting a Document (Exercise 1)

2. Typography: Figure 2.18 displays a completed version of the *Chapter 2 Practice 2* document that exists on the data disk. We want you to retrieve the original document from the data disk, then change the document so that it matches Figure 2.18. No editing is required as the text in the original document is identical to the finished document.

   The only changes are in formatting, but you will have to compare the documents in order to determine the nature of the changes. Color is a nice touch (which depends on the availability of a color printer) and is not required. Add your name somewhere in the document, then print the revised document and submit it to your instructor.

3. The Preamble: Create a simple document containing the text of the Preamble to the Constitution as shown in Figure 2.19.
   a. Set the Preamble in 12 point Times New Roman.
   b. Use single spacing and left alignment.
   c. Copy the Preamble to a new page, then change to a larger point size and more interesting typeface.
   d. Create a title page for your assignment, containing your name, course name, and appropriate title.
   e. Use a different typeface for the title page than in the rest of the document, and set the title in at least 24 points.
   f. Submit all three pages (the title page and both versions of the Preamble) to your instructor.

TYPOGRAPHY

The art of formatting a document is more than just knowing definitions, but knowing the definitions is definitely a starting point. A **typeface** is a complete set of characters with the same general appearance, and can be *serif* (cross lines at the end of the main strokes of each letter) or *sans serif* (without the cross lines). A **type size** is a vertical measurement, made from the top of the tallest letter in the character set to the bottom of the lowest letter in the character set. **Type style** refers to variations in the typeface, such as boldface and italics.

Several typefaces are shipped with Windows, including **Times New Roman,** a serif typeface, and **Arial**, a sans serif typeface. Times New Roman should be used for large amounts of text, whereas Arial is best used for titles and subtitles. It is best not to use too many different typefaces in the same document, but rather to use only one or two and then make the document interesting by varying their size and style.

FIGURE 2.18   Typography (Exercise 2)

𝔚e, the people of the United States, in order to form a more perfect Union, establish justice, insure domestic tranquillity, provide for the common defense, promote the general welfare, and secure the blessings of liberty to ourselves and our posterity, do ordain and establish this Constitution for the United States of America.

FIGURE 2.19   The Preamble (Exercise 3)

4. Tab Stops: Anyone who has used a typewriter is familiar with the function of the Tab key; that is, press Tab and the insertion point moves to the next tab stop (a measured position to align text at a specific place). The Tab key is more powerful in Word because you can choose from four different types of tab stops (left, center, right, and decimal). You can also specify a leader character, typically dots or hyphens, to draw the reader's eye across the page.

Create the document in Figure 2.20 and add your name in the indicated position. (Use the Help facility to discover how to work with tab stops.) Submit the completed document to your instructor as proof that you have mastered the Tab key.

EXAMPLES OF TAB STOPS

Example 1 - Right tab at 6":

CIS 120   **Maryann Barber**
Fall 1999   **September 21, 1999**

Example 2 - Right tab with a dot leader at 6":

Chapter 1...1
Chapter 2...31
Chapter 3...56

Example 3 - Right tab at 1" and left tab at 1.25":

                To: Maryann Barber
          From: Joel Stutz
Department: Computer Information Systems
   Subject: Exams

Example 4 - Left tab at 2" and a decimal tab at 3.5":

                  Rent $375.38
                  Utilities $125.59
                  Phone $56.92
                  Cable $42.45

FIGURE 2.20   Tab Stops (Exercise 4)

5. The Page Borders Command: Figure 2.21 illustrates a hypothetical title page for a paper describing the capabilities of borders and shading. The Borders and Shading command is applied at the paragraph level as indicated in the chapter. You can, however, select the Page Border tab within the Borders and Shading dialog box to create an unusual and attractive document. Experiment with the command to create a title page similar to Figure 2.21. Submit the document to your instructor as proof you did the exercise.

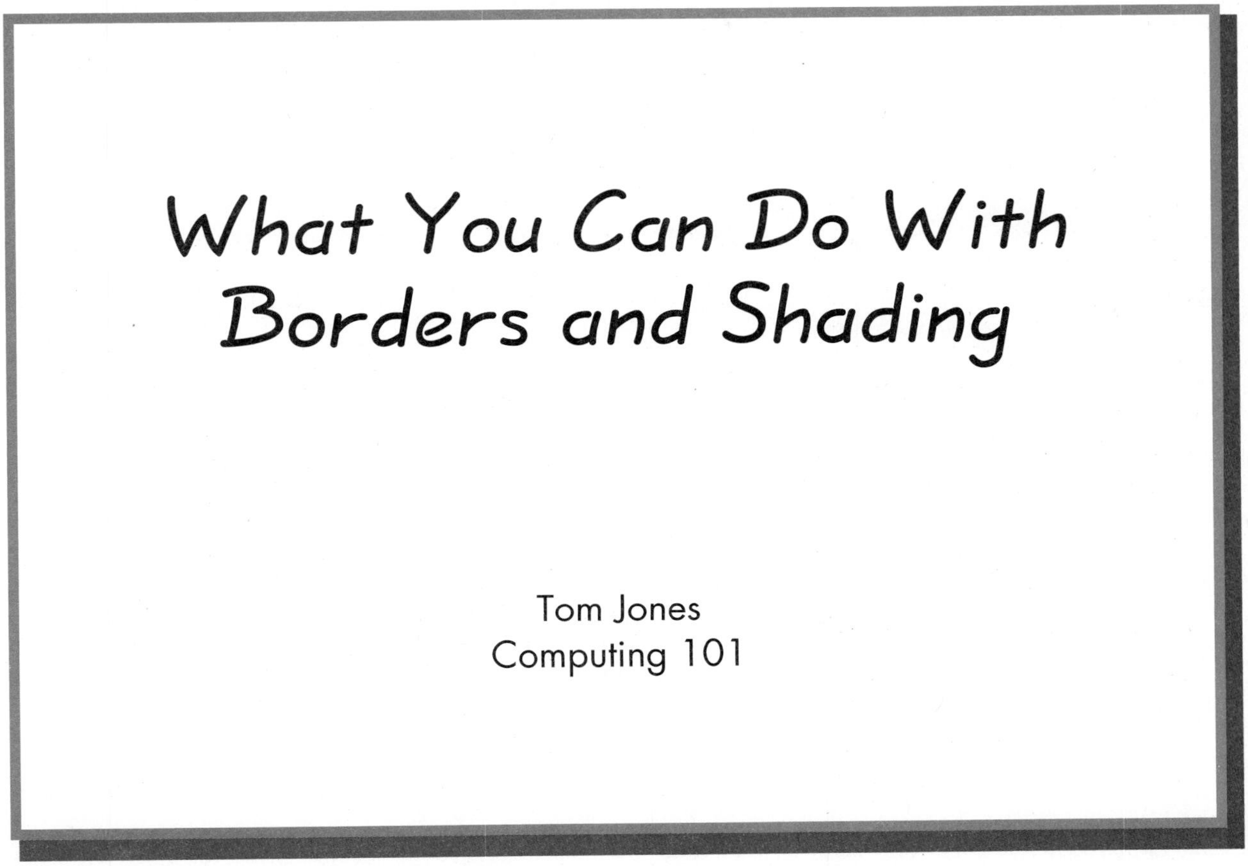

What You Can Do With Borders and Shading

Tom Jones
Computing 101

FIGURE 2.21   The Page Borders Command (Exercise 5)

6. Exploring Fonts: The Font Folder within the Control Panel displays the names of the fonts available on a system and enables you to obtain a printed sample of any specific font. Click the Start button, click (or point to) the Settings command, click (or point to) Control Panel, then double click the Fonts icon to open the font folder and display the fonts on your system.

   a. Double click a font you want to view, then click the Print button to print a sample of the selected font.

   b. Click the Fonts button on the Taskbar to return to the Fonts window and open a different font. Print a sample page of this font as well.

   c. Start Word. Create a title page containing your name, class, date, and the title of this assignment (My Favorite Fonts). Center the title. Use boldface or italics as you see fit. Be sure to use appropriate type sizes.

   d. Staple the three pages together (the title page and two font samples), then submit them to your instructor.

7. Inserting the Date and Time: Create a document similar to Figure 2.22 that describes the Insert Date and Time command. You need not duplicate our document exactly, but you are asked to print the dates in several formats. Use the columns feature to separate the two sets of dates. Note the keyboard shortcut that is described in the document to go to the next column. You will also have to insert a section break before and after the dates to change the number of columns in the document. Create your document on one day, then open it a day later, to be sure that the dates that were entered as fields were updated appropriately.

Inserting the Date and Time

The *Insert Date and Time command* puts the date (and/or time) into a document. The date can be inserted as a specific value (the date and time on which the command is executed) or as a *field*. The latter is updated automatically from the computer's internal clock whenever the document is opened or when the document is printed. You can also update a field manually, by selecting the appropriate command from a shortcut menu. Either way, the date may be printed in a variety of formats as shown below.

Update field box is clear	Update field box is checked
January 21, 1999	February 15, 1999
Thursday, January 21, 1999	Monday, February 15, 1999
1/21/99	2/15/99
21 January 1999	15 February 1999
1/21/99 10:08 AM	2/15/1999

Any date that is entered as a field is shaded by default. You can change that, however, by using the Options command in the Tools menu. (Select the View tab and click the drop-down arrow in the Field Shading list box to choose the option you want.) Note, too, that I created this document using the columns feature. My document has three sections, with the section in the middle containing two columns. (I pressed **Ctrl+Shift+Enter** to go from the bottom of one column to the top of the next.)

Maryann Coulter
January 21, 1999

FIGURE 2.22   Inserting the Date and Time (Exercise 7)

CASE STUDIES

Computers Past and Present

The ENIAC was the scientific marvel of its day and the world's first operational electronic computer. It could perform 5,000 additions per second, weighed 30 tons, and took 1,500 square feet of floor space. The price was a modest $486,000 in 1946 dollars. The story of the ENIAC and other influential computers of the author's choosing is found in the file *History of Computers*, which we forgot to format, so we are asking you to do it for us.

Be sure to use appropriate emphasis for the names of the various computers. Create a title page in front of the document, then submit the completed assignment to your instructor. If you are ambitious, you can enhance this assignment by using your favorite search engine to look for computer museums on the Web. Visit one or two sites, and include this information on a separate page at the end of the document. One last task, and that is to update the description of Today's PC (the last computer in the document).

Your First Consultant's Job

Go to a real installation, such as a doctor's or an attorney's office, the company where you work, or the computer lab at school. Determine the backup procedures that are in effect, then write a one-page report indicating whether the policy is adequate and, if necessary, offering suggestions for improvement. Your report should be addressed to the individual in charge of the business, and it should cover all aspects of the backup strategy—that is, which files are backed up and how often, and what software is used for the backup operation. Use appropriate emphasis (for example, bold italics) to identify any potential problems. This is a professional document (it is your first consultant's job), and its appearance must be perfect in every way.

To Hyphenate or Not to Hyphenate

The best way to learn about hyphenation is to experiment with an existing document. Open the *To Hyphenate or Not to Hyphenate* document that is on the data disk. The document is currently set in 12-point type with hyphenation in effect. Experiment with various formatting changes that will change the soft line breaks to see the effect on the hyphenation within the document. You can change the point size, the number of columns, and/or the right indent. You can also suppress hyphenation altogether, as described within the document. Summarize your findings in a short note to your instructor.

Paper Makes a Difference

Most of us take paper for granted, but the right paper can make a significant difference in the effectiveness of the document. Reports and formal correspondence are usually printed on white paper, but you would be surprised how many different shades of white there are. Other types of documents lend themselves to colored paper for additional impact. In short, which paper you use is far from an automatic decision. Walk into a local copy store and see if they have any specialty papers available. Our favorite source for paper is a company called *Paper Direct* (1-800-APAPERS). Ask for a catalog, then consider the use of a specialty paper the next time you have an important project.

The Invitation

Choose an event and produce the perfect invitation. The possibilities are endless and limited only by your imagination. You can invite people to your wedding or to a fraternity party. Your laser printer and abundance of fancy fonts enable you to do anything a professional printer can do. Special paper (see previous case study) will add the finishing touch. Go to it—this assignment is a lot of fun.

One Space After a Period

Touch typing classes typically teach the student to place two spaces after a period. The technique worked well in the days of the typewriter and monospaced fonts, but it creates an artificially large space when used with proportional fonts and a word processor. Select any document that is at least several paragraphs in length and print the document with the current spacing. Use the Find and Replace commands to change to the alternate spacing, then print the document a second time. Which spacing looks better to you? Submit both versions of the document to your instructor with a brief note summarizing your findings.

The Contest

Almost everyone enjoys some form of competition. Ask your instructor to choose a specific type of document, such as a flyer or résumé, and declare a contest in the class to produce the "best" document. Submit your entry, but write your name on the back of the document so that it can be judged anonymously. Your instructor may want to select a set of semifinalists and then distribute copies of those documents so that the class can vote on the winner.

chapter 3

ENHANCING A DOCUMENT: THE WEB AND OTHER RESOURCES

OBJECTIVES

After reading this chapter you will be able to:

1. Describe object linking and embedding; explain how it is used to create a compound document.
2. Describe the resources in the Microsoft Clip Gallery; insert clip art and/or a photograph into a document.
3. Use the Format Picture command to wrap text around a clip art image.
4. Use WordArt to insert decorative text into a document.
5. Describe the Internet and World Wide Web; download resources from the Web for inclusion in a Word document.
6. Insert a hyperlink into a Word document; save a Word document as a Web page.
7. Use the Drawing toolbar to create and modify lines and objects.
8. Insert a footnote or endnote into a document to cite a reference.
9. Use wizards and templates to create a document.

OVERVIEW

This chapter describes how to enhance a document using applications within Microsoft Office Professional as well as resources on the Internet and World Wide Web. We begin with a discussion of the Microsoft Clip Gallery, a collection of clip art, sound files, and motion clips that can be inserted into any office document. We describe how Microsoft WordArt can be used to create special effects with text and how to create lines and objects through the Drawing toolbar.

These resources pale, however, in comparison to what is available via the Internet. Thus, we also show you how to download an object from the Web and include it in an Office document. We describe how to add footnotes to give appropriate credit to your sources and how to further enhance a document through inclusion of hyperlinks. We also explain how to save a Word document as a Web page so that you can post the documents you create to a Web server or local area network.

The chapter also describes the various wizards and templates that are built into Microsoft Word to help you create professionally formatted documents. We believe this to be a very enjoyable chapter that will add significantly to your capability in Microsoft Word. As always, learning is best accomplished by doing, and the hands-on exercises are essential to master the material.

A COMPOUND DOCUMENT

The applications in Microsoft Office are thoroughly integrated with one another. Equally important, they share information through a technology known as *Object Linking and Embedding (OLE),* which enables you to create a *compound document* containing data (objects) from multiple applications.

Consider, for example, the compound document in Figure 3.1, which was created in Microsoft Word but contains objects (data) from other applications. The *clip art* (a graphic as opposed to a photograph) was taken from the Microsoft Clip Gallery. The title of the document was created using Microsoft WordArt. The document also illustrates the Insert Symbol command to insert special characters such as the Windows logo.

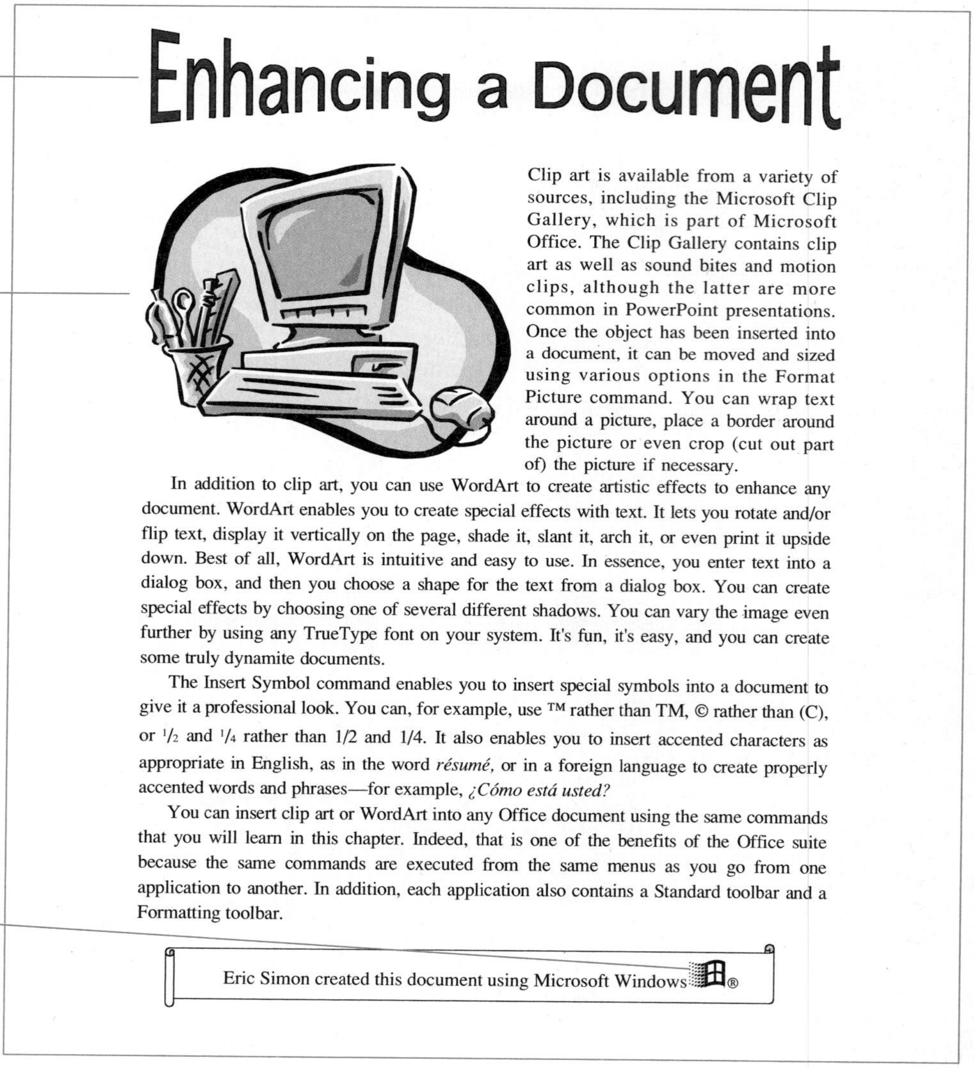

WordArt ————

Enhancing a Document

Clip art ————

Clip art is available from a variety of sources, including the Microsoft Clip Gallery, which is part of Microsoft Office. The Clip Gallery contains clip art as well as sound bites and motion clips, although the latter are more common in PowerPoint presentations. Once the object has been inserted into a document, it can be moved and sized using various options in the Format Picture command. You can wrap text around a picture, place a border around the picture or even crop (cut out part of) the picture if necessary.

In addition to clip art, you can use WordArt to create artistic effects to enhance any document. WordArt enables you to create special effects with text. It lets you rotate and/or flip text, display it vertically on the page, shade it, slant it, arch it, or even print it upside down. Best of all, WordArt is intuitive and easy to use. In essence, you enter text into a dialog box, and then you choose a shape for the text from a dialog box. You can create special effects by choosing one of several different shadows. You can vary the image even further by using any TrueType font on your system. It's fun, it's easy, and you can create some truly dynamite documents.

The Insert Symbol command enables you to insert special symbols into a document to give it a professional look. You can, for example, use ™ rather than TM, © rather than (C), or $\frac{1}{2}$ and $\frac{1}{4}$ rather than 1/2 and 1/4. It also enables you to insert accented characters as appropriate in English, as in the word *résumé,* or in a foreign language to create properly accented words and phrases—for example, *¿Cómo está usted?*

You can insert clip art or WordArt into any Office document using the same commands that you will learn in this chapter. Indeed, that is one of the benefits of the Office suite because the same commands are executed from the same menus as you go from one application to another. In addition, each application also contains a Standard toolbar and a Formatting toolbar.

Eric Simon created this document using Microsoft Windows ⊞ ®

Windows logo added through
Insert Symbol command ————

FIGURE 3.1 A Compound Document

Microsoft Clip Gallery

The **Microsoft Clip Gallery** contains clip art, sound files, and motion clips and it is accessible from any application in Microsoft Office. Clip art is inserted into a document in one of two ways—through the **Insert Object command** or more directly through the **Insert Picture command** as shown in Figure 3.2. Choose the type of object and the category (such as a picture in the Animals category in Figure 3.2a), then select the image (the lion in Figure 3.2b) and insert it into the document. After a picture has been placed into a document, it can be moved and sized just like any Windows object.

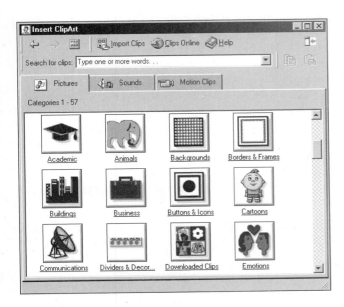

(a) Choose the Category

(b) Choose the Image

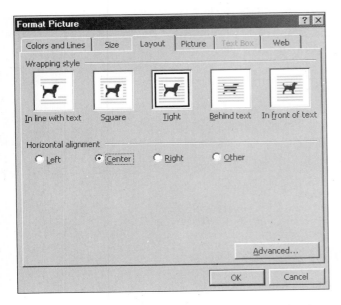

(c) Format the Picture

(d) The Completed Document

FIGURE 3.2 Microsoft Clip Gallery

The ***Format Picture command*** enables you to further customize the picture. The Layout tab in Figure 3.2c determines the position of the picture with respect to the text. We chose the tight wrapping style, which means that the text comes to the border of the picture. You can also use the ***Picture Toolbar*** (not shown in Figure 3.2) to ***crop*** (cut out part of) the picture if necessary. Figure 3.2d shows how the selected object appears in the completed document. Note, too, the ***sizing handles*** on the graphic that enable you to move and size the picture within the document.

The Insert Symbol Command

One characteristic of a professional document is the use of typographic symbols in place of ordinary typing—for example, ® rather than (R), © rather than (C), or ½ and ¼ rather than 1/2 and 1/4. Much of this formatting is implemented automatically by Word through substitutions built into the ***AutoCorrect*** feature. Other characters, especially accented characters such as the "é" in résumé, or those in a foreign language (e.g., ¿Cómo está usted?), have to be inserted manually into a document.

Look carefully at the last line of Figure 3.1, and notice the Windows logo at the end of the sentence. The latter was created through the ***Insert Symbol command,*** as shown in Figure 3.3. You select the font containing the desired character (e.g., Wingdings in Figure 3.3), then you select the character, and finally you click the Insert command button to place the character in the document.

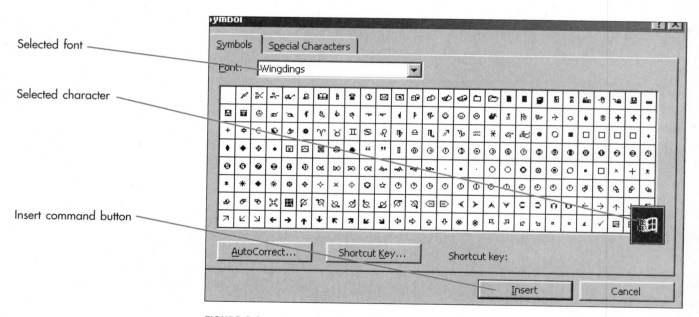

FIGURE 3.3   The Insert Symbol Command

THE WINGDINGS AND SYMBOLS FONTS

The Wingdings and Symbols fonts are two of the best-kept secrets in Windows 95. Both fonts contain a variety of special characters that can be inserted into a document through the Insert Symbol command. These fonts are scaleable to any point size, enabling you to create some truly unusual documents. (See practice exercise 3 at the end of the chapter.)

Microsoft WordArt

Microsoft WordArt is an application within Microsoft Office that creates decorative text to add interest to a document. You can use WordArt in addition to clip art, as was done in Figure 3.1, or in place of clip art if the right image is not available. You're limited only by your imagination, as you can rotate text in any direction, add three-dimensional effects, display the text vertically down the page, shade it, slant it, arch it, or even print it upside down.

WordArt is intuitive and easy to use. In essence, you choose a style for the text from among the selections in the dialog box of Figure 3.4a, then you enter your specific text as shown in Figure 3.4b. You can modify the style through various special effects, you can use any TrueType font on your system, and you can change the color or shading. Figure 3.4c shows the completed WordArt object. It's fun, it's easy, and you can create some truly dynamite documents.

Selected WordArt style

Selected font

Enter text

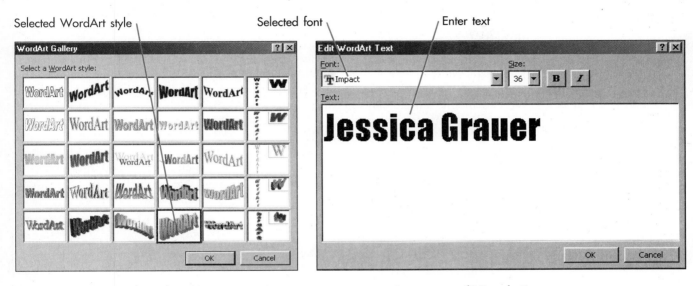

(a) Choose the Style

(b) Enter the Text

(c) Completed WordArt

FIGURE 3.4   Microsoft WordArt

Did you ever stop to think how the images in the Clip Gallery were developed? Undoubtedly they were drawn by someone with artistic ability who used basic shapes, such as lines and curves in various combinations, to create the images. The *Drawing toolbar* in Figure 3.5 contains all of the tools necessary to create original clip art. As with any toolbar, you can point to a button to display a Screen-Tip containing the name of the button that is indicative of its function.

To draw an object, select the appropriate tool, then click and drag in the document to create the object. Select the Line tool, for example, then draw the line. After the line has been created, you can select it and change its properties (such as thickness, style, or color) by using other tools on the Drawing toolbar. To create a drawing, you add other objects such as lines and curves, and soon you have a piece of original clip art.

Once you learn the basics, there are other techniques to master. The Shift key, for example, has special significance when used in conjunction with the Line, Rectangle, and Oval tools. Press and hold the Shift key as you drag the line tool horizontally or vertically to create a perfectly straight line in either direction. Press and hold the Shift key as you drag the Rectangle and Oval tool to create a square or circle, respectively. We don't expect you to create clip art comparable to the images within the Clip Gallery, but you can use the tools on the Drawing toolbar to modify an existing image and/or create simple shapes of your own that can enhance any document.

One tool that is especially useful is the *AutoShapes button* that displays a series of selected shapes such as the callout or banner. And, as with any object, you can change the thickness, color, or fill by selecting the object and choosing the appropriate tool. It's fun, it's easy—just be flexible and willing to experiment. We think you will be pleased at what you will be able to do.

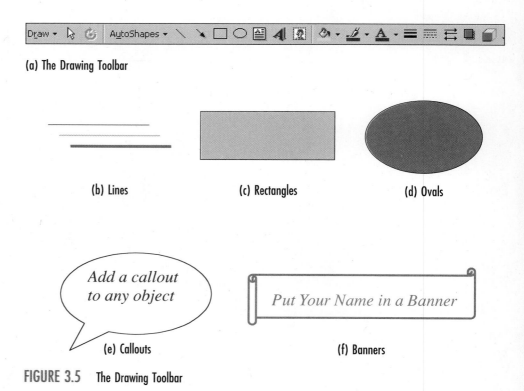

(a) The Drawing Toolbar

(b) Lines   (c) Rectangles   (d) Ovals

(e) Callouts   (f) Banners

FIGURE 3.5 The Drawing Toolbar

Creating a Compound Document

Objective: To create a compound document containing clip art and WordArt; to illustrate the Insert Symbol command to place typographical symbols into a document. Use Figure 3.6 as a guide in the exercise.

STEP 1: Insert the Clip Art

➤ Start Word. Open the **Clip Art and WordArt** document in the Exploring Word folder. Save the document as **Modified Clip Art and WordArt.**

➤ Check that the insertion point is at the beginning of the document. Pull down the **Insert menu,** click **Picture,** then click **Clip Art** to display the Insert Clip Art dialog box as shown in Figure 3.6a.

➤ If necessary, click the **Pictures tab** and select (click) the **Science and Technology category.** Select the **Computers graphic** (or a different image if you prefer), then click the **Insert Clip button** on the shortcut menu.

➤ The picture should appear in the document where it can be moved and sized as described in the next several steps.

➤ Click the **Close button** on the Insert Clip Art dialog box.

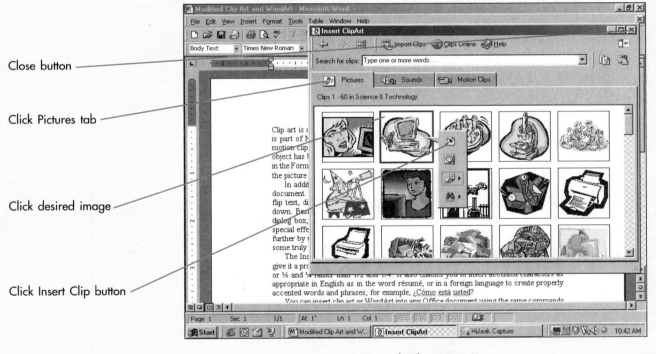

Close button

Click Pictures tab

Click desired image

Click Insert Clip button

(a) Insert the Clip Art (step 1)

FIGURE 3.6   Hands-on Exercise 1

STEP 2: Move and Size the Picture

➤ Change to the Print Layout view in Figure 3.6b. Move and size the image.

➤ To size an object:

- Click the object to display the sizing handles.
- Drag a corner handle (the mouse pointer changes to a double arrow) to change the length and width of the picture simultaneously; this keeps the graphic in proportion as it sizes it.
- Drag a handle on the horizontal or vertical border to change one dimension only; this distorts the picture.

➤ To move an object:

- Click the object to display the sizing handles.
- Point to any part of the image except a sizing handle (the mouse pointer changes to a four-sided arrow), then click and drag to move the image elsewhere in the document. You cannot wrap text around the image until you execute the Format Picture command in step 3.

➤ Save the document.

Picture toolbar is displayed when image is selected

Click and drag sizing handle to size object

Click and drag to move object

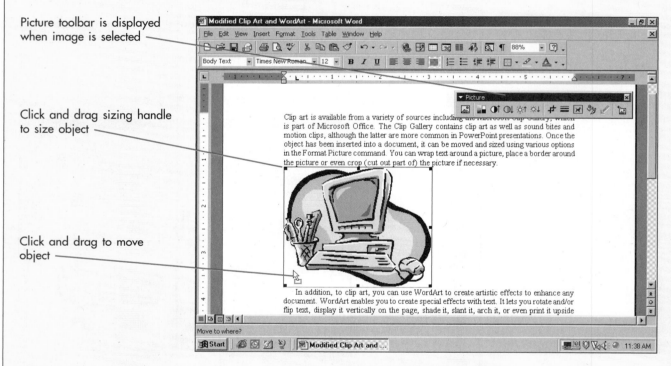

(b) Move and Size the Picture (step 2)

FIGURE 3.6   Hands-on Exercise 1 (continued)

FIND THE RIGHT CLIP ART

Use the search capability within the Clip Gallery to find the right image. Pull down the Insert menu, click Picture, then click Clip Art to display the Insert Clip Art dialog box. Click in the Search for text box, enter a key word such as "women," then press the enter key to display all of the images, regardless of category, that list "women" as a key word.

STEP 3: Format the Picture

➤ Be sure the clip art is still selected, then pull down the **Format menu** and select the **Picture command** to display the Format Picture dialog box in Figure 3.6c.

➤ Click the **Layout tab,** select **Square** as the wrapping style, and choose the **left option button** under horizontal alignment.

➤ The text should be wrapped to the right of the image. Move and size the image until you are satisfied with its position. Note, however, that the image will always be positioned (wrapped) according to the settings in the Format Picture command.

➤ Save the document.

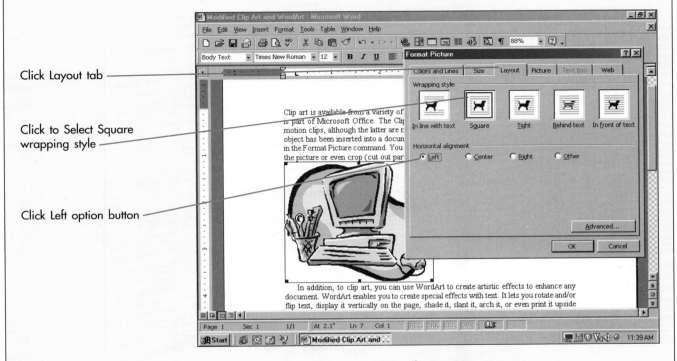

Click Layout tab

Click to Select Square wrapping style

Click Left option button

(c) Format the Picture (step 3)

FIGURE 3.6   Hands-on Exercise 1 (continued)

CLIP PROPERTIES

Every clip art image has multiple properties that determine the category (or categories) in which it is listed as well as key words that are reflected in a search of the Clip Gallery. Right click any image within the Insert Clip Art dialog box and click the Click Properties command to display the Clip Properties dialog box. Click the Categories tab, then check any additional categories under which the image should appear. Click the Keywords tab to add (delete) the entries for this item. Click OK to accept the changes and close the Properties dialog box. Check the additional categories or search on a new key word within the Insert Clip Art dialog box to verify the effect of your changes.

STEP 4: WordArt

➤ Press **Ctrl+End** to move to the end of the document. Pull down the **Insert menu,** click **Picture,** then click **WordArt** to display the WordArt Gallery dialog box.

➤ Select the WordArt style you like (you can change it later). Click **OK.** You will see a second dialog box in which you enter the text. Enter **Enhancing a Document.** Click **OK.**

➤ The WordArt object appears in your document in the style you selected. Point to the WordArt object and click the **right mouse button** to display the shortcut menu in Figure 3.6d. Click **Format WordArt** to display the Format WordArt dialog box.

➤ Click the **Layout tab,** then select **Square** as the Wrapping style. Click **OK.** It is important to select this wrapping option to facilitate placing the WordArt at the top of the document. Save the document.

WordArt toolbar is displayed
when WordArt object is
selected

Point to WordArt object and
click right mouse button to
display shortcut menu

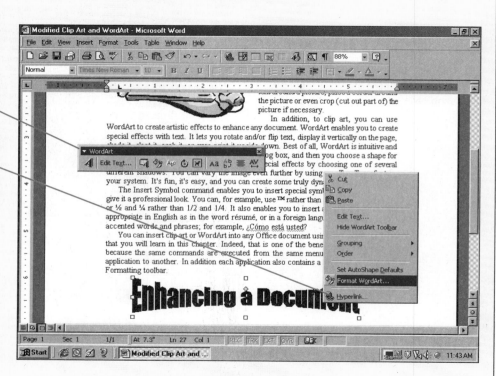

(d) WordArt (step 4)

FIGURE 3.6   Hands-on Exercise 1 (continued)

FORMATTING WORDART

The WordArt toolbar offers the easiest way to execute various commands associated with a WordArt object. It is displayed automatically when a WordArt object is selected, and suppressed otherwise. As with any toolbar, you can point to a button to display a ScreenTip containing the name of the button, which is indicative of its function. You will find buttons to display the text vertically, change the style or shape, and/or edit the text.

STEP 5: WordArt (continued)

➤ Click and drag the WordArt object to move it the top of the document as shown in Figure 3.6e. (The Format WordArt dialog box is not yet visible.)

➤ Point to the WordArt object, click the **right mouse button** to display a short-cut menu, then click **Format WordArt** to display the Format WordArt dialog box.

➤ Click the **Colors and Lines tab,** then click the **Fill Color drop-down arrow** to display the available colors. Select a different color (e.g., blue). Click **OK**.

➤ Move and/or size the WordArt object as necessary.

➤ Save the document.

Click Colors and Lines tab

Move WordArt object to top of document

Click Fill color drop-down arrow

Select a color

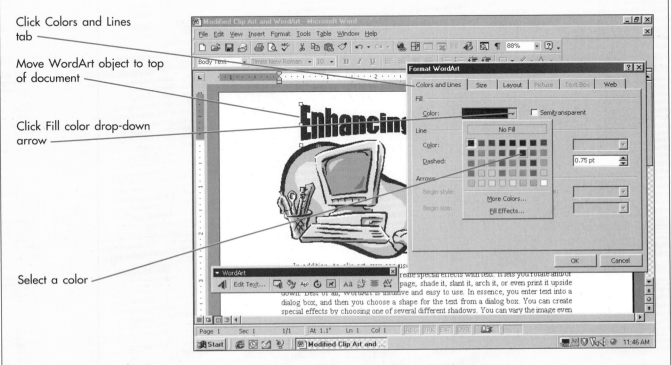

(e) WordArt, Continued (step 5)

FIGURE 3.6   Hands-on Exercise 1 (continued)

THE THIRD DIMENSION

You can make your WordArt images even more dramatic by adding 3-D effects. You can tilt the text up or down, right or left, increase or decrease the depth, and change the shading. Pull down the View menu, click Toolbars, click Customize to display the complete list of available toolbars, click the Toolbars tab, check the box to display the 3-D Settings toolbar, and click the Close button. Select the WordArt object, then experiment with various tools and special effects. The results are even better if you have a color printer.

STEP 6: The Insert Symbol Command

➤ Press **Ctrl+End** to move to the end of the document as shown in Figure 3.6f. Press the **enter key** to insert a blank line at the end of the document.

➤ Type the sentence, **Eric Simon created this document using Microsoft Windows,** substituting your name for Eric Simon. Click the **Center button** on the Formatting toolbar to center the sentence.

➤ Pull down the **Insert menu,** click **Symbol,** then choose **Wingdings** from the Font list box. Click the **Windows logo** (the last character in the last line), click **Insert,** then close the Symbol dialog box.

➤ Click and drag to select the newly inserted symbol, click the **drop-down arrow** on the **Font Size box,** then change the font to **24** points. Press the **right arrow key** to deselect the symbol.

➤ Click the **drop-down arrow** on the **Font Size box** and change to **10 point type** so that subsequent text is entered in this size. Type **(r)** after the Windows logo and try to watch the monitor as you enter the text. The (r) will be converted automatically to ® because of the AutoFormat command.

Font size box

Center button

Press Ctrl+End to move insertion point to end of document

Click to display additional fonts

Click to select symbol

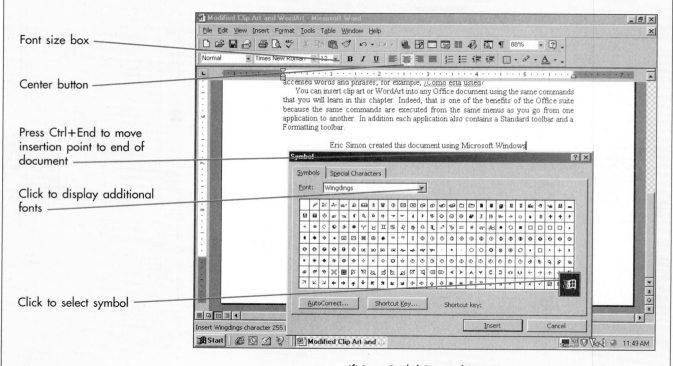

(f) Insert Symbol Command (step 6)

FIGURE 3.6   Hands-on Exercise 1 (continued)

AUTOCORRECT AND AUTOFORMAT

The AutoCorrect feature not only corrects mistakes as you type by substituting one character string for another (e.g., *the* for *teh*), but it will also substitute symbols for typewritten equivalents such as © for (c), provided the entries are included in the table of substitutions. The AutoFormat feature is similar in concept and replaces common fractions such as 1/2 or 1/4 with ½ or ¼. It also converts ordinal numbers such as 1st to 1st.

STEP 7: Create the AutoShape

➤ Pull down the **View menu,** click (or point to) the **Toolbars command** to display the list of available toolbars, then click the **Drawing toolbar.**

➤ Press **Ctrl+End** to move to the end of the document. Move up one line and press **enter** to create a blank line. Click the **down arrow** on the AutoShapes button to display the AutoShapes menu. Click the **Stars and Banners submenu** and select (click) the **Horizontal scroll.**

➤ The mouse pointer changes to a tiny crosshair. Click and drag the mouse over the last sentence (that has Eric Simon's name) to create the scroll as shown in Figure 3.6g (the shortcut menus are not yet visible). Release the mouse.

➤ The scroll is still selected but the underlying text has disappeared. Click the **right mouse button** to display a context-sensitive menu, click the **Order command,** then click **Send Behind Text.** The text is now visible.

➤ Click the **Line Style** and/or **Line Color** tools to change the thickness and color of the line, respectively.

➤ Click elsewhere in the document to deselect the scroll. Save the document.

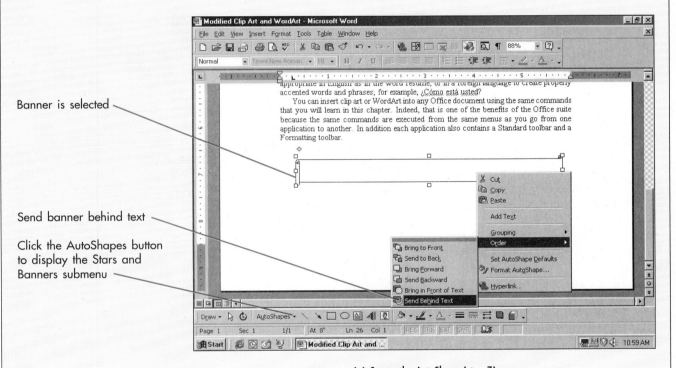

Banner is selected

Send banner behind text

Click the AutoShapes button to display the Stars and Banners submenu

(g) Create the AutoShape (step 7)

FIGURE 3.5   Hands-on Exercise 1 (continued)

DISPLAY THE AUTOSHAPE TOOLBAR

Click the down arrow on the AutoShapes button on the Drawing toolbar to display a cascaded menu listing the various types of AutoShapes, then click and drag the menu's title bar to display the menu as a floating toolbar. Click any tool on the AutoShapes toolbar (such as Stars and Banners), then click and drag its title bar to display the various stars and banners in their own floating toolbar.

STEP 8: The Completed Document

➤ Pull down the **File menu** and click the **Page Setup command** to display the Page Setup dialog box. Click the **Margins tab** and change the top margin to **1.5 inches** (to accommodate the WordArt at the top of the document). Click **OK.**

➤ Click the **drop-down arrow** on the Zoom box and select **Whole Page** to preview the completed document as shown in Figure 3.6h. You can change the size and position of the objects from within this view. For example:

  • Click the WordArt to select the object and display the sizing handles and WordArt toolbar.

  • Click the banner to deselect the WordArt and display the sizing handles for the banner.

➤ Move and size either object as necessary; then save the document a final time.

➤ Print the document and submit it to your instructor as proof that you did the exercise. Close the document. Exit Word if you do not want to continue with the next exercise at this time.

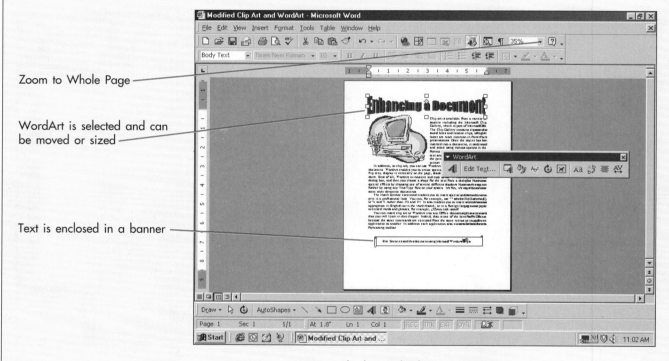

Zoom to Whole Page

WordArt is selected and can be moved or sized

Text is enclosed in a banner

(h) The Completed Document (step 8)

FIGURE 3.6   Hands-on Exercise 1 (continued)

HIGHLIGHT IMPORTANT TEXT

You will love the Highlight text tool, especially if you are in the habit of highlighting text in with a pen. Click the tool to turn the feature on (the button is depressed and the mouse pointer changes to a pen), then paint as many sections as you like. Click the tool a second time to turn the feature off. Click the drop-down arrow on the tool to change the highlighting color.

WORD 2000 AND THE INTERNET

The emergence of the Internet and World Wide Web has totally changed our society. Perhaps you are already familiar with the basic concepts that underlie the Internet, but if not, a brief review is in order. The ***Internet*** is a network of networks that connects computers anywhere in the world. The ***World Wide Web*** (WWW or simply, the Web) is a very large subset of the Internet, consisting of those computers that store a special type of document known as a ***Web page*** or ***HTML document.***

The interesting thing about a Web page is that it contains references called ***hyperlinks*** to other Web pages, which may in turn be stored on a different computer that may be located anywhere in the world. And therein lies the fascination of the Web, in that you simply click on link after link to go effortlessly from one document to the next. You can start your journey on your professor's home page, then browse through any set of links you wish to follow.

The Internet and World Wide Web are thoroughly integrated into Office 2000 in three important ways. First, you can download resources from any Web page for inclusion in an Office document. Second, you can insert hyperlinks into an Office document, then click those links within Office to display the associated Web page. And finally, you can convert any Office document into a Web page as we will do in Figure 3.7.

All Web pages are developed in a special language called ***HTML (Hyper-Text Markup Language).*** Initially, the only way to create a Web page was to learn HTML. As indicated, Office 2000 simplifies the process because you can create the document in Word, then simply save it as a Web page. In other words, you start Word in the usual fashion and enter the text of the document with basic formatting. However, instead of saving the document in the default format (as a Word document), you use the ***Save As Web Page command*** to convert the document to HTML. Microsoft Word does the rest and generates the HTML statements for you.

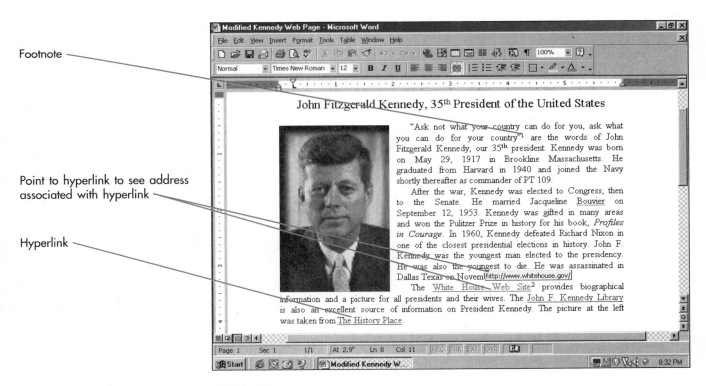

FIGURE 3.7   Creating a Web Page

Figure 3.7 contains the Web page you will create in the next hands-on exercise. The exercise begins by having you search the Web to locate a suitable photograph of President Kennedy for inclusion into the document. You then download the picture to your PC and use the Insert Picture command to insert the photograph into your document. You add formatting, hyperlinks, and footnotes as appropriate, then you save the document as a Web page. The exercise is easy to do and it will give you an appreciation for the various Web capabilities that are built into Office 2000.

Realize, however, that even if you do not place your page on the Web, you can still view it locally on your PC. This is the approach we follow in the next hands-on exercise, which shows you how to save a Word document as a Web page, then see the results of your effort in a Web browser. The Web page is stored on a local drive (e.g., on drive A or drive C) rather than on an Internet server, but it can still be viewed through Internet Explorer (or any other browser).

The ability to create links to local documents and to view those pages through a Web browser has created an entirely new way to disseminate information. Organizations of every size are taking advantage of this capability to develop an **intranet,** in which Web pages are placed on a local area network for use within the organizations. The documents on an intranet are available only to individuals with access to the local area network on which the documents are stored. This is in contrast to loading pages onto a Web server, where they can be viewed by anyone with access to the Web.

THE WEB PAGE WIZARD

The Save As Web Page command converts a Word document to the equivalent HTML document for posting on a Web server. The Web Page Wizard extends the process to create a multipage Web site, complete with navigation and a professionally designed theme. The navigation options let you choose between horizontal and vertical frames so that the user can see the links and content at the same time. The design themes are quite varied and include every element on a Web page. The Wizard is an incredibly powerful tool that rivals any Web-authoring tool we have seen. Try it if a Web project is in your future!

Copyright Protection

A **copyright** provides legal protection for a written or artistic work, giving the author exclusive rights to its use and reproduction, except as governed under the fair use exclusion as explained below. Anything on the Internet or World Wide Web should be considered copyrighted unless the document specifically says it is in the **public domain,** in which case the author is giving everyone the right to freely reproduce and distribute the material.

Does copyright protection mean you cannot quote in your term papers statistics and other facts you find while browsing the Web? Does it mean you cannot download an image to include in your report? The answer to both questions depends on the amount of the material and on your intended use of the information. It is considered **fair use,** and thus not an infringement of copyright, to use a portion of the work for educational, nonprofit purposes, or for the purpose of critical review or commentary. In other words, you can use a quote, downloaded image, or other information from the Web *if* you cite the original work in your footnotes and/or bibliography. Facts themselves are not covered by copyright, so you can use statistical and other data without fear of infringement. You should, however, cite the original source in your document.

Footnotes and Endnotes

A *footnote* provides additional information about an item, such as its source, and appears at the bottom of the page where the reference occurs. An *endnote* is similar in concept but appears at the end of a document. A horizontal line separates the notes from the rest of the document.

The ***Insert Footnote command*** inserts a note into a document, and automatically assigns the next sequential number to that note. To create a note, position the insertion point where you want the reference, pull down the Insert menu, click Footnote to display the dialog box in Figure 3.8a, then choose either the Footnote or Endnote option button. A superscript reference is inserted into the document, and you will be positioned at the bottom of the page (a footnote) or at the end of the document (an endnote) where you enter the text of the note.

The Options command button in the Footnote and Endnote dialog box enables you to modify the formatting of either type of note as shown in Figure 3.8b. You can change the numbering format (e.g., to Roman numerals) and/or start numbering from a number other than 1. You can also convert footnotes to endnotes or vice versa.

The Insert Footnote command adjusts for last-minute changes, either in your writing or in your professor's requirements. It will, for example, renumber all existing notes to accommodate the addition or deletion of a footnote or endnote. Existing notes are moved (or deleted) within a document by moving (deleting) the reference mark rather than the text of the footnote.

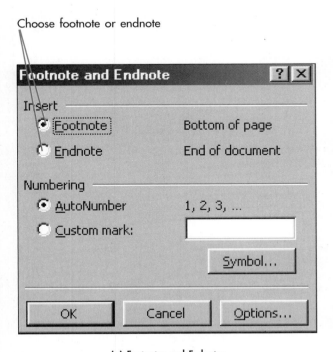

Choose footnote or endnote

Enter initial footnote number

Click to select format of footnote number

(a) Footnotes and Endnotes

(b) Options

FIGURE 3.8   Footnotes and Endnotes

Word 2000 and the Web

Objective: To download a picture from the Internet for use in a Word document; to insert a hyperlink into a Word document; to save a Word document as a Web page. The exercise requires an Internet connection.

STEP 1: Search the Web

➤ Start **Internet Explorer.** Click the **Maximize button** so that Internet Explorer takes the entire screen.

➤ Click the **Search button** on the Internet Explorer toolbar to open the Explorer bar. The option button to find a Web page is selected by default. Enter **John Kennedy** in the text box, then click the **Search button.**

➤ The results of the search are displayed in the left pane. You can follow any of the links returned by your search engine, or you can attempt to duplicate our results using **Yahoo.** Click the **down arrow** on the **Next button,** then select **Yahoo** as the search engine.

➤ The list of hits is displayed at the bottom of the left pane as shown in Figure 3.9a. (Your list may be different from ours.) Click any link and the associated page is displayed in the right pane. We chose the first category. The links for that category are displayed in the right pane, where we chose the link to **Photo History of JFK.**

➤ Close the left pane to give yourself more room to browse through the site containing the Kennedy photographs. (You can click the **Search button** at any time to reopen the Explorer bar to choose a different site.)

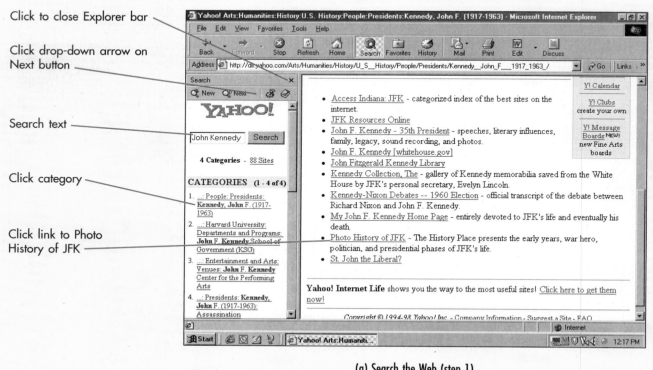

Click to close Explorer bar

Click drop-down arrow on Next button

Search text

Click category

Click link to Photo History of JFK

(a) Search the Web (step 1)

FIGURE 3.9   Hands-on Exercise 2

STEP 2: Save the Picture

➤ Point to the picture of President Kennedy you want to use in your document. Click the **right mouse button** to display a shortcut menu, then click the **Save Picture As command** to display the Save As dialog box in Figure 3.9b.

- Click the **drop-down arrow** in the Save in list box to specify the drive and folder in which you want to save the graphic.
- Internet Explorer supplies the file name and file type for you. You may change the name, but you cannot change the file type.
- Click the **Save button** to download the image. Remember the file name and location, as you will need to access the file in the next step.

➤ The Save As dialog box will close automatically after the picture has been downloaded. Click the **Minimize button** in the Internet Explorer window, since you are temporarily finished using the browser.

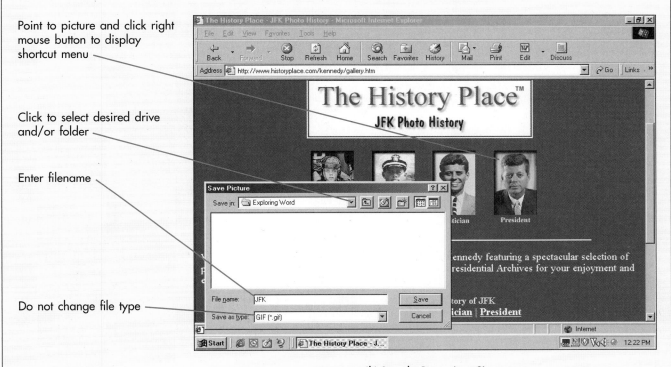

Point to picture and click right mouse button to display shortcut menu

Click to select desired drive and/or folder

Enter filename

Do not change file type

(b) Save the Picture (step 2)

FIGURE 3.9   Hands-on Exercise 2 (continued)

MINIMIZING VERSUS CLOSING AN APPLICATION

Minimizing an application is different from closing it, and you should understand the difference. Minimizing an application leaves the application open in memory, but shrinks its window to a button on the Windows taskbar so that you can return to it later in the session. Closing an application removes the application from memory, so that you have to restart the application if you need it. The advantage to closing an application, however, is that you free system resources, so that your remaining applications will run more efficiently.

STEP 3: Insert the Picture

➤ Start Word and open the **Kennedy document** in the **Exploring Word folder.** Save the document as **Modified Kennedy.**

➤ Pull down the **View menu** to be sure that you are in the **Print Layout view** (or else you will not see the picture after it is inserted into the document). Pull down the **Insert menu,** point to (or click) **Picture command,** then click **From File** to display the Insert Picture dialog box shown in Figure 3.9c.

➤ Click the **drop-down arrow** on the Look in text box to select the drive and folder where you previously saved the picture.

➤ Select (click) **JFK,** which is the file containing the picture of President Kennedy. Click the **drop-down arrow** on the **Views button** to switch to the **Preview button** and display the picture prior to inserting it into the document. Click **Insert.**

➤ Save the document.

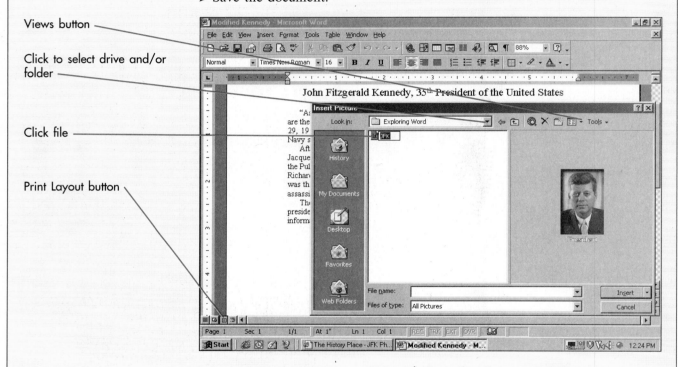

Views button

Click to select drive and/or folder

Click file

Print Layout button

(c) Insert the Picture (step 3)

FIGURE 3.9   Hands-on Exercise 2 (continued)

THE VIEWS BUTTON

Click the Views button to cycle through the four available views, each with a flavor of its own. The Details view shows the file size as well as the date and time the file was last modified. The Preview view displays the beginning of the file without having to open it. The Properties view shows additional characteristics about the file, such as the author's name. The List view displays only icons and file names, but enables you to see the largest number of files without having to scroll. Choose the view that is appropriate for your current task.

STEP 4: Move and Size the Picture

➤ Point to the picture after it is inserted into the document, click the **right mouse button** to display a shortcut menu, then click the **Format Picture command** to display the Format Picture dialog box.

➤ Click the **Layout tab,** choose **Square** as the Wrapping Style, then click the **Left option button** under Horizontal Alignment. Click **OK** to accept the settings and close the Format Picture dialog box. Move and/or size the picture so that it approximates the position in Figure 3.9d.

➤ Check that the picture is still selected, then click the **Crop tool** on the Picture toolbar. The mouse pointer changes to interlocking lines. Click and drag the sizing handle on the bottom of the picture upward to delete the label in the picture. Resize the picture as necessary.

➤ Save the document.

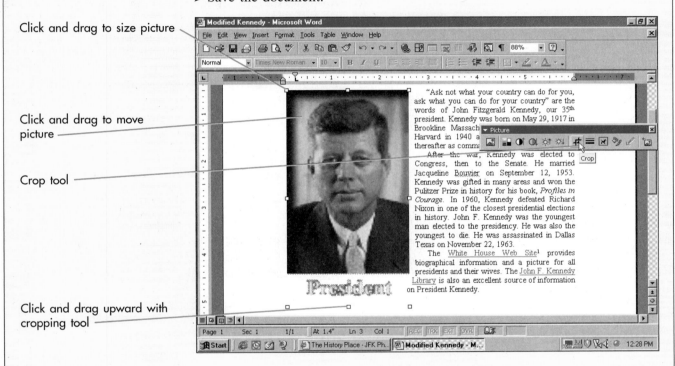

Click and drag to size picture

Click and drag to move picture

Crop tool

Click and drag upward with cropping tool

(d) Move and Size the Picture (step 4)

FIGURE 3.9   Hands-on Exercise 2 (continued)

THE PICTURE TOOLBAR

The Picture Toolbar is displayed automatically when a picture is selected, and suppressed otherwise. As with any toolbar, it may be docked along the edge of the application window or floating within the window. You can move a floating toolbar by dragging its title bar. You can move a docked toolbar by dragging the move handle (the line at the left of the toolbar). If by chance you do not see the Picture toolbar when a picture is selected, pull down the View menu, click the Toolbars command, and check the Picture toolbar. Point to any toolbar button to display a Screen-Tip that is indicative of its function.

STEP 5: Insert a Hyperlink

➤ Press **Ctrl+End** to move to the end of the document, where you will add a sentence to identify the photograph. Enter the text, **The picture at the left was taken from** (the sentence will end with a hyperlink).

➤ Pull down the **Insert menu** and click the **Hyperlink command** (or click the **Insert Hyperlink button** on the Standard toolbar) to display the Insert Hyperlink dialog box as shown in Figure 3.9e.

➤ Click in the **Text to display** text box and enter **The History Place.** Press **Tab.** Enter **www.historyplace.com/kennedy/gallery.htm.** Click **OK.** The hyperlink should appear as an underlined entry in the document. Type a period after the hyperlink. Save the document.

Insert Hyperlink button ——

Enter text of hyperlink ——

Enter Web address ——

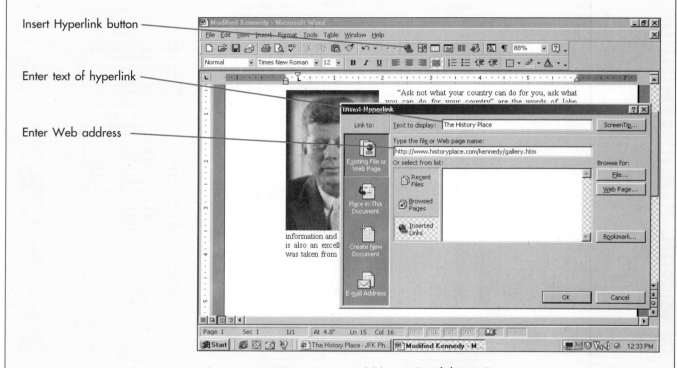

(e) Insert a Hyperlink (step 5)

FIGURE 3.9   Hands-on Exercise 2 (continued)

COPY THE WEB ADDRESS

Use the Copy command to enter a Web address from Internet Explorer into a Word document or dialog box. Not only do you save time by not having to type the address yourself, but you also ensure that it is entered correctly. Click in the Address bar of Internet Explorer to select the URL, then pull down the Edit menu and click the Copy command (or use the Ctrl+C keyboard shortcut). Switch to the Word document, click at the place in the document where you want to insert the URL, pull down the Edit menu and click the Paste command (or use the Ctrl+V keyboard shortcut). You must, however, use the keyboard shortcut if you are pasting the address into a dialog box.

STEP 6: Insert a Footnote

➤ Press **Ctrl+Home** to move to the beginning of the document. Click at the end of the quotation in the first paragraph, where you will insert a new footnote.

➤ Pull down the **Insert menu.** Click **Footnote** to display the Footnote and Endnote dialog as shown in Figure 3.9f. Check that the option buttons for **Footnote** and **AutoNumber** are selected, then click **OK.**

➤ The insertion point moves to the bottom of the page, where you type the text of the footnote. Enter **Inaugural Address, John F. Kennedy, January 20, 1961.** You can expand the footnote to include a Web site that contains the text at **www.cc.columbia.edu/acis/bartleby/inaugural/pres56.html.**

➤ Press **Ctrl+Home** to move to the beginning of the page, where you will see a reference for the footnote you just created. If necessary, you can move (or delete) a footnote by moving (deleting) the reference mark. Save the document.

Click at end of quotation

Click Footnote

Click AutoNunmber

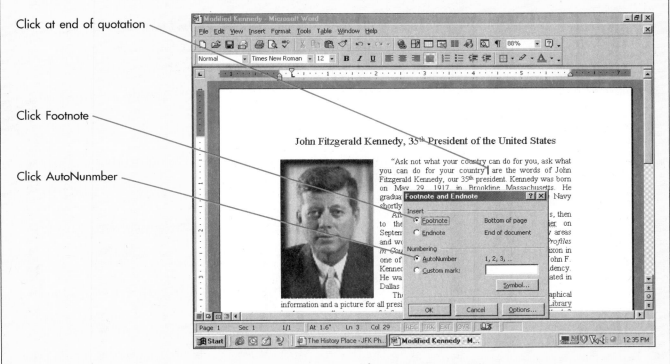

(f) Insert a Footnote (step 6)

FIGURE 3.9 Hands-on Exercise 2 (continued)

CREATE A HYPERLINK AUTOMATICALLY

Type any Internet path (i.e., any text that begins with http:// or www) or e-mail address, and Word will automatically convert the entry to a hyperlink. (If this does not work on your system, pull down the Tools menu, click AutoCorrect, then click the AutoFormat as you Type tab. Check the box in the Replace as you type area for Internet and Network paths, and click OK.) To modify the hyperlink after it is created, right click the link to display a shortcut menu, click the Hyperlink command, then select the Edit Hyperlink command to display the associated dialog box.

STEP 7: Create the Web Page

➤ Pull down the **File menu** and click the **Save as Web Page** command to display the Save as dialog box as shown in Figure 3.9g. Click the drop-down arrow in the Save In list box to select the appropriate drive, then open the **Exploring Word folder** that contains the documents you are using.

➤ Change the name of the Web page to **Modified Kennedy Web Page** (to differentiate it from the Word document). Click the **Save button.**

➤ The title bar changes to reflect the name of the Web page. There are now two versions of this document in the Exploring Word folder—Modified Kennedy, and Modified Kennedy Web Page. The latter has been saved as a Web page (in HTML format).

➤ Print this page for your instructor.

Print button

Click to select drive and/or folder

Enter filename

Internet Explorer button

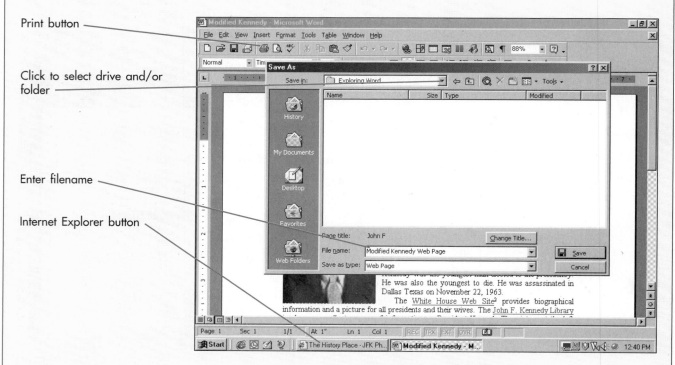

(g) Create the Web Page (step 7)

FIGURE 3.9   Hands-on Exercise 2 (continued)

CHANGE THE DEFAULT FILE LOCATION

The default file location is the folder Word uses to open and save a document unless it is otherwise instructed. To change the default location, pull down the Tools menu, click Options, click the File Locations tab, click the desired File type (documents), then click the Modify command button to display the Modify Location dialog box. Click the drop-down arrow in the Look In box to select the new folder (e.g., C:\Exploring Word). Click OK to accept this selection. Click OK to close the Options dialog box. The next time you access the Open or Save command from the File menu, the Look In text box will reflect the change.

STEP 8: Preview the Web Page

➤ The easiest way to start Internet Explorer is to pull down the **File menu** and click the **Web Page Preview command.** However, we want you to see the extra folder that was created with your Web page. Thus, click the button for Internet Explorer on the Windows taskbar.

➤ Pull down the **File menu** and click the **Open command** to display the Open dialog box. Click the **Browse button,** then select the folder (e.g., Exploring Word) where you saved the Web page. Select (click) the **Modified Kennedy as Web Page** document, click **Open,** then click **OK** to open the document.

➤ You should see the Web page that was created earlier as shown in Figure 3.9h, except that you are viewing the page in Internet Explorer.

➤ Click the **Print button** on the Internet Explorer toolbar to print this page for your instructor. Does this printed document differ from the version that was printed at the end of step 7? Close Internet Explorer.

➤ Exit Word if you do not want to continue with the next exercise at this time.

Print button

Address bar reflects local address

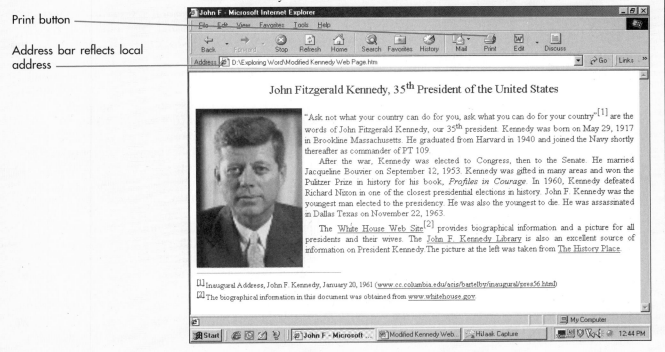

(h) Preview the Web Page (step 8)

FIGURE 3.9   Hands-on Exercise 2 (continued)

AN EXTRA FOLDER

Look carefully at the contents of the Exploring Word folder within the Open dialog box. You see the HTML document you just created, as well as a folder that was created automatically by the Save as Web page command. The latter folder contains the objects that are referenced by the page such as the Kennedy picture and a horizontal line above the footnotes. Be sure to copy the contents of this folder to the Web server in addition to your Web page if you decide to post the page.

We have created some very interesting documents throughout the text, but in every instance we have formatted the document entirely on our own. It is time now to see what is available to "jump start" the process by borrowing professional designs from others. Accordingly, we discuss the wizards and templates that are built into Microsoft Word.

A *template* is a partially completed document that contains formatting, text, and/or graphics. It may be as simple as a memo or as complex as a résumé or newsletter. Microsoft Word provides a variety of templates for common documents including a résumé, agenda, and fax cover sheet. You simply open the template, then modify the existing text as necessary, while retaining the formatting in the template. A *wizard* makes the process even easier by asking a series of questions, then creating a customized document based on your answers. A template or wizard creates the initial document for you. It's then up to you to complete the document by entering the appropriate information.

Figure 3.10 illustrates the use of wizards and templates in conjunction with a résumé. You can choose from one of three existing templates (contemporary, elegant, and professional) to which you add personal information. Alternatively, you can select the *Résumé Wizard* to create a customized résumé, as was done in Figure 3.10a.

After the Résumé Wizard is selected, it prompts you for the information it needs to create a basic résumé. You specify the style in Figure 3.10b, enter the requested information in Figure 3.10c, and choose the headings in Figure 3.10d. The wizard continues to ask additional questions (not shown in Figure 3.10), after which it displays the (partially) completed résumé based on your responses. You then complete the résumé by entering the specifics of your employment and/or additional information. As you edit the document, you can copy and paste information within the résumé, just as you would with a regular document. It takes a little practice, but the end result is a professionally formatted résumé in a minimum of time.

Microsoft Word contains templates and wizards for a variety of other documents. (Look carefully at the tabs within the dialog box of Figure 3.10a and you can infer that Word will help you to create letters, faxes, memos, reports, legal pleadings, publications, and even Web pages.) Consider, too, Figure 3.11, which displays four attractive documents that were created using the respective wizards. Realize, however, that while wizards and templates will help you to create professionally designed documents, they are only a beginning. *The content is still up to you.*

THIRTY SECONDS IS ALL YOU HAVE

Thirty seconds is the average amount of time a personnel manager spends skimming your résumé and deciding whether or not to call you for an interview. It doesn't matter how much training you have had or how good you are if your résumé and cover letter fail to project a professional image. Know your audience and use the vocabulary of your targeted field. Be positive and describe your experience from an accomplishment point of view. Maintain a separate list of references and have it available on request. Be sure that all information is accurate. Be conscientious about the design of your résumé, and proofread the final documents very carefully.

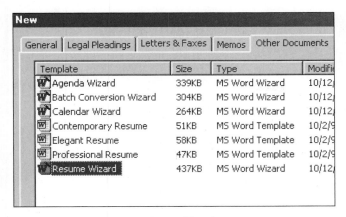

(a) Résumé Wizard

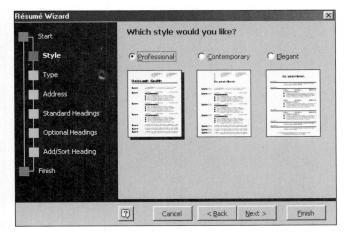

(b) Choose the Style

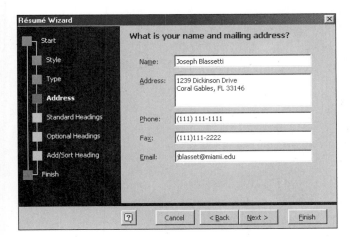

(c) Supply the Information

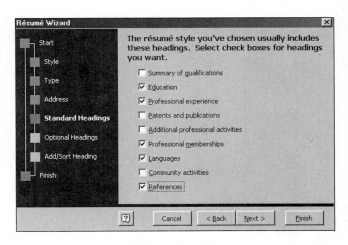

(d) Choose the Headings

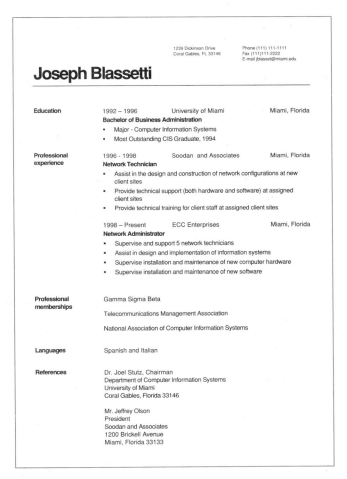

(e) The Completed Résumé

FIGURE 3.10   Creating a Résumé

	Sun	Mon	Tue	Wed	Thu	Fri	Sat
May							1
	2	3	4	5	6	7	8
	9	10	11	12	13	14	15
	16	17	18	19	20	21	22
	23	24	25	26	27	28	29
1999	30	31					

(a) Calendar

Agenda

Initial Study Group Session

2/20/99
7:30 PM to 8:15 PM
Joe's Place

Note taker:	Jennifer
Attendees:	Jennifer, Susan, Joe, and Paul
Please bring:	Text book, class notes, calendar

Agenda topics

10	Introduction	Susan
20	Semester Plan	Joe
15	Review current assignment	Paul

Special notes:	As you can see, the meeting should not take any longer than 45-50 minutes, if everyone is prepared. We can order pizza afterwards, if anyone is interested.

(b) Agenda

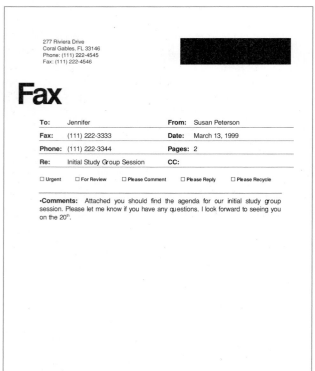

277 Riviera Drive
Coral Gables, FL 33146
Phone: (111) 222-4545
Fax: (111) 222-4546

Fax

To:	Jennifer	**From:**	Susan Peterson
Fax:	(111) 222-3333	**Date:**	March 13, 1999
Phone:	(111) 222-3344	**Pages:**	2
Re:	Initial Study Group Session	**CC:**	

☐ Urgent　　☐ For Review　　☐ Please Comment　　☐ Please Reply　　☐ Please Recycle

•Comments: Attached you should find the agenda for our initial study group session. Please let me know if you have any questions. I look forward to seeing you on the 20th.

(c) Fax Cover Sheet

Interoffice Memo

Date: 2/15/99
To: Dr. Robert Plant, Dr. John Stewart
From: Jenn Sheridan
RE: CIS 120 Final Exam

The meeting to prepare the final exam for CIS 120 will be on Friday, February 19, 1999 at 3:00PM in my office. I have attached a copy of last semester's final, which I would like for you to review prior to the meeting. In addition, if you could take a few minutes and create approximately 20 new questions for this semester's test, it would make our job at the meeting a lot easier. The meeting should last no longer than an hour, provided that we all do our homework before the meeting. If you have any questions before that time, please let me know.

Attachments

2/15/99　　　　　　　Confidential　　　　　　1

(d) Memo

FIGURE 3.11　What You Can Do With Wizards

Objective: To use the Agenda Wizard to create an agenda for a study group, then use the Fax Wizard to fax the agenda to your group. Use Figure 3.12 as a guide in the exercise.

STEP 1: The File New Command

➤ Start Word. Pull down the **File menu.** Click **New** to display the New dialog box shown in Figure 3.12a. Click the **Other Documents tab.**

➤ Click the **Details button** to switch to the Details view to see the file name, type, size, and date of last modification. Click and drag the vertical line between the Template and Size columns, to increase the size of the Template column, so that you can see the complete document name.

➤ Select (click) **Agenda Wizard.** If necessary, click the option button to **Create New Document** (as opposed to a template). Click **OK.**

Details button

Click Other Documents tab

Click and drag to change size of column

Click to select Agenda Wizard

Click Document option button

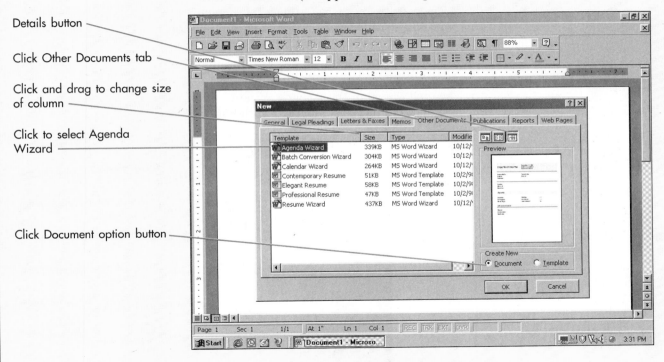

(a) The File New Command (step 1)

FIGURE 3.12   Hands-on Exercise 3

SORT BY NAME, DATE, OR FILE SIZE

The files in the Save As, Open, and New dialog boxes can be displayed in ascending or descending sequence by name, date modified, or size. Change to the Details view, then click the heading of the desired column; e.g., click the Type column to list the files according to file type (to separate the documents from the templates).

STEP 2: The Agenda Wizard

➤ You should see the main screen of the Agenda Wizard as shown in Figure 3.12b. Click **Next** to begin. The Wizard will take you through a series of questions, from start to finish. To create the desired agenda:

- Click **Modern** as the style of the agenda. Click **Next.**

- Enter the date and time of your meeting. Enter **Initial Study Group Session** as the title. Enter **Joe's Place** as the location. Click **Next.**

- The Wizard asks which headings you want and supplies a check box next to each heading. The check boxes function as toggle switches to select (deselect) each heading. We suggest you clear all entries except **Please bring.** Click **Next.**

- The Wizard asks which names you want in the agenda. Clear all headings except **Note Taker** and **Attendees.** Click **Next.**

- Enter at least three topics for the agenda. Press the **Tab key** to move from one text box to the next (e.g., from Agenda topic, to Person, to Minutes). Click the **Add** button when you have completed the information for one topic.

- If necessary, reorder the topics by clicking the desired topic, then clicking the **Move Up** or **Move Down** command button. Click **Next** when you are satisfied with the agenda.

- Click **No** when asked whether you want a form to record the minutes of the meeting. Click **Next.**

➤ The final screen of the Agenda Wizard indicates that the Wizard has all the information it needs. Click the **Finish button.**

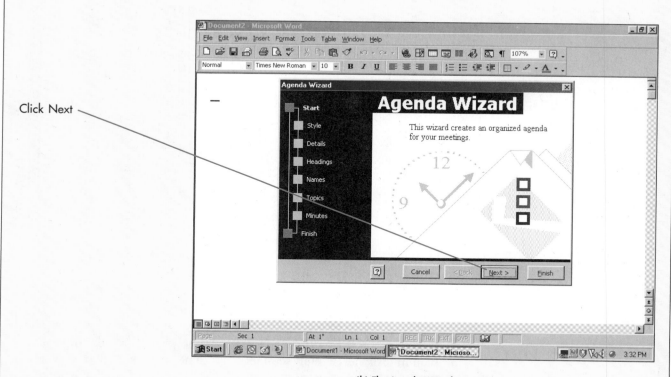

(b) The Agenda Wizard (step 2)

FIGURE 3.12   Hands-on Exercise 3 (continued)

STEP 3: Complete the Agenda

➤ You should see an initial agenda similar to the document in Figure 3.12c. Cancel the Office Assistant if it appears (or you can leave it open and request help as necessary).

➤ Save the agenda as **Initial Study Group Session** in the **Exploring Word** folder. If necessary, change to the **Print Layout view** and zoom to **Page Width** so that your document more closely matches ours.

➤ Complete the Agenda by entering the additional information, such as the names of the note taker and attendees as well as the specifics of what to read or bring, as shown in the figure. Click at the indicated position on the figure prior to entering the text, so that your entries align properly.

➤ Click the **Spelling and Grammar button** to check the agenda for spelling.

➤ Save the document but do not close it.

➤ Click the **Print button** on the Standard toolbar to print the completed document and submit it to your instructor.

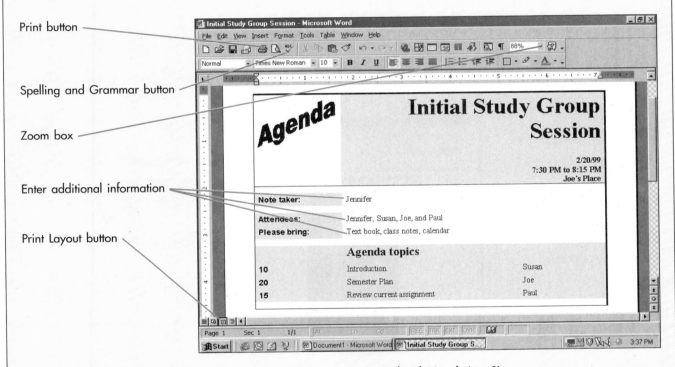

(c) Complete the Agenda (step 3)

FIGURE 3.12   Hands-on Exercise 3 (continued)

RETRACE YOUR STEPS

The Agenda Wizard guides you every step of the way, but what if you make a mistake or change your mind? Click the Back command button at any time to return to a previous screen in order to enter different information, then continue working with the Wizard.

STEP 4: The Fax Wizard

➤ Pull down the **File menu** and click **New** to display the New dialog box. Click the **Letters & Faxes tab** to display the indicated wizards and templates. Check that the **Document option button** is selected. Double click the **Fax Wizard** to start it.

➤ You should see the main screen of the Fax Wizard as shown in Figure 3.12d. Click **Next** to begin.

- The Fax Wizard suggests Initial Study Group as the name of the document you want to fax (because the document is still open). The option button **With a Cover Sheet** is selected. Click **Next.**

- Do not be concerned about the fax software that is installed on your computer, because you're not going to send the fax. Thus, click the option button to print the document (as though you were going to send it from a fax machine). Click **Next.**

- Enter the name and fax number of one person in your group. Complete this entry even if you do not intend to send an actual fax. Click **Next.**

- Choose the style of the cover sheet. We selected **Professional.** Click **Next.**

- If necessary, complete and/or modify the information about the sender so that it reflects your name and telephone number. Click **Next.**

- Read the last screen reminding you about how to list phone numbers correctly. Click **Finish.**

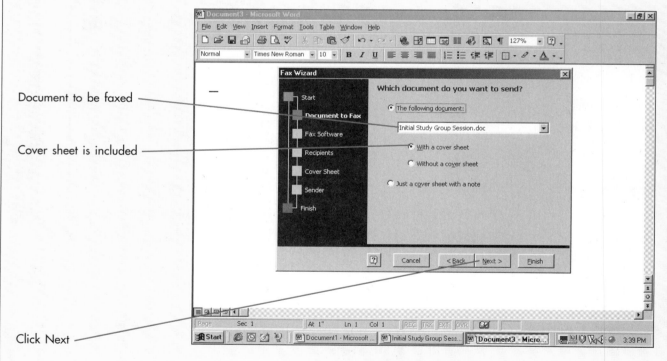

Document to be faxed

Cover sheet is included

Click Next

(d) The Fax Wizard (step 4)

FIGURE 3.12   Hands-on Exercise 3 (continued)

STEP 5: Complete the Fax

➤ You should see a fax cover sheet similar to the document in Figure 3.12e.

➤ Save the cover sheet as **Fax Cover Sheet** in the **Exploring Word** folder. If necessary, change to the **Normal view** and zoom to **Page Width** so that your document more closely matches ours.

➤ Complete the cover sheet by entering the additional information as appropriate. Click at the indicated position in Figure 3.12e prior to entering the text, so that your entries align properly.

➤ Click the **Spelling and Grammar button** to check the agenda for spelling.

➤ Save the document a final time. Click the **Print button** on the Standard toolbar to print the completed document, and submit it to your instructor.

➤ Exit Word. Congratulations on a job well done.

Print button

Spelling and Grammar button

Zoom box

Print Layout button

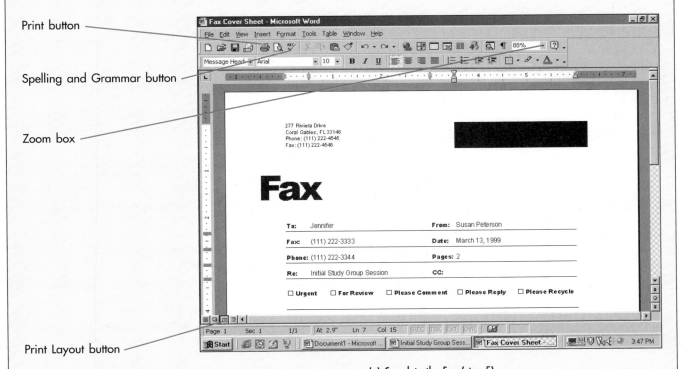

(e) Complete the Fax (step 5)

FIGURE 3.12   Hands-on Exercise 3 (continued)

CHANGING THE VIEW

Word provides different views of a document and different magnifications of each view. The Normal view suppresses the margins, giving you more room in which to work. The Print Layout view, on the other hand, displays the margins, so that what you see on the monitor more closely resembles the printed page. The easiest way to change from one view to the other is by clicking the appropriate icon above the status bar. The easiest way to change the magnification is to click the drop-down arrow in the Zoom box on the Standard toolbar.

The applications in Microsoft Office are thoroughly integrated with one another. They look alike and work alike. Equally important, they share information through a technology known as Object Linking and Embedding (OLE), which enables you to create a compound document containing data (objects) from multiple applications.

The Microsoft Clip Gallery contains clip art, sound files, and motion clips and it is accessible from any application in Microsoft Office. Clip art is inserted into a document in one of two ways—through the Insert Object command or more directly through the Insert Picture command. Either way, you choose the type of object and the category, then select the image and insert it into the document. Microsoft WordArt is an application within Microsoft Office that creates decorative text, which can be used to add interest to a document.

The Insert Symbol command provides access to special characters, making it easy to place typographic characters into a document. The symbols can be taken from any TrueType font and can be displayed in any point size.

The Internet is a network of networks. The World Wide Web (WWW, or simply the Web) is a very large subset of the Internet, consisting of those computers containing hypertext and/or hypermedia documents. Resources (e.g., clip art or photographs) can be downloaded from the Web for inclusion in a Word document. All Web pages are written in a language called HTML (HyperText Markup Language). The Save As Web Page command saves a Word document as a Web page.

A copyright provides legal protection to a written or artistic work, giving the author exclusive rights to its use and reproduction except as governed under the fair use exclusion. Anything on the Internet or World Wide Web should be considered copyrighted unless the document specifically says it is in the public domain. The fair use exclusion enables you to use a portion of the work for educational, nonprofit purposes, or for the purpose of critical review or commentary.

A footnote provides additional information about an item, such as its source, and appears at the bottom of the page where the reference occurs. The Insert Footnote command inserts a footnote into a document and automatically assigns the next sequential number to that note.

Wizards and templates help create professionally designed documents with a minimum of time and effort. A template is a partially completed document that contains formatting and other information. A wizard is an interactive program that creates a customized template based on the answers you supply.

OBJECT LINKING AND EMBEDDING

Object Linking and Embedding (OLE) enables you to create a compound document containing objects (data) from multiple Windows applications. Each of the techniques, linking and embedding, can be implemented in various ways. Althogh OLE is one of the major benefits of working in the Windows environment, it would be impossible to illustrate all of the techniques in a single exercise. Accordingly, we have created the icon at the left to help you identify the many OLE examples that appear throughout the *Exploring Windows* series.

Agenda Wizard
AutoCorrect
AutoFormat
Clip art
Clipboard
Compound document
Copyright
Crop
Drawing toolbar
Endnote
Fair use exclusion
Fax Wizard
Footnote
Format Picture
   command

HTML document
Hyperlink
Insert Footnote
   command
Insert Hyperlink
   command
Insert Picture command
Insert Symbol
   command
Internet
Intranet
Microsoft Clip Gallery
Microsoft WordArt
Object Linking and
   Embedding (OLE)

Picture toolbar
Public domain
Résumé Wizard
Save as Web Page
   command
Sizing handle
Template
Web page
Wizard
WordArt
WordArt toolbar
World Wide Web

MULTIPLE CHOICE

1. How do you change the size of a selected object so that the height and width change in proportion to one another?
   - (a) Click and drag any of the four corner handles in the direction you want to go
   - (b) Click and drag the sizing handle on the top border, then click and drag the sizing handle on the left side
   - (c) Click and drag the sizing handle on the bottom border, then click and drag the sizing handle on the right side
   - (d) All of the above

2. The Microsoft Clip Galley:
   - (a) Is accessed through the Insert Picture command
   - (b) Is available to every application in the Microsoft Office
   - (c) Enables you to search for a specific piece of clip art by specifying a key word in the description of the clip art
   - (d) All of the above

3. Which view, and which magnification, offers the most convenient way to position a graphic within a document?
   - (a) Page Width in the Print Layout view
   - (b) Full Page in the Print Layout view
   - (c) Page Width in the Normal view
   - (d) Full Page in the Normal view

4. Which of the following can be inserted from the Microsoft Clip Gallery?
   - (a) Clip art
   - (b) Sound
   - (c) Motion clips
   - (d) All of the above

5. How do you insert special characters such as the accented letters or typo-graphical symbols into a Word document?

   (a) Use the Insert WordArt command to draw the character
   (b) Use the Insert Picture command to draw the character
   (c) Use the Insert Symbol command
   (d) All of the above

6. How do you format a document so that text in the document wraps around a clip art image?

   (a) Select the text, then use the Format Text command or the Format Text toolbar to specify the desired layout
   (b) Select the picture, then use the Format Picture command or the Format Picture toolbar to specify the desired layout
   (c) Select the text, then click and drag a sizing handle to obtain the desired layout
   (d) You cannot wrap the text around the picture

7. Which of the following is true about footnotes or endnotes?

   (a) The addition of a footnote or endnote automatically renumbers the notes that follow
   (b) The deletion of a footnote or endnote automatically renumbers the notes that follow
   (c) Both (a) and (b)
   (d) Neither (a) nor (b)

8. Which of the following is true about the Insert Symbol command?

   (a) It can insert a symbol in different type sizes
   (b) It can access any TrueType font installed on the system
   (c) Both (a) and (b)
   (d) Neither (a) nor (b)

9. Which of the following is a true statement regarding objects and the tool-bars associated with those objects?

   (a) Clicking on a WordArt object displays the WordArt toolbar
   (b) Clicking on a Picture displays the Picture Toolbar
   (c) Both (a) and (b)
   (d) Neither (a) nor (b)

10. How do you insert a hyperlink into a Word document?

   (a) Pull down the Insert menu and click the Hyperlink command
   (b) Click the Insert Hyperlink button on the Standard toolbar
   (c) Both (a) and (b)
   (d) Neither (a) nor (b)

11. A Web browser such as Internet Explorer can display a page from:

   (a) A local drive such as drive A or drive C
   (b) A drive on a local area network
   (c) The World Wide Web
   (d) All of the above

12. What happens if you enter the text *www.intel.com* into a document?
    (a) The entry is converted to a hyperlink, and the text will be underlined and displayed in a different color
    (b) The associated page will be opened, provided your computer has access to the Internet
    (c) Both (a) and (b)
    (d) Neither (a) nor (b)

13. Which of the following is a true statement about wizards?
    (a) They are accessed through the New command in the File menu
    (b) They always produce a finished document
    (c) Both (a) and (b)
    (d) Neither (a) nor (b)

14. How do you access the wizards built into Microsoft Word?
    (a) Pull down the Wizards and Templates menu
    (b) Pull down the Insert menu and choose the Wizards and Templates command
    (c) Pull down the File menu and choose the New command
    (d) None of the above

15. Which of the following is true regarding wizards and templates?
    (a) A wizard may create a template
    (b) A template may create a wizard
    (c) Both (a) and (b)
    (d) Neither (a) nor (b)

Answers

1. a	**6.** b	**11.** d
2. d	**7.** c	**12.** a
3. b	**8.** c	**13.** a
4. d	**9.** c	**14.** c
5. c	**10.** c	**15.** a

PRACTICE WITH MICROSOFT WORD

1. Inserting Objects: Figure 3.13 illustrates a flyer that we created for a hypothetical computer sale. We embedded clip art and WordArt and created what we believe is an attractive flyer. Try to duplicate our advertisement, or better yet, create your own. Include your name somewhere in the document as a sales associate. Be sure to spell check your ad, then print the completed flyer and submit it to your instructor.

2. Exploring TrueType: The installation of Microsoft Windows and/or Office 2000 also installs several TrueType fonts, which in turn are accessible from any application. Two of the fonts, Symbols and Wingdings, contain a variety of special characters that can be used to create some unusual documents. Use the Insert Symbol command, your imagination, and the fact that TrueType fonts are scaleable to any point size to re-create the documents in Figure 3.14. Better yet, use your imagination to create your own documents.

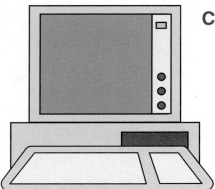

Computer World's Annual Pre-Inventory Sale

When: **June 21, 1999**
                     8:00AM - 10:00PM

Where: **13640 South Dixie Highway**

Computer World

Computers
Printers
Fax/Modems
CD-ROM drives
Sound Systems
Software
Etc.

Pre-Inventory Sale

Sales Associate: Bianca Costo

FIGURE 3.13   Inserting Objects (Exercise 1)

Valentine's Day
We'll serenade your sweetheart
Call 284-LOVE

STUDENT COMPUTER LAB
Fall Semester Hours

FIGURE 3.14   Exploring TrueType (Exercise 2)

3. Automatic Formatting: The document in Figure 3.15 was created to illustrate the automatic formatting and correction facilities that are built into Microsoft Word. We want you to create the document, include your name at the bottom, then submit the completed document to your instructor as proof that you did the exercise. All you have to do is follow the instructions within the document and let Word do the formatting and correcting for you.

The only potential difficulty is that the options on your system may be set to negate some of the features to which we refer. Accordingly, you need to pull down the Tools menu, click the AutoCorrect command, and click the AutoFormat As You Type tab. Verify that the options referenced in the document are in effect. You also need to review the table of predefined substitutions on the AutoCorrect tab to learn the typewritten characters that will trigger the smiley faces, copyright, and registered trademark substitutions.

It's Easier Than It Looks

This document was created to demonstrate the AutoCorrect and AutoFormat features that are built into Microsoft Word. In essence, you type as you always did and enter traditional characters, then let Word perform its "magic" by substituting symbols and other formatting for you. Among the many features included in these powerful commands are the:

1. Automatic creation of numbered lists by typing a number followed by a period, tab, or right parenthesis. Just remember to press the return key twice to turn off this feature.
2. Symbols for common fractions such as $\frac{1}{2}$ or $\frac{1}{4}$.
3. Ordinal numbers with superscripts created automatically such as 1st, 2nd, or 3rd.
4. Copyright © and Registered trademark ® symbols.

AutoFormat will even add a border to a paragraph any time you type three or more hyphens, equal signs, or underscores on a line by itself.

And finally, the AutoCorrect feature has built-in substitution for smiley faces that look best when set in a larger point size such as 72 points.

FIGURE 3.15   Automatic Formatting (Exercise 3)

4. Create an Envelope: The Résumé Wizard will take you through the process of creating a résumé, but you need an envelope in which to mail it. Pull down the Tools menu, click the Envelopes and Labels command, click the Envelopes command, then enter the indicated information. Look closely at the dialog box and note that Word will even append a bar code to the envelope if you request it.

You can print the envelope and/or include it permanently in the document as shown in Figure 3.16. *Do not, however, do this exercise in a Computer Lab at school unless envelopes are available for the printer.*

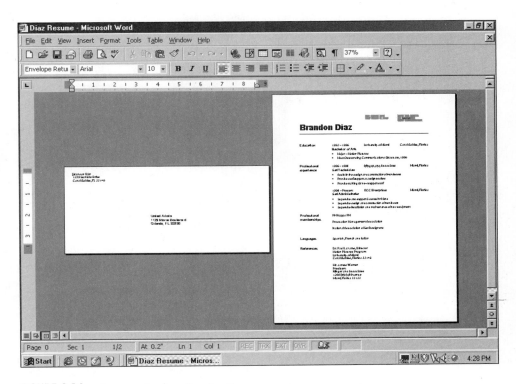

FIGURE 3.16   Create an Envelope (Exercise 4)

5. Presidential Anecdotes: Figure 3.17 displays the finished version of a document containing 10 presidential anecdotes. The anecdotes were taken from the book *Presidential Anecdotes,* by Paul F. Boller, Jr., published by Penguin Books (New York, NY, 1981). Open the *Chapter 3 Practice 5* document that is found on the data disk, then make the following changes:

a. Add a footnote after Mr. Boller's name, which appears at the end of the second sentence, citing the information about the book. This, in turn, renumbers all existing footnotes in the document.

b. Switch the order of the anecdotes for Lincoln and Jefferson so that the presidents appear in order. The footnotes for these references are changed automatically.

c. Convert all of the footnotes to endnotes, as shown in the figure.

d. Go to the White House Web site and download a picture of any of the 10 presidents, then incorporate that picture into a cover page. Remember to cite the reference with an appropriate footnote.

e. Submit the completed document to your instructor.

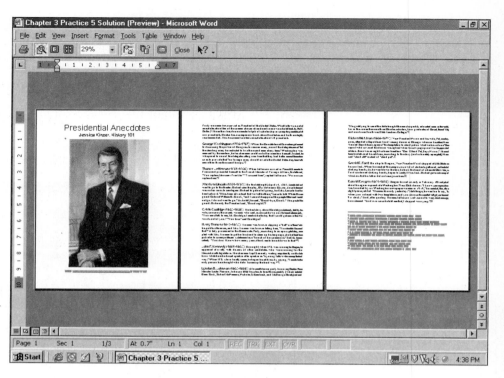

FIGURE 3.17 Presidential Anecdotes (Exercise 5)

6. Photographs Online: The Smithsonian Institution is a priceless resource. Go to the home page of the Smithsonian (www.si.edu), select photography from the subject area, then go to Smithsonian Photographs online to display the page in Figure 3.18. (You can also go to this page directly at photo2.si.edu). Click the link to search the image database, then choose one or two photographs on any subject that you find interesting.

Use the technique described in the chapter to download those photographs to your PC, then use the Insert Picture command to incorporate those pictures into a Word document. Write a short paper (250 to 500 words) describing those photographs and submit the paper to your professor as proof you did this exercise. Be sure to include an appropriate footnote to cite the source of the photographs.

7. Music on the Web: The World Wide Web is a source of infinite variety, including music from your favorite rock group. You can find biographical information and/or photographs such as the one in Figure 3.19. You can even find music, which you can download and play, provided you have the necessary hardware. It's fun, it's easy, so go to it. Use any search engine to find documents about your favorite rock group. Try to find biographical information as well as a picture, then incorporate the results of your research into a short paper to submit to your instructor.

8. The iCOMP Index: The iCOMP index was developed by Intel to compare the speeds of various microprocessors. We want you to search the Web and find a chart showing values in the current iCOMP index. (The chart you find need not be the same as the one in Figure 3.20.) Once you find the chart, download the graphic and incorporate it into a memo to your instructor. Add a paragraph or two describing the purpose of the index as shown in Figure 3.20.

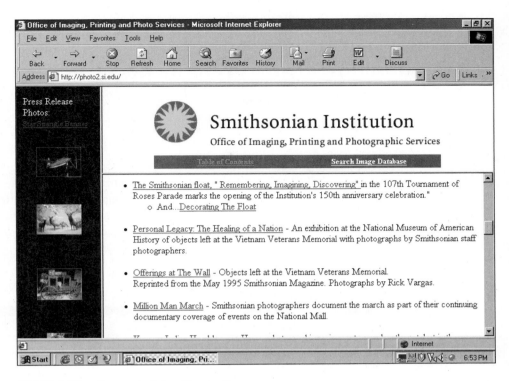

FIGURE 3.18   Photographs Online (Exercise 6)

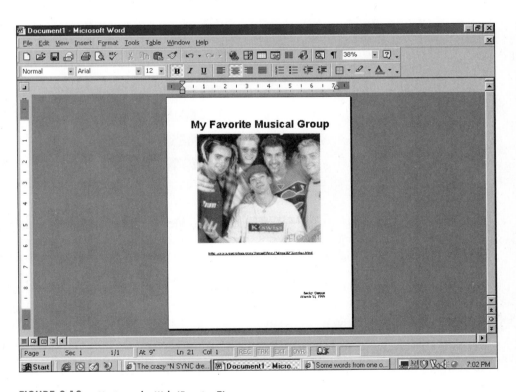

FIGURE 3.19   Music on the Web (Exercise 7)

A Comparison of Microcomputers

James Warren, CIS 120
(http://pentium.intel.com/procs/perf/icomp/index.htm)

The capability of a PC depends on the microprocessor on which it is based. Intel microprocessors are currently in their sixth generation, with each generation giving rise to increasingly powerful personal computers. All generations are upward compatible; that is, software written for one generation will automatically run on the next. This upward compatibility is crucial because it protects your investment in software when you upgrade to a faster computer.

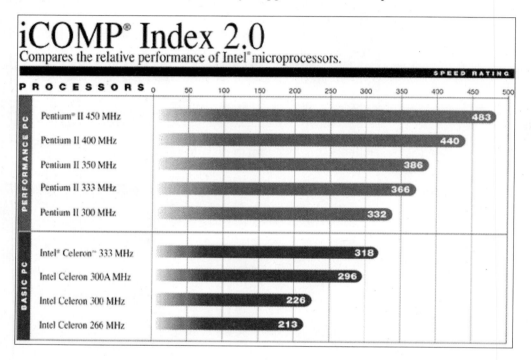

Each generation has multiple microprocessors which are differentiated by *clock speed*, an indication of how fast instructions are executed. Clock speed is measured in *megahertz* (MHz). The higher the clock speed the faster the machine. Thus, all Pentiums are not created equal, because they operate at different clock speeds. The *Intel CPU Performance Index* (see chart) was created to compare the performance of one microprocessor to another. The index consists of a single number to indicate the relative performance of the microprocessor; the higher the number, the faster the processor.

FIGURE 3.20   The iCOMP Index (Exercise 8)

9. Create a Home Page: Creating a home page has never been easier. Start Word, click the File menu, then click the New command to display the New Page dialog box. Select the Web Pages tab, then open the Personal Web page template in Figure 3.21. Add your personal information to the appropriate sections in the template and you have your home page. Pull down the Format menu, click the Themes command, then select a professionally chosen design for your Web page. You can view the completed page locally, or better yet, ask your instructor whether the page can be posted to a Web server.

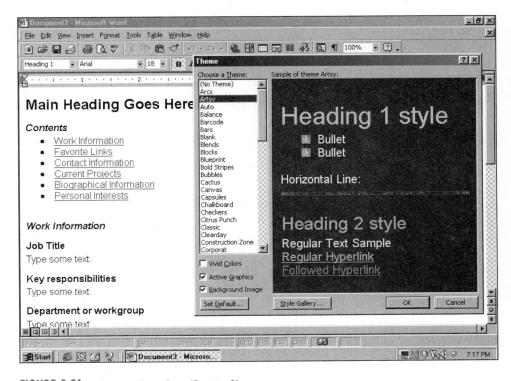

FIGURE 3.21   Create a Home Page (Exercise 9)

CASE STUDIES

The Letterhead

Collect samples of professional stationery, then design your own letterhead, which includes your name, address, phone, and any other information you deem relevant. Try different fonts and/or the Format Border command to add horizontal line(s) under the text. Consider a graphic logo, but keep it simple. You might also want to decrease the top margin so that the letterhead prints closer to the top of the page.

The Cover Page

Use WordArt and/or the Clip Gallery to create a truly original cover page that you can use with all of your assignments. The cover page should include the title of the assignment, your name, course information, and date. (Use the Insert Date and Time command to insert the date as a field so that it will be updated automatically every time you retrieve the document.) The formatting is up to you.

The Résumé

Use your imagination to create a résumé for Benjamin Franklin or Leonardo da Vinci, two acknowledged geniuses. The résumé is limited to one page and will be judged for content (yes, you have to do a little research on the Web) as well as appearance. You can intersperse fact and fiction as appropriate; for example, you may want to leave space for a telephone and/or a fax number, but could indicate that these devices have not yet been invented. You can choose a format for the résumé using the Résumé Wizard, or better yet, design your own.

File Compression

Photographs add significantly to the appearance of a document, but they also add to its size. Accordingly, you might want to consider acquiring a file compression program to facilitate copying large documents to a floppy disk in order to transport your documents to and from school, home, or work. You can download an evaluation copy of the popular WinZip program at *www.winzip.com*. Investigate the subject of file compression, then submit a summary of your findings to your instructor.

Copyright Infringement

It's fun to download images from the Web for inclusion in a document, but is it legal? Copyright protection (infringement) is one of the most pressing legal issues on the Web. Search the Web for sites that provide information on current copyright law. One excellent site is the copyright page at the Institute for Learning Technologies at *www.ilt.columbia.edu/projects/copyright*. Another excellent reference is the page at *www.benedict.com*. Research these and other sites, then summarize your findings in a short note to your instructor.

Macros

The Insert Symbol command can be used to insert foreign characters into a document, but this technique is too slow if you use these characters with any frequency. It is much more efficient to develop a series of macros (keyboard shortcuts) that will insert the characters for you. You could, for example, create a macro to insert an accented *e,* then invoke that macro through the Ctrl+e keyboard shortcut. Parallel macros could be developed for the other vowels or special characters that you use frequently. Use the Help menu to learn about macros, then summarize your findings in a short note to your instructor.

chapter 4

ADVANCED FEATURES: OUTLINES, TABLES, STYLES, AND SECTIONS

After reading this chapter you will be able to:

1. Create a bulleted or numbered list; create an outline using a multi-level list.

2. Describe the Outline view; explain how this view facilitates moving text within a document.

3. Describe the tables feature; create a table and insert it into a document.

4. Explain how styles automate the formatting process and provide a consistent appearance to common elements in a document.

5. Use the AutoFormat command to apply styles to an existing document; create, modify, and apply a style to selected elements of a document.

6. Define a section; explain how section formatting differs from character and paragraph formatting.

7. Create a header and/or a footer; establish different headers or footers for the first, odd, or even pages in the same document.

8. Insert page numbers into a document; use the Edit menu's Go To command to move directly to a specific page in a document.

9. Create an index and a table of contents.

OVERVIEW

This chapter presents a series of advanced features that will be especially useful the next time you have to write a term paper with specific formatting requirements. We show you how to create a bulleted or numbered list to emphasize important items within a term paper, and how to create an outline for that paper. We also introduce the tables feature, which is one of the most powerful features in Microsoft Word as it provides an easy way to arrange text, numbers, and/or graphics.

The second half of the chapter develops the use of styles, or sets of formatting instructions that provide a consistent appearance to similar elements in a document. We describe the AutoFormat command that assigns styles to an existing document and greatly simplifies the formatting process. We show you how to create a new style, how to modify an existing style, and how to apply those styles to text within a document. We introduce the Outline view, which is used in conjunction with styles to provide a condensed view of a document. We also discuss several items associated with longer documents, such as page numbers, headers and footers, a table of contents, and an index.

The chapter contains four hands-on exercises to apply the material at the computer. This is one more exercise than in our earlier chapters, but we think you will appreciate the practical application of these very important capabilities within Microsoft Word.

BULLETS AND LISTS

A list helps you organize information by highlighting important topics. A **bulleted list** emphasizes (and separates) the items. A **numbered list** sequences (and prioritizes) the items and is automatically updated to accommodate additions or deletions. An **outline** (or outline numbered list) extends a numbered list to several levels, and it too is updated automatically when topics are added or deleted. Each of these lists is created through the **Bullets and Numbering command** in the Format menu, which displays the Bullets and Numbering dialog box in Figure 4.1.

The tabs within the Bullets and Numbering dialog box are used to choose the type of list and customize its appearance. The Bulleted tab selected in Figure 4.1a enables you to specify one of several predefined symbols for the bullet. Typically, that is all you do, although you can use the Customize button to change the default spacing (of ¼ inch) of the text from the bullet and/or to choose a different symbol for the bullet.

The Numbered tab in Figure 4.1b lets you choose Arabic or Roman numerals, or upper- or lowercase letters, for a Numbered list. As with a bulleted list, the Customize button lets you change the default spacing, the numbering style, and/or the punctuation before or after the number or letter. Note, too, the option buttons to restart or continue numbering, which become important if a list appears in multiple places within a document. In other words, each occurrence of a list can start numbering anew, or it can continue from where the previous list left off.

The Outline Numbered tab in Figure 4.1c enables you to create an outline to organize your thoughts. As with the other types of lists, you can choose one of several default styles, and/or modify a style through the Customize command button. You can also specify whether each outline within a document is to restart its numbering, or whether it is to continue numbering from the previous outline.

CREATING AN OUTLINE

The following exercise explores the Bullets and Numbering command in conjunction with creating an outline for a hypothetical paper on the United States Constitution. The exercise begins by having you create a bulleted list, then asking you to convert it to a numbered list, and finally to an outline. The end result is the type of outline your professor may ask you to create prior to writing a term paper.

As you do the exercise, remember that a conventional outline is created as an outline numbered list within the Bullets and Numbering command. Text for the outline is entered in the Print Layout or Normal view, *not* the Outline view. The latter provides a completely different capability—a condensed view of a document that is used in conjunction with styles and is discussed later in the chapter. We mention this to avoid confusion should you stumble into the Outline view.

Select Bullet symbol

Click to choose a different bullet symbol or change the default spacing

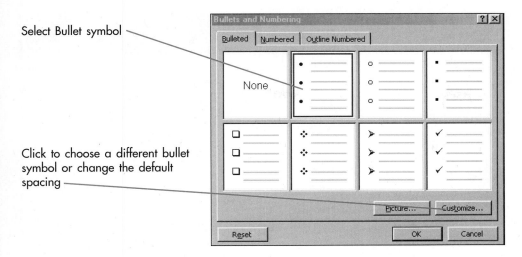

(a) Bulleted List

Select Number style

Restarts numbering for each new list within document

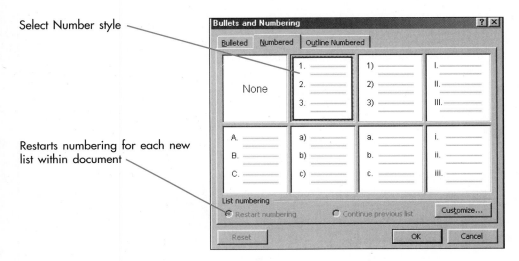

(b) Numbered List

Select Outline style

Click Customize to modify the Outline style

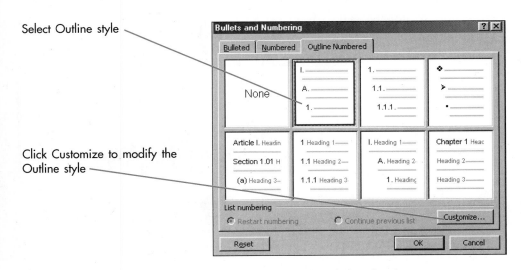

(c) Outline Numbered List

FIGURE 4.1   Bullets and Numbering

Bullets, Lists, and Outlines

Objective: To use the Bullets and Numbering command to create a bulleted list, a numbered list, and an outline. Use Figure 4.2 as a guide in doing the exercise.

STEP 1: Create a Bulleted List

➤ Start Word and begin a new document. Type **Preamble,** the first topic in our list, and press **enter.**

➤ Type the three remaining topics, **Article I—Legislative Branch, Article II—Executive Branch,** and **Article III—Judicial Branch.** Do not press enter after the last item.

➤ Click and drag to select all four topics as shown in Figure 4.2a. Pull down the **Format menu** and click the **Bullets and Numbering command** to display the Bullets and Numbering dialog box.

➤ If necessary, click the **Bulleted tab,** select the type of bullet you want, then click **OK** to accept this setting and close the dialog box. Bullets have been added to the list.

➤ Click after the words **Judicial Branch** to deselect the list and also to position the insertion point at the end of the list. Press **enter** to begin a new line. A bullet appears automatically since Word copies the formatting from one paragraph to the next.

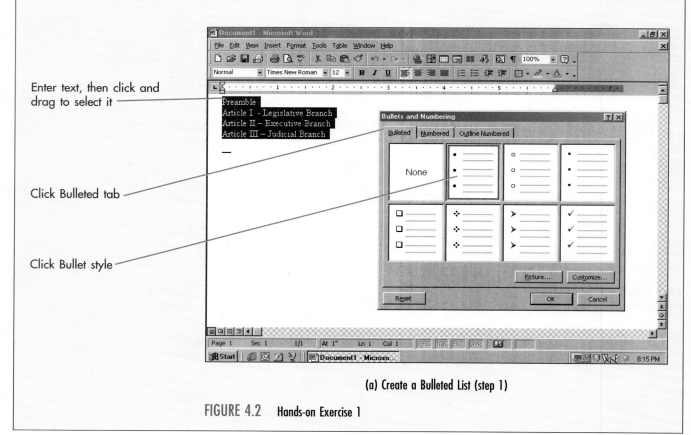

Enter text, then click and drag to select it

Click Bulleted tab

Click Bullet style

(a) Create a Bulleted List (step 1)

FIGURE 4.2   Hands-on Exercise 1

➤ Type **Amendments.** Press **enter** to end this line and begin the next, which already has a bullet. Press **enter** a second time to terminate the bulleted list.

➤ Save the document as **US Constitution** in the **Exploring Word folder.**

THE BULLETS AND NUMBERING BUTTONS

Select the items for which you want to create a list, then click the Numbering or Bullets button on the Formatting toolbar to create a numbered or bulleted list, respectively. The buttons function as toggle switches; that is, click the button once (when the items are selected) and the list formatting is in effect. Click the button a second time and the bullets or numbers disappear. The buttons also enable you to switch from one type of list to another; that is, selecting a bulleted list and clicking the Numbering button changes the list to a numbered list, and vice versa.

STEP 2: Modify a Numbered List

➤ Click and drag to select the five items in the bulleted list, then click the **Numbering button** on the Standard toolbar.

➤ The bulleted list has been converted to a numbered list as shown in Figure 4.2b. (The last two items have not yet been added to the list.)

Numbering button

Click and drag selected text to left of "Preamble"

Click in selection bar to select line

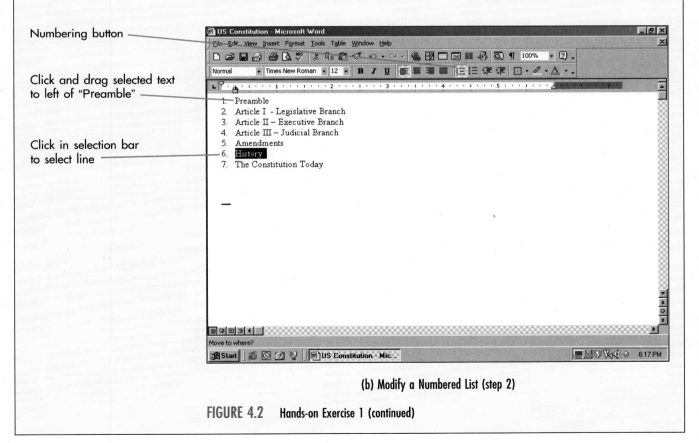

(b) Modify a Numbered List (step 2)

FIGURE 4.2   Hands-on Exercise 1 (continued)

- ➤ Click immediately after the last item in the list and press **enter** to begin a new line. Word automatically adds the next sequential number to the list.
- ➤ Type **History** and press **enter.** Type **The Constitution Today** as the seventh (and last) item.
- ➤ Click in the selection area to the left of the sixth item, **History** (only the text is selected). Now drag the selected text to the beginning of the list, in front of *Preamble.* Release the mouse.
- ➤ The list is automatically renumbered. *History* is now the first item, *Preamble* is the second item, and so on.
- ➤ Save the document.

AUTOMATIC CREATION OF A NUMBERED LIST

Word automatically creates a numbered list whenever you begin a paragraph with a number or letter, followed by a period, tab, or right parenthesis. Once the list is started, press the enter key at the end of a line, and Word generates the next sequential number or letter in the list. To end the list, press the backspace key once, or press the enter key twice. To turn the autonumbering feature on or off, pull down the Tools menu, click AutoCorrect to display the AutoCorrect dialog box, click the AutoFormat as you Type tab, then check (clear) the box for Automatic Numbered lists.

STEP 3: Convert to an Outline

- ➤ Click and drag to select the entire list, then click the **right mouse button** to display a context-sensitive menu.
- ➤ Click the **Bullets and Numbering command** to display the Bullets and Numbering dialog box in Figure 4.2c.
- ➤ Click the **Outline Numbered tab,** then select the type of outline you want. (Do not be concerned if the selected formatting does not display Roman numerals as we customize the outline later in the exercise.)
- ➤ Click **OK** to accept the formatting and close the dialog box. The numbered list has been converted to an outline, although that is difficult to see at this point.
- ➤ Click at the end of the third item, **Article I—Legislative Branch.** Press **enter.** The number 4 is generated automatically for the next item in the list.
- ➤ Press the **Tab key** to indent this item and automatically move to the next level of numbering (a lowercase *a*). Type **House of Representatives.**
- ➤ Press **enter.** The next sequential number (a lowercase *b*) is generated automatically. Type **Senate.**
- ➤ Save the document.

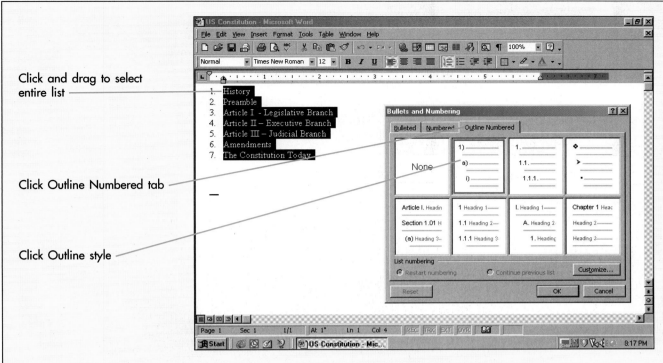

Click and drag to select entire list

Click Outline Numbered tab

Click Outline style

(c) Convert to an Outline (step 3)

FIGURE 4.2 Hands-on Exercise 1 (continued)

THE TAB AND SHIFT+TAB KEYS

The easiest way to enter text into an outline is to type continually from one line to the next, using the Tab and Shift+Tab keys as necessary. Press the enter key after completing an item to move to the next item, which is automatically created at the same level, then continue typing if the item is to remain at this level. To change the level, press the Tab key to demote the item (move it to the next lower level), or the Shift+Tab combination to promote the item (move it to the next higher level).

STEP 4: Enter Text into the Outline

➤ Your outline should be similar in appearance to Figure 4.2d, except that you have not yet entered most of the text. Click at the end of the line containing *House of Representatives*.

➤ Press **enter** to start a new item (which begins with a lowercase *b*). Press **Tab** to indent one level, changing the number to a lowercase *i*. Type **Length of term.** Press **enter.** Type **Requirements for office.** Enter these two items for the Senate as well.

➤ Enter the remaining text as shown in Figure 4.2.d, using the **Tab** and **Shift+Tab** keys to demote and promote the items. Save the document.

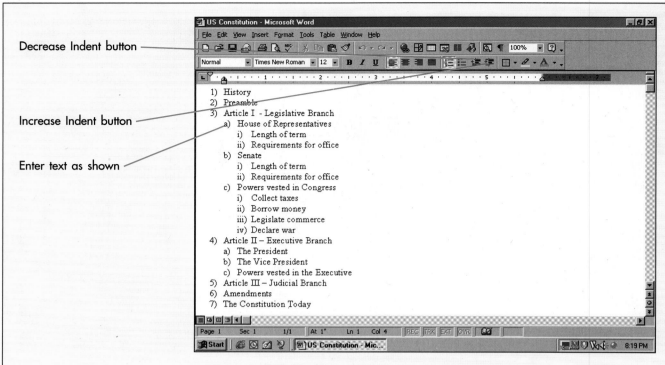

Decrease Indent button

Increase Indent button

Enter text as shown

(d) Enter Text into the Outline (step 4)

FIGURE 4.2   Hands-on Exercise 1 (continued)

THE INCREASE AND DECREASE INDENT BUTTONS

The Increase and Decrease Indent buttons on the Standard toolbar are another way to change the level within an outline. Click anywhere within an item, then click the appropriate button to change the level within the outline. Indentation is implemented at the paragraph level, and hence you can click the button without selecting the entire item. You can also click and drag to select multiple item(s), then click the desired button.

STEP 5: Customize the Outline

➤ Select the entire outline, pull down the **Format menu,** then click **Bullets and Numbering** to display the Bullets and Numbering dialog box.

➤ If necessary, click the Outline Numbered tab and click **Customize** to display the Customize dialog box as shown in Figure 4.2e. Level **1** should be selected in the Level list box.

- Click the **drop-down arrow** in the Number style list box and select **I, II, III** as the style.

- Click in the Number format text box, which now contains the Roman numeral I followed by a right parenthesis. Click and drag to select the parenthesis and replace it with a period.

- Click the **drop-down arrow** in the Number position list box. Click **right** to right-align the Roman numerals that will appear in your outline.

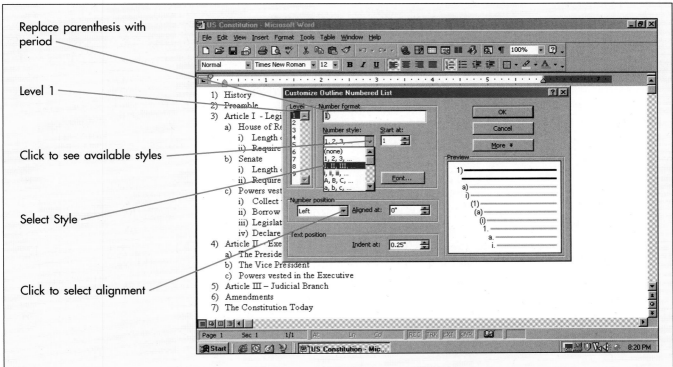

Replace parenthesis with period

Level 1

Click to see available styles

Select Style

Click to select alignment

(e) Customize the Outline (step 5)

FIGURE 4.2   Hands-on Exercise 1 (continued)

➤ Click the number **2** in the Level list box and select **A, B, C** as the Number style. Click in the Number format text box and replace the right parenthesis with a period.

➤ Click the number **3** in the Level list box and select **1, 2, 3** as the Number style. Click in the Number format text box and replace the right parenthesis with a period.

➤ Click **OK** to accept these settings and close the dialog box. The formatting of your outline has changed to match the customization in this step.

CHANGE THE FORMATTING

Word provides several types of default formatting for an outline. Surprisingly, however, Roman numerals are not provided as the default and hence you may want to change the formatting to meet your exact requirements. The formats are changed one level at a time by selecting the style for a level, then changing the punctuation (e.g., by substituting a period for a right parenthesis). If you make a mistake, you can return to the default format by closing the Custom Outline Numbered List dialog box, then clicking the Reset button from within the Bullets and Numbering dialog box.

STEP 6: The Completed Outline

➤ Your outline should reflect the style in Figure 4.2f. The major headings begin with Roman numerals, the second level headings with uppercase letters, and so on.

➤ Press **Ctrl+Home** to move to the beginning of the outline. The insertion point is after Roman numeral I, in front of the word *History*. Type **The United States Constitution.** Press **enter.**

➤ The new text appears as Roman numeral I and all existing entries have been renumbered appropriately.

➤ The insertion point is immediately before the word *History*. Press **enter** to create a blank line (for your name).

➤ The blank line is now Roman numeral II and *History* has been moved to Roman numeral III. Move the insertion point to the blank line.

➤ Press the **Tab** key so that the blank line (which will contain your name) is item A. This also renumbers *History* as Roman numeral II.

➤ Enter your name as shown in Figure 4.2f. Save the document, then print the outline and submit it to your instructor as proof you did this exercise.

➤ Close the document. Exit Word if you do not want to continue with the next exercise at this time.

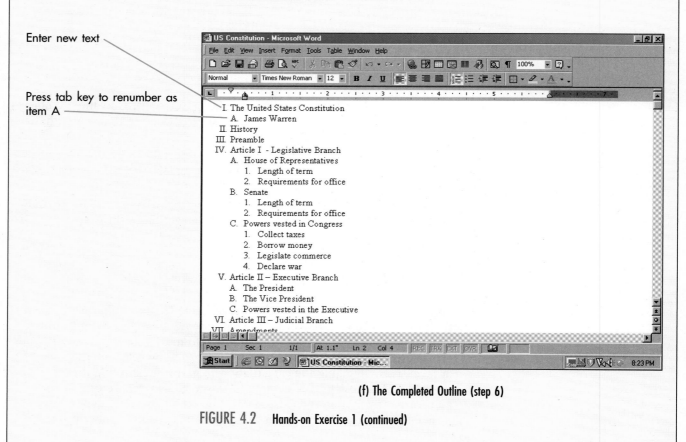

(f) The Completed Outline (step 6)

FIGURE 4.2   Hands-on Exercise 1 (continued)

The *tables feature* is one of the most powerful in Word and is the basis for an almost limitless variety of documents. The study schedule in Figure 4.3a, for example, is actually a 12 × 8 (12 rows and 8 columns) table as can be seen from the underlying structure in Figure 4.3b. The completed table looks quite impressive, but it is very easy to create once you understand how a table works. (See the practice exercises at the end of the chapter for other examples.)

The rows and columns in a table intersect to form *cells.* Each cell is formatted independently of every other cell and may contain text, numbers and/or graphics. Commands operate on one or more cells. Individual cells can be joined together to form a larger cell as was done in the first and last rows of Figure 4.3a. Conversely, a single cell can be split into multiple cells. The rows within a table can be different heights, just as each column can be a different width. You can specify the height or width explicitly, or you can let Word determine it for you.

A cell can contain anything, even clip art as in the bottom right corner of Figure 4.3a. Just click in the cell where you want the clip art to go, then use the Insert Picture command as you have throughout the text. Use the sizing handles once the clip art has been inserted to move and/or position it within the cell.

A table is created through the *Insert Table command* in the *Table menu.* The command produces a dialog box in which you enter the number of rows and columns. Once the table has been defined, you enter text in individual cells. Text wraps as it is entered within a cell, so that you can add or delete text in a cell without affecting the entries in other cells. You can format the contents of an individual cell the same way you format an ordinary paragraph; that is, you can change the font, use boldface or italics, change the alignment, or apply any other formatting command. You can select multiple cells and apply the formatting to all selected cells at once.

You can also modify the structure of a table after it has been created. The Insert and Delete commands in the Table menu enable you to add new rows or columns, or delete existing rows or columns. You can invoke other commands to shade and/or border selected cells or the entire table.

You can work with a table using commands in the Table menu, or you can use the various tools on the Tables and Borders toolbar. (Just point to a button to display a ScreenTip indicative of its function.) Some of the buttons are simply shortcuts for commands within the Table menu. Other buttons offer new and intriguing possibilities, such as the button to Change Text Direction.

It's easy, and as you might have guessed, it's time for another hands-on exercise in which you create the table in Figure 4.3.

LEFT	**CENTER**	**RIGHT**

Many documents call for left, centered, and/or right aligned text on the same line, an effect that is achieved through setting tabs, or more easily through a table. To achieve the effect shown in the heading of this box, create a 1 × 3 table (one row and three columns), type the text in the three cells as needed, then use the buttons on the Formatting toolbar to left-align, center, and right-align the respective cells. Select the table, pull down the Format menu, click Borders and Shading, then specify None as the Border setting.

Weekly Class and Study Schedule

	Monday	Tuesday	Wednesday	Thursday	Friday	Saturday	Sunday
8:00AM							
9:00AM							
10:00AM							
11:00AM							
12:00PM							
1:00PM							
2:00PM							
3:00PM							
4:00PM							

Notes:

James Warren

(a) Completed Table

(b) Underlying Structure

FIGURE 4.3   The Tables Feature

Tables

Objective: To create a table; to change row heights and column widths; to join cells together; to apply borders and shading to selected cells. Use Figure 4.4 as a guide in the exercise.

STEP 1: The Page Setup Command

➤ Start Word. Click the **Tables and Borders button** on the Standard toolbar to display the Tables and Borders toolbar as shown in Figure 4.4a.

➤ The button functions as a toggle switch—click it once and the toolbar is displayed. Click the button a second time and the toolbar is suppressed.

➤ Pull down the **File menu.** Click **Page Setup.** Click the **Paper Size tab** to display the dialog box in Figure 4.4a. Click the **Landscape option button.**

➤ Click the **Margins tab.** Change the top and bottom margins to **.75** inch. Change the left and right margins to **.5** inch each. Click **OK** to accept the settings and close the dialog box.

➤ Change to the **Print Layout** view. Zoom to **Page Width.**

➤ Save the document as **My Study Schedule** in the Exploring Word folder.

Tables and Borders button

Tables and Borders toolbar

Paper Size tab

Click Landscape

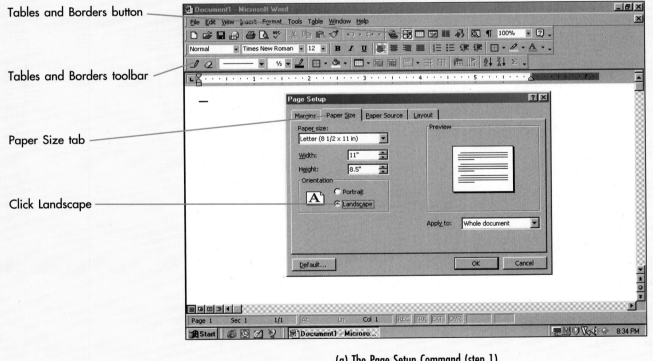

(a) The Page Setup Command (step 1)

FIGURE 4.4   Hands-on Exercise 2

THE TABLES AND BORDERS TOOLBAR

The Tables and Borders toolbar contains a variety of tools for use in creating and/or modifying a table. Some of the buttons are simply shortcuts for commands within the Table menu. Other buttons offer new and intriguing possibilities, such as the button to Change Text Direction. You can point to any button to display a ScreenTip to show the name of the button, which is indicative of its function. You can also use the Help command for additional information.

STEP 2: Create the Table

➤ Pull down the **Table menu.** Click **Insert,** then click **Table** to display the dialog box in Figure 4.4b.

➤ Enter **8** as the number of columns. Enter **12** as the number of rows. Click **OK** and the table will be inserted into the document.

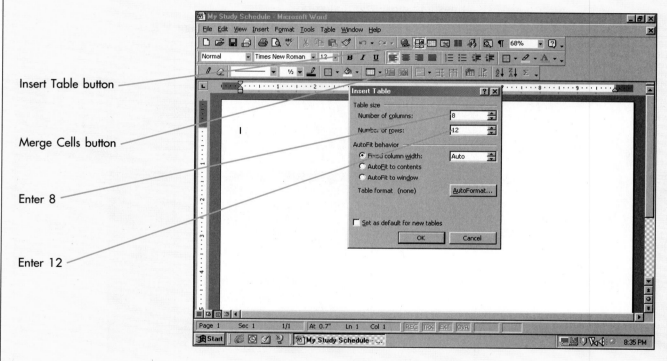

Insert Table button

Merge Cells button

Enter 8

Enter 12

(b) Create the Table (step 2)

FIGURE 4.4   Hands-on Exercise 2 (continued)

THE INSERT TABLE BUTTON

The fastest way to create a table is to use the Insert Table button on the Standard toolbar. Click the Insert Table button to display a grid, then drag the mouse across and down the grid until you have the desired number of rows and columns. Release the mouse to create the table.

STEP 3: Table Basics

➤ Practice moving within the table:

- If the cells in the table are empty (as they are now), press the **left** and **right arrow keys** to move from cell to cell.
- If the cells contain text (as they will later in the exercise), you must press **Tab** and **Shift+Tab** to move from cell to cell.
- Press the **up** and **down arrow keys** to move from row to row. This works for both empty cells and cells with text.

➤ Select a cell row, column, or block of contiguous cells:

- To select a single cell, click immediately to the right of the left cell border (the pointer changes to an arrow when you are in the proper position).
- To select an entire row, click outside the table to the left of the first cell in that row.
- To select a column, click just above the top of the column (the pointer changes to a small black arrow).
- To select adjacent cells, drag the mouse over the cells.
- To select the entire table, drag the mouse over the table.

➤ You can also pull down the **Table menu,** click the **Select command,** then choose table, column, row, or cell as appropriate.

TABS AND TABLES

The Tab key functions differently in a table than in a regular document. Press the Tab key to move to the next cell in the current row (or to the first cell in the next row if you are at the end of a row). Press Tab when you are in the last cell of a table to add a new blank row to the bottom of the table. Press Shift+Tab to move to the previous cell in the current row (or to the last cell in the previous row). You must press Ctrl+Tab to insert a regular tab character within a cell.

STEP 4: Merge the Cells

➤ Click outside the table to the left of the first cell in the first row to select the entire first row as shown in Figure 4.4c.

➤ Pull down the **Table menu** and click **Merge Cells** (or click the **Merge Cells button** on the Tables and Borders toolbar).

➤ Type **Weekly Class and Study Schedule** and format the text in 24 point Arial bold. Center the text within the cell.

➤ Click outside the table to the left of the first cell in the last row to select the entire row. Click the **Merge Cells button** to join the cells into a single cell.

➤ Type **Notes:** and format the entry in 12 point Arial bold.

➤ Save the table.

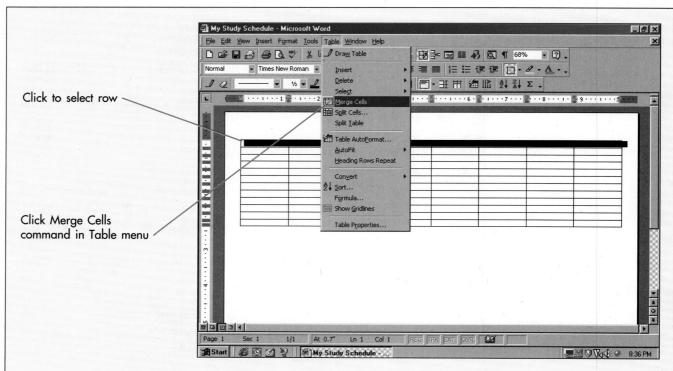

Click to select row

Click Merge Cells
command in Table menu

(c) Merge the Cells (step 4)

FIGURE 4.4   Hands-on Exercise 2 (continued)

STEP 5: Enter the Days and Hours

➤ Click the second cell in the second row. Type **Monday.**

➤ Press the **Tab** (or **right arrow**) **key** to move to the next cell. Type **Tuesday.**
Continue until the days of the week have been entered.

➤ Use the Formatting Toolbar to change the font and alignment for the days
of the week:

• Select the entire row. Click the **Bold button.**

• Click the **Font List box** to choose an appropriate font such as **Arial.**

• Click the **Font Size List box** to choose an appropriate size such as **10** point.

• Click the **Center button** on the Formatting toolbar.

➤ Click anywhere in the table to deselect the text and see the effect of the formatting change.

➤ Click the first cell in the third row. Type **8:00AM.** Press the **down arrow key**
to move to the first cell in the fourth row. Type **9:00AM.**

➤ Continue in this fashion until you have entered the hourly periods up to
3:00PM. Select the row containing the entry for 3:00PM. Pull down the **Table
menu,** click the **Insert command,** then click **Rows Below** to insert a new row.
Enter 4:00PM.

➤ Format as appropriate. (We right aligned the time periods and changed the
font to 10-point Arial bold.) Your table should match Figure 4.4d. Save the
table.

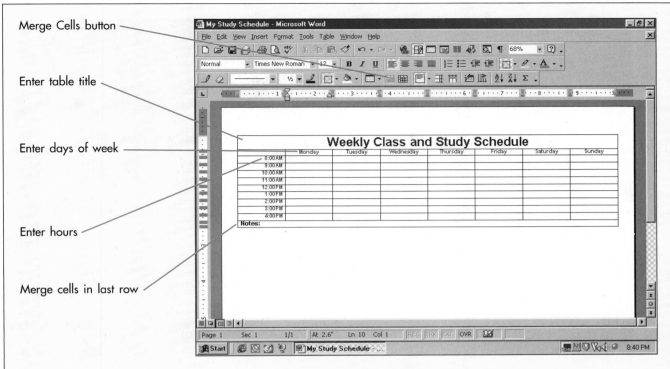

Merge Cells button

Enter table title

Enter days of week

Enter hours

Merge cells in last row

(d) Enter the Days and Hours (step 5)

FIGURE 4.4   Hands-on Exercise 2 (continued)

INSERTING OR DELETING ROWS AND COLUMNS

You can insert or delete rows and columns after a table has been created. To insert a row, select the entire row, pull down the Table menu, click the Insert command, then choose Rows Above or Below as appropriate. Follow a similar procedure to insert columns, then choose whether the column is to go to the left or right of the selected column. You can also right click a row or column, then select the Insert or Delete command from the context-sensitive menu.

STEP 6: Change the Row Heights

➤ Click immediately after the word *notes*. Press the **enter key** five times. The height of the cell increases automatically to accommodate the blank lines.

➤ Select the cells containing the hours of the day. Pull down the **Table menu.** Click **Table Properties,** then click the **Row tab** to display the Table Properties dialog box in Figure 4.4e.

➤ Click the **Specify height** check box. Click the **up arrow** until the height is **.5″,** then click the **drop-down arrow** on the Row Heights list box and select **Exactly.**

➤ Click the **Cell tab** in the Tables Properties dialog box, then click the **Center button.** Click **OK** to accept the settings and close the dialog box.

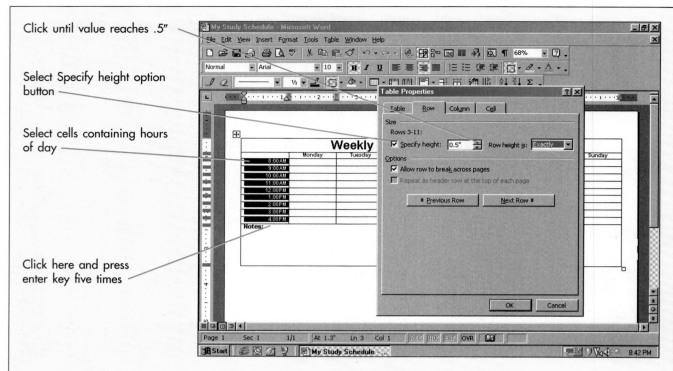

Click until value reaches .5"

Select Specify height option button

Select cells containing hours of day

Click here and press enter key five times

(e) Change the Row Heights (step 6)

FIGURE 4.4   Hands-on Exercise 2 (continued)

STEP 7: Borders and Shading

➤ Click outside the first row (the cell containing the title of the table) to select the cell. Pull down the **Format menu,** click the **Borders and Shading** command to display the Borders and Shading dialog box as shown in Figure 4.4f.

➤ Click the **Shading tab.** Click the **drop-down arrow** on the Style list box, then select **solid (100%)** as the Style pattern. Click **OK.**

➤ Click outside the cell to see the effect of this command. You should see white letters on a solid black background. Save the document.

USE COLOR REVERSES FOR EMPHASIS

White letters on a solid background (technically called a reverse) is a favorite technique of desktop publishers. It looks even better in color. Select the text, click the Shading button on the Tables and Borders toolbar, then click the desired background color (e.g., red) to create the solid background. Next, click the drop-down arrow on the Font Color list box, click white for the text color, and click the Bold button to emphasize the white text. Click elsewhere in the document to see the result.

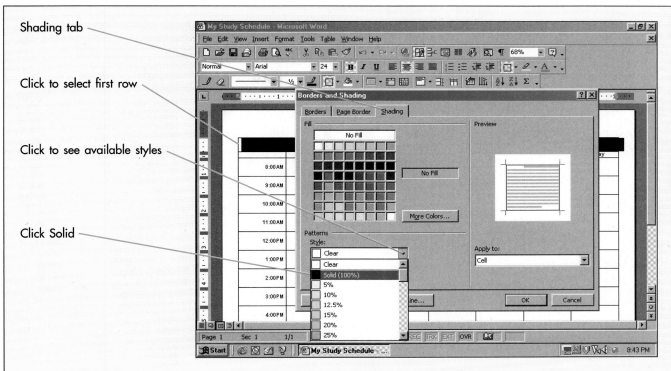

Shading tab

Click to select first row

Click to see available styles

Click Solid

(f) Borders and Shading (step 7)

FIGURE 4.4   Hands-on Exercise 2 (continued)

STEP 8: Insert the Clip Art

➤ Click the **drop-down arrow** on the Zoom list box and zoom to **Whole Page.** Click in the last cell in the table, the cell for your notes.

➤ Pull down the **Insert menu,** click **Picture,** then click **ClipArt** to display the Insert ClipArt dialog box as shown in Figure 4.4g. Click **OK** if you see a dialog box reminding you that additional clip art is available on the Office CD.

➤ If necessary, click the **Pictures tab** and select (click) the **Academic category.** Select the Books (or a different image if you prefer). Click the **Insert Clip** icon.

➤ Close the Insert ClipArt dialog box and the picture will be inserted into the table, where it can be moved and sized as described in step 9. Do not be concerned if the clip art is too large for your table or if it spills to a second page.

FIND THE RIGHT CLIP ART

You can manually search the individual categories within the Clip Gallery to find the image you are looking for. It's faster, however, to use the automated search capability. Pull down the Insert menu, click Picture, then click Clip Art to display the Insert ClipArt dialog box. Click in the Search for text box, enter a key word such as "women," then press the enter key to display all of the images, regardless of category, that list "women" as a key word.

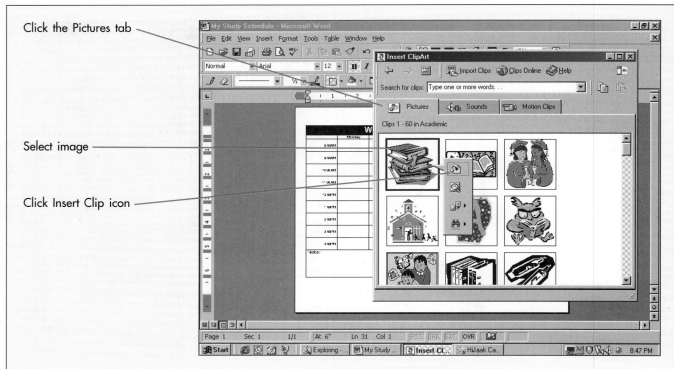

Click the Pictures tab

Select image

Click Insert Clip icon

(g) Insert the Clip Art (step 8)

FIGURE 4.4 Hands-on Exercise 2 (continued)

STEP 9: Complete the Table

➤ Click the picture to select it and display the Picture toolbar. Click the **Format Picture** tool to display the Format Picture dialog box.

➤ Click the **Layout tab,** then click the **Advanced button** to display the Advanced Layout dialog box. Select **In Front of Text** and click **OK.** Click **OK** a second time to close the Format Picture dialog box.

➤ The clip art should still be selected as indicated by the sizing handles in Figure 4.4h. Move and size the clip art until you are satisfied with its position within the table.

➤ Add your name somewhere in the table. Add other finishing touches (especially color if you have a color printer) to further personalize your table. Save the document.

➤ Print the completed table and submit it to your instructor as proof you did this exercise. Close the document. Exit Word if you do not want to continue with the next exercise at this time.

ROTATE TEXT IN A TABLE

Take advantage of the Text Direction command to display text vertically within a cell. Select the cell, pull down the Format menu, and click the Text Direction command to display the Text Direction dialog box. Choose the desired orientation and click OK to accept the settings. The effect is interesting but only in moderation.

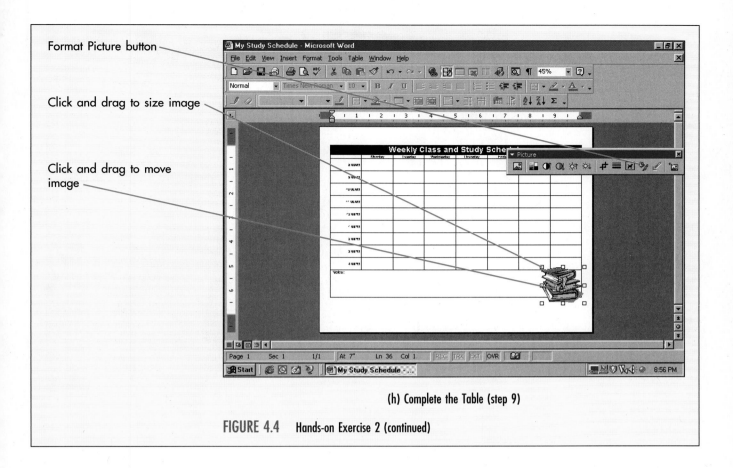

Format Picture button

Click and drag to size image

Click and drag to move image

(h) Complete the Table (step 9)

FIGURE 4.4   Hands-on Exercise 2 (continued)

STYLES

A characteristic of professional documents is the use of uniform formatting for each element. Different elements can have different formatting; for example, headings may be set in one font and the text under those headings in a different font. You may want the headings centered and the text fully justified.

If you are like most people, you will change your mind several times before arriving at a satisfactory design, after which you will want consistent formatting for each element in the document. You can use the Format Painter on the Standard toolbar to copy the formatting from one occurrence of an element to another, but it still requires you to select the individual elements and paint each one whenever formatting changes.

A much easier way to achieve uniformity is to store the formatting information as a *style,* then apply that style to multiple occurrences of the same element within the document. Change the style and you automatically change all text defined by that style.

Styles are created on the character or paragraph level. A ***character style*** stores character formatting (font, size, and style) and affects only the selected text. A ***paragraph style*** stores paragraph formatting (alignment, line spacing, indents, tabs, text flow, and borders and shading, as well as the font, size, and style of the text in the paragraph). A paragraph style affects the current paragraph or multiple paragraphs if several paragraphs are selected. The ***Style command*** in the Format menu is used to create and/or modify either type of style, then enables you to apply that style within a document.

Execution of the Style command displays the dialog box shown in Figure 4.5, which lists the styles in use within a document. The ***Normal style*** contains the

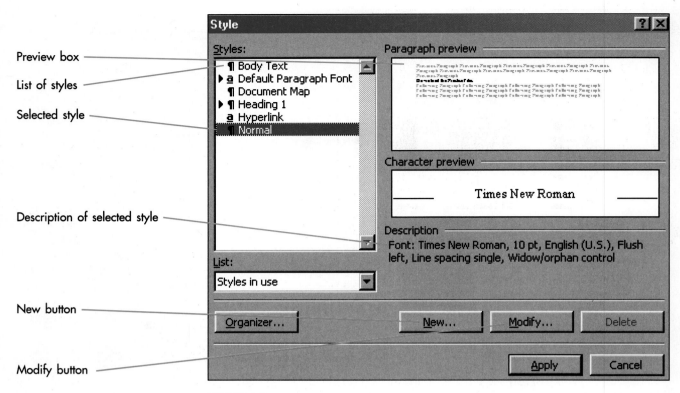

Preview box

List of styles

Selected style

Description of selected style

New button

Modify button

FIGURE 4.5   The Normal Style

default paragraph settings (left aligned, single spacing, and the default font) and is automatically assigned to every paragraph unless a different style is specified. The **Heading 1** and **Body Text** styles are used in conjunction with the AutoFormat command, which applies these styles throughout a document. (The AutoFormat command is illustrated in the next hands-on exercise.) The **Default Paragraph Font** is a character style that specifies the (default) font for new text.

The Description box displays the style definition; for example, Times New Roman, 10 point, flush left, single spacing, and widow/orphan control. The Paragraph Preview box shows how paragraphs formatted in that style will appear. The Modify command button provides access to the Format Paragraph and Format Font commands to change the characteristics of the selected style. The Apply command button applies the style to all selected paragraphs or to the current paragraph. The New command button enables you to define a new style.

Styles automate the formatting process and provide a consistent appearance to a document. Any type of character or paragraph formatting can be stored within a style, and once a style has been defined, it can be applied to multiple occurrences of the same element within a document to produce identical formatting.

STYLES AND PARAGRAPHS

A paragraph style affects the entire paragraph; that is, you cannot apply a paragraph style to only part of a paragraph. To apply a style to an existing paragraph, place the insertion point anywhere within the paragraph, pull down the Style list box on the Formatting toolbar, then click the name of the style you want.

One additional advantage of styles is that they enable you to view a document in the *Outline view.* The Outline view does not display a conventional outline (such as the multilevel list created earlier in the chapter), but rather a structural view of a document that can be collapsed or expanded as necessary. Consider, for example, Figure 4.6, which displays the Outline view of a document that will be the basis of the next hands-on exercise. The document consists of a series of tips for Word 2000. The heading for each tip is formatted according to the Heading 1 style. The text of each tip is formatted according to the Body Text style.

The advantage of the Outline view is that you can collapse or expand portions of a document to provide varying amounts of detail. We have, for example, collapsed almost the entire document in Figure 4.6, displaying the headings while suppressing the body text. We also expanded the text for two tips (Download the Practice Files and Moving Within a Document) for purposes of illustration.

Now assume that you want to move the latter tip from its present position to immediately below the first tip. Without the Outline view, the text would stretch over two pages, making it difficult to see the text of both tips at the same time. Using the Outline view, however, you can collapse what you don't need to see, then simply click and drag the headings to rearrange the text within the document.

Outline toolbar

Tip has been expanded (body text is displayed)

Tips are collapsed (body text is not displayed)

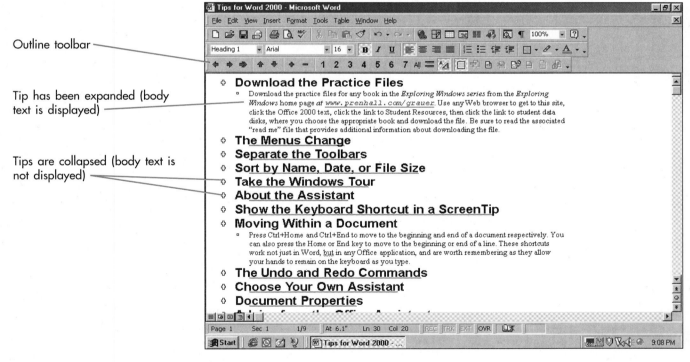

FIGURE 4.6 The Outline View

THE OUTLINE VERSUS THE OUTLINE VIEW

A conventional outline is created as a multilevel list within the Bullets and Numbering command. Text for the outline is entered in the Print Layout or Normal view, *not* the Outline view. The latter provides a condensed view of a document that is used in conjunction with styles.

The AutoFormat Command

Styles are extremely powerful. They enable you to impose uniform formatting within a document and they let you take advantage of the Outline view. What if, however, you have an existing and/or lengthy document that does not contain any styles (other than the default Normal style, which is applied to every paragraph)? Do you have to manually go through every paragraph in order to apply the appropriate style? The AutoFormat command provides a quick solution.

The *AutoFormat command* enables you to format lengthy documents quickly, easily, and in a consistent fashion. In essence, the command analyzes a document and formats it for you. Its most important capability is the application of styles to individual paragraphs; that is, the command goes through an entire document, determines how each paragraph is used, then applies an appropriate style to each paragraph. The formatting process assumes that one-line paragraphs are headings and applies the predefined Heading 1 style to those paragraphs. It applies the Body Text style to ordinary paragraphs and can also detect lists and apply a numbered or bullet style to those lists.

The AutoFormat command will also add special touches to a document if you request those options. It can replace "ordinary quotation marks" with "smart quotation marks" that curl and face each other. It will replace ordinal numbers (1st, 2nd, or 3rd) with the corresponding superscripts (1st, 2nd, or 3rd), or common fractions (1/2 or 1/4) with typographical symbols (½ or ¼).

The AutoFormat command will also replace Internet references (Web addresses and e-mail addresses) with hyperlinks. It will recognize, for example, any entry beginning with http: or www. as a hyperlink and display the entry as underlined blue text (www.microsoft.com). This is not merely a change in formatting, but an actual hyperlink to a document on the Web or corporate Intranet. It also converts entries containing an @ sign, such as rgrauer@umiami.miami.edu to a hyperlink as well. All Office 2000 documents are Web-enabled. Thus, clicking on a hyperlink or e-mail address within a Word document displays the Web page or starts your e-mail program, respectively.

The options for the AutoFormat command are controlled through the Auto-Correct command in the Tools menu as shown in Figure 4.7. Once the options have been set, all formatting is done automatically by selecting the AutoFormat command from the Format menu. The changes are not final, however, as the command gives you the opportunity to review each formatting change individually, then accept the change or reject it as appropriate. (You can also format text automatically as it is entered according to the options specified under the AutoFormat As You Type tab.)

AUTOMATIC BORDERS AND LISTS

The AutoFormat As You Type option applies sophisticated formatting as text is entered. It automatically creates a numbered list any time a number is followed by a period, tab, or right parenthesis (press enter twice in a row to turn off the feature). It will also add a border to a paragraph any time you type three or more hyphens, equal signs, or underscores followed by the enter key. Pull down the Tools menu, click the AutoCorrect command, then click the AutoFormat As You Type tab and select the desired features.

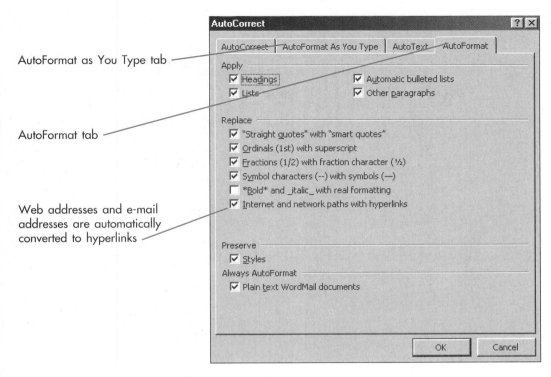

AutoFormat as You Type tab

AutoFormat tab

Web addresses and e-mail addresses are automatically converted to hyperlinks

FIGURE 4.7   The AutoFormat Command

HANDS-ON EXERCISE 3

Styles

Objective: To use the AutoFormat command on an existing document; to modify existing styles; to create a new style. Use Figure 4.8 as a guide.

STEP 1: Load the Practice Document

➤ Start Word. Pull down the **File menu.** Open the document **Tips for Word 2000** from the Exploring Word folder.

➤ Pull down the **File menu** a second time. Save the document as **Modified Tips for Word 2000** so that you can return to the original if necessary.

➤ If necessary, pull down the **View menu** and click **Normal** (or click the **Normal View button** above the status bar). Pull down the **View menu** a second time, click **Zoom,** click **Page Width,** and click **OK** (or click the **arrow** on the **Zoom Control box** on the Standard toolbar and select **Page Width**).

CREATE A NEW FOLDER

Do you work with a large number of documents? If so, it may be useful for you to store those documents in different folders. Pull down the File menu, click the Save As command to display the Save As dialog box, then click the Create New Folder button to display the New Folder dialog box. Enter the name of the folder, then click OK to create the folder.

STEP 2: The AutoFormat Command

➤ Press **Ctrl+Home** to move to the beginning of the document. Pull down the **Format menu.** Click **AutoFormat** to display the AutoFormat dialog box in Figure 4.8a.

➤ Click the **Options command button** to display the AutoCorrect dialog box. Be sure that every check box is selected to implement the maximum amount of automatic formatting. Click **OK.**

➤ Click the **OK command button** in the AutoFormat dialog box to format the document. You will see a message at the left side of the status bar as the formatting is taking place, then you will see the newly formatted document.

➤ Click the title of any tip and you will see the Heading 1 style in the Style box. Click the text of any tip. You will see the Body Text style in the Style box.

➤ Save the document.

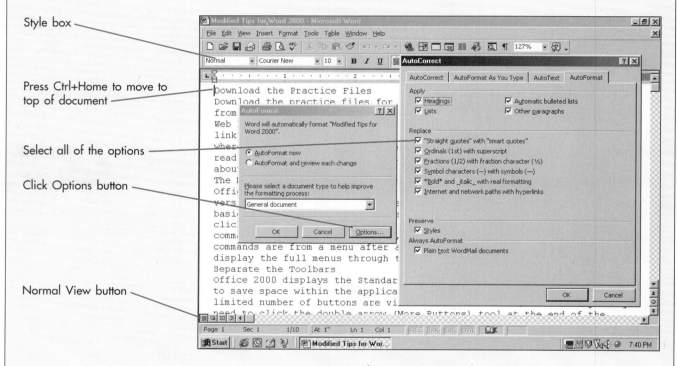

Style box

Press Ctrl+Home to move to top of document

Select all of the options

Click Options button

Normal View button

(a) The AutoFormat Command (step 2)

FIGURE 4.8   Hands-on Exercise 3

STEP 3: Modify the Body Text Style

➤ Press **Ctrl+Home** to move to the beginning of the document. Click anywhere in the text of the first tip (except within the hyperlink).

➤ Pull down the **Format menu.** Click **Style.** The Body Text style is automatically selected, and its characteristics are displayed within the description box.

➤ Click the **Modify command button** to display the Modify Style dialog box in Figure 4.8b.

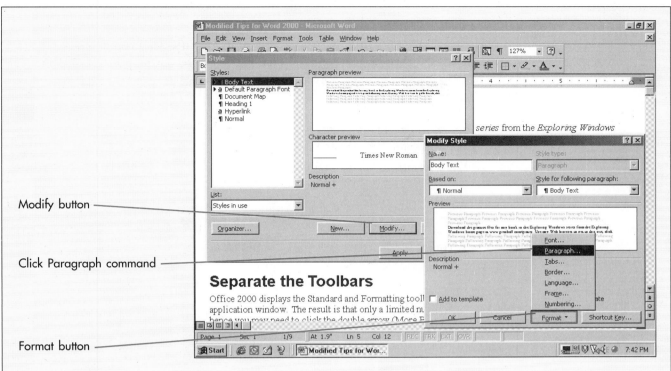

Modify button

Click Paragraph command

Format button

(b) Modify the Body Text Style (step 3)

FIGURE 4.8   Hands-on Exercise 3 (continued)

➤ Click the **Format command button.**

- Click **Paragraph** to produce the Paragraph dialog box.

- Click the **Indents and Spacing** tab.

- Click the **arrow** on the **Alignment list box.** Click **Justified.**

- Change the **Spacing After** to **12.**

- Click the **Line and Page Breaks tab** on the Paragraph dialog box.

- Click the **Keep Lines Together** check box so an individual tip will not be broken over two pages. Click **OK** to close the Paragraph dialog box.

➤ Click **OK** to close the Modify Style dialog box. Click the **Close command button** to return to the document.

➤ All paragraphs in the document change automatically to reflect the new definition of the Body Text style.

SPACE BEFORE AND AFTER

It's common practice to press the enter key twice at the end of a paragraph (once to end the paragraph, and a second time to insert a blank line before the next paragraph). The same effect can be achieved by setting the spacing before or after the paragraph using the Spacing Before or After list boxes in the Format Paragraph command. The latter technique gives you greater flexibility in that you can specify any amount of spacing (e.g., 6 points to leave only half a line) before or after a paragraph. It also enables you to change the spacing between paragraphs more easily because the information is stored within the paragraph style.

STEP 4: Review the Formatting

➤ Pull down the **Help menu** and click the **What's This command** (or press **Shift+F1**). The mouse pointer changes to a large question mark.

➤ Click in any paragraph to display the formatting in effect for that paragraph as shown in Figure 4.8c.

➤ You will see formatting specifications for the Body Text style—Indent: Left 0″, Right 0″, Justified, Space After 12 pt, Keep Lines Together, Font Times New Roman, 10 pt, and English (US).

➤ Click in any other paragraph to see the formatting in effect for that paragraph. Press **Esc** to return to normal editing.

Style in effect

Paragraph formatting specifications for Body Text style

Click in paragraph

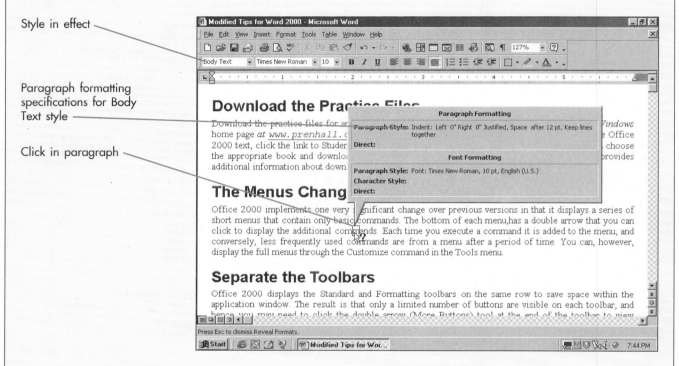

(c) Review the Formatting (step 4)

FIGURE 4.8   Hands-on Exercise 3 (continued)

USE THE DOCUMENT ORGANIZER

Use the Document Organizer to copy styles from one document to another. Start with the document that contains the style you want to copy, pull down the Format menu, and click the Style command to display the Style dialog box. Click the Organizer command button to display the Organizer dialog box. Select (click) the styles you want to copy from your document, then click the Copy button to copy those styles to the Normal template in the right side of the Organizer dialog box. Close the dialog box. The copied styles will now be available to any document that is based on the Normal template.

STEP 5: Modify the Heading 1 Style

➤ Click anywhere in the title of the first tip. The Style box on the Formatting toolbar contains Heading 1 to indicate that this style has been applied to the current paragraph.

➤ Pull down the **Format menu.** Click **Style.** The Heading 1 style is automatically selected, and its characteristics are displayed within the description box.

➤ Click the **Modify command button** to display the Modify Style dialog box.

➤ Click the **Format command button.**

- Click **Paragraph** to display the Paragraph dialog box. Click the **Indents and Spacing tab.**

- Change the **Spacing After** to **0** (there should be no space separating the heading and the paragraph).

- Change the **Spacing Before** to **0** (since there are already 12 points after the Body Text style as per the settings in step 4). Click **OK.**

- Click the **Format command button** a second time.

- Click **Font** to display the Font dialog box.

- Click **10** in the Font size box. Click **OK.**

➤ Click **OK** to close the Modify Style dialog box. Click the **Close command button** to return to the document and view the changes.

➤ Save the document.

MODIFY STYLES BY EXAMPLE

The Modify command button in the Format Style command is one way to change a style, but it prevents the use of the toolbar buttons. Thus it's easier to modify an existing style by example. Select any text that is defined by the style you want to modify, then reformat that text using the Formatting toolbar, shortcut keys, or pull-down menus. Click the Style box on the Formatting toolbar, make sure the selected style is the correct one, press enter, then click OK when asked if you want to update the style to reflect recent changes.

STEP 6: The Outline View

➤ Pull down the **View menu** and click **Outline** (or click the **Outline view button** above the status bar) to display the document in the Outline view.

➤ Pull down the **Edit menu** and click **Select All** (or press **Ctrl+A**) to select the entire document. Click the **Collapse button** on the Outlining toolbar to collapse the entire document so that only the headings are visible.

➤ Click in the heading of the first tip (Download the Practice Files) as shown in Figure 4.7d. Click the **Expand button** on the Outlining toolbar to see the subordinate items under this heading.

➤ Experiment with the Collapse and Expand buttons to display different levels of information in the outline.

Style box

Expand button

Collapse button

Click in heading for first tip

Outline View button

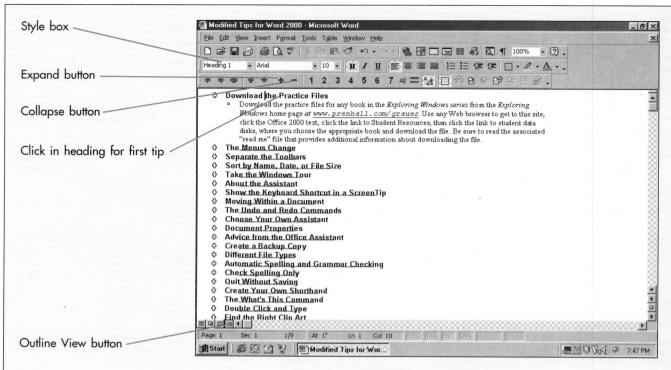

(d) The Outline View (step 6)

FIGURE 4.8   Hands-on Exercise 3 (continued)

STEP 7: Moving Text

➤ The advantage of the Outline view is that it facilitates moving text in a large document. You can move either an expanded or collapsed item, but the latter is generally easier, as you see the overall structure of the document.

➤ Click the **down arrow** on the vertical scroll bar until you see the tip, **Create Your Own Shorthand.** Click and drag to select the tip as shown in Figure 4.7e.

➤ Point to the **plus sign** next to the selected tip (the mouse pointer changes to a double arrow), then click and drag to move the tip below the **Different File Types** as shown in Figure 4.7e. Release the mouse.

➤ Change to the Print Layout view. Change the magnification to **Page Width.** Save the document.

THE DOCUMENT MAP

The Document Map helps you to navigate within a large document. Click the Document Map button on the Standard toolbar to divide the screen into two panes. The headings in a document are displayed in the left pane and the text of the document is visible in the right pane. To go to a specific point in a document, click its heading in the left pane, and the insertion point is moved automatically to that point in the document, which is visible in the right pane. Click the Map button a second time to turn the feature off.

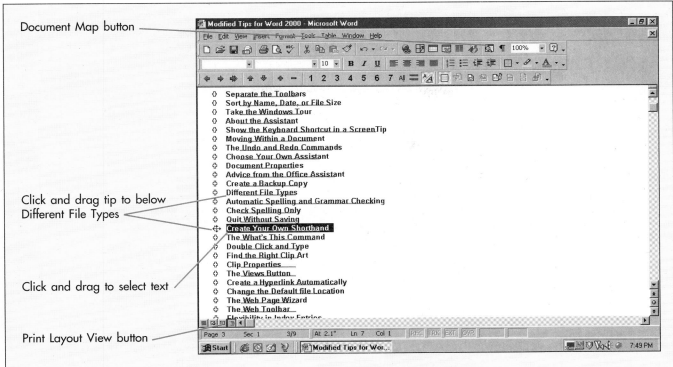

Document Map button

Click and drag tip to below Different File Types

Click and drag to select text

Print Layout View button

(e) Moving Text (step 7)

FIGURE 4.8   Hands-on Exercise 3 (continued)

STEP 8: Create a New Style

➤ Press **Ctrl+Home** to move to the beginning of the document. Press **Ctrl+enter** to create a page break for a title page.

➤ Move the insertion point on to the new page. Press the **enter key** five to ten times to move to an appropriate position for the title.

➤ Click the **Show/Hide ¶ button** on the Standard toolbar to display the non-printing characters. Select the paragraph marks, pull down the **Style list** on the Formatting toolbar, and click **Normal.**

➤ Deselect the paragraph marks to continue editing.

➤ Place the insertion point immediately to the left of the last hard return above the page break.

➤ Enter the title, **Tips for Microsoft Word 2000,** and format it in 28 Point Arial Bold as shown in Figure 4.8f.

➤ Click the **Center button** on the Formatting toolbar.

➤ Check that the title is still selected, then click in the **Styles List box** on the Formatting toolbar. The style name, Normal, is selected.

➤ Type **My Style** (the name of the new style). Press **enter.** You have just created a new style that we will use in the next exercise.

➤ Save the document.

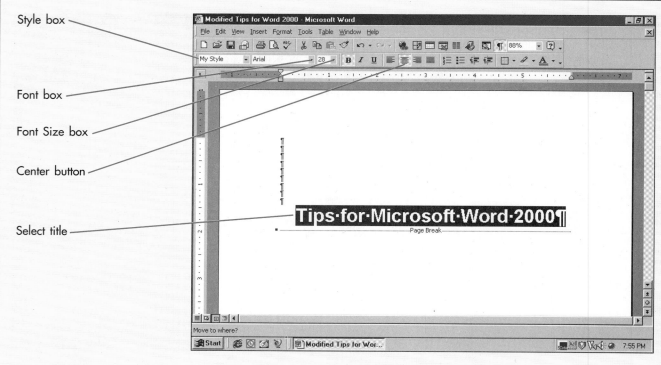

Style box
Font box
Font Size box
Center button
Select title

(f) Create a New Style (step 8)

FIGURE 4.8   Hands-on Exercise 3 (continued)

STEP 9: Complete the Title Page

➤ Click the **arrow** on the **Zoom box** on the Standard toolbar. Click **Two Pages.**

➤ Scroll through the document to see the effects of your formatting.

➤ Press **Ctrl+Home** to return to the beginning of the document, then change the magnification to **Page Width** so that you can read what you are typing. Complete the title page as shown in Figure 4.8g.

➤ Click immediately to the left of the ¶ after the title. Press **enter** once or twice.

➤ Click the **arrow** on the **Font Size box** on the Formatting toolbar. Click **12.** Type **by Robert Grauer and Maryann Barber.** Press **enter.**

➤ Save the document. Exit Word if you do not want to continue with the next exercise at this time.

THE PAGE BORDER COMMAND

Add interest to a title page with a border. Click anywhere on the page, pull down the Format menu, click the Borders and Shading command, then click the Page Border tab in the Borders and Shading dialog box. You can choose a box, shadow, or 3-D style in similar fashion to placing a border around a paragraph. You can also click the drop-down arrow on the Art text box to create a border consisting of a repeating clip art image.

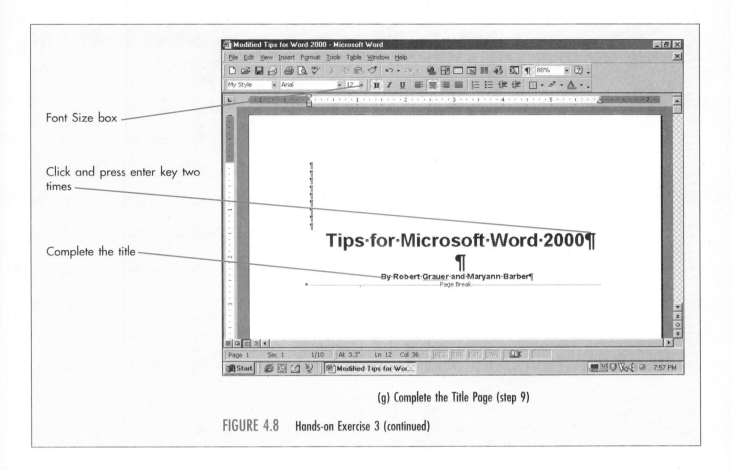

Font Size box

Click and press enter key two times

Complete the title

(g) Complete the Title Page (step 9)

FIGURE 4.8   Hands-on Exercise 3 (continued)

WORKING IN LONG DOCUMENTS

Long documents, such as term papers or reports, require additional formatting for better organization. These documents typically contain page numbers, headers and/or footers, a table of contents, and an index. Each of these elements is discussed in turn and will be illustrated in a hands-on exercise.

Page Numbers

The ***Insert Page Numbers command*** is the easiest way to place ***page numbers*** into a document and is illustrated in Figure 4.9. The page numbers can appear at the top or bottom of a page, and can be left, centered, or right-aligned. Word provides additional flexibility in that you can use Roman rather than Arabic numerals, and you need not start at page number one.

The Insert Page Number command is limited, however, in that it does not provide for additional text next to the page number. You can overcome this restriction by creating a header or footer which contains the page number.

Headers and Footers

Headers and footers give a professional appearance to a document. A ***header*** consists of one or more lines that are printed at the top of every page. A ***footer*** is printed at the bottom of the page. A document may contain headers but not footers, footers but not headers, or both headers and footers.

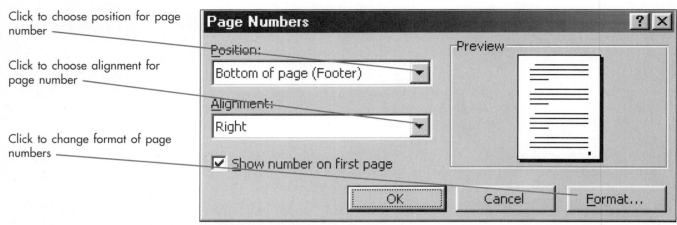

Click to choose position for page number

Click to choose alignment for page number

Click to change format of page numbers

FIGURE 4.9   Page Numbers

Headers and footers are created from the View menu. (A simple header or footer is also created automatically by the Insert Page Number command, depending on whether the page number is at the top or bottom of a page.) Headers and footers are formatted like any other paragraph and can be centered, left- or right-aligned. They can be formatted in any typeface or point size and can include special codes to automatically insert the page number, date, and/or time a document is printed.

The advantage of using a header or footer (over typing the text yourself at the top or bottom of every page) is that you type the text only once, after which it appears automatically according to your specifications. In addition, the placement of the headers and footers is adjusted for changes in page breaks caused by the insertion or deletion of text in the body of the document.

Headers and footers can change continually throughout a document. The Page Setup dialog box (in the File menu) enables you to specify a different header or footer for the first page, and/or different headers and footers for the odd and even pages. If, however, you wanted to change the header (or footer) midway through a document, you would need to insert a section break at the point where the new header (or footer) is to begin.

Sections

Formatting in Word occurs on three levels. You are already familiar with formatting at the character and paragraph levels that have been used throughout the text. Formatting at the section level controls headers and footers, page numbering, page size and orientation, margins, and columns. All of the documents in the text so far have consisted of a single *section,* and thus any section formatting applied to the entire document. You can, however, divide a document into sections and format each section independently.

Formatting at the section level gives you the ability to create more sophisticated documents. You can use section formatting to:

➤ Change the margins within a multipage letter, where the first page (the letterhead) requires a larger top margin than the other pages in the letter.

➤ Change the orientation from portrait to landscape to accommodate a wide table at the end of the document.

➤ Change the page numbering to use Roman numerals at the beginning of the document for a table of contents and Arabic numerals thereafter.

➤ Change the number of columns in a newsletter, which may contain a single column at the top of a page for the masthead, then two or three columns in the body of the newsletter.

In all instances, you determine where one section ends and another begins by using the *Insert menu* to create a *section break.* You also have the option of deciding how the section break will be implemented on the printed page; that is, you can specify that the new section continue on the same page, that it begin on a new page, or that it begin on the next odd or even page even if a blank page has to be inserted.

Word stores the formatting characteristics of each section in the section break at the end of a section. Thus, deleting a section break also deletes the section formatting, causing the text above the break to assume the formatting characteristics of the next section.

Figure 4.10 displays a multipage view of a ten-page document. The document has been divided into two sections, and the insertion point is currently on the fourth page of the document (page four of ten), which is also the first page of the second section. Note the corresponding indications on the status bar and the position of the headers and footers throughout the document.

Figure 4.10 also displays the Headers and Footers toolbar, which contains various icons associated with these elements. As indicated, a header or footer may contain text and/or special codes—for example, the word "page" followed by a code for the page number. The latter is inserted into the header by clicking the appropriate button on the Headers and Footers toolbar. Remember, headers and footers are implemented at the section level. Thus, changing a header or footer within a document requires the insertion of a section break.

Insertion point is on page 4

Header area

Footer area

Header and Footer toolbar

Page Numbers button

Insertion point is on page 1 of second section

Insertion point is on page 4 of a 10-page document

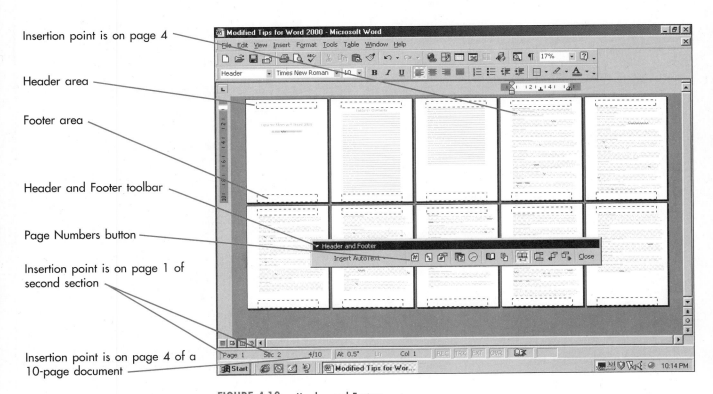

FIGURE 4.10   Headers and Footers

Table of Contents

A ***table of contents*** lists headings in the order they appear in a document and the page numbers where the entries begin. Word will create the table of contents automatically, provided you have identified each heading in the document with a built-in heading style (Heading 1 through Heading 9). Word will also update the table automatically to accommodate the addition or deletion of headings and/or changes in page numbers brought about through changes in the document.

The table of contents is created through the ***Index and Tables command*** from the Insert menu as shown in Figure 4.11a. You have your choice of several

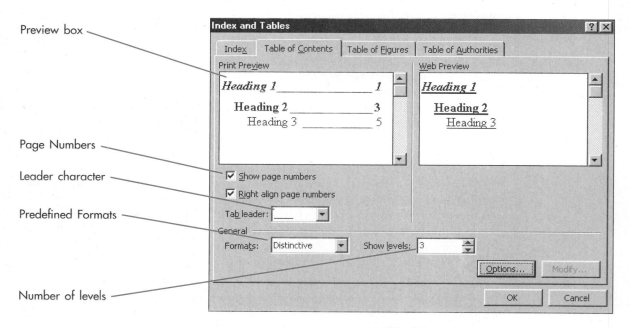

(a) Table of Contents

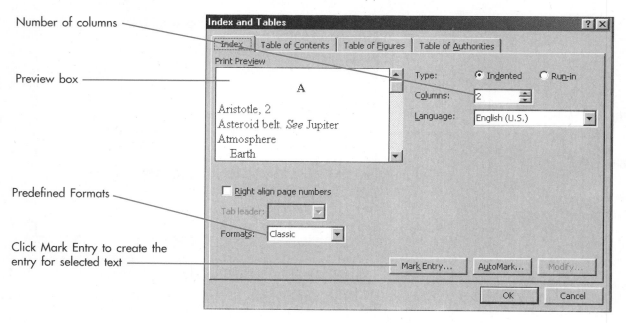

(b) Index

FIGURE 4.11   Index and Tables Command

predefined formats and the number of levels within each format; the latter correspond to the heading styles used within the document. You can also choose the *leader character* and whether or not to right align the page numbers.

Creating an Index

An *index* is the finishing touch in a long document. Word will create an index automatically provided that the entries for the index have been previously marked. This, in turn, requires you to go through a document, and one by one, select the terms to be included in the index and mark them accordingly. It's not as tedious as it sounds. You can, for example, select a single occurrence of an entry and tell Word to mark all occurrences of that entry for the index. You can also create cross-references, such as "see also Internet."

After the entries have been specified, you create the index by choosing the appropriate settings in the Index and Tables command as shown in Figure 4.11b. You can choose a variety of styles for the index just as you can for the table of contents. Word will put the index entries in alphabetical order and will enter the appropriate page references. You can also create additional index entries and/or move text within a document, then update the index with the click of a mouse.

The Go To Command

The *Go To command* moves the insertion point to the top of a designated page. The command is accessed from the Edit menu by pressing the F5 function key, or by double clicking the Page number on the status bar. After the command has been executed, you are presented with a dialog box in which you enter the desired page number. You can also specify a relative page number—for example, P +2 to move forward two pages, or P −1 to move back one page.

HANDS-ON EXERCISE 4

Working in Long Documents

Objective: To create a header (footer) that includes page numbers; to insert and update a table of contents; to add an index entry; to insert a section break and demonstrate the Go To command; to view multiple pages of a document. Use Figure 4.12 as a guide for the exercise.

STEP 1: Applying a Style

➤ Open the **Modified Tips for Word 2000 document** from the previous exercise. Scroll to the top of the second page. Click to the left of the first tip title. (If necessary, click the **Show/Hide ¶ button** on the Standard toolbar to hide the paragraph marks.)

➤ Type **Table of Contents**. Press the **enter key** two times.

➤ Click anywhere within the phrase "Table of Contents". Click the **down arrow** on the **Styles list box** to pull down the styles for this document as shown in Figure 4.12a.

➤ Click **My Style** (the style you created at the end of the previous exercise). "Table of Contents" is centered in 28 point Arial bold according to the definition of My Style.

Click down arrow on styles box

Click My Style

Click in text

Print Layout View button

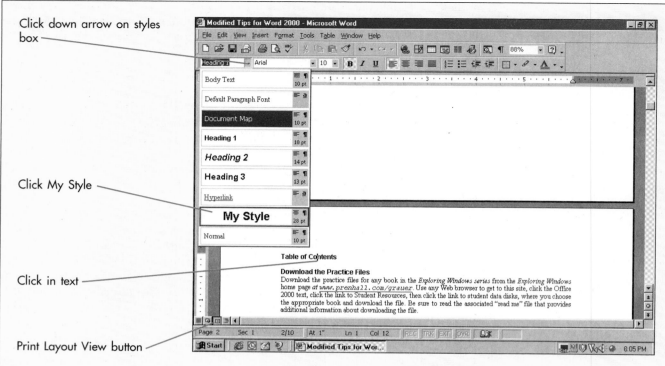

(a) Applying a Style (step 1)

FIGURE 4.12   Hands-on Exercise 4

STEP 2: View Many Pages

➤ If necessary, change to the Print Layout view. Click the line immediately under the title for the table of contents. Pull down the **View menu.** Click **Zoom** to display the dialog box in Figure 4.12b.

➤ Click the **monitor icon.** Click and drag the **page icons** to display two pages down by five pages across as shown in the figure. Release the mouse.

➤ Click **OK.** The display changes to show all ten pages in the document.

STEP 3: Create the Table of Contents

➤ Pull down the **Insert menu.** Click **Index and Tables.** If necessary, click the **Table of Contents tab** to display the dialog box in Figure 4.12c.

➤ Check the boxes to **Show Page Numbers** and to **Right Align Page Numbers.**

➤ Click the **down arrow** on the Formats list box, then click **Distinctive.** Click the **arrow** in the **Tab Leader list box.** Choose a dot leader. Click **OK.** Word takes a moment to create the table of contents, which extends to two pages.

AUTOFORMAT AND THE TABLE OF CONTENTS

Word will create a table of contents automatically, provided you use the built-in heading styles to define the items for inclusion. If you have not applied the styles to the document, the AutoFormat command will do it for you. Once the heading styles are in the document, pull down the Insert command, click Index and Tables, then click the Table of Contents command.

Click Monitor icon

Click and drag 5 pages
across by 2 pages down

Text is in My Style style

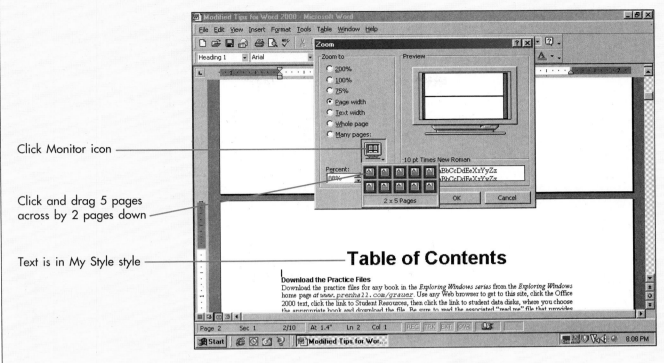

(b) View Many Pages (step 2)

Click Table of Contents tab

Select both options

Click to select dot leader

Click to select Distinctive style

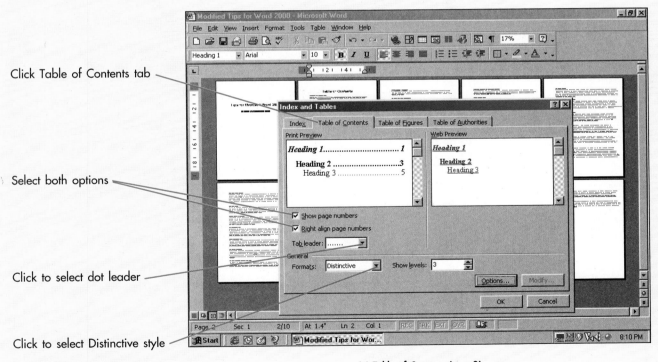

(c) Table of Contents (step 3)

FIGURE 4.12   Hands-on Exercise 4 (continued)

STEP 4: Field Codes versus Field Text

➤ Click the **arrow** on the **Zoom Control box** on the Standard toolbar. Click **Page Width** in order to read the table of contents as in Figure 4.12d.

➤ Use the **up arrow key** to scroll to the beginning of the table of contents. Press **Alt+F9.** The table of contents is replaced by an entry similar to {TOC \o "1-3"} to indicate a field code. The exact code depends on the selections you made in step 4.

➤ Press **Alt+F9** a second time. The field code for the table of contents is replaced by text.

➤ Pull down the **Edit menu.** Click **Go To** to display the dialog box in Figure 4.12d.

➤ Type **3** and press the **enter key** to go to page 3, which contains the bottom portion of the table of contents. Click **Close.**

Click Go To tab

Enter 3

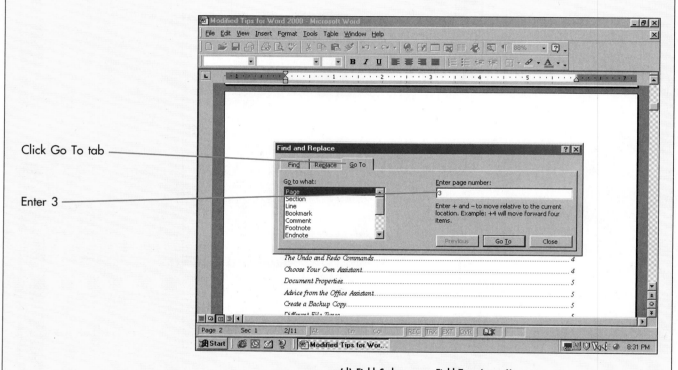

(d) Field Codes versus Field Text (step 4)

FIGURE 4.12   Hands-on Exercise 4 (continued)

THE GO TO AND GO BACK COMMANDS

The F5 key is the shortcut equivalent of the Go To command and displays a dialog box to move to a specific location (a page or section) within a document. The Shift+F5 combination executes the Go Back command and returns to a previous location of the insertion point; press Shift+F5 repeatedly to cycle through the last three locations of the insertion point.

STEP 5: Insert a Section Break

➤ Scroll down page three until you are at the end of the table of contents. Click to the left of the first tip heading as shown in Figure 4.12e.

➤ Pull down the **Insert menu.** Click **Break** to display the Break dialog box. Click the **Next Page button** under Section Breaks. Click **OK** to create a section break, simultaneously forcing the first tip to begin on a new page.

➤ The first tip, Download the Practice Files, moves to the top of the next page (page 4 in the document). If the status bar already displays Page 1 Section 2, a previous user has changed the default numbering to begin each section on its own page and you can go to step 6. If not you need to change the page numbering.

➤ Pull down the **Insert menu** and click **Page Numbers** to display the Page Numbers dialog box. Click the **drop-down arrow** in the Position list box to position the page number at the top of page (in the header).

➤ Click the **Format command button** to display the Page Number Format dialog box. Click the option button to **Start at** page 1 (i.e., you want the first page in the second section to be numbered as page 1), and click **OK** to close the Page Number Format box.

➤ Close the Page Numbers dialog box. The status bar now displays page 1 Sec 2 to indicate that you are on page 1 in the second section. The entry 4/12 indicates that you are physically on the fourth page of a 12-page document.

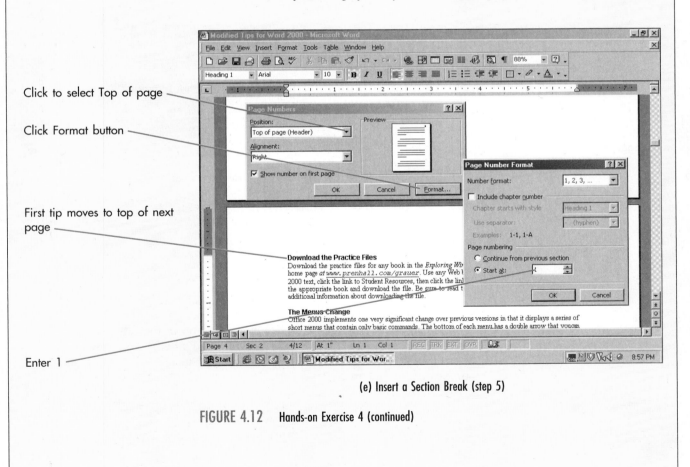

Click to select Top of page

Click Format button

First tip moves to top of next page

Enter 1

(e) Insert a Section Break (step 5)

FIGURE 4.12   Hands-on Exercise 4 (continued)

STEP 6: The Page Setup Command

➤ Pull down the **File menu** and click the **Page Setup** command (or double click the ruler) to display the Page Setup dialog box.

➤ Click the **Layout tab** to display the dialog box in Figure 4.12f.

➤ If necessary, clear the box for Different Odd and Even Pages and for Different First Page, as all pages in this section (section two) are to have the same header. Click **OK.**

➤ Save the document.

Click Layout tab

Check boxes should not be selected

Insertion point is on page 1 of section 2

Insertion point is on page 4 of 12-page document

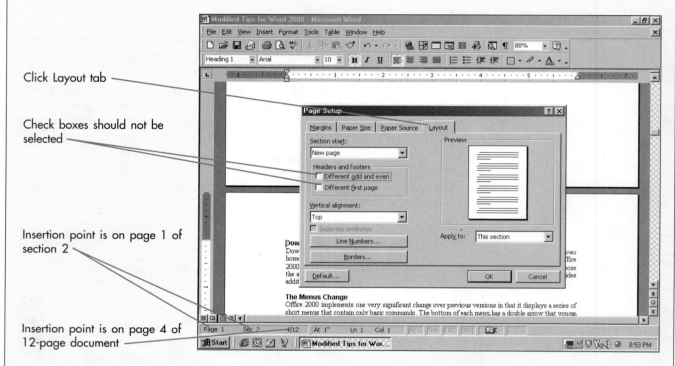

(f) The Page Setup Command (step 6)

FIGURE 4.12   Hands-on Exercise 4 (continued)

MOVING WITHIN LONG DOCUMENTS

Double click the page indicator on the status bar to display the dialog box for the Go To command from where you can go directly to any page within the document. You can also click an entry in the table of contents to go directly to the text of that entry. And finally, you can use the Ctrl+Home and Ctrl+End keyboard shortcuts to move to the beginning or end of the document, respectively.

STEP 7: Create the Header

➤ Pull down the **View menu.** Click **Header and Footer** to produce the screen in Figure 4.12g. The text in the document is faded to indicate that you are editing the header, as opposed to the document.

➤ The "Same as Previous" indicator is on since Word automatically uses the header from the previous section.

➤ Click the **Same as Previous button** on the Header and Footer toolbar to toggle the indicator off and to create a different header for this section.

➤ If necessary, click in the header. Click the **arrow** on the **Font list box** on the Formatting toolbar. Click **Arial.** Click the **arrow** on the Font size box. Click **8.** Type **Tips for Microsoft Word 2000.**

➤ Press the **Tab key** twice. Type **PAGE.** Press the **space bar.** Click the **Insert Page Number button** on the Header and Footer toolbar.

➤ Click the **Close button** on the Header and Footer toolbar. The header is faded, and the document text is available for editing.

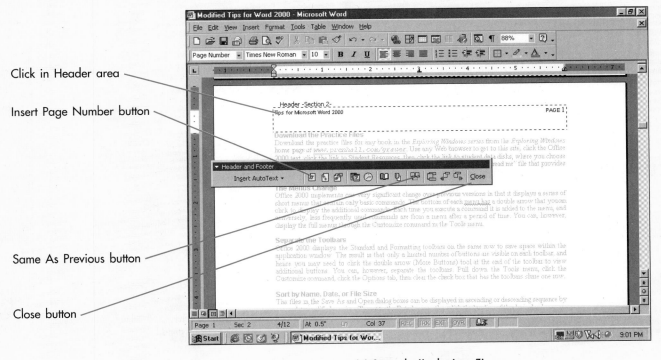

Click in Header area

Insert Page Number button

Same As Previous button

Close button

(g) Create the Header (step 7)

FIGURE 4.12   Hands-on Exercise 4 (continued)

HEADERS AND FOOTERS

If you do not see a header or footer, it is most likely because you are in the wrong view. Headers and footers are displayed in the Print Layout view but not in the Normal view. (Click the Print Layout button on the status bar to change the view.)

STEP 8: Update the Table of Contents

➤ Press **Ctrl+Home** to move to the beginning of the document. The status bar indicates Page 1, Sec 1.

➤ Click the **Select Browse Object button** on the Vertical scroll bar, then click the **Browse by Page** icon.

➤ If necessary, click the **Next Page button** or **Previous Page button** on the vertical scroll bar (or press **Ctrl+PgDn**) to move to the page containing the table of contents.

➤ Click to the left of the first entry in the Table of Contents. Press the **F9 key** to update the table of contents. If necessary, click the **Update Entire Table button** as shown in Figure 4.12h, then click **OK**.

➤ The pages are renumbered to reflect the actual page numbers in the second section.

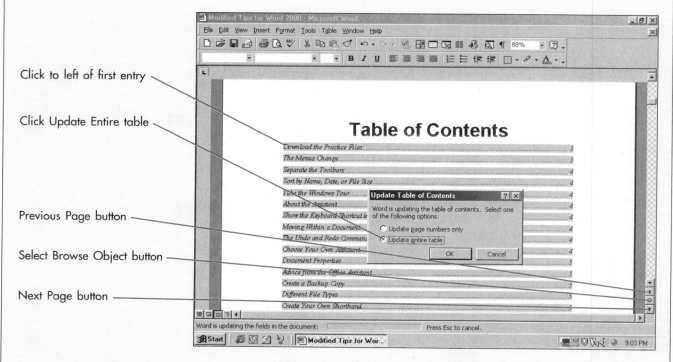

(h) Update the Table of Contents (step 8)

FIGURE 4.12   Hands-on Exercise 4 (continued)

SELECT BROWSE OBJECT

Click the Select Browse Object button toward the bottom of the vertical scroll bar to display a menu in which you specify how to browse through a document. Typically you browse from one page to the next, but you can browse by footnote, section, graphic, table, or any of the other objects listed. Once you select the object, click the Next or Previous buttons on the vertical scroll bar (or press Ctrl+PgDn or Ctrl+PgUp) to move to the next or previous occurrence of the selected object.

STEP 9: Create an Index Entry

➤ Press **Ctrl+Home** to move to the beginning of the document. Pull down the **Edit menu** and click the **Find command.** Search for the first occurrence of the text "Ctrl+Home" within the document, as shown in Figure 4.12i. Close the Find and Replace dialog box.

➤ Click the **Show/Hide ¶ button** so you can see the nonprinting characters in the document, which include the index entries that have been previously created by the authors. (The index entries appear in curly brackets and begin with the letters XE.)

➤ Check that the text "Ctrl+Home" is selected within the document, then press **Alt+Shift+X** to display the Mark Index Entry dialog box. (Should you forget the shortcut, pull down the Insert menu, click the **Index and Tables command,** then click the Mark Entry command button.)

➤ Click the **Mark command button** to create the index entry, after which you see the field code, {XE "Ctrl+Home"} to indicate that the index entry has been created.

➤ The Mark Index Entry dialog box stays open so that you can create additional entries by selecting additional text.

➤ Click the option button to create a **cross-reference.** Type **keyboard shortcut** in the associated text box. Click **Mark.**

➤ Click in the document, click and drag to select the text "Ctrl+End," then click in the dialog box, and the Main entry changes to Ctrl+End automatically. Click the **Mark command button** to create the index entry. Close the Mark Index Entry dialog box. Save the document.

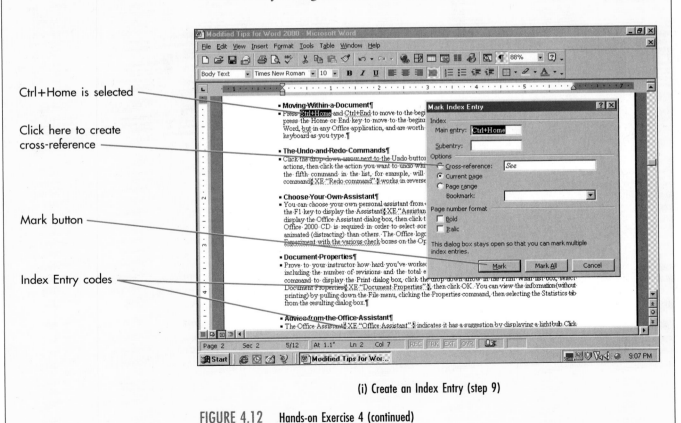

Ctrl+Home is selected

Click here to create cross-reference

Mark button

Index Entry codes

(i) Create an Index Entry (step 9)

FIGURE 4.12   Hands-on Exercise 4 (continued)

STEP 10: Create the Index

➤ Press **Ctrl+End** to move to the end of the document where you will insert the index. Pull down the **Insert menu** and click the **Index and Tables command** to display the Index and Tables dialog box in Figure 4.12j. Click the **Index tab** if necessary.

➤ Choose the type of index you want. We selected a **classic format** over **two columns.** Click **OK** to create the index. Click the **Undo command** if you are not satisfied with the appearance of the index, then repeat the process to create an index with a different style.

➤ Save the document.

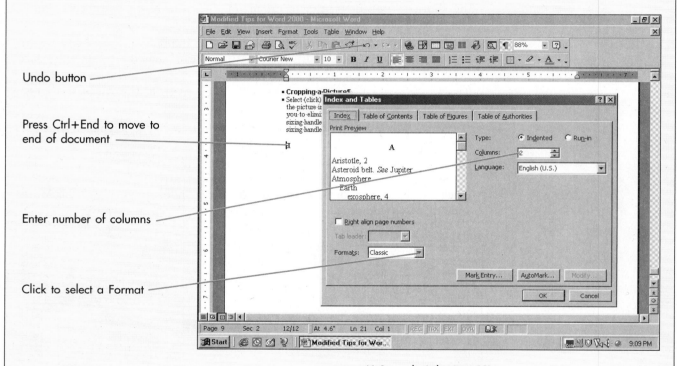

Undo button

Press Ctrl+End to move to end of document

Enter number of columns

Click to select a Format

(j) Create the Index (step 10)

FIGURE 4.12   Hands-on Exercise 4 (continued)

AUTOMARK INDEX ENTRIES

The AutoMark command will, as the name implies, automatically mark all occurrences of all entries for inclusion in an index. To use the feature, you have to create a separate document that lists the terms you want to reference, then you execute the AutoMark command from the Index and Tables dialog box. The advantage is that it is fast. The disadvantage is that every occurrence of an entry is marked in the index so that a commonly used term may have too many page references. You can, however, delete superfluous entries by manually deleting the field codes. Click the Show/Hide button if you do not see the entries in the document.

STEP 11: Complete the Index

➤ Scroll to the beginning of the index and click to the left of the letter "A." Pull down the **File menu** and click the **Page Setup command** to display the Page Setup dialog box and click the **Layout tab.**

➤ Click the **down arrow** in the Section start list box and specify **New page.** Click the **down arrow** in the Apply to list box and specify **This section.** Click **OK.** The index moves to the top of a new page.

➤ Click anywhere in the index, which is contained in its own section since it is displayed over two columns. The status bar displays Page 1, Section 3, 13/13 as shown in Figure 4.12k.

➤ Save the document.

Click Layout tab

Click to select New Page

Click to select This section

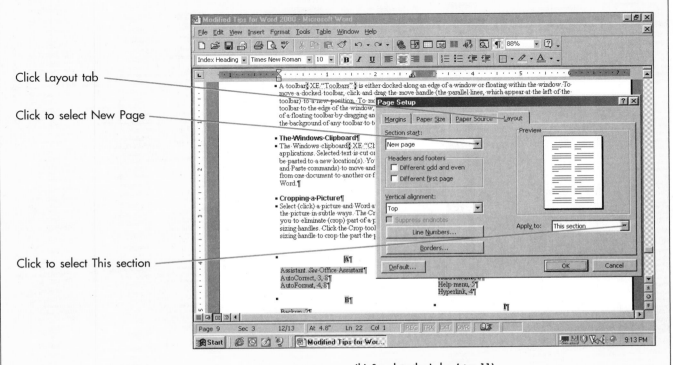

(k) Complete the Index (step 11)

FIGURE 4.12   Hands-on Exercise 4 (continued)

SECTION FORMATTING

Page numbering and orientation, headers, footers, and columns are implemented at the section level. Thus the index is automatically placed in its own section because it contains a different number of columns from the rest of the document. The notation on the status bar, Page 1, Section 3, 13/13 indicates that the insertion point is on the first page of section three, corresponding to the 13th page of a 13-page document.

STEP 12: The Completed Document

➤ Pull down the **View menu.** Click **Zoom.** Click **Many Pages.** Click the **monitor icon.** Click and drag the page icon within the monitor to display two pages down by five pages. Release the mouse. Click **OK.**

➤ The completed document is shown in Figure 4.12l. The index appears by itself on the last (13th) page of the document.

➤ Save the document, then print the completed document to prove to your instructor that you have completed the exercise.

➤ Congratulations on a job well done. Exit Word.

Index is on last page

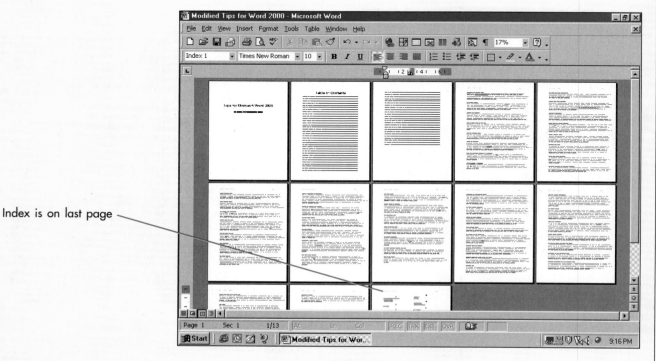

(l) The Completed Document (step 12)

FIGURE 4.12   Hands-on Exercise 4 (continued)

UPDATING THE TABLE OF CONTENTS

Use a Shortcut menu to update the table of contents. Point to any entry in the table of contents, then press the right mouse button to display a shortcut menu. Click Update Field, click the Update Entire Table command button, and click OK. The table of contents will be adjusted automatically to reflect page number changes as well as the addition or deletion of any items defined by any built-in heading style.

A list helps to organize information by emphasizing important topics. A bulleted or numbered list can be created by clicking the appropriate button on the Formatting toolbar or by executing the Bullets and Numbering command in the Format menu. An outline extends a numbered list to several levels.

Tables represent a very powerful capability within Word and are created through the Insert Table command in the Table menu or by using the Insert Table button on the Standard toolbar. Each cell in a table is formatted independently and may contain text, numbers, and/or graphics.

A style is a set of formatting instructions that has been saved under a distinct name. Styles are created at the character or paragraph level and provide a consistent appearance to similar elements throughout a document. Existing styles can be modified to change the formatting of all text defined by that style.

The Outline view displays a condensed view of a document based on styles within the document. Text may be collapsed or expanded as necessary to facilitate moving text within long documents.

The AutoFormat command analyzes a document and formats it for you. The command goes through an entire document, determines how each paragraph is used, then applies an appropriate style to each paragraph.

Formatting occurs at the character, paragraph, or section level. Section formatting controls margins, columns, page orientation and size, page numbering, and headers and footers. A header consists of one or more lines that are printed at the top of every (designated) page in a document. A footer is text that is printed at the bottom of designated pages. Page numbers may be added to either a header or footer.

A table of contents lists headings in the order they appear in a document with their respective page numbers. It can be created automatically, provided the built-in heading styles were previously applied to the items for inclusion. Word will create an index automatically, provided that the entries for the index have been previously marked. This, in turn, requires you to go through a document, select the appropriate text, and mark the entries accordingly. The Edit Go To command enables you to move directly to a specific page, section, or bookmark within a document.

KEY WORDS AND CONCEPTS

AutoFormat command	Go To command	Normal style
AutoMark	Header	Numbered list
Body Text style	Heading 1 style	Outline
Bookmark	Index	Outline view
Bulleted list	Index and Tables command	Page numbers
Bullets and Numbering command	Insert menu	Paragraph style
Cell	Insert Page Numbers command	Section
Character style	Insert Table command	Section break
Default Paragraph Font style	Leader character	Style
Footer	Mark Index entry	Style command
Format Style command	Outline numbered list	Table menu
		Table of contents
		Tables feature

1. Which of the following can be stored within a paragraph style?
   (a) Tabs and indents
   (b) Line spacing and alignment
   (c) Shading and borders
   (d) All of the above

2. What is the easiest way to change the alignment of five paragraphs scattered throughout a document, each of which has been formatted with the same style?
   (a) Select the paragraphs individually, then click the appropriate alignment button on the Formatting toolbar
   (b) Select the paragraphs at the same time, then click the appropriate alignment button on the Formatting toolbar
   (c) Change the format of the existing style, which changes the paragraphs
   (d) Retype the paragraphs according to the new specifications

3. The AutoFormat command will do all of the following except:
   (a) Apply styles to individual paragraphs
   (b) Apply boldface italics to terms that require additional emphasis
   (c) Replace ordinary quotes with smart quotes
   (d) Substitute typographic symbols for ordinary letters—such as © for (C)

4. Which of the following is used to create a conventional outline?
   (a) The Bullets and Numbering command
   (b) The Outline view
   (c) Both (a) and (b)
   (d) Neither (a) nor (b)

5. In which view do you see headers and/or footers?
   (a) Print Layout view
   (b) Normal view
   (c) Both (a) and (b)
   (d) Neither (a) nor (b)

6. Which of the following numbering schemes can be used with page numbers?
   (a) Roman numerals (I, II, III . . . or i, ii, iii)
   (b) Regular numbers (1, 2, 3, . . .)
   (c) Letters (A, B, C . . . or a, b, c)
   (d) All of the above

7. Which of the following is true regarding headers and footers?
   (a) Every document must have at least one header
   (b) Every document must have at least one footer
   (c) Both (a) and (b)
   (d) Neither (a) nor (b)

8. Which of the following is a *false* statement regarding lists?
   (a) A bulleted list can be changed to a numbered list and vice versa
   (b) The symbol for the bulleted list can be changed to a different character
   (c) The numbers in a numbered list can be changed to letters or roman numerals
   (d) The bullets or numbers cannot be removed

9. Page numbers can be specified in:
   (a) A header but not a footer
   (b) A footer but not a header
   (c) A header or a footer
   (d) Neither a header nor a footer

10. Which of the following is true regarding the formatting within a document?
    (a) Line spacing and alignment are implemented at the section level
    (b) Margins, headers, and footers are implemented at the paragraph level
    (c) Both (a) and (b)
    (d) Neither (a) nor (b)

11. What happens when you press the Tab key from within a table?
    (a) A Tab character is inserted just as it would be for ordinary text
    (b) The insertion point moves to the next column in the same row or the first column in the next row if you are at the end of the row
    (c) Both (a) and (b)
    (d) Neither (a) nor (b)

12. Which of the following is true, given that the status bar displays Page 1, Section 3, followed by 7/9?
    (a) The document has a maximum of three sections
    (b) The third section begins on page 7
    (c) The insertion point is on the very first page of the document
    (d) All of the above

13. The Edit Go To command enables you to move the insertion point to:
    (a) A specific page
    (b) A relative page forward or backward from the current page
    (c) A specific section
    (d) Any of the above

14. Once a table of contents has been created and inserted into a document:
    (a) Any subsequent page changes arising from the insertion or deletion of text to existing paragraphs must be entered manually
    (b) Any additions to the entries in the table arising due to the insertion of new paragraphs defined by a heading style must be entered manually
    (c) Both (a) and (b)
    (d) Neither (a) nor (b)

15. Which of the following is *false* about the Outline view?
    (a) It can be collapsed to display only headings
    (b) It can be expanded to show the entire document
    (c) It requires the application of styles
    (d) It is used to create a conventional outline

Answers

1. d		**6.** d		**11.** b
2. c		**7.** d		**12.** b
3. b		**8.** d		**13.** d
4. a		**9.** c		**14.** d
5. a		**10.** d		**15.** d

PRACTICE WITH MICROSOFT WORD

1. Use your favorite search engine to locate the text of the United States Constitution. There are many available sites and associated documents. Once you locate the text of the Constitution, expand the outline created in the first hands-on exercise to include information about the other provisions of the Constitution (Articles IV through VII, the Bill of Rights, and the other amendments). Submit the completed outline to your professor.

2. Sections and Page Orientation: Formatting in Word takes place at the character, paragraph, or section level. The latter controls the margins and page orientation within a document and is illustrated in Figure 4.13. Create the study schedule as described in the second hands-on exercise, then insert a title page in front of the table. Note, however, that the title page and table must appear in different sections so that you can use the portrait and landscape orientations, respectively. Print the two-page document, consisting of the title page and table, and submit it to your instructor.

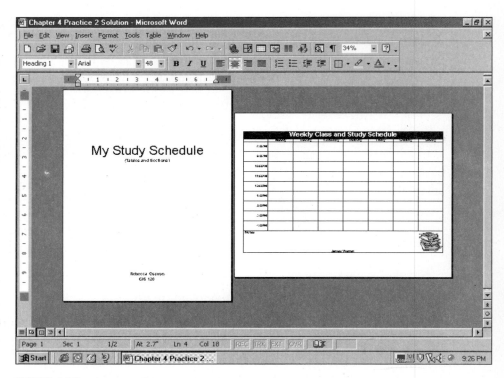

FIGURE 4.13   Sections and Page Orientation (Exercise 2)

3. For the health conscious: Open the *Chapter 4 Practice 3 document* in the *Exploring Word folder,* which consists of a series of tips for healthy living. Modify the document as follows:

   a. Use the AutoFormat command to apply the Heading 1 and Body Text styles throughout the document.

   b. Change the specifications for the Body Text and Heading 1 styles as follows. The Heading 1 style calls for 12 point Arial bold with a blue top border (which requires a color printer). The Body Text style is 12 point Times New Roman, justified, with a ¼ inch left indent.

   c. Create a title page for the document consisting of the title, *Tips for Healthy Living,* the author, *Marion B. Grauer,* and an additional line, indicating that the document was prepared for you.

   d. Create a header for the document consisting of the title, *Tips for Healthy Living,* and a page number. The header is not to appear on the title page, nor should the title page be included in the page numbering.

   e. Print the entire document for your instructor.

4. Graphics: A table may contain anything—text, graphics, or numbers as shown by the document in Figure 4.14. It's not complicated; in fact, it was really very easy; just follow the steps below:

   a. Create a 7 × 4 table.

   b. Merge all of the cells in row one and enter the heading. Merge all of the cells in row two and type the text describing the sale.

   c. Use the Clip Gallery to insert a picture into the table.

   d. Enter the sales data in rows three through seven of the table; all entries are centered within the respective cells.

   e. Change the font, colors, and formatting, then print the completed document. Use any format you think is appropriate.

Of course, it isn't quite as simple as it sounds, but we think you get the idea. Good luck and feel free to improve on our design. Color is a nice touch, but it is definitely not required.

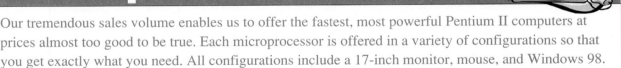

Computers To Go

Our tremendous sales volume enables us to offer the fastest, most powerful Pentium II computers at prices almost too good to be true. Each microprocessor is offered in a variety of configurations so that you get exactly what you need. All configurations include a 17-inch monitor, mouse, and Windows 98.

Capacity	Configuration 1 128 Mb RAM 12 Gb Hard Drive	Configuration 2 96 Mb RAM 10 Gb Hard Drive	Configuration 3 64 Mb RAM 8 Gb Hard Drive
Pentium II – 450 MHz	$2,655	$2,437	$2,341
Pentium II – 400 MHz	$2,367	$2,249	$2,053
Pentium II – 350 MHz	$1,970	$1,769	$1,554
Pentium II – 333 MHz	$1,693	$1,492	$1,277

FIGURE 4.14   Graphics (Exercise 6)

Tips for Windows 98

Open the *Tips for Windows 98* document that can be found in the Exploring Windows folder. The tips are not formatted so we would like you to use the Auto-Format command to create an attractive document. There are lots of tips so a table of contents is also appropriate. Add a cover page with your name and date, then submit the completed document to your instructor.

Milestones in Communications

We take for granted immediate news of everything that is going on in the world, but it was not always that way. Did you know, for example, that it took five months for Queen Isabella to hear of Columbus' discovery, or that it took two weeks for Europe to learn of Lincoln's assassination? We've done some research on milestones in communications and left the file for you (Milestones in Communications). It runs for two, three, or four pages, depending on the formatting, which we leave to you. We would like you to include a header, and we think you should box the quotations that appear at the end of the document (it's your call as to whether to separate the quotations or group them together). Please be sure to number the completed document and don't forget a title page.

The Term Paper

Go to your most demanding professor and obtain the formatting requirements for the submission of a term paper. Be as precise as possible; for example, ask about margins, type size, and so on. What are the requirements for a title page? Is there a table of contents? Are there footnotes or endnotes, headers or footers? What is the format for the bibliography? Summarize the requirements, then indicate the precise means of implementation within Microsoft Word.

Word Outlines and PowerPoint Presentations

A Word document can be the basis of a PowerPoint presentation, provided the document has been formatted to include styles. Each paragraph formatted according to the Heading 1 style becomes the title of a slide, each paragraph formatted with the Heading 2 style becomes the first level of text, and so on.

Use the *Milestones in Communications* document in the Exploring Word folder as the basis of a PowerPoint presentation (see the first case study). Use the AutoFormat command to apply the necessary styles, pull down the File menu, select the Send To command, then choose Microsoft PowerPoint. Your system will start PowerPoint, then convert the styles in the Word document to a PowerPoint outline. Complete the presentation based on facts in the Word document, then submit the completed presentation to your instructor.

chapter 5

DESKTOP PUBLISHING: CREATING A NEWSLETTER

OVERVIEW

Desktop publishing evolved through a combination of technologies including faster computers, laser printers, and sophisticated page composition software to manipulate text and graphics. Desktop publishing was initially considered a separate application, but today's generation of word processors has matured to such a degree, that it is difficult to tell where word processing ends and desktop publishing begins. Microsoft Word is, for all practical purposes, a desktop publishing program that can be used to create all types of documents.

The essence of *desktop publishing* is the merger of text with graphics to produce a professional-looking document without reliance on external services. Desktop publishing will save you time and money because you are doing the work yourself rather than sending it out as you did in traditional publishing. That is the good news. The bad news is that desktop publishing is not as easy as it sounds, precisely because you are doing work that was done previously by skilled professionals. Nevertheless, with a little practice, and a basic knowledge of graphic design, you will be able to create effective and attractive documents.

Our chapter begins with the development of a simple newsletter in which we create a multicolumn document, import clip art and other objects, and position those objects within a document. The newsletter also reviews material from earlier chapters on bullets and lists, borders and shading, and section formatting. The second half of the chapter presents additional tools that you can use to enhance your documents. We describe the Drawing toolbar and explain how it is used to add objects to a Word document. We also introduce Microsoft Graph, an application that creates (and modifies) a graph based on numerical data that you enter or import from another application.

THE NEWSLETTER

The newsletter in Figure 5.1 demonstrates the basics of desktop publishing and provides an overview of the chapter. The material is presented conceptually, after which you implement the design in two hands-on exercises. We provide the text and you do the formatting. The first exercise creates a simple newsletter from copy that we provide. The second exercise uses more sophisticated formatting as described by the various techniques mentioned within the newsletter. Many of the terms are new, and we define them briefly in the next few paragraphs.

A *reverse* (light text on a dark background) is a favorite technique of desktop publishers to emphasize a specific element. It is used in the *masthead* (the identifying information) at the top of the newsletter and provides a distinctive look to the publication. The number of the newsletter and the date of publication also appear in the masthead in smaller letters.

A *pull quote* is a phrase or sentence taken from an article to emphasize a key point. It is typically set in larger type, often in a different typeface and/or italics, and may be offset with parallel lines at the top and bottom.

A *dropped-capital letter* is a large capital letter at the beginning of a paragraph. It, too, catches the reader's eye and calls attention to the associated text.

Clip art, used in moderation, will catch the reader's eye and enhance almost any newsletter. It is available from a variety of sources including the *Microsoft Clip Gallery,* which is included in Office 2000. Clip art can also be downloaded from the Web, but be sure you are allowed to reprint the image. The banner at the bottom of the newsletter is not a clip art image per se, but was created using various tools on the *Drawing toolbar.*

Borders and shading are effective individually, or in combination with one another, to emphasize important stories within the newsletter. Simple vertical and/or horizontal lines are also effective. The techniques are especially useful in the absence of clip art or other graphics and are a favorite of desktop publishers.

Lists, whether bulleted or numbered, help to organize information by emphasizing important topics. A *bulleted list* emphasizes (and separates) the items. A *numbered list* sequences (and prioritizes) the items and is automatically updated to accommodate additions or deletions.

All of these techniques can be implemented with commands you already know, as you will see in the hands-on exercise, which follows shortly.

Creating a Newsletter

Volume I, Number 2   Spring 1999

Desktop publishing is easy, but there are several points to remember. This chapter will take you through the steps in creating a newsletter. The first hands-on exercise creates a simple newsletter with a masthead and three-column design. The second exercise creates a more attractive document by exploring different ways to emphasize the text.

Clip Art and Other Objects

Clip art is available from a variety of sources. You can also use other types of objects such as maps, charts, or organization charts, which are created by other applications, then brought into a document through the Insert Object command. A single dominant graphic is usually more appealing than multiple smaller graphics.

Techniques to Consider

Our finished newsletter contains one or more examples of each of the following desktop publishing techniques. Can you find where each technique is used, and further, explain, how to implement that technique in Microsoft Word?

1. Pull Quotes
2. Reverse
3. Drop Caps
4. Tables
5. Styles
6. Bullets and Numbering
7. Borders and Shading
8. The Drawing Toolbar

Newspaper-Style Columns

The essence of a newsletter is the implementation of columns in which text flows continuously from the bottom of one column to the top of the next. You specify the number of columns, and optionally, the space between columns. Microsoft Word does the rest. It will compute the width of each column based on the number of columns and the margins.

Beginners often specify margins that are too large and implement too much space between the columns. Another way to achieve a more sophisticated look is to avoid the standard two-column design. You can implement columns of varying width and/or insert vertical lines between the columns.

The number of columns will vary in different parts of a document. The masthead is typically a single column, but the body of the newsletter will have two or three. Remember, too, that columns are implemented at the section level and hence, section breaks are required throughout a document.

Typography

Typography is the process of selecting typefaces, type styles, and type sizes, and is a critical element in the success of any document. Type should reinforce the message and should be consistent with the information you want to convey. More is not better, especially in the case of too many typefaces and styles, which produce cluttered documents that impress no one. Try to limit yourself to a maximum of two typefaces per document, but choose multiple sizes and/or styles within those typefaces. Use boldface or italics for emphasis, but do so in moderation, because if you use too many different elements, the effect is lost.

A pull quote adds interest to a document while simultaneously emphasizing a key point. It is implemented by increasing the point size, changing to italics, centering the text, and displaying a top and bottom border on the paragraph.

Use Styles as Appropriate

Styles were covered in the previous chapter, but that does not mean you cannot use them in conjunction with a newsletter. A style stores character and/or paragraph formatting and can be applied to multiple occurrences of the same element within a document. Change the style and you automatically change all text defined by that style. You can also use styles from one edition of your newsletter to the next to insure consistency.

Borders and Shading

Borders and shading are effective individually or in combination with one another. Use a thin rule (one point or less) and light shading (five or ten percent) for best results. The techniques are especially useful in the absence of clip art or other graphics and are a favorite of desktop publishers.

All the News that Fits

FIGURE 5.1   The Newsletter

Typography

Typography is the process of selecting typefaces, type styles, and type sizes, and it is a critical, often subtle, element in the success of a document. Good typography goes almost unnoticed, whereas poor typography calls attention to itself and detracts from a document. Our discussion presents the basic concepts and terminology.

A *typeface* (or *font*) is a complete set of characters (upper- and lowercase letters, numbers, punctuation marks, and special symbols). Typefaces are divided into two general categories, serif and sans serif. A *serif typeface* has tiny cross lines at the ends of the characters to help the eye connect one letter with the next. A *sans serif typeface* (sans from the French for *without*) does not have these lines. A commonly accepted practice is to use serif typefaces with large amounts of text and sans serif typefaces for smaller amounts. The newsletter in Figure 5.1, for example, uses *Times New Roman* (a serif typeface) for the text and *Arial* (a sans serif typeface) for the headings.

A second characteristic of a typeface is whether it is monospaced or proportional. A *monospaced typeface* (e.g., Courier New) uses the same amount of space for every character regardless of its width. A *proportional typeface* (e.g., Times New Roman or Arial) allocates space according to the width of the character. Mono-spaced fonts are used in tables and financial projections where items must be precisely lined up, one beneath the other. Proportional typefaces create a more professional appearance and are appropriate for most documents.

Any typeface can be set in different styles (e.g. regular, bold or italic). A *font* (as the term is used in Windows) is a specific typeface in a specific style; for example, *Times New Roman Italic,* **Arial bold** or `Courier New Bold Italic.`

Type size is a vertical measurement and is specified in points. One *point* is equal to $\frac{1}{72}$ of an inch. The text in most documents is set in 10- or 12-point type. (The book you are reading is set in 10-point.) Different elements in the same document are often set in different type sizes to provide suitable emphasis. A variation of at least two points, however, is necessary for the difference to be noticeable. The headings in the newsletter, for example, were set in 12-point type, whereas the text of the articles is in 10-point type. The introduction of columns into a document poses another concern in that the type size should be consistent with the width of a column. Nine-point type, for example, is appropriate in columns that are two inches wide, but much too small in a single-column term paper. In other words, longer lines or wider columns require larger type sizes.

There are no hard and fast rules for the selection of type, only guidelines and common sense. You will find that the design that worked so well in one document may not work at all in a different document. Indeed, good typography is often the result of trial and error, and we encourage you to experiment freely.

TYPOGRAPHY TIP: USE RESTRAINT

More is not better, especially in the case of too many typefaces and styles, which produce cluttered documents that impress no one. Try to limit yourself to a maximum of two typefaces per document, but choose multiple sizes and/or styles within those typefaces. Use boldface or italics for emphasis, but do so in moderation, because if you emphasize too many elements the effect is lost.

The Columns Command

The columnar formatting in a newsletter is implemented through the **Columns command** as shown in Figure 5.2. Start by selecting one of the preset designs and Microsoft Word takes care of everything else. It calculates the width of each column based on the number of columns, the left and right margins on the page, and the specified (default) space between columns.

Consider, for example, the dialog box in Figure 5.2 in which a design of three equal columns is selected with a spacing of ¼ inch between each column. The 2-inch width of each column is computed automatically based on left and right margins of 1 inch each and the ¼-inch spacing between columns. The width of each column is computed by subtracting the sum of the margins and the space between the columns (a total of 2½ inches in this example) from the page width of 8½ inches. The result of the subtraction is 6 inches, which is divided by 3, resulting in a column width of 2 inches.

You can change any of the settings in the Columns dialog box and Word will automatically make the necessary adjustments. The newsletter in Figure 5.1, for example, uses a two-column layout with wide and narrow columns. We prefer this design to columns of uniform width, as we think it adds interest to our document. Note, too, that once columns have been defined, text will flow continuously from the bottom of one column to the top of the next

Return for a minute to the newsletter in Figure 5.1, and notice that the number of columns varies from one part of the newsletter to another. The masthead is displayed over a single column at the top of the page, whereas the remainder of the newsletter is formatted in two columns of different widths. The number of columns is specified at the section level, and thus a **section break** is required whenever the column specification changes. A section break is also required at the end of the last column to balance the text within the columns.

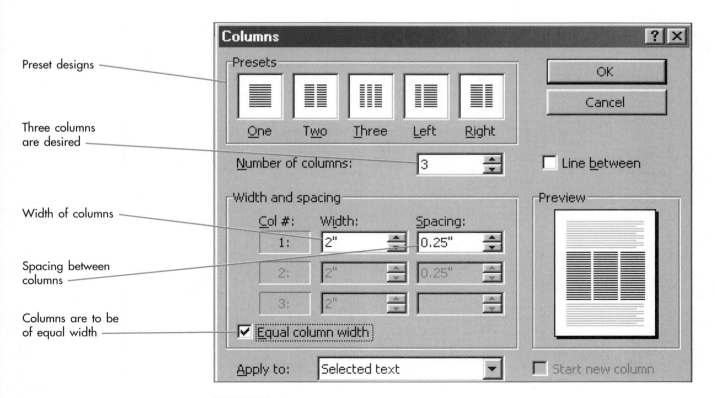

FIGURE 5.2   The Columns Command

Newspaper Columns

Objective: To create a basic newsletter through the Format columns command; to use section breaks to change the number of columns. Use Figure 5.3.

STEP 1: The Page Setup Command

➤ Start Word. Open the **Text for Newsletter document** in the Exploring Word folder. Save the document as **Modified Newsletter.**

➤ Pull down the **File menu.** Click **Page Setup** to display the Page Setup dialog box in Figure 5.3a. Change the top, bottom, left, and right margins to .75.

➤ Click **OK** to accept these settings and close the Page Setup dialog box. If necessary, click the **Print Layout View button** above the status bar. Set the magnification (zoom) to **Page Width.**

Zoom box

Change all margins to .75"

Print Layout View button

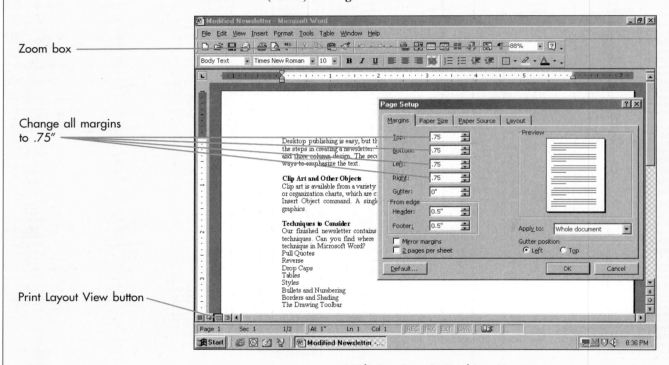

(a) The Page Setup Command (step 1)

FIGURE 5.3   Hands-on Exercise 1

CHANGE THE MARGINS

The default margins of 1 inch at the top and bottom of a page, and 1¼ inches on the sides, are fine for a typical document. A multicolumn newsletter, however, looks better with smaller margins, which in turn enables you to create wider columns. Margins are defined at the section level, and hence it's easiest to change the margins at the very beginning, when a document consists of only a single section.

STEP 2: Check the Document

➤ Pull down the **Tools menu,** click **Options,** click the **Spelling and Grammar tab,** and select the option for **Standard writing style.** Click **OK** to close the Options dialog box.

➤ Click the **Spelling and Grammar button** on the Standard toolbar to check the document for errors.

➤ The first error detected by the spelling and grammar check is the omitted hyphen between the words *three* and *column* as shown in Figure 5.3b. (This is a subtle mistake and emphasizes the need to check a document using the tools provided by Word.) Click **Change** to accept the indicated suggestion.

➤ Continue checking the document, accepting (or rejecting) the suggested corrections as you see fit.

➤ Save the document.

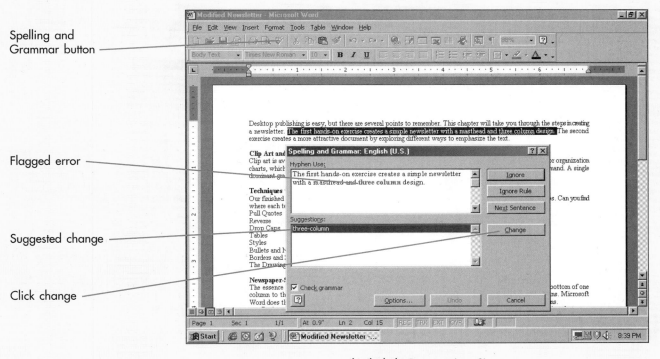

Spelling and Grammar button

Flagged error

Suggested change

Click change

(b) Check the Document (step 2)

FIGURE 5.3   Hands-on Exercise 1 (continued)

USE THE SPELLING AND GRAMMAR CHECK

Our eyes are less discriminating than we would like to believe, allowing misspellings and simple typos to go unnoticed. To prove the point, count the number of times the letter f appears in this sentence, *"Finished files are the result of years of scientific study combined with the experience of years."* The correct answer is six, but most people find only four or five. Checking your document takes only a few minutes. Do it!

STEP 3: Implement Newspaper Columns

➤ Pull down the **Format menu.** Click **Columns** to display the dialog box in Figure 5.4c. Click the **Presets icon** for **Two.** The column width for each column and the spacing between columns will be determined automatically from the existing margins.

➤ If necessary, clear the **Line Between box.** Click **OK** to accept the settings and close the Columns dialog box.

➤ The text of the newsletter should be displayed in two columns. If you do not see the columns, it is probably because you are in the wrong view. Click the **Print Layout View button** above the status bar to change to this view.

Click preset design for 2 columns

Clear check box for line between the columns

Preview of column design

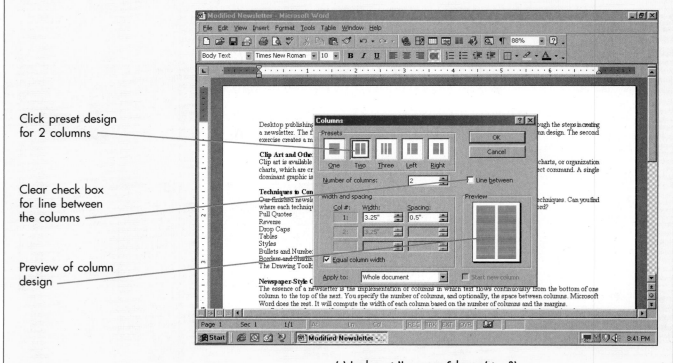

(c) Implement Newspaper Columns (step 3)

FIGURE 5.3   Hands-on Exercise 1 (continued)

THE COLUMNS BUTTON

The Columns button on the Standard toolbar is the fastest way to create columns in a document. Click the button, drag the mouse to choose the number of columns, then release the mouse to create the columns. The toolbar lets you change the number of columns, but not the spacing between columns. The toolbar is also limited in that you cannot create columns of different widths or select a line between columns.

STEP 4: Balance the Columns

➤ Use the **Zoom box** on the Standard toolbar to zoom to **Whole Page** to see the entire newsletter as shown in Figure 5.3d. Do not be concerned if the columns are of different lengths.

➤ Press **Ctrl+End** to move the insertion point to the end of the document. Pull down the **Insert menu.** Click **Break** to display the Break dialog box in Figure 5.3d. Select the **Continuous option button** under Section breaks.

➤ Click **OK** to accept the settings and close the dialog box. The columns should be balanced, although one column may be one line longer than the other.

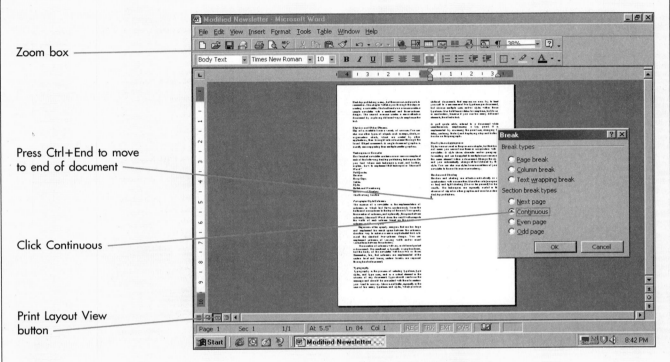

Zoom box

Press Ctrl+End to move to end of document

Click Continuous

Print Layout View button

(d) Balance the Columns (step 4)

FIGURE 5.3 Hands-on Exercise 1 (continued)

USE THE RULER TO CHANGE COLUMN WIDTH

Click anywhere within the column whose width you want to change, then point to the ruler and click and drag the right column margin (the mouse pointer changes to a double arrow) to change the column width. Changing the width of one column in a document with equal-sized columns changes the width of all other columns so that they remain equal. Changing the width in a document with unequal columns changes only that column. You can also double click the ruler to display the Page Setup dialog box, then click the Margins tab to change the left and right margins, which in turn will change the column width.

STEP 5: Create the Masthead

➤ Use the Zoom box on the Standard toolbar to change to **Page Width.** Click the **Show/Hide ¶ button** to display the paragraph and section marks.

➤ Press **Ctrl+Home** to move the insertion point to the beginning of the document. Pull down the **Insert menu,** click **Break,** select the **Continuous option button,** and click **OK.** You should see a double dotted line indicating a section break as shown in Figure 5.3e.

➤ Click immediately to the left of the dotted line, which will place the insertion point to the left of the line. Check the status bar to be sure you are in section one.

➤ Change the format for this section to a single column by clicking the **Columns button** on the Standard toolbar and selecting one column. (Alternatively, you can pull down the **Format menu,** click **Columns,** and choose **One** from the Presets column formats.)

➤ Type **Creating a Newsletter** and press the **enter key** twice. Select the newly entered text, click the **Center button** on the Formatting toolbar. Change the font to **48 point Arial Bold.**

➤ Click underneath the masthead (to the left of the section break). Pull down the **Table menu,** click **Insert** to display a submenu, then click **Table.** Insert a table with one row and two columns as shown in Figure 5.3e.

➤ Click in the left cell of the table. Type **Volume I, Number 1.** Click in the right cell (or press the **Tab key** to move to this cell and type the current semester (for example, **Spring 1999**). Click the **Align Right button.**

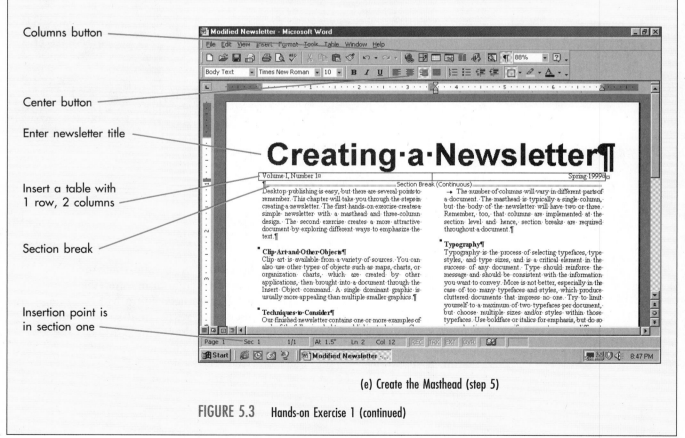

(e) Create the Masthead (step 5)

FIGURE 5.3   Hands-on Exercise 1 (continued)

STEP 6: Create a Reverse

➤ Press **Ctrl+Home** to move the insertion point to the beginning of the newsletter. Click anywhere within the title of the newsletter.

➤ Pull down the **Format menu,** click **Borders and Shading** to display the Borders and Shading dialog box, then click the **Shading tab** in Figure 5.4f.

➤ Click the **drop-down arrow** in the Style list box (in the Patterns area) and select **Solid (100%)** shading. Click **OK** to accept the setting and close the dialog box. Click elsewhere in the document to see the results.

➤ The final step is to remove the default border that appears around the table. Click in the selection area to the left of the table to select the entire table.

➤ Pull down the **Format menu,** click **Borders and Shading,** and if necessary click the **Borders tab.** Click the **None icon** in the Presets area. Click **OK.** Click elsewhere in the document to see the result.

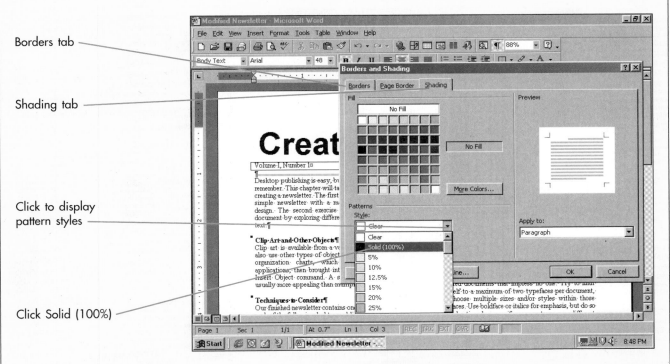

Borders tab

Shading tab

Click to display pattern styles

Click Solid (100%)

(f) Create a Reverse (step 6)

FIGURE 5.3   Hands-on Exercise 1 (continued)

LEFT ALIGNED	CENTERED	RIGHT ALIGNED

Many documents call for left, centered, and/or right aligned text on the same line, an effect that is achieved through setting tabs, or more easily through a table. To achieve the effect shown at the top of this box, create a 1 × 3 table (one row and three columns), type the text in the cells, then use the buttons on the Formatting toolbar to left-align, center, and right-align the cells. Select the table, pull down the Format menu, click Borders and Shading, then specify None as the Border setting.

STEP 7: Modify the Heading Style

➤ Two styles have been implemented for you in the newsletter. Click in any text paragraph and you see the Body Text style name displayed in the Style box on the Formatting toolbar. Click in any heading and you see the Heading 1 style.

➤ Click and drag to select the heading **Clip Art and Other Objects.** Click the **drop-down arrow** on the Font list box and change the font to **Arial.** Change the **Font Size** to **12** point.

➤ Click the Style list box on the Formatting toolbar to select the **Heading 1** style. Press **enter** to select this style and display the Modify Style dialog box as shown in Figure 5.3g.

➤ The option button to update the style according to the current formatting is selected. Click **OK** to change the style, which automatically reformats every element defined by this style.

➤ Save the newsletter.

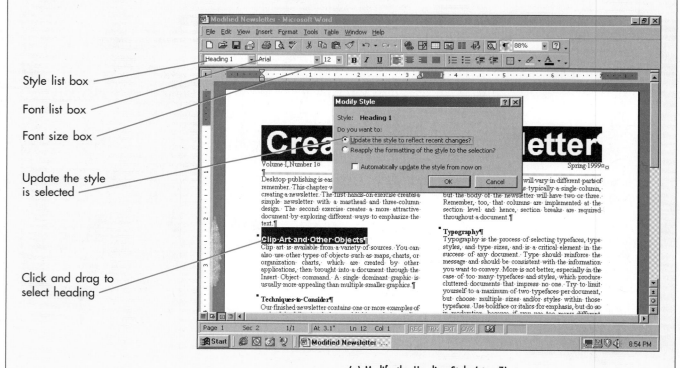

Style list box

Font list box

Font size box

Update the style is selected

Click and drag to select heading

(g) Modify the Heading Style (step 7)

FIGURE 5.3   Hands-on Exercise 1 (continued)

USE STYLES AS APPROPRIATE

Styles were covered in the previous chapter, but that does not mean you cannot use them in conjunction with a newsletter. A style stores character and/or paragraph formatting and can be applied to multiple occurrences of the same element within a document. Change the style and you automatically change all text defined by that style. Use the same styles from one edition of your newsletter to the next to ensure consistency.

STEP 8: The Print Preview Command

➤ Pull down the **File menu** and click **Print Preview** (or click the **Print Preview button** on the Standard toolbar) to view the newsletter as in Figure 5.3h. This is a basic two-column newsletter with the masthead appearing as a reverse and stretching over a single column.

➤ Click the **Print button** to print the newsletter at this stage so that you can compare this version with the finished newsletter at the end of the next exercise. Click the **Close button** on the Print Preview toolbar to close the Preview view and return to the Page Layout view.

➤ Exit Word if you do not want to continue with the next exercise at this time.

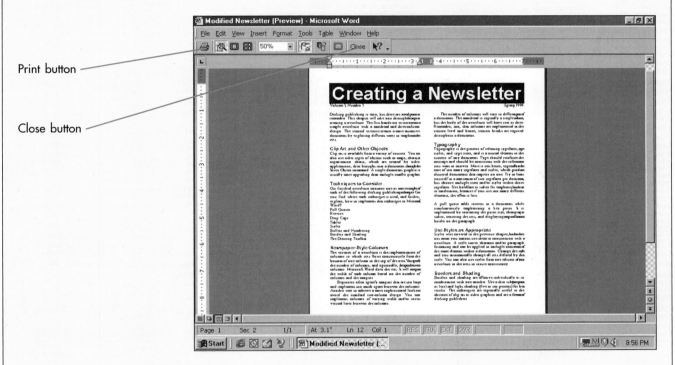

Print button

Close button

(h) The Print Preview Command (step 8)

FIGURE 5.3   Hands-on Exercise 1 (continued)

THE PRINT PREVIEW TOOLBAR

Click the Context Sensitive Help button on the extreme right of the Print Preview toolbar (the mouse pointer changes to an arrow and a question mark), then click any other button for an explanation of its function. The Shrink to Fit button is especially useful if a small portion of the newsletter spills over to a second page—click the button and it uniformly reduces the fonts throughout the document to eliminate the second page.

We trust you have completed the first hands-on exercise without difficulty and that you were able to duplicate the initial version of the newsletter. That, however, is the easy part of desktop publishing. The more difficult aspect is to develop the design in the first place because the mere availability of a desktop publishing program does not guarantee an effective document, any more than a word processor will turn its author into another Shakespeare. Other skills are necessary, and so we continue with a brief introduction to graphic design.

Much of what we say is subjective, and what works in one situation will not necessarily work in another. Your eye is the best judge of all, and you should follow your own instincts. Experiment freely and realize that successful design is the result of trial and error. Seek inspiration from others by collecting samples of real documents that you find attractive, then use those documents as the basis for your own designs.

The Grid

The design of a document is developed on a **grid,** an underlying, but *invisible,* set of horizontal and vertical lines that determine the placement of the major elements. A grid establishes the overall structure of a document by indicating the number of columns, the space between columns, the size of the margins, the placement of headlines, art, and so on. The grid does *not* appear in the printed document or on the screen.

Figure 5.4 shows the "same" document in three different designs. The left half of each design displays the underlying grid, whereas the right half displays the completed document.

(a) Three-column Grid

FIGURE 5.4   The Grid System of Design

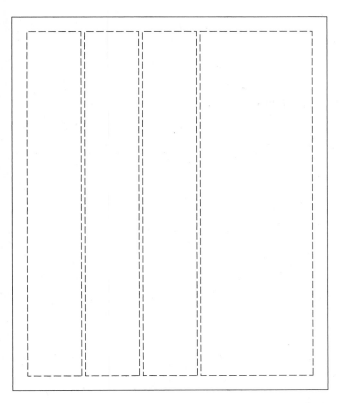

No Can Do

He felt more and more pressure to play the game of not playing. Maybe that's why he stepped in front of that truck.

People wonder why people do things like this, but all you have to do is look around and see all the stress and insanity each person in responsibility is required to put up with. There is no help or end in sight. It seems that managers are managing less and shoveling the workloads on to their underlings. This seems to be the overall response to the absence of raises or benefit packages they feel are their entitlement. Something must be done now!

People wonder why people do things like this, but all you have to do is look around and

see all the stress and insanity each person in responsibility is required to put up with. There is no help or end in sight. It seems that managers are managing less and shoveling the workloads on to their underlings. This seems to be the overall response to the absence of raises or benefit packages they feel are their entitlement. Something must be done now!

People wonder why people do things like this, but all you have to do is look around and see all the stress and insanity each person in responsibility is

required to put up with. There is no help or end in sight. It seems that managers are managing less and shoveling the workloads on to their underlings. This seems to be the overall response to the absence of raises or benefit packages they feel are their entitlement.

People wonder why people do things like this, but all you have to do is look around and see all the stress and insanity each person in responsibility is required to put up with. There is no help or end in sight. It seems that managers are

managing less and shoveling the workloads on to their underlings. This seems to be the overall response to the absence of raises or benefit packages they feel are their entitlement. Some-thing must be done now!

People wonder why people do things like this, but all you have to do is look around and see all the stress and insanity each person in responsibility is required to put up with. There is no help or end in sight. It seems that managers are managing less. Something must be done now!

People wonder why people do things like this, but all you have to do is look around and see all the stress and insanity each person in responsibility is required to put up with. There is no help or end in sight. It seems that managers are managing less and shoveling the workloads on to their underlings. This seems to be the overall response to the ▼

(b) Four-column Grid

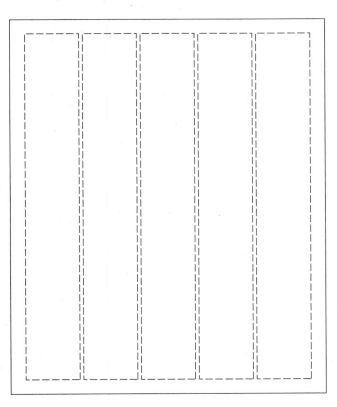

People wonder why people do things like this, but all you have to do is look around and see all the stress and insanity each person in responsibility is required to put up with. There is no help or end in sight. It seems that managers are managing less and shoveling the workloads on to their underlings. This seems to be the overall response to the absence of raises or benefit packages they feel are their entitlement. Something must be done!

People wonder why people do things like this, but all you have to do is look around and see all the stress and insanity each person in responsibility is required to put up with. There is no help or end in sight. It seems that managers are managing less and shoveling the workloads on to their underlings. This seems to be the overall response to the absence of raises or benefit packages they feel are their entitlement. Something must be done!

People wonder why people do things like this, but all you have to do is look around and see all the stress and insanity each person in responsibility is required to put up with. There is no help or end in sight. It seems that managers are managing less and shoveling the

He felt more and more pressure to play the game of not playing. Maybe that's why he stepped in front of that truck.

workloads on to their underlings. This seems to be the overall re-sponse to the absence of raises or benefit packages they feel are their

is look around and see all the stress and insanity each person in responsibility is required to put up with. There is no help or end in sight. It seems that managers are managing less and shoveling the

entitlement. Some-thing must be done now!

People wonder why people do things like this, but all you have to do is look around and see all the stress and insanity each person in responsibility is required to put up with. There is no help or end in sight. It seems that managers are managing less and shoveling the workloads on to their underlings. This seems to be the overall re-sponse to the absence of raises or benefit packages they feel are their entitlement. Some-thing

must be done!

People wonder why people do things like this, but all you have to do is look around and see all the stress and insanity each person in responsibility is required to put up with. There is no help or end in sight. It seems that managers are managing less and shoveling the workloads on to their underlings. This seems to be the overall response to the absence of rais-es or benefit pack-ages they feel are their entitlement. Something must be done!

People wonder why people do things like this, but all you have to do is look around and see all the stress and insanity each person in responsibility is required to put up with. There is no help or end in sight. It seems that man-agers are managing less and shoveling the workloads on to their underlings. Something must be done now!

People wonder why people do things like this, but all you have to do ▼

(c) Five-column Grid

FIGURE 5.4   **The Grid System of Design (continued)**

A grid may be simple or complex, but is always distinguished by the number of columns it contains. The three-column grid of Figure 5.4a is one of the most common and utilitarian designs. Figure 5.4b shows a four-column design for the same document, with unequal column widths to provide interest. Figure 5.4c illustrates a five-column grid that is often used with large amounts of text. Many other designs are possible as well. A one-column grid is used for term papers and letters. A two-column, wide and narrow format is appropriate for textbooks and manuals. Two- and three-column formats are used for newsletters and magazines.

The simple concept of a grid should make the underlying design of any document obvious, which in turn gives you an immediate understanding of page composition. Moreover, the conscious use of a grid will help you organize your material and result in a more polished and professional-looking publication. It will also help you to achieve consistency from page to page within a document (or from issue to issue of a newsletter). Indeed, much of what goes wrong in desktop publishing stems from failing to follow or use the underlying grid.

Emphasis

Good design makes it easy for the reader to determine what is important. As indicated earlier, emphasis can be achieved in several ways, the easiest being variations in type size and/or type style. Headings should be set in type sizes (at least two points) larger than body copy. The use of **boldface** is effective as are *italics,* but both should be done in moderation. (UPPERCASE LETTERS and underlining are alternative techniques that we believe are less effective.)

Boxes and/or shading call attention to selected articles. Horizontal lines are effective to separate one topic from another or to call attention to a pull quote. A reverse can be striking for a small amount of text. Clip art, used in moderation, will catch the reader's eye and enhance almost any newsletter.

Clip Art

Clip art is available from a variety of sources including the Microsoft Clip Gallery and Microsoft Web site. The Clip Gallery can be accessed in a variety of ways, most easily through the ***Insert Picture command.*** Once clip art has been inserted into a document, it can be moved and sized just like any other Windows object, as will be illustrated in our next hands-on exercise.

The ***Format Picture command*** provides additional flexibility in the placement of clip art. The Text Wrapping tab, in the Advanced Layout dialog box, determines the way text is positioned around a picture. The Top and Bottom option (no wrapping) is selected in Figure 5.5a and the resulting document is shown in Figure 5.5b. The sizing handles around the clip art indicate that it is currently selected, enabling you to move and/or resize the clip art using the mouse. (You can also use the Size and Position tabs in the Format Picture dialog box for more precision with either setting.) Changing the size or position of the object, however, does not affect the way in which text wraps around the clip art.

The document in Figure 5.5c illustrates a different wrapping selection in which text is wrapped on both sides. Figure 5.5c also uses an option on the Colors and Lines tab to draw a blue border around the clip art. The document in Figure 5.5d eliminates the border and chooses the tight wrapping style so that the text is positioned as closely as possible to the figure in a free-form design. Choosing among the various documents in Figure 5.5 is one of personal preference. Our point is simply that Word provides multiple options, and it is up to you, the desktop publisher, to choose the design that best suits your requirements.

Top and bottom
wrapping style

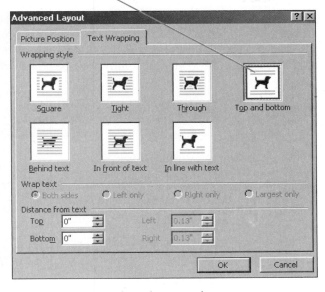

(a) Advanced Layout Dialog Box

(b) Top and Bottom Wrapping

(c) Square Wrapping (both sides)

(d) Tight Wrapping (both sides)

FIGURE 5.5   The Format Picture Command

Did you ever stop to think how the images in the Clip Gallery were developed? Undoubtedly they were drawn by someone with artistic ability who used basic shapes, such as lines and curves in various combinations, to create the images. The ***Drawing toolbar*** in Figure 5.6a contains all of the tools necessary to create original clip art. Select the Line tool for example, then click and drag to create the line. Once the line has been created, you can select it, then change its properties (such as thickness, style, or color) by using other tools on the Drawing toolbar. Draw a second line, or a curve, then depending on your ability, you have a piece of original clip art.

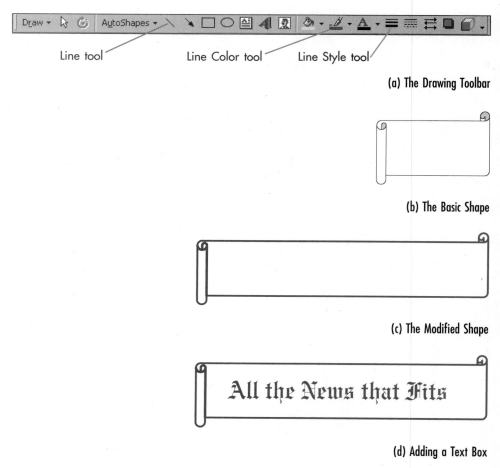

(a) The Drawing Toolbar

(b) The Basic Shape

(c) The Modified Shape

All the News that Fits

(d) Adding a Text Box

FIGURE 5.6   The Drawing Toolbar

We don't expect you to create clip art comparable to the images within the Clip Gallery. You can, however, use the tools on the Drawing toolbar to modify an existing image and/or create simple shapes of your own that can enhance any document. One tool that is especially useful is the AutoShapes button that displays a series of pre-designed shapes. Choose a shape (the banner in figure 5.6b), change its size and color (Figure 5.6c), then use the Textbox tool to add an appropriate message.

The Drawing toolbar is displayed through the Toolbars command in the View menu. The following exercise has you use the toolbar to create the banner and text in Figure 5.6d. It's fun, it's easy; just be flexible and willing to experiment. We think you will be pleased at what you will be able to do.

Complete the Newsletter

Objective: To insert clip art into a newsletter; to format a newsletter using styles, borders and shading, pull quotes, and lists. Use Figure 5.7a as a guide in the exercise.

STEP 1: Change the Column Layout

➤ Open the **Modified Newsletter** from the previous exercise. Click in the masthead and change the number of this edition from 1 to **2.**

➤ Click anywhere in the body of the newsletter. The status bar should indicate that you are in the second section. Pull down the **Format menu.** Click **Columns** to display the dialog box in Figure 5.7a. Click the **Left Preset icon.**

➤ Change the width of the first column to **2.25** and the space between columns to **.25.** Check (click) the **Line Between box.** Click **OK.** Save the newsletter.

Click Left
Preset design

Click Line
Between Columns

Change column
width to 2.25"

Change spacing between
columns to .25"

Insertion point
is in section 2

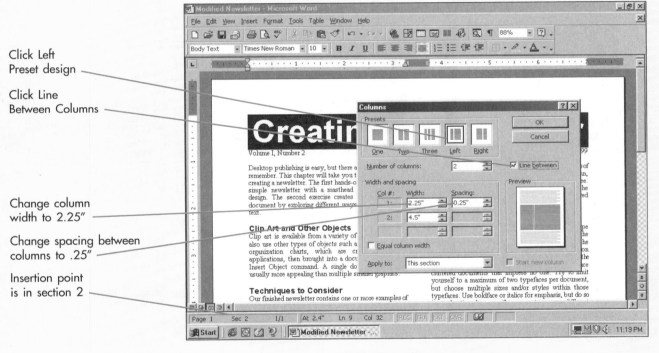

(a) Change the Column Layout (step 1)

FIGURE 5.7 Hands-on Exercise 2

EXPERIMENT WITH THE DESIGN

The number and width of the columns in a newsletter is the single most important element in its design. Experiment freely. Good design is often the result of trial and error.

STEP 2: Bullets and Numbering

➤ Scroll in the document until you come to the list within the **Techniques to Consider** paragraph. Select the entire list as shown in Figure 5.7b.

➤ Pull down the **Format menu** and click **Bullets and Numbering** to display the Bullets and Numbering dialog box. If necessary, click the **Numbered tab** and choose the numbering style with Arabic numbers followed by periods. Click **OK** to accept these settings and close the Bullets and Numbering dialog box.

➤ Click anywhere in the newsletter to deselect the text. Save the newsletter.

Numbered tab

Choose style for numbers

Click and drag to select list

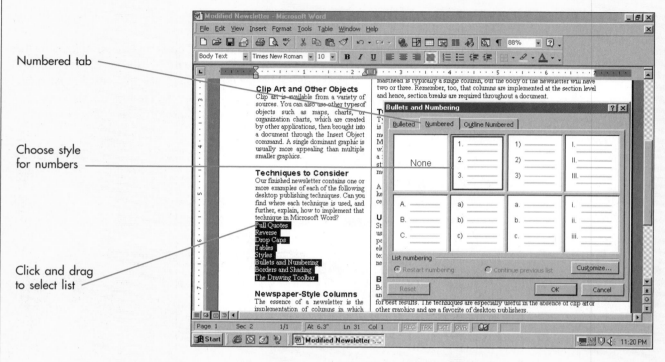

(b) Bullets and Numbering (step 2)

FIGURE 5.7   Hands-on Exercise 2 (continued)

LISTS AND THE FORMATTING TOOLBAR

The Formatting toolbar contains four buttons for use with bulleted and numbered lists. The Increase Indent and Decrease Indent buttons move the selected items one tab stop to the right and left, respectively. The Bullets button creates a bulleted list from unnumbered items or converts a numbered list to a bulleted list. The Numbering button creates a numbered list or converts a bulleted list to numbers. The Bullets and Numbering buttons also function as toggle switches; for example, clicking the Bullets button when a bulleted list is already in effect will remove the bullets.

STEP 3: Insert the Clip Art

➤ Click immediately to the left of the article beginning **Clip Art and Other Objects.** Pull down the **Insert menu,** click **Picture,** then click **Clip Art** to display the Insert Clip Art dialog box.

➤ If necessary, click the **Pictures tab** and select (click) the **Buildings category.** Select the **goals image** or a different image if you prefer, then click the **Insert Clip button** on the shortcut menu.

➤ The picture should appear in the document, where it can be moved and sized as described in the next several steps. Click the **Close button** on the Insert Clip Art dialog box.

Position insertion point

Pictures tab

Click image

Click Insert Clip button

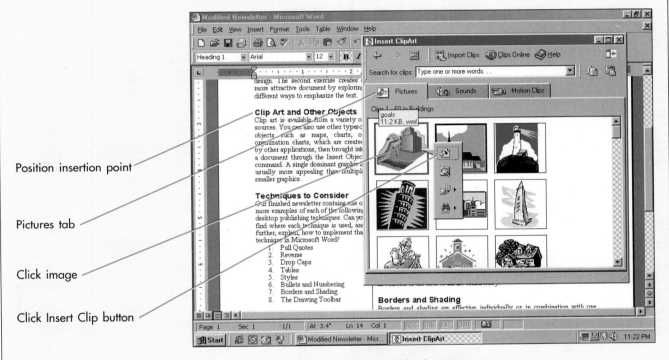

(c) Insert the Clip Art (step 3)

FIGURE 5.7   Hands-on Exercise 2 (continued)

CLIP GALLERY LIVE

Why settle for the same old clip art when you can get new images from the Microsoft Web site? Pull down the Insert menu, click the Picture command, then choose Clip Art to display the Insert Clip Art dialog box. Click the Clips Online button to connect to the Microsoft site where you have your choice of clip art, photographs, sounds, and motion clips in a variety of categories. Click any image to see a preview, then click the preview box to download the image to your PC. Click the image after it has been downloaded to display a shortcut menu from where you insert the image into your document.

STEP 4: Move and Size the Clip Art

➤ Click the **drop-down arrow** on the Zoom list box and select **Whole Page.**

➤ Point to the picture, click the **right mouse button** to display a context-sensitive menu, then click the **Format Picture command** to display the Format Picture dialog box as shown in Figure 5.7d.

➤ Click the **Layout tab,** choose the **Square layout,** then click the option button for left or right alignment. Click **OK** to close the dialog box. You can now move and size the clip art just like any other Windows object

➤ To size the clip art, click anywhere within the clip art to select it and display the sizing handles. Drag a corner handle (the mouse pointer changes to a double arrow) to change the length and width of the picture simultaneously and keep the object in proportion.

➤ To move the clip art, click the object to select it and display the sizing handles. Point to any part of the object except a sizing handle (the mouse pointer changes to a four-sided arrow), then click and drag to move the clip art.

➤ Save the document.

Show/Hide button

Click Layout tab

Click Square style

Sizing handle

Point to picture and click right
mouse button to display
shortcut menu

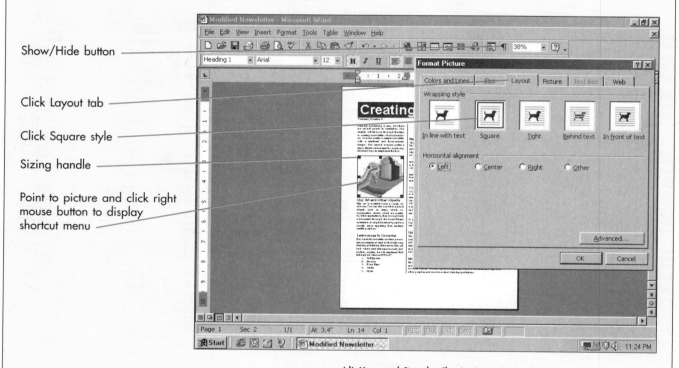

(d) Move and Size the Clip Art (step 4)

FIGURE 5.7   Hands-on Exercise 2 (continued)

CROPPING A PICTURE

Select a picture and Word automatically displays the Picture toolbar, which enables you to modify the picture in subtle ways. The Crop tool enables you to eliminate (crop) part of a picture. Select the picture to display the Picture toolbar and display the sizing handles. Click the Crop tool (the ScreenTip will display the name of the tool), then click and drag a sizing handle to crop the part of the picture you want to eliminate.

STEP 5: Borders and Shading

➤ Change to **Page Width** and click the **Show/Hide ¶ button** to display the paragraph marks. Press **Ctrl+End** to move to the end of the document, then select the heading and associated paragraph for Borders and Shading. (Do not select the ending paragraph mark.)

➤ Pull down the **Format menu.** Click **Borders and Shading.** If necessary click the **Borders tab** to display the dialog box in Figure 5.4e. Click the **Box icon** in the Setting area. Click the **drop-down arrow** in the Width list box and select the **1 point** line style.

➤ Click the **Shading tab.** Click the **drop-down arrow** in the Style list box (in the Patterns area) and select 5% shading. Click **OK** to accept the setting.

➤ Click elsewhere in the document to see the results. The heading and paragraph should be enclosed in a border with light shading.

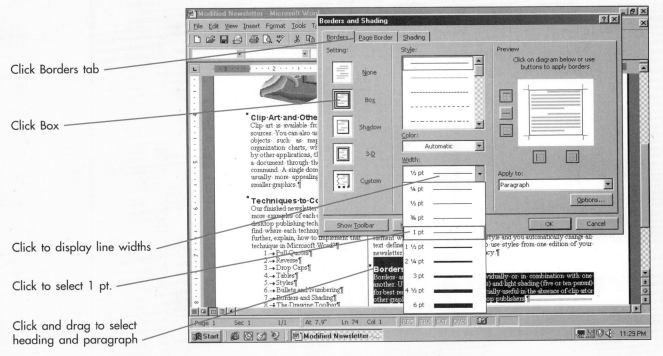

(e) Borders and Shading (step 5)

FIGURE 5.7 Hands-on Exercise 2 (continued)

THE TABLES AND BORDERS TOOLBAR

The Tables and Borders toolbar contains all of the tools to change the line style, thickness, or shading within a table. Point to any visible toolbar, click the right mouse button to display the list of toolbars, then check the Tables and Borders toolbar to display it on your screen.

STEP 6: Create a Pull Quote

➤ Scroll to the bottom of the document until you find the paragraph describing a pull quote. Select the entire paragraph and change the text to **14-point Arial italic.**

➤ Click in the paragraph to deselect the text, then click the **Center button** to center the paragraph.

➤ Click the **drop-down arrow** on the **Border button** to display the different border styles as shown in Figure 5.7f.

➤ Click the **Top Border button** to add a top border to the paragraph.

➤ Click the **Bottom border button** to create a bottom border and complete the pull quote.

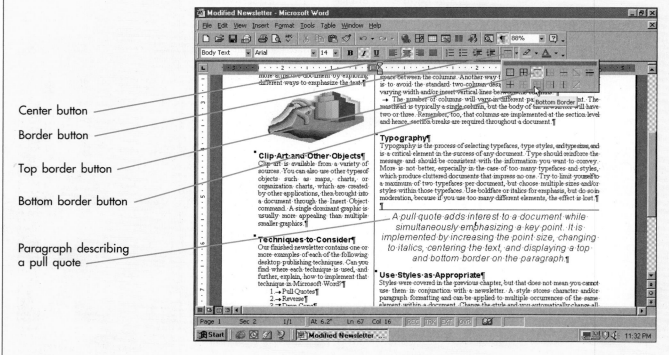

(f) Create a Pull Quote (step 6)

FIGURE 5.7   Hands-on Exercise 2 (continued)

EMPHASIZE WHAT'S IMPORTANT

Good design makes it easy for the reader to determine what is important. A pull quote (a phrase or sentence taken from an article) adds interest to a document while simultaneously emphasizing a key point. Boxes and shading are also effective in catching the reader's attention. A simple change in typography, such as increasing the point size, changing the typeface, and/or the use of boldface or italics, calls attention to a heading and visually separates it from the associated text.

STEP 7: Create a Drop Cap

➤ Scroll to the beginning of the newsletter. Click immediately before the D in *Desktop publishing.*

➤ Pull down the **Format menu.** Click the **Drop Cap command** to display the dialog box in Figure 5.7g.

➤ Click the **Position icon** for **Dropped** as shown in the figure. We used the default settings, but you can change the font, size (lines to drop), or distance from the text by clicking the arrow on the appropriate list box.

➤ Click **OK** to create the Drop Cap dialog box. Click outside the frame around the drop cap.

➤ Save the newsletter.

Click Dropped

Position insertion point to left of D

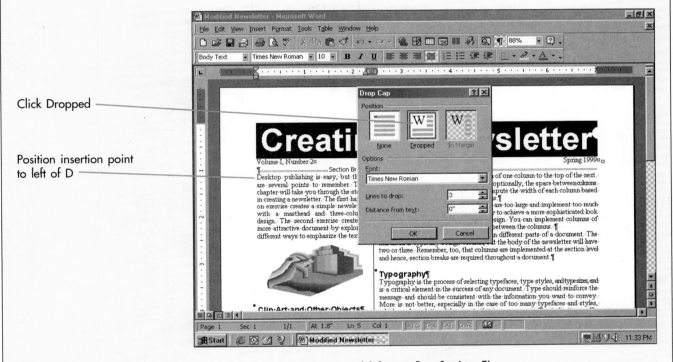

(g) Create a Drop Cap (step 7)

FIGURE 5.7   Hands-on Exercise 2 (continued)

MODIFYING A DROP CAP

Select (click) a dropped capital letter to display a thatched border known as a frame, then click the border or frame to display its sizing handles. You can move and size a frame just as you can any Windows object; for example, click and drag a corner sizing handle to change the size of the frame (and the drop cap it contains). To delete the frame (and remove the drop cap) press the delete key.

STEP 8: Create the AutoShape

➤ Click the **Show/Hide button** to hide the nonprintin characters. Pull down the **View menu,** click (or point to) the **Toolbars command** to display the list of available toolbars, then click the **Drawing toolbar** to display this toolbar.

➤ Press **Ctrl+End** to move to the end of the document. Click the **down arrow** on the AutoShapes button to display the AutoShapes menu. Click the **Stars and Banners submenu** and select (click) the **Horizontal scroll.**

➤ The mouse pointer changes to a tiny crosshair. Click and drag the mouse at the bottom of the newsletter to create the scroll as shown in Figure 5.7h.

➤ Release the mouse. The scroll is still selected as can be seen by the sizing handles. (You can click and drag the yellow diamond to change the thickness of the scroll.)

➤ Click the **Line Style tool** to display this menu as shown in Figure 5.7h. Select a thicker line (we chose **3 points**). Click the **down arrow** on the **Line color tool** to display the list of colors (if you have access to a color printer. We selected **blue**).

Click 3 pt. line

Click yellow diamond to change the width of autoshape

Sizing handles

Shadow tool

Line style tool

Line color tool

Click to display AutoShapes menu

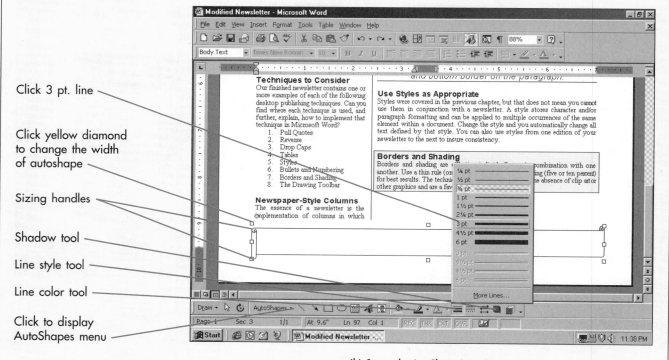

(h) Create the AutoShape (step 8)

FIGURE 5.7 Hands-on Exercise 2 (continued)

DISPLAY THE AUTOSHAPE TOOLBARS

Click the down arrow on the AutoShapes button on the Drawing toolbar to display a cascaded menu listing the various types of AutoShapes, then click and drag the menu's title bar to display the menu as a floating toolbar. Click any tool on the AutoShapes toolbar (such as Stars and Banners), then click and drag its title bar to display the various stars and banners in their own floating toolbar.

STEP 9: Add the Text Box

➤ Click the **Text Box tool,** then click and drag within the banner to create a text box as shown in Figure 5.7i. Type **All the News that Fits** as the text of the banner. Click the **Center button** on the Standard toolbar.

➤ Click and drag to select the text, click the **down arrow** on the **Font Size list box,** and select a larger point size (26 or 28 points). If necessary, click and drag the bottom border of the text box, and/or the bottom border of the AutoShape, in order to see all of the text. Click the **down arrow** on the **Font list box** and choose a different font.

➤ Right click the text box to display a context-sensitive menu, then click the Format Textbox command to display the **Format Textbox dialog** box as shown in Figure 5.7i. Click the **Colors and Lines tab** (if necessary), click the **down arrow** next to Color in the Line section, click **No Line,** then click **OK** to accept the settings and close the dialog box.

➤ Click anywhere in the document to deselect the text box. Save the document.

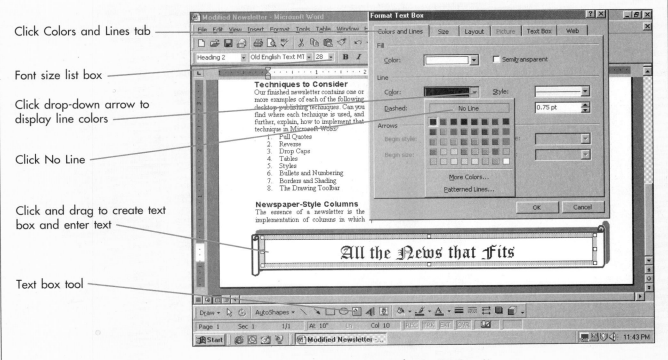

Click Colors and Lines tab

Font size list box

Click drop-down arrow to
display line colors

Click No Line

Click and drag to create text
box and enter text

Text box tool

(i) Create the Text Box (step 9)

FIGURE 5.7   Hands-on Exercise 2 (continued)

DON'T FORGET WORDART

Microsoft WordArt is another way to create decorative text to add interest to a document. Pull down the Insert menu, click Picture, click WordArt, choose the WordArt style, and click OK. Enter the desired text then click OK to create the WordArt object. You can click and drag the sizing handles to change the size or proportion of the text. Use any tool on the WordArt toolbar to further change the appearance of the object.

STEP 10: The Completed Newsletter

➤ Zoom to **Whole Page** to view the completed newsletter as shown in Figure 5.7j. The newsletter should fit on a single page, but if not, there are several techniques that you can use:

- Pull down the **File menu,** click the **Page Setup command,** click the **Margins tab,** then reduce the top and/or bottom margins to .5 inch. Be sure to apply this change to the **Whole document** within the Page Setup dialog box.

- Change the **Heading 1 style** to reduce the point size to **10 points** and/or the space before the heading to **6 points.**

- Click the **Print Preview button** on the Standard toolbar, then click the **Shrink to Fit button** on the Print Preview toolbar.

- Save the document a final time. Print the completed newsletter and submit it to your instructor as proof you did this exercise. Congratulations on a job well done.

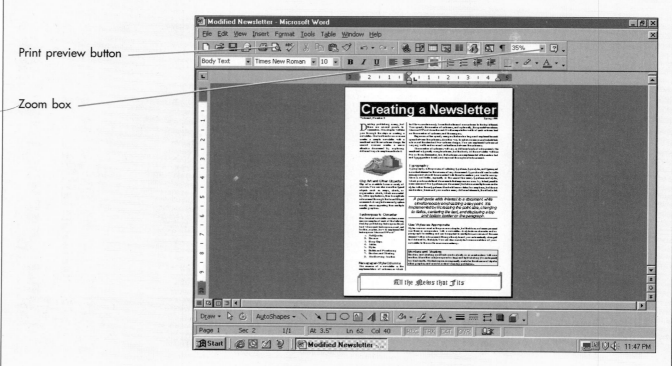

Print preview button

Zoom box

(j) The Completed Newsletter (step 10)

FIGURE 5.7   Hands-on Exercise 2 (continued)

A FINAL WORD OF ADVICE

Desktop publishing is not a carefree operation. It is time-consuming to implement and you will be amazed at the effort required for even a simple document. Computers are supposed to save time, not waste it, and while desktop publishing is clearly justified for some documents, the extensive formatting is not necessary for most documents. And finally, remember that the content of a document is its most important element.

MICROSOFT GRAPH

Clip art is only one type of object that can be inserted into a newsletter or other Word document. Another frequently used object is a graph (or chart), which is easily created through Microsoft Graph, an application that is part of Office 2000. The chart is created from within a Word document through the Insert Object command. Figure 5.8 illustrates the basics of the Microsoft Graph application, as it will be used in our next hands-on exercise. (The program has many of the same commands and capabilities as the charting component of Microsoft Excel.)

A graph (also called a chart) is based on numerical data that is stored in an associated *datasheet* as shown in Figure 5.8. The program supplies the default datasheet in Figure 5.8, but you can modify the data to create your own chart. Our example shows the quarterly sales for each of three regions, East, West, and North. The datasheet contains 12 *data points* (four quarterly values for each of three regions). The data points are grouped into *data series* that appear as rows or columns in the datasheet.

The graph may be plotted in one of two ways, by rows or columns, depending on the message you want to convey. If you elect to plot the data by rows, then the first row in the datasheet will appear on the X-axis. Conversely, if you plot the data by columns, then the first column appears on the X-axis. The choice between rows and columns depends on the message you want to convey. Figure 5.8b, for example, plots the data in columns to show the progress of each region over the course of the year.

Look closely at Figure 5.8b to see the correspondence between the graph and the datasheet. There are four data series, corresponding to the values in columns A, B, C, and D (the sales for 1st, 2nd, 3rd, and 4th quarters in each region). Each data series has three data points (one each for East, West, and North). The text in the first column of the datasheet appears on the X-axis. The entries in the first row of the datasheet appear in the legend to distinguish the series from one another..

Once the graph is created, it can be incorporated into a Word document as shown in Figure 5.8c. The graph in Figure 5.8d also plots the data series in columns, but it uses a different graph type, a stacked column rather than side-by-side columns. Once again, the choice between the types of graphs depends on your message. If, for example, you want your focus on each region's sales with separate numbers for each quarter, the side-by-side graph is more appropriate. If, on the other hand, you want to emphasize the total sales for each region, the stacked column graph is preferable. Note, too, the different scale on the Y-axis in the two graphs. The side-by-side graph in Figure 5.8c shows the sales in each quarter and so the Y-axis goes only to $90,000. The stacked bars in Figure 5.8d, however, reflect the total sales for each salesperson and thus the scale goes to $200,000.

The document in Figure 5.8d also contains a *watermark,* a text (or graphical) entry that appears on each page of a document, but in a lighter color or background. The watermark is created through the View Header/Footer command and can be used to lend interest or to supply additional information. In this example, the watermark reminds the reader that the financial data is confidential.

EMPHASIZE YOUR MESSAGE

A graph exists to deliver a message. One way to help put your point across is to choose a title that leads the audience. A neutral title such as *Sales Data* does nothing and requires the audience to reach its own conclusion. A better title might be *Eastern Region Has Record 3rd Quarter* to emphasize the results in the individual sales offices.

Click in any cell to enter or
modify the data

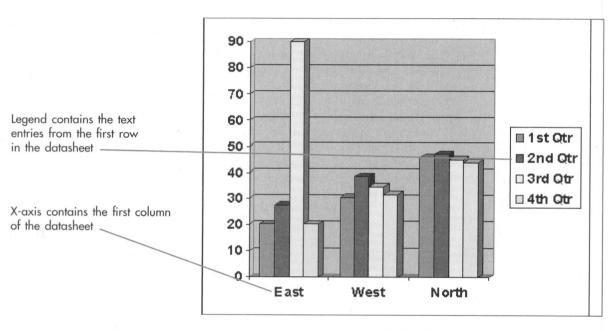

(a) Datasheet

Legend contains the text
entries from the first row
in the datasheet

X-axis contains the first column
of the datasheet

(b) Data Series in Columns

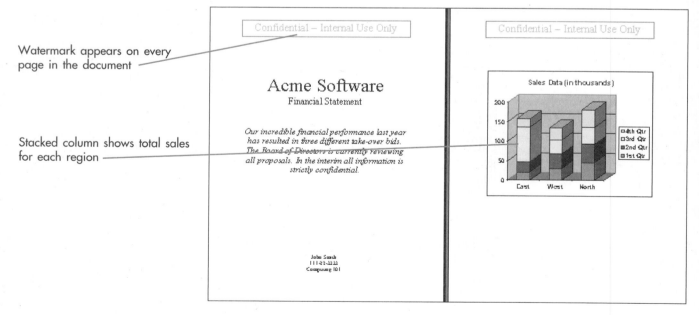

Watermark appears on every
page in the document

Stacked column shows total sales
for each region

(c) Word Document

FIGURE 5.8   Microsoft Graph

Microsoft Graph

Objective: Create a Watermark. Use Microsoft Graph to insert a graph into a document; modify the graph to display the data in rows or columns; change the graph format and underlying data. Use Figure 5.9 as a guide.

STEP 1: Create the Watermark

➤ Start Word and open a new document. Press the **enter key** several times. Enter the title of the document, **Acme Software Financial Statement,** as well as your name and class. Save the document as **Confidential Memo.**

➤ If necessary, click the **Print Layout View button** above the status bar, then click the **down arrow** on the Zoom list box and select **Two Pages.** Your document should take only a single page, however, as shown in Figure 5.9a.

➤ Pull down the **View menu** and click the **Header and Footer command** to display the Header and Footer toolbar. The text in the document (its title and your name, social security number, and class) is now dim since you are working in the header and footer area of the document.

➤ Pull down the **Insert menu** and click the **Text Box command.** Click and drag near the top of the document to create a text box.

➤ Click the **down arrow** on the Font Size box and change to **28** points. Click inside the text box. Enter **Confidential—Internal Use Only.** Center the text.

➤ Click the **Close button** on the Header and Footer toolbar to close the toolbar. The watermark (the text box you just created) is visible, but dim.

Zoom box

Font size box

Click and drag to create text box

Text in document is dim

Header and Footer toolbar

Close button

Print Layout View button

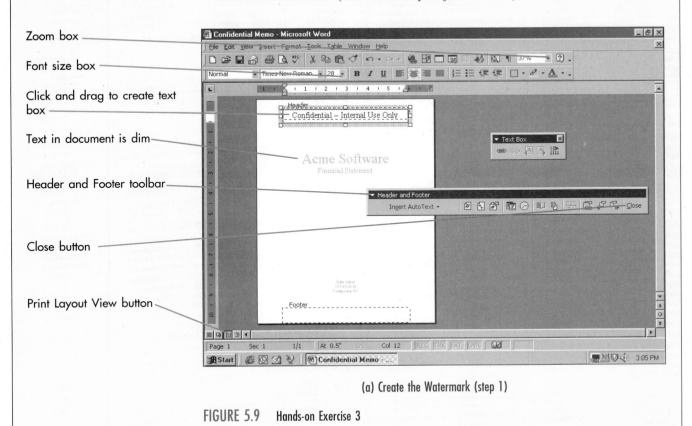

(a) Create the Watermark (step 1)

FIGURE 5.9   Hands-on Exercise 3

STEP 2: The Default Graph

➤ Press **Ctrl+End** to move to the end of the document, then press **Ctrl+Enter** to insert a page break and create a second page. The watermark appears automatically on this page and will appear on any other pages that are added to the document.

➤ Click at the top of the second page, then press the **enter key** several times to move down the page. Pull down the **Insert menu,** click the **Object command** to display the Insert Object dialog box.

➤ Click the **down arrow** in the Object type list box until you can select **Microsoft Graph 2000 Chart.** Click **OK.**

➤ The default datasheet and graph should be displayed on your monitor, as shown in Figure 5.9b. Do not be concerned if the numbers in your datasheet are different from those in the figure. Note that the menus and toolbar have changed to reflect the Microsoft Graph application.

➤ Click and drag the **title bar** of the datasheet so that you can see more of the graph, as in the figure. Click in cell **B1** of the datasheet (the value for East in the 2nd Quarter). Type **50** and press the **enter key.** The graph changes automatically to reflect the new data.

➤ Click in cell **D1.** Type **75** and press the **enter key.** Again the graph changes. Finally, click in cell **D3,** type **12** and press the **enter key.**

➤ Check that all of the values in your data sheet match those in Figure 5.9b. Click the **close button** to close the datasheet.

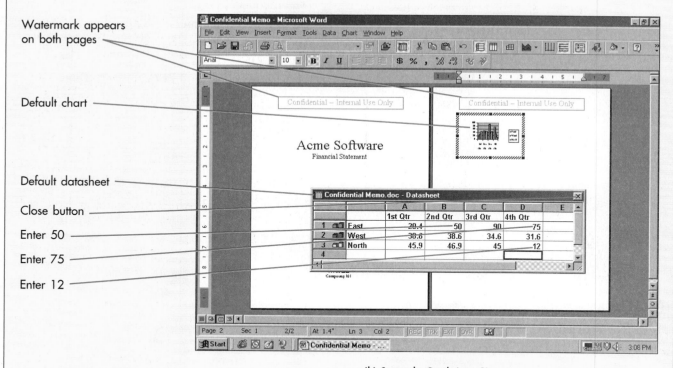

(b) Create the Graph (step 2)

FIGURE 5.9   Hands-on Exercise 3 (continued)

STEP 3: Move and Size the Graph

➤ Click outside the graph to exit from Microsoft Graph. The hashed line disappears from the graph to indicate that you are back in Word. The menus and toolbars are those of Microsoft Word.

➤ Click inside the graph to select the graph and display the sizing handles. The graph is selected as an object in a Word document and may be moved and/or sized just like any other object

- To size the graph, click and drag a corner handle.

- To move the graph, right click the graph, then click the **Format Object** command to change the wrapping option. Point anywhere inside the graph (the mouse pointer changes to a double arrow), then click and drag the graph so that it is positioned as shown in Figure 5.9c.

➤ Click outside the graph to deselect it, which causes the sizing handles to disappear. Save the document.

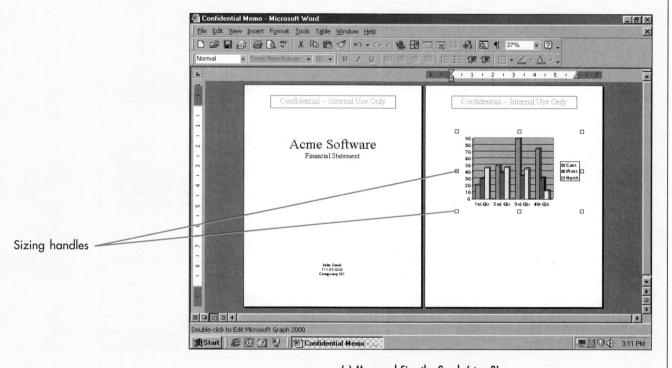

Sizing handles

(c) Move and Size the Graph (step 3)

FIGURE 5.9   Hands-on Exercise 3 (continued)

TO CLICK OR DOUBLE CLICK

A graph is an embedded object within a Word document, but retains its connection to Microsoft Graph for easy editing. Click the graph to select it, then move and size the graph just like any other object. (You can also press the Del key to delete the graph from a document.) Click outside the graph to deselect it, then double click the graph to restart Microsoft Graph (the graph is bordered by a hashed line) at which point you can edit the graph using the tools of the original application.

STEP 4: Change the Orientation and Graph Type

➤ Double click the graph to restart Microsoft Graph. The datasheet is displayed, a hashed line borders the graph, and the menus and toolbar are those of the Microsoft Graph application. Close the Datasheet window.

➤ Pull down the **Data menu** and click the **Series in Columns command** to change the data series from rows to columns as shown in Figure 5.9d. The X-axis changes automatically and now displays the names of the regions. The legend also changes and indicates the quarter.

➤ Pull down the **Data** menu and click the **Series in Rows command** to change the data series back to rows. Click the **Undo button** to return to columns and match the orientation in Figure 5.9d.

➤ Pull down the **Chart menu.** Click **Chart Type** to display the Chart Type dialog box. Close the Office Assistant if it appears.

➤ Select the **Stacked Column with a 3-D visual effect.** Click **OK.** The chart type changes to a stacked column graph. Save the document.

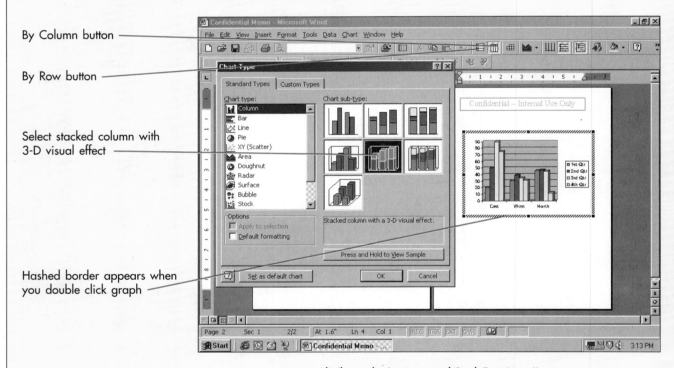

(d) Change the Orientation and Graph Type (step 4)

FIGURE 5.9   Hands-on Exercise 3 (continued)

DON'T FORGET HELP

Microsoft Graph includes its own Help system that functions identically to the Help in any other application. Pull down the Help menu and search on any topic for which you want additional information. Remember, too, that you can print the contents of a Help screen by pulling down the File menu and selecting the Print Topic command.

STEP 5: Add a Data Series

➤ Pull down the View menu and click **Datasheet** to display the datasheet (or click the **View Datasheet** button on the toolbar). The command and toolbar button function as a toggle switch; thus execute the command or click the button a second time and the datasheet closes.

➤ If necessary, click and drag the title bar of the datasheet so you can see more of the graph. Add an additional data series as follows:

- Click in the cell under North. Type **Central** then press the **right arrow key** to move to cell A4. Central appears as a category name on the X-axis.

- Enter **10, 15, 20,** and **25** in cells A4, B4, C4, and D4 respectively. Notice that as you complete each entry the graph adjusts automatically to reflect the value you just entered.

➤ The data for the Central region are plotted automatically as shown in Figure 5.9e. Close the datasheet.

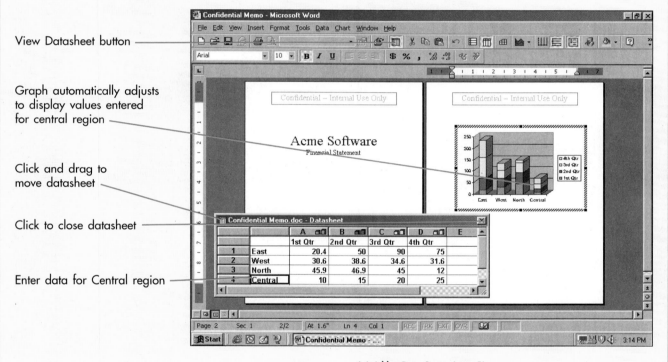

View Datasheet button

Graph automatically adjusts to display values entered for central region

Click and drag to move datasheet

Click to close datasheet

Enter data for Central region

(e) Add a Data Series (step 5)

FIGURE 5.9   Hands-on Exercise 3 (continued)

IMPORT THE DATA

Microsoft Graph enables you to import data from another application (e.g., Microsoft Excel) and use that data as the basis for the graph. Click in the upper left cell (the cell above row 1 and to the left of column A) to select the entire datasheet. Click the Import File button on the Microsoft Graph toolbar to produce an Import Data dialog box. Select the appropriate drive and folder, select the file, select the worksheet or specify a range to import, then click OK.

STEP 6: Chart Options

➤ Pull down the **Chart menu.** Click **Chart Options** to display the Chart Options dialog box. If necessary, click the **Title tab** and enter **Sales Data (in millions)** as the chart title as shown in Figure 5.9f. Click **OK** to accept the title and close the dialog box.

➤ Point to any value on the vertical axis, click the **right mouse button** to display a context-sensitive menu, then click the **Format Axis** command to display the Format Axis dialog box.

➤ Click the **Number tab,** then select the **Currency format.** Specify **zero** as the number of decimal places. Click **OK.** The format of the axis has been changed to include the dollar sign.

➤ Save the document.

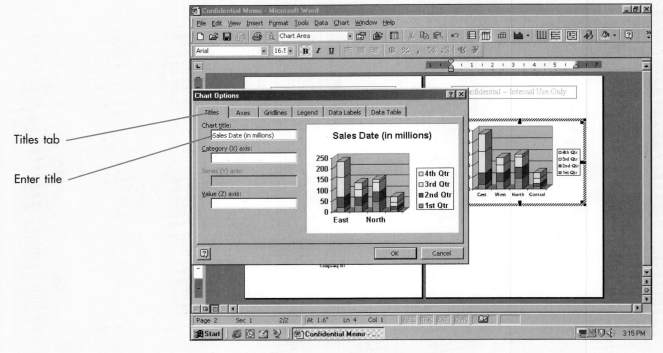

Titles tab

Enter title

(f) Chart Options (step 6)

FIGURE 5.9   Hands-on Exercise 3 (continued)

KEEP IT SIMPLE

Microsoft Graph provides unlimited flexibility with respect to the charts it creates. You can, for example, right click any data series within a graph and click the Format Data Series command to change the color, fill pattern, or shape of a data series. There are other options such as the 3-D View command that lets you fine-tune the graph by controlling the rotation, elevation, and other parameters. It's fun to experiment, but the best advice is to keep it simple and set a time limit at which point the project is finished.

STEP 7: Complete the Document

➤ Complete the document by adding text as appropriate, as shown in Figure 5.9g. You can use the text in our document that describes a confidential takeover, or make up your own. The text can appear on either page (or both pages) of the document.

➤ Place a border around the graph. Click the graph to select it, pull down the **Format menu,** click the **Object command,** and click the **Colors and Lines tab.** Click the **down arrow** on the color text box (in the Line section of the dialog box and select a line color. Click **OK.** Click elsewhere in the document to deselect the graph.

➤ Save the document a final time. Click the **Print button** on the standard toolbar to print the document and prove to your instructor that you completed this exercise.

Print button

Add text on title page

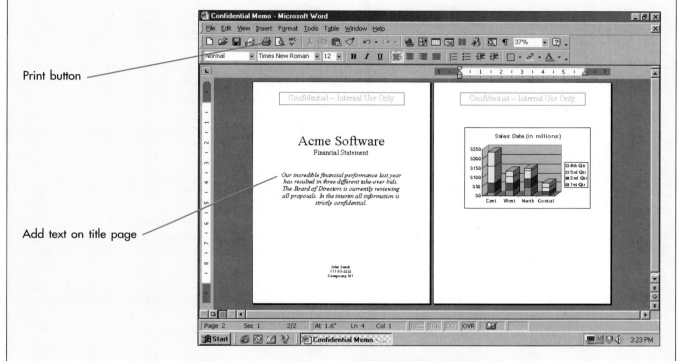

(g) The Finished Document (step 7)

FIGURE 5.9   Hands-on Exercise 3 (continued)

WRAPPING TEXT AROUND A WATERMARK

Text can be made to wrap around a watermark or it can appear directly over a watermark depending on the wrapping property in effect. Pull down the View menu and click the Header and Footer command so that you can modify the watermark. Point to the watermark, click the right mouse button to display a context-sensitive menu, and select the Format Text Box command to display the Format Text dialog box. Click the wrapping tab, then select the desired option, just as you do with clip art.

SUMMARY

The essence of desktop publishing is the merger of text with graphics to produce a professional-looking document. Proficiency in desktop publishing requires knowledge of the associated commands in Microsoft Word, as well as familiarity with the basics of graphic design.

Typography is the process of selecting typefaces, type styles, and type sizes. A typeface (or font) is a complete set of characters (upper- and lowercase letters, numbers, punctuation marks, and special symbols). Type size is a vertical measurement and is specified in points. One point is equal to $\frac{1}{72}$ of an inch.

The design of a document is developed on a grid, an underlying but invisible set of horizontal and vertical lines that determine the placement of the major elements. A newsletter can be divided into any number of newspaper-style columns in which text flows from the bottom of one column to the top of the next. Columns are implemented by clicking the Columns button on the Standard toolbar or by selecting the Columns command from the Format menu. Sections are required if different column arrangements are present in the same document. The Page Layout view is required to see the columns displayed side by side.

Emphasis can be achieved in several ways, the easiest being variations in type size and/or type style. Boxes and/or shading call attention to selected articles in a document. Horizontal lines are effective in separating one topic from another or calling attention to a pull quote (a phrase or sentence taken from an article to emphasize a key point). A reverse (light text on a solid background) is striking for a small amount of text. Clip art, used in moderation, will catch the reader's eye and enhance almost any newsletter.

Clip art is available from a variety of sources including the Microsoft Clip Gallery, which is accessed most easily through the Insert Picture command. Once clip art has been inserted into a document, it can be moved and sized just like any other Windows object. The Format Picture command provides additional flexibility and precision in the placement of an object. The Drawing toolbar contains various tools that are used to insert and/or modify objects into a Word document.

Graphic design does not have hard and fast rules, only guidelines and common sense. Creating an effective document is an iterative process and reflects the result of trial and error. We encourage you to experiment freely with different designs.

Microsoft Graph enables you to create a graph for inclusion in any Office document. It is a powerful graphing program that has many of the same capabilities as the charting component in Microsoft Excel.

A watermark is a text (or graphical) entry that appears on each page of a document. It is created through the View Header/Footer command and can be used to lend interest to a document or to supply additional information.

KEY WORDS AND CONCEPTS

Arial
AutoShape
AutoShapes toolbar
Borders and Shading command
Bulleted list
Category names
Clip art

Columns command
Data points
Data series
Datasheet
Desktop publishing
Drawing toolbar
Drop cap
Emphasis

Font
Format Picture command
Grid
Insert Picture command
Masthead
Microsoft Clip Gallery
Microsoft Graph

Monospaced typeface   Proportional typeface   Text box
Newsletter Wizard   Pull quote   Times New Roman
Newspaper-style   Reverse   Type size
  columns   Sans serif typeface   Typeface
Numbered list   Section break   Typography
Point size   Serif typeface   Watermark

MULTIPLE CHOICE

1. Which of the following is a commonly accepted guideline in typography?
   (a) Use a serif typeface for headings and a sans serif typeface for text
   (b) Use a sans serif typeface for headings and a serif typeface for text
   (c) Use a sans serif typeface for both headings and text
   (d) Use a serif typeface for both headings and text

2. Which of the following best enables you to see a multicolumn document as it will appear on the printed page?
   (a) Normal view at 100% magnification
   (b) Normal view at whole page magnification
   (c) Print Layout view at 100% magnification
   (d) Print Layout view at whole page magnification

3. What is the width of each column in a document with two uniform columns, given 1¼-inch margins and ½-inch spacing between the columns?
   (a) 2½ inches
   (b) 2¾ inches
   (c) 3 inches
   (d) Impossible to determine

4. What is the minimum number of sections in a three-column newsletter whose masthead extends across all three columns?
   (a) One
   (b) Two
   (c) Three
   (d) Four

5. Which of the following describes the Arial and Times New Roman fonts?
   (a) Arial is a sans serif font, Times New Roman is a serif font
   (b) Arial is a serif font, Times New Roman is a sans serif font
   (c) Both are serif fonts
   (d) Both are sans serif fonts

6. How do you balance the columns in a newsletter so that each column contains the same amount of text?
   (a) Check the Balance Columns box in the Format Columns command
   (b) Visually determine where the break should go, then insert a column break at the appropriate place
   (c) Insert a continuous section break at the end of the last column
   (d) All of the above

7. What is the effect of dragging one of the four corner handles on a selected object?
   (a) The length of the object is changed but the width remains constant
   (b) The width of the object is changed but the length remains constant
   (c) The length and width of the object are changed in proportion to one another
   (d) Neither the length nor width of the object is changed

8. Which type size is the most reasonable for columns of text, such as those appearing in the newsletter created in the chapter?
   (a) 6 point
   (b) 10 point
   (c) 14 point
   (d) 18 point

9. A grid is applicable to the design of:
   (a) Documents with one, two, or three columns and moderate clip art
   (b) Documents with four or more columns and no clip art
   (c) Both (a) and (b)
   (d) Neither (a) nor (b)

10. Which of the following can be used to add emphasis to a document?
    (a) Borders and shading
    (b) Pull quotes and reverses
    (c) Both (a) and (b)
    (d) Neither (a) nor (b)

11. Which of the following is a recommended guideline in the design of a document?
    (a) Use at least three different clip art images in every newsletter
    (b) Use at least three different typefaces in a document to maintain interest
    (c) Use the same type size for the heading and text of an article
    (d) None of the above

12. Which of the following is implemented at the section level?
    (a) Columns
    (b) Margins
    (c) Both (a) and (b)
    (d) Neither (a) nor (b)

13. How do you size an object so that it maintains the original proportion between height and width?
    (a) Drag a sizing handle on the left or right side of the object to change its width, then drag a sizing handle on the top or bottom edge to change the height
    (b) Drag a sizing handle on any of the corners
    (c) Both (a) and (b)
    (d) Neither (a) nor (b)

14. A reverse is implemented:
    (a) By selecting 100% shading in the Borders and Shading command
    (b) By changing the Font color to black
    (c) Both (a) and (b)
    (d) Neither (a) nor (b)

15. The Format Picture command enables you to:

    (a) Change the way in which text is wrapped around a figure

    (b) Change the size of a figure

    (c) Place a border around a figure

    (d) All of the above

Answers

1. b	**6.** c	**11.** d
2. d	**6.** c	**12.** c
3. b	**8.** b	**13.** b
4. b	**9.** c	**14.** a
5. a	**10.** c	**15.** d

PRACTICE WITH MICROSOFT WORD

1. Create a newsletter containing at least one graphic image from the Microsoft Clip Gallery. The intent of this problem is simply to provide practice in graphic design. There is no requirement to write meaningful text, but the headings in the newsletter should follow the theme of the graphic. Do the following:

    a. Select a graphic, then write one or two sentences in support of that graphic. If, for example, you choose a clip art image of a dog or cat, write a sentence about your pet.

    b. As indicated, there is no requirement to write meaningful text for the newsletter; just copy the sentences from part (a) once or twice to create a paragraph, then copy the paragraph several times to create the newsletter. You should, however, create meaningful headings to add interest to the document.

    c. Develop an overall design away from the computer—that is, with pencil and paper. Use a grid to indicate the placement of the articles, headings, clip art, and masthead. You may be surprised to find that it is easier to master commands in Word than it is to design the newsletter; do not, however, underestimate the importance of graphic design in the ultimate success of your document.

2. The flyers in Figure 5.10 were created using clip art from the Microsoft Clip Gallery. Once the clip art was brought into the document, it was moved and sized as necessary to create the documents in the figure.

    Recreate either or both of our flyers, or better yet, design your own with our text but your own layout. Alternatively, you can create a flyer for a hypothetical intramural sporting event or a fraternity or sorority rushing function. (Use the Insert Symbol command to select Greek letters from the Symbols font.) The flyers are simpler to create than a newsletter. Submit your flyers and a cover sheet to your instructor as proof you did this exercise. Look at the documents submitted by your classmates to see additional samples of graphic design.

UM Jazz Band
Plays Dixieland

Where: Gusman Hall

When: Wednesday
        November 10

Time: 8:00 PM

(a)

CIS 120 Study Sessions

For those who don't know a bit from a byte
Come to Stanford College this Tuesday night
We'll study the concepts that aren't always clear
And memorize terms that hackers hold dear

We'll hit the books from 7 to 10
And then Thursday night, we'll do it again
It can't hurt to try us - so come on by
And give the CIS tutors that old college try!

(b)

FIGURE 5.10   The Flyer (Exercise 2)

3. The Masthead: Figure 5.11 displays three additional mastheads suitable for the newsletter that was developed in the chapter. Each masthead was created as follows:

a. A two-by-two table was used in Figure 5.11a in order to right justify the date of the newsletter.

b. Microsoft WordArt was used to create the masthead in Figure 5.11c.

c. A different font was used for the masthead in Figure 5.11b.

Choose the masthead you like best, then modify the newsletter as it existed at the end of the second hands-on exercise to include the new masthead. Submit the modified newsletter to your instructor.

Creating a Newsletter
Volume 1, Number 1   Spring 1999

Creating a Newsletter

Creating a Newsletter

FIGURE 5.11   The Masthead (Exercise 3)

4. A Guide to Smart Shopping: This problem is more challenging than the previous exercises in that you are asked to consider content as well as design. The objective is to develop a one- (or two-) page document with helpful tips to the novice on buying a computer. We have, however, written the copy for you and put the file on the data disk.

a. Open and print the *Chapter 5 Practice 4* document on the data disk, which takes approximately a page and a half as presently formatted. Read our text and determine the tips you want to retain and those you want to delete. Add other tips as you see fit.

b. Examine the available clip art through the Insert Picture command or through the Microsoft Clip Gallery. There is no requirement, however, to include a graphic; that is, use clip art only if you think it will enhance the document.

c. Consult a current computer magazine (or another source) to determine actual prices for one or more configurations, then include this information prominently in your document.

d. Create the masthead for the document, then develop with pencil and paper a rough sketch of the completed document showing the masthead, the placement of the text, clip art, and the special of the month (the configuration in part c).

e. Print the completed document for your instructor.

5. The Equation Editor: Create a simple newsletter such as the two-column design in Figure 5.12. There is no requirement to write meaningful text, as the intent of this exercise is to illustrate the Equation Editor. Thus all you need to do is write a sentence or two, then copy that sentence so that it fills the newsletter.

To create the equation, pull down the Insert menu, click the Object command, click the Create New tab, then select Microsoft Equation 3.0 to start the Equation Editor. This is a new application and we do not provide instruction in its use. It does, however, follow the conventions of other Office applications, and through trial and error, and reference to the Help menu, you should be able to duplicate our equation. Print the document for your instructor.

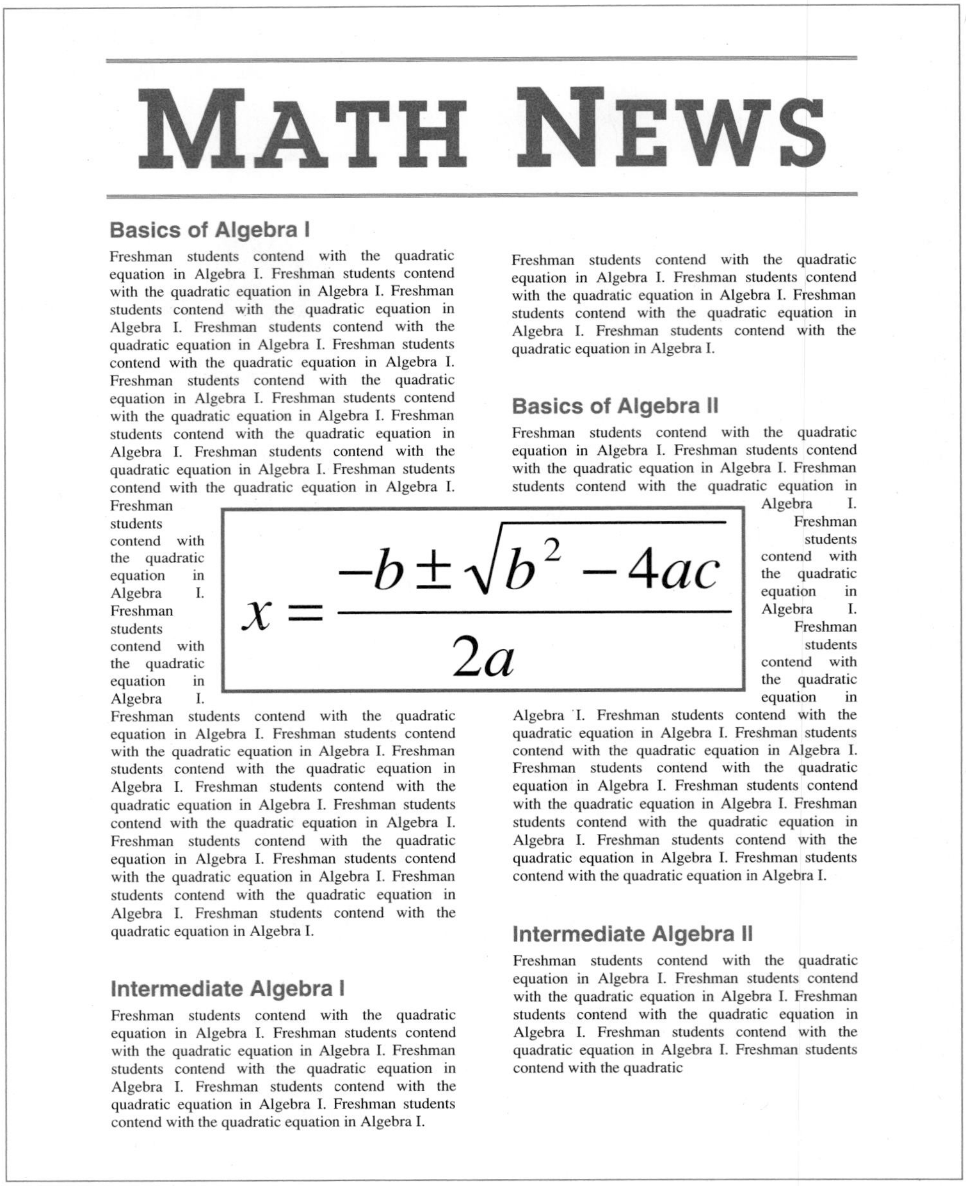

MATH NEWS

Basics of Algebra I

Freshman students contend with the quadratic equation in Algebra I. Freshman students contend with the quadratic equation in Algebra I. Freshman students contend with the quadratic equation in Algebra I. Freshman students contend with the quadratic equation in Algebra I. Freshman students contend with the quadratic equation in Algebra I. Freshman students contend with the quadratic equation in Algebra I. Freshman students contend with the quadratic equation in Algebra I. Freshman students contend with the quadratic equation in Algebra I. Freshman students contend with the quadratic equation in Algebra I. Freshman students contend with the quadratic equation in Algebra I. Freshman students contend with the quadratic equation in Algebra I. Freshman students contend with the quadratic equation in Algebra I.

$$x = \frac{-b \pm \sqrt{b^2 - 4ac}}{2a}$$

Freshman students contend with the quadratic equation in Algebra I. Freshman students contend with the quadratic equation in Algebra I. Freshman students contend with the quadratic equation in Algebra I. Freshman students contend with the quadratic equation in Algebra I. Freshman students contend with the quadratic equation in Algebra I. Freshman students contend with the quadratic equation in Algebra I. Freshman students contend with the quadratic equation in Algebra I. Freshman students contend with the quadratic equation in Algebra I.

Intermediate Algebra I

Freshman students contend with the quadratic equation in Algebra I. Freshman students contend with the quadratic equation in Algebra I. Freshman students contend with the quadratic equation in Algebra I. Freshman students contend with the quadratic equation in Algebra I. Freshman students contend with the quadratic equation in Algebra I.

Freshman students contend with the quadratic equation in Algebra I. Freshman students contend with the quadratic equation in Algebra I. Freshman students contend with the quadratic equation in Algebra I. Freshman students contend with the quadratic equation in Algebra I. Freshman students contend with the quadratic equation in Algebra I.

Basics of Algebra II

Freshman students contend with the quadratic equation in Algebra I. Freshman students contend with the quadratic equation in Algebra I. Freshman students contend with the quadratic equation in Algebra I. Freshman students contend with the quadratic equation in Algebra I. Freshman students contend with the quadratic equation in Algebra I. Freshman students contend with the quadratic equation in Algebra I. Freshman students contend with the quadratic equation in Algebra I. Freshman students contend with the quadratic equation in Algebra I. Freshman students contend with the quadratic equation in Algebra I. Freshman students contend with the quadratic equation in Algebra I. Freshman students contend with the quadratic equation in Algebra I.

Intermediate Algebra II

Freshman students contend with the quadratic equation in Algebra I. Freshman students contend with the quadratic equation in Algebra I. Freshman students contend with the quadratic equation in Algebra I. Freshman students contend with the quadratic equation in Algebra I. Freshman students contend with the quadratic

FIGURE 5.12   The Equation Editor (Exercise 5)

6. Microsoft Graph: Figure 5.13 displays a modified version of the confidential memo that was created in the fourth hands-on exercise. To create the new document, we removed the legend from the chart, included the associated data table, then enlarged the chart and repositioned it on the page. We also moved the watermark to the bottom of the page so it would not interfere with the chart. Complete the hands-on exercise in the chapter, then make the necessary modifications so that your finished document matches Figure 5.13. (Use any wording you like for the statement on the first page.)

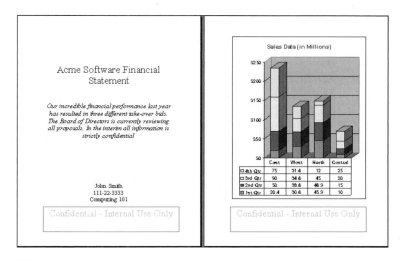

FIGURE 5.13 Corporate Takeover (Exercise 6)

CASE STUDIES

Before and After

The best way to learn about the do's and don'ts of desktop publishing is to study the work of others. Choose a particular type of document—for example, a newsletter, résumé, or advertising flyer, then collect samples of that document. Choose one sample that is particularly bad and redesign the document. You need not enter the actual text, but you should keep all of the major headings so that the document retains its identity. Add or delete clip art as appropriate. Bring the before and after samples to class for your professor.

Clip Art

Clip art—you see it all the time, but where do you get it, and how much does it cost? Scan the computer magazines and find at least two sources for additional clip art. Better yet, use your favorite search engine to locate additional sources of clip art on the Web. Return to class with specific information on prices and types of the clip art.

Color Separations

It's difficult to tell where word processing stops and desktop publishing begins. One distinguishing characteristic of a desktop publishing program, however, is the ability to create color separations, which in turn enable you to print a document in full color. Use your favorite search engine to learn more about the process of color separations. Summarize the results of your research in a short paper to your instructor.

Photographs versus Clip Art

The right clip art can enhance any document, but there are times when clip art just won't do. It may be too juvenile or simply inappropriate. Photographs offer an alternative and are inserted into a presentation through the Insert Picture command. Once inserted into a presentation, photographs can be moved or sized just like any other Windows object. Use your favorite search engine to locate a photograph, then incorporate that photograph into the newsletter that was developed in this chapter.

Microsoft Organization Chart

Microsoft Organization Chart is yet another application that is included in Microsoft Office 2000. To insert an organization chart into a document, pull down the Insert menu, click Object, and choose MS Organization Chart. We won't tell you any more about the application, other than it's easy to use, and that it follows the same conventions as Microsoft Graph with respect to placing it within a Word document. Imagine yourself as the CEO of a small company and use MS Organization Chart to develop your organization. Print the completed chart for your instructor.

chapter 6

CREATING A HOME PAGE: INTRODUCTION TO HTML

OBJECTIVES

After reading this chapter you will be able to:

1. Define HTML and its role on the World Wide Web; describe the nature of HTML codes and explain how they control the appearance of a Web document.

2. Use the Insert Hyperlink command to include hyperlinks, bookmarks, and/or an e-mail address in a Word document.

3. Use the Save As Web page command to convert a Word document to HTML.

4. Use the Format Theme command to enhance the appearance of a Web document.

5. Use the FTP capability in Office 2000 to upload a document to a Web server; add a Web page to the catalog of a search engine.

6. Explain how to view HTML codes from within Internet Explorer; describe the use of the Telnet program that is built into Windows.

7. Use the Web Page Wizard in Microsoft Word 2000 to create a Web site with multiple pages.

8. Explain how the use of frames and/or bookmarks facilitates navigation between multiple documents.

OVERVIEW

Sooner or later anyone who cruises the World Wide Web wants to create a home page and/or a Web site of their own. That, in turn, requires an appreciation for *HyperText Markup Language (HTML),* the language in which all Web pages are written. A Web page (HTML document) consists of text and graphics, together with a set of codes (or tags) that describe how the document is to appear when viewed in a Web browser such as Internet Explorer.

In the early days of the Web, anyone creating a Web document (home page) had to learn each of these codes and enter it explicitly. Today, however, it's much easier as you can create a Web document directly in any application in Microsoft Office 2000. In essence, you enter the text of a document, apply basic formatting such as boldface or italics, then simply save the file as a Web document. Office 2000 also provides an FTP (File Transfer Protocol) capability that lets you upload your documents directly on to a Web server.

There are, of course, other commands that you will need to learn, but all commands are executed from within Word, through pull-down menus, toolbars, or keyboard shortcuts. You can create a single document (called a home page) or you can create multiple documents to build a simple Web site. Either way, the document(s) can be viewed locally within a Web browser such as Internet Explorer, and/or they can be placed on a Web server where they can be accessed by anyone with an Internet connection.

As always, the hands-on exercises are essential to our learn-by-doing philosophy since they enable you to apply the conceptual material at the computer. The exercises are structured in such a way that you can view the Web pages you create, even if you do not have access to the Internet. If you have an account on a Web server, however, you will want to read the section that describes the FTP capabilities in Microsoft Word, in order to save your documents directly on the Web. The last exercise introduces the Web Page Wizard to create a Web site that contains multiple Web pages.

LEARN MORE ABOUT HTML

Use your favorite Web search engine to search for additional information about HTML. One excellent place to begin is the resource page on HTML that is maintained by the Library of Congress at http://lcweb.loc.gov/global/html.html. This site contains links to several HTML tutorials and also provides you with information about the latest HTML standard.

INTRODUCTION TO HTML

Figure 6.1 displays a simple Web page that is similar to the one you will create in the hands-on exercise that follows shortly. Our page has the look and feel of Web pages you see when you access the World Wide Web. It includes different types of formatting, a bulleted list, underlined links, and a heading displayed in a larger font. All of these elements are associated with specific HTML codes that identify the appearance and characteristics of the item. Figure 6.1a displays the document, as it would appear when viewed in Internet Explorer. Figure 6.1b shows the underlying HTML codes (tags) that are necessary to format the page.

Fortunately, however, it is not necessary to memorize the HTML tags since you can usually determine their meaning from the codes themselves. Nor is it even necessary for you to enter the tags, as Word will create the HTML tags for you based on the formatting in the document. Nevertheless, we think it worthwhile for you to gain an appreciation for HTML by comparing the two views of the document.

HTML codes become less intimidating when you realize that they are enclosed in angle brackets and are used consistently from document to document. Most tags occur in pairs, at the beginning and end of the text to be formatted, with the ending code preceded by a slash, such as <p and </p> to indicate the beginning and end of a paragraph. Links to other pages (which are known as hyperlinks) are enclosed within a pair of anchor tags <A and </A> in which you specify the URL address of the document through the HREF parameter.

Heading in a larger font

Underlined links

Bulleted List

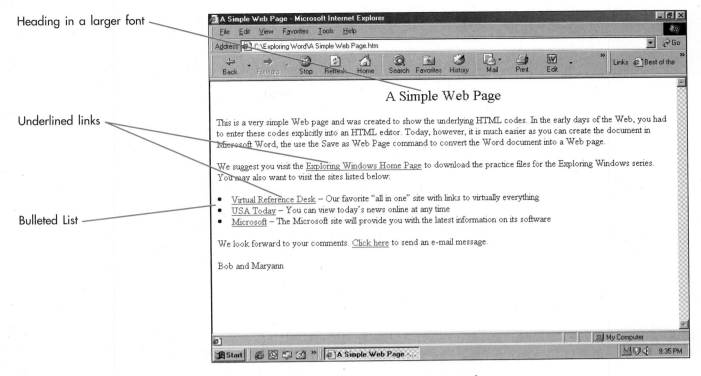

(a) Internet Explorer

Paragraph tags

Anchor tags enclose
URL address of link

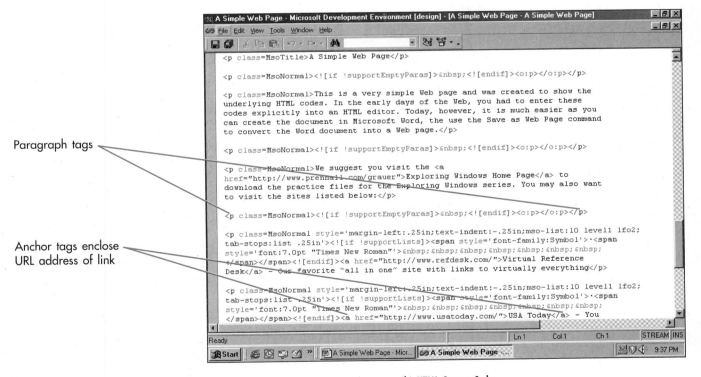

(b) HTML Source Code

FIGURE 6.1   Introduction to HTML

As indicated, there are different ways to create an HTML document. The original (and more difficult) method was to enter the codes explicitly in a text editor such as the Notepad accessory that is built into Windows. An easier way (and the only method you need to consider) is to use Microsoft Word 2000 to create the document for you, without having to enter or reference the HTML codes at all.

Figure 6.2 displays Jessica Kinzer's home page in Microsoft Word 2000. You can create a similar page by entering the text and formatting just as you would enter the text of an ordinary document. The only difference is that instead of saving the document in the default format (as a Word 2000 document), you use the *Save As Web Page command* to specify the HTML format. Microsoft Word does the rest, generating the HTML codes needed to create the document.

Hyperlinks are added through the Insert Hyperlink button on the Standard toolbar or through the corresponding *Insert Hyperlink command* in the Insert menu. You can format the elements of the document (the heading, bullets, text and so on) individually, or you can select a *theme* from those provided by Microsoft Word. A theme (or template) is a set of unified design elements and color schemes that will save you time, while making your document more attractive.

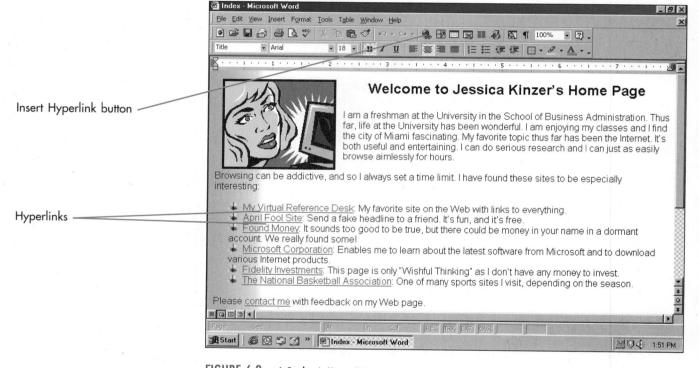

FIGURE 6.2   A Student's Home Page

ROUND-TRIP HTML

Each application in Microsoft Office 2000 lets you open an HTML document in both Internet Explorer and the application that created the Web page initially. In other words, you can start with a Word document and use the Save As Web Page command to convert the document to Web page, then view that page in a Web browser. You can then reopen the Web page in Word (the original Office application) with full access to all Word commands, should you want to modify the document.

Introduction to HTML

Objective: To use Microsoft Word to create a simple home page with clip art and multiple hyperlinks; to format a Web page by selecting a theme. Use Figure 6.3 as a guide in the exercise.

STEP 1: Enter the Text

➤ Start Microsoft Word. Pull down the **View menu** and click the **Web Layout command.** Enter the text of your home page as shown in Figure 6.3a. Use any text you like and choose an appropriate font and type size. Center and enlarge the title for your page.

➤ Enter the text for our links (e.g., My Virtual Reference Desk and the April Fool site) or choose your own. You do not enter the URL addresses at this time.

➤ Click and drag to select all of your links, then click the **Bullets button** on the Formatting toolbar to precede each link with a bullet. The Bullets button functions as a toggle switch; that is, click it a second time and the bullets disappear. Click anywhere to deselect the text.

➤ Click the **Spelling and Grammar button** to check the document for spelling. (There is absolutely no excuse for not checking the spelling and grammar in a document, be it a printed document or a Web page.)

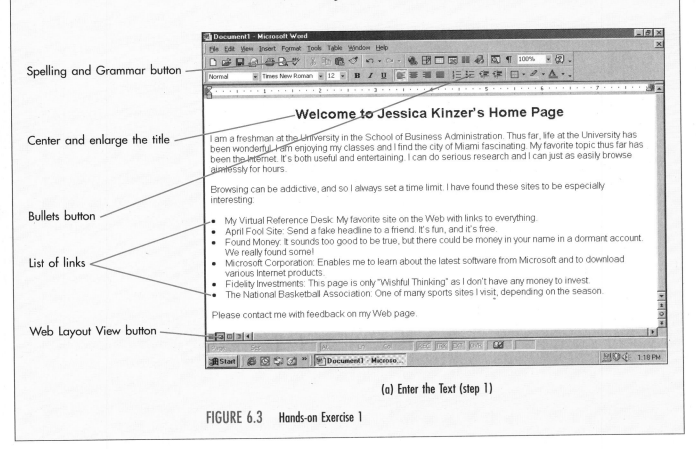

(a) Enter the Text (step 1)

FIGURE 6.3 Hands-on Exercise 1

STEP 2: Save the Document

➤ Pull down the **File menu** and click the **Save As Web Page** command to display the Save As dialog box in Figure 6.3b.

➤ Click the drop-down arrow in the Save In list box to select the appropriate drive—drive C or drive A. Click to open the **Exploring Word folder** that contains the documents you have used throughout the text.

➤ Change the name of the Web page to **Index.** (Index is chosen as the name of the document to be consistent with the convention used by a Web browser; i.e., to automatically display the Index document, if it exists.)

➤ Click the **Change Title button** if you want to change the title of the Web page as it will appear in the Title bar of the Web browser. (The default title is the opening text in your document.)

➤ Click the **Save button.** The title bar reflects the name of the Web page (Index), but the screen does not change in any other way.

Click to select drive/folder

Enter new name for Web page

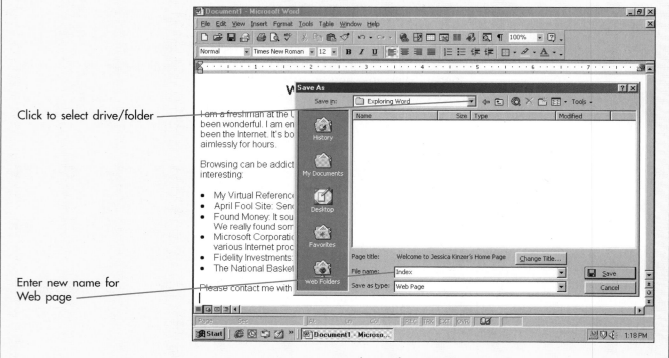

(b) Save the Document (step 2)

FIGURE 6.3   Hands-on Exercise 1 (continued)

THE FILE TYPES ARE DIFFERENT

Click the Start button, click (or point to) the Programs command, then start Windows Explorer. Select the drive and folder where you saved the Index document. If necessary, pull down the View menu and change to the Details view. Look for the Index document you just created, and note that it is displayed with the icon of a Web browser (Internet Explorer or Netscape Navigator) to indicate that it is an HTML document, rather than a Word document.

STEP 3: Add the Clip Art

➤ Pull down the **Insert menu,** click (or point to) **Picture,** then click **Clip Art** to display the Insert Clip Art dialog box in Figure 6.3c.

➤ Click in the **Search for Clips text box,** type **woman** (man) to search for any clip art image that has this property, then press the **enter key.** Select (click) the image you want, then click the **Insert Clip button** on the shortcut menu. Close the Insert Clip Art dialog box.

➤ The picture should appear in the document. Point to the picture, click the **right mouse** button to display the context-sensitive menu, then click the **Format Picture command** to display the Format Picture dialog box.

➤ Click the **Layout tab,** choose the **Square layout,** then click the option button for Left or Right alignment. Click **OK** to close the dialog box. Click and drag the sizing handles on the picture as appropriate. Save the document.

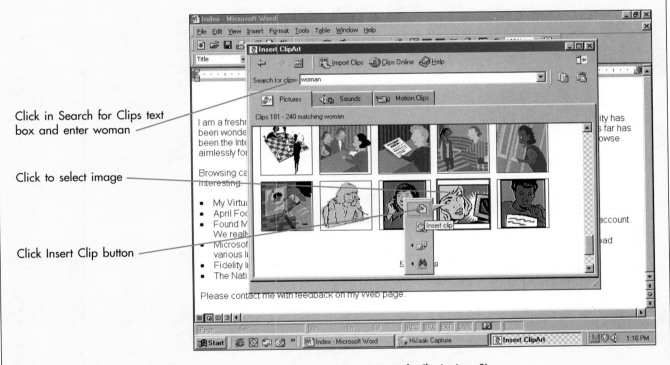

Click in Search for Clips text box and enter woman

Click to select image

Click Insert Clip button

(c) Insert the Clip Art (step 3)

FIGURE 6.3   Hands-on Exercise 1 (continued)

CLIP PROPERTIES

Every clip art image has multiple properties that determine the category (or categories) in which it is listed as well as key words that are reflected in a search of the Clip Gallery. Right click any image within the Insert Clip Art dialog box and click the Clip Properties command to display the Clip Properties dialog box. Click the Categories tab, then check any additional categories under which the image should appear. Click the Keywords tab to add (delete) the entries for this item. Click OK to accept the changes and close the Properties dialog box.

STEP 4: Add the Hyperlinks

➤ Select **My Virtual Reference Desk** (the text for the first hyperlink). Pull down the **Insert menu** and click **Hyperlink** (or click the **Insert Hyperlink button**) to display the Insert Hyperlink dialog box in Figure 6.3d.

➤ The text to display (My Virtual Reference Desk) is already entered because the text was selected prior to executing the Insert Hyperlink command. If necessary, click the icon for **Existing File** or **Web Page.**

➤ Click in the second text box and enter the address **www.refdesk.com** (the http is assumed). Click **OK**.

➤ Add the additional links in similar fashion. The addresses in our document are: **www.aprilfool.com, www.foundmoney.com, www.microsoft.com, www.fidelity.com,** and **www.nba.com.**

➤ Click and drag to select the words, **contact me,** then click the **Insert Hyperlink button** to display the Insert Hyperlink dialog box.

➤ Click the **E-mail Address icon** then click in the E-mail Address text box and enter your e-mail address. Click **OK**.

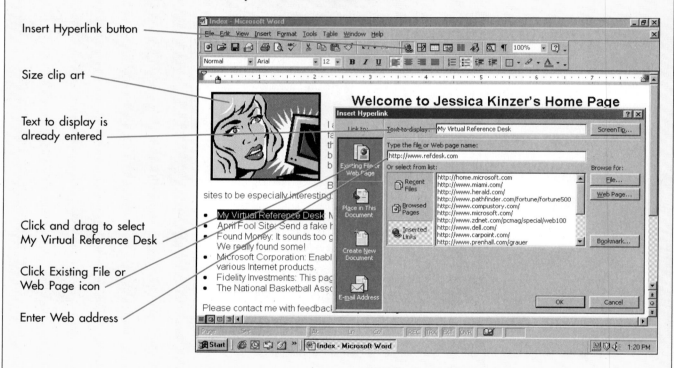

Insert Hyperlink button

Size clip art

Text to display is already entered

Click and drag to select My Virtual Reference Desk

Click Existing File or Web Page icon

Enter Web address

(d) Add the Hyperlinks (step 4)

FIGURE 6.3 Hands-on Exercise 1 (continued)

SELECTING (EDITING) A HYPERLINK

You cannot select a hyperlink by clicking it, because that displays the associated Web page. You can, however, right click the text of the hyperlink to display a context-sensitive menu. Click the Hyperlink command from that menu, then select the Edit Hyperlink command to display the associated dialog box in which to make the necessary changes.

STEP 5: Apply a Theme

➤ You should see underlined hyperlinks in your document. Pull down the **Format menu** and click the **Theme command** to display the Theme dialog box in Figure 6.3e.

➤ Select (click) a theme from the list box on the left and a sample of the design appears in the right. Only a limited number of the listed themes are installed by default, however, and thus you may be prompted for the Microsoft Office 2000 CD depending on your selection. Click **OK.**

➤ You can go from one theme to the next by clicking the new theme. There are approximately 65 themes to choose from, and they are all visually appealing. Every theme offers a professionally designed set of formatting specifications for the various headings, horizontal lines, bullets, and links.

➤ Make your decision as to which theme you will use. Save the document.

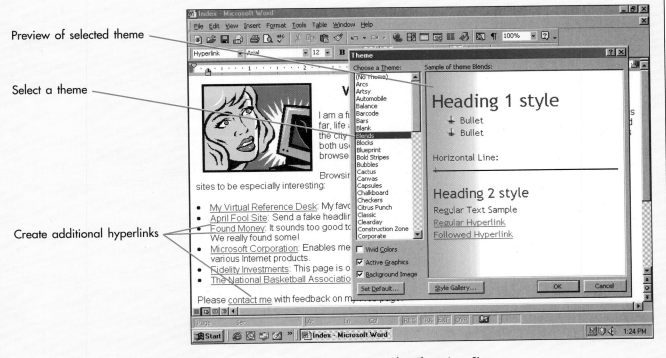

Preview of selected theme

Select a theme

Create additional hyperlinks

(e) Apply a Theme (step 5)

FIGURE 6.3   Hands-on Exercise 1 (continued)

KEEP IT SIMPLE

Too many would-be designers clutter a page unnecessarily by importing a complex background, which tends to obscure the text. The best design is a simple design—either no background or a very simple pattern. We also prefer light backgrounds with dark text (e.g., black or dark blue text on a white background) as opposed to the other way around. Design, however, is subjective and there is no consensus as to what makes an attractive page. Variety is indeed the spice of life.

STEP 6: View the Web Page

➤ Start your Web browser. Pull down the **File menu** and click the **Open command** to display the Open dialog box in Figure 6.3f. Click the **Browse button,** then select the drive folder (e.g., Exploring Word on drive C) where you saved the Web page.

➤ Select (click) the **Index document,** click **Open,** then click **OK** to open the document. You should see the Web page that was just created except that you are viewing it in your browser rather than Microsoft Word.

➤ The Address bar shows the local address (C:\Exploring Word\Index.htm) of the document. (You can also open the document from the address bar, by clicking in the address bar, then typing the address of the document; e.g., c:\Exploring word\Index.htm.)

➤ Click the **Print button** on the Internet Explorer toolbar to print this page for your instructor.

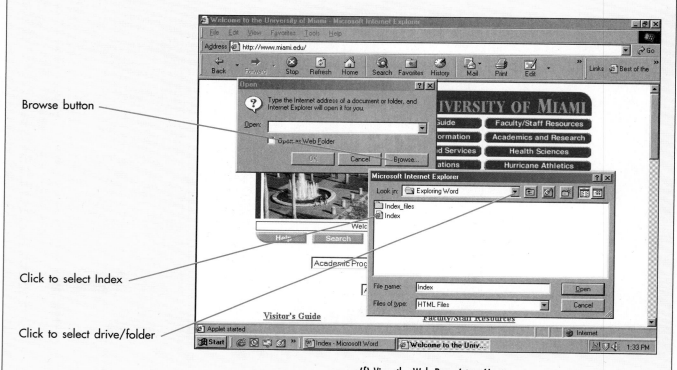

Browse button

Click to select Index

Click to select drive/folder

(f) View the Web Page (step 6)

FIGURE 6.3 Hands-on Exercise 1 (continued)

AN EXTRA FOLDER

Look carefully at the contents of the Exploring Word folder within the Open dialog box. You see the HTML document you just created as well as a folder that was created automatically by the Save As Web Page command. The latter folder contains the various objects that are referenced by the Web page. Be sure to copy the contents of this folder to the Web server in addition to your Web page if you decide to post the page.

STEP 7: Test the Web Page

➤ This step requires an Internet connection because you will be verifying the addresses you entered earlier.

➤ Click the hyperlink to the **Found Money** Web site to display the Web page in Figure 6.3g. The URL address displayed by the browser corresponds to the address you entered in step 4.

➤ If you are unable to connect, it is most likely because you entered the URL incorrectly, the site is temporarily down, or you are not connected to the Internet. Click a second hyperlink to see if you can connect to that site.

➤ If you connect to one site, but not the other, you may have to return to your original document to correct the URL:

- Click the **Microsoft Word button** on the Windows taskbar to return to your home page, **right click the hyperlink** as described in the boxed tip for step 4 and make the necessary correction. **Save the corrected document.**

- Click the **browser button** on the Windows taskbar to return to the browser, click the **Refresh button** to load the corrected page, then try the hyperlink a second time.

➤ If you link successfully, click the **Back button** in your browser to return to your home page, then test the various other links to be sure that they are working.

➤ Exit Word and Internet Explorer if you do not want to continue with the next exercise at this time.

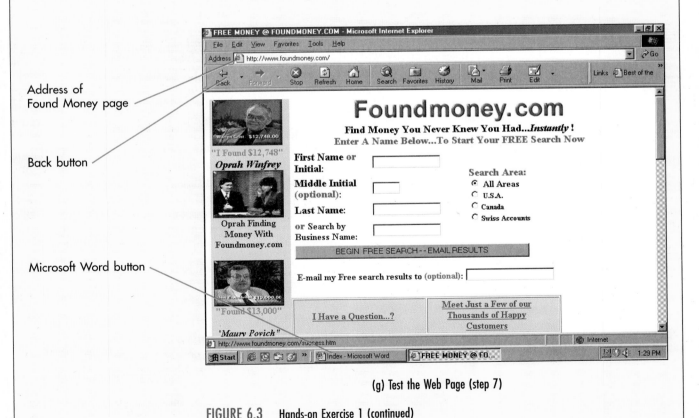

(g) Test the Web Page (step 7)

FIGURE 6.3   Hands-on Exercise 1 (continued)

The previous exercise described how to create a Web document and view it through a browser such as Internet Explorer. The document was stored locally and thus you are the only one who can view it. It's more fun, however, to place the document on a Web server, where it becomes part of the World Wide Web and is therefore accessible by anyone with an Internet connection. The next several pages tell you how.

In order to place your page on the Web you will need Internet access, and further, you will need permission to store your document on a computer connected to the Internet. Thus, you will need the address of the server, a username, and a password. You will also need the name of the folder where you are to store your document (typically the public_html folder) as well as the path to that folder. Your instructor will provide this information for you if, in fact, your school is able to offer you this service. If not, you can still do the exercise if you have a computer at home and your Internet Service Provider enables you to store documents on its server.

The procedure to place your document on the Web is straightforward. First you create the document as you did in the previous exercise. However, in addition to (and/or instead of) storing the document locally, you have to upload it to your Web server. This can be done through the Save As command by specifying a remote location corresponding to the address of your Web server. Word will then upload the file from your PC to the server using the **FTP (File Transfer Protocol)** capability that is built into Office 2000. Once the file has been saved on the Web server it may be viewed by anyone with Internet access.

The following exercise takes you through the procedure in detail as we upload Jessica Kinzer's home page to the Web server at the University of Miami. We use *jkinzer* as the username and *homer.bus.miami.edu* as the address of the Web server. (You will, however, have to use your own account.) The combination of the Web server and username provides the address of the page; for example, Jessica's home page can be viewed at *homer.bus.miami.edu/~jkinzer*. Your server may have a different convention. The University of Miami uses the ~ symbol in front of the username to indicate that the complete path on the server to the folder called *jkinzer* need not be specified.

You can upload and maintain a Web page entirely through Office 2000. Occasionally, however, it is advantageous to connect directly to the Web server and execute commands as though you were attached directly to that computer. This is known as a **terminal session** and it is established through a program called **Telnet.** (A terminal, unlike a PC, is a device without memory or disk storage that communicates with a computer via a keyboard and display.) Telnet is illustrated in the last step of the hands-on exercise.

THE INTRANET

The ability to create links to local documents and to view those pages through a Web browser has created an entirely new way to disseminate information. Indeed, many organizations are taking advantage of this capability to develop an Intranet, in which Web pages are placed on a local area network for use within the organization. The documents on an Intranet are available only to individuals with access to the LAN on which the documents are stored. This is in contrast to loading the pages onto a Web server where they can be viewed by anyone with access to the Web.

Publishing Your Home Page

Objective: To use the FTP capability in Microsoft Word to upload an HTML document onto a Web server; to demonstrate Telnet. Use Figure 6.4 as a guide in the exercise.

STEP 1: Add the FTP Location

➤ Start Word. Pull down the **File menu** and click **Open** (or click the **Open button** on the Standard toolbar). If necessary, change to the appropriate drive and folder (e.g., the Exploring Word folder on drive C).

➤ Click the **drop-down arrow** on the Files of type list box, then select **All Files.** Scroll until you can select **Index** (the Web document created in the first exercise), then click **Open** to open the document.

➤ Pull down the **File menu** a second time and click the **Save As command** to display the Save As dialog box. Click the **down arrow** on the Save In list box, then click the command to **Add/Modify FTP Locations** to display the associated dialog box in Figure 6.4a.

➤ Click in the Name of FTP site text box and enter the name of your server. Click the **User option button** then enter your **username.** Do not, however, enter your password if this is not your own computer or else your account will be accessible to anyone else who uses that computer.

➤ Click the **Add button.** Click **OK** to close the Add/Modify FTP Locations dialog box. Your site should appear in the list of FTP sites. The Save As dialog box is open with the name of your server.

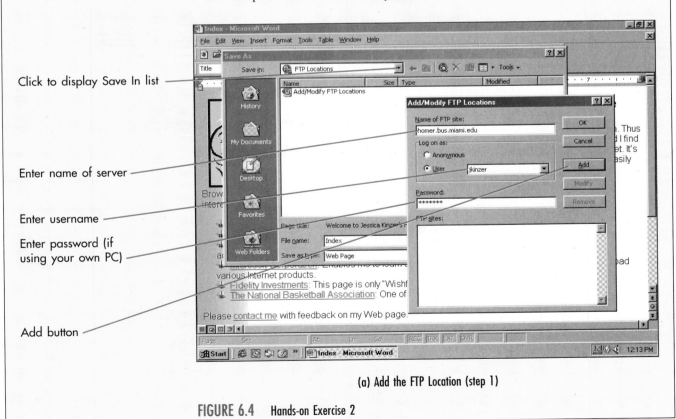

Click to display Save In list

Enter name of server

Enter username

Enter password (if using your own PC)

Add button

(a) Add the FTP Location (step 1)

FIGURE 6.4   Hands-on Exercise 2

STEP 2: Upload (Save) the Document

➤ This step requires an Internet connection. Double click the name of your server from within the Save As dialog box. If necessary, pull down the **File menu,** click **the Save As command,** click the down arrow in the Save In list box, then click the name of your server. Enter your password if prompted.

➤ You must now navigate the precise route on your server to your account. The route to Jessica's folder on our system can be seen in Figure 6.4b.

➤ Your route will be different, but you will wind up in a public_html folder. **Be patient.** It can take several seconds via a modem.

➤ Check that you are saving your home page as **Index** with a **Web Page** file type. Click the **Save button.** Again, you must **be patient** because you are uploading your home page (via a modem if you are connecting from home).

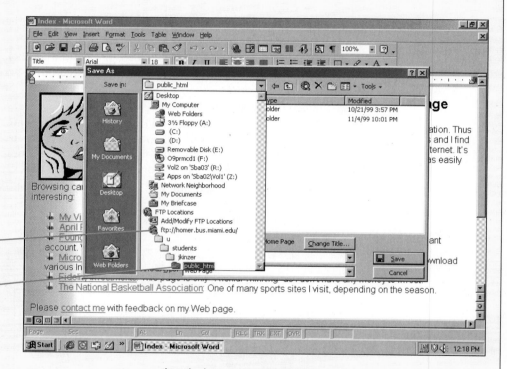

Route to folder is displayed

public_html folder

(b) Upload (Save) Your Home Page (step 2)

FIGURE 6.4   Hands-on Exercise 2 (continued)

FTP FOR WINDOWS

Office 2000 simplifies the process of uploading a page to a Web server by including a basic FTP capability. That is the good news. The bad news is that the capability is limited when compared to stand-alone FTP programs. One advantage of the latter is the ability to display the progress of a file transfer. In Word, for example, you click the Save button to upload a document, then you wait several seconds (or longer) before the system displays any additional information. An FTP program, however, will display the progress of the file transfer as it takes place. See the case study at the end of the chapter for additional information.

STEP 3: View Your Home Page

➤ Start your Internet browser. Click in the Address bar and enter the name of your server followed by your username (preceded by the ~ character); for example, homer.bus.miami.edu/~jkinzer. Your server may follow a different convention.

➤ You should see your home page as shown in Figure 6.4c. You do not have to specify the document name because the browser will automatically display a document called Index.html if that document is present in the public_html folder.

➤ Click the hyperlinks on your page to be sure that they work as intended. (You should have tested the hyperlinks in the first exercise, but we suggest that you try one or two at this time anyway.)

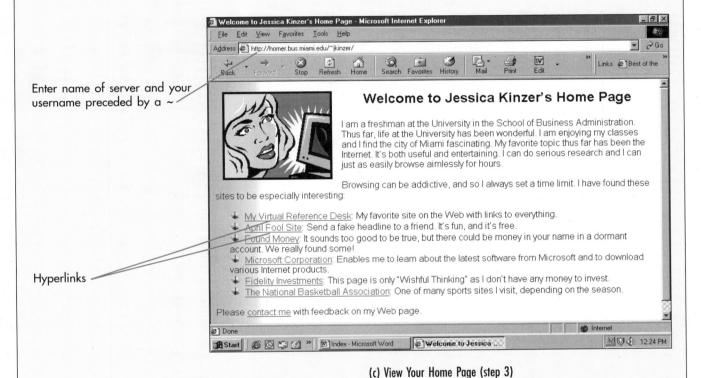

Enter name of server and your username preceded by a ~

Hyperlinks

(c) View Your Home Page (step 3)

FIGURE 6.4   Hands-on Exercise 2 (continued)

HYPERLINKS BEFORE AND AFTER (INTERNET EXPLORER)

Hyperlinks are displayed in different colors depending on whether (or not) the associated page has been displayed. You can change the default colors, however, to suit your personal preference. Pull down the Tools menu, click the Internet Options command to display the Internet Options dialog box, and click the General tab. Click the Colors button, then click the color box next to the visited or unvisited links to display a color palette. Select (click) the desired color, click OK to close the palette, click OK to close the Colors dialog box, then click OK to close the Internet Options dialog box.

STEP 4: Add Your Home Page to a Search Engine Database

➤ Click in the address bar, enter **www.lycos.com/addasite.html,** then press the **enter key.** Scroll down the page until you see the section to add your site as shown in Figure 6.4d.

➤ Enter your URL (the address of your home page) and your e-mail address. Click the button to **Add Site to Lycos** then read the additional information that is displayed on the screen.

➤ Wait a week or two, then see if your Web page has been entered into the Lycos database. Start Internet Explorer, then type **www.lycos.com** to access the Lycos search engine. (You can also access the Lycos search engine by clicking the Search button on the Internet Explorer toolbar.)

➤ Enter your name in the Search for text box at the top of the page, then click the **Go Get It button,** to see if your page is recognized by the Lycos search engine. Try a different search engine and compare the results.

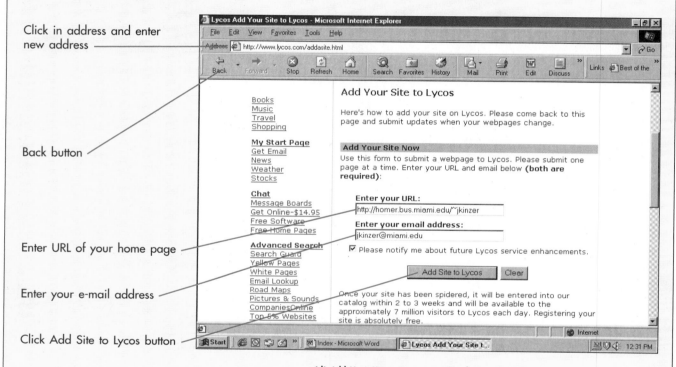

(d) Add Your Home Page to a Search Engine (step 4)

FIGURE 6.4   Hands-on Exercise 2 (continued)

ADD YOUR E-MAIL ADDRESS TO A DIRECTORY

Add your personal information to various directories on the Internet. Click the Address bar, type www.whowhere.com, press the enter key to display the form for one such directory, then enter your name and other information as appropriate. Click the Go Get It button to see whether you are listed. If not, scroll down the page until you can click Adding Your Listing to add your e-mail address to the directory. As with all directories, there are advantages/disadvantages to an unlisted address.

STEP 5: Print the Web Document

➤ Right click the **Back button,** then click the address of your home page. Pull down the **File menu,** click the **File menu** and click the **Print command** to display the dialog box in Figure 6.4e.

➤ Check the box to **Print table of links,** then click **OK** to print your home page.

➤ Look closely at the printed document. You will see the text of your home page (as you did in the previous exercise). You will also see a list of the hyperlinks in your document together with the associated URLs (Web addresses).

➤ Look at the header and/or footer of the printed page. You should see the address of your Web page as well as today's date. If not, you can modify this information through the Page Setup command.

➤ Submit the printed document to your instructor.

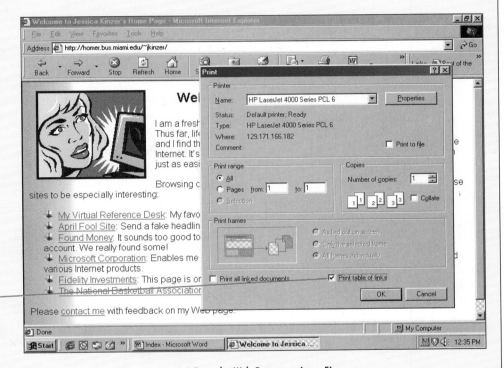

Check box to Print table of links

(e) Print the Web Document (step 5)

FIGURE 6.4   Hands-on Exercise 2 (continued)

THE PAGE SETUP COMMAND

Pull down the File menu and click the Page Setup command to display the Page Setup dialog box that controls the appearance of the printed page. The contents of the header and footer text boxes are especially interesting as they contain information such as the URL of the page and/or the date the page was printed. The precise information that is printed is a function of the code that is entered in the text box; e.g., &u and &d for the URL and date, respectively. Click the Help button (the question mark at the right of the title bar), then point to the Header or Footer text boxes to see the meaning of the various codes, then modify the codes as necessary.

STEP 6: Telnet to the Web Server

➤ Click the **Start button** on the Windows taskbar, click the **Run command** to display the Run dialog box, type **Telnet,** then click **OK** to start Telnet and display the window in Figure 6.4f.

➤ Pull down the **Connect menu,** click the **Remote Server command,** then enter the address of your Web server (homer.bus.miami.edu in our example) in the Host Name text box. Click **Connect.**

➤ Enter your username and password (the same entries you supplied earlier). The system will then display an opening message (e.g., University of Miami on our system), followed by a prompt (homer> on our system). Our Web server uses the Unix operating system.

➤ Type the command **ls −l** to display the files and folders that are stored in your account. You should see the public_html folder (the folder you specified when you uploaded your Web page).

➤ Type the command **cd public_html** to change to this directory, then type the command **pwd** to print the name of the working directory. You should see /u/students/jkinzer/public_html corresponding to the path you specified when you saved your Web page.

➤ Type the command **ls −l** to see the contents of the public_html directory. You should see Index.htm (the name of your home page) and Index files (the folder that contains the graphic elements on that page).

➤ Type **exit** to log out; you will then see a dialog box indicating that the connection to the host is lost. Click **OK.**

➤ Close the Telnet window. Close Internet Explorer. Close Microsoft Word if you do not want to do the next exercise at this time.

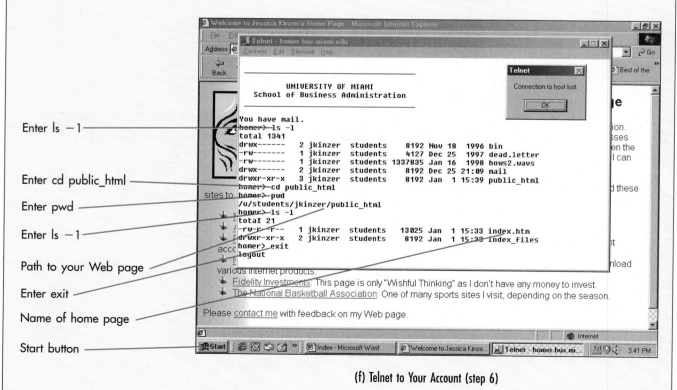

(f) Telnet to Your Account (step 6)

FIGURE 6.4   Hands-on Exercise 2 (continued)

Thus far, you have created a home page and have placed it on a Web server. The next logical task is to extend your home page to reference additional pages that are stored on the server. In other words, you want to create a *Web* site, as opposed to a single home page.

Figure 6.5 displays a Web site for a hypothetical travel agency. The address bar in both Figures 6.5a and 6.5b shows that the document (named default.htm) is stored in the World Wide Travel folder on drive C. (The document would be subsequently renamed to Index.htm prior to uploading it on a Web.) The reference to drive C indicates that the site is being developed on a local machine and has not yet been uploaded to a Web server.

The default.htm document is divided into two vertical *frames,* each of which displays a different document. The left frame is the same in both Figure 6.5a and 6.5b and it contains a series of hyperlinks that are associated with other pages at the site. Click the About the Agency link in the left pane of Figure 6.5a, for example, and you display information about the agency in the right pane. Click the New York Weekend in Figure 6.5b, however, and you display a page describing a trip to New York. Note, too, that each frame has its own vertical scroll bar. The scroll bars function independently of one another. Thus you can click the vertical scroll bar in the left pane to view additional links or you can click the scroll bar in the right pane to see additional information about the agency itself.

The document in the right pane of Figure 6.5a also illustrates the use of a *bookmark* or link to a location within the same document. A bookmark is a useful navigation aid in long documents, as it lets you jump from one place to another (within the same document) without having to manually scroll through the document. Thus, you can click the link that says, "click here for travel tips" and the browser will scroll automatically to the paragraph about travel tips and display that entire paragraph on the screen.

Creation of the Web site will require that you develop separate documents for the agency, as well as for each destination. There is no shortcut because the content of every site is unique and must be created specifically for that site. You can, however, use the *Web Page Wizard* to simplify the creation of the site itself as shown in Figure 6.6 on page 275. The Wizard asks you a series of questions, then it creates the site based on the answers you supply. The Wizard takes care of the navigation and design. The content is up to you.

The Wizard begins by asking for the name of the site and its location (Figure 6.6a). It's easiest to specify a local folder such as the World Wide Travel folder on drive C and then upload the entire folder to the Web server once the site is complete. Next you choose the means of navigation through the site (Figure 6.6b). Vertical frames are the most common but you can also choose horizontal frames or a separate window for each document.

The essence of the Wizard, however, is in the specification of the pages as shown in Figures 6.6c and 6.6d. The Wizard suggests three pages initially (Figure 6.6c), but you can add additional pages or remove the suggested pages. The Wizard gives you the opportunity to rename any of the pages and/or change the order in which they will appear in Figure 6.6d.

You choose the theme for your site in Figure 6.6e. The Wizard then has all of the information it needs and it creates the default page in Figure 6.6f. This page is much simpler than the completed site we saw in Figure 6.5. Nevertheless, the Wizard has proved invaluable because it has created the site and established the navigation. It's now your task to complete and/or enhance the individual pages. The ease with which you create the documents in Figure 6.6 depends on your proficiency in Microsoft Word. Even if you have only limited experience with Microsoft Word, however, our instructions are sufficiently detailed that you should be able to complete our next exercise with little difficulty.

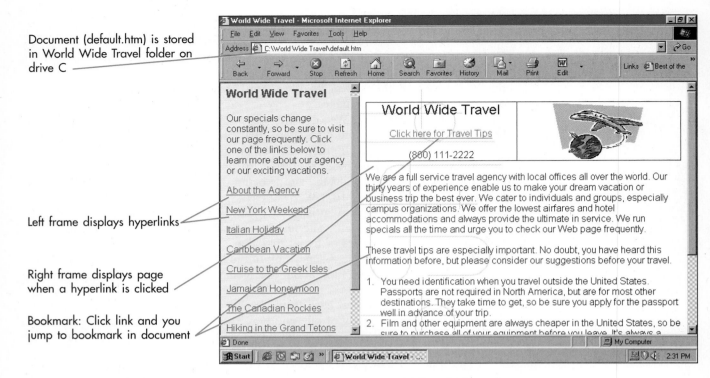

Document (default.htm) is stored in World Wide Travel folder on drive C

Left frame displays hyperlinks

Right frame displays page when a hyperlink is clicked

Bookmark: Click link and you jump to bookmark in document

(a) About the Agency Page

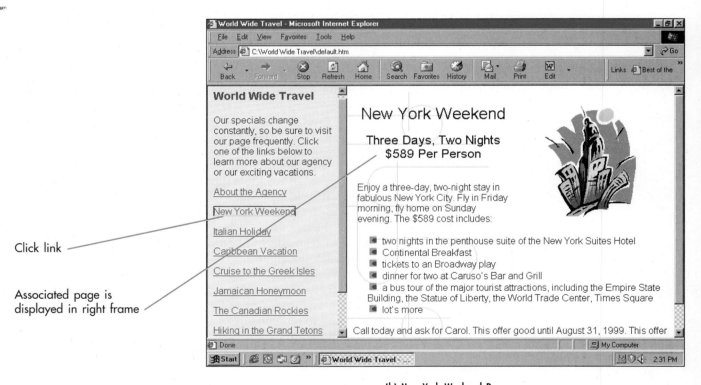

Click link

Associated page is displayed in right frame

(b) New York Weekend Page

FIGURE 6.5   A Web Site

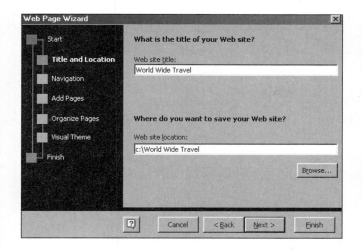

(a) Create the Site

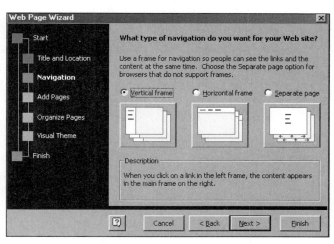

(b) Choose the Navigation

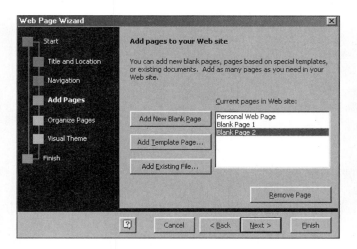

(c) Add the Pages

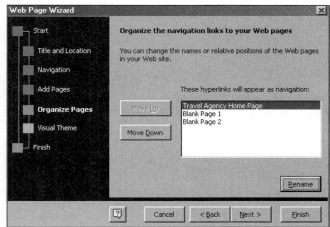

(d) Organize the Pages

(e) Choose the Theme

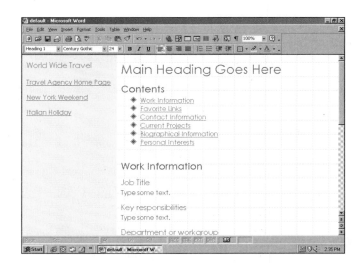

(f) The Initial Site

FIGURE 6.6   The Web Page Wizard

Creating a Web Site

Objective: To use the Web Page Wizard to create a Web site; to facilitate navigation within a document by creating a bookmark. Use Figure 6.7.

STEP 1: The Web Page Wizard

➤ Start Word. Pull down the **File menu,** click the **New command** to display the New dialog box, then click the **Web Pages tab.** Double click the **Web Page Wizard** to start the Wizard and display the opening screen. Click **Next.**

➤ Enter **World Wide Travel** as the title of the Web site. Choose a separate folder to hold all of the documents for the site. We suggest **C:\World Wide Travel** as shown in Figure 6.7a. Click **Next.**

➤ The option button for **Vertical frame** as the means of navigation is already selected. Click **Next.**

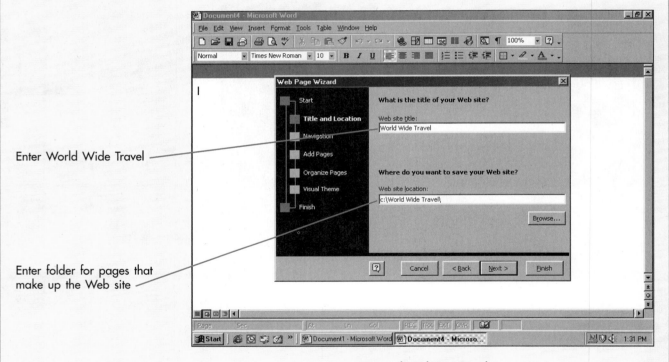

Enter World Wide Travel

Enter folder for pages that make up the Web site

(a) Start the Web Page Wizard

FIGURE 6.7   Hands-on Exercise 3

WIZARDS AND TEMPLATES

Microsoft Word 2000 includes wizards and templates for a variety of documents. A template is a partially completed document that contains formatting, text, and/or graphics. A wizard introduces additional flexibility by first asking you a series of questions, then creating a template based on your answers.

STEP 2: Specify the Pages

➤ The Web Page Wizard creates a site with three pages: Personal Web Page, Blank Page 1, and Blank Page 2. You can, however, add, remove, and/or rename these pages as appropriate for your site.

➤ Select (click) **Personal Web page** and click the **Remove Page button.** Click the **Add New Blank Page button** to add Blank Page 3. Click **Next** to display the screen in Figure 6.7b.

➤ Select **Blank Page 1** and click the **Rename button** (or simply double click Blank Page 1) to display the Rename Hyperlink dialog box. Enter **About the Agency** and click **OK.** Rename Blank Page 2 and Blank Page 3 to **New York Weekend** and **Italian Holiday,** respectively.

➤ Check that the order of pages is what you intend (About the Agency, New York Weekend, and Italian Holiday). Click **Next.**

➤ Click the **Browse Themes button** and choose a suitable theme. We chose **Capsules.** Click **OK.** Click **Next.** Click **Finish.**

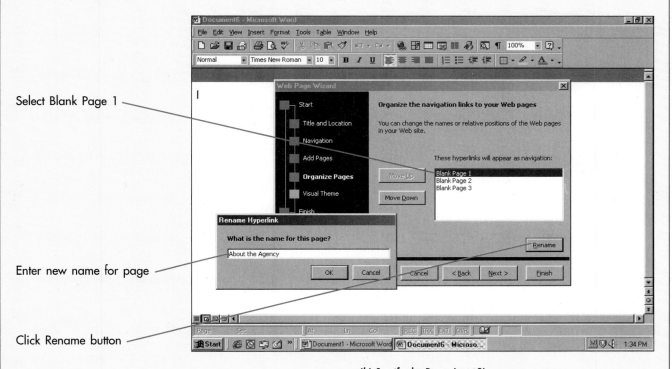

(b) Specify the Pages (step 2)

FIGURE 6.7   Hands-on Exercise 3 (continued)

CHANGING THE WEB SITE

The Web Page Wizard is intended to get you up and running as quickly as possible. It takes you through all of the steps to create a Web site and it builds the appropriate links to all of the pages on that site. You will, however, need to modify the site after it has been created by adding text, adding new links, and/or deleting or modifying existing links.

STEP 3: Modify the Default Page

➤ You should see the default page for the World Wide Travel site as shown in Figure 6.7c. Our figure, however, already reflects the changes that you will make to the default page. Close the Frames toolbar.

➤ Click and drag to select **World Wide Travel.** Click the **Bold button.** Click to the right of the text to deselect it. Press the **enter key** twice. Enter the text shown in Figure 6.7c.

➤ Click the **Save button** to save the changes to the default page. Pull down the **File menu** and click the **Close command** to close the default page but remain in Microsoft Word.

➤ We will reopen the default page in Internet Explorer later in the exercise in order to view the page as it will appear to others.

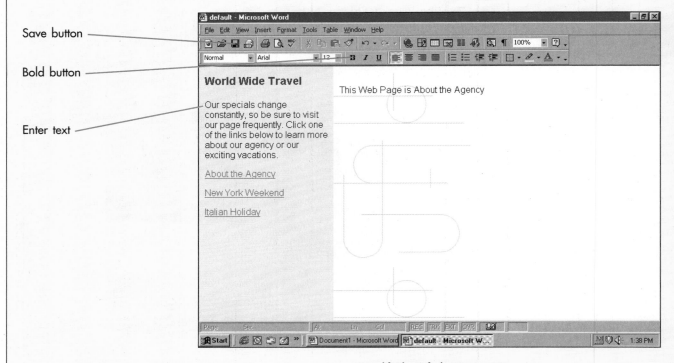

(c) Modify the Default Page (step 3)

FIGURE 6.7   Hands-on Exercise 3 (continued)

OBTAINING A PASSPORT

You can't obtain a passport online, but you can get all of the information you need. Go to travel.state.gov, the home page of the Bureau of Consular Affairs in the U.S. Department of State, then scroll down the page until you can click the link to Passport Information. You will be able to download an actual passport application with detailed instructions including a list of the documents you need to supply. You can also access a nationwide list of where to apply.

STEP 4: Open the Agency Page

➤ You should still be in Microsoft Word. Click the **Open button** on the Standard toolbar to display the Open dialog box. Click the **down arrow** on the Look In text box, then double click the **World Wide Travel folder** on **drive C** (the location you specified when you created the Web site).

➤ Double click the **About the Agency document** that currently consists of a single line of text. Click at the end of this sentence and press the **enter key.**

➤ Pull down the **Insert menu** and click the **File command** to display the Insert File dialog box. Change to the **Exploring Word folder** and insert the **Text for Travel document.**

➤ Your document should match the document in Figure 6.7d. Click and drag to select the original sentence as shown in the figure. Press the **Del key** to delete this sentence. Delete the blank line as well. Save the document.

Open button

Click and drag to select the original sentence, then press the Del key

Click here and insert the Text for Travel document

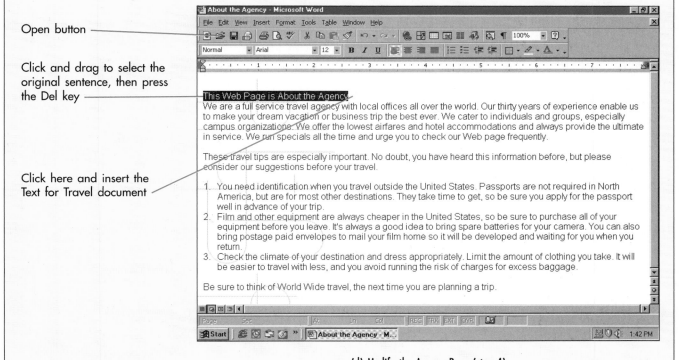

(d) Modify the Agency Page (step 4)

FIGURE 6.7   Hands-on Exercise 3 (continued)

THE WORLD WIDE TRAVEL FOLDER

A Web site consists of multiple Web pages, each of which is saved as a separate document. Each document in turn may contain graphical elements that are also saved separately. Thus the World Wide Travel folder contains an About the Agency document that in turn references graphic elements in its own folder. The other pages (e.g., Italian Holiday and New York Weekend) have their own folders. The World Wide Travel folder also contains additional documents such as a default page and a TOC (table of contents) frame that is displayed in the left pane.

STEP 5: Test the Navigation

➤ Start your Web browser. Pull down the **File menu** and click the **Open command** to display the Open dialog box. Click the **Browse button,** then select the drive (e.g., drive C) and folder (e.g., World Wide Travel).

➤ Select (click) the **default** document, then click **OK** to display the document in Figure 6.7e. You should see the Web page that was created earlier, except that you are viewing it in your browser rather than Microsoft Word. The Address bar reflects the local address of the document (C:\World Wide Travel\default.htm).

➤ Click the link to **New York Weekend** to display this page in the right pane. The page is not yet complete, but the link works properly. Click the link to **Italian Holiday** to display this page. Again, the page is not complete, but the link works properly.

➤ Click the link to **About the Agency** to access this page.

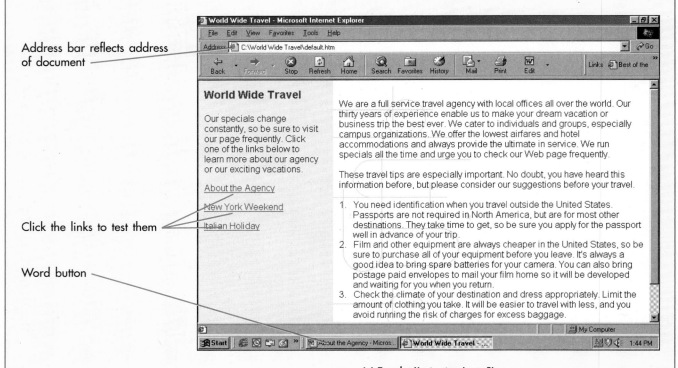

(e) Test the Navigation (step 5)

FIGURE 6.7   Hands-on Exercise 3 (continued)

PROTOTYPING

Prototyping enables an end user to experience the "look and feel" of a site before the site has been completed. The user is shown the opening document, and is provided with a set of links to partially completed documents. The user gets the sense of the eventual site even though the latter is far from finished. Prototyping also provides valuable feedback to the developer, who is able to make the necessary adjustments before any extensive work has been done.

STEP 6: Insert the Clip Art

➤ Click the **Word button** on the Windows taskbar. The About the Agency document should still be open. Press **Ctrl+Home** to move to the beginning of the document. Press the **enter** key to add a blank line.

➤ Click the **Insert Table button** on the Standard toolbar, then click and drag to select a one-by-two grid. Release the mouse. Click in the left cell. Type **World Wide Travel.**

➤ Press the **enter key** twice. Type the sentence **Click here for Travel Tips** (we will create the link later), press the **enter key** twice, and enter the agency's phone number, **(800) 111-2222.**

➤ Select all three lines and click the **Center button.** Choose a suitable point size. We suggest 18 point for the first line and 12 point for the other text.

➤ Click in the right pane. Pull down the **Insert menu,** click **Picture,** then click **Clip Art** to display the Insert Clip Art dialog box in Figure 6.7f.

➤ If necessary, click the **Pictures tab** and select (click) the **Maps category.** Click the **Airplane and Globe** (or a different image if you prefer), then click the **Insert Clip button** on the shortcut menu. Close the Insert Clip Art dialog box.

➤ The picture should appear in the document. Click the picture to select it, then click and drag the sizing handle to make the picture smaller.

➤ Click the **Internet Explorer button** on the Windows taskbar. Click the **Refresh button** on the Internet Explorer toolbar to display the new version of the page.

➤ If necessary, return to the Word document to resize the picture. Save the document, then return to Internet Explorer. Remember to click the **Refresh button** in Internet Explorer to see the most recent version.

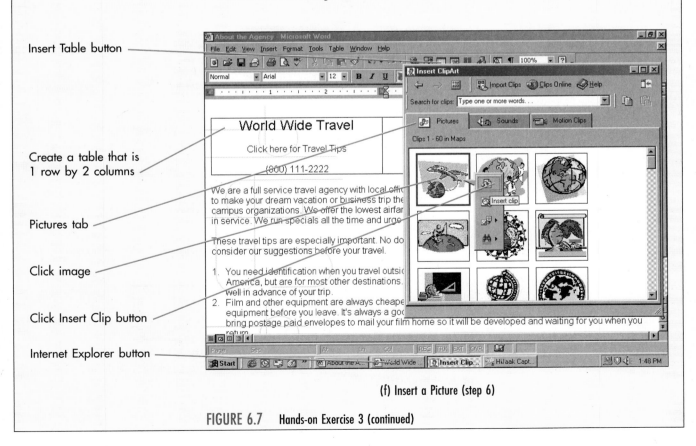

(f) Insert a Picture (step 6)

FIGURE 6.7   Hands-on Exercise 3 (continued)

STEP 7: Insert a Bookmark

➤ Return to the Agency page in Microsoft Word in order to create a bookmark.

➤ To create the bookmark:

- Click at the beginning of the second paragraph. Pull down the **Insert menu** and click **Bookmark** to display the Bookmark dialog box.

- Enter **TravelTips** (spaces are not allowed) as the name of the bookmark, then click the **Add button** to add the bookmark and close the dialog box.

➤ To create the link to the bookmark:

- Click and drag the text **Click here for Travel Tips** as shown in Figure 6.7g, then click the **Insert Hyperlink button** to display the dialog box.

- Click the icon for **Place in This Document,** click the **plus sign** next to Bookmarks, then click **TravelTips.** Click **OK.**

➤ The sentence, Click here for Travel Tips, should appear as underlined text to indicate that it is now a hyperlink. Save the document.

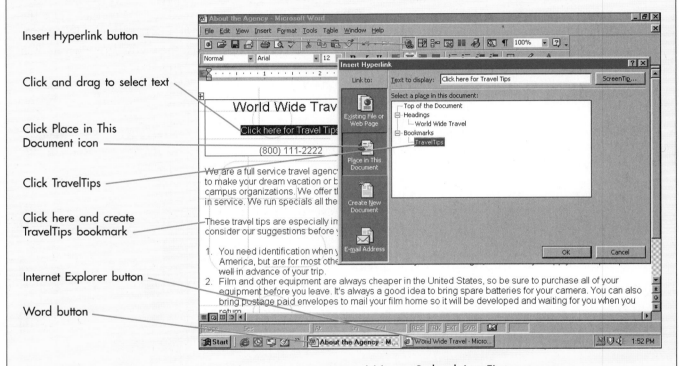

Insert Hyperlink button

Click and drag to select text

Click Place in This Document icon

Click TravelTips

Click here and create TravelTips bookmark

Internet Explorer button

Word button

(g) Insert a Bookmark (step 7)

FIGURE 6.7   Hands-on Exercise 3 (continued)

THE TOP OF DOCUMENT BOOKMARK

Simplify the navigation within a long page with a link to the top of the document. Press Ctrl+End to move to the bottom of the document (one of several places where you can insert this link), then click the Insert Hyperlink button to display the Insert Hyperlink dialog box. Click the icon for Place in This Document, click Top of the Document from the list of bookmarks (Word creates this bookmark automatically), then click OK. You will see the underlined text, Top of Document, as a hyperlink.

STEP 8: View the Completed Page

➤ Click the **Internet Explorer button** on the Windows taskbar. Click the **Refresh button** to view the completed document as shown in Figure 6.7h.

➤ If necessary, click the link to **About the Agency** to display the completed Agency page. There is a scroll bar in the right frame, because you cannot see the entire agency page at one time. Note, however, that you do not see a scroll bar in the left frame because this page can be seen in its entirety.

➤ Click in the right pane. Pull down the **File menu** and click the **Print command** to display the Print dialog box in Figure 6.7h. Click the option button to print **Only the selected frame** but check the box to **Print all linked documents** (which effectively prints every document in the site).

➤ Click **OK,** then submit the printed pages to your instructor as proof that you did this exercise.

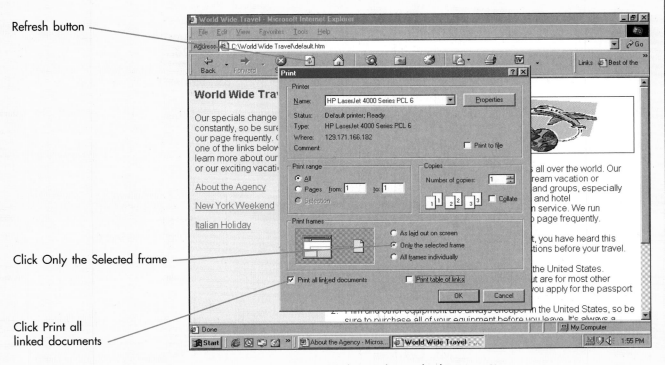

Refresh button

Click Only the Selected frame

Click Print all linked documents

(h) View the Completed Site (step 8)

FIGURE 6.7   Hands-on Exercise 3 (continued)

CHANGE THE FONT SIZE

Internet Explorer enables you to view and/or print a page in one of five font settings (smallest, small, medium, large, and largest). Pull down the View menu, click the Text Size command, then choose the desired font size. The setting pertains to both the displayed page as well as the printed page.

All Web documents are written in HyperText Markup Language (HTML), a language that consists of codes (or tags) that format a document for display on the World Wide Web. The easiest way to create an HTML document is through Microsoft Word. You start Word in the usual fashion and enter the text of the document with basic formatting. Then you pull down the File menu and click the Save As Web Page command.

Microsoft Word does the rest, generating the HTML tags that are needed to create the document. The resulting document can be modified with respect to its content and/or appearance just like an ordinary Word document. The Insert Hyperlink command is used to link a document to other pages. Graphics may come from a variety of sources and are inserted into a document through the Insert Picture command. The Format Theme command applies a professional design to the document

After a Web document has been created, it can be placed on a server or local area network so that other people will be able to access it. This, in turn, requires you to check with your professor or system administrator to obtain the necessary username and password. Once you have this information, you can use the FTP (File Transfer Protocol) capability within Office 2000 to upload your page. Even if your page is not placed on the Web, you can still view it locally on your PC through a Web browser.

The Web Page Wizard simplifies the creation of a multipage site. The Wizard asks you a series of questions, then it creates the site based on the answers you supply. The Wizard takes care of the navigation and design. The content is up to you.

KEY WORDS AND CONCEPTS

Bookmark
File Transfer Protocol
  (FTP)
Frame
Graphics
Home page
HTML
Hyperlink
Hypertext Markup
  Language (HTML)

Insert Bookmark
  command
Insert Hyperlink
  command
Insert Picture
  command
Internet Explorer
Intranet
Save As Web Page
  command

Server
Source code
Tag
Telnet
Terminal session
Theme
Web Page Wizard
Web site

MULTIPLE CHOICE

1. Which of the following requires you to enter HTML tags explicitly in order to create a Web document?

(a) A text editor such as the Notepad accessory

(b) Microsoft Word 2000

(c) Both (a) and (b)

(d) Neither (a) nor (b)

2. What is the easiest way to switch back and forth between Word and Internet Explorer, given that both are open?
   (a) Click the appropriate button on the Windows taskbar
   (b) Click the Start button, click Programs, then choose the appropriate program
   (c) Minimize all applications to display the Windows desktop, then double click the icon for the appropriate application
   (d) All of the above are equally convenient

3. When should you click the Refresh button on the Internet Explorer toolbar?
   (a) Whenever you visit a new Web site
   (b) Whenever you return to a Web site within a session
   (c) Whenever you view a document on a corporate Intranet
   (d) Whenever you return to a document that has changed during the session

4. How do you view the HTML tags for a Web document from Internet Explorer?
   (a) Pull down the View menu and select the Source command
   (b) Pull down the File menu, click the Save As command, and specify HTML as the file type
   (c) Click the Web Page Preview button on the Standard toolbar
   (d) All of the above

5. Internet Explorer can display an HTML page that is stored on:
   (a) A local area network
   (b) A Web server
   (c) Drive A or drive C of a stand-alone PC
   (d) All of the above

6. How do you save a Word document as a Web page?
   (a) Pull down the Tools menu and click the Convert to Web Page command
   (b) Pull down the File menu and click the Save As Web Page command
   (c) Both (a) and (b)
   (d) Neither (a) nor (b)

7. How do you upload a Web page onto a Web server from within Microsoft Word?
   (a) Use the Web Page Wizard
   (b) Specify the FTP location from within the Save As dialog box
   (c) Use the Upload Server Wizard
   (d) It cannot be done

8. Which of the following requires an Internet connection?
   (a) Using Internet Explorer to view a document that is stored locally
   (b) Using Internet Explorer to view the Microsoft home page
   (c) Both (a) and (b)
   (d) Neither (a) nor (b)

9. Which of the following requires an Internet connection?
   (a) Telnet
   (b) FTP
   (c) Both (a) and (b)
   (d) Neither (a) nor (b)

10. Assume that you have an account on the server, www.myserver.edu, under the username, jdoe. What is the most likely Web address to view your home page?
    (a) www.myserver.edu
    (b) www.jdoe.edu
    (c) www.myserver.edu/~jdoe
    (d) www.myserver.edu.jdoe.html

11. The Insert Hyperlink command can reference:
    (a) An e-mail address
    (b) A bookmark
    (c) A Web page
    (d) All of the above

12. The Format Theme command:
    (a) Is required in order to save a Word document as a Web page
    (b) Applies a uniform design to the links and other elements within a document
    (c) Both (a) and (b)
    (d) Neither (a) nor (b)

13. The Web Page Wizard creates a default Web site and enables you to specify the:
    (a) Means of navigation such as vertical or horizontal frames
    (b) The number of pages (links) that found on the default page
    (c) The theme (design) of the Web site
    (d) All of the above

14. The Web Page Wizard creates a site with a Personal Web page, Blank Page 1, and Blank Page 2, but you can
    (a) Delete any of these pages
    (b) Add new pages to those it creates for you
    (c) Rename any pages it supplies
    (d) All of the above

15. Assume that the Web Page Wizard was used to create a site called Personal Computer Store, and further, that the site contains links to four separate pages, each of which contains one or more graphics. Which of the following is true?
    (a) You can expect to see a Personal Computer Store folder on your system
    (b) The Personal Computer Store folder will contain a separate document for each of the four pages
    (c) The Personal Computer Store folder will contain a separate folder for each of the four pages
    (d) All of the above

ANSWERS

1. a	**6.** b	**11.** d
2. a	**7.** b	**12.** b
3. d	**8.** b	**13.** d
4. a	**9.** c	**14.** d
5. d	**10.** c	**15.** d

PRACTICE WITH MICROSOFT WORD

1. New York Weekend: Create the World Wide Travel Web site as described in the third hands-on exercise. Test the site to be sure that the navigation works. The About the Agency page is complete, but the New York Weekend and Italian Holiday documents exist only as one-sentence documents. Open either document and complete the page. Our suggestion for the New York weekend is shown in Figure 6.8, but feel free to improve on our page. Print the additional page(s) and submit them to your instructor as proof you did this exercise.

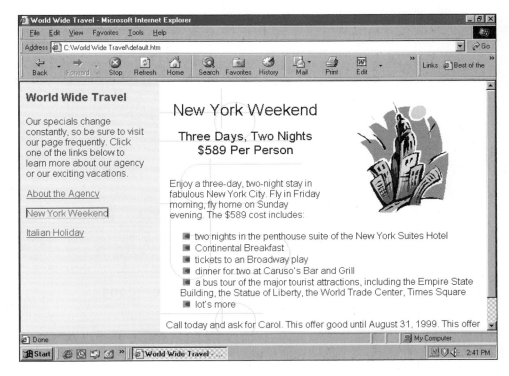

FIGURE 6.8   New York Weekend (Exercise 1)

2. Adding an External Link: Open the default.htm document in the World Wide Travel folder and add the link to the State Department page (travel.state.gov) as shown in Figure 6.9. This is a real page and it contains a wealth of information for the would-be traveler, including information on how to obtain a passport. Print the document called TOC Frame that was created for you by the Web Page Wizard to prove to your instructor that you have added the additional link.

3. Frequently Asked Questions: Pull down the File menu, click the New command, and click the Web Pages tab to display a dialog box containing several templates for use as Web pages. Open the Frequently Asked Questions template, and use it to create a document with questions and answers about any subject that interests you. You could, for example, create a document with questions about travel, then add a link to this document to your World Wide Travel site. Print the completed document for your instructor as proof you did this exercise. Be sure to explore the bookmarks on the page that are created automatically within the template.

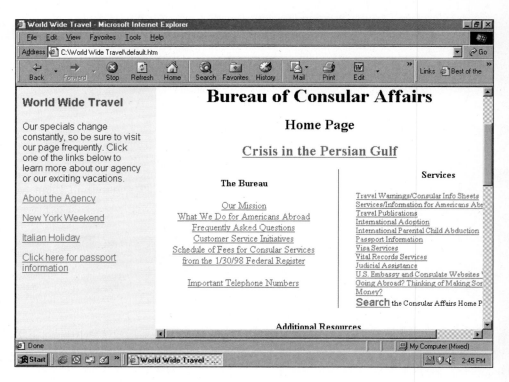

FIGURE 6.9   Adding an External Link (Exercise 2)

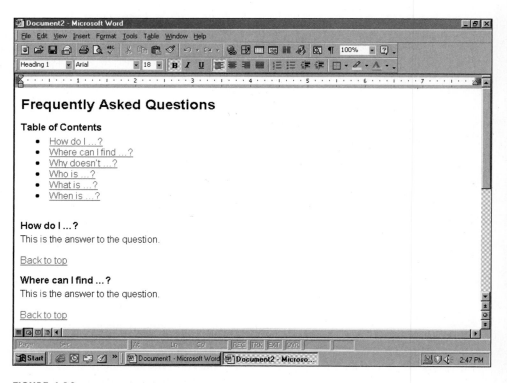

FIGURE 6.10   Frequently Asked Questions (Exercise 3)

4. Milestones in Communications: The use of hyperlinks enables the creation of interactive documents such as the document in Figure 6.11. Open the Chapter 6 Practice 4 document in the Exploring Word folder, a document with very little formatting, pull down the Format menu, click the AutoFormat command to display the AutoFormat dialog box, verify that the Auto-Format option is selected, and click OK.

Once the document has been formatted, you can change the Body Text style and/or the Heading 1 style as you see fit. The most important task, however, is to create the hyperlinks at the beginning of the document that let you branch to the various headings within the document. You also need to insert a hyperlink after each article to return to the top of the document. The result is an interactive document that lets the user browse through the document in any sequence you choose. Complete the formatting, save the document as a Web page, then view it in a Web browser. Print the completed document for your instructor.

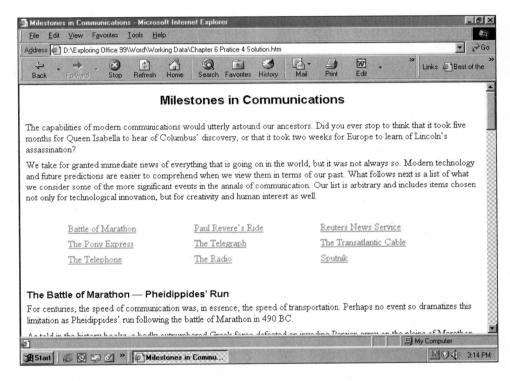

FIGURE 6.11   Milestones in Communications (Exercise 4)

CASE STUDIES

Designer Home Pages

Everyone has a personal list of favorite Web sites, but have you ever thought seriously about what makes an attractive Web page? Is an attractive page the same as a useful page? Try to develop a set of guidelines for a designer to follow as he or she creates a Web site, then incorporate these guidelines into a brief report for your instructor. Support your suggestions by referring to specific Web pages that you think qualify for your personal "Best (Worst) of the Web" award.

Employment Opportunities

The Internet abounds with employment opportunities, help-wanted listings, and places to post your résumé. Your home page reflects your skills and experience to the entire world, and represents an incredible opportunity never before available to college students. You can encourage prospective employers to visit your home page, and make contact with hundreds more companies than would otherwise be possible. Update your home page to include a link to your résumé, and then surf the Net to find places to register it.

Front Page

Microsoft Word 2000 is an excellent way to begin creating Web documents. It is only a beginning, however, and there are many specialty programs with significantly more capability. One such product is Front Page, a product aimed at creating a Web site as opposed to isolated documents. Search the Microsoft Web site for information on Front Page, then summarize your findings in a short note to your instructor. Be sure to include information on capabilities that are included in Front Page which are not found in Word.

UNIX Permissions

As a developer, you need to be able to log on to your account, to add or modify documents. You also want others to be able to go to your URL to view the page, but you want to prevent the world at large from being able to modify the documents. This is controlled on the Web server through the operating system by setting appropriate permissions for each document. Return to the second hands-on exercise that described how to Telnet to a Web server and view the associated documents on that server. Look to the left of the listed files and note the various letters that indicate different levels of permission for different users.

FTP for Windows

Use your favorite search engine to locate an FTP program. There are many such programs available, and many permit a free trial period. Locate a specific program, then compare its capabilities to the FTP capability in Office 2000. Summarize your findings in a short note to your instructor.

Forms in HTML Documents

Many Web pages require you to enter information into a text box, then submit that information to a Web server. Every time you use a search engine, for example, you enter key words into a form that transmits your request to the search engine. Other common forms include a guest book where you register as having visited the site. Including a form on a page is not difficult but it does require additional knowledge of HTML. Use an appropriate search engine to see what you can find about forms, then summarize your results in a brief note to your instructor.

chapter 7

THE EXPERT USER: WORKGROUPS, FORMS, MASTER DOCUMENTS, AND MACROS

OBJECTIVES

After reading this chapter you will be able to:

1. Describe how to highlight editing changes in a document, and how to review, accept, or reject those changes.
2. Save multiple versions of a document and/or save a document with password protection.
3. Create and modify a form containing text fields, check boxes, and a drop-down list.
4. Create and modify a table; perform calculations within a table.
5. Arrange (sort) the rows in a table in ascending or descending sequence according to the value of a specific column in the table.
6. Create a master document; add and/or modify subdocuments.
7. Explain how macros facilitate the execution of repetitive tasks; record and run a macro; view and edit the statements in a simple macro.
8. Use the Copy and Paste commands to duplicate an existing macro; modify the copied macro to create an entirely new macro.

OVERVIEW

This chapter introduces several capabilities that will make you a true expert in Microsoft Word. The features go beyond the needs of the typical student and extend to capabilities that you will appreciate in the workplace, as you work with others on a collaborative project. We begin with a discussion of workgroup editing, whereby suggested revisions from one or more individuals can be stored electronically within a document. This enables the original author to review each suggestion individually before it is incorporated into the document, and further, allows multiple people to work on a document in collaboration with one another.

The forms feature is covered as a means to facilitate data entry. Forms are ideal for documents that are used repetitively, where much of the text is constant but where there is variation in specific places (fields) within the document. The chapter also extends the earlier discussion on tables to include both sorting and calculations within a table, giving a Word document the power of a simple spreadsheet. We also describe the creation of a master document, a special type of structure that references one or more subdocuments, each of which is saved under a different name. A master document is useful when many individuals work on a common project, with each person assigned to a different task within the project.

The chapter ends with a discussion of macros, a technique that lets you automate the execution of any type of repetitive task. We create a simple macro to insert your name into a document, then we expand that macro to create a title page for any document. As always, the hands-on exercises enable you to implement the conceptual material at the computer.

WORKGROUPS

As a student, you have the final say in the content of your documents. In the workplace, however, it's common for several people to work on the same document. You may create the initial draft, then submit your work to a supervisor who suggests various changes and revisions. Word facilitates this process by enabling the revisions to be stored electronically within the document. The revisions can come from a single individual or from several persons working together on a project team or workgroup.

Consider, for example, Figure 7.1, which displays two different versions of a document. Figure 7.1a contains the original document with suggested revisions, whereas Figure 7.1b shows the finished document after the changes have been made. The persons who entered the revisions could have made the changes directly in the document, but decided instead to give the original author the opportunity to accept or reject each change individually. The suggestions are entered into the Word document and appear on screen and/or the printed page, just as they might appear if they had been marked with pencil and paper.

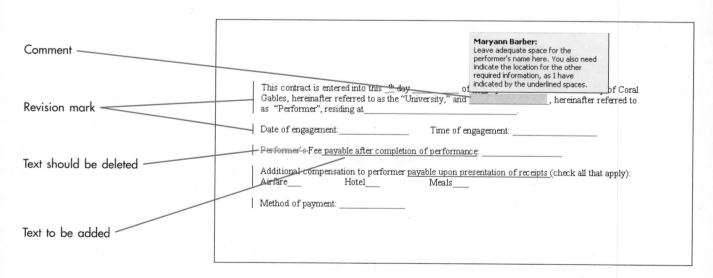

(a) Suggested Changes

FIGURE 7.1   Workgroup Editing

```
This contract is entered into this __th day _____ of 19__, by and between the University of
Coral Gables, hereinafter referred to as the "University," and _____,
hereinafter referred to as "Performer", residing at _____.

Date of engagement: _____        Time of engagement: _____

Fee payable after completion of performance: _____

Additional compensation to performer payable upon presentation of receipts (check all that apply):
Airfare ___          Hotel ___          Meals ___

Method of payment: _____
```

(b) Revised Document

FIGURE 7.1   Workgroup Editing (continued)

The notation is simple and intuitive. A ***revision mark*** (a vertical line outside the left margin) signifies a change (an addition or deletion) has been made at that point in the document. A line through existing text indicates that the text should be deleted, whereas text that is underlined is to be added. The suggestions of multiple reviewers appear in different colors, with each reviewer assigned a different color. Yellow highlighting denotes a comment indicating that the reviewer has added a descriptive note without making a specific change. The comment appears on the screen when the cursor is moved over the highlighted text. (Comments can be printed at the end of a document.)

The review process is straightforward. The initial document is sent for review to one or more individuals, who enter their changes through tools on the ***Reviewing toolbar*** or through the ***Track Changes command*** in the Tools menu. The author of the original document receives the corrected document, then uses the ***Accept and Review Changes command*** to review the document and implement the suggested changes.

Versions

The Save command is one of the most basic in Microsoft Office. Each time you execute the command, the contents in memory are saved to disk under the designated filename, and the previous contents of the file are erased. What if, however, you wanted to retain the previous version of the file in addition to the current version that was just saved? You could use the Save As command to create a second file. It's easier to use the ***Versions command*** in the File menu because it lets you save multiple versions of a document in a single file.

The existence of multiple versions is transparent in that the latest version is opened automatically when you open the file at the start of a session. You can, however, review previous versions to see the changes that were made. Word displays the date and time each version was saved as well as the name of the person who saved each version.

Word provides two different levels of ***password protection*** in conjunction with saving a document. You can establish one password to open the document and a different password to modify it. A password can contain any combination of letters, numbers, and symbols, and can be 15 characters long. Passwords are case-sensitive.

Forms are ubiquitous in the workplace and our society. You complete a form, for example, when you apply for a job or open any type of account. The form may be electronic and completed online, or it may exist as a printed document. All forms, however, are designed for some type of data entry. Microsoft Word lets you create a special type of document called a *form,* which allows the user to enter data in specific places, but precludes editing the document in any other way. The process requires you to create the form and save it to disk, where it serves as a template for future documents. Then, when you need to enter data for a specific document, you open the original form, enter the data, and save the completed form as a new document.

Figure 7.2 displays two additional versions of the document shown earlier in Figure 7.1. The form in Figure 7.2a does not contain specific data, but it does contain the text of a document (a contract in this example) that is to be completed by the user. The form also contains shaded entries, or *fields,* that represent the locations where the user will enter the data. To complete the form, the user presses the Tab key to go from one field to the next and enters data as appropriate. Then, when all fields have been entered, the form is printed to produce the finished document (a contract for a specific event) in Figure 7.2b. The data that was entered into the various fields in Figure 7.2a appears as regular text in Figure 7.2b.

The form is created as a regular document with the various fields added through tools on the *Forms toolbar.* Word enables you to create three types of fields—text boxes, check boxes, and drop-down list boxes. A *text field* is the most common and is used to enter any type of text. The length of a text field can be set exactly; for example, to two positions for the day in the first line of the document. The length can also be left unspecified, in which case the field will expand to the exact number of positions that are required as the data are entered. A *check box,* as the name implies, consists of a box, which is checked or not. The Airfare and Hotel boxes are checked in Figure 7.2b, whereas the Meals box is left unchecked. A *drop-down list box* enables the user to choose from one of several existing entries.

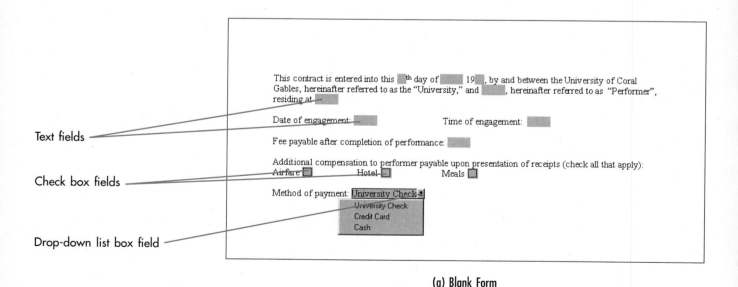

(a) Blank Form

FIGURE 7.2   Forms

This contract is entered into this 30ᵗʰ day of March 1999, by and between the University of Coral Gables, hereinafter referred to as the "University," and Benjamin Lee, hereinafter referred to as "Performer", residing at 1000 Main Street, Orlando, FL 32835

Date of engagement: December 20, 1999   Time of engagement: 8:00PM

Fee payable after completion of performance: $1,000 (One thousand dollars)

Additional compensation to performer payable upon presentation of receipts (check all that apply):
Airfare ☒   Hotel ☒   Meals ☐

Method of payment: University Check

Data appears as regular text after it is entered

(b) Completed Form

FIGURE 7.2   Forms (continued)

After the form is created, it is protected to prevent further modification other than data entry. Our next exercise has you open an existing document, review changes to that document as suggested by members of a workgroup, accept the changes as appropriate, then convert the revised document into a form for data entry.

HANDS-ON EXERCISE 1

Workgroups and Forms

Objective: To review the editing comments within a document and revise a document based on those comments; to create a form containing text fields, check boxes, and a drop-down list. Use Figure 7.3 as a guide in the exercise.

STEP 1: Display the Forms and Reviewing Toolbars

➤ Start Word. If Word is already open, pull down the **File menu** and click the **Close command** to close any open documents.

➤ Point to any visible toolbar, click the **right mouse button** to display a context-sensitive menu, then click the **Customize command** to display the Customize dialog box as shown in Figure 7.3a.

➤ If necessary, click the **Toolbars tab** in the Customize dialog box. The boxes for the Standard and Formatting toolbars should be checked, as these toolbars are displayed by default.

➤ Check the boxes to display the **Forms** and **Reviewing toolbars** as shown in Figure 7.3a. Click the **close button** to close the Customize dialog box.

➤ Click and drag the **move handle** and/or the title bar to arrange the toolbars as you see fit.

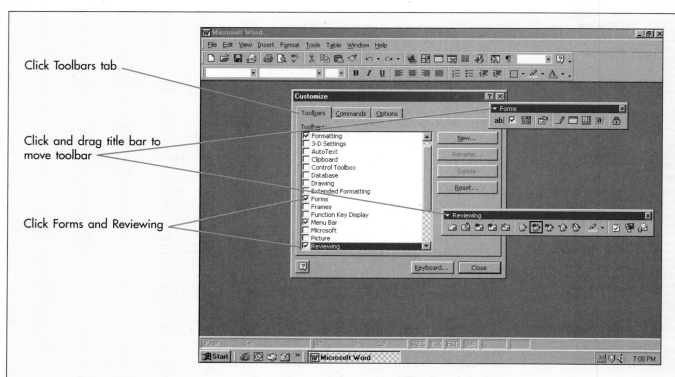

Click Toolbars tab

Click and drag title bar to
move toolbar

Click Forms and Reviewing

(a) Display the Forms and Reviewing Toolbars (step 1)

FIGURE 7.3   Hands-on Exercise 1

DOCKED VERSUS FLOATING TOOLBARS

A toolbar is either docked along an edge of a window or floating within
the window. To move a docked toolbar, click and drag the move handle
(the vertical line that appears at the left of the toolbar) to a new position.
To move a floating toolbar click and drag its title bar—if you drag a floating toolbar to the edge of the window, it becomes a docked toolbar and
vice versa. You can also change the shape of a floating toolbar by dragging any border in the direction you want to go. And finally, you can double click the background of any toolbar to toggle between a floating toolbar and a docked (fixed) toolbar.

STEP 2: Highlight Changes

➤ Open the document called **Contract** in the **Exploring Word folder** as shown
in Figure 7.3b. The Highlight Changes dialog box is not yet visible, but the
document contains several changes from a previous editing session.

➤ Save the document as **Modified Contract** so that you can return to the original document if necessary.

➤ Pull down the **Tools menu,** click (or point to) the **Track Changes command,**
then click **Highlight Changes** to display the Highlight Changes dialog box in
Figure 7.3b. Check the box to **Track changes while editing.**

➤ Click **OK** to close the Highlight Changes dialog box. The **TRK** indicator should be displayed on the status bar so that all of your subsequent changes will be highlighted in the document.

➤ Press **Ctrl+Home** to move to the beginning of the document. Press the **Del key** three times to delete the word "The". As you do, the text changes to red with a line through the deleted word.

➤ Move to the end of the address (immediately after the zip code). Press the space bar three or four times, then enter the phone number, **(305) 111-2222.** The new text is also in red, but is underlined to indicate that it is an addition to the document.

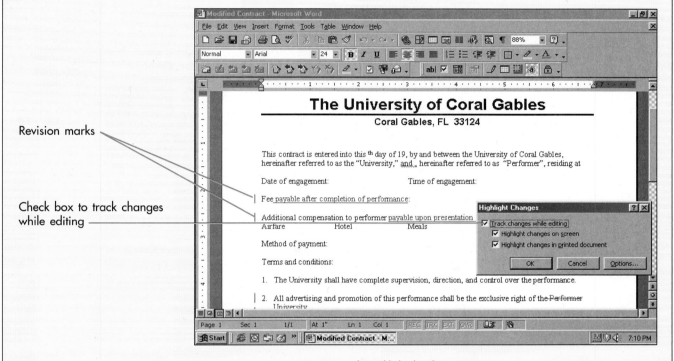

Revision marks

Check box to track changes while editing

(b) Highlight the Changes (step 2)

FIGURE 7.3   Hands-on Exercise 1 (continued)

CHANGE THE EDITING MARKS

Red is the default color used to indicate changes to a document. Text that is added to a document is underlined in red, whereas text that is deleted is shown with a line through the deleted portion. You can, however, change either the color or the editing marks. Pull down the Tools menu, click the Track Changes command, click Highlight Changes to display the Highlight Changes dialog box, then click the Options buttons to display the Track Changes dialog box. Enter your editing preferences, click OK to close the Track Changes dialog box, then click OK a second time to close the Highlight Changes dialog box.

STEP 3: Accept or Reject Changes

➤ Press **Ctrl+Home** to move to the beginning of the document. Pull down the **Tools menu,** click (or point to) the **Track Changes command,** then click **Accept or Reject Changes** to display the Accept or Reject Changes dialog box in Figure 7.3c.

➤ Click the **Find Forward button** to move to the first change. The word "The" is selected at the beginning of the document. Click the **Accept button** to accept the change and automatically move to the next change.

➤ You can review the changes individually or (in this case) you can click the **Accept All button** since we know in advance that all changes are to be accepted. Click **Yes** if asked whether to accept all changes without reviewing. Close the dialog box.

➤ Save the document.

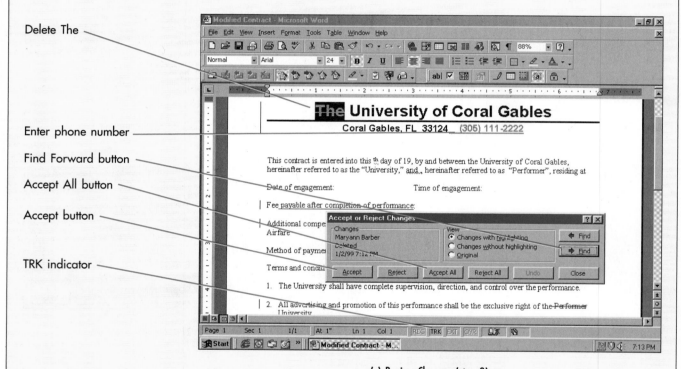

(c) Review Changes (step 3)

FIGURE 7.3   Hands-on Exercise 1 (continued)

INSERT COMMENTS INTO A DOCUMENT

Add comments to a document to remind yourself (or a reviewer) of action that needs to be taken. Click in the document where you want the comment to appear, then pull down the Insert menu and click the Comment command to open the Comments window. Enter the text of the comment, then close the Comments window. The word containing the insertion point is highlighted in yellow to indicate that a comment has been added. Point to the highlighted entry and the text of the comment is displayed in a ScreenTip. Edit or delete existing comments by right clicking the comment, then choosing the Edit Comment or Delete Comment command.

STEP 4: Create the Text and Check Box Fields

➤ Click the **Track Changes button** on the Reviewing toolbar to stop tracking changes, which removes the TRK indicator from the status bar. Click the button a second time and tracking is again in effect. (You can also double click the **TRK indicator** on the status bar to toggle tracking on or off.)

➤ Move to the first line of text in the contract, then click to the right of the space following the second occurrence of the word "this".

➤ Click the **Text Form Field button** on the Forms toolbar to create a text field as shown in Figure 7.3d. The field should appear in the document as a shaded entry (see boxed tip). Do not worry, however, about the length of this field as we adjust it shortly via the Text Form Field Options dialog box (which is not yet visible).

➤ Click after the word **of** on the same line and insert a second text field followed by a blank space. Insert the six additional text fields as shown in Figure 7.3d. Add blank spaces as needed before each field.

➤ Click immediately after the word **Airfare.** Add a blank, then click the **Check Box Form Field** to create a check box as shown in the Figure. Create additional check boxes after the words **Hotel** and **Meals.**

➤ Click in the first text field (after the word "this"), then click the **Form Field Options button** on the Forms toolbar to display the Text Form Field Options dialog box. Click the **down arrow** in the Type list box and choose **Number.** Enter **2** in the Maximum Length box.

➤ Click **OK** to accept these settings and close the dialog box. The length of the form field changes automatically to two positions. Change the options for the Year (Number, 2 positions) and Date of Engagement fields (Date, MMMM d, yyyy format) in similar fashion. Save the document.

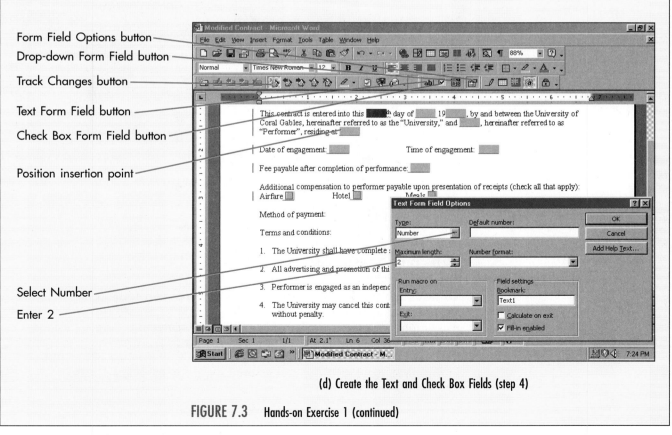

Form Field Options button
Drop-down Form Field button
Track Changes button
Text Form Field button
Check Box Form Field button
Position insertion point
Select Number
Enter 2

(d) Create the Text and Check Box Fields (step 4)

FIGURE 7.3   Hands-on Exercise 1 (continued)

STEP 5: Add the Drop-Down List Box

➤ Double click the **TRK indicator** on the status bar to stop tracking changes. (The indicator should be dim after double clicking.)

➤ Pull down the **Tools menu,** click **Track Changes,** then click **Accept or Reject Changes** to display the associated dialog box. Click **Accept All,** then click **Yes.** Close the dialog box.

➤ Click in the document after the words **Method of Payment,** then click the **Drop-down Form Field button** to create a drop-down list box. **Double click** the newly created field to display the dialog box in Figure 7.3e.

➤ Click in the Drop-down Item text box, type **University Check,** and click the **Add button** to move this entry to the Items in drop-down list box. Type **Credit Card** and click the **Add button.** Type **Cash** then click the **Add button** to complete the entries for the drop-down list box.

➤ Click **OK** to accept the settings and close the dialog box. Save the document.

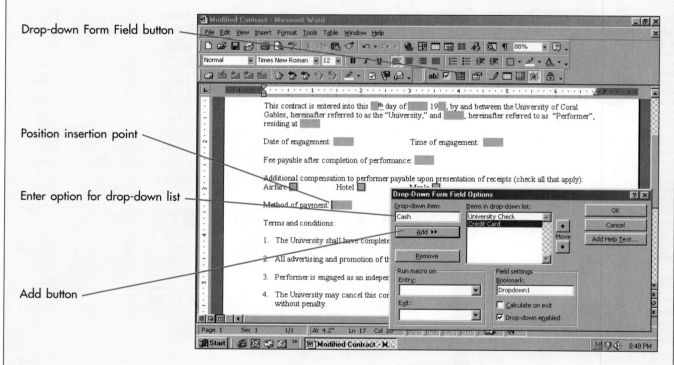

(e) Add the Drop-Down List Box (step 5)

FIGURE 7.3 Hands-on Exercise 1 (continued)

FIELD CODES VERSUS FIELD RESULTS

All fields are displayed in a document in one of two formats, as a field code or as a field result. A field code appears in braces and indicates instructions to insert variable data when the document is printed; a field result displays the information as it will appear in the printed document. (The field results of a form field are blank until the data are entered into a form.) You can toggle the display between the field code and field result by selecting the field and pressing Shift+F9 during editing.

STEP 6: Save This Version

➤ Proofread the document to be sure that it is correct. Once you are satisfied with the finished document, click the **Protect Form button** on the Forms toolbar to prevent further changes to the form. (You can still enter data into the fields on the form, as we will do in the next step.)

➤ Pull down the **File menu** and click the **Versions command** to display the Versions dialog box for this document. There is currently one previous version, the one created by Robert Grauer on August 28, 1998.

➤ Click the **Save Now button** to display the Save Version dialog box in Figure 7.3f. Enter the text of a comment you want to associate with this version. The author's name will be different on your screen and will reflect the person who registered the version of Microsoft Word you are using.

➤ Click **OK** to save the version and close the dialog box.

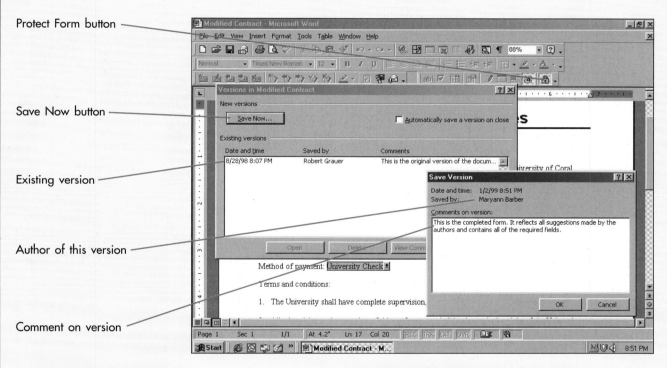

Protect Form button

Save Now button

Existing version

Author of this version

Comment on version

(f) Save a New Version (step 6)

FIGURE 7.3   Hands-on Exercise 1 (continued)

CREATE A BACKUP COPY

Microsoft Word enables you to automatically create a backup copy of a document in conjunction with the Save command. Pull down the Tools menu, click the Options button, click the Save tab, then check the box to Always create backup copy. The next time you save the file, the previously saved version is renamed "Backup of document" after which the document in memory is saved as the current version. In other words, the disk will contain the two most recent versions of the document.

STEP 7: Fill In the Form

➤ Be sure that the form is protected; that is, that all buttons are dim on the Forms toolbar except for the Protect Form and Form Field Shading buttons. Press **Ctrl+Home** to move to the first field.

➤ Enter today's date, press the **Tab key** (to move to the next field), enter today's month, press the **Tab key** and enter the year.

➤ Continue to press the **Tab key** to complete the form. Enter your name as the performer. Press the **space bar** on the keyboard to check or clear the various check boxes. Check the boxes for airfare, hotel, and meals, and enter a fee of $1,000. Click the **down arrow** on the Method of Payment list box and choose University Check.

➤ Your completed form should be similar to our form as shown in Figure 7.3g. You can make changes to the text of the contract by unprotecting the form. Do not**,** however, click the Protect Form button after data has been entered or you will lose the data.

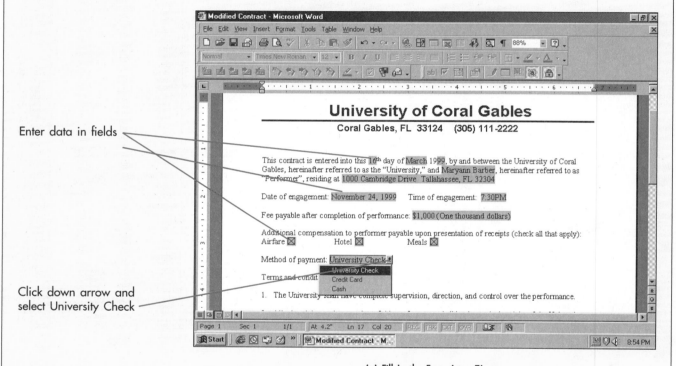

(g) Fill In the Form (step 7)

FIGURE 7.3   Hands-on Exercise 1 (continued)

PROTECTING AND UNPROTECTING A FORM

The Protect Form button toggles protection on and off. Click the button once and the form is protected; data can be entered into the various fields, but the form itself cannot be modified. Click the button a second time and the form is unprotected and can be fully modified. Be careful, however, about unprotecting a form once data has been entered. That action will not create a problem in and of itself, but protecting a form a second time (after the data was previously entered) will reset all of its fields.

STEP 8: Password-Protect the Executed Contract

➤ Pull down the **File menu,** click the **Save As command** to display the Save As dialog box, then type **Executed Contract** as the filename.

➤ Click the **drop-down arrow** next to the Tools button and click the **General Options command** to display the Save dialog box in Figure 7.3h. Click in the **Password to open** text box and enter **password** (the password is case-sensitive) as the password. Click **OK.**

➤ A Confirm Password dialog box will open asking you to reenter the password and warning you not to forget the password; i.e., once a document is protected by a password, it cannot be opened without that password. Reenter the password and click **OK** to establish the password.

➤ Click **Save** to save the document and close the Save As dialog box. Exit Word if you do not want to continue with the next exercise at this time.

Click down arrow on Tools button ────

Enter new name of file ────

Enter password to open file ────

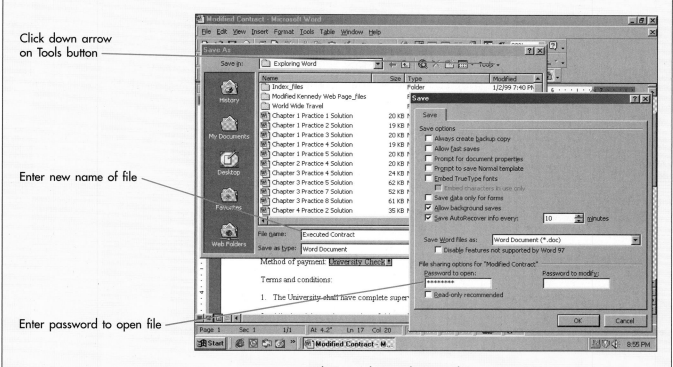

(h) Password-Protect the Executed Contract (step 8)

FIGURE 7.3   Hands-on Exercise 1 (continued)

THE FORM VERSUS THE EXECUTED CONTRACT

The form created in this exercise is a general form that can be used for any contract. Once data has been entered into the form, however, it pertains to a specific agreement and should be saved as a separate document. Pull down the File menu and click the Save As command to save the completed form that is currently in memory under a different name (Executed Contract in this example). The generalized version of the form is stored on disk under its original name and can be used as the basis for all future contracts.

Tables were introduced in an earlier chapter and provide an easy way to arrange text, numbers, and/or graphics within a document. This section extends that discussion to include calculations within a table, giving a Word document the power of a simple spreadsheet. We also describe how to *sort* the rows within a table in a different sequence, according to the entries in a specific column of the table.

We begin by reviewing a few basic concepts. The rows and columns in a table intersect to form *cells,* each of which can contain text, numbers, and/or graphics. Text is entered into each cell individually, enabling you to add, delete, or format text in one cell without affecting the text in other cells. The rows within a table can be different heights, and each row may contain a different number of columns.

The commands in the *Tables menu* or the *Tables and Borders toolbar* operate on one or more cells. The Insert and Delete commands add new rows or columns, or delete existing rows or columns, respectively. Other commands shade and/or border selected cells or the entire table. You can also select multiple cells and merge them into a single cell. All of this was presented earlier, and should be familiar.

Figure 7.4 displays a table of expenses that is associated with the performer's contract. The table also illustrates two additional capabilities that are associated with a table. First, you can sort the rows in a table to display the data in different

Header row

Expenses are in alphabetical order

Totals are displayed

Expense	Number of Days	Per Diem Amount	Amount
Airfare			$349.00
Hotel	2	$129.99	$259.98
Meals	2	$75.00	$150.00
Performance Fee			$1000.00
Total			**$1758.98**

(a) Expenses (Alphabetical Order by Expense)

Descending order by amount

Expense	Number of Days	Per Diem Amount	Amount
Performance Fee			$1000.00
Airfare			$349.00
Hotel	2	$129.99	$259.98
Meals	2	$75.00	$150.00
Total			**$1758.98**

(b) Expenses (Descending Order by Amount)

Column labels

Row labels

	A	B	C	D
1	Expense	Number of Days	Per Diem Amount	Amount
2	Performance Fee			$1000.00
3	Airfare			$349.00
4	Hotel	2	$129.99	{=b4*c4}
5	Meals	2	$75.00	{=b5*c5}
6	Total			{=SUM(ABOVE)}

Field codes

(c) Field codes

FIGURE 7.4 Sorting and Table Math

sequences as shown in Figures 7.4a and 7.4b. Both figures display the same 6×4 table (six rows and four columns). The first row in each figure is a header row and contains the field names for each column. The next four rows contain data for a specific expense, while the last row displays the total for all expenses

Figure 7.4a lists the expenses in alphabetical order—airfare, hotel, meals, and performance fee. Figure 7.4b, however, lists the expenses in descending (high to low) sequence according to the amount. Thus the performance fee (the largest expense) is listed first, and the meals (the smallest expense) appear last. Note, too, that the sort has been done in such a way as to affect only the four middle rows; that is the header and total rows have not moved. This is accomplished according to the select-then-do methodology that is used for many operations in Microsoft Word. You select the rows that are to be sorted, then you execute the command (the Sort command in the Tables menu in this example).

Figure 7.4c displays the same table as in Figure 7.4b, albeit in a different format that displays the field codes rather than the field results. The entries consist of formulas that were entered into the table to perform a calculation. The entries are similar to those in a spreadsheet. Thus, the rows in the table are numbered from one to six while the columns are labeled from A to D. The row and column labels do not appear in the table per se, but are used to enter the formulas.

The intersection of a row and column forms a cell. Cell D4, for example, contains the entry to compute the total hotel expense by multiplying the number of days (in cell B4) by the per diem amount (in cell C4). In similar fashion, the entry in cell D5 computes the total expense for meals by multiplying the values in cells B5 and C5, respectively. The formula is not entered (typed) into the cell explicitly, but is created through the Formula command in the Tables menu.

The formula in cell D6 has a different syntax and sums the value of all cells directly above it. You do not need to know the syntax since Word provides a dialog box which supplies the entry for you. It's easy, as you shall see in our next hands-on exercise.

HANDS-ON EXERCISE 2

Table Math

Objective: To open a password-protected document and remove the password protection; to create a table containing various cell formulas. Use Figure 7.5 as a guide in the exercise.

STEP 1: Open the Document

➤ Start Word and open the **Executed Contract** in the **Exploring Word folder** that was created in the last exercise. You will be prompted for a password as shown in Figure 7.5a.

➤ Type **password** (in lowercase) since this was the password that was specified when you saved the document originally.

➤ Pull down the **File menu** and click the **Save As command** to display the Save As dialog box. Click the **Tools button,** click **General Options,** then click in the Password to open text box.

➤ Click and drag to select the existing password (which appears as a string of eight asterisks). Press the **Del key** to remove the password. Click **OK** to close the Save dialog box. Click the **Save command button** to close the Save As dialog box. The document is no longer password protected.

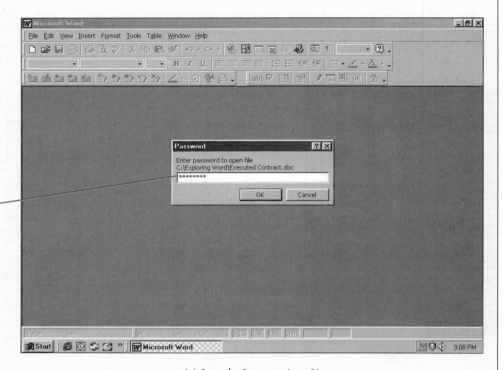

Enter Password

(a) Open the Document (step 1)

FIGURE 7.5   Hands-on Exercise 2

CHANGE THE DEFAULT FOLDER

The default folder is the folder where Word saves and retrieves documents unless it is otherwise instructed. To change the default folder, pull down the Tools menu, click Options, click the File Locations tab, click Documents, and click the Modify command button. Enter the name of the new folder (for example, C:\Exploring Word), click OK, then click the Close button. The next time you access the File menu the default folder will reflect these changes.

STEP 2: Review the Contract

➤ You should see the executed contract from the previous exercise. If necessary, click the **Protect Form button** on the Forms toolbar to unprotect the document so that its context can be modified.

➤ Do **not** click the Protect Form button a second time or else the data will disappear. (You can quit the document without saving the changes, as described in the boxed tip below.)

➤ Point to any toolbar, and click the **right mouse button** to display the list of toolbars shown in Figure 7.5b. Click the **Forms toolbar** to toggle the toolbar off (the check will disappear). Right click any toolbar a second time, and toggle the Reviewing toolbar off as well.

Right click an existing toolbar to display a shortcut menu

Click to toggle Forms toolbar off

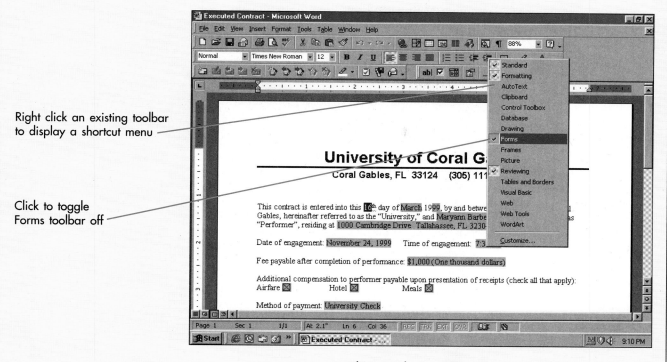

(b) Review the Contract (step 2)

FIGURE 7.5   Hands-on Exercise 2

QUIT WITHOUT SAVING

There will be times when you do not want to save the changes to a document; for example, when you have edited it beyond recognition and wish you had never started. Pull down the File menu and click the Close command, then click No in response to the message asking whether you want to save the changes to the document. Pull down the File menu and reopen the file (it should be the first file in the list of most recently edited documents), then start over from the beginning.

STEP 3: Create the Table

➤ Press **Ctrl+End** to move to the end of the contract, then press **Ctrl+Enter** to create a page break. You should be at the top of page two of the document.

➤ Press the **enter key** three times and then enter **Summary of Expenses** in **24-point Arial bold** as shown in Figure 7.5c. Center the text. Press **enter** twice to add a blank line under the heading.

➤ Change to **12-point Times New Roman.** Click the **Insert Table button** on the Standard toolbar to display a grid, then drag the mouse across and down the grid to create a 6 × 4 table (six rows and four columns). Release the mouse to create the table.

➤ Enter data into the table as shown in Figure 7.5c. You can format the column headings by selecting multiple cells, then clicking the **Center button** on the Standard toolbar. In similar fashion, you can right justify the numerical data by selecting the cells and clicking the **Align Right button.**

➤ Save the document.

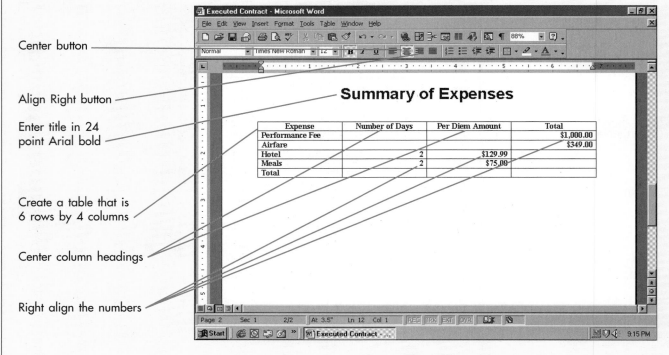

(c) Create the Table (step 3)

FIGURE 7.5   Hands-on Exercise 2 (continued)

TABS AND TABLES

The Tab key functions differently in a table than in a regular document. Press the Tab key to move to the next cell in the current row (or to the first cell in the next row if you are at the end of a row). Press Tab when you are in the last cell of a table to add a new blank row to the bottom of the table. Press Shift+Tab to move to the previous cell in the current row (or to the last cell in the previous row). You must press Ctrl+Tab to insert a regular tab character within a cell.

STEP 4: Sort the Table

➤ Click and drag to select the entire table except for the last row. Pull down the **Table menu** and click the **Sort command** to display the Sort dialog box in Figure 7.5d.

➤ Click the **drop-down arrow** in the Sort by list box and select **Expense** (the column heading for the first column). The **Ascending option button** is selected by default.

➤ Verify that the option button to include a Header row is selected. Click **OK.** The entries in the table are rearranged alphabetically according to the entry in the Expenses column. The Total row remains at the bottom of the table since it was not included in the selected rows for the Sort command.

➤ Save the document.

Click and drag to select everything except the last row

Click to select Expense

Click Ascending button

Header row should be selected

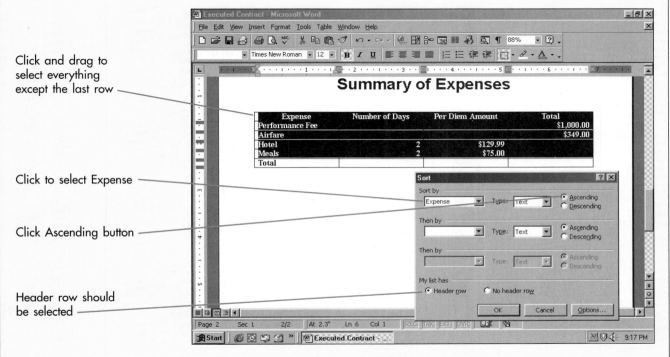

(d) Sort the Table (step 4)

FIGURE 7.5   Hands-on Exercise 2 (continued)

THE HEADER ROW

The first row in a table is known as the header row and contains the column names (headings) that describe the value in each column of the table. The header row is typically included in the range selected for the sort so that the Sort by list box displays the column names. The header row must remain at the top of the table, however, and thus it is important that the option button that indicates a header row be selected. In similar fashion, the last row typically contains the totals and should remain as the bottom row of the table. Hence it (the total row) is not included in the rows that are selected for sorting.

STEP 5: Enter the Formulas for Row Totals

➤ Click in cell **D3** (the cell in the fourth column and third row). Pull down the **Table menu** and click the **Formula command** to display the Formula dialog box.

➤ Click and drag to select the =SUM(ABOVE) function which is entered by default. Type **=b3*c3** as shown in Figure 7.5e to compute the total hotel expense. The total is computed by multiplying the number of days (in cell B3) by the per diem amount (in cell C3). Click **OK**. You should see $259.98 in cell D3.

➤ Click in cell **D4** and repeat the procedure to enter the formula **=b4*c4** to compute the total expense for meals. You should see $150.00 (two days at $75.00 per day). Save the document.

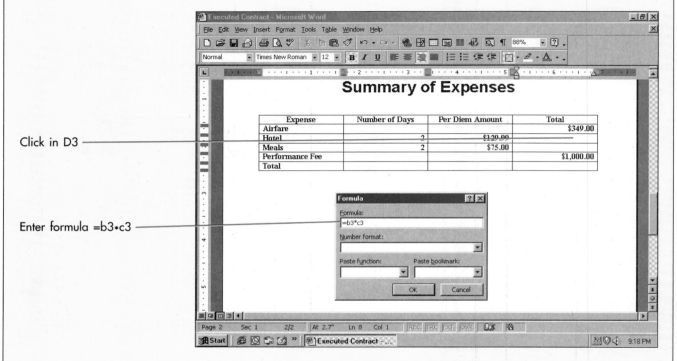

Click in D3

Enter formula =b3*c3

(e) Enter the Formulas for Row Totals (step 5)

FIGURE 7.5   Hands-on Exercise 2 (continued)

IT'S NOT EXCEL

Your opinion of table math within Microsoft Word depends on what you know about a spreadsheet. If you have never used Excel, then you will find table math to be very useful, especially when simple calculations are necessary within a Word document. If, on the other hand, you know Excel, you will find table math to be rather limited; for example, you cannot copy a formula from one cell to another, but must enter it explicitly in every cell. Nevertheless, the feature enables simple calculations to be performed entirely within Word, without having to link an Excel worksheet to a Word document.

STEP 6: Enter the SUM(ABOVE) Formula

➤ Click in cell **D6** (the cell in row 6, column 4) which is to contain the total of all expenses. Pull down the **Table menu** and click the **Formula command** to display the Formula dialog box in Figure 7.5f.

➤ The =SUM(ABOVE) function is entered by default. Click **OK** to accept the formula and close the dialog box. You should see $1,758.98 (the sum of the cells in the last column) displayed in the selected cell.

➤ Select the formula and press **Shift+F9** to display the code {=SUM (ABOVE)}. Press **Shift+F9** a second time to display the field value ($1,758.98).

➤ Click in cell **D2** (the cell containing the airfare). Replace $349 with **549.00** and press the **Tab key** to move out of the cell. The total expenses are *not* yet updated in cell D6.

➤ Point to cell **D6,** click the **right mouse button** to display a context-sensitive menu, and click the **Update Field** command. Cell D6 displays $1,958.98, the correct total for all expenses.

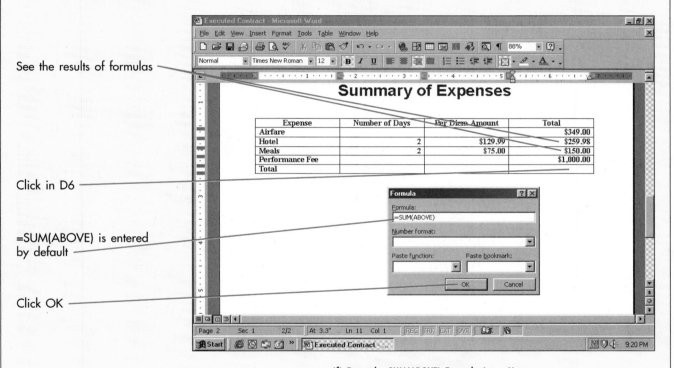

(f) Enter the SUM(ABOVE) Formula (step 6)

FIGURE 7.5   Hands-on Exercise 2 (continued)

FORMATTING A CALCULATED VALUE

Word does its best to format a calculation according to the way you want it. You can, however, change the default format by clicking the down arrow on the Number format list box and choosing a different format. You can also enter a format directly in the Number format text box. To display a dollar sign and comma without a decimal point, enter $#,##0 in the text box. You can use trial and error to experiment with other formats.

STEP 7: Print the Completed Contract

➤ Zoom to two pages to preview the completed document. The first page contains the text of the executed contract that was completed in the previous exercise. The second page contains the table of expenses from this contract.

➤ Pull down the **File Menu** and click the **Print command** to display the Print dialog box in Figure 7.5g. Click the **Options command button** to display the second Print dialog box.

➤ Check the box to include **Field Codes** with the document. Click **OK** to close that dialog box, then click **OK** to print the document.

➤ Repeat the process to print the document a second time, but this time with field values, rather than field codes. Thus, pull down the **File Menu,** click the **Print command** to display the Print dialog box, and click the **Options command button** to display a second Print dialog box.

➤ Clear the box to include **Field Codes** with the document. Click **OK** to close that dialog box, then click **OK** to print the document.

➤ Exit Word if you do not want to continue with the next exercise at this time. Click **Yes** if asked to save the changes.

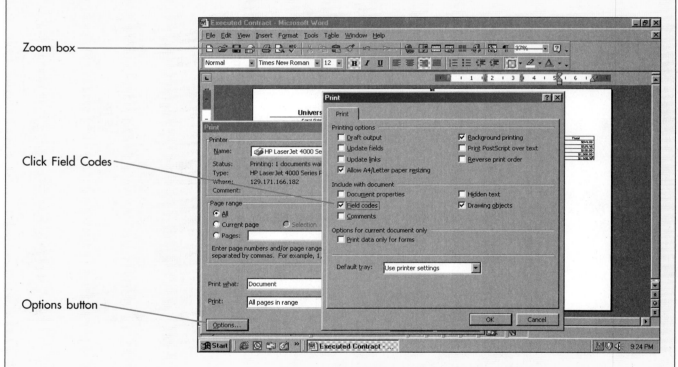

Zoom box

Click Field Codes

Options button

(g) Print the Completed Contract (step 7)

FIGURE 7.5 Hands-on Exercise 2 (continued)

DOCUMENT PROPERTIES

Prove to your instructor how hard you've worked by printing various statistics about your document including the number of revisions and the total editing time. Pull down the File menu, click the Print command to display the Print dialog box, click the drop down arrow in the Print What list box, select Document properties, then click OK.

MASTER DOCUMENTS

A *master document* is composed of multiple *subdocuments,* each of which is stored as a separate file. The advantage of the master document is that you can work with several smaller documents as opposed to a single large document. Thus, you edit the subdocuments individually and more efficiently, than if they were all part of the same document. You can create a master document to hold the chapters of a book, where each chapter is stored as a subdocument. You can also use a master document to hold multiple documents created by others, such as a group project, where each member of the group is responsible for a section of the document.

Figure 7.6 displays a master document with five subdocuments. The subdocuments are collapsed in Figure 7.6a and expanded in Figure 7.6b. (The *Outlining toolbar* contains the Collapse and Expand Subdocument buttons, as well as other tools associated with master documents.) The collapsed structure in Figure 7.6a enables you to see at a glance the subdocuments that comprise the master document. You can insert additional subdocuments and/or remove existing subdocuments from the master document. Deleting a subdocument from within a master document does *not* delete the subdocument from disk.

The expanded structure in Figure 7.6b enables you to view and/or edit the contents of the subdocuments. Look carefully, however, at the first two subdocuments in Figure 7.6b. A padlock appears to the left of the first line in the first subdocument whereas it is absent from the second subdocument. These subdocuments are locked and unlocked respectively, and the distinction determines how changes made within the master document are saved. (All subdocuments are locked when collapsed as in Figure 7.6a.) Changes made to the locked subdocument will be saved in the master document, but not in the subdocument. Changes to the unlocked subdocument, however, will be saved in both the master document and the underlying subdocument. (The Lock Subdocuments button on the Outlining toolbar toggles between locked and unlocked subdocuments.) Either approach is acceptable. You just need to understand the difference, as you may want to use one technique or the other.

Regardless of how you edit the subdocuments, the attraction of a master document is the ability to work with multiple subdocuments simultaneously. The subdocuments are created independently of one another, with each subdocument stored in its own file. Then, when all of the subdocuments are finished, the master document is created and the subdocuments are inserted into the master document, from where they are easily accessed. Inserting page numbers into the master document, for example, causes the numbers to run consecutively from one subdocument to the next. You can also create a table of contents or index for the master document that will reflect the entries in all of the subdocuments. And finally you can print all of the subdocuments from within the master document with a single command.

Alternatively, you can reverse the process by starting with an empty master document and using it as the basis to create the subdocuments. This is ideal for organizing a group project in school or at work. Start with a new document, enter the topics assigned to each group member as headings within the master document, then use the *Create Subdocument command* to create subdocuments based on those headings. Saving the master document will automatically save each subdocument in its own file. This is the approach that we will follow in our next hands-on exercise.

The exercise also illustrates the *Create New Folder command* that lets you create a new folder on your hard drive (or floppy disk) from within Microsoft Word as opposed to using Windows Explorer. The new folder can then be used to store the master document and all of its subdocuments in a single location apart from any other documents.

Subdocuments are collapsed

Subdocuments are locked

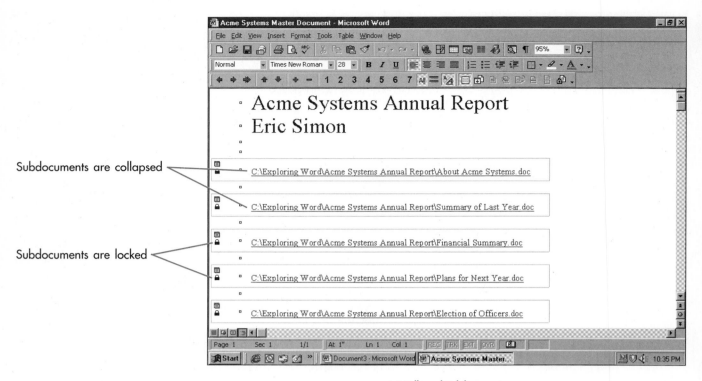

(a) Collapsed Subdocuments

Subdocument is locked

Subdocuments are expanded

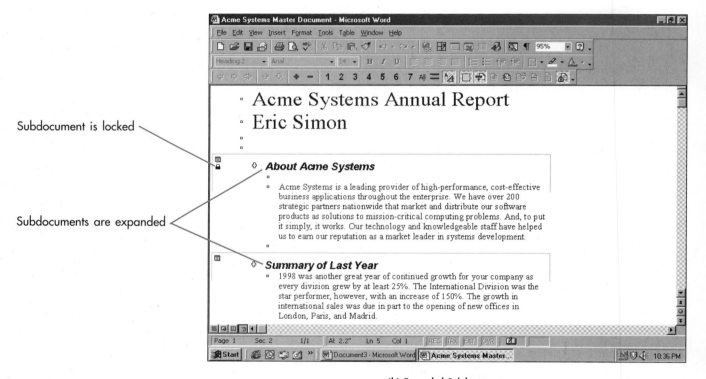

(b) Expanded Subdocuments

FIGURE 7.6   A Master Document

Master Documents

Objective: To create a master document and various subdocuments; to create a new folder from within the Save As dialog box in Microsoft Word. Use Figure 7.7 as a guide in the exercise.

STEP 1: Create a New Folder

➤ Start Word. If necessary, click the **New button** on the Standard toolbar to begin a new document. Enter the text of the document in Figure 7.7a in **12 point Times New Roman.**

➤ Press **Ctrl+Home** to move to the beginning of the document. Pull down the **Style List box** on the Formatting toolbar, then select **Heading 2** as the style for the document title.

➤ Click the **Save button** to display the Save As dialog box. If necessary click the **drop-down arrow** on the Save in list box to select the **Exploring Word folder** you have used throughout the text.

➤ Click the **Create New Folder** button to display the New Folder dialog box. Type **Acme Systems Annual Report** as the name of the new folder. Click **OK** to create the folder and close the New Folder dialog box.

➤ The Save in list box indicates that the Acme Systems Annual Report folder is the current folder. The name of the document, **About Acme Systems,** is entered by default (since this text appears at the beginning of the document).

➤ Click the **Save button** to save the document and close the Save As dialog box.

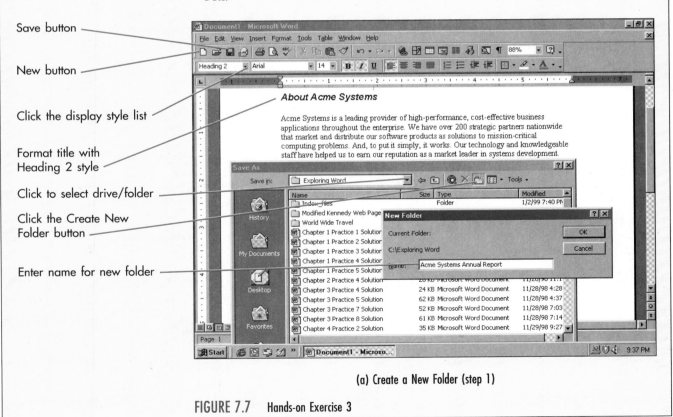

(a) Create a New Folder (step 1)

FIGURE 7.7   Hands-on Exercise 3

STEP 2: Create the Master Document

➤ Click the **New button** on the Standard toolbar. Enter **Acme Systems Annual Report** as the first line of the document. Enter your name under the title.

➤ Press the **enter key** twice to leave a blank line or two after your name before the first subdocument. Type **Summary of Last Year** in the default typeface and size. Press **enter.** Enter the remaining topics, **Financial Summary, Plans for Next Year,** and **Election of Officers.**

➤ Change the format of the title and your name to **28 pt Times New Roman.**

➤ Pull down the **View menu** and click **Outline** to change to the Outline view. Click and drag to select the four headings as shown in Figure 7.7b. Click the **drop-down arrow** on the Style List box and select **Heading 2**.

➤ Be sure that all four headings are still selected. Press **Create Subdocument button.** Each heading expands automatically into a subdocument.

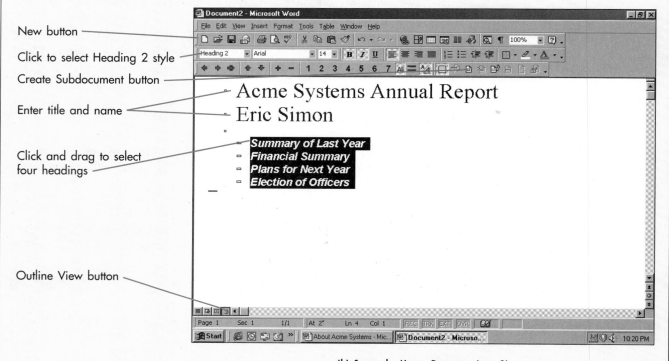

New button

Click to select Heading 2 style

Create Subdocument button

Enter title and name

Click and drag to select four headings

Outline View button

(b) Create the Master Document (step 2)

FIGURE 7.7   Hands-on Exercise 3 (continued)

THE CREATE SUBDOCUMENT BUTTON

You can enter subdocuments into a master document in one of two ways, through the Insert Subdocuments button if the subdocuments already exist, or through the Create Subdocument button to create the subdocuments from within the master document. Start a new document, enter the title of each subdocument on a line by itself that is formatted in a heading style, then click the Create Subdocument button to create the subdocuments. Save the master document. The subdocuments are saved automatically as individual files in the same folder.

STEP 3: Save the Master Document

➤ Click the **Save button** to display the Save As dialog box in Figure 7.7c. If necessary, click the **drop-down arrow** on the Save In list box to select the **Acme Systems Annual Report folder** that was created in step one. You should see the About Acme Systems document in this folder.

➤ Enter **Acme Systems Master Document** in the File Name list box, then click the **Save button** within the Save As dialog box to save the master document (which automatically saves the subdocuments in the same folder).

➤ Press the **Collapse Subdocuments button** to collapse the subdocuments. You will see the name of each subdocument as it appears on disk, with the drive and folder information. Press the **Expand Subdocuments button** and the subdocuments are reopened within the master document.

Save button

Click to select folder

Enter new file name

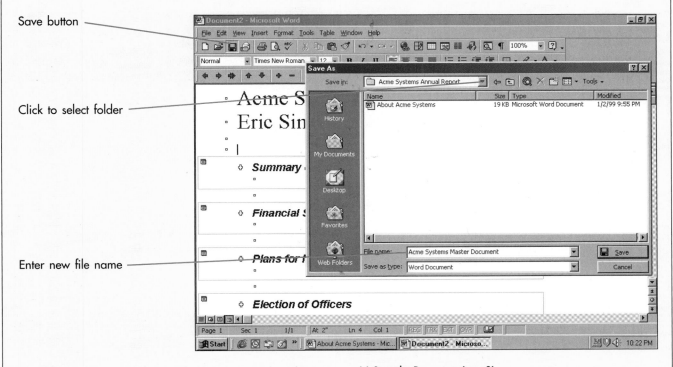

(c) Save the Documents (step 3)

FIGURE 7.7   Hands-on Exercise 3 (continued

HELP WITH TOOLBAR BUTTONS

The Outlining toolbar is displayed automatically in the Outline view and suppressed otherwise. As with every toolbar you can point to any button to see a ToolTip with the name of the button. You can also press Shift+F1 to change the mouse pointer to a large arrow next to a question mark, then click any button to learn more about its function. The Outlining toolbar contains buttons that pertain specifically to master documents such as buttons to expand and collapse subdocuments, or insert and remove subdocuments. The Outlining toolbar also contains buttons to promote and demote items, to display or suppress formatting, and/or to collapse and expand the outline.

STEP 4: Insert a Subdocument

➤ Click below your name, but above the first subdocument. Click the **Insert Subdocument button** to display the Insert Subdocument dialog box in Figure 7.7d. If necessary click the **drop-down arrow** on the Look in list box to change to the Acme Systems Annual Report folder.

➤ There are six documents, which include the About Acme Systems document from step one, the Acme Systems Master document that you just saved, and the four subdocuments that were created automatically in conjunction with the master document.

➤ Select the **About Acme Systems** document then click the **Open button** to insert this document into the master document. Save the master document.

Click to select folder

Click About Acme Systems

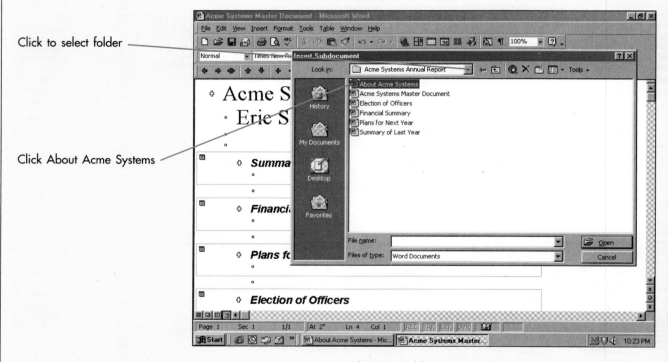

(d) Insert a Subdocument (step 4)

FIGURE 7.7   Hands-on Exercise 3 (continued

CHANGE THE VIEW

The Outline view is used to create and/or modify a master document through insertion, repositioning, or deletion of its subdocuments. You can also modify the text of a subdocument within the Outline view and/or implement formatting changes at the character level such as a change in font, type size, or style. More sophisticated formatting, however, such as changes in alignment, indentation, or line spacing has to be implemented in the Normal or Print Layout views.

STEP 5: Modify a Subdocument

➤ Click within the second subdocument, which will summarize the activities of last year. (The text of the document has not yet been entered).

➤ Click the **Lock Document button** on the Outlining toolbar to display the padlock for this document. Click the **Lock Document button** a second time, which unlocks the document.

➤ Enter the text of the document as shown in Figure 7.7e, then click the **Save button** to save the changes to the master document. Be sure the subdocument is unlocked so that the changes you have made will be reflected in the subdocument file as well.

Save button

Padlock indicates subdocuments is locked

Collapse/Expand Subdocuments button

Insert Subdocuments button

Lock Subdocuments button

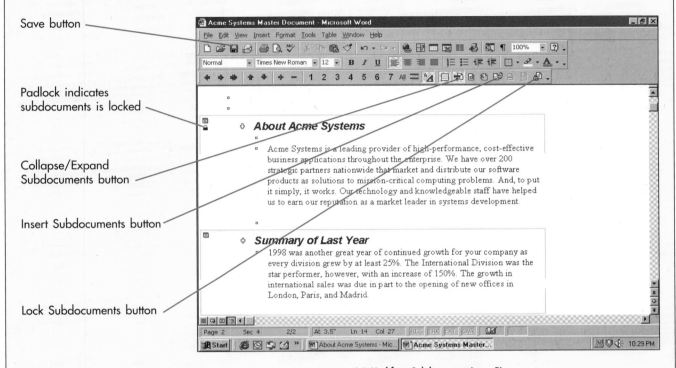

(e) Modify a Subdocument (step 5)

FIGURE 7.7   Hands-on Exercise 3 (continued)

OPEN THE SUBDOCUMENT

You can edit the text of a subdocument from within a master document, but it is often more convenient to open the subdocument when the editing is extensive. You can open a subdocument in one of two ways, by double clicking the document icon in the Outline view when the master document is expanded, or by clicking the hyperlink to the document when the Master Document is collapsed. Either way, the subdocument opens in its own windows. Enter the changes into the subdocument, then save the subdocument and close its window to return to the master document, which now reflects the modified subdocument.

STEP 6: Print the Completed Document

➤ Click the **Collapse Subdocuments button** to collapse the subdocuments as shown in Figure 7.7f. Click **OK** if asked to save the changes in the master document.

➤ Click the **Print button** on the Standard toolbar to print the document. Click **No** when asked whether to open the subdocuments before printing. The entire document appears on a single page. The text of the subdocuments is not printed, only the address of the documents.

➤ Click the **Print button** a second time, but click **Yes** when asked whether to open the subdocuments before printing.

➤ Submit both versions of the printed document to your instructor as proof that you did this exercise. Exit Word if you do not want to continue with the next exercise at this time.

Print button

Collapse/Expand subdocuments button

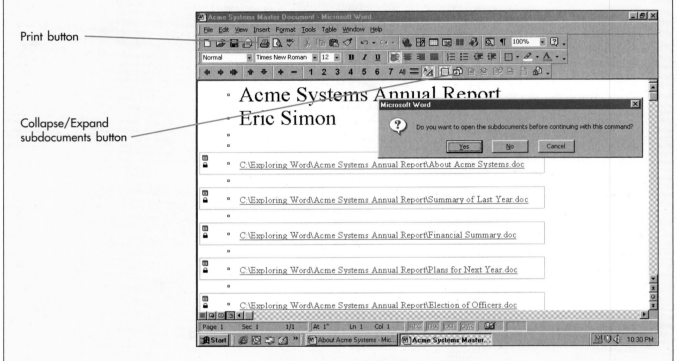

(f) Print the Document (step 6)

FIGURE 7.7   Hands-on Exercise 3 (continued)

THE DOCUMENT MAP

The Document Map is one of our favorite features when working with large documents. Be sure that the master document is expanded to display the text of the subdocuments, then click the Document Map button on the Standard toolbar to divide the screen into two panes. The headings in a document are displayed in the left pane and the text of the document is visible in the right pane. To go to a specific point in a document, click its heading in the left pane, and the insertion point is moved automatically to that point in the document, which is visible in the right pane. Click the Document Map button a second time to turn the feature off.

INTRODUCTION TO MACROS

Have you ever pulled down the same menus and clicked the same sequence of commands over and over? Easy as the commands may be to execute, it is still burdensome to continually repeat the same mouse clicks or keystrokes. If you can think of any task that you do repeatedly, whether in one document or in a series of documents, you are a perfect candidate to use macros.

A *macro* is a set of instructions (that is, a program) that executes a specific task. It is written in *Visual Basic for Applications (VBA),* a programming language that is built into Microsoft Office. Fortunately, however, you don't have to be a programmer to use VBA. Instead, you use the *macro recorder* within Word to record your actions, which are then translated automatically into VBA. You get results that are immediately usable and you can learn a good deal about VBA through observation and intuition.

Figure 7.8 illustrates a simple macro to enter your name, date, and class into a Word document. We don't expect you to be able to write the VBA code by yourself, but, as indicated, you don't have to. You just invoke the macro recorder and let it create the VBA statements for you. It is important, however, for you to understand the individual statements so that you can modify them as necessary. Do not be concerned with the precise syntax of every statement, but try instead to get an overall appreciation of what the statements do.

Every macro begins and ends with a Sub and End Sub statement, respectively. These statements identify the macro and convert it to a VBA procedure. The Sub statement contains the name of the macro such as NameAndCourse in Figure 7.8. (Spaces are not allowed in a macro name.) The End Sub statement is always the last statement in a VBA procedure. Sub and End Sub are Visual Basic key words and appear in blue.

The next several statements begin with an apostrophe, appear in green, and are known as *comments.* Comments provide information about the procedure, but

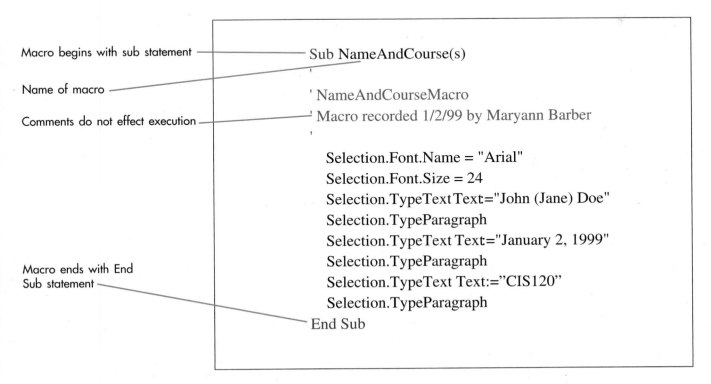

Macro begins with sub statement

Name of macro

Comments do not effect execution

```
Sub NameAndCourse(s)
    '
    ' NameAndCourseMacro
    ' Macro recorded 1/2/99 by Maryann Barber
    '
    Selection.Font.Name = "Arial"
    Selection.Font.Size = 24
    Selection.TypeText Text="John (Jane) Doe"
    Selection.TypeParagraph
    Selection.TypeText Text="January 2, 1999"
    Selection.TypeParagraph
    Selection.TypeText Text:="CIS120"
    Selection.TypeParagraph
End Sub
```

Macro ends with End Sub statement

FIGURE 7.8   The NameAndCourse Macro

do not affect its execution. In other words, the results of a procedure are the same, whether or not the comments are included. The comments are inserted automatically by the macro recorder and include the name of the macro, the date it was recorded, and the author. Additional comments can be inserted at any time as long as each line begins with an apostrophe.

Every other statement in the procedure corresponds directly to a command that was executed in Microsoft Word. It doesn't matter how the commands were executed—whether from a pull-down menu, toolbar, or keyboard shortcut, because the end results, the VBA statements that are generated by the commands, are the same. In this example, the user began by changing the font and font size, and these commands were converted by the macro recorder to the VBA statements that specify Arial and 24-point, respectively. Next, the user entered his name and pressed the enter key to begin a new paragraph. Again, the macro recorder converts these actions to the equivalent VBA statements. The user entered the date, pressed the enter key, entered the class, and pressed the enter key. Each of these actions resulted in additional VBA statements.

You do not have to write VBA statements from scratch, but you should understand their function once they have been recorded. You can also edit the statements after they have been recorded, to change the selected text and/or its appearance. It's easy, for example, to change the procedure to include your name instead of John Smith. You can also change the font or point size by changing the appropriate statement. All changes to a macro (VBA procedure) are done through the Visual Basic Editor.

The Visual Basic Editor

Figure 7.9a displays the NameAndCourse macro as it appears within the *Visual Basic Editor* (VBE). The Visual Basic Editor is a separate application (as can be determined from its button on the taskbar in Figure 7.9) and it is accessible from any application in Office 97. The left side of the VBE window displays the *Project Explorer,* which is similar in concept and appearance to the Windows Explorer, except that it displays the open Word documents and/or other Visual Basic projects. Macros are stored by default in the Normal template, which is available to all Word documents. The VBA code is stored in the NewMacros module. (A module contains one or more procedures.)

The macros for the selected module (NewMacros in Figure 7.9) appear in the Code Window in the right pane. (Additional macros, if any, are separated from one another by a horizontal line.) The VBA statements are identical to what we described earlier. The difference between Figure 7.8 and 7.9a is that the latter shows the macro within the Visual Basic Editor that is used to create, edit, execute, and debug macros.

Figure 7.9b displays the TitlePage macro, which is built from to the NameAndCourse macro. The new macro (a VBA procedure) is more complicated than its predecessor. "Complicated" is an intimidating word, however, and we prefer to use "powerful" instead. In essence, the TitlePage procedure moves the insertion point to the beginning of a Word document, inserts three blank lines at the beginning of the document, then enters three additional lines that center the student's name, date, and course in 24-point Arial. The last statement creates a page break within the document so that the title appears on a page by itself. The macro recorder created these statements for us, as we executed the corresponding actions from within Microsoft Word.

Note, too, that the TitlePage macro changed the way in which the date is entered in order to make the macro more general. The NameAndCourse macro in Figure 7.9a specified a date (January 2, 1999). The TitlePage macro, however, uses the VBA InsertDateTime command to insert the current date. We did not

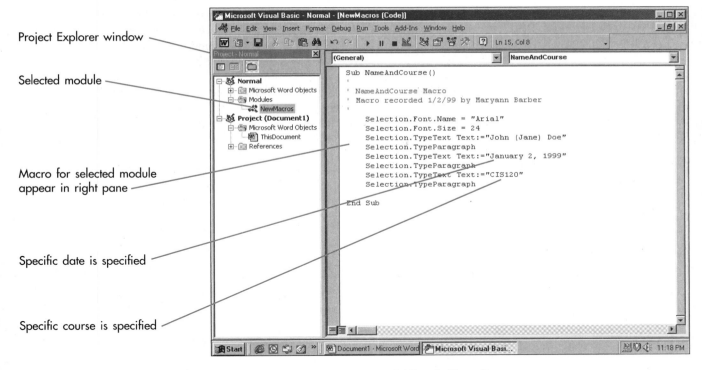

Project Explorer window

Selected module

Macro for selected module appear in right pane

Specific date is specified

Specific course is specified

(a) NameAndCourse Macro

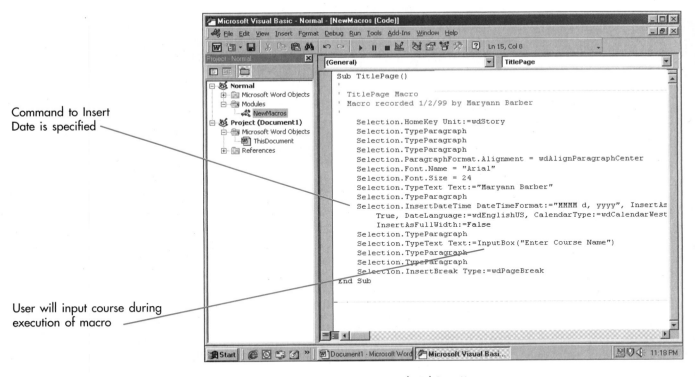

Command to Insert Date is specified

User will input course during execution of macro

(b) TitlePage Macro

FIGURE 7.9   The Visual Basic Editor

know the syntax of this statement, but we didn't have to. Instead we pulled down the Insert menu from within Word, and chose the Date and Time command. The macro recorder kept track of our actions and created the appropriate VBA statement for us. In similar fashion, the macro recorder kept track of our actions when we moved to the beginning of the document and when we inserted a page break.

As we have indicated throughout, you do not have to know the precise syntax of VBA statements in order to use the Visual Basic Editor to make changes. It is a simple matter, for example, to modify the student's name, typeface, font size, or alignment. As you learn more about VBA, you can add additional statements that extend the scope of the procedure beyond the actions that can be recorded in Word.

Macros in Word can be made even more powerful through inclusion of additional VBA statements. Look carefully at the statement to enter the course name in the TitlePage macro, as compared to the way it was done originally in the NameAndCourse macro. The NameAndCourse macro entered a specific course—CIS120. The TitlePage macro, however, uses the VBA **InputBox statement** to prompt the user for the course, then enters the user's response in the document. This requires you to enter the InputBox statement explicitly, but it's not as complicated as it sounds and you get a chance to practice in the next hands-on exercise.

A SENSE OF FAMILIARITY

Visual Basic for Applications has the basic capabilities found in any other programming language. If you have programmed before, whether in Pascal, C, or even COBOL, you will find all of the logic structures you are used to. These include the Do While and Do Until statements, the If-Then-Else statement for decision making, nested If statements, a Case statement, and calls to subprograms.

HANDS-ON EXERCISE 4

Introduction to Macros

Objective: To record, run, view, and edit simple macros; to run a macro from an existing Word document via a keyboard shortcut. Use Figure 7.10 as a guide in the exercise.

STEP 1: Create a Macro

➤ Start Word as you have throughout the text. Open a new document if one is not already open. There is no need to save this document, as it will not contain any useful text.

➤ Pull down the **Tools menu,** click (or point to) the **Macro command,** then click **Record New Macro** to display the Record Macro dialog box in Figure 7.10a.

➤ Enter **NameAndCourse** as the name of the macro. Do not leave any spaces in the macro name. The description is entered automatically and contains today's date and the name of the person in whose name this copy of Word is registered. If necessary, change the description to include your name.

➤ Click **Yes** if asked whether you want to replace the existing macro. (The existing macro may have been created by another student or if you previously attempted the exercise. Either way, you want to replace the existing macro.)

➤ Click **OK** to begin recording the macro. The mouse pointer changes to include a recording icon and the Stop Recording toolbar is displayed.

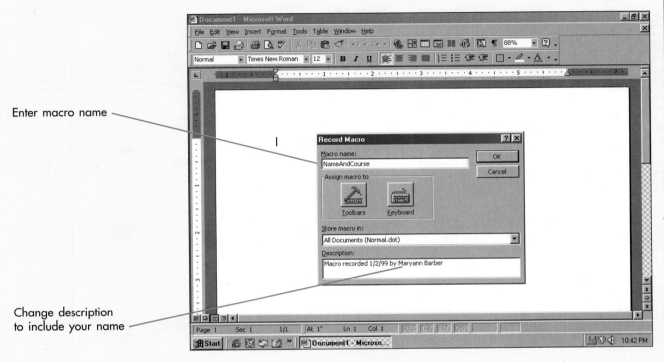

Enter macro name

Change description to include your name

(a) Create a Macro (step 1)

FIGURE 7.10   Hands-on Exercise 4

MACRO NAMES

Macro names are not allowed to contain spaces or punctuation except for the underscore character. To create a macro name containing more than one word, capitalize the first letter of each word to make the words stand out and/or use the underscore character; for example, NameAndCourse or Name_And_Course.

STEP 2: Record the Macro

➤ Do this command even if the default type matches our specification, because you want the instructions to change to this typeface included within the macro. Click the **drop-down arrows** on the Font list and Font Size box and select **Times New Roman 12-point** type.

➤ Type your name and press the **enter key.**

➤ Pull down the **Insert menu** and click the **Date and Time command** to display the Date and Time dialog box in Figure 7.10b. Choose the format of the date that you prefer. Check the box to **Update Automatically** then click **OK** to accept the settings and close the dialog box. Press the **enter key.**

➤ Enter the course you are taking this semester. Press the **enter key** a final time. Click the **Stop Recording button** to end the macro.

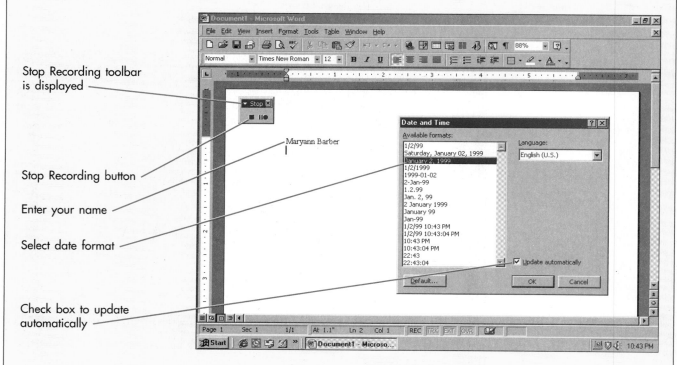

(b) Record the Macro (step 2)

FIGURE 7.10   Hands-on Exercise 4

THE INSERT DATE COMMAND

A date is inserted into a document in one of two ways—as a field that is updated automatically to reflect the current date or as a specific value (the date and time on which the command is executed). The determination of which way the date is entered depends on whether the Update Automatically check box is checked or cleared, respectively. Be sure to choose the option that reflects your requirements.

STEP 3: Run (Test) the Macro

➤ Click and drag to select your name, date, and class, then press the **Del key** to erase this information from the document.

➤ Pull down the **Tools menu.** Click **Macro,** then click the **Macros . . . command** to display the Macros dialog box in Figure 7.10c. Select **NameAndCourse** (the macro you just recorded) and click **Run.**

➤ Your name and class information should appear in the document. The type-face is 12 point Times New Roman, which corresponds to your selection when you recorded the macro initially. Do not be dismayed if the macro did not work properly as we show you how to correct it in the next several steps.

➤ Press the **enter key** a few times. Press **Alt+F8** (a keyboard shortcut) to display the Macros dialog box.

➤ Double click the **NameAndCourse** macro to execute the macro. Your name and class information is entered a second time.

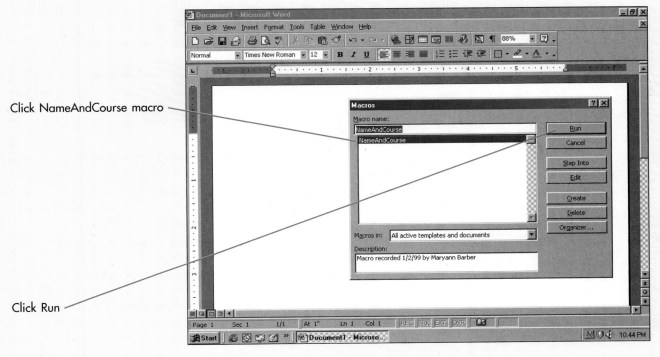

Click NameAndCourse macro

Click Run

(c) Test the Macro (step 3)

FIGURE 7.10   Hands-on Exercise 4 (continued)

KEYBOARD SHORTCUTS

Take advantage of built-in shortcuts to facilitate the creation and testing of a macro. Press Alt+F11 to toggle between the VBA editor and the Word document. Use the Alt+F8 shortcut to display the Macros dialog box, then double click a macro to run it. You can also assign your own keyboard shortcut to a macro, as will be shown later in the exercise.

STEP 4: View the Macro

➤ Pull down the **Tools menu,** click the **Macro command,** then click **Visual Basic Editor** (or press **Alt+F11**) to open the Visual Basic Editor. Maximize the VBE window. If necessary, pull down the **View menu** and click **Project Explorer** to open the Project window in the left pane. Close the Properties window if it is open.

➤ There is currently one project open, Document1, corresponding to the Word document on which you are working. Click the **plus sign** next to the Normal folder to expand that folder. Click the **plus sign** next to the **Modules folder** (within the Normal folder) then click **NewMacros.**

➤ Pull down the **View menu,** and click **Code** to open the Code window in the right pane. If necessary, click the maximize button in the Code window.

➤ Your screen should be similar to the one in Figure 7.10d except that it will reflect your name rather than John Smith within the macro. The name in the comment statement may be different, however, (especially if you are doing the exercise at school) as it corresponds to the person in whose name the program is registered.

Click + next to Normal folder (+ becomes −)

Click + next to Modules folder

Click NewMacros

Macro code is displayed

Name of Macro

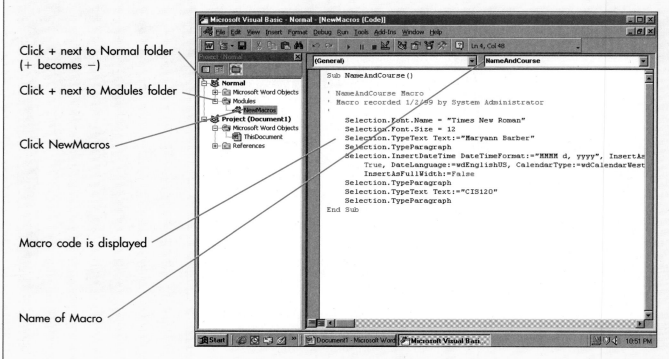

(d) View the Macro (step 4)

FIGURE 7.10   Hands-on Exercise 4 (continued)

RED, GREEN, AND BLUE

Visual Basic automatically assigns different colors to different types of statements (or a portion of those statements). Comments appear in green and are nonexecutable (i.e., they do not affect the outcome of a macro). Any statement containing a syntax error appears in red. Key words such as Sub and End Sub, With and End With, and True and False, appear in blue.

STEP 5: Edit the Macro

➤ If necessary, change the name in the comment statement to reflect your name. The macro will run identically regardless of the changes in the comments. Changes to the statements within the macro, however, affect its execution.

➤ Click and drag to select the existing font name, Times New Roman, then enter **Arial** as shown in Figure 7.10e. Be sure that the Arial appears within quotation marks. Change the font size to **24.**

➤ Click and drag to select the name of the course which is "CIS120" in our example. Type **InputBox("Enter Course Name")** to replace the selected text.

➤ Note that as you enter the Visual Basic key word, InputBox, a prompt (containing the correct syntax) is displayed on the screen as shown in Figure 7.10e.

➤ Ignore the prompt and keep typing to complete the entry. Be sure you enter a closing parenthesis. Click the **Save button.**

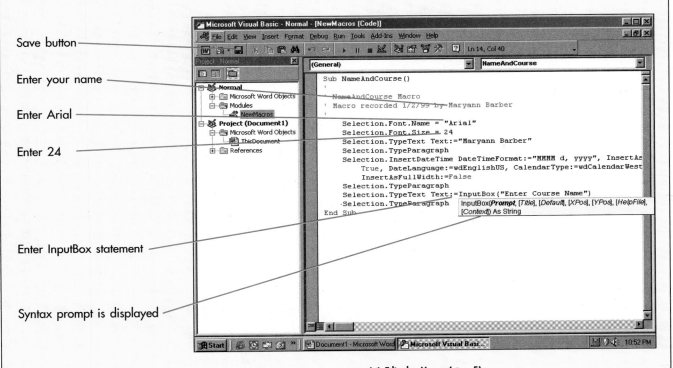

Save button

Enter your name

Enter Arial

Enter 24

Enter InputBox statement

Syntax prompt is displayed

(e) Edit the Macro (step 5)

FIGURE 7.10   Hands-on Exercise 4 (continued)

COPY, RENAME, AND DELETE MACRO

You can copy a macro, rename it, then use the duplicate macro as the basis of a new macro. Click and drag to select the entire macro, click the Copy button, click after the End Sub statement, and click the Paste button to copy the macro. Click and drag to select the macro name in the Sub statement, type a new name, and you have a new (duplicate) macro. To delete a macro, click and drag to select the entire macro and press the Del key.

STEP 6: Test the Revised Macro

➤ Press **Alt+F11** to toggle back to the Word document (or click the **Word button** on the taskbar). **Delete any text that is in the document.** If necessary, press **Ctrl+Home** to move to the beginning of the Word document.

➤ Press the **Alt+F8** key to display the Macros dialog box, then double click the **NameAndCourse** macro. The macro enters your name and date, then displays the input dialog box shown in Figure 7.10f.

➤ Enter any appropriate course and click **OK** (or press the **enter key**). You should see your name, today's date, and the course you entered in 24 point Arial type.

➤ Press **Alt+F11** to return to the Visual Basic Editor if the macro does not work as intended. Correct your macro so that its statements match those in step 5.

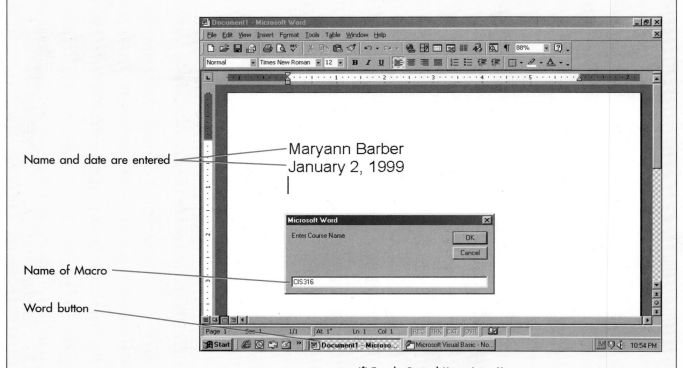

Name and date are entered

Name of Macro

Word button

(f) Test the Revised Macro (step 6)

FIGURE 7.10   Hands-on Exercise 4 (continued)

HELP FOR VISUAL BASIC

Click within any Visual Basic key word, then press the F1 key for context-sensitive help. You will see a help screen containing a description of the statement, its syntax, key elements, and several examples. You can print the help screen by clicking the Options command button and selecting Print. (If you do not see the help screens, ask your instructor to install Visual Basic Help.)

STEP 7: Record the TitlePage Macro

➤ If necessary, return to Word and delete the existing text in the document. Pull down the **Tools menu.** Click the **Macro command,** then click **Record New Macro** from the cascaded menu. You will see Record Macro dialog box as described earlier.

➤ Enter **TitlePage** as the name of the macro. Do not leave any spaces in the macro name. Click the **Keyboard button** in the Record Macro dialog box to display the Customize Keyboard dialog box in Figure 7.10g. The insertion point is positioned in the Press New Shortcut Key text box.

➤ Press **Ctrl+T** to enter this keystroke combination as the new shortcut; note, however, that this shortcut is currently assigned to the Hanging Indent command:

• Click the **Assign button** if you do not use the Hanging Indent shortcut,

• *Or,* choose a different shortcut for the macro (or omit the shortcut altogether) if you are already using Ctrl+T for the Hanging Indent command.

➤ Close the Customize Keyboard dialog box.

➤ You are back in your document and can begin recording your macro:

• Press **Ctrl+Home** to move to the beginning of the document.

• Press the **enter key** three times to insert three blank lines.

• Click the **Center button** to center the text that will be subsequently typed.

• Press the **enter key** to create an additional blank line

• Press **Ctrl+Enter** to create a page break.

➤ Click the **Stop Recording button** to end the macro.

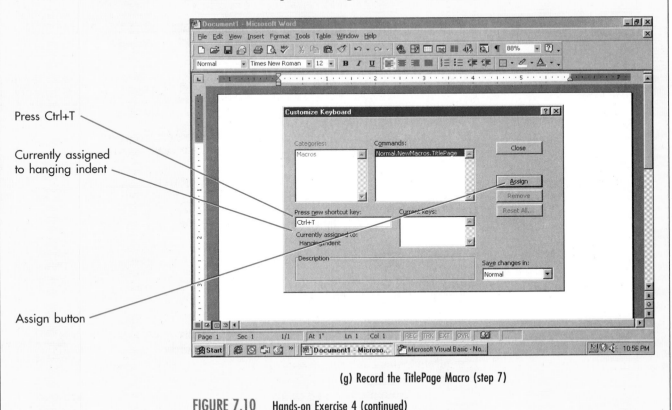

(g) Record the TitlePage Macro (step 7)

FIGURE 7.10   Hands-on Exercise 4 (continued)

STEP 8: Complete the TitlePage Macro

➤ Press **Alt+F11** to return to the Visual Basic Editor. You should see two macros, NameAndCourse and TitlePage. Click and drag to select the statements in the NameAndCourse macro as shown in Figure 7.10h.

➤ Click the **Copy button** on the Standard toolbar (or use the **Ctrl+C** shortcut) to copy these statements to the clipboard.

➤ Move to the TitlePage macro and click after the VBA statement to center a paragraph. Press **enter** to start a new line. Click the **Paste button** on the Standard toolbar (or use the **Ctrl+V** shortcut) to paste the statements from the NameAndCourse macro into the TitlePage macro.

➤ You can see the completed macro by looking at Figure 7.10j, the screen in step 10. Click the **Save button** to save your macros.

➤ Press **Alt+F11** to return to Word. Pull down the File menu and click the **Close command** to close the document you were using to create the macros in this exercise. There is no need to save that document.

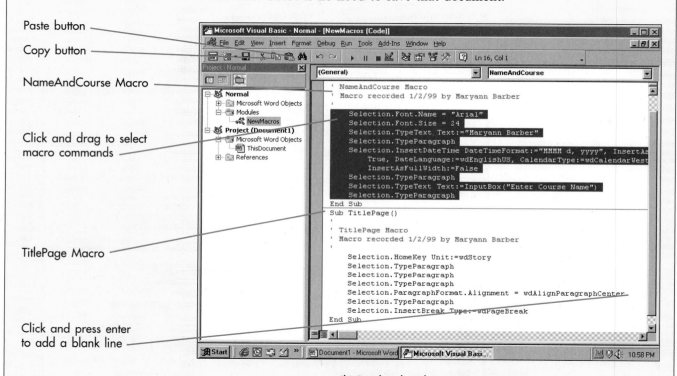

(h) Complete the TitlePage Macro (step 8)

FIGURE 7.10   Hands-on Exercise 4 (continued)

THE PAGE BORDER COMMAND

Add interest to a title page with a border. Click anywhere on the page, pull down the Format menu, click the Borders and Shading command, then click the Page Border tab in the Borders and Shading dialog box. You can choose a box, shadow, or 3-D style in similar fashion to placing a border around a paragraph. You can also click the drop-down arrow on the Art list box to create a border consisting of a repeating clipart image.

STEP 9: Test the TitlePage Macro

➤ Open the completed Word document (Executed Contract) from the second hands-on exercise. Click anywhere in the document, then press **Ctrl+T** to execute the TitlePage macro.

➤ Your name and date should appear, after which you will be prompted for your course. Enter the course you are taking and the macro will complete the title page.

➤ Pull down the **View menu** and change to the **Print Layout view.** Pull down the **View menu** a second time, click the **Zoom command,** click the option button for **Many Pages,** then click and drag the monitor to display three pages.

➤ You should see the executed contract with a title page as shown in Figure 7.10i. Print this document for your instructor. Save the document.

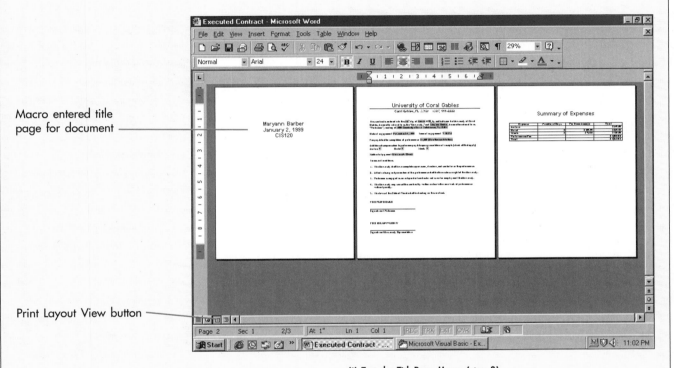

Macro entered title page for document —

Print Layout View button —

(i) Test the TitlePage Macro (step 9)

FIGURE 7.10   Hands-on Exercise 4 (continued)

TROUBLESHOOTING

If the shortcut keys do not work, it is probably because they were not defined properly. Pull down the View menu, click Toolbars, click Customize, then click the Keyboard command button to display the Customize Keyboard dialog box. Drag the scroll box in the Categories list box until you can select the Macros category. Select (click) the macro that is to receive the shortcut and click in the Press New Shortcut Key text box. Enter the desired shortcut, click the Assign button to assign the shortcut, then click the Close button to close the dialog box.

STEP 10: Print the Module

➤ Press **Alt+F11** to return to the Visual Basic Editor. Delete the second Selection.TypeParagraph line, as it is unnecessary.

➤ Pull down the **File menu.** Click **Print** to display the Print dialog box in Figure 7.10j. Click the option button to print the current module. Click **OK.** Submit the listing of the current module, which contains the procedures for both macros, to your instructor as proof you did this exercise.

➤ Delete all of the macros you have created in this exercise if you are not working on your own machine. Pull down the **File menu.** Click the **Close and Return to Word command.**

➤ Exit Word. The Title Page macro will be waiting for you the next time you use Microsoft Word provided you did the exercise on your own computer.

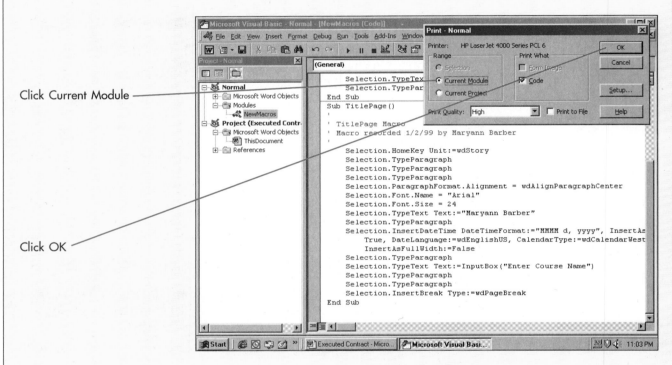

Click Current Module

Click OK

(j) Print the Macros (step 10)

FIGURE 7.10   Hands-on Exercise 4 (continued)

INVEST IN MACROS

Creating a macro takes time, but that time can be viewed as an investment, because a well-designed macro will simplify the creation of subsequent documents. A macro is recorded once, tested and corrected as necessary, then run (executed) many times. It is stored by default in the Normal template where it is available to every Word document. Yes, it takes time to create a meaningful macro, but once that's done, it is only a keystroke away.

Multiple persons within a workgroup can review a document and have their revisions stored electronically within that document. The changes are entered via various tools on the Reviewing toolbar. A red line through existing text indicates that the text should be deleted, whereas text that is underlined is to be added. Yellow highlighting indicates a comment where the reviewer has added a descriptive note without making a specific change.

A form facilitates data entry when the document is made available to multiple individuals via a network. It is created as a regular document with the various fields added through tools on the Forms toolbar. Word enables you to create three types of fields—text boxes, check boxes, and drop-down list boxes. After the form is created, it is protected to prevent further modification other than data entry.

The rows in a table can be sorted to display the data in ascending or descending sequence, according to the values in one or more columns in the table. Sorting is accomplished by selecting the rows within the table that are to be sorted, then executing the Sort command in the Tables menu. Calculations can be performed within a table using the Formula command in the Tables menu.

A master document consists of multiple subdocuments, each of which is stored as a separate file. It is especially useful for very large documents such as a book or dissertation, which can be divided into smaller, more manageable documents. The attraction of a master document is that you can work with multiple subdocuments simultaneously.

A macro is a set of instructions that automates a repetitive task. It is in essence a program, and its instructions are written in Visual Basic for Applications (VBA), a programming language. A macro is created initially through the macro recorder in Microsoft Word, which records your commands and generates the corresponding VBA statements. Once a macro has been created, it can be edited manually by inserting, deleting, or changing its statements. A macro is run (executed) by the Run command in the Tools menu or more easily through a keyboard shortcut.

KEY WORDS AND CONCEPTS

Accept and Review
    Changes command
Ascending sequence
Check box
Code window
Comment statement
Create New Folder
    command
Create Subdocument
    command
Date field
Descending sequence
Drop-down list box
End Sub statement
Field
Form
Forms toolbar

Header row
InputBox statement
Insert Date command
Insert Subdocument
    command
Keyboard shortcut
Macro
Macro recorder
Master document
Module
Password protection
Procedure
Project Explorer
Reviewing toolbar
Revision mark
Shortcut key
Sort command

Sub statement
Subdocument
Text field
Track Changes
    command
VBA
Versions command
Visual Basic for
    Applications
Workgroup

1. Which of the following is a true statement regarding password protection?
   (a) All documents are automatically saved with a default password
   (b) The password is case-sensitive
   (c) A password cannot be changed once it has been implemented
   (d) All of the above

2. Which statement describes the way revisions are marked in a document?
   (a) A red line appears through text that is to be deleted
   (b) A red underline appears beneath text that is to be added
   (c) Yellow highlighting indicates a comment, where the user has made a suggestion, but has not indicated the actual revision in the document
   (d) All of the above

3. Which of the following types of fields *cannot* be inserted into a form?
   (a) Check boxes
   (b) Text fields
   (c) A drop-down list
   (d) Radio buttons

4. Which of the following is true about a protected form (i.e., a form where the Protect Form button on the Forms toolbar is toggled on and is assumed to remain in that position)?
   (a) Data can be entered into the form
   (b) The text of the form cannot be modified
   (c) Both (a) and (b)
   (d) Neither (a) nor (b)

5. Which of the following describes the function of the Form Field Shading button on the Forms toolbar?
   (a) Clicking the button shades every field in the form
   (b) Clicking the button shades every field in the form and also prevents further modification to the form
   (c) Clicking the button removes the shading from every field
   (d) Clicking the button toggles the shading on or off

6. You have created a table containing numerical values and have entered the SUM(ABOVE) function at the bottom of a column. You then delete one of the rows included in the sum. Which of the following is true?
   (a) The row cannot be deleted because it contains a cell that is included in the sum function
   (b) The sum is updated automatically
   (c) The sum cannot be updated unless the Form Protect button is toggled off
   (d) The sum will be updated provided you right click the cell and select the Update field command

7. Which of the following is suitable for use as a master document?
   (a) An in-depth proposal that contains component documents that were created by different individuals
   (b) A lengthy newsletter with stories submitted by several people

(c) A book

(d) All of the above

8. Which of the following is true regarding changes made to a subdocument from within a master document?

   (a) The changes will be saved in the master document only

   (b) The changes will be saved in both the master document and the subdocument provided the subdocument is unlocked

   (c) The changes will be saved in both the master document and the subdocument provided the subdocument is locked

   (d) Changes cannot be made to a subdocument from within a master document

9. What happens if you click inside a subdocument, then click the Lock button on the Outlining toolbar?

   (a) The subdocument is locked

   (b) The subdocument is unlocked

   (c) The subdocument is locked or unlocked depending on its status prior to clicking the button

   (d) All editing to the subdocument is disabled

10. Which of the following describes the storage of a master document and the associated subdocuments?

    (a) Each document is saved under its own name as a separate file

    (b) All of the subdocuments must be stored in the same folder

    (c) Both (a) and (b)

    (d) Neither (a) nor (b)

11. Which of the following best describes the recording and execution of a macro?

    (a) A macro is recorded once and executed once

    (b) A macro is recorded once and executed many times

    (c) A macro is recorded many times and executed once

    (d) A macro is recorded many times and executed many times

12. Which of the following is true regarding comments in Visual Basic?

    (a) A comment is not executable; that is, its inclusion or omission does not affect the outcome of a macro

    (b) A comment begins with an apostrophe

    (c) Both (a) and (b)

    (d) Neither (a) nor (b)

13. Which commands are used to copy an existing macro so that it can become the basis of a new macro?

    (a) Copy command

    (b) Paste command

    (c) Both (a) and (b)

    (d) Neither (a) nor (b)

14. What is the default location for a macro created in Microsoft Word?

    (a) In the Normal template where it is available to every Word document

    (b) In the document in which it was created where it is available only to that document

    (c) In the Macros folder on your hard drive

    (d) In the Office folder on your hard drive

15. Which of the following correctly matches the shortcut to the associated task?
   (a) Alt+F11 toggles between Word and the Visual Basic Editor
   (b) Alt+F8 displays the Macros dialog box
   (c) Both (a) and (b)
   (d) Neither (a) nor (b)

ANSWERS

1. b	**6.** d	**11.** b
2. d	**7.** d	**12.** c
3. d	**8.** b	**13.** c
4. a	**9.** c	**14.** a
5. d	**10.** a	**15.** c

PRACTICE WITH MICROSOFT WORD

1. Reviewing a Document: Open the Chapter 7 Practice 1 document shown in Figure 7.11, then revise that document by incorporating all of the suggested revisions. Delete the existing comment, which appears as a screen tip in Figure 7.11, then insert your own comment indicating that you have completed the necessary revisions.

   Save the revised document as its own version within the Chapter 7 Practice 1 document. Print both versions of the document, the original and the one you created, and include the associated comments and properties for each version. These elements can be included with the printed document by clicking the Options button within the Print command.

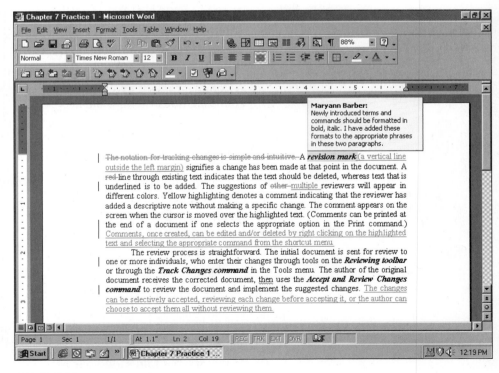

FIGURE 7.11   Reviewing a Document (Exercise 1)

2. Route a Document for Review: Do the two hands-on exercises as described in the text, then send a copy of the executed contract to your instructor as shown in Figure 7.12. You can use the Send To Mail Recipient button on the Reviewing toolbar to start your e-mail program, which in turn attaches the document automatically. Alternatively, you can start your e-mail program independently, then use the Insert Attachment command to select the appropriate document.

Either way, you will be sending an attached file to an e-mail recipient. You can include multiple attachments in the same message and/or send attachments of any file type. It's faster and cheaper than sending an overnight package.

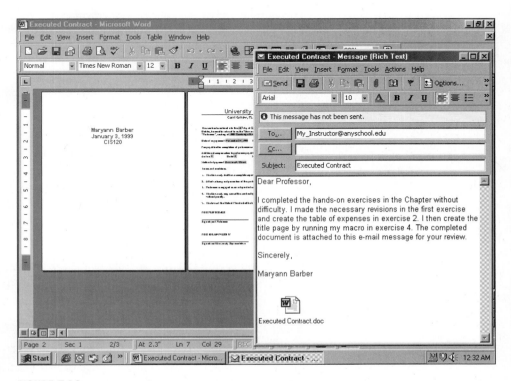

FIGURE 7.12   Route (Attach) Documents (Exercise 2)

3. Table Math: Figure 7.13 displays two versions of a table. Figure 7.13a shows the original table prior to any modification, whereas Figure 7.13b displays the table at the end of the exercise.

   a. Open the Chapter 7 Practice 3 file in the Exploring Windows folder.

   b. Click in the cell containing "Enter your name" and enter your last name. (White was the person added in our exercise.)

   c. Sort the table so that the names appear in alphabetical order. (By coincidence the names are in the same sequence after sorting.)

   d. Enter the appropriate formula for each cell person to compute the gain in sales over last year.

   e. Enter the appropriate formulas in the total row to complete the totals as shown in Figure 7.13b.

   f. Add a short memo to your instructor indicating that you have completed the table. Print the memo twice, once with displayed values as shown in Figure 7.13b, then a second time to show the cell formulas.

Sales Person	Last Year	This Year	Gain
Brown	200	225	
Jones	200	300	
Smith	125	140	
Your name goes here	100	450	
Total			

(a) Original Table (as it exists on disk)

Sales Person	Last Year	This Year	Gain
Brown	200	225	25
Jones	200	300	100
Smith	125	140	15
White	100	450	350
Total	625	1115	490

(b) Completed Table

FIGURE 7.13   Table Math (Exercise 3)

4. The Master Document: Do the third hands-on exercise as described in the chapter, then modify the master document as follows:

    a. Complete the subdocument, "Election of Offices" in which you propose nominations for the Board of Directors. Nominate yourself as the CEO and various classmates to fill the other positions.

    b. Delete the subdocument, "Plans for Next Year".

    c. Modify the Financial Summary document to include the table of fiscal results shown in Figure 7.14.

    d. Print the completed master document for your instructor. Print the document twice, in both the expanded and collapsed format.

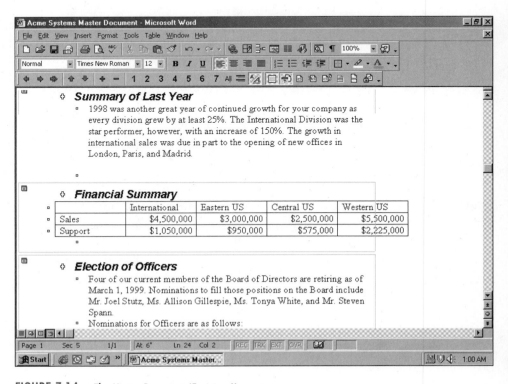

FIGURE 7.14   The Master Document (Exercise 4)

5. Customizing a Toolbar—Add a macro button: The chapter illustrated different ways to execute a macro—from the Tools menu in Word, by pressing Alt+F8 to display the Macros dialog box, and via a keyboard shortcut. You can also add a customized button to a toolbar as shown in Figure 7.15. Do the following:

a. Pull down the View menu, click Toolbars, then click Customize to display the Customize dialog box in Figure 7.15. Click the Commands tab, click the down arrow in the Categories list box until you see the Macros category, then click and drag the TitlePage macro from the Commands area in the Customize dialog box (it is not visible in Figure 7.15) to an existing toolbar.

b. Click the Modify Selection command button, click the Change Button Image command, then click the image you want for the toolbar button. Click the Modify Selection command button a second time, then click the Default style option to display just the image on the button as opposed to the image and the text. Click the Close button to accept the settings and close the Customize dialog box.

c. Open an existing Word document, then click the button to test it. Experiment with other options in the Customize dialog box, then summarize your findings in a brief note to your instructor.

d. See the case study on customizing a toolbar to add additional buttons corresponding to existing commands in Microsoft Word.

e. Read the Toolbar appendix to learn more about toolbars. You can change the ScreenTip for any button and / or modify its image. You can even create your own toolbars.

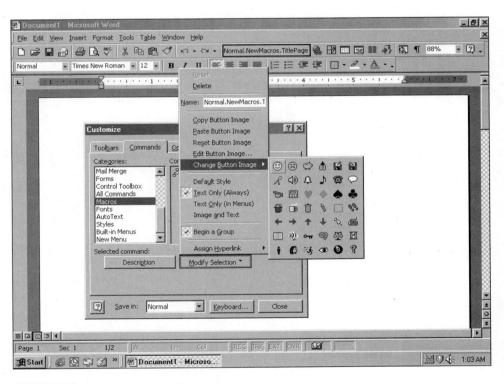

FIGURE 7.15   Customizing the Toolbar (Exercise 5)

6. **Debugging a Macro:** A "bug" is a mistake in a computer program; hence "debugging" refers to the process of correcting a programming error. One useful tool for debugging macro is the STEP Into command, in which you execute a macro one statement at a time as shown in Figure 7.16:

   a. Open any Word document, the press Alt+F11 to open VBE window. Click the Close button in the left pane to close the Project window within the Visual Basic Editor. The Code window expands to take the entire Visual Basic Editor window.

   b. Point to an empty area on the Windows taskbar, then click the right mouse button to display a shortcut menu. Click Tile Windows Vertically to tile the open windows (Word and the Visual Basic Editor). Your desktop should be similar to Figure 7.16. It doesn't matter if the document is in the left or right window. (If additional windows are open on the desktop, minimize the other windows, then repeat the previous step to tile the open windows.)

   c. Click in the Visual Basic Editor window, then click anywhere within the TitlePage macro. Pull down the Debug menu and click the STEP Into command (or press the F8 key) to enter the macro. The Sub statement is highlighted. Press the F8 key a second time to move to the first executable statement (the comments are skipped). The statement is selected (highlighted), but it has not yet been executed. Press the F8 key again to execute this statement and moves to the next statement.

   d. Continue to press the F8 key to execute the statements in the macro one at a time. You can see the effect of each statement as it is executed in the Word window.

   e. Do you think this procedure is useful in finding any bugs that might exist? Summarize the steps in debugging a macro in a short note to your instructor.

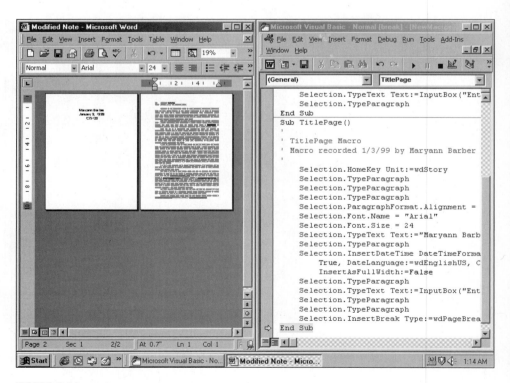

FIGURE 7.16   Debugging a Macro (Exercise 6)

Customize the Toolbar

The Create Envelope button is a perfect addition to the Standard toolbar if you print envelopes frequently. Pull down the Tools menu, click Customize, then click the Toolbars tab in the dialog box. If necessary, click the arrow in the Categories list box, select Tools, then drag the Create Envelope button to the Standard toolbar. Close the Customize dialog box. The Create Envelope button appears on the Standard toolbar and can be used the next time you need to create an envelope or label.

¿Cómo Está Usted?

The Insert Symbol command can be used to insert foreign characters into a document, but this technique is too slow if you use these characters with any frequency. Alternatively, you can use the predefined shortcut keys; for example, Ctrl+' followed by the letter "a" will insert á into a document. It's cumbersome, however, to remember the apostrophe, and we find it easier to create a macro and assign the shortcut Ctrl+A. Parallel macros can be developed for the other vowels or special characters, such as Ctrl+q for ¿. Try creating the appropriate macros, then summarize the utility of this technique in a short note to your instructor. Be sure to address the issue of using shortcuts that are already assigned to other macros; Ctrl+A, for example, is assigned to the Select All command by default.

Object Linking and Embedding

Table math is fine for simple calculations, but it is exceedingly limited when compared to Microsoft Excel. Thus, if you know Excel, you would be wise to explore the ability to link or embed an Excel workbook into a Word document. What is the difference between linking and embedding? Can the same workbook be associated with multiple Word documents? Does Object Linking and Embedding (OLE) pertain to applications other than Word and Excel? Use Appendix B as a starting point to learn about OLE, then summarize your findings in a short note to your instructor.

File Management in Microsoft Office

Most newcomers to Microsoft Office take the Open and Save As dialog boxes for granted. Look closely, however, and you will discover that these dialog boxes provide access to virtually all of the file management capabilities in Windows. You can create a folder, as was done in the chapter. You can also search for specific documents or create entries in the Favorites list. Write a short note to your instructor that summarizes the file management capabilities within the Open and Save dialog boxes. What additional capabilities are available through Windows Explorer that are not found within these dialog boxes?

appendix a

MAIL MERGE: SENDING FORM LETTERS

OVERVIEW

A *mail merge* can create any type of standardized document, but it is used most frequently to create a set of *form letters.* In essence, it creates the same letter many times, changing the name, address, and other information as appropriate from letter to letter. You might use a mail merge to look for a job upon graduation, when you send essentially the same cover letter to many different companies. The concept is illustrated in Figure A.1, in which John Smith has written a letter describing his qualifications, then merges that letter with a set of names and addresses to produce the individual letters.

The mail merge process uses two files as input, a main document and a data source. A set of form letters is created as output. The *main document* (e.g., the cover letter in Figure A.1a) contains standardized text, together with one or more *merge fields* that serve as placeholders for the variable data that will be inserted in the individual letters. The *data source* (the set of names and addresses in Figure A.1b) contains the information that varies from letter to letter. (You can also send the same document to an *alternative data source,* in which case the letter will go to a different set of names and addresses.)

The first row in the data source is called the *header row* and identifies the fields in the remaining rows. Each additional row contains the data to create one letter and is called a data record. Every data record contains the same fields in the same order; for example, Title, FirstName, LastName, and so on.

The main document and the data source work in conjunction with one another, with the merge fields in the main document referencing the corresponding fields in the data source. The first line in the address of Figure A.1a, for example, contains three entries in angle brackets, *«Title» «FirstName» «LastName».* (These entries are not typed explicitly but are entered through special commands, as described in the hands-on exercise that follows shortly.) The merge process examines each record in the data source and substitutes the appropriate field values for the corresponding merge fields as it creates the individual form letters. For example, the first three fields in the first record will produce *Mr. Jason Frasher.* The same fields in the second record will produce *Ms. Elizabeth Schery,* and so on.

John H. Smith

426 Jenny Lake Drive • Coral Gables, FL 33146 • (305) 666-4801

August 27, 1999

«Title» «FirstName» «LastName»
«JobTitle»
«Company»
«Address1»
«City», «State» «PostalCode»

Dear «Title» «LastName»:

I am writing to inquire about a position with «Company» as an entry-level computer programmer. I have just graduated from the University of Miami with a Bachelor's Degree in Computer Information Systems (May 1999) and I am very interested in working for you. I have a background in microcomputer applications (Windows 98, Word, Excel, PowerPoint, and Access) as well as extensive experience with programming languages (Visual Basic, C++, and COBOL). I feel that I am well qualified to join your staff as over the past two years I have had a great deal of experience designing and implementing computer programs, both as a part of my educational program and during my internship with Personalized Computer Designs, Inc.

I am eager to put my skills to work and would like to talk with you at your earliest convenience. I have enclosed a copy of my résumé and will be happy to furnish the names and addresses of my references. You may reach me at the above address and phone number. I look forward to hearing from you.

Sincerely,

John Smith

(a) The Main Document

FIGURE A.1   The Mail Merge

In similar fashion, the second line in the address of the main document contains the *«JobTitle»* field. The third line contains the *«Company»* field. The fourth line references the *«Address1»* field, and the last line contains the *«City», «State»,* and *«PostalCode»* fields. The salutation repeats the *«Title»* and *«LastName»* fields. The first sentence in the letter uses the *«Company»* field a second time. The mail merge prepares the letters one at a time, with one letter created for every record in the data source until the file of names and addresses is exhausted. The individual form letters are shown in Figure A.1c. Each letter begins automatically on a new page.

Title	FirstName	LastName	JobTitle	Company	Address1	City	State	PostalCode
Mr.	Jason	Frasher	President	Frasher Systems	1000 South Main Street	Miami	FL	33103
Ms.	Elizabeth	Schery	Director of Personnel	Custom Computing	1000 Federal Highway	Fort Lauderdale	FL	33124
Ms.	Lauren	Howard	President	Unique Systems	475 Le Jeune Road	Coral Gables	FL	33146
Mr.	Frank	Barber	President	Barber Systems, Inc	100 Las Olas Boulevard	Fort Lauderdale	FL	33124

(b) The Data Source

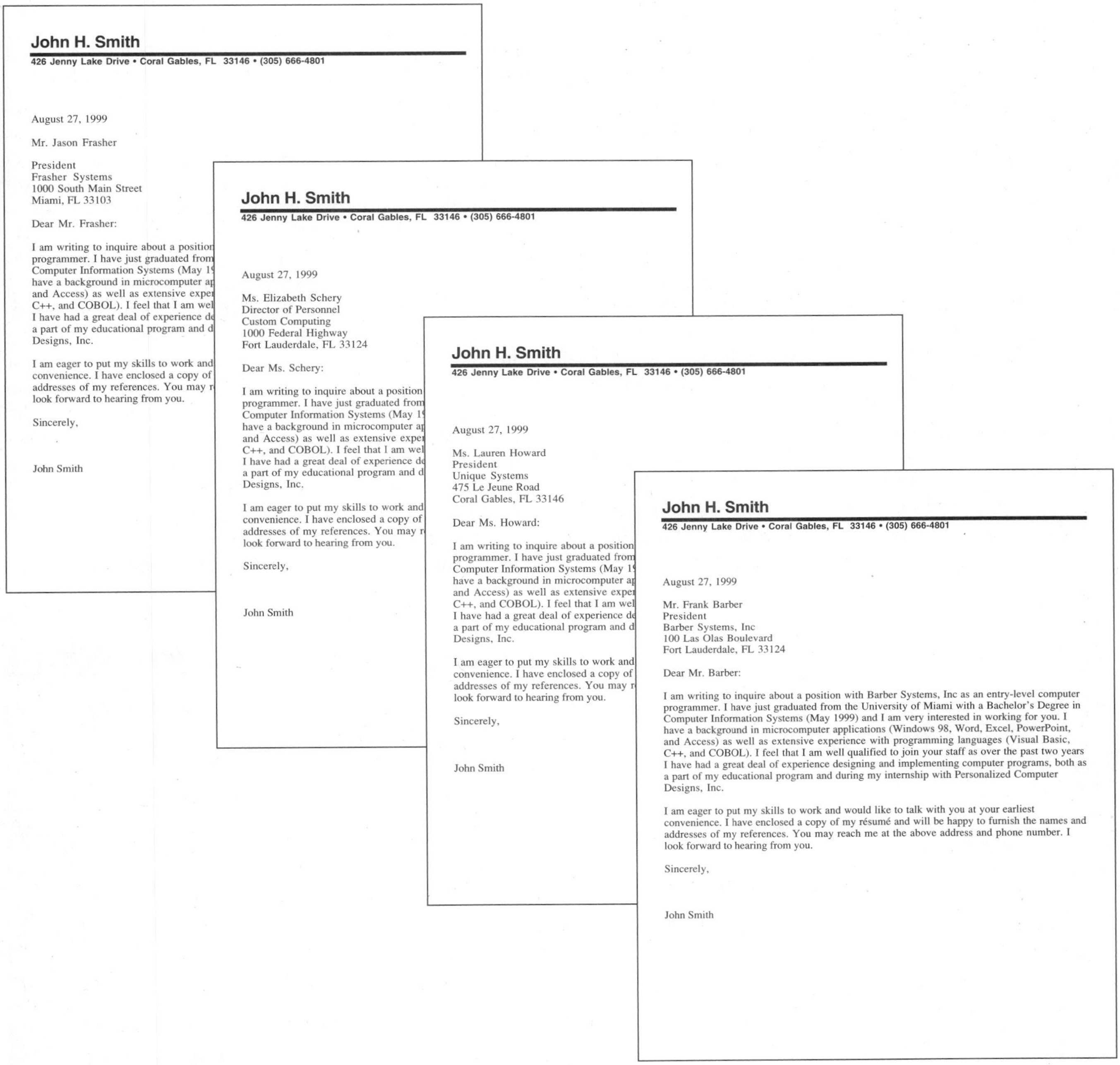

(c) The Printed Letters

FIGURE A.1   The Mail Merge (continued)

The implementation of a mail merge is accomplished through the **Mail Merge Helper** that lists the steps in the mail merge process and guides you through it. In essence there are three things you must do:

1. Create and save the main document
2. Create and save the data source
3. Merge the main document and data source to create the individual letters

The screen in Figure A.2 shows the Mail Merge Helper as it appears after steps 1 and 2 have been completed. The main document is the file *Form Letter.doc.* The data source is the file *Names and Addresses.doc.* All that remains is to merge the files and create the individual form letters. The options in effect indicate that the letters will be created in a new document and that blank lines, if any, in addresses (e.g., a missing company or title) will be suppressed. The **Query Options command** button lets you filter and/or sort the records in the data source prior to the merge.

The same data source can be used to create multiple sets of form letters through the application of different filters and/or sorts. A *filter* limits the set of form letters that are created in the mail merge to those records that satisfy a specified condition. You could, for example, create a filter to send records to only the individuals in Miami. The filter could also be expanded to include a logical Or and/or And condition. Thus, you could send letters to only the individuals in Miami and Fort Lauderdale. You could also create a different filter to restrict the mailing to persons in Orlando whose job title was president. A *sort* can be implemented regardless of whether a filter is in effect to print the letters in a specified sequence, such as zip code, to take advantage of bulk mail.

The form letters have to be mailed, which leads in turn to the creation of envelopes or mailing labels. This requires a second mail merge that is based on the same data source (the set of names and addresses used to create the form letters), but a different main document.

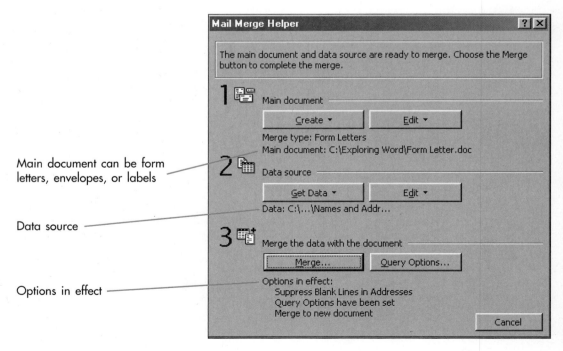

FIGURE A.2   Mail Merge Helper

Mail Merge

Objective: To create a main document and associated data source; to implement a mail merge and produce a set of form letters and associated envelopes; to illustrate filters and sorting. Use Figure A.3 as a guide.

STEP 1: Open the Cover Letter

➤ Open the **Form Letter** document in the **Exploring Word folder.** If necessary, change to the **Print Layout view** and zoom to **Page Width** as shown in Figure A.3a.

➤ Modify the letterhead to reflect your name and address. Click to the left of the "D" in Dear Sir, then press the **enter key** twice to insert two lines. Press the **up arrow** two times to return to the first line you inserted.

➤ Pull down the **Insert menu** and click the **Date and Time** command to display the dialog box in Figure A.3a. Select (click) the date format you prefer and, if necessary, check the box to update automatically. Click **OK** to close the dialog box.

➤ Save the document as **Modified Form Letter** so that you can return to the original document if necessary.

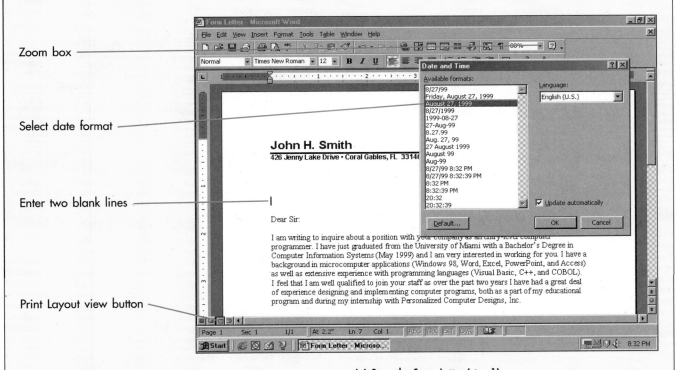

Zoom box

Select date format

Enter two blank lines

Print Layout view button

(a) Open the Cover Letter (step 1)

FIGURE A.3   Hands-on Exercise 1

STEP 2: Mail Merge Helper

➤ Pull down the **Tools menu.** Click **Mail Merge** to display the Mail Merge Helper shown in Figure A.3b. Click the **Create command button.**

➤ Click **Form Letters,** then click **Active Window** to indicate that you will use the Modified Form Letter (the document in the active window).

➤ Click **Get Data** under step 2 of the Mail Merge Helper, then click **Create Data Source** to display the Create Data Source dialog box. Word provides commonly used field names for the data source, but not all of the data fields are necessary. Click **Address2,** then click the **Remove Field Name** command button. Delete the **Country, HomePhone,** and **WorkPhone** fields.

➤ Click **OK** to complete the definition of the data source. You will then be presented with the Save As dialog box, as you need to save the data source.

➤ Type **Names and Addresses** in the File name text box as the name of the data source. Click **Save.** Click **Edit Data Source** in order to add records at this time.

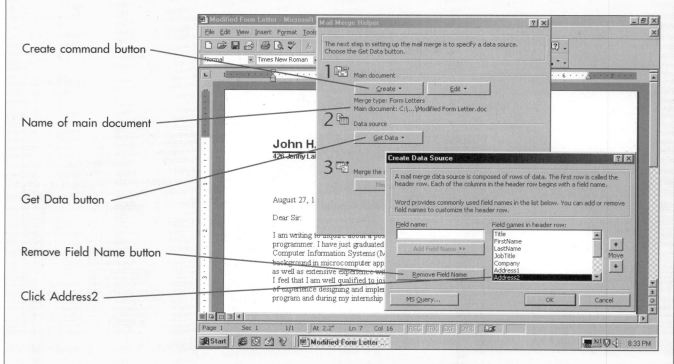

(b) Mail Merge Helper (step 2)

FIGURE A.3   Hands-on Exercise 1 (continued)

CATALOGS VERSUS FORM LETTERS

A catalog is similar in concept to a set of form letters except that the merged records do not begin on a new page. You could use this option to create a product catalog or employee list. The records in the data source might contain data about individual products or employees. The main document would include common text to describe the data. The merged document (i.e., the catalog) would consist of a single Word document, with each page containing data for one or more products or employees.

STEP 3: Add the Data

➤ Enter data for the first record. Type **Mr.** in the Title field. Press **Tab** to move to the next (FirstName) field and type **Jason.** Complete the first record as shown in Figure A.3c.

➤ Click the **Add New button** to enter the data for the next person to receive the letter. This is Ms. Elizabeth Schery, Director of Personnel, Custom Computing, 1000 Federal Highway, Fort Lauderdale, FL 33124.

➤ Click **Add New** to enter the next record. This is Ms. Lauren Howard, President, Unique Systems, 475 LeJeune Road, Coral Gables, FL 33146.

➤ And finally, click **Add New** to enter the data for the fourth and last recipient. This is Mr. Frank Barber, President, Barber Systems, Inc., 100 Las Olas Boulevard, Fort Lauderdale, FL 33124.

➤ Click **OK** to end the data entry and return to the main document. The Mail Merge toolbar is displayed immediately below the Formatting toolbar.

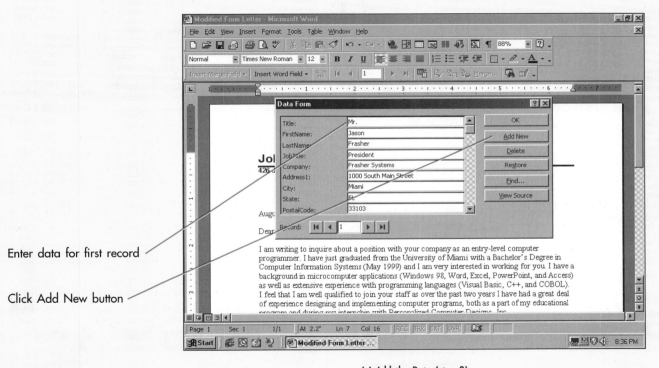

Enter data for first record

Click Add New button

(c) Add the Data (step 3)

FIGURE A.3   Hands-on Exercise 1 (continued)

THREE DIFFERENT FILES

A mail merge works with three different files. The main document and data source are input to the mail merge, creating a set of merged letters as output. You can use the same data source (e.g., a set of names and addresses) with different main documents (a form letter and an envelope) and/or use the same main document with multiple data sources. All three documents can be open at one time. Use the Windows menu (or click the corresponding button on the taskbar) to switch documents.

STEP 4: Insert the Merge Fields

➤ Click in the main document immediately below the date. Press **enter** to leave a blank line between the date and the first line of the address.

➤ Click the **Insert Merge Field button** on the Merge toolbar. Click **Title** from the list of fields within the data source. The title field is inserted into the main document and enclosed in angle brackets as shown in Figure A.3d.

➤ Press the **space bar** to add a space between the words. Click the **Insert Merge Field button** a second time. Click **FirstName.** Press the **space bar.** Click the **Insert Merge Field button** again. Click **LastName.**

➤ Press **enter** to move to the next line. Enter the remaining fields in the address as shown in Figure A.3d. Be sure to add a comma after the **City field** as well as a space.

➤ Delete the word "Sir" in the salutation and replace it with the **Title** and **Last Name fields.** Delete the words "your company" in the first sentence and replace them with the **Company field.** Save the main document.

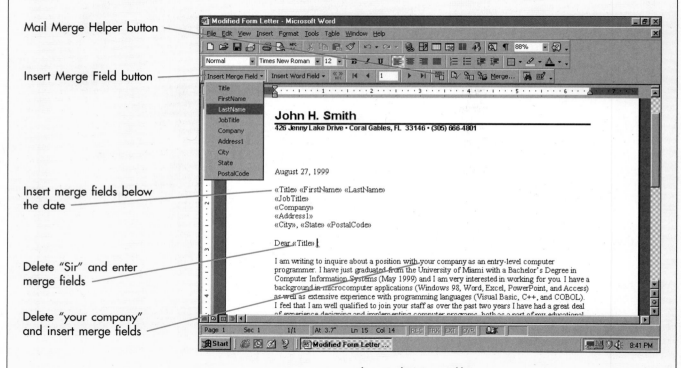

Mail Merge Helper button

Insert Merge Field button

Insert merge fields below the date

Delete "Sir" and enter merge fields

Delete "your company" and insert merge fields

(d) Insert the Merge Fields (step 4)

FIGURE A.3   Hands-on Exercise 1 (continued)

THE MAIL MERGE TOOLBAR

The Mail Merge toolbar lets you preview the form letters before they are created. Click the <<abc>> button to display field values rather than field codes. Click the button a second time and you switch back to field codes from field values. Use the navigation buttons to view the different letters. Click the ► button, for example, and you move to the next letter. Click the ►| button to display the form letter for the last record.

STEP 5: The Merge

➤ Click the **Mail Merge Helper button** to review your progress thus far:
  - The main document has been created and saved as Modified Form Letter.
  - The data source has been created and saved as Names and Addresses.

➤ Click the **Merge button** to display the Merge dialog box in Figure A.3e:
  - If necessary, click the down arrow in the Merge To list box and select **New document.**
  - If necessary, click the **All options button** to include all records in the data source.
  - If necessary, click the option button to **suppress (don't print) blank lines when data fields are empty.**

➤ Click the **Merge button** in the Merge dialog box. Word pauses momentarily, then generates the four form letters in a new document.

Name of main document

Name of data source

Merge button

Merge button

Select New document

Select All

Select Don't print blank lines

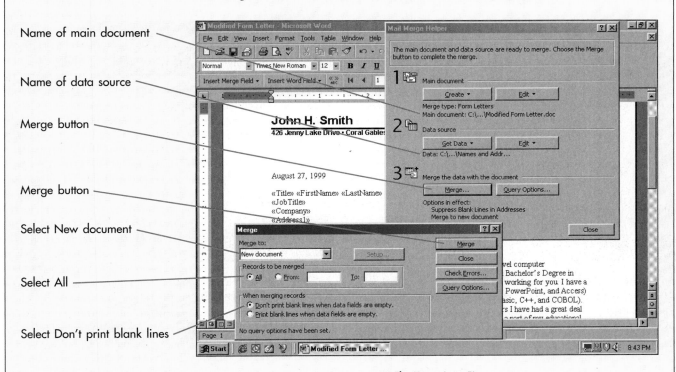

(e) The Merge (step 5)

FIGURE A.3   Hands-on Exercise 1 (continued)

EDIT THE DATA SOURCE

Click the Edit Data Source button on the Mail Merge toolbar to display the Data Form dialog box where you can view, add, edit, or delete records in the data source one at a time. You can also click the View Source button within the Data Form dialog box to see multiple records simultaneously. Edit the data source as necessary, then pull down the Window menu and click the name of the file containing the main document to continue working on the mail merge.

STEP 6: View the Form Letters

➤ The title bar of the active window changes to show Form Letters1, the document that contains the individual form letters. You are looking at the letter to Jason Frasher as shown in Figure A.3f. The status bar indicates that you are on the first for four pages in the active document.

➤ Click the **Next Page button** (or press **Ctrl+PgDn**) on the vertical scroll bar to view the next letter. This is the letter to Elizabeth Schery, the second person entered in the Names and Addresses file. The status bar indicates you are on page 2 of the document.

➤ View the letters for the other two persons in the file. We will not ask you to print the individual letters, although this could be easily done at this time.

➤ Close the **Form Letters1** document, as you will not need it further. There is no need to save this document, since you can always recreate it from the main document and data source.

Form Letters1 is in title bar

Letter to Mr. Jason Frasher

Next Page button

Current page is one of four pages

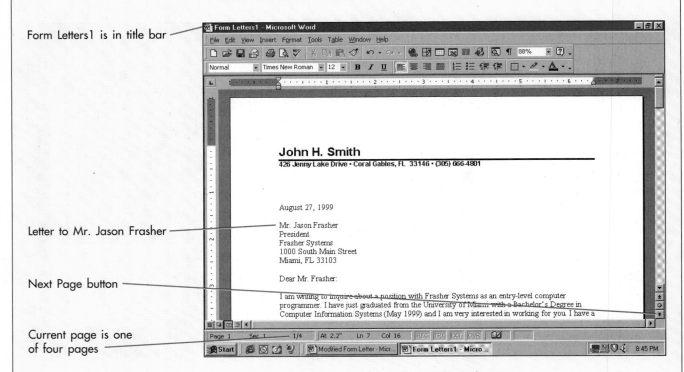

(f) View the Form Letters (step 6)

FIGURE A.3   Hands-on Exercise 1 (continued)

PAPER MAKES A DIFFERENCE

Most of us take paper for granted, but the right paper can make a significant difference in the effectiveness of the document, especially when you are trying to be noticed. Reports and formal correspondence are usually printed on white paper, but you would be surprised how many different shades of white there are. Other types of documents lend themselves to a specialty paper for additional impact. In short, the paper you use is far from an automatic decision. Consider the use of a specialty paper the next time you have an important project.

STEP 7: Sort and Filter

➤ Click the **Mail Merge Helper button** on the Mail Merge toolbar to display the Mail Merge Helper dialog box. Click the **Query Options command button** to display the Query Options dialog box as shown in Figure A.3g.

➤ If necessary, click the **Filter Records tab.** Click the **down arrow** on the Field list box and select the **City** field. Choose **Equal to** as the comparison and specify **Fort Lauderdale** as the city.

➤ Click the **Sort Records tab.** Click the **down arrow** in the first Sort by list box, choose the **LastName** field, and specify an **Ascending sort.** Click **OK.**

➤ Click the **Merge button** and use the same settings as before—a new document, include all the letters in the data source, and suppress blank lines if the data fields are empty. Click **Merge,** and once again Word pauses momentarily, then generates the form letters in a new document.

➤ The document is called **FormLetters2.** This time there are two letters, for Frank Barber and Elizabeth Schery, since these are the only two records where the city is Fort Lauderdale. The letters are in sequence by last name.

➤ Print both letters to submit to your instructor.

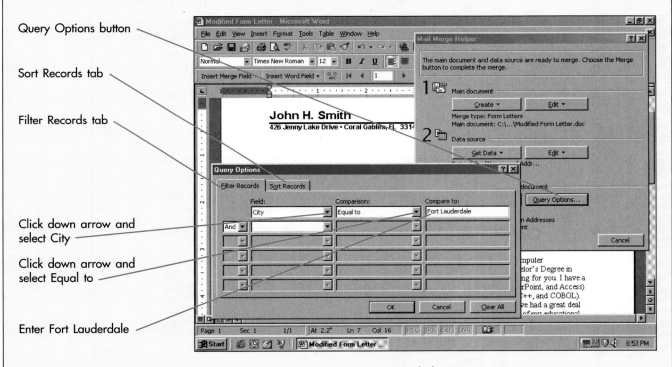

(g) Sort and Filter (step 7)

FIGURE A.3   Hands-on Exercise 1 (continued)

THE LETTERHEAD

A well-designed letterhead adds impact to your correspondence. Collect samples of professional stationery, then design your own letterhead. Consider a graphic logo, but keep it simple. You might also want to decrease the top margin so that the letterhead prints closer to the top of the page.

STEP 8: Create the Envelope

➤ Pull down the **Window menu** and click the **Modified Form Letter document** to return to the main document (or click its button on the Windows taskbar). Click the **Mail Merge Helper button** on the Mail Merge toolbar.

➤ Click the **Create button** (under step 1), select **Envelopes** as the type of document, then choose **New Main Document,** since we want to retain the existing form letter. Click the **Get Data button,** then choose the command to **Open Data Source.** Open the **Names and Addresses file** you created earlier.

➤ Click the **Set Up Main Document button.** Choose the type of envelope (a size 10 envelope is the default size for a business letter). Click **OK.**

➤ Click **OK** a second time when you see the Envelope Options dialog box. You should see the Envelope Address dialog box in Figure A.3h. Insert the merge fields as shown. Click **OK.**

➤ Click the **Query Options button** in the Mail Merge Helper dialog box. Use the same filter (City equals Fort Lauderdale) and sort (alphabetically by last name) as for the form letters you created in the previous step. Click **OK** to close the Query Options dialog box

➤ Click the **Merge button,** then click the second **Merge button** to create the envelopes in a new document. Do *not,* however, attempt to print the envelopes, since envelopes are not available in a computer lab.

➤ Close Envelopes1, the document containing the individual envelopes. There is no need to save this document, since you can always recreate it.

➤ Close Document3 (your number may differ) corresponding to the main document used to create the envelopes. Save this document as **Envelope Main Document.**

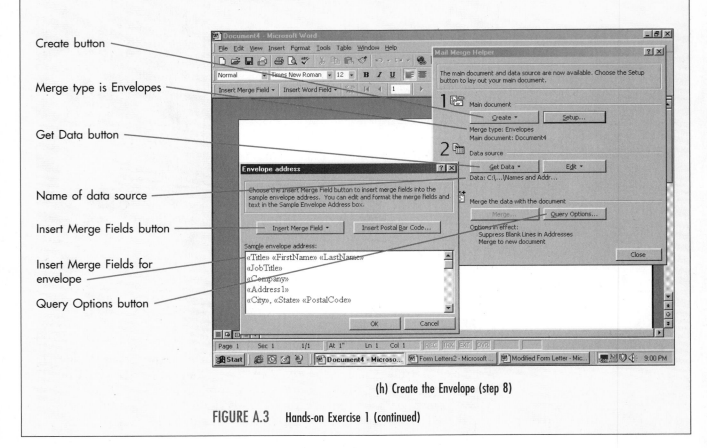

(h) Create the Envelope (step 8)

FIGURE A.3   Hands-on Exercise 1 (continued)

Step 9: Create the Mailing Labels

➤ Pull down the **Window menu** and click the **Modified Form Letter document** to return to the main document (or click its button on the Windows taskbar). Click the **Mail Merge Helper button** on the Mail Merge toolbar.

➤ Click the **Create button** (under step 1), select **Mailing Labels** as the type of document, then choose **New Main Document,** since we want to retain the existing form letter.

➤ Click the **Get Data button,** then choose the command to **Open Data Source.** Open the **Names and Addresses file** you created earlier.

➤ Click the **Set Up Main Document** button as instructed. There are many different types of labels available that can be purchased from an office supply store.

➤ Click the **down arrow** in the Product Number list box and select **5160—Address.** Click **OK** to open the Create Labels dialog box.

➤ Click the **Insert Merge button** to insert the various fields in each label. Click **OK** when you have completed the label. You will see a main document similar to Figure A.3i.

➤ Click the **Merge button** in the Mail Merge Helper dialog box, then click the second **Merge button** to create the mailing labels in a new document.

➤ Do not attempt to print the labels since mailing labels are not available in a computer lab.

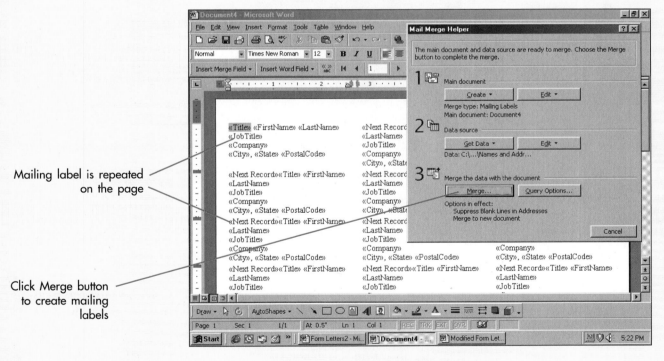

(i) Create the Mailing Labels (step 9)

FIGURE A.3   Hands-on Exercise 1 (continued)

Step 10: Choose an Alternate Data Source

➤ Pull down the **Window menu** and click **Document4** (your document may have a different number) to return to the main document for the mailing labels.

➤ Click the **Mail Merge Helper button** on the Mail Merge toolbar to display the Mail Merge Helper window. Click the **Get Data button** in step 2.

➤ Select **Open Data Source,** then open the **More Names** document in the **Exploring Word folder.**

➤ Click the **Merge button** in the Mail Merge Helper dialog box, then click the second **Merge button** to create a second set of mailing labels.

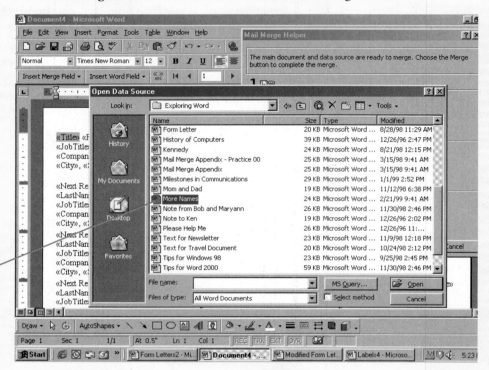

Select the More Names file as the alternate data source

(j) Choose an Alternate Data Source (step 10)

FIGURE A.3   Hands-on Exercise 1 (continued)

CUSTOMIZE THE TOOLBAR

Use the Envelopes and Labels command in the Tools menu to print a single envelope outside of a mail merge. You can even customize the Standard toolbar to include the Create Envelope button if you print envelopes frequently. Pull down the Tools menu, click Customize, then click the Commands tab in the dialog box. If necessary, click the down arrow in the Categories list box, select Tools, then drag the Envelopes and Labels button to the Standard toolbar. Close the Customize dialog box. The Envelopes and Labels button appears on the Standard toolbar and can be used the next time you need to create an envelope or label.

Step 11: Exit Word

➤ You should see a new document that contains the mailing labels based on the alternate data source, as shown in Figure A.3k. Once again, do not attempt to print these labels in a computer lab.

➤ Pull down the **File menu** and click **Exit** to exit Word. Pay close attention to the informational messages that ask whether to save the modified file(s):

  • There is no need to save either of the merged documents (Form Letters2 or Labels4), since you can always recreate the merged documents from the main document and data source.

  • Save the Modified Form Letter and Names and Addresses documents if you are asked to do so. Save the main document that was created to generate the mailing labels as **Mailing Labels Main Document.**

➤ Congratulations on a job well done. Good luck in your job hunting!

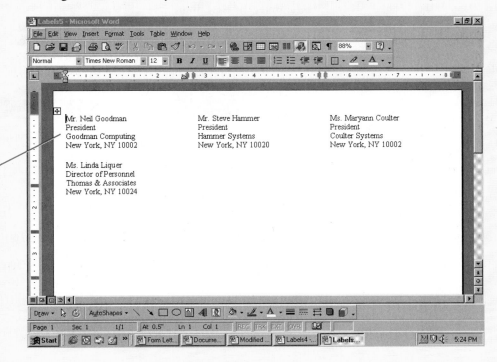

Four mailing labels were printed from the alternate data source

(k) Exit Word (step 11)

FIGURE A.3   Hands-on Exercise 1 (continued)

THIRTY SECONDS IS ALL YOU HAVE

Thirty seconds is the average amount of time a personnel manager spends skimming your résumé and deciding whether or not to call you for an interview. It doesn't matter how much you know or how good you are if your résumé and cover letter do not project a professional image. Know your audience and use the vocabulary of your targeted field. Be positive and describe your experience from an accomplishment point of view. Maintain a separate list of references and have it available on request. Be sure all information is accurate. Be conscientious about the design of your résumé and proofread the final documents very carefully

SUMMARY

A mail merge creates the same letter many times, changing only the variable data, such as the addressee's name and address, from letter to letter. It is performed in conjunction with a main document and a data source, which are stored as separate documents. The mail merge can be used to create a form letter for selected records, and/or print the form letters in a sequence different from the way the records are stored in the data source.

The same data source can be used to create multiple sets of form letters through the application of different filters and/or sorts. A filter limits the set of form letters that are created in the mail merge to those records that satisfy a specified condition. A sort can be implemented regardless of whether a filter is in effect to print the letters in a specified sequence, such as zip code to take advantage of bulk mail.

The Mail Merge Helper enables you to create envelopes or mailing labels in support of form letters. Microsoft Word also contains an Envelopes and Labels command for use in creating envelopes or labels outside of a mail merge

KEY WORDS AND CONCEPTS

Alternative data
  source
Catalog
Data source
Envelopes and Labels
  command
Field

Field code
Field result
Filter
Form letter
Header row
Mail merge
Mail Merge Helper

Main document
Merge field
Query Options
  command
Record
Sort

appendix b

OBJECT LINKING
AND EMBEDDING

OVERVIEW

The ability to create a document containing data (objects) from multiple applications is one of the primary advantages of the Windows environment. The memo in Figure B.1, for example, was created in Microsoft Word, and it contains a worksheet from Microsoft Excel. *Object Linking and Embedding* (abbreviated OLE and pronounced "OH-lay") is the means by which you insert an object from a source file (e.g., an Excel workbook) into a destination file (e.g., a Word document).

The essential difference between linking and embedding is whether the object in the destination file maintains a connection to the source file. A *linked object* maintains the connection. An *embedded object* does not. A linked object can be associated with many different destination files that do not contain the object per se, but only a representation of the object as well as a pointer (link) to the source file containing the object. Any change to the object in the source file is reflected automatically in every destination file that is linked to that object. An embedded object, however, is contained entirely within the destination file. Changes to the object in the destination file are *not* reflected in the source file.

The choice between linking and embedding depends on how the object will be used. Linking is preferable if the object is likely to change and the destination file requires the latest version. Linking should also be used when the same object is placed in many documents, so that any change to the object has to be made in only one place. Embedding is preferable if you intend to edit the destination file on a computer other than the one on which it was created.

The exercise that follows shows you how to create the compound document in Figure B.1. The exercise uses the *Insert Object command* to embed a copy of the Excel worksheet into a Word document. Once an object has been embedded into a document, it can be modified through *in-place editing.* In-place editing enables you to double click an embedded object (the worksheet) and change it, using the tools of the source application (Excel). In other words, you remain in Microsoft Word, but you have access to the Excel toolbar and pull-down menus. In-place editing modifies the copy of the embedded object in the destination file. It does *not* change the original object because there is no connection (or link) between the source file (if indeed there is a source file) and the destination file.

Lionel Douglas

402 Mahoney Hall • Coral Gables, Florida 33124

January 3, 1999

Dear Folks,

I heard from Mr. Black, the manager at University Commons, and the apartment is a definite for next semester. Ken and I are very excited, and can't wait to get out of the dorm. The food is poisonous, not that either of us is a cook, but anything will be better than this! I have been checking into car prices (we are definitely too far away from campus to walk!), and have done some estimating on what it will cost. The figures below are for a Jeep Wrangler, the car of my dreams:

Price of car	$11,995			
Manufacturer's rebate	$1,000			
Down payment	$3,000	**My assumptions**		
Amount to be financed	$7,995	Interest rate		7.90%
Monthly payment	$195	Term (years)		4
Gas	$40			
Maintenance	$50			
Insurance	$100			
Total per month	$385			

My initial estimate was $471 based on a $2,000 down payment and a three-year loan at 7.9%. I know this is too much so I plan on earning an additional $1,000 and extending the loan to four years. That will bring the total cost down to a more manageable level (see the above calculations). If that won't do it, I'll look at other cars.

Lionel

FIGURE B.1   A Compound Document

Embedding

Objective: To embed an Excel worksheet into a Word document; to use in-place editing to modify the worksheet within Word. Use Figure B.2 as a guide in the exercise.

STEP 1: Open the Word Document

➤ Start Word. Open the **Car Request document** in the **Exploring Word folder.** Zoom to **Page Width** so that the display on your monitor matches ours.

➤ Save the document as **Modified Car Request** so that you can return to the original document if you edit the duplicated file beyond redemption.

➤ Point to the date field, click the **right mouse button** to display the shortcut menu in Figure B.2a, then click the **Update Field command.**

Point to date and click right mouse button to display shortcut menu

Click Update Field

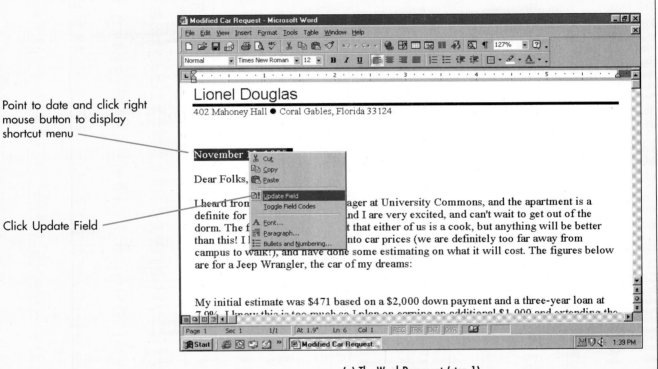

(a) The Word Document (step 1)

FIGURE B.2   Hands-on Exercise 1

THE DATE FIELD

The Insert Date and Time command enables you to insert the date as a specific value (the date on which a document is created) or as a field. The latter will be updated automatically whenever the document is printed or when the document is opened in Page Layout view. Opening the document in the Normal view requires the date field to be updated manually.

STEP 2: Insert an Object

➤ Click the blank line above paragraph two as shown in Figure B.2b. This is the place in the document where the worksheet is to go.

➤ Pull down the **Insert menu**, and click the **Object command** to display the Object dialog box in Figure B.2b.

➤ Click the **Create from File tab,** then click the **Browse command button** in order to open the Browse dialog box and select the object.

➤ Click (select) the **Car Budget workbook** (note the Excel icon), which is in the Exploring Word folder.

➤ Click **Insert** to select the workbook and close the Browse dialog box.

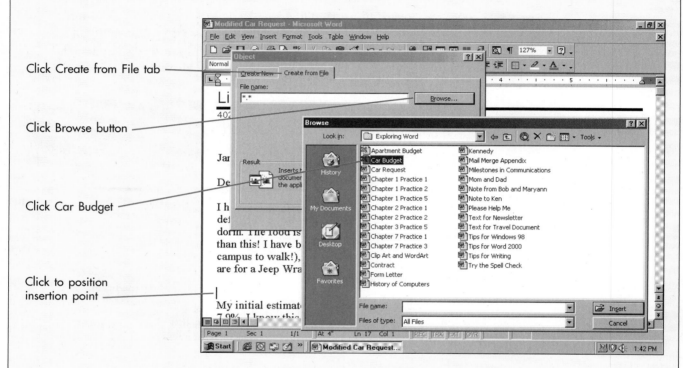

Click Create from File tab

Click Browse button

Click Car Budget

Click to position insertion point

(b) Insert Object Command (step 2)

FIGURE B.2   Hands-on Exercise 1 (continued)

STEP 3: Insert an Object (continued)

➤ The file name of the object (Car Budget.xls) has been placed into the File Name text box, as shown in Figure B.2c.

➤ Verify that the Link to File and Display as Icon check boxes are clear.

➤ Note the description at the bottom of the Object dialog box, which indicates that you will be able to edit the object using the application that created the source file.

➤ Click **OK** to insert the Excel worksheet into the Word document. Save the document.

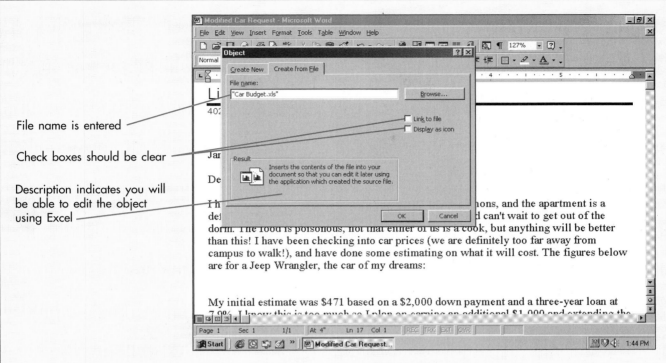

File name is entered

Check boxes should be clear

Description indicates you will be able to edit the object using Excel

(c) Insert Object Command (step 3)

FIGURE B.2   Hands-on Exercise 1 (continued)

STEP 4: Position the Worksheet

➤ The worksheet should appear within the Word document. If necessary, click (select) the worksheet to display the sizing handles as shown in Figure B.2d.

➤ To move the worksheet:
  • Point anywhere on the worksheet except a sizing handle (the mouse pointer changes to a four-sided arrow), then click and drag to move the worksheet.

➤ To size the worksheet:
  • Drag a corner handle (the mouse pointer changes to a double arrow) to change the length and width simultaneously.
  • Drag a handle on any border to change one dimension.

➤ Click anywhere in the document, except for the worksheet. The sizing handles disappear and the worksheet is no longer selected.

➤ If necessary, click above and/or below the worksheet, then press the **enter key** to insert a blank line(s) for better spacing. Save the document.

THE FORMAT OBJECT DIALOG BOX

An Excel workbook has only limited movement within a Word document unless its properties are changed through the Format Object command. Point to the worksheet, click the right mouse button to display a shortcut menu, click the Format Object command, then click the Advanced command button. Click the Text Wrapping tab, then click the icon for Top and Bottom wrapping style. Click OK to close the Advanced Layout dialog box. Click OK a second time to close the Format Object dialog box.

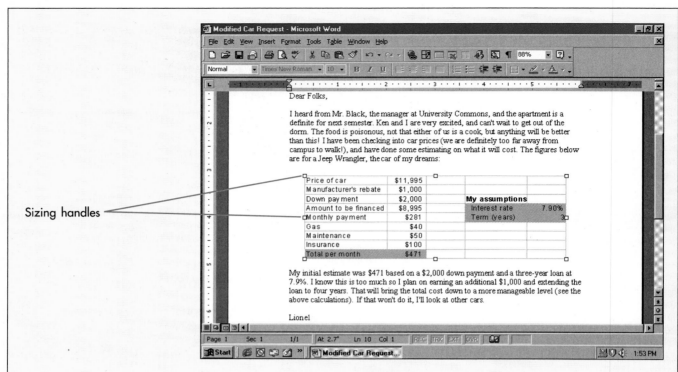

Sizing handles

(d) Position the Worksheet (step 4)

FIGURE B.2   Hands-on Exercise 1 (continued)

STEP 5: In-place Editing

➤ We will change the worksheet to reflect Lionel's additional $1,000 for the down payment. Double click the worksheet object to edit the worksheet in place.

➤ Be patient as this step takes a while, even on a fast machine. The Excel grid, consisting of the row and column labels, will appear around the worksheet, as shown in Figure B.2e.

➤ You are still in Word, as indicated by the title bar (Modified Car Request—Microsoft Word), but the Excel toolbars are displayed.

➤ Click in cell **B3,** type the new down payment of **$3,000,** and press **enter.**

➤ Click in cell **E5,** type **4,** and press **enter.** The Monthly payment (cell B5) and Total per month (cell B9) drop to $195 and $385, respectively.

IN-PLACE EDITING

In-place editing enables you to edit an embedded object using the toolbar and pull-down menus of the original application. Thus, when editing an Excel worksheet embedded into a Word document, the title bar is that of Microsoft Word, but the toolbars and pull-down menus are from Excel. There are, however, two exceptions; the File and Window menus are from Microsoft Word, so that you can save the compound document and/or arrange multiple documents.

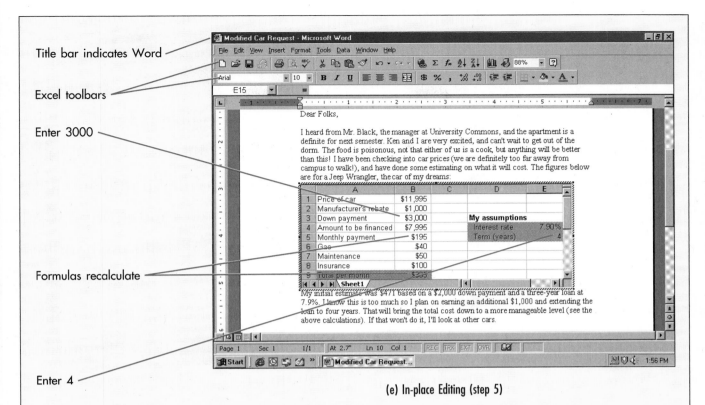

Title bar indicates Word

Excel toolbars

Enter 3000

Formulas recalculate

Enter 4

(e) In-place Editing (step 5)

FIGURE B.2   Hands-on Exercise 1 (continued)

STEP 6: The Completed Document

➤ Click anywhere outside the worksheet to deselect it. Press **Ctrl+Home** to move to the beginning of the document, then scroll as necessary to view the completed Word document as shown in Figure B.2f.

➤ Pull down the **File menu** and click **Save** (or click the **Save button** on the Standard toolbar).

➤ Pull down the **File menu** a second time. Click **Exit** if you do not want to continue with the next hands-on exercise once this exercise is completed. Otherwise click **Close** to remove the document from memory but leave Word open.

TO CLICK OR DOUBLE CLICK

Clicking an object selects the object and displays the sizing handles, which let you move and/or size the object. Double clicking an object starts the application that created the object and enables you to modify the object using that application. Double click a worksheet, for example, and you start Microsoft Excel from where you can modify the worksheet without exiting from Microsoft Word.

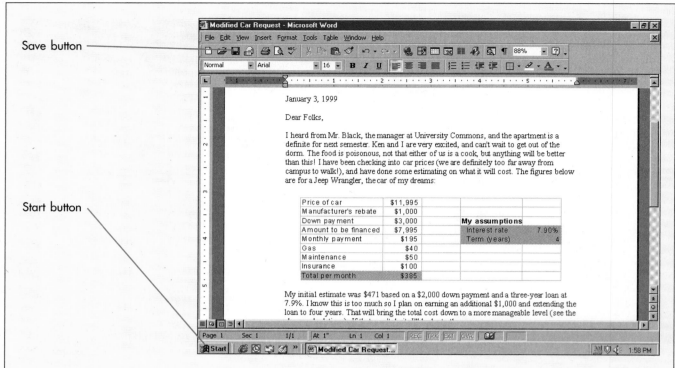

Save button ——

Start button ——

(f) The Completed Word Document (step 6)

FIGURE B.2 Hands-on Exercise 1 (continued)

STEP 7: View the Original Object

➤ Click the **Start Button,** click (or point to) the **Programs menu,** then click **Microsoft Excel** to open the program.

➤ If necessary, click the **Maximize button** in the application window so that Excel takes the entire desktop, as shown in Figure B.2g.

➤ Pull down the **File menu** and click **Open** (or click the **Open button** on the Standard toolbar) to display the Open dialog box.

• Click the **drop-down arrow** on the Look In list box. Click the appropriate drive, drive C or drive A, depending on the location of your data.

• Double click the **Exploring Word folder** to make it the active folder.

• Click (select) **Car Budget** to select the workbook that we have used throughout the exercise.

• Click the **Open command button** to open the workbook, as shown in Figure B.2g.

• Click the **Maximize button** in the document window (if necessary) so that the document window is as large as possible.

➤ You should see the original (unmodified) worksheet, with a down payment of $2,000, a three-year loan, a monthly car payment of $281, and total expenses per month of $471. The changes that were made in step 6 were made to the compound document and are *not* reflected in the source file.

➤ Pull down the **File menu.** Click **Exit** to exit Microsoft Excel.

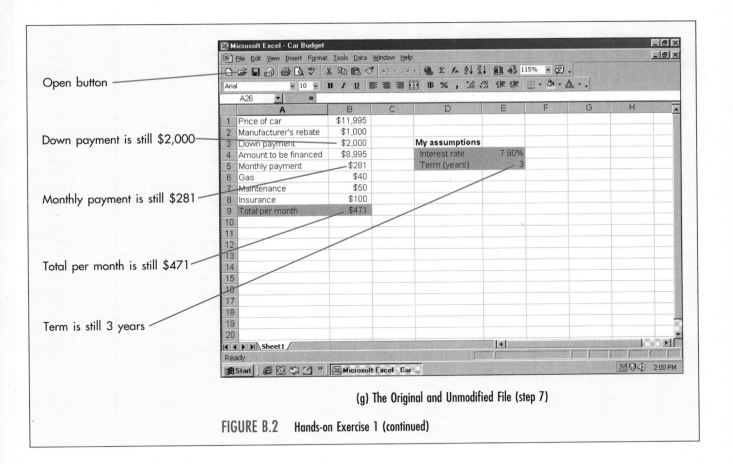

Open button

Down payment is still $2,000

Monthly payment is still $281

Total per month is still $471

Term is still 3 years

(g) The Original and Unmodified File (step 7)

FIGURE B.2   Hands-on Exercise 1 (continued)

LINKING

The exercise just completed used embedding rather than linking to place a copy of the Excel worksheet into the Word document. The last step in the exercise demonstrated that the original worksheet was unaffected by changes made to the embedded copy within the compound document (destination file).

Linking is very different from embedding as you shall see in the next exercise. Linking maintains a dynamic connection between the source and destination files. Embedding does not. With linking, the object created by the source application (e.g., an Excel worksheet) is tied to the destination file (e.g., a Word document) in such a way that any changes in the Excel worksheet are automatically reflected in the Word document. The Word document does not contain the worksheet per se, but only a representation of the worksheet, as well as a pointer (or link) to the Excel workbook.

Linking requires that an object be saved in its own file because the object does not actually exist within the destination file. Embedding, on the other hand, lets you place the object directly in a destination file without having to save it as a separate file. (The embedded object simply becomes part of the destination file.)

Consider now Figure B.3, in which the same worksheet is linked to two different documents. Both documents contain a pointer to the worksheet, which may be edited by double clicking the object in either document. Alternatively, you may open the source application and edit the object directly. In either case, changes to the Excel workbook are reflected in every destination file that is linked to the workbook.

Lionel Douglas

402 Mahoney Hall • Coral Gables, Florida 33124

Dear Mom and Dad,

Enclosed please find the budget for my apartment at University Commons. As I told you before, it's a great apartment and I can't wait to move.

	Total	Individual
Rent	$895	$298
Utilities	$125	$42
Cable	$45	$15
Phone	$60	$20
Food	$600	$200
Total		$575
Persons	3	

I really appreciate everything that you and Dad are doing for me. I'll be home next week after finals.

Lionel

(a) First Document (Mom and Dad)

Lionel Douglas

402 Mahoney Hall • Coral Gables, Florida 33124

Dear Ken,

I just got the final figures for our apartment next year and am sending you an estimate of our monthly costs. I included the rent, utilities, phone, cable, and food. I figure that food is the most likely place for the budget to fall apart, so learning to cook this summer is critical. I'll be taking lessons from the Galloping Gourmet, and suggest you do the same. Enjoy your summer and Bon Appetit.

	Total	Individual
Rent	$895	$298
Utilities	$125	$42
Cable	$45	$15
Phone	$60	$20
Food	$600	$200
Total		$575
Persons	3	

Guess what - the three bedroom apartment just became available which saves us more than $100 per month over the two bedroom we had planned to take. Jason Adler has decided to transfer and he can be our third roommate.

Lionel

(b) Second Document (Note to Ken)

	Total	Individual
Rent	$895	$298
Utilities	$125	$42
Cable	$45	$15
Phone	$60	$20
Food	$600	$200
Total		$575
Persons	3	

(c) Worksheet (Apartment Budget)

FIGURE B.3 Linking

The next exercise links a single Excel worksheet to two different Word documents. During the course of the exercise both applications (Word and Excel) will be explicitly open, and it will be necessary to switch back and forth between the two. Thus, the exercise also demonstrates the multitasking capability within Windows and the use of the taskbar to switch between the open applications.

Linking

Objective: To demonstrate multitasking and the ability to switch between applications; to link an Excel worksheet to multiple Word documents. Use Figure B.4 as a guide in the exercise.

STEP 1: Open the Word Document

➤ Check the taskbar to see whether there is a button for Microsoft Word indicating that the application is already active in memory. Start Word if you do not see its button on the taskbar.

➤ Open the **Mom and Dad document** in the **Exploring Word folder** as shown in Figure B.4a. The document opens in the Normal view (the view in which it was last saved). If necessary, zoom to **Page Width** so that the display on your monitor matches ours.

➤ Save the document as **Modified Mom and Dad.**

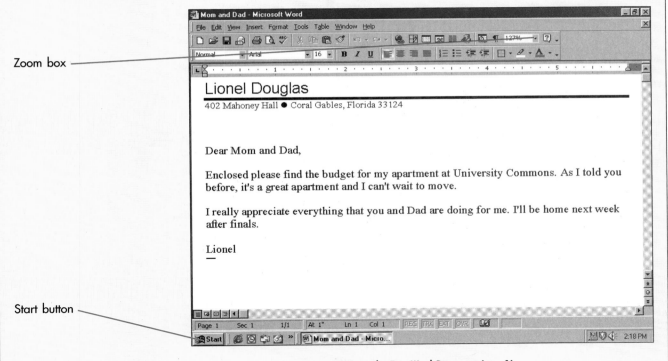

Zoom box

Start button

(a) Open the First Word Document (step 1)

FIGURE B.4   Hands-on Exercise 2

STEP 2: Open the Excel Worksheet

➤ Click the **Start button,** click (or point to) the **Programs menu,** then click **Microsoft Excel** to open the program.

➤ If necessary, click the **Maximize button** in the application window so that Excel takes the entire desktop. Click the **Maximize button** in the document window (if necessary) so that the document window is as large as possible.

➤ The taskbar should now contain buttons for both Microsoft Word and Microsoft Excel. Click either button to move back and forth between the open applications. End by clicking the Microsoft Excel button, since you want to work in that application.

➤ Pull down the **File menu** and click **Open** (or click the **Open button** on the Standard toolbar) to display the Open dialog box in Figure B.4b.

➤ Click the **drop-down arrow** on the Look In list box. Click the appropriate drive, drive C or drive A, depending on the location of your data. Double click the **Exploring Word folder** to make it the active folder. Double click **Apartment Budget** to open the workbook.

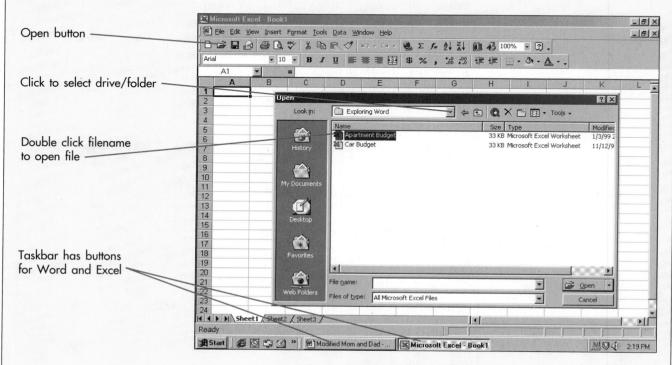

Open button

Click to select drive/folder

Double click filename to open file

Taskbar has buttons for Word and Excel

(b) Open the Excel Workbook (step 2)

FIGURE B.4   Hands-on Exercise 2 (continued)

THE COMMON USER INTERFACE

The common user interface provides a sense of familiarity from one Windows application to the next. Even if you have never used Excel, you will recognize many of the elements present in Word. Both applications share a common menu structure with consistent ways to execute commands from those menus. The Standard and Formatting toolbars are present in both applications. Many keyboard shortcuts are also common—for example Ctrl+Home and Ctrl+End to move to the beginning and end of a document.

STEP 3: Copy the Worksheet to the Clipboard

➤ Click in cell **A1.** Drag the mouse over cells **A1 through C9** so that the entire worksheet is selected as shown in Figure B.4c.

➤ Point to the selected cells, then click the **right mouse button** to display the shortcut menu shown in the figure. Click **Copy.** A moving border appears around the selected area in the worksheet, indicating that it has been copied to the clipboard.

➤ Click the **Microsoft Word button** on the Windows taskbar to return to the Word document.

Click and drag to select A1:C9

Point to selected cells and click right mouse button to display shortcut menu

Click copy

Click Word button

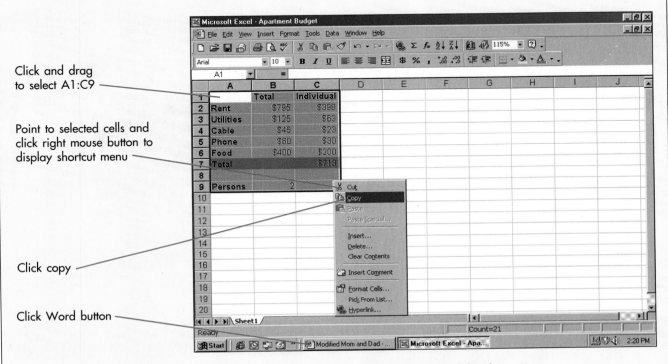

(c) Copy the Worksheet to the Clipboard (step 3)

FIGURE B.4   Hands-on Exercise 2 (continued)

THE WINDOWS TASKBAR

Multitasking, the ability to run multiple applications at the same time, is one of the primary advantages of the Windows environment. Each button on the taskbar appears automatically when its application or folder is opened and disappears upon closing. (The buttons on are resized automatically according to the number of open windows.) You can customize the taskbar by right clicking an empty area to display a shortcut menu, then clicking the Properties command. You can resize the taskbar by pointing to its inside edge, then dragging when you see a double-headed arrow. You can also move the taskbar to the left or right edge of the desktop, or to the top of the desktop, by dragging a blank area of the taskbar to the desired position.

STEP 4: Create the Link

➤ Click in the document between the two paragraphs. Press **enter** to enter an additional blank line.

➤ Pull down the **Edit menu.** Click **Paste Special** to produce the dialog box in Figure B.4d.

➤ Click the **Paste Link option button.** Click **Microsoft Excel Worksheet Object.** Click **OK** to insert the worksheet into the document. You may want to insert a blank line before and/or after the worksheet to make it easier to read.

➤ Save the document containing the letter to Mom and Dad.

Click Microsoft Excel Worksheet Object

Click Paste Link option button

Click to position insertion point

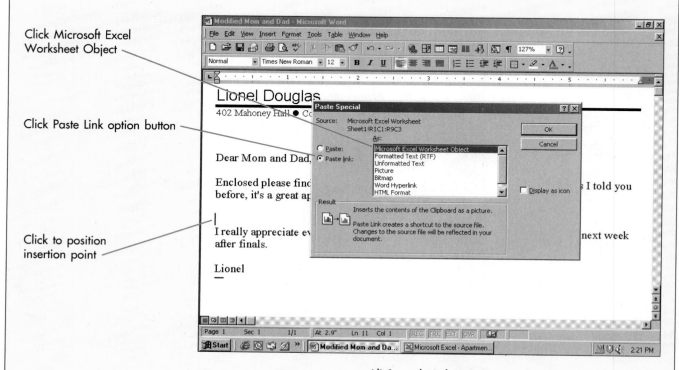

(d) Create the Link (step 4)

FIGURE B.4   Hands-on Exercise 2 (continued)

LINKING VERSUS EMBEDDING

The Paste Special command will link or embed an object, depending on whether the Paste Link or Paste option button is checked. Linking stores a pointer to the source file containing the object together with a reference to the source application. Changes to the object are automatically reflected in all destination files that are linked to the object. Embedding stores a copy of the object with a reference to the source application. Changes to the object within the destination file, however, are not reflected in the original object. Linking and embedding both allow you to double click the object in the destination file to edit the object by using the tools of the source application.

STEP 5: Open the Second Word Document

➤ Open the **Note to Ken document** in the **Exploring Word folder.** Save the document as **Modified Note to Ken** so that you can always return to the original document.

➤ The Apartment Budget worksheet is still in the clipboard since the contents of the clipboard have not been changed. Click at the end of the first paragraph (after the words Bon Appetit). Press the **enter key** to insert a blank line after the paragraph.

➤ Pull down the **Edit menu.** Click **Paste Special.** Click the **Paste Link option button.** Click **Microsoft Excel Worksheet Object.** Click **OK** to insert the worksheet into the document, as shown in Figure B.4e.

➤ If necessary, enter a blank line before or after the object to improve the appearance of the document. Save the document.

➤ Click anywhere on the worksheet to select the worksheet, as shown in Figure B.4e. The message on the status bar indicates you can double click the worksheet to edit the object.

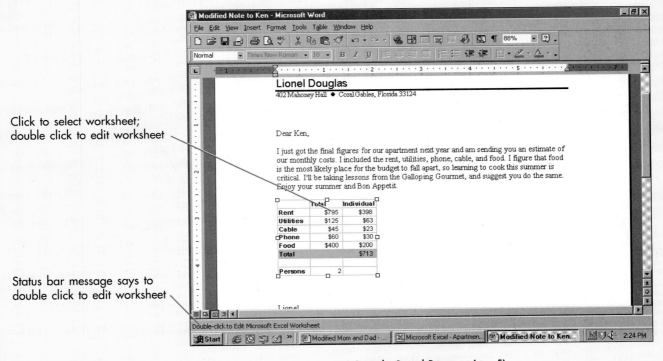

Click to select worksheet;
double click to edit worksheet

Status bar message says to
double click to edit worksheet

(e) Open the Second Document (step 5)

FIGURE B.4   Hands-on Exercise 2 (continued)

STEP 6: Modify the Worksheet

➤ The existing spreadsheet indicates the cost of a two-bedroom apartment, but you want to show the cost of a three-bedroom apartment. Double click the worksheet in order to change it.

➤ The system pauses (the faster your computer, the better) as it switches back to Excel. Maximize the document window.

➤ Cells **A1 through C9** are still selected from step 3. Click outside the selected range to deselect the worksheet. Press **Esc** to remove the moving border.

➤ Click in cell **B2.** Type **$895** (the rent for a three-bedroom apartment).

➤ Click in cell **B6.** Type **$600** (the increased amount for food).

➤ Click in cell **B9.** Type **3** to change the number of people sharing the apartment. Press **enter.** The total expenses (in cell C9) change to $575, as shown in Figure B.4f.

➤ Save the worksheet.

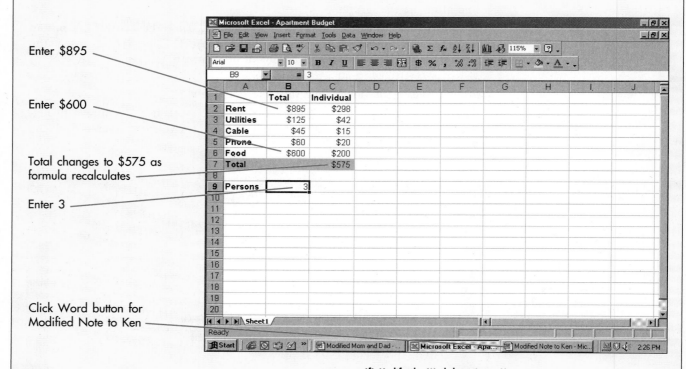

Enter $895

Enter $600

Total changes to $575 as formula recalculates

Enter 3

Click Word button for Modified Note to Ken

(f) Modify the Worksheet (step 6)

FIGURE B.4   Hands-on Exercise 2 (continued)

STEP 7: View the Modified Document

➤ Click the **Modified Note to Ken button** on the taskbar to return to Microsoft Word and the note to Ken, as shown in Figure B.4g.

➤ The note to Ken displays the modified worksheet because of the link established earlier.

➤ Click below the worksheet and add the additional text shown in Figure B.4g to let Ken know about the new apartment.

➤ Save the document.

STEP 8: View the Completed Note to Mom and Dad

➤ Click the **Modified Mom and Dad button** on the Windows taskbar to switch to this document as shown in Figure B.4h.

➤ The note to your parents also contains the updated worksheet (with three roommates) because of the link established earlier.

➤ Save the completed document.

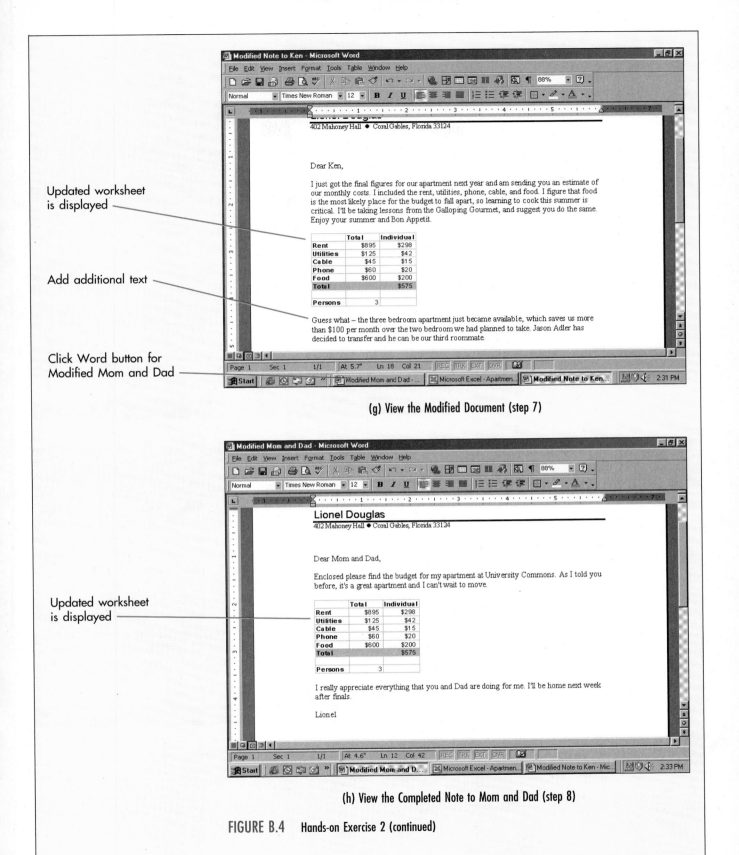

Updated worksheet is displayed

Add additional text

Click Word button for Modified Mom and Dad

(g) View the Modified Document (step 7)

Updated worksheet is displayed

(h) View the Completed Note to Mom and Dad (step 8)

FIGURE B.4 Hands-on Exercise 2 (continued)

ALT+TAB STILL WORKS

Alt+Tab was a treasured shortcut in Windows 3.1 that enabled users to switch back and forth between open applications. The shortcut also works in Windows 95. Press and hold the Alt key while you press and release the Tab key repeatedly to cycle through the open applications. Note that each time you release the Tab key, the icon of a different application is selected in the small rectangular window that is displayed in the middle of the screen. Release the Alt key when you have selected the icon for the application you want.

STEP 9: Exit Word

➤ Exit Word. Save the files if you are requested to do so. The button for Microsoft Word disappears from the taskbar.

➤ Exit Excel. Save the files if you are requested to do so. The button for Microsoft Excel disappears from the taskbar.

SUMMARY

The essential difference between linking and embedding is that linking does not place an object into the destination file (compound document), but only a pointer (link) to that object. Embedding, on the other hand, places (a copy of) the object into the destination file. Linking is dynamic whereas embedding is not.

Linking requires that an object be saved in its own (source) file, and further that the link between the source file and the destination file be maintained. Linking is especially useful when the same object is present in multiple documents, because any subsequent change to the object is made in only one place (the source file), but will be automatically reflected in the multiple destination files.

Embedding does not require an object to be saved in its own file because the object is contained entirely within the destination file. Thus, embedding lets you distribute a copy of the destination file, without including a copy of the source file, and indeed, there need not be a separate source file. You would not, however, want to embed the same object into multiple documents because any subsequent change to the object would have to be made in every document.

KEY WORDS AND CONCEPTS

Common user interface
Compound document
Embedding
In-place editing

Insert Object command
Linking
Multitasking

Object linking and
  embedding (OLE)
Paste Special command

appendix c

TOOLBARS

OVERVIEW

Microsoft Word has 21 predefined toolbars that provide access to commonly used commands. The toolbars are displayed in Figure A.1 and are listed here for convenience. They are: the Standard, Formatting, 3-D Settings, AutoText, Clipboard, Control Toolbox, Database, Drawing, Extended Formatting, Forms, Frames, Function Key Display, Microsoft, Picture, Reviewing, Shadow Settings, Tables and Borders, Visual Basic, Web, Web Tools, and WordArt. The Standard and Formatting toolbars are displayed by default and appear on the same row immediately below the menu bar. The other predefined toolbars are displayed (hidden) at the discretion of the user.

Four other toolbars are displayed automatically when their corresponding features are in use. These toolbars appear (and disappear) automatically and are shown in Figure C.2. They are: the Equation Editor, Header/Footer, Mail Merge, and Outlining toolbars.

The buttons on the toolbars are intended to indicate their functions. Clicking the Printer button (the fifth button from the left on the Standard toolbar), for example, executes the Print command. If you are unsure of the purpose of any toolbar button, point to it, and a ScreenTip will appear that displays its name.

You can display multiple toolbars at one time, move them to new locations on the screen, customize their appearance, or suppress their display.

➤ To separate the Standard and Formatting toolbars and simultaneously display all of the buttons for each toolbar, pull down the Tools menu, click the Customize command, click the Options tab, then clear the check box that has the toolbars share one row. Alternatively, the toolbars appear on the same row so that only a limited number of buttons are visible on each toolbar and hence you may need to click the double arrow (More Buttons) tool at the end of the toolbar to view additional buttons. Additional buttons will be added to either toolbar as you use the associated feature, and conversely, buttons will be removed from the toolbar if the feature is not used.

➤ To display or hide a toolbar, pull down the View menu and click the Toolbars command. Select (deselect) the toolbar(s) that you want to display (hide). The selected toolbar(s) will be displayed in the same position as when last displayed. You may also point to any toolbar and click with the right mouse button to bring up a shortcut menu, after which you can select the toolbar to be displayed (hidden).

➤ To change the size of the buttons, suppress the display of the ScreenTips, or display the associated shortcut key (if available), pull down the View menu, click Toolbars, and click Customize to display the Customize dialog box. If necessary, click the Options tab, then select (deselect) the appropriate check box. Alternatively, you can right click on any toolbar, click the Customize command from the context-sensitive menu, then select (deselect) the appropriate check box from within the Options tab in the Customize dialog box.

➤ Toolbars are either docked (along the edge of the window) or floating (in their own window). A toolbar moved to the edge of the window will dock along that edge. A toolbar moved anywhere else in the window will float in its own window. Docked toolbars are one tool wide (high), whereas floating toolbars can be resized by clicking and dragging a border or corner as you would with any window.

  • To move a docked toolbar, click anywhere in the gray background area and drag the toolbar to its new location. You can also click and drag the move handle (the vertical line) at the left of the toolbar

  • To move a floating toolbar, drag its title bar to its new location.

➤ To customize one or more toolbars, display the toolbar(s) on the screen. Then pull down the View menu, click Toolbars and click Customize to display the Customize dialog box. Alternatively, you can click on any toolbar with the right mouse button and select Customize from the shortcut menu.

  • To move a button, drag the button to its new location on that toolbar or any other displayed toolbar.

  • To copy a button, press the Ctrl key as you drag the button to its new location on that toolbar or any other displayed toolbar.

  • To delete a button, drag the button off the toolbar and release the mouse button.

  • To add a button, click the Commands tab in the Customize dialog box, select the category from the Categories list box that contains the button you want to add, then drag the button to the desired location on the toolbar. (To see a description of a tool's function prior to adding it to a toolbar, select the tool, then click the Description command button.)

  • To restore a predefined toolbar to its default appearance, click the Toolbars tab, select (highlight) the desired toolbar, and click the Reset command button.

➤ Buttons can also be moved, copied, or deleted without displaying the Customize dialog box.

  • To move a button, press the Alt key as you drag the button to the new location.

  • To copy a button, press the Alt and Ctrl keys as you drag the button to the new location.

  • To delete a button, press the Alt key as you drag the button off the toolbar.

➤ To create your own toolbar, pull down the View menu, click Toolbars, click Customize, click the Toolbars tab, then click the New command button. Alternatively, you can click on any toolbar with the right mouse button, select Customize from the shortcut menu, click the Toolbars tab, and then click the New command button.

  • Enter a name for the toolbar in the dialog box that follows. The name can be any length and can contain spaces. Click OK.

- The new toolbar will appear on the screen. Initially it will be big enough to hold only one button, but you can add, move, and delete buttons following the same procedures as for an existing toolbar. The toolbar will automatically size itself as new buttons are added and deleted.
- To delete a custom toolbar, pull down the View menu, click Toolbars, click Customize, and click the Toolbars tab. *Verify that the custom toolbar to be deleted is the only one selected (highlighted).* Click the Delete command button. Click OK to confirm the deletion. (Note that a predefined toolbar cannot be deleted.)

Standard Toolbar

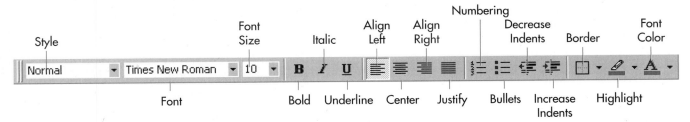

Formatting Toolbar

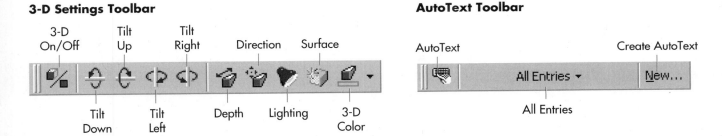

3-D Settings Toolbar   **AutoText Toolbar**

Clipboard Toolbar   **Control Toolbox**

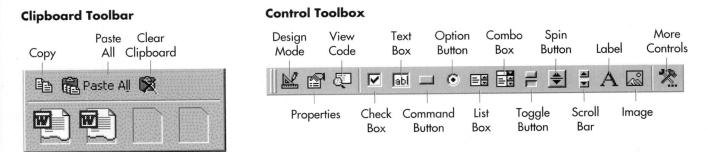

FIGURE C.1

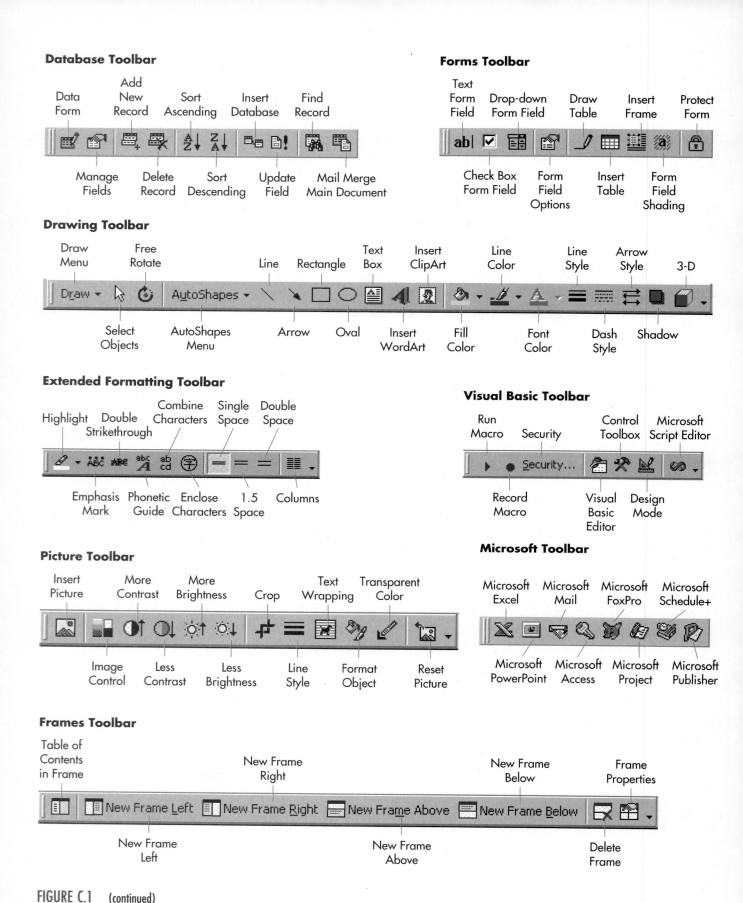

Database Toolbar

Data Form · Add New Record · Sort Ascending · Insert Database · Find Record

Manage Fields · Delete Record · Sort Descending · Update Field · Mail Merge Main Document

Forms Toolbar

Text Form Field · Drop-down Form Field · Draw Table · Insert Frame · Protect Form

Check Box Form Field · Form Field Options · Insert Table · Form Field Shading

Drawing Toolbar

Draw Menu · Free Rotate · Line · Rectangle · Text Box · Insert ClipArt · Line Color · Line Style · Arrow Style · 3-D

Select Objects · AutoShapes Menu · Arrow · Oval · Insert WordArt · Fill Color · Font Color · Dash Style · Shadow

Extended Formatting Toolbar

Highlight · Double Strikethrough · Combine Characters · Single Space · Double Space

Emphasis Mark · Phonetic Guide · Enclose Characters · 1.5 Space · Columns

Visual Basic Toolbar

Run Macro · Security · Control Toolbox · Microsoft Script Editor

Record Macro · Visual Basic Editor · Design Mode

Picture Toolbar

Insert Picture · More Contrast · More Brightness · Crop · Text Wrapping · Transparent Color

Image Control · Less Contrast · Less Brightness · Line Style · Format Object · Reset Picture

Microsoft Toolbar

Microsoft Excel · Microsoft Mail · Microsoft FoxPro · Microsoft Schedule+

Microsoft PowerPoint · Microsoft Access · Microsoft Project · Microsoft Publisher

Frames Toolbar

Table of Contents in Frame · New Frame Right · New Frame Below · Frame Properties

New Frame Left · New Frame Above · Delete Frame

FIGURE C.1   (continued)

Function Key Display Toolbar

F1 Help	F2 Move Text	F3 Insert Auto...
F4 Repeat	F5 Go To...	F6 Other Pane
F7 Spelling and ...	F8	F9 Update Field
F10 Menu Mode	F11 Next Field	F12 Save As...

WordArt Toolbar

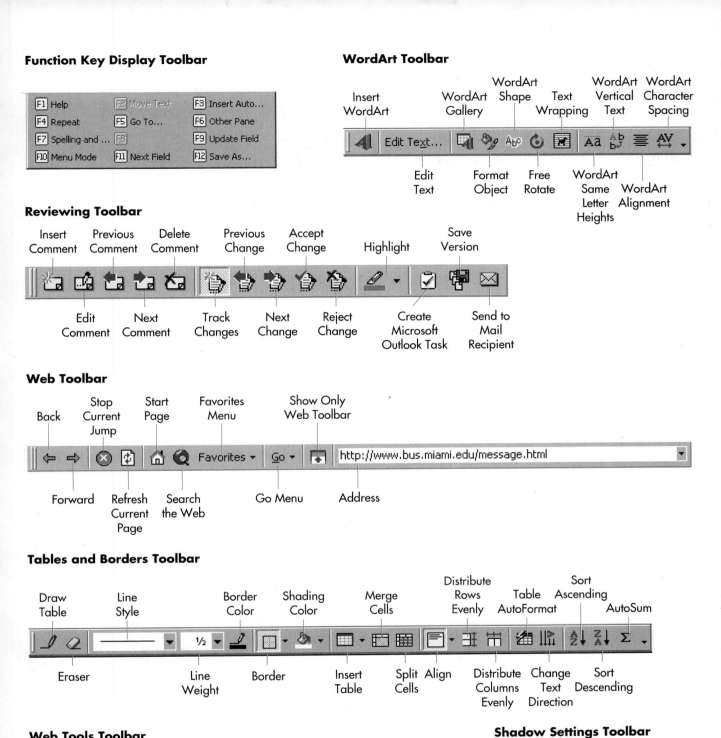

Insert WordArt — Edit Text — WordArt Gallery — WordArt Shape — Text Wrapping — WordArt Vertical Text — WordArt Character Spacing — Edit Text — Format Object — Free Rotate — WordArt Same Letter Heights — WordArt Alignment

Reviewing Toolbar

Insert Comment — Previous Comment — Delete Comment — Previous Change — Accept Change — Highlight — Save Version — Edit Comment — Next Comment — Track Changes — Next Change — Reject Change — Create Microsoft Outlook Task — Send to Mail Recipient

Web Toolbar

Back — Stop Current Jump — Start Page — Favorites Menu — Show Only Web Toolbar — Forward — Refresh Current Page — Search the Web — Go Menu — Address

http://www.bus.miami.edu/message.html

Tables and Borders Toolbar

Draw Table — Line Style — Border Color — Shading Color — Merge Cells — Distribute Rows Evenly — Table AutoFormat — Sort Ascending — AutoSum — Eraser — Line Weight — Border — Insert Table — Split Cells — Align — Distribute Columns Evenly — Change Text Direction — Sort Descending

Web Tools Toolbar

Design Mode — Microsoft Script Editor — Option Button — List Box — Text Area — Submit with Image — Hidden — Movie — Scrolling Text — Properties — Check Box — Drop-down Box — Text Box — Submit — Reset — Password — Sound

Shadow Settings Toolbar

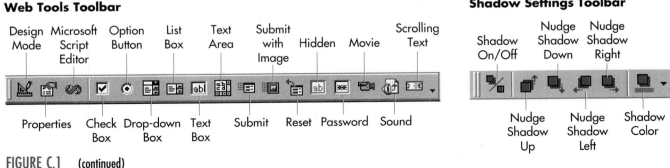

Shadow On/Off — Nudge Shadow Down — Nudge Shadow Right — Nudge Shadow Up — Nudge Shadow Left — Shadow Color

FIGURE C.1   (continued)

Equation Editor Toolbar

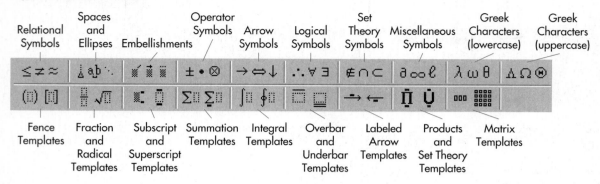

Relational Symbols · Spaces and Ellipses · Embellishments · Operator Symbols · Arrow Symbols · Logical Symbols · Set Theory Symbols · Miscellaneous Symbols · Greek Characters (lowercase) · Greek Characters (uppercase)

Fence Templates · Fraction and Radical Templates · Subscript and Superscript Templates · Summation Templates · Integral Templates · Overbar and Underbar Templates · Labeled Arrow Templates · Products and Set Theory Templates · Matrix Templates

Header/Footer Toolbar

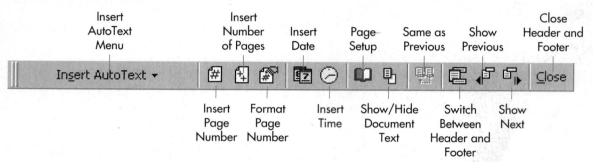

Insert AutoText Menu · Insert Number of Pages · Insert Date · Page Setup · Same as Previous · Show Previous · Close Header and Footer

Insert Page Number · Format Page Number · Insert Time · Show/Hide Document Text · Switch Between Header and Footer · Show Next

Mail Merge Toolbar

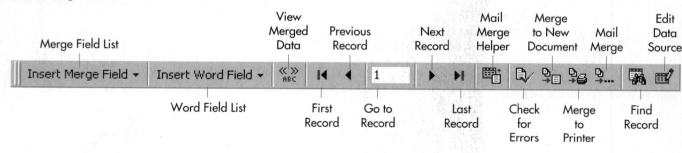

Merge Field List · View Merged Data · Previous Record · Next Record · Mail Merge Helper · Merge to New Document · Mail Merge · Edit Data Source

Word Field List · First Record · Go to Record · Last Record · Check for Errors · Merge to Printer · Find Record

Outlining Toolbar

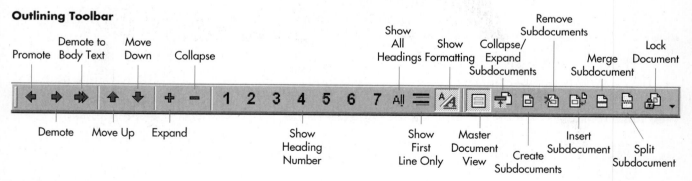

Promote · Demote to Body Text · Move Down · Collapse · Show All Headings · Show Formatting · Collapse/Expand Subdocuments · Remove Subdocuments · Merge Subdocument · Lock Document

Demote · Move Up · Expand · Show Heading Number · Show First Line Only · Master Document View · Create Subdocuments · Insert Subdocument · Split Subdocument

FIGURE C.2

prerequisites

ESSENTIALS OF WINDOWS 95/98: DISK AND FILE MANAGEMENT

OBJECTIVES

After reading this supplement you will be able to:

1. Describe the objects on the Windows desktop; distinguish between the Classic style and the Web style.

2. Explain the significance of the common user interface; identify several elements that are present in every window.

3. Use the Help command to learn about Windows 98.

4. Format a floppy disk.

5. Define a file; differentiate between a program file and a data file; describe the rules for naming a file.

6. Explain how folders are used to organize the files on a disk; explain how to compress and expand a folder or drive within Windows Explorer.

7. Distinguish between My Computer and Windows Explorer with respect to viewing files and folders; explain the advantages of the hierarchical view available within Windows Explorer.

8. Use Internet Explorer to access the Internet and download the practice files for the Exploring Windows series.

9. Copy and/or move a file from one folder to another; delete a file, then recover the deleted file from the Recycle Bin.

10. Describe how to view a Web page from within Windows Explorer.

OVERVIEW

Windows 98 is a computer program (actually many programs) that controls the operation of a computer and its peripherals. Windows 98 is the third major release of the Windows operating system and it improves upon its immediate predecessor, Windows 95, in two important ways. First, there are many enhancements "under the surface" that make the PC run more efficiently. Second, Windows 98 brings the Internet to the desktop. Unlike Windows 95, however, Windows 98 has two distinct interfaces, a "Classic Style" and a "Web Style." The Classic style works identically to Windows 95, and thus we have titled this section, "Essentials of Windows 95/98" in that the Classic Style applies to both operating systems.

We begin with a discussion of the Windows desktop and describe the common user interface and consistent command structure that is present in every Windows application. We identify the basic components of a window and discuss how to execute commands and supply information through different elements in a dialog box. We introduce you to My Computer, an icon on the Windows desktop, and show you how to use My Computer to access the various components of your system. We also describe how to access the Help command.

The supplement focuses, however, on disk and file management. We present the basic definitions of a file and a folder, then describe how to use My Computer to look for a specific file or folder. We introduce Windows Explorer, which provides a more efficient way of finding data on your system, then show you how to move or copy a file from one folder to another. We discuss other basic operations such as renaming and deleting a file. We also describe how to recover a deleted file (if necessary) from the Recycle Bin.

There are also four hands-on exercises that enable you to apply the conceptual discussion in the text at the computer. The exercises refer to a set of practice files (known as a data disk) that we have created for you. You can obtain the practice files from our Web site (www.prenhall.com/grauer) or from a local area network if your professor has downloaded the files for you.

WINDOWS NT VERSUS WINDOWS 98

The computer you purchase for home use will have Windows 98. The computer you use at school or the office, however, will most likely have **Windows NT**, a more secure version of Windows that is intended for networked environments. This is significant to system personnel, but transparent to the user because Windows NT 5.0 (which will be called **Windows 2000**) has the same user interface as Windows 98. There are subtle differences, but for the most part, the screens are identical, and thus you will be able to use this text with either operating system.

THE DESKTOP

All versions of Windows create a working environment for your computer that parallels the working environment at home or in an office. You work at a desk. Windows operations take place on the **desktop.** There are physical objects on a desk such as folders, a dictionary, a calculator, or a phone. The computer equivalents of those objects appear as **icons** (pictorial symbols) on the desktop. Each object on a real desk has attributes (properties) such as size, weight, and color. In similar fashion, Windows assigns properties to every object on its desktop. And just as you can move the objects on a real desk, you can rearrange the objects on the Windows desktop.

Figure 1 displays three different versions of the **Windows 98** desktop. Figures 1a and 1b illustrate the desktop when Windows 98 is first installed on a new computer. These desktops have only a few objects and are similar to the desk in a new office, just after you move in. Figure 1a is displayed in the **Classic style,** which for all practical purposes is identical to the **Windows 95** desktop. Figure 1b

Click icon to select it; double click icon to open it

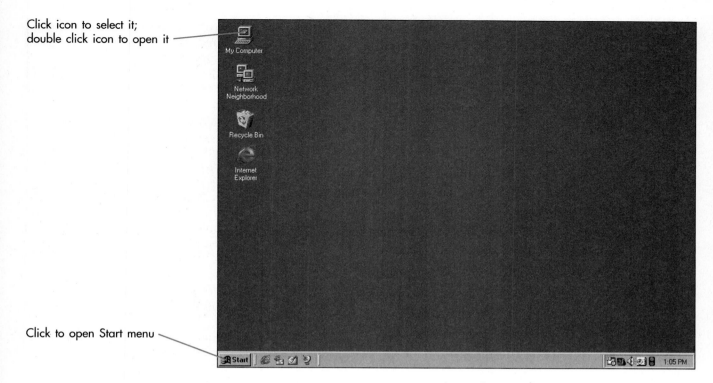

(a) Classic Style

Point to icon to select it; click icon to open it

Click to open Start menu

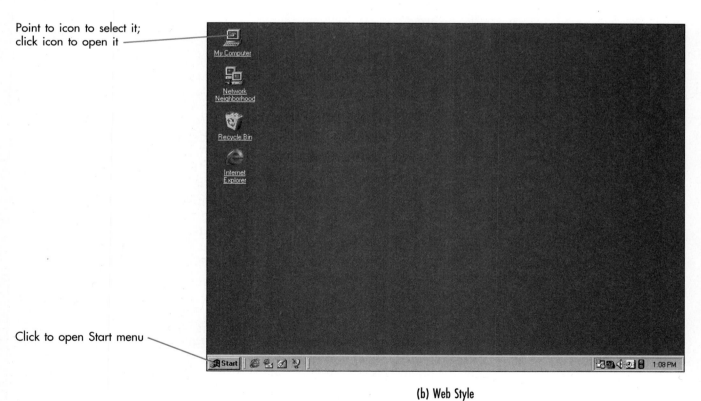

(b) Web Style

FIGURE 1   The Different Faces of Windows 98

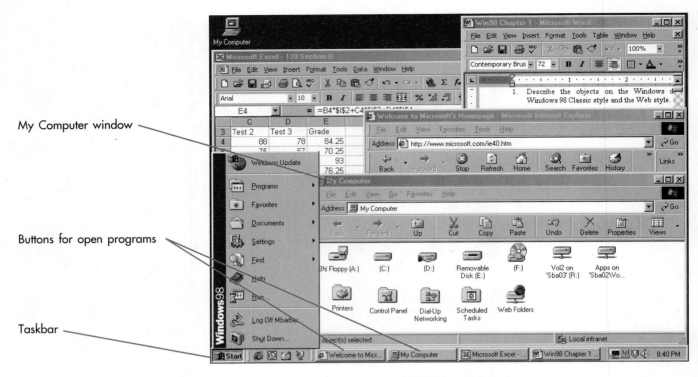

My Computer window

Buttons for open programs

Taskbar

(c) A Working Desktop

FIGURE 1   The Different Faces of Windows 98 (continued)

is displayed in the **Web style,** which is new to Windows 98. The icons on a Web style desktop are underlined and function identically to the hyperlinks within a browser such as Internet Explorer or Netscape Communicator.

The styles differ in visual appearance and in the way the icons work. In the Classic style, you click an icon to select it (mouse operations are described on page 10), and you double click the icon to open it. In the Web style, however, you point to an icon to select it, and you click the icon to open it. These operations mimic those of a Web browser—hence the term, "Web style." (It is a misnomer of sorts, in that the Web style has nothing to do with the Web per se, as you are not necessarily connected to the Internet nor are you viewing any Web pages.) You can display your desktop in either style by setting the appropriate option through the View menu in My Computer, as will be described later in a hands-on exercise. The choice depends entirely on personal preference.

Do not be concerned if your desktop is different from ours. Your real desk is arranged differently from those of your friends, and so your Windows desktop will also be different. What is important is that you recognize the capabilities inherent in Windows 98, as illustrated in Figure 1. Thus, it is the simplicity of the desktops in Figures 1a and 1b that helps you to focus on what is important. The **Start button,** as its name suggests, is where you begin. Click the Start button and you see a menu that lets you start any program installed on your computer. Starting a program opens a window on the desktop and from there you go to work.

Look now at Figure 1c, which displays an entirely different desktop, one with four open windows, that is similar to a desk in the middle of a working day. Each window in Figure 1c displays a program that is currently in use. The ability to run several programs at the same time is known as **multitasking,** and it is a major benefit of the Windows environment. Multitasking enables you to run a word processor in one window, create a spreadsheet in a second window, surf the Internet in a third window, play a game in a fourth window, and so on. You can work in a program as long as you want, then change to a different program by clicking its program.

You can also change from one program to another by using the taskbar at the bottom of the desktop. The *taskbar* contains a button for each open program, and it enables you to switch back and forth between those programs by clicking the appropriate button. The taskbars in Figures 1a and 1b do not contain any buttons (other than the Start button) since there are no open applications. The taskbar in Figure 1c, however, contains four additional buttons, one for each open program.

The icons on the desktop in Figures 1a and 1b are used to access programs or other functions in Windows 98. The *My Computer* icon is the most basic, and it enables you to view the devices on your system. Open My Computer in either Figure 1a or 1b, for example, and you see the objects in the My Computer window of Figure 1c. The contents of the My Computer window depend on the hardware of the specific computer system. Our system, for example, has one floppy drive, two hard (fixed) disks, a removable disk (an Iomega Zip drive), a CD-ROM, and access to two network drives. The My Computer window also contains the Control Panel, Printers, Dial-Up Networking, Web Folders, and Scheduled Tasks folders, which allow access to functions that control other elements in the environment on your computer. (These capabilities are not used by beginners and are generally "off limits" in a lab environment, and thus are not discussed further.)

The other icons on the desktop in Figures 1a and 1b are also noteworthy. *Network Neighborhood* extends your view of the computer to include the accessible drives on the network to which your machine is attached, if indeed it is part of a network. (You will not see this icon if you are not connected to a network.) The *Recycle Bin* allows you to restore a file that was previously deleted. The Internet Explorer icon starts *Internet Explorer,* the Web browser that is built into Windows 98. Indeed, the single biggest difference between Windows 98 and its predecessor, Windows 95, is the tight integration with the Internet and the World Wide Web.

THE COMMON USER INTERFACE

All Windows applications share a *common user interface* and possess a consistent command structure. This is a critically important concept and one of the most significant benefits of the Windows environment, as it provides a sense of familiarity from one application to the next. In essence, every Windows application follows the same conventions and works essentially the same way. Thus, once you learn the basic concepts and techniques in one application, you can apply that knowledge to every other application. The next several pages present this material, after which you will have an opportunity to practice in a hands-on exercise.

Anatomy of a Window

Figure 2 displays a typical window and labels its essential elements. Figure 2a displays the window in the Classic style. Figure 2b shows the identical window using the Web style. Regardless of the style, each window has a title bar, a minimize button, a maximize or restore button, and a close button. Other elements, which may or may not be visible, include a horizontal and/or vertical scroll bar, a menu bar, a status bar, and one or more toolbars. A window may also contain additional objects (icons) that pertain specifically to the programs or data associated with that window.

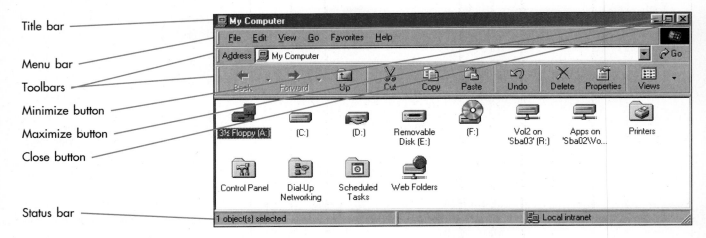

Title bar

Menu bar

Toolbars

Minimize button

Maximize button

Close button

Status bar

(a) Classic Style

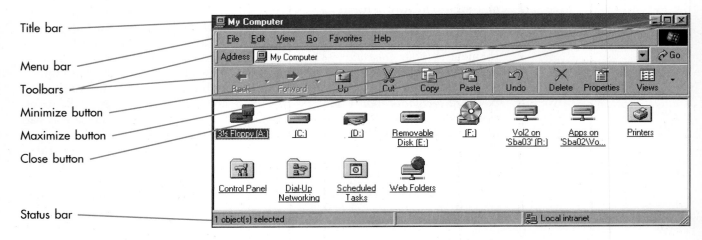

Title bar

Menu bar

Toolbars

Minimize button

Maximize button

Close button

Status bar

(b) Web Style

FIGURE 2   Anatomy of a Window

The *title bar* appears at the top of the window and displays the name of the window; for example, My Computer in both Figures 2a and 2b. The icon at the extreme left of the title bar provides access to a control menu that lets you select operations relevant to the window such as moving it or sizing it. The *minimize button* shrinks the window to a button on the taskbar, but leaves the application in memory. The *maximize button* enlarges the window so that it takes up the entire desktop. The *restore button* (not shown in Figure 2) appears instead of the maximize button after a window has been maximized, and restores the window to its previous size. The *close button* closes the window and removes it from memory and the desktop.

The *menu bar* appears immediately below the title bar and provides access to pull-down menus (as discussed later). Two toolbars, the *Address bar* and *Standard Buttons bar,* appear below the menu bar. The *status bar* at the bottom of the window displays information about the window as a whole or about a selected object within a window.

A *vertical* (or *horizontal*) *scroll bar* appears at the right (or bottom) border of a window when its contents are not completely visible and provides access to the unseen areas. Scroll bars do not appear in Figure 2 since all of the objects in the window are visible at the same time.

Moving and Sizing a Window

A window can be sized or moved on the desktop through appropriate actions with the mouse. To **size a window,** point to any border (the mouse pointer changes to a double arrow), then drag the border in the direction you want to go—inward to shrink the window or outward to enlarge it. You can also drag a corner (instead of a border) to change both dimensions at the same time. To **move a window** while retaining its current size, click and drag the title bar to a new position on the desktop.

Pull-down Menus

The menu bar provides access to **pull-down menus** that enable you to execute commands within an application (program). A pull-down menu is accessed by clicking the menu name or by pressing the Alt key plus the underlined letter in the menu name; for example, press Alt+V to pull down the View menu. Three pull-down menus associated with My Computer are shown in Figure 3.

Commands within a menu are executed by clicking the command or by typing the underlined letter (for example, C to execute the Close command in the File menu) once the menu has been pulled down. Alternatively, you can bypass the menu entirely if you know the equivalent keystrokes shown to the right of the command in the menu (e.g., Ctrl+X, Ctrl+C, or Ctrl+V to cut, copy, or paste as shown within the Edit menu). A **dimmed command** (e.g., the Paste command in the Edit menu) means the command is not currently executable, and that some additional action has to be taken for the command to become available.

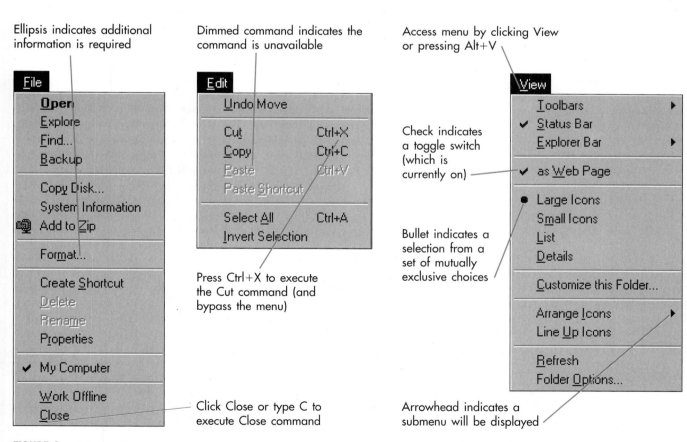

Ellipsis indicates additional information is required

Dimmed command indicates the command is unavailable

Access menu by clicking View or pressing Alt+V

Press Ctrl+X to execute the Cut command (and bypass the menu)

Check indicates a toggle switch (which is currently on)

Bullet indicates a selection from a set of mutually exclusive choices

Click Close or type C to execute Close command

Arrowhead indicates a submenu will be displayed

FIGURE 3   Pull-down Menus

An *ellipsis* (. . .) following a command indicates that additional information is required to execute the command; for example, selection of the Format command in the File menu requires the user to specify additional information about the formatting process. This information is entered into a dialog box (discussed in the next section) which appears immediately after the command has been selected.

A *check* next to a command indicates a toggle switch, whereby the command is either on or off. There is a check next to the Status Bar command in the View menu of Figure 3, which means the command is in effect (and thus the status bar will be displayed). Click the Status Bar command, and the check disappears, which suppresses the display of the status bar. Click the command a second time, and the check reappears, as does the status bar in the associated window.

A *bullet* next to an item (e.g., Large Icons in Figure 3c) indicates a selection from a set of mutually exclusive choices. Click another option within the group (e.g., Small Icons), and the bullet will disappear from the previous selection (Large Icons) and appear next to the new selection (Small Icons).

An *arrowhead* after a command (e.g., the Arrange Icons command in the View menu) indicates that a *submenu* (also known as a cascaded menu) will be displayed with additional menu options.

Dialog Boxes

A *dialog box* appears when additional information is needed to execute a command. The Format command, for example, requires information about which drive to format and the type of formatting desired.

Option (radio) buttons indicate mutually exclusive choices, one of which must be chosen; for example, one of three Format Type options in Figure 4a. Click a button to select an option, which automatically deselects the previously selected option.

Check boxes are used instead of option buttons if the choices are not mutually exclusive or if an option is not required. Multiple boxes can be checked as in Figure 4a, or no boxes may be checked as in Figure 4b. Individual options are selected and cleared by clicking the appropriate check box.

A *text box* is used to enter descriptive information—for example, Bob's Disk in Figure 4a. A flashing vertical bar (an I-beam) appears within the text box when the text box is active, to mark the insertion point for the text you will enter.

A *list box* displays some or all of the available choices, any one of which is selected by clicking the desired item. A *drop-down list box,* such as the Capacity list box in Figure 4a, conserves space by showing only the current selection. Click the arrow of a drop-down list box to display the list of available options. An *open list box,* such as those in Figure 4b, displays multiple choices at one time. (A scroll bar appears within an open list box if all of the choices are not visible and provides access to the hidden choices.)

A *tabbed dialog box* provides multiple sets of options. The dialog box in Figure 4c, for example, has six tabs, each with its own set of options. Click a tab (the Web tab is currently selected) to display the associated options.

The *Help button* (a question mark at the right end of the title bar) provides help for any item in the dialog box. Click the button, then click the item in the dialog box for which you want additional information. The close button (the X at the extreme right of the title bar) closes the dialog box.

All dialog boxes also contain one or more *command buttons,* the function of which is generally apparent from the button's name. The Start button, in Figure 4a, for example, initiates the formatting process. The OK command button in Figure 4b accepts the settings and closes the dialog box. The Cancel button does just the opposite, and ignores (cancels) any changes made to the settings, then closes the dialog box without further action.

Drop-down list box shows current selection (click arrow to see list of available options)

Start button begins formatting (executes command)

Option buttons indicate mutually exclusive choices

Text box is used to enter descriptive information

Check boxes indicate choices that are not mutually exclusive

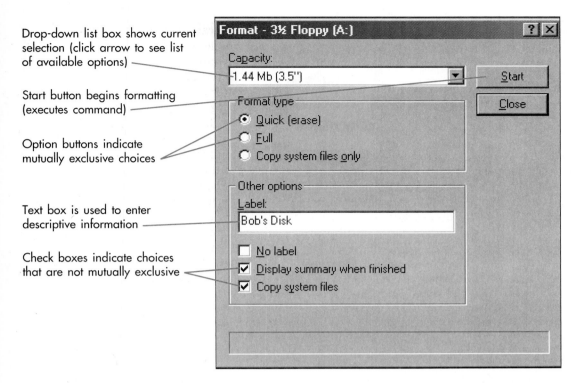

(a) Option Boxes and Check Boxes

Open list box displays multiple options

Scroll bar indicates that not all choices are visible

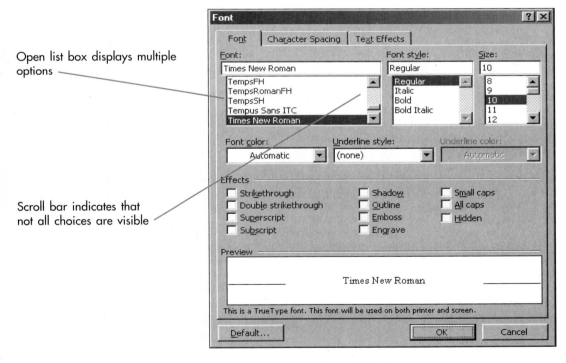

(b) List Boxes

FIGURE 4   Dialog Boxes

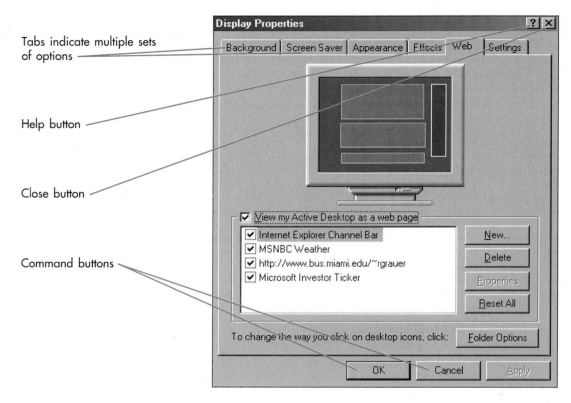

Tabs indicate multiple sets of options

Help button

Close button

Command buttons

(c) Tabbed Dialog Box

FIGURE 4   Dialog Boxes (continued)

THE MOUSE

The mouse is indispensable to Windows and is referenced continually in the hands-on exercises throughout the text. There are five basic operations with which you must become familiar:

- To *point* to an object, move the mouse pointer onto the object.
- To *click* an object, point to it, then press and release the left mouse button.
- To *right click* an object, point to the object, then press and release the right mouse button.
- To *double click* an object, point to it, then quickly click the left button twice in succession.
- To *drag* an object, move the pointer to the object, then press and hold the left button while you move the mouse to a new position.

The mouse is a pointing device—move the mouse on your desk and the *mouse pointer,* typically a small arrowhead, moves on the monitor. The mouse pointer assumes different shapes according to the location of the pointer or the nature of the current action. You will see a double arrow when you change the size of a window, an I-beam as you insert text, a hand to jump from one help topic to the next, or a circle with a line through it to indicate that an attempted action is invalid.

The mouse pointer will also change to an hourglass to indicate Windows is processing your command, and that no further commands may be issued until the action is completed. The more powerful your computer, the less frequently the hourglass will appear.

The Mouse versus the Keyboard

Almost every command in Windows can be executed in different ways, using either the mouse or the keyboard. Most people start with the mouse and add keyboard shortcuts as they become more proficient. There is no right or wrong technique, just different techniques, and the one you choose depends entirely on personal preference in a specific situation. If, for example, your hands are already on the keyboard, it is faster to use the keyboard equivalent. Other times, your hand will be on the mouse and that will be the fastest way. Toolbars provide still other ways to execute common commands.

In the beginning, you may wonder why there are so many different ways to do the same thing, but you will eventually recognize the many options as part of Windows' charm. It is not necessary to memorize anything, nor should you even try; just be flexible and willing to experiment. The more you practice, the faster all of this will become second nature to you.

THE HELP COMMAND

Windows 98 includes extensive documentation with detailed information about virtually every area in Windows. It is accessed through the **Help command** on the Start menu, which provides three different ways to search for information.

The **Contents tab** in Figure 5a is analogous to the table of contents in an ordinary book. The topics are listed in the left pane, and the information for the selected topic is displayed in the right pane. The list of topics can be displayed in varying amounts of detail, by opening and closing the various book icons that appear.

A closed book (e.g., Troubleshooting) indicates that there are subtopics that can be seen by opening (clicking) the book. An open book (e.g., How the Screen Looks) indicates that all of the subtopics are visible. (You can click an open book to close it and gain additional space in the left pane.) A question mark (e.g., Set up a screen saver) indicates the actual topic, the contents of which are displayed in the right side of the screen. An underlined entry (e.g., Related Topics) indicates a hyperlink, which you can click to display additional information. You can also print the information in the right pane by pulling down the Options menu and selecting the Print command.

The **Index tab** in Figure 5b is analogous to the index of an ordinary book. You enter the first several letters of the topic to look up (e.g., Internet), choose a topic from the resulting list, and then click the Display button to view the information in the right pane. The underlined entries represent hyperlinks, which you can click to display additional topics. And, as in the Contents window, you can print the information in the right pane by pulling down the Options menu and selecting the Print command.

The **Search tab** (not shown in Figure 5) contains a more extensive listing of entries than does the Index tab. It lets you enter a specific word or phrase, then it returns every topic containing that word or phrase.

GET HELP ONLINE

The Windows 98 Help file is a powerful tool, but it may not have the answer to every question. Click the Start button, click Help to display the Windows Help dialog box, then click the Web Help button on the toolbar. Click the link to Support online and you will be connected to the Microsoft technical support site, where you can search the Microsoft Knowledge base.

Index tab

Search tab

Open book indicates that
subtopics are listed; click to
close book and hide subtopics

Selected topic; contents
displayed in right pane

Hyperlink; click to display
additional information

Click to open book and
see list of subtopics

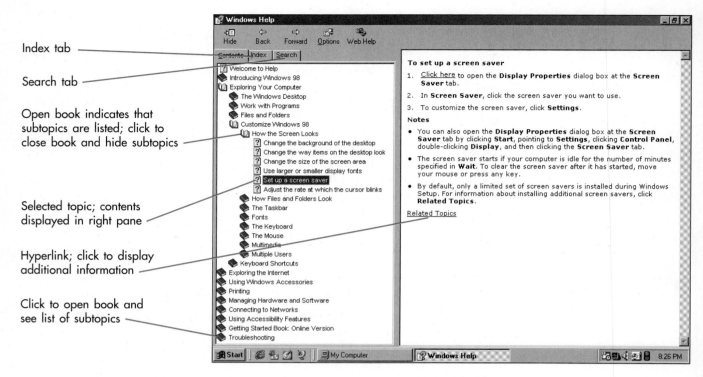

(a) Contents Tab

Enter topic

Click specific topic

Click specific topic

Click display

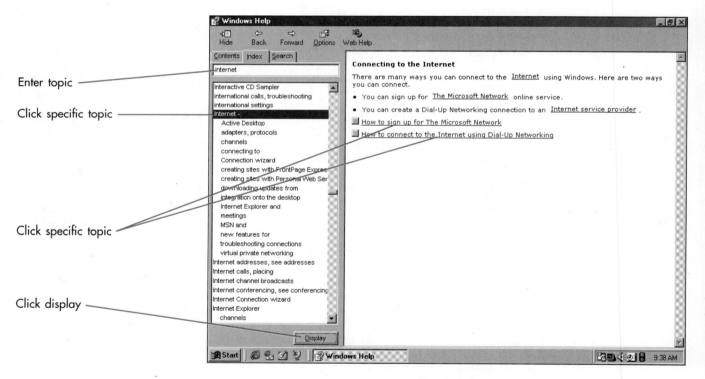

(b) Index Tab

FIGURE 5   The Help Command

FORMATTING A FLOPPY DISK

You will soon begin to work on the computer, which means that you will be using various applications to create different types of documents. Each document is saved in its own file and stored on disk, either on a hard disk (e.g., drive C) if you have your own computer, or on a floppy disk (drive A) if you are working in a computer lab at school.

All disks have to be formatted before they can hold data. The formatting process divides a disk into concentric circles called tracks, then further divides each track into sectors. You don't have to worry about formatting a hard disk, as that is done at the factory prior to the machine being sold. You do, however, have to format a floppy disk in order to write to that disk. Realize, too, that you will need to use one or more floppy disks even if you have your own computer in order to copy important files (such as your term paper) from your hard drive to the floppy disks. The latter will serve as backup should anything happen to the file on the hard disk.

In any event, you need to purchase floppy disks, and format them so that they will be able to store the files you create. (You can purchase preformatted floppy disks, but it is very easy to format your own, and we provide instructions in the hands-on exercise that follows.) Be aware, however, that formatting erases any data that was previously on a disk, so be careful not to format a disk with important data (e.g., one containing today's homework assignment).

Formatting is accomplished through the *Format command.* The process is straightforward and has you enter all of the necessary information into a dialog box. One of the box's options is to copy system files onto the disk while formatting it. These files are necessary to start (boot) your computer, and if your hard disk were to fail, you would need a floppy disk with the system (and other) files in order to start the machine. (See Help for information on creating a *boot disk* containing the system files.) For ordinary purposes, however, you do not put the system files on a floppy disk because they take up space you could use to store data.

FORMAT AT THE PROPER CAPACITY

A floppy disk should be formatted at its rated capacity, or else you may be unable to read the disk. There are two types of 3½-inch floppy disks, double-density (720KB and obsolete) and high-density (1.44MB). The easiest way to determine the type of disk you have is to look at the disk itself for the label DD or HD, for double- and high-density, respectively. You can also check the number of square holes in the disk; a double-density disk has one, whereas a high-density disk has two.

LEARNING BY DOING

Learning is best accomplished by doing, and so we come to the first of two hands-on exercises in this chapter. The exercises enable you to apply the concepts you have learned, then extend those concepts to further exploration on your own. Our opening exercise welcomes you to the Windows desktop, directs you to open My Computer, then has you move and size a window. It describes how to format a floppy disk and how to use the Help command. The exercise provides instructions for both the Classic style and Web style and illustrates how to switch between the two.

Objective: To turn on the computer, start Windows, and open My Computer; to move and size a window; to format a floppy disk and use the Help command. Use Figure 6 as a guide in the exercise.

STEP 1: Open My Computer

➤ Start the computer by turning on the various switches appropriate to your system. Your system will take a minute or so to boot up, after which you should see the desktop in Figure 6a. (The My Computer window is not yet open.) Close the Welcome to Windows 98 window if it appears.

➤ Do not be concerned if your desktop differs from ours. The way in which you open My Computer depends on the style in effect on your desktop. Thus:

- In the Classic style, double click the **My Computer icon** (shown in Figure 6a).
- In the Web style, click the **My Computer icon** (not shown in Figure 6a).
- In either style, right click the **My Computer icon** to display a context-sensitive menu, then click the **Open command.**

➤ The My Computer window will open as shown in Figure 6a. The contents of your window and/or its size and position on the desktop will be different from ours.

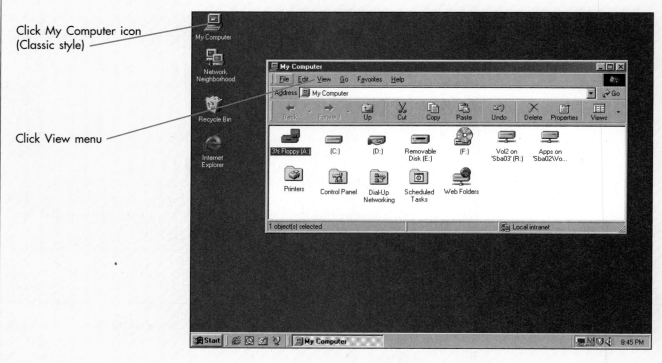

Click My Computer icon (Classic style)

Click View menu

(a) Open My Computer (step 1)

FIGURE 6   Hands-on Exercise 1

STARTING YOUR COMPUTER

The number and location of the on/off switches depend on the nature and manufacturer of the devices connected to the computer. The easiest possible setup is when all components of the system are plugged into a surge protector, in which case only a single switch has to be turned on. In any event, turn on the monitor, printer, and system unit. Note, too, that newcomers to computing often forget that the floppy drive should be empty prior to starting a computer. This ensures that the system starts by reading files from the hard disk (which contains the Windows files) as opposed to a floppy disk (which does not).

STEP 2: Customize My Computer

➤ Pull down the **View menu,** then click (or point to) the **Toolbars command** to display a cascaded menu as shown in Figure 6b. If necessary, check the commands for the **Standard Buttons** and **Address Bar,** and clear the commands for Links and Text Labels.

➤ If necessary, pull down the **View menu** a second time to make or verify the selections in Figure 6b. (You have to pull down the menu each time you choose a different command.)

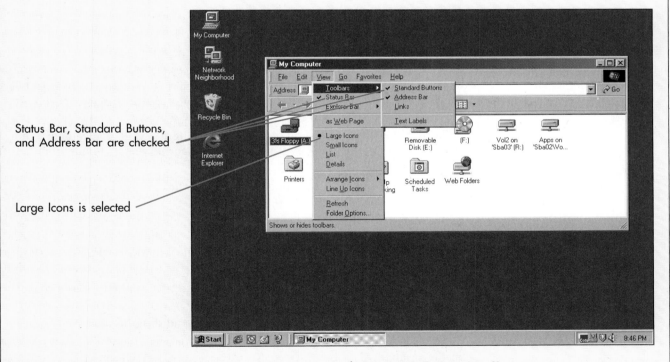

Status Bar, Standard Buttons, and Address Bar are checked

Large Icons is selected

(b) Customize My Computer (step 2)

FIGURE 6   Hands-on Exercise 1 (continued)

- The **Status Bar command** should be checked. The Status Bar command functions as a toggle switch. Click the command, and the status bar is displayed; click the command a second time, and the status bar disappears.
- **Large Icons** should be selected as the current view. (The Large Icons view is one of four mutually exclusive views in My Computer.)

➤ Pull down the **View menu** once again, click (or point to) the **Explorer Bar command** and verify that none of the options are checked. Each option functions as a toggle switch; i.e., click an option to check it, and click it a second time to remove the check.

➤ Pull down the **View menu** a final time. Click (or point to) the **Arrange Icons command** and (if necessary) click the **AutoArrange command** so that a check appears. Click outside the menu (or press the **Esc key**) if the command is already checked.

DESIGNATING THE DEVICES ON A SYSTEM

The first (usually only) floppy drive is always designated as drive A. (A second floppy drive, if it were present, would be drive B.) The first (often only) hard disk on a system is always drive C, whether or not there are one or two floppy drives. A system with one floppy drive and one hard disk (today's most common configuration) will contain icons for drive A and drive C. Additional hard drives (if any) and/or the CD-ROM are labeled from D on.

STEP 3: Move and Size a Window

➤ Click the **maximize button** so that the My Computer window expands to fill the entire screen. Click the **restore button** (which replaces the maximize button and is not shown in Figure 6c) to return the window to its previous size.

➤ Pull down the **View menu** and click **Details**. (Alternatively, you can click the **Down Arrow** for the **Views button** on the toolbar and select **Details** from the resulting menu.)

➤ Move and size the My Computer window on your desktop to match the display in Figure 6c.
- To change the width or height of the window, click and drag a border (the mouse pointer changes to a double arrow) in the direction you want to go. Thus you drag the border inward to shrink the window or drag it outward to enlarge it.
- To change the width and height at the same time, click and drag a corner rather than a border.
- To change the position of the window, click and drag the title bar.

➤ Click the **minimize button** to shrink the My Computer window to a button on the taskbar. My Computer is still active in memory although its window is no longer visible.

➤ Click the **My Computer button** on the taskbar to reopen the window.

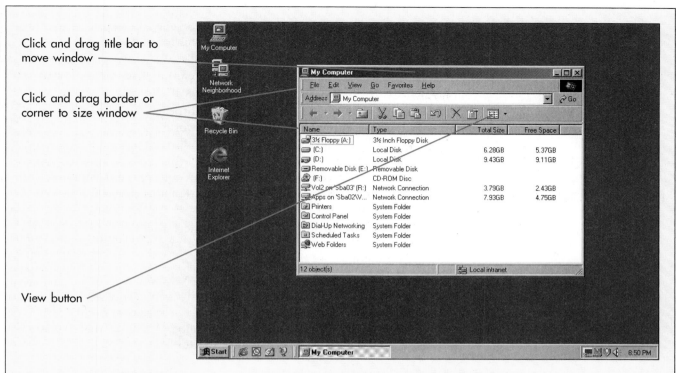

Click and drag title bar to move window

Click and drag border or corner to size window

View button

(c) Move and Size a Window (step 3)

FIGURE 6   Hands-on Exercise 1 (continued)

MINIMIZING VERSUS CLOSING AN APPLICATION

Minimizing an application leaves the application open in memory and available at the click of the taskbar button. Closing it, however, removes the application from memory, which also causes it to disappear from the taskbar. The advantage of minimizing an application is that you can return to the application immediately. The disadvantage is that leaving too many applications open will degrade the performance of your system.

STEP 4: Format a Floppy Disk

➤ Place a floppy disk in drive A. The formatting process erases anything that is on the disk, so be sure that you do not need anything on the disk.

➤ The way you select drive A and display the Format dialog box depends on the style in effect. Thus:

  • In the Classic style, click (do not double click) the icon for **drive A,** then pull down the **File menu** and click the **Format command.**

  • In the Web style, point to (do not click) the icon for **drive A,** then pull down the **File menu** and click the **Format command.**

  • In either style, right click the icon for **drive A** to select it and display a context-sensitive menu, then click the **Format command.**

➤ Move the Format dialog box by clicking and dragging its **title bar** so that the display on your desktop matches ours. Set the formatting parameters as shown in Figure 6d:

• Set the **Capacity** to match the floppy disk you purchased (1.44MB for a high-density disk and 720KB for a double-density disk).

• Click the **Full option button** to choose a full format, which checks a disk for errors as it is formatted. This option is worth the extra time as compared to a quick format; the latter erases the files on a previously formatted disk but does not check for errors.

• Click the **Label text box** if it's empty or click and drag over the existing label if there is an entry. Enter a new label (containing up to 11 characters) such as **Bob's Disk.**

• Click the **Start command button** to begin the formatting operation. This will take a minute or two. You can see the progress of the formatting process at the bottom of the dialog box.

➤ After the formatting process is complete, you will see the Format Results message box. Read the information, then click the **Close command button** to close the informational dialog box.

➤ Click the **close button** to close the Format dialog box. Save the formatted disk for use with various exercises later in the text.

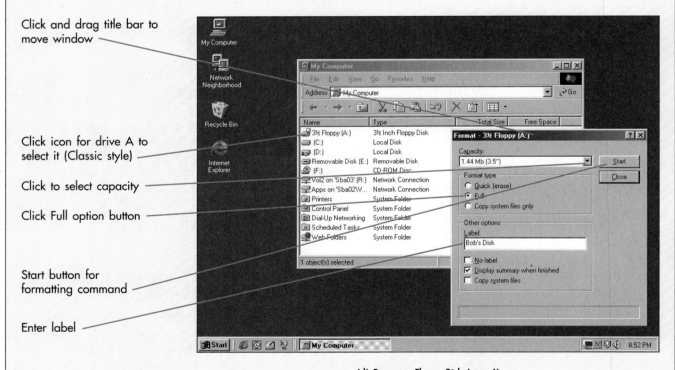

(d) Format a Floppy Disk (step 4)

FIGURE 6   Hands-on Exercise 1 (continued)

THE HELP BUTTON

The Help button (a question mark) appears in the title bar of almost every dialog box. Click the question mark, then click the item you want information about (which then appears in a pop-up window). To print the contents of the pop-up window, click the right mouse button inside the window, and click Print Topic. Click outside the pop-up window to close the window and continue working.

STEP 5: Change the Style

➤ Pull down the **View menu** and click the **Folder Options command** to display the Folder Options dialog box in Figure 6e. Click the **General tab,** click the option button for **Web style,** then click **OK** to accept the settings and close the Folder Options dialog box.

➤ The icons in the My Computer window should be underlined because you have changed to the Web style. Click the icon for **drive A** to view the contents of the floppy disk. The contents of the Address bar change to reflect drive A. The disk is empty, so you do not see any files.

➤ Close the My Computer window. Click the (underlined) **My Computer icon** on the desktop to open My Computer. You click (rather than double click) the icon to open it because you are in the Web style.

➤ Close My Computer.

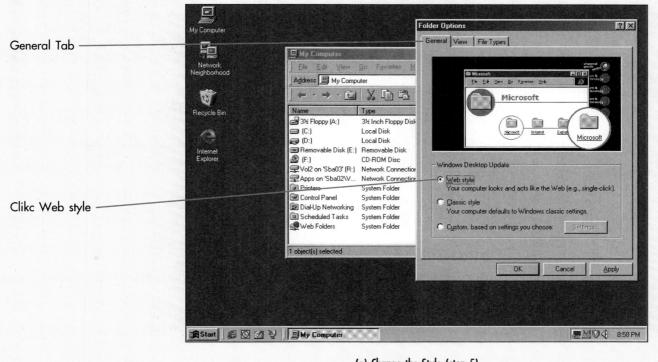

General Tab

Clikc Web style

(e) Change the Style (step 5)

FIGURE 6   Hands-on Exercise 1 (continued)

STEP 6: The Help Command

➤ Click the **Start button** on the taskbar, then click the **Help command** to display the Help window in Figure 6f. Do not be concerned if the size or position of your window is different from ours.

➤ Click the **Index tab,** then click in the text box to enter the desired topic. Type **Web st** (the first letters in "Web style," the topic you are searching for). Note that when you enter the last letter, the Help window displays "Web style folders" in the list of topics.

➤ Click (select) **Web style mouse selection,** then click the **Display button** to view the information in Figure 6f. Read the instructions carefully.

➤ Pull down the **Options menu** and click the **Print command** to display the Print dialog box. Click **OK** to print the selected page.

➤ Click the **close button** to close the Help window.

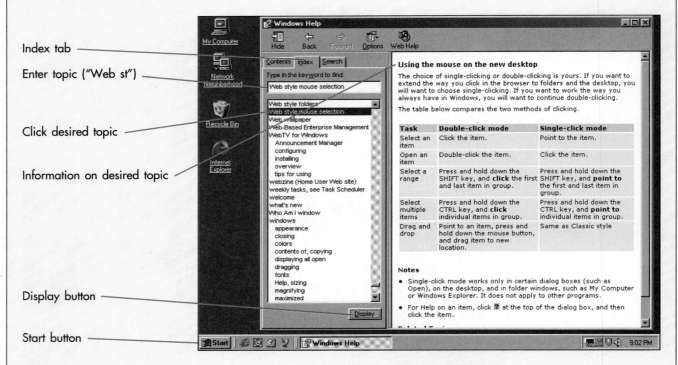

Index tab

Enter topic ("Web st")

Click desired topic

Information on desired topic

Display button

Start button

(f) The Help Command (step 6)

FIGURE 6   Hands-on Exercise 1 (continued)

STEP 7: Shut Down the Computer

➤ Click the **Start button,** click the **Shut Down command** to display the Shut Down Windows dialog box, and if necessary, click the option button to shut down the computer.

➤ Click the **Yes command button,** then wait as Windows gets ready to shut down your system. Wait until you see another screen indicating that it is OK to turn off the computer.

FILES AND FOLDERS

A *file* is a set of instructions or data that has been given a name and stored on disk. There are two basic types of files, program files and data files. Microsoft Word and Microsoft Excel are examples of program files. The documents and workbooks created by these programs are examples of data files.

A **program file** is an executable file because it contains instructions that tell the computer what to do. A **data file** is not executable and can be used only in conjunction with a specific program. As a student, you execute (run) program files, then you use those programs to create and/or modify the associated data files.

Every file must have a **file name** so that it can be identified. The file name may contain up to 255 characters and may include spaces and other punctuation. (This is very different from the rules that existed under MS-DOS, which limited file names to eight characters followed by an optional three-character extension.) Long file names permit descriptive entries such as *Term Paper for Western Civilization* (as opposed to *TPWCIV* that would be required under MS-DOS).

Files are stored in **folders** to better organize the hundreds (often thousands) of files on a hard disk. A Windows folder is similar in concept to a manila folder in a filing cabinet into which you put one or more documents (files) that are somehow related to each other. An office worker stores his or her documents in manila folders. In Windows, you store your files (documents) in electronic folders on disk.

Folders are the keys to the Windows storage system. Some folders are created automatically; for example, the installation of a program such as Microsoft Office automatically creates one or more folders to hold the various program files. Other folders are created by the user to hold the documents he or she creates. You could, for example, create one folder for your word processing documents and a second folder for your spreadsheets. Alternatively, you can create a folder to hold all of your work for a specific class, which may contain a combination of word processing documents and spreadsheets. Anything at all can go into a folder—program files, data files, even other folders.

Figure 7 displays a My Computer window for a folder containing six documents. Figure 7a shows the folder in the Classic style whereas Figure 7b shows it in the Web style. The choice between the two is one of personal preference and has to do with the action of the mouse. In the Classic style, you click an icon to select it, and you double click the icon to open it. In the Web style, you point to an icon to select it, and you click the icon to open it. (These operations mimic those of a Web browser.)

Regardless of the style in effect, the name of the folder (Homework) appears in the title bar next to the icon of an open folder. The minimize, maximize, and close buttons appear at the right of the title bar. A menu bar with six pull-down menus appears below the title bar. The Address bar appears below the menu bar and the toolbar appears below that. As with any toolbar, you can point to any button to display a ScreenTip that is indicative of the button's function. A status bar appears at the bottom of both windows, indicating that the Homework folder contains six objects (documents) and that the total file size is 333KB.

The Homework folder in both Figures 7a and 7b is displayed in *Details view,* one of four views available in My Computer. (The other views are Large Icons, Small Icons, and List view. The choice of view depends on your personal preference.) The Details view contains the maximum amount of information for each file and is used more frequently than the other views. It shows the file size, the type of file, and the date and time the file was last modified. The Details view also displays a small icon to the left of each file name that represents the application that is associated with the file. The Views button is the easiest way to switch from one view to another.

Name of folder

Menu bar

Address bar

Tool bar

Views button

Icon indicates associated application

Status bar

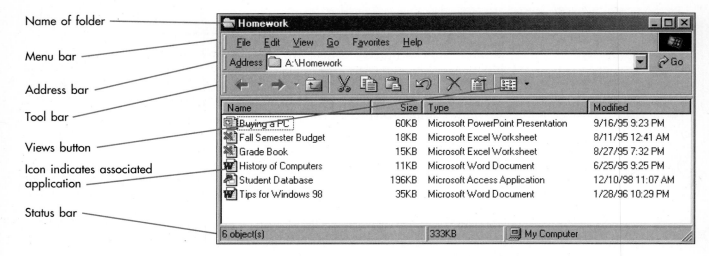

(a) Classic Style

Type column

Web Style has underlined icons

Icon indicates a Word document

Number of objects in window

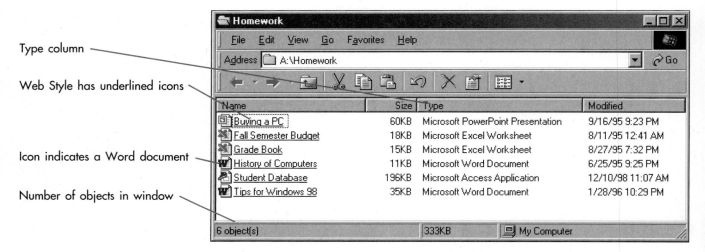

(b) Web Style

FIGURE 7   The Homework Folder

CLASSIC STYLE OR WEB STYLE

The Classic style and Web style are very different from one another, but neither style is a "better" style. The choice is one of personal preference, and depends on how you want to view the desktop and how you want to open its objects, by double clicking or clicking, respectively. We encourage you to experiment with both styles, and indeed, we find ourselves switching back and forth between the two. Use the Folder Options command in the View menu to change the style.

File Type

Every data file has a specific *file type* that is determined by the application used to create the file. One way to recognize the file type is to examine the Type column in the Details view as shown in Figure 7a. The History of Computers file, for example, is a Microsoft Word document. The Grade Book is a Microsoft Excel worksheet.

You can also determine the file type (or associated application) in any view by examining the application icon displayed next to the file name. Look carefully at the icon next to the History of Computers document in Figure 7a or 7b, for example, and you will recognize the icon for Microsoft Word. The application icon is recognized more easily in Large Icons view, as shown in Figure 8. Each application in Microsoft Office has a distinct icon.

Still another way to determine the file type is through a three-character *extension,* which is appended to the file name, but which is not shown in Figure 7. (A period separates the file name from the extension.) Each application has a unique extension that is automatically assigned to the file name when the file is created. DOC and XLS, for example, are the extensions for Microsoft Word and Excel, respectively. The extension may be suppressed or displayed according to an option in the View menu, but is better left suppressed.

My Computer

My Computer enables you to browse through the various folders on your system so that you can locate a document and go to work. Let's assume that you're looking for your term paper on the History of Computers, which you began yesterday, and which you saved in a folder called Homework.

My Computer can be used to locate the Homework file, and as indicated earlier, you can use either the Classic style in Figure 8a or the Web style in Figure 8b. The concepts are identical, but there are differences in the appearance of the icons (they are underlined in the Web style) and in the way the commands are executed. One other difference is that the Classic style opens a new window for each open folder, whereas the Web style uses a single window throughout the process.

In the Classic style in Figure 8a, you begin by double clicking the My Computer icon on the desktop to open the My Computer window, which in turn displays the devices on your system. Next, you double click the icon for drive C to open a second window that displays the folders on drive C. From there, you double click the icon for the Homework folder to open a third window containing the documents in the Homework folder. Once in the Homework folder, you can double click the icon of an existing document, which starts the associated application and opens the document, enabling you to begin work.

The Web style in Figure 8b follows the same sequence, but has you click rather than double click. Equally important, it uses a single window throughout the process as opposed to the multiple windows in the Classic style. You begin by clicking the My Computer icon on the desktop to display the contents of My Computer, which includes an icon for drive C. Then you click the icon for drive C, which in turn lets you click the Homework folder, from which you can click the icon for the data file to start the associated application and open the document. Note, too, the back arrow on the toolbar in Figure 8b, which is active throughout the Web style. You can click the back arrow to return to the previous folder (drive C in this example), just as you can click the back arrow on a Web browser to return to the previous Web page.

Double click My Computer icon

Double click icon for Drive C

Double click icon for Homework folder

Double click to start Excel and open Grade Book file

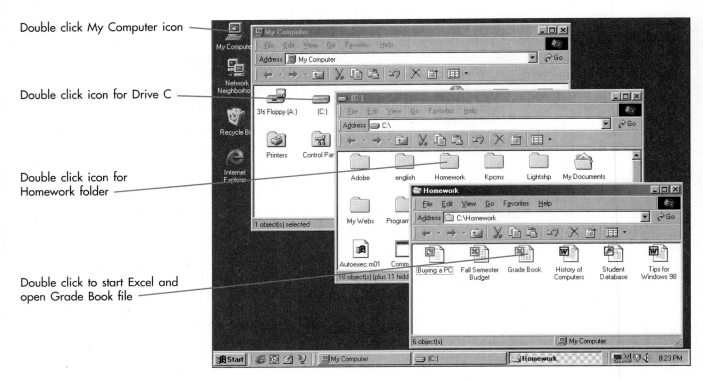

(a) Classic Style

Click to open My computer

Click Back arrow to return to previous folder

Click to start Excel and open Grade Book file

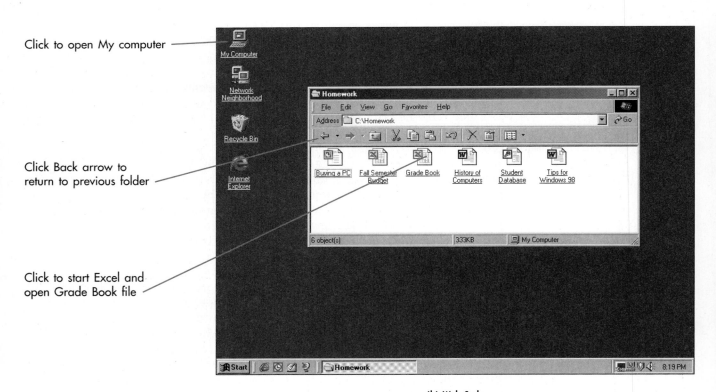

(b) Web Style

FIGURE 8   Browsing My Computer

HANDS-ON EXERCISE 2

The Exploring Windows Home Page

Objective: To download a file from the Web to a PC using the Classic and/or Web style. The exercise requires a formatted floppy disk and access to the Internet. Use Figure 9 as a guide in the exercise.

STEP 1: Start Internet Explorer

➤ Start Internet Explorer by clicking its icon on the desktop. If necessary, click the **maximize button** so that Internet Explorer takes the entire desktop.

➤ Enter the address of the site you want to visit:

- Pull down the **File menu,** click the **Open command** to display the Open dialog box, and enter **www.prenhall.com/grauer** (the http:// is assumed). Click **OK.**

- *Or, c*lick in the **Address bar** below the toolbar, which automatically selects the current address (so that whatever you type replaces the current address). Enter the address of the site, **www.prenhall.com/grauer** (the http:// is assumed). Press **Enter.**

➤ You should see the Exploring Windows series home page as shown in Figure 9a. Click the book for **Office 2000,** which takes you to the Office 2000 home page. Click the **Student Resources link** (at the top of the window) to go to the Student Resources page.

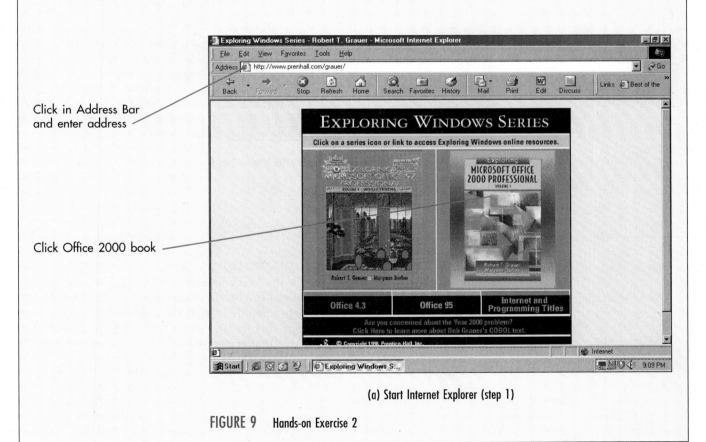

Click in Address Bar and enter address

Click Office 2000 book

(a) Start Internet Explorer (step 1)

FIGURE 9   Hands-on Exercise 2

STEP 2: Download the Practice Files

➤ Click the link to **Student Data Disk** (in the left frame), then scroll down the page until you see Windows 98 Prerequisites. Click the indicated link to download the student data disk as shown in Figure 9b.

➤ You will see the File Download dialog box asking what you want to do. The option button to save this program to disk is selected. Click **OK.** The Save As dialog box appears.

➤ Place a formatted floppy disk in drive A, click the **drop-down arrow** on the Save in list box, and select (click) **drive A.** Click **Save** to begin downloading the file.

Click Student Resources link

Click link to Student Data Disk

Click Save

Click link to download Windows 98 Prerequisites Data Disk

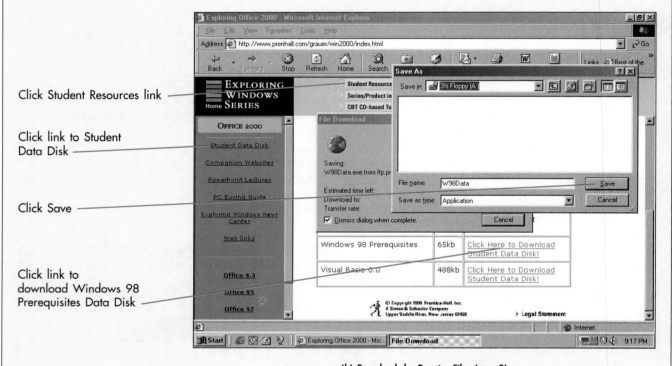

(b) Download the Practice Files (step 2)

FIGURE 9   Hands-on Exercise 2 (continued)

REMEMBER THE LOCATION

It's easy to download a file from the Web. The only tricky part, if any, is remembering where you have saved the file. This exercise is written for a laboratory setting, and thus we specified drive A as the destination, so that you will have the file on a floppy disk at the end of the exercise. If you have your own computer, however, it's faster to save the file to the desktop or in a temporary folder on drive C. Just remember where you save the file so that you can access it after it has been downloaded. And, if you really lose a file, click the Start button, then click the Find command. Use Help to learn more about searching for files on your PC.

➤ The File Download window will reappear on your screen and show you the status of the downloading operation. Be patient as this may take a few minutes.

➤ The File Download window will close automatically when the downloading is complete. If necessary, click **Close** when you see the dialog box indicating that the download is complete. Close Internet Explorer.

STEP 3: Classic Style or Web Style

➤ The instructions for opening My Computer and installing the practice files vary slightly, depending on which style is in effect on your desktop.

- In the Classic style you click an icon to select it, and you double click the icon to open it.

- In the Web style you point to an icon to select it, and you click the icon to open it. These operations mimic those of a Web browser—hence the term "Web style."

➤ You can switch from one style to the other using **My Computer.** Pull down the **View menu,** click the **Folder Options command,** then click the **General tab.** Select the option button for **Web style** or **Classic style** as desired, then click **OK** to accept the settings and close the Folder Options dialog box.

➤ Go to **step 4** or **step 6,** depending on which style is in effect on your desktop. You might even want to do the exercise both ways, in order to determine which style you prefer.

TO CLICK OR DOUBLE CLICK

The choice between Web style and Classic style is personal and depends on how you want to open a document, by clicking or double clicking, respectively. One way to change from one style to the other is to point to the desktop, click the right mouse button to display a context-sensitive menu, then click the Properties command to open the Display Properties dialog box. Click the Web tab, click the Folder Options command button, click Yes when prompted whether to view the folder options, then choose the style you want.

STEP 4: Install the Practice Files in Classic Style

➤ Double click the **My Computer icon** on the desktop to open the My Computer window. Double click the icon for **drive A** to open a second window as shown in Figure 9c. The size and/or position of these windows on your desktop may differ from ours; the second window, for example, may appear directly on top of the existing window.

➤ Double click the **W98Data icon** to install the data disk. You will see a dialog box thanking you for selecting the Exploring Windows series. Click **OK** when you have finished reading the dialog box to continue the installation and display the WinZip Self-Extractor dialog box in Figure 9c.

➤ Check that the Unzip To Folder text box specifies **A:**, which will extract the files to the floppy disk. (You can enter a different drive and/or folder if you prefer.)

➤ Click the **Unzip button** to extract (uncompress) the practice files and copy them onto the designated drive. Click **OK** after you see the message indicating that the files have been unzipped successfully. Close the WinZip dialog box.

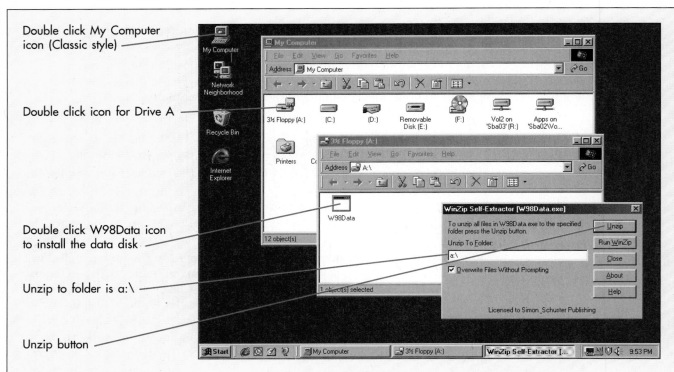

Double click My Computer icon (Classic style)

Double click icon for Drive A

Double click W98Data icon to install the data disk

Unzip to folder is a:\

Unzip button

(c) Install the Practice Files in Classic Style (step 4)

FIGURE 9 Hands-on Exercise 2 (continued)

CUSTOMIZE MY COMPUTER

You can customize the My Computer window regardless of whether you choose the Classic style or Web style. Pull down the View menu, click the Toolbars command to display a cascaded menu, then check the commands for the Standard Buttons and Address Bar, and clear the commands for Links and Text Labels. Pull down the View menu a second time and select (click) the desired view. Pull down the View menu a final time, click the Arrange Icons command, and (if necessary) click the AutoArrange command so that a check appears. Click outside the menu (or press the Esc key) if the command is already checked.

STEP 5: Delete the Compressed File in Classic Style

➤ The practice files have been extracted to drive A and should appear in the drive A window. If you do not see the files, pull down the **View menu** and click the **Refresh command.**

➤ You should see a total of six files in the drive A window. Five of these are the practice files on the data disk; the sixth is the original file that you downloaded earlier.

➤ If necessary, pull down the **View menu** and click **Details** (or click the **Views button** repeatedly) to change to the Details view. Your display should match Figure 9d.

➤ Select (click) the **W98Data icon.** Pull down the **File menu** and click the **Delete command** or click the **Delete button** on the toolbar. Click **Yes** when asked to confirm the deletion. The ie4datadisk file disappears from the drive A window.

➤ Go to **step 8** to complete this exercise; that is, you can skip steps 6 and 7, which illustrate the Web style.

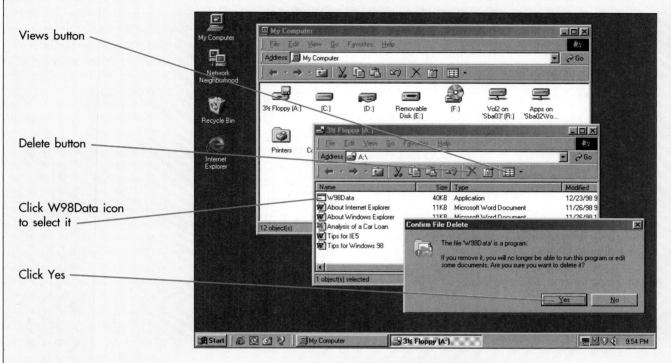

Views button

Delete button

Click W98Data icon
to select it

Click Yes

(d) Delete the Compressed File in Classic Style (step 5)

FIGURE 9   Hands-on Exercise 2 (continued)

ONE WINDOW OR MANY

The Classic style opens a new window every time you open a new drive or folder using My Computer, which can quickly lead to a cluttered desktop. You can, however, customize the Classic style to display the objects in a single window. Pull down the View menu, click the Folder Options command, click the option button for Custom based on the settings you choose, then click the Settings command button to display the Custom Settings dialog box. Click the option button in the Browse folders area to open each folder in the same window, click OK to close the Custom Settings dialog box, then click OK to close the Folder Options dialog box.

STEP 6: Install the Practice Files in Web Style

➤ Click the **My Computer icon** on the desktop to open the My Computer window, then click the icon for **drive A** within My Computer. Click the **W98Data icon** to install the data disk.

➤ You will see a dialog box thanking you for selecting the Exploring Windows series. Click **OK** when you have finished reading the dialog box to continue the installation and display the WinZip Self-Extractor dialog box in Figure 9e.

➤ Check that the Unzip To Folder text box specifies **A:**, which will extract the files to the floppy disk. (You can enter a different drive and/or folder if you prefer.)

➤ Click the **Unzip button** to extract the practice files and copy them onto the designated drive. Click **OK** after you see the message indicating that the files have been unzipped successfully. Close the WinZip dialog box.

➤ The practice files have been extracted to drive A and should appear in the drive A window. If you do not see the files, pull down the **View menu** and click the **Refresh command.**

➤ Pull down the **View menu.** Toggle the command **as Web Page** on or off as you prefer. The command is off in Figure 9e.

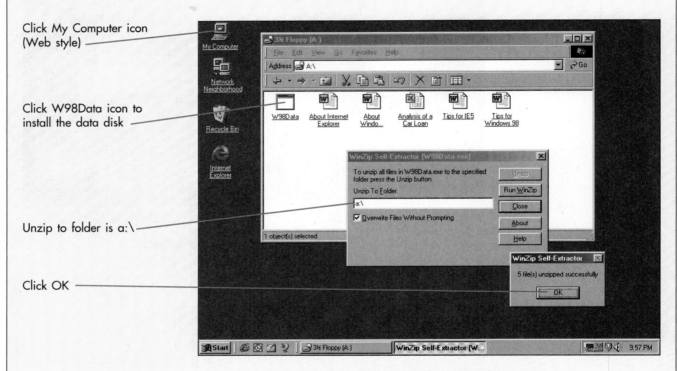

Click My Computer icon (Web style)

Click W98Data icon to install the data disk

Unzip to folder is a:\

Click OK

(e) Install the Practice Files in Web Style (step 6)

FIGURE 9   Hands-on Exercise 2 (continued)

THE BACK AND FORWARD BUTTONS IN MY COMPUTER

The Web style is so named because it follows the conventions of a Web browser. Unlike the Classic style, which displays a separate window for each drive or folder, the Web style uses a single window throughout. Thus, you can click the Back button on the My Computer toolbar to return to a previous folder. In similar fashion you can click the Forward button from a previously viewed folder to go to the next folder.

STEP 7: Delete the Compressed File in Web Style

➤ You should see a total of six files in the drive A window. Five of these are the practice files on the data disk; the sixth is the original file that you downloaded earlier.

➤ If necessary, pull down the **View menu** and click **Details** to change to the Details view in Figure 9f so that your display matches ours.

➤ Point to the **W98Data icon,** which in turn selects the file. Pull down the **File menu** and click the **Delete command** or click the **Delete button** on the toolbar. Click **Yes** when asked to confirm the deletion. The W98Data file disappears from the drive A window.

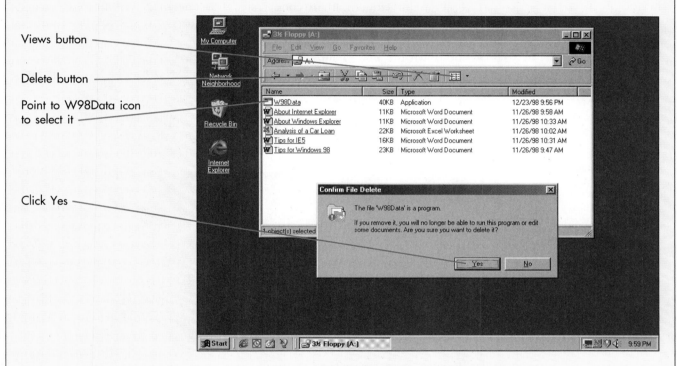

(f) Delete the Compressed File in Web Style (step 7)

FIGURE 9   Hands-on Exercise 2 (continued)

CHANGE THE VIEW

The contents of drive A are displayed in the Details view, one of four views available in My Computer. Details view displays the maximum amount of information for each file and is our general preference. You can, however, click the Views button on the My Computer toolbar to cycle through the other views (Large Icons, Small Icons, and List). You can also pull down the View menu and toggle the As Web Page command on, which will display additional information in the My Computer window.

STEP 8: Modify a File

➤ It doesn't matter whether you are in the Web style or the Classic style. (Our figure displays the Web style.) What is important, however, is that you have successfully downloaded the practice files.

➤ Open the **About Internet Explorer** document:

- Click the icon in Web style.

- Double click the document icon in Classic style.

➤ If necessary, maximize the window for Microsoft Word. (The document will open in the WordPad accessory if Microsoft Word is not installed on your machine.)

➤ Read the document, then click inside the document window and press **Ctrl+End** to move to the end of the document. Add the sentence shown in Figure 9g followed by your name.

➤ Pull down the **File menu,** click **Print,** then click **OK** to print the document and prove to your instructor that you did the exercise. Pull down the **File menu** and click **Exit** to close the application. Click **Yes** if prompted whether to save the file.

➤ Exit Windows if you do not want to continue with the next exercise at this time.

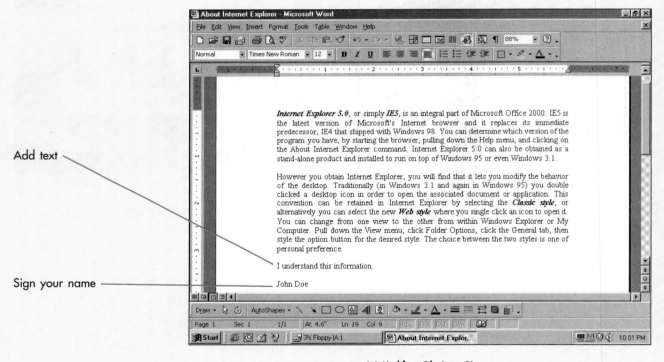

(g) Modify a File (step 8)

FIGURE 9   Hands-on Exercise 2 (continued)

There are two programs that manage the files and folders on your system, My Computer and Windows Explorer. My Computer is intuitive, but less efficient, as you have to open each folder in succession. Windows Explorer is more sophisticated, as it provides a hierarchical view of the entire system in a single window. A beginner might prefer My Computer whereas a more experienced user will most likely opt for Windows Explorer.

Assume, for example, that you are taking four classes this semester, and that you are using the computer in each course. You've created a separate folder to hold the work for each class and have stored the contents of all four folders on a single floppy disk. Assume further that you need to retrieve your third English assignment so that you can modify the assignment, then submit the revised version to your instructor.

Figure 10 illustrates how *Windows Explorer* could be used to locate your assignment. As with My Computer, you can display Windows Explorer in either the Classic style or the Web style. The concepts are identical, but there are differences in the appearance of the icons (they are underlined in the Web style) and in the way the commands are executed. The choice is one of personal preference and you can switch back and forth between the two. (Pull down the View menu and click the Folder Options command to change from one style to the other.)

The Explorer window in both Figure 10a and Figure 10b is divided into two panes. The left pane contains a tree diagram (or hierarchical view) of the entire system showing all drives and, optionally, the folders in each drive. The right pane shows the contents of the active (open) drive or folder. Only one object (a drive or folder) can be active in the left pane, and its contents are displayed automatically in the right pane.

Look carefully at the icon for the English folder in the left pane of either figure. The folder is open, whereas the icon for every other folder is closed. The open folder indicates that the English folder is the active folder. (The name of the active folder also appears in the title bar of Windows Explorer and in the address bar on the toolbar.) The contents of the active folder (three Word documents in this example) are displayed in the right pane. The right pane is displayed in Details view, but could just as easily have been displayed in another view (e.g., Large or Small Icons).

As indicated, only one folder can be open (active) at a time in the left pane. Thus, to see the contents of a different folder such as Accounting, you would open (click on) the Accounting folder, which automatically closes the English folder. The contents of the Accounting folder would then appear in the right pane.

Look carefully at the tree structure in either Figure 10a or Figure 10b and note that it contains an icon for Internet Explorer, which when selected, starts Internet Explorer and displays a Web page in the contents pane of Windows Explorer. Thus you can use Windows Explorer to view Web pages, and conversely, you can use Internet Explorer to view documents and/or folders that are stored locally.

ORGANIZE YOUR WORK

Organize your folder in ways that make sense to you, such as a separate folder for every class you are taking. You can also create folders within folders; for example, a correspondence folder may contain two folders of its own, one for business correspondence and one for personal letters.

Name of active folder

Minus indicates object is expanded

Selected folder

Contents of selected folder

Plus signs indicate drives are collapsed

Icon for Internet Explorer

Click to display Web page in right pane

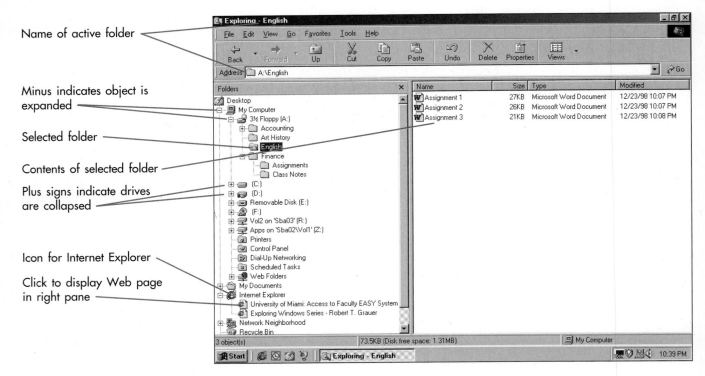

(a) Classic Style (Details view)

Name of active folder

Selected folder

Click minus to collapse folder

Contents of selected folder

Click plus to expand drive

Icon for Internet Explorer

Click to display Web page in right pane

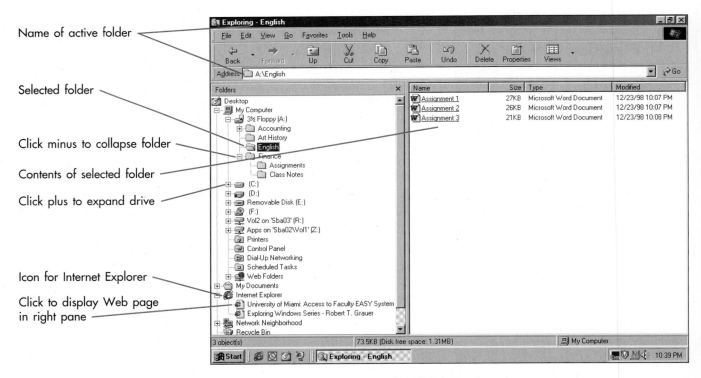

(b) Web Style (Details view)

FIGURE 10   Windows Explorer

Expanding and Collapsing a Drive

The tree diagram in Windows Explorer displays the devices on your system in hierarchical fashion. The desktop is always at the top of the hierarchy, and it contains various icons such as My Computer, the Recycle Bin, Internet Explorer, and Network Neighborhood. My Computer in turn contains the various drives that are accessible from your system, each of which contains folders, which in turn contain documents and/or additional folders. Each *icon* may be *expanded* or *collapsed* by clicking the plus or minus sign, respectively. Click either sign to toggle to the other. Clicking a plus sign, for example, expands the drive, then displays a minus sign next to the drive to indicate that its subordinates are visible.

Return to either Figure 10a or 10b and look at the icon next to My Computer. It is a minus sign (as opposed to a plus sign), and it indicates that My Computer has been expanded to show the devices on the system. There is also a minus sign next to the icon for drive A to indicate that it too has been expanded to show the folders on the disk. There is also a minus sign next to the Internet Explorer icon, which displays the Web sites that were visited in this session. Note, however, the plus sign next to drives C and D, indicating that these parts of the tree are currently collapsed and thus their subordinates (in this case, folders) are not visible.

A folder may contain additional folders, and thus individual folders may also be expanded or collapsed. The minus sign next to the Finance folder, for example, indicates that the folder has been expanded and contains two additional folders, for Assignments and Class Notes, respectively. The plus sign next to the Accounting folder, however, indicates the opposite; that is, the folder is collapsed and its subordinate folders are not currently visible. A folder with neither a plus or minus sign, such as Art History, does not contain additional folders and cannot be expanded or collapsed.

The hierarchical view within Windows Explorer, and the ability to expand and collapse the various folders on a system, enables the user to quickly locate a specific file or folder. If, for example, you wanted to see the contents of the Art History folder, all you would do is click its icon in the left pane, which automatically changes the display in the right pane to show the documents in that folder.

Windows Explorer is ideal for moving or copying files from one folder or drive to another. You simply select (open) the folder that contains the files, use the scroll bar in the left pane (if necessary) so that the destination folder is visible, then click and drag the files from the right pane to the destination folder. Windows Explorer is a powerful tool, but it takes practice to master. It's time for another hands-on exercise in which we use Windows Explorer to copy the practice files from a network drive to a floppy disk. (The exercise assumes that your instructor has placed our files on your local area network.)

THE DOCUMENT, NOT THE APPLICATION

Windows 98 is document oriented, meaning that you are able to think in terms of the document rather than the application that created it. You can still open a document in traditional fashion, by starting the application that created the document, then using the File Open command in that program to retrieve the document. It's often easier, however, to open the document from within My Computer (or Windows Explorer) by clicking its icon in Web view, or double clicking the icon in Classic view. Windows then starts the application and opens the data file. In other words, you can open a document without explicitly starting the application.

The Practice Files (via a local area network)

Objective: To use Windows Explorer to copy the practice files from a network drive to a floppy disk. The exercise requires a formatted floppy disk and access to a local area network. Use Figure 11 as a guide in the exercise.

CONVERGENCE OF THE EXPLORERS

Windows Explorer and Internet Explorer are separate programs, but each includes some functionality of the other. You can use Windows Explorer to display a Web page by clicking the Internet Explorer icon within the tree structure in the left pane. Conversely, you can use Internet Explorer to display a local drive, document, or folder. Start Internet Explorer in the usual fashion, click in the Address bar, then enter the appropriate address such as C: to display the contents of drive C.

STEP 1: Start Windows Explorer

➤ Click the **Start button,** click (or point to) the **Programs command,** then click **Windows Explorer** to start this program. Click the **maximize button.**

➤ Make or verify the following selections using the **View menu** as shown in Figure 11a. You have to pull down the **View menu** each time you choose a different command.

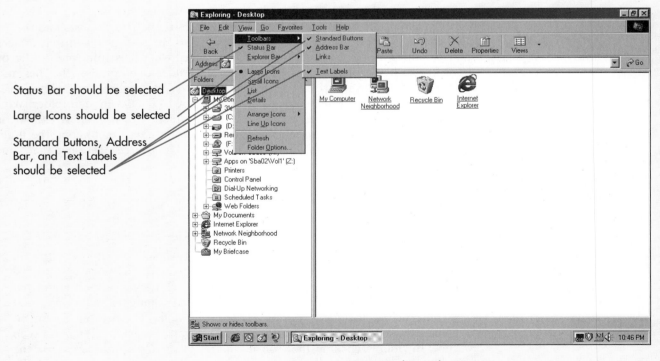

Status Bar should be selected

Large Icons should be selected

Standard Buttons, Address Bar, and Text Labels should be selected

(a) Start Windows Explorer (step 1)

FIGURE 11   Hands-on Exercise 3

- The **Standard Buttons, Address Bar,** and **Text Labels** should be checked.
- The **Status Bar command** should be checked.
- The **Large Icons view** should be selected.

➤ Click (select) the **Desktop icon** in the left pane to display the contents of the desktop in the right pane. Our desktop contains icons for My Computer, Network Neighborhood, the Recycle Bin, and Internet Explorer.

➤ Your desktop may have different icons from ours, but your screen should otherwise match the one in Figure 11a, given that you are in Web style.

CLASSIC STYLE OR WEB STYLE

Which do you prefer, Coke or Pepsi? They are both good, and the choice is one of personal preference. So it is with Classic style and Web style. They are different, but neither is clearly better than the other, and indeed we find ourselves switching between the two. This exercise is written for the Classic style.

STEP 2: Change to Classic Style (if necessary)

➤ You can skip this step if your desktop is already in Classic style. Pull down the **View menu,** click the **Folder Options command** to display the Folder Options dialog box, then click the **General tab** as shown in Figure 11b.

➤ Click the **Classic style option button,** then click **OK** to accept this setting and close the Folder Options dialog box. The icons within Windows Explorer should be displayed in Classic style.

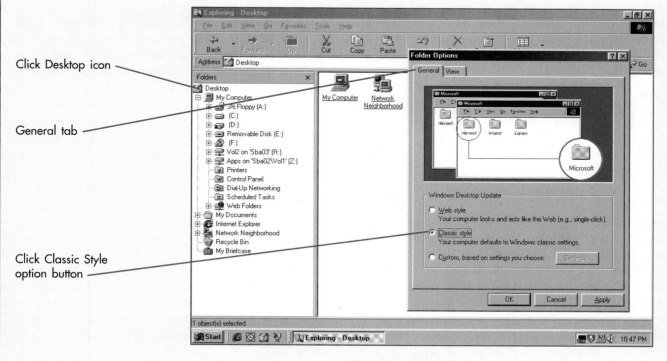

(b) Change to Classic Style (step 2)

FIGURE 11   Hands-on Exercise 3 (continued)

FILE EXTENSIONS

Long-time DOS users remember a three-character extension at the end of a file name to indicate the file type; for example, DOC or XLS to indicate a Word document or Excel workbook, respectively. The extensions are displayed or hidden according to the option you choose through the View menu of Windows Explorer. Pull down the View menu, click the Folder Options command to display the Folder Options dialog box, click the View tab, then check (or clear) the box to hide (or show) file extensions for known file types. Click OK to accept the setting and exit the dialog box.

STEP 3: Collapse the Individual Drives

➤ Click the **minus** (or the **plus**) **sign** next to My Computer to collapse (or expand) My Computer. Toggle the signs back and forth a few times for practice. End with a minus sign next to My Computer.

➤ Place a formatted floppy disk in drive A. Click the drive icon next to **drive A** to select the drive and display its contents in the right pane as shown in Figure 11c. The disk does not contain any files, and hence the right pane is empty.

➤ Click the **plus sign** next to drive A. The plus sign disappears, as drive A does not have any folders.

➤ Click the **sign** next to the other drives to toggle back and forth between expanding and collapsing the individual drives on your system. End this step with every drive collapsed; that is, there should be a **plus sign** next to every drive except drive A, as shown in Figure 11c.

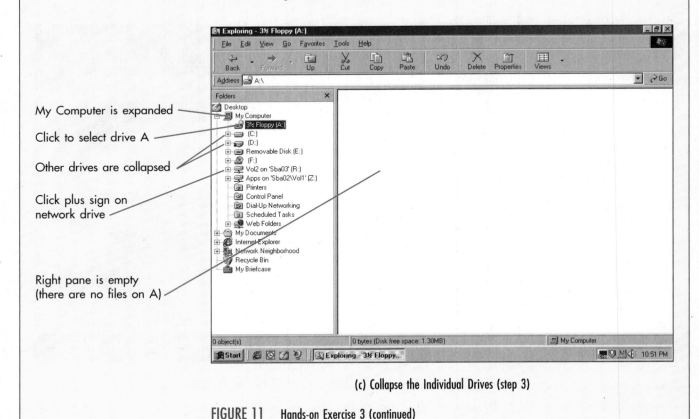

My Computer is expanded

Click to select drive A

Other drives are collapsed

Click plus sign on network drive

Right pane is empty (there are no files on A)

(c) Collapse the Individual Drives (step 3)

FIGURE 11   Hands-on Exercise 3 (continued)

THE PLUS AND MINUS SIGNS

Any drive, be it local or on the network, may be expanded or collapsed to display or hide its folders. A minus sign indicates that the drive has been expanded and that its folders are visible. A plus sign indicates the reverse; that is, the device is collapsed and its folders are not visible. Click either sign to toggle to the other. Clicking a plus sign, for example, expands the drive, then displays a minus sign next to the drive to indicate that the folders are visible. Clicking a minus sign has the reverse effect; that is, it collapses the drive, hiding its folders.

STEP 4: Select the Network Drive

➤ Click the **plus sign** for the network drive that contains the files you are to copy (e.g., **drive R** in Figure 11d). Select (click) the **Exploring Windows 98 folder** to open this folder.

➤ You may need to expand other folders on the network drive (such as the Datadisk folder on our network) as per instructions from your professor. Note the following:

• The Exploring Windows 98 folder is highlighted in the left pane, its icon has changed to an open folder, and its contents are displayed in the right pane.

• The status bar indicates that the folder contains five objects and the total file size is 82.5KB.

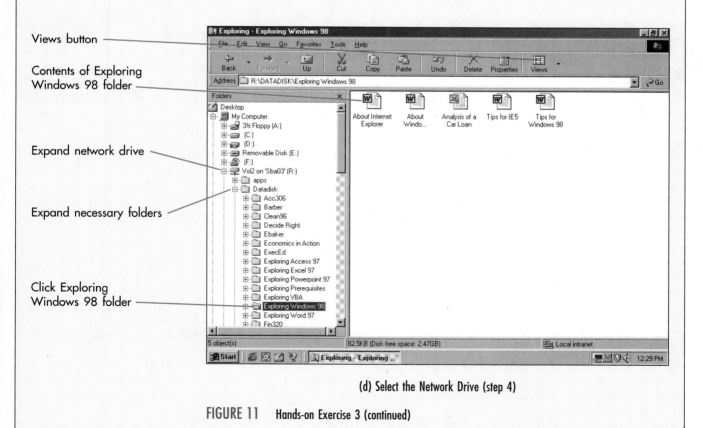

(d) Select the Network Drive (step 4)

FIGURE 11   Hands-on Exercise 3 (continued)

➤ Click the icon next to any other folder to select the folder, which in turn deselects the Exploring Windows 98 folder. (Only one folder in the left pane can be active at a time.)

➤ Reselect (click) the **Exploring Windows 98 folder,** and its contents are again visible in the right pane.

➤ Pull down the **View menu** and select **Details** (or click the arrow on the **Views button** on the toolbar to display the different views, then **Details**). This enables you to see the file sizes of the individual files.

SORT BY NAME, DATE, FILE TYPE, OR SIZE

The files within a folder can be displayed in ascending or descending sequence by name, date modified, file type, or size. Change to the Details view. Select the desired folder in the left pane, then click the desired column heading in the right pane; click size, for example, to display the contents of the selected folder according to the size of the individual files. Click the column heading a second time to reverse the sequence—that is, to switch from ascending to descending, and vice versa.

STEP 5: Copy the Individual Files

➤ Select (click) the file called **About Windows Explorer,** which highlights the file as shown in Figure 11e. The Exploring Windows 98 folder is no longer highlighted because a different object has been selected. The folder is still open, however, and its contents are displayed in the right pane.

➤ Click and drag the selected file in the right pane to the **drive A icon** in the left pane:

  • You will see the ⊘ symbol as you drag the file until you reach a suitable destination (e.g., until you point to the icon for drive A). The ⊘ symbol will change to a plus sign when the icon for drive A is highlighted, indicating that the file can be copied successfully.

  • Release the mouse to complete the copy operation. You will see a pop-up window, which indicates the status of the copy operation. This may take several seconds depending on the size of the file.

➤ Select (click) the file **Tips for Windows 98,** which automatically deselects the previously selected file (About Windows Explorer). Copy the selected file to drive A by dragging its icon from the right pane to the drive A icon in the left pane.

➤ Copy the three remaining files to drive A as well. (You can select multiple files at the same time by pressing and holding the **Ctrl key** as you click each file in turn. Point to any of the selected files, then click and drag the files as a group.)

➤ Select (click) **drive A** in the left pane, which in turn displays the contents of the floppy disk in the right pane. You should see the five files you have copied to drive A.

Click About Windows
Explorer to select it

Drag file to icon for drive A

Click minus to
collapse network drive

+ indicates file is
being copied

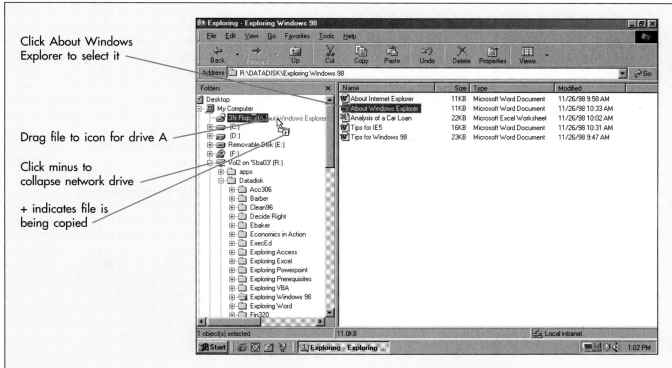

(e) Copy the Individual Files (step 5)

FIGURE 11   Hands-on Exercise 3 (continued)

SELECT MULTIPLE FILES

Selecting (clicking) one file automatically deselects the previously selected
file. You can, however, select multiple files by pressing and holding the
Ctrl key as you click each file in succession. You can also select multiple
files that are adjacent to one another by using the Shift key; that is, click
the icon of the first file, then press and hold the Shift key as you click the
icon of the last file. You can also select every file in a folder through the
Select All command in the Edit menu (or by clicking in the right pane
and pressing Ctrl+A). The same commands work in the Web style, except
that you hover over an icon (point to it and pause) rather than click it;
for example, point to the first file, then press the Ctrl key as you hover
over each subsequent file that you want to select.

STEP 6: Display a Web Page
➤ This step requires an Internet connection. Click the **minus sign** next to the
network drive to collapse that drive. Click the **minus sign** next to any other
expanded drive so that the left pane in Windows Explorer is similar to Figure 11f.
➤ Click the **Internet Explorer icon** to start Internet Explorer and display the
starting page for your configuration. Click in the Address bar near the top of
the window. Type **www.prenhall.com/grauer** to go to the *Exploring Windows*
home page.

➤ Look closely at the icons on the toolbar, which have changed to reflect the tools associated with viewing a Web page.

➤ Click the **Back button** to return to drive A, which was the previously displayed item in Windows Explorer. The icons on the toolbar return to those associated with a folder.

➤ Click the **Forward button** to return to the Web page. The icons on the toolbar change back to those associated with the Internet.

➤ Close Windows Explorer. Shut down the computer if you do not want to continue with the next exercise at this time.

Icons on toolbar reflect those associated with a Web page

Back button

Forward button

Click Internet Explorer icon to display your start page

Click a site to display Web page in right pane

Web page is displayed

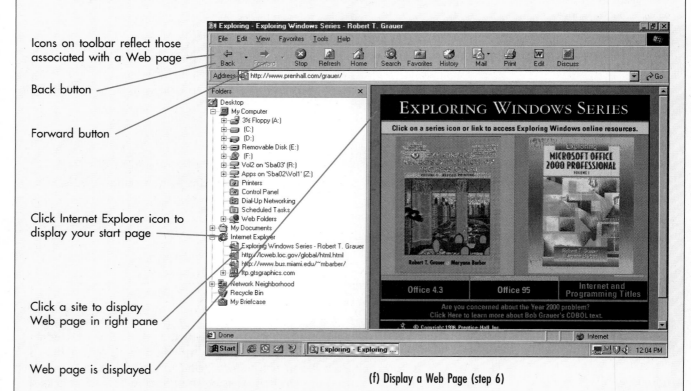

(f) Display a Web Page (step 6)

FIGURE 11   Hands-on Exercise 3 (continued)

THE SMART TOOLBAR

The toolbar in Windows Explorer recognizes whether you are viewing a Web page or a set of files and folders, and changes accordingly. The icons that are displayed when viewing a Web page are identical to those in Internet Explorer and include the Search, History, Favorites, and buttons that show various sets of Internet links. The buttons that are displayed when viewing a file or folder include the Undo, Delete, and Views buttons that are used in file management. Both sets of icons include the Back button to return to the previous object.

THE BASICS OF FILE MANAGEMENT

As you grow to depend on the computer, you will create a variety of files in applications such as Microsoft Word or Excel. Learning how to manage those files is one of the most important skills you can acquire. The purpose of Hands-on Exercises 2 and 3 was to give you a set of files with which to practice. That way, when you have your own files, you will be comfortable executing the various file management commands you will need on a daily basis. Accordingly, we discuss the basic commands you will use, then present another hands-on exercise in which you apply those commands.

Moving and Copying a File

Moving and copying a file from one location to another is the essence of file management. It is accomplished most easily by clicking and dragging the file icon from the source drive or folder to the destination drive or folder, within Windows Explorer. There is a subtlety, however, in that the result of dragging a file (i.e., whether the file is moved or copied) depends on whether the source and destination are on the same or different drives. Dragging a file from one folder to another folder on the same drive moves the file. Dragging a file to a folder on a different drive copies the file. The same rules apply to dragging a folder, where the folder and every file in it are moved or copied as per the rules for an individual file.

   This process is not as arbitrary as it may seem. Windows assumes that if you drag an object (a file or folder) to a different drive (e.g., from drive C to drive A), you want the object to appear in both places. Hence, the default action when you click and drag an object to a different drive is to copy the object. You can, however, override the default and move the object by pressing and holding the Shift key as you drag.

   Windows also assumes that you do not want two copies of an object on the same drive, as that would result in wasted disk space. Thus, the default action when you click and drag an object to a different folder on the same drive is to move the object. You can override the default and copy the object by pressing and holding the Ctrl key as you drag.

   You don't have to remember these conventions, however. Just click and drag with the right mouse button and you will be presented with a context-sensitive menu asking whether to move or copy the files. It's not as complicated as it sounds, and you get a chance to practice in the hands-on exercise, which follows shortly.

Deleting a File

The **Delete command** deletes (removes) a file from a disk. The command can be executed in different ways, most easily by selecting a file, then pressing the Del key. Even after a file is deleted, however, you can usually get it back because it is not physically deleted from the hard disk, but moved instead to the Recycle Bin from where it can be recovered.

   The **Recycle Bin** is a special folder that contains all files that were previously deleted from any hard disk on your system. Think of the Recycle Bin as similar to the wastebasket in your room. You throw out (delete) a report by tossing it into a wastebasket. The report is gone (deleted) from your desk, but you can still get it back by taking it out of the wastebasket as long as the basket wasn't emptied. The Recycle Bin works the same way. Files are not deleted from the hard disk per se, but moved instead to the Recycle Bin from where they can be restored to their original location.

   The Recycle Bin will eventually run out of space, in which case the files that have been in the Recycle Bin the longest are deleted to make room for additional files. Accordingly, once a file is removed from the Recycle Bin, it can no longer be restored, as it has been physically deleted from the hard disk. Note, too, that the protection afforded by the Recycle Bin does not extend to files deleted from a floppy disk. Such files can be recovered, but only through utility programs outside of Windows 98.

Backup

It's not a question of *if* it will happen, but *when*—hard disks die, files are lost, or viruses may infect a system. It has happened to us and it will happen to you, but you can prepare for the inevitable by creating adequate backup *before* the problem occurs. The essence of a ***backup strategy*** is to decide which files to back up, how often to do the backup, and where to keep the backup. Once you decide on a strategy, follow it, and follow it faithfully!

Our strategy is very simple—back up what you can't afford to lose, do so on a daily basis, and store the backup away from your computer. You need not copy every file, every day. Instead, copy just the files that changed during the current session. Realize, too, that it is much more important to back up your data files than your program files. You can always reinstall the application from the original disks or CD, or if necessary, go to the vendor for another copy of an application. You, however, are the only one who has a copy of the term paper that is due tomorrow.

We cannot overemphasize the importance of adequate backup and urge you to copy your data files to floppy disks and store those disks away from your computer. You might also want to write-protect your backup disks so that you cannot accidentally erase a file. It takes only a few minutes, but you will thank us, when (not if) you lose an important file and wish you had another copy.

Write-protection

A floppy disk is normally ***write-enabled*** (the square hole is covered with the movable tab) so that you can change the contents of the disk. Thus, you can create (save) new files to a write-enabled disk and/or edit or delete existing files. Occasionally, however, you may want to ***write-protect*** a floppy disk (by sliding the tab to expose the square hole) so that its contents cannot be modified. This is typically done with a backup disk where you want to prevent the accidental deletion of a file and/or the threat of virus infection.

Our Next Exercise

As we have indicated throughout this supplement, the ability to move and copy files is of paramount importance. The only way to master these skills is through practice, and so we offer our next exercise in which you execute various commands for file management.

The exercise begins with the floppy disk containing the five practice files in drive A. We ask you to create two folders on drive A (step 1) and to move the various files into these folders (step 2). Next, you copy a folder from drive A to drive C (step 3), modify one of the files in the folder on drive C (step 4), then copy the modified file back to drive A (step 5). We ask you to delete a file in step 6, then recover it from the Recycle Bin in step 7. We also show you how to write-protect a floppy disk in step 8. Disk and file management is a critical skill, and you will want to master the exercise in its entirety. There is a lot to do, so let's get started.

HANDS-ON EXERCISE 4

Windows Explorer

Objective: Use Windows Explorer to move, copy, and delete a file. Use Figure 12, which was done using the Classic style, as a guide.

STEP 1: Create a New Folder

➤ Start Windows Explorer. Place the floppy disk from Hands-on Exercise 2 or 3 in drive A. Select (click) the icon for **drive A** in the left pane of the Explorer window. Drive A should contain the files shown in Figure 12a.

➤ You will create two folders on drive A, using two different techniques:

- Point to a blank area anywhere in the **right pane,** click the **right mouse button** to display a context-sensitive menu, click (or point to) the **New command,** then click **Folder** as the type of object to create. The icon for a new folder will appear with the name of the folder (New Folder) highlighted. Type **Computing 101** to change the name of the folder. Press **Enter.**

- Click the icon for **drive A** once again. Pull down the **File menu,** click (or point to) the **New command,** and click **Folder** as the type of object to create. Type **IE Documents** to change the name of the folder. Press **Enter.** The right pane should now contain five documents and two folders.

➤ Pull down the **View menu.** Click (or point to) the **Arrange Icons command** to display a submenu, then click the **By Name command.**

Click Folder

Click icon for drive A

Point to a blank area in right pane and click right mouse button to display shortcut menu

Click new

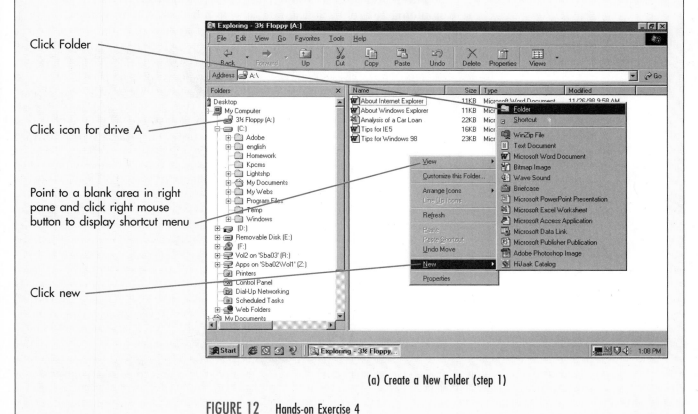

(a) Create a New Folder (step 1)

FIGURE 12   Hands-on Exercise 4

RENAME COMMAND

Every file or folder is assigned a name at the time it is created, but you may want to change that name at some point in the future. Point to a file or a folder, then click the right mouse button to display a menu with commands pertaining to the object. Click the Rename command. The name of the file or folder will be highlighted with the insertion point (a flashing vertical line) positioned at the end of the name. Enter a new name to replace the selected name, or click anywhere within the name to change the insertion point and edit the name.

STEP 2: Move a File

➤ Pull down the **View** menu and click **Refresh.** Click the **plus sign** next to drive A to expand the drive as shown in Figure 12b. Note the following:

- The left pane shows that drive A is selected. The right pane displays the contents of drive A (the selected object in the left pane). The folders are shown first and appear in alphabetical order. The file names are displayed after the folders and are also in alphabetical order.

- There is a minus sign next to the icon for drive A in the left pane, indicating that it has been expanded and that its folders are visible. Thus, the folder names also appear under drive A in the left pane.

➤ Click and drag the icon for **About Windows Explorer** from the right pane to the **Computing 101 folder** in the left pane to move the file into that folder.

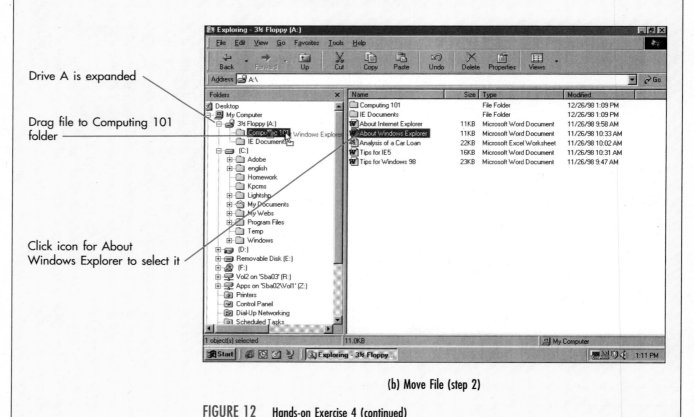

(b) Move File (step 2)

FIGURE 12   Hands-on Exercise 4 (continued)

➤ Click and drag the **Tips for Windows 98 icon** and the **Analysis of a Car Loan icon** to the **Computing 101 folder** in similar fashion.

➤ Click the **Computing 101 icon** in the left pane to select the folder and display its contents in the right pane. You should see the three files.

➤ Click the icon for **drive A** in the left pane, then click and drag the remaining files, **About Internet Explorer** and **Tips for IE5,** to the **IE Documents folder.**

RIGHT CLICK AND DRAG

The result of dragging a file with the left mouse button depends on whether the source and destination folders are on the same or different drives. Dragging a file to a folder on a different drive copies the file. Dragging the file to a folder on the same drive moves the file. If you find this hard to remember, click and drag with the right mouse button to display a shortcut menu asking whether you want to copy or move the file. This simple tip can save you from making a careless (and potentially serious) error.

STEP 3: Copy a Folder

➤ If necessary, click the **plus sign** next to the icon for drive C to expand the drive and display its folders as shown in Figure 12c.

➤ Do *not* click the icon for drive C, as drive A is to remain selected. (You can expand or collapse an object without selecting it.)

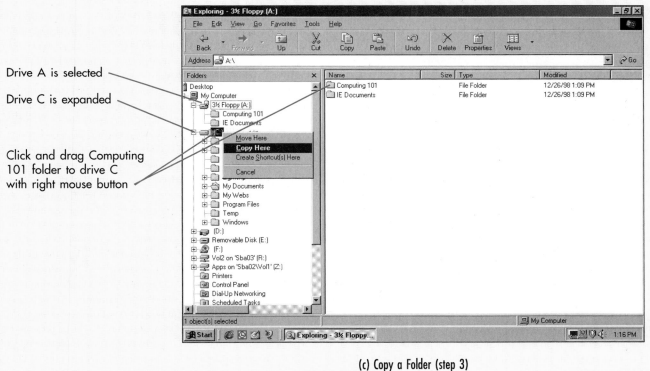

(c) Copy a Folder (step 3)

FIGURE 12   Hands-on Exercise 4 (continued)

➤ Point to the **Computing 101 folder** in either pane, click the **right mouse button,** and drag the folder to the icon for **drive C** in the left pane, then release the mouse to display a shortcut menu. Click the **Copy Here command.**

- You may see a Copy files dialog box as the individual files within the folder are copied from drive A to drive C.

- If you see the Confirm Folder Replace dialog box, it means that the previous student forgot to delete the Computing 101 folder when he or she did this exercise. Click the **Yes to All button** so that the files on your floppy disk will replace the previous versions on drive C.

➤ Please remember to **delete** the Computing 101 folder on drive C, when you get to step 9 at the end of the exercise.

CUSTOMIZE WINDOWS EXPLORER

Increase or decrease the size of the left pane within Windows Explorer by dragging the vertical line separating the left and right panes in the appropriate direction. You can also drag the right border of the various column headings (Name, Size, Type, and Modified) in the right pane to increase or decrease the width of the column and see more or less information in that column. And best of all, you can click any column heading to display the contents of the selected folder in sequence by that column. Click the heading a second time, and the sequence changes from ascending to descending and vice versa.

STEP 4: Modify a Document

➤ Click the **Computing 101 folder** on drive C to make this folder the active folder and display its contents in the right pane. Open the **About Windows Explorer** document:

- Double click the document icon in Classic style.
- Click the icon in Web style.

➤ Do not be concerned if the size and/or position of the Microsoft Word window is different from ours. All that matters is that you see the document. If necessary, click inside the document window, then press **Ctrl+End** to move to the end of the document.

➤ Add the sentence shown in Figure 12d followed by your name. Pull down the **File menu** and click **Save** to save the modified file (or click the **Save button** on the Standard toolbar). Pull down the **File menu** and click **Exit** to exit from Microsoft Word.

➤ Pull down the **View menu** in Windows Explorer and click **Refresh** (or press the **F5 key**) to update the contents of the right pane. The date and time associated with the About Windows Explorer file has been changed to indicate that the file has just been modified.

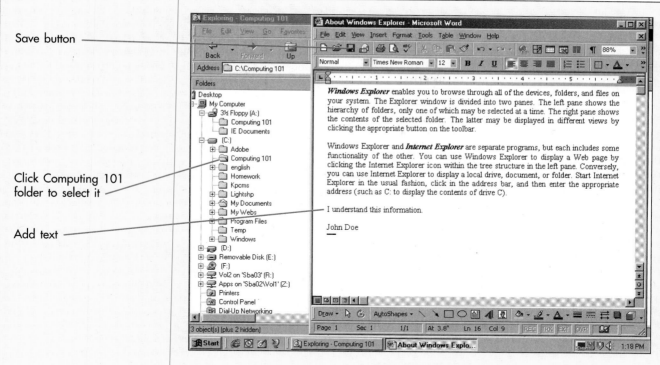

Save button

Click Computing 101 folder to select it

Add text

(d) Modify a Document (step 4)

FIGURE 12 Hands-on Exercise 4 (continued)

KEYBOARD SHORTCUTS

Most people begin with the mouse, but add keyboard shortcuts as they become more proficient. Ctrl+B, Ctrl+I, and Ctrl+U are shortcuts to boldface, italicize, and underline, respectively. Ctrl+X (the X is supposed to remind you of a pair of scissors), Ctrl+C, and Ctrl+V correspond to Cut, Copy, and Paste, respectively. Ctrl+Home and Ctrl+End move to the beginning or end of a document. These shortcuts are not unique to Microsoft Word, but are recognized in virtually every Windows application.

STEP 5: Copy (Back Up) a File

➤ Verify that the **Computing 101 folder** on drive C is the active folder as denoted by the open folder icon. Click and drag the icon for the **About Windows Explorer** file from the right pane to the **Computing 101 folder** on **drive A** in the left pane.

➤ You will see the message in Figure 12e, indicating that the folder (drive A) already contains a file called About Windows Explorer and asking whether you want to replace the existing file. Click **Yes** because you want to replace the previous version of the file on drive A with the updated version from drive C.

➤ You have just backed up the file; in other words, you have created a copy of the file on drive C on the disk in drive A. Thus, you can use the floppy disk to restore the file on drive C should anything happen to it. We cannot overemphasize the importance of adequate backup!

Click and drag About Windows Explorer file to Computing 101 folder on drive A

Computing 101 folder on drive C is selected

Click Yes

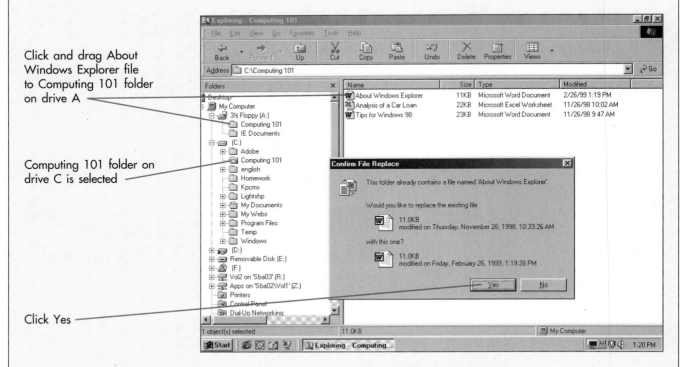

(e) Copy (Back Up) a File (step 5)

FIGURE 12   Hands-on Exercise 4 (continued)

COPYING FROM ONE FLOPPY DISK TO ANOTHER

You've learned how to copy a file from drive C to drive A, or from drive A to drive C, but how do you copy a file from one floppy disk to another? It's easy when you know how. Place the first floppy disk in drive A, select drive A in the left pane of the Explorer window, then copy the file from the right pane to a temporary folder on drive C in the left pane. Remove the first floppy disk, and replace it with the second. Select the temporary folder on drive C in the left pane, then click and drag the file from the right pane to the floppy disk in the left pane.

STEP 6: Delete a Folder

➤ Select (click) the **Computing 101 folder** on drive C in the left pane. Pull down the **File menu** and click **Delete** (or press the **Del key**).

➤ You will see the dialog box in Figure 12f asking whether you are sure you want to delete the folder (i.e., send the folder and its contents to the Recycle Bin). Note the green recycle logo within the box, which implies that you will be able to restore the file.

➤ Click **Yes** to delete the folder. The folder disappears from drive C. Pull down the **Edit menu.** Click **Undo Delete.**

➤ The deletion is cancelled and the folder reappears in the left pane. If you don't see the folder, pull down the **View menu** and click the **Refresh command.**

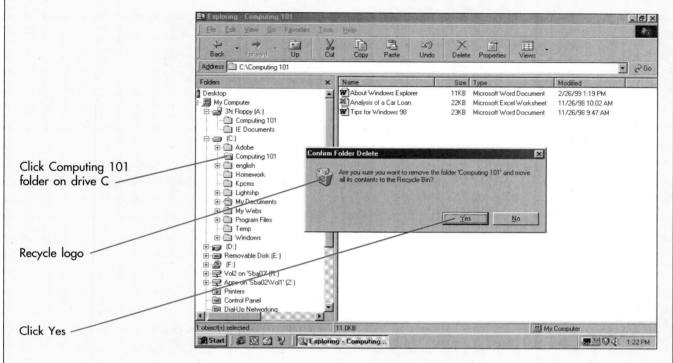

Click Computing 101 folder on drive C

Recycle logo

Click Yes

(f) Delete a Folder (step 6)

FIGURE 12   Hands-on Exercise 4 (continued)

THE UNDO COMMAND

The Undo command is present not only in application programs such as Word or Excel, but in Windows Explorer as well. You can use the command to undelete a file if it is executed immediately (within a few commands) after the Delete command. To execute the Undo command, right click anywhere in the right pane to display a shortcut menu, then select the Undo action. You can also pull down the Edit menu and click Undo to reverse (undo) the last command. Some operations cannot be undone (in which case the command will be dimmed), but Undo is always worth a try.

STEP 7: The Recycle Bin

➤ The Recycle Bin can also be used to recover a deleted file provided that the network administrator has not disabled this function.

➤ If necessary, select the **Computing 101 folder** on drive C in the left pane. Select (click) the **About Windows Explorer** file in the right pane. Press the **Del key,** then click **Yes** when asked whether to send the file to the Recycle Bin.

➤ Click the **down arrow** in the vertical scroll bar in the left pane until you see the icon for the **Recycle Bin.** (You can also open the Recycle Bin from the desktop.) Click the icon to make the Recycle Bin the active folder and display its contents in the right pane.

➤ The Recycle Bin contains all files that have been previously deleted from drive C, and hence you will see a different set of files than those displayed in Figure 12g. Pull down the **View menu,** click (or point to) **Arrange Icons,** then click **By Delete Date** to display the files in this sequence.

➤ Click in the **right pane.** Press **Ctrl+End** or scroll to the bottom of the window. Point to the **About Windows Explorer** file, click the **right mouse button** to display the shortcut menu in Figure 12g, then click **Restore.**

➤ The file disappears from the Recycle Bin because it has been returned to the Computing 101 folder. You can open the Computing 101 folder on drive C to confirm that the file has been restored.

Click Restore

Point to About Windows Explorer and click right mouse button to display shortcut menu

Click Recycle Bin

Click down arrow until you can see Recycle Bin

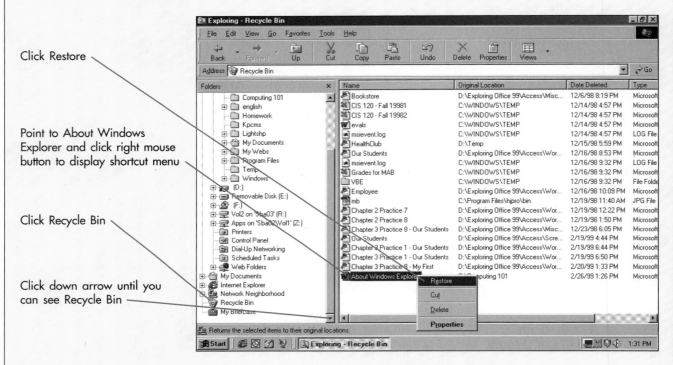

(g) The Recycle Bin (step 7)

FIGURE 12   Hands-on Exercise 4 (continued)

THE SHOW DESKTOP BUTTON

The Show Desktop button on the taskbar enables you to minimize all open windows with a single click. The button functions as a toggle switch. Click it once and all windows are minimized. Click it a second time and the open windows are restored to their position on the desktop. If you do not see the Show Desktop button, right click a blank area of the taskbar to display a context-sensitive menu, click Toolbars, then check the Quick Launch toolbar, which contains the Show Desktop button.

STEP 8: Write-protect a Floppy Disk

➤ You can write-protect a floppy disk so that its contents cannot be modified. Remove the floppy disk from drive A, then move the built-in tab on the disk so that the square hole on the disk is open. The disk is now write-protected.

➤ If necessary, expand drive A in the left pane, select the **Computing 101 folder,** select the **Analysis of a Car Loan document** in the right pane, then press the **Del key.** Click **Yes** when asked whether to delete the file.

➤ You will see the message in Figure 12h indicating that the file cannot be deleted because the disk is write-protected. Click **OK.** Remove the write-protection by moving the built-in tab to cover the square hole.

➤ Repeat the procedure to delete the **Analysis of a Car Loan document.** Click **Yes** in response to the confirmation message asking whether you want to delete the file. Note, however, the icon that appears in this dialog box is a red exclamation point, rather than a recycle emblem, indicating you cannot (easily) recover a deleted file from a floppy disk.

➤ The file disappears from the right pane indicating it has been deleted. The Computing 101 folder on drive A should contain only two files.

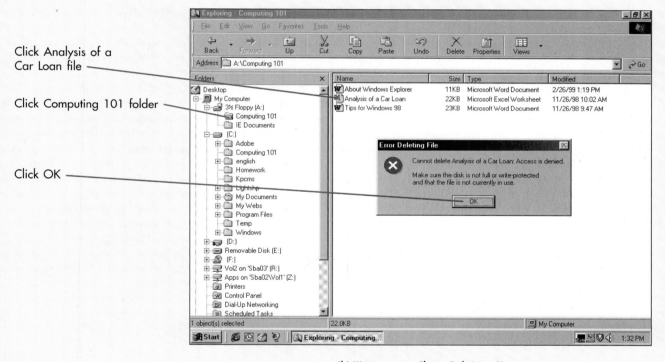

Click Analysis of a Car Loan file

Click Computing 101 folder

Click OK

(h) Write-protect a Floppy Disk (step 8)

FIGURE 12   Hands-on Exercise 4 (continued)

STEP 9: Complete the Exercise

➤ Delete the **Computing 101 folder** on drive C as a courtesy to the next student in the Computer Lab.

➤ Exit Windows Explorer. Welcome to Windows 98!

Windows 98 is a computer program (actually many programs) that controls the operation of your computer and its peripherals. It is the third major release of the Windows operating system, following Windows 3.1 and Windows 95.

All Windows operations take place on the desktop, which is displayed in either the Classic style or the Web style. The choice between the two is one of personal preference. The Classic style is virtually identical to the Windows 95 desktop and requires you to click an icon to select it, and double click the icon to open it. The Web style uses underlined icons that function identically to the hyperlinks in a browser; thus you point to an icon to select it, and click the icon to open it.

All Windows applications share a common user interface and possess a consistent command structure. Every window on the desktop contains the same basic elements, which include a title bar, a minimize button, a maximize or restore button, and a close button. Other elements that may be present include a menu bar, vertical and/or horizontal scroll bars, a status bar, and a toolbar. All windows may be moved and sized.

Multitasking is a major benefit of the Windows environment as it enables you to run several programs at the same time. The taskbar contains a button for each open program and enables you to switch back and forth between those programs by clicking the appropriate button.

The mouse is essential to Windows and has five basic actions: pointing, clicking, right clicking, double clicking, and dragging. The mouse pointer assumes different shapes according to the nature of the current action.

A dialog box supplies information needed to execute a command. Option buttons indicate mutually exclusive choices, one of which must be chosen. Check boxes are used if the choices are not mutually exclusive or if an option is not required. A text box supplies descriptive information. A (drop-down or open) list box displays multiple choices, any of which may be selected. A tabbed dialog box provides access to multiple sets of options.

The Help command on the Start menu provides access to detailed information about Windows 98. You can search for information three ways—through the Contents, Index, and Find tabs. You can also go to the Microsoft Web site, where you have access to the Windows Knowledge Base of current information.

A floppy disk must be formatted before it can store data. Formatting is accomplished through the Format command within the My Computer window. My Computer enables you to browse the disk drives and other devices attached to your system. My Computer is present on every desktop, but its contents depend on your specific configuration.

A file is a set of data or set of instructions that has been given a name and stored on disk. There are two basic types of files—program files and data files. A program file is an executable file, whereas a data file can be used only in conjunction with a specific program. Every file has a file name and a file type. The file name can be up to 255 characters in length and may include spaces.

Files are stored in folders to better organize the hundreds (or thousands) of files on a disk. A folder may contain program files, data files, and/or other folders. There are two basic ways to search through the folders on your system—My Computer and Windows Explorer. My Computer is intuitive but less efficient than Windows Explorer, as you have to open each folder in succession. Windows Explorer is more sophisticated as it provides a hierarchical view of the entire system.

Windows Explorer is divided into two panes. The left pane displays all of the devices and, optionally, the folders on each device. The right pane shows the contents of the active (open) drive or folder. Only one drive or folder can be active in the left pane. Any device, be it local or on the network, may be expanded or collapsed to display or hide its folders. A minus sign indicates that the drive has been expanded and that its folders are visible. A plus sign indicates the reverse; that is, the device is collapsed and its folders are not visible.

The result of dragging a file (or folder) from one location to another depends on whether the source and destination folders are on the same or different drives. Dragging the file to a folder on the same drive moves the file. Dragging the file to a folder on a different drive copies the file. It's easier, therefore, to click and drag with the right mouse button to display a menu from which you can select the desired operation.

The Delete command deletes (removes) a file from a disk. A file deleted from a hard disk can be restored from the Recycle Bin. This is not true, however, for files that are deleted from a floppy disk.

The choice between Web style and Classic style is strictly one of personal preference and depends on how you want to open a document, by clicking or double clicking, respectively. The Folder Options command in the View menu of My Computer or Windows Explorer enables you to switch from one style to the other.

KEY WORDS AND CONCEPTS

Backup strategy	Folder	Rename a file
Check box	Format command	Restore a file
Classic style	Help command	Restore button
Close button	Horizontal scroll bar	Search tab
Collapsed icon	Index tab	Smart toolbar
Command button	Internet Explorer	Start button
Common user interface	List box	Status bar
Contents tab	Maximize button	Tabbed dialog box
Copy a file	Menu bar	Taskbar
Data file	Minimize button	Text box
Delete a file	Mouse operations	Title bar
Desktop	Move a file	Vertical scroll bar
Dialog box	Multitasking	Web style
Dimmed command	My Computer	Windows 2000
Drop-down list box	Network Neighborhood	Windows 95
Expanded icon	Option button	Windows 98
Extension	Program file	Windows NT
File	Pull-down menu	Windows Explorer
File name	Radio button	Write-enabled
File type	Recycle Bin	Write-protected

1. What is the significance of a faded (dimmed) command in a pull-down menu?
   (a) The command is not currently accessible
   (b) A dialog box will appear if the command is selected
   (c) A Help window will appear if the command is selected
   (d) There are no equivalent keystrokes for the particular command

2. Which of the following is true regarding a dialog box?
   (a) Option buttons indicate mutually exclusive choices
   (b) Check boxes imply that multiple options may be selected
   (c) Both (a) and (b)
   (d) Neither (a) nor (b)

3. Which of the following is the first step in sizing a window?
   (a) Point to the title bar
   (b) Pull down the View menu to display the toolbar
   (c) Point to any corner or border
   (d) Pull down the View menu and change to large icons

4. Which of the following is the first step in moving a window?
   (a) Point to the title bar
   (b) Pull down the View menu to display the toolbar
   (c) Point to any corner or border
   (d) Pull down the View menu and change to large icons

5. How do you exit Windows?
   (a) Click the Start button, then click the Shut Down command
   (b) Right click the Start button, then click the Shut Down command
   (c) Click the End button, then click the Shut Down command
   (d) Right click the End button, then click the Shut Down command

6. How do you open My Computer?
   (a) Double click the My Computer icon in the Windows 98 Classic style
   (b) Click the My Computer icon in the Windows 98 Web style
   (c) Both (a) and (b)
   (d) Neither (a) nor (b)

7. Which button appears immediately after a window has been maximized?
   (a) The close button
   (b) The restore button
   (c) The maximize button
   (d) All of the above

8. What happens to a window that has been minimized?
   (a) The window is still visible but it no longer has a minimize button
   (b) The window shrinks to a button on the taskbar
   (c) The window is closed and the application is removed from memory
   (d) The window is still open but the application has been removed from memory

9. What is the significance of three dots next to a command in a pull-down menu?
    (a) The command is not currently accessible
    (b) A dialog box will appear if the command is selected
    (c) A Help window will appear if the command is selected
    (d) There are no equivalent keystrokes for the particular command

10. The Recycle Bin enables you to restore a file that was deleted from:
    (a) Drive A
    (b) Drive C
    (c) Both (a) and (b)
    (d) Neither (a) nor (b)

11. The left pane of Windows Explorer may contain:
    (a) One or more folders with a plus sign
    (b) One or more folders with a minus sign
    (c) Both (a) and (b)
    (d) Neither (a) nor (b)

12. Which of the following was suggested as essential to a backup strategy?
    (a) Back up all program files at the end of every session
    (b) Store backup files at another location
    (c) Both (a) and (b)
    (d) Neither (a) nor (b)

13. Which of the following is true regarding a disk that has been write protected?
    (a) Existing files cannot be modified or erased
    (b) A new file cannot be added to the disk
    (c) Both (a) and (b)
    (d) Neither (a) nor (b)

14. How do you open a file from within My Computer or Windows Explorer?
    (a) Click the file icon if you are in the Classic style
    (b) Double click the file icon if you are in the Web style
    (c) Both (a) and (b)
    (d) Neither (a) nor (b)

15. How do you change from the Web style to the Classic style?
    (a) Open My Computer, pull down the View menu, click Options, click the General tab, and specify Classic style
    (b) Open Windows Explorer, pull down the View menu, click Folder Options, click the General tab, and specify Classic style
    (c) Both (a) and (b)
    (d) Neither (a) nor (b)

Answers

1. a	6. c	11. c
2. c	7. b	12. b
3. c	8. b	13. c
4. a	9. b	14. d
5. a	10. b	15. c

1. My Computer: Figure 13 displays a document that was created using the WordPad program, a simple word processor that is included in Windows 98. You can do the exercise using WordPad, or alternatively you can use Microsoft Word. Our directions are for WordPad:

   a. Open My Computer. Pull down the View menu and switch to the Details view. Size the window as necessary.

   b. Press Alt+Print Screen to copy the My Computer window to the clipboard.

   c. Click the Start menu, click Programs, click Accessories, then click Word-Pad to open the word processor. Maximize the window.

   d. Pull down the Edit menu. Click the Paste command to copy the contents of the clipboard to the document you are about to create. The My Computer window should be pasted into your document.

   e. Click below the graphic, press Ctrl+End to move to the end of your document. Press the enter key three times (to leave three blank lines).

   f. Type a modified form of the memo in Figure 13 so that it conforms to your configuration. Type just as you would on a regular typewriter except do not press the enter key at the end of a line as the program will automatically wrap from one line to the next. If you make a mistake, just press the backspace key to erase the last character, and continue typing.

   g. Finish the memo and sign your name. Pull down the File menu, click the Print command, then click OK in the dialog box to print the document.

2. Windows Explorer: Prove to your instructor that you have completed the four hands-on exercises by capturing a screen similar to Figure 14 that displays the contents of the floppy disk at the end of the exercise. Follow these instructions to create the document in Figure 14 on page 60:

   a. Do the hands-on exercises as described in the text. Place the floppy disk used in the exercise in drive A, and select the Computing 101 folder to display its contents in the right pane of Windows Explorer. If necessary, change to Details view.

   b. Press the Print Screen key to copy the screen to the clipboard (an area of memory that is available to every Windows application).

   c. Click the Start button, click Programs, click Accessories, then click Paint to open the Paint accessory. If necessary, click the maximize button so that the Paint window takes the entire desktop.

   d. Pull down the Edit menu. Click Paste to copy the screen from the clipboard to the drawing. Click Yes if you are asked to enlarge the bitmap.

   e. Click the text tool (the capital A), then click and drag in the drawing area to create a dotted rectangle that will contain the message to your instructor. Type the text indicating that you did your homework. (If necessary, pull down the View menu and check the command for the Text toolbar. This enables you to change the font and/or point size). Click outside the text to deselect it.

   f. Pull down the File menu and click the Page Setup command to display the Page Setup dialog box. Click the Landscape option button. Change the margins to one inch all around. Click OK.

   g. Pull down the File menu a second time. Click Print. Click OK.

   h. Exit Paint. You do not have to save the file. Submit the document to your instructor.

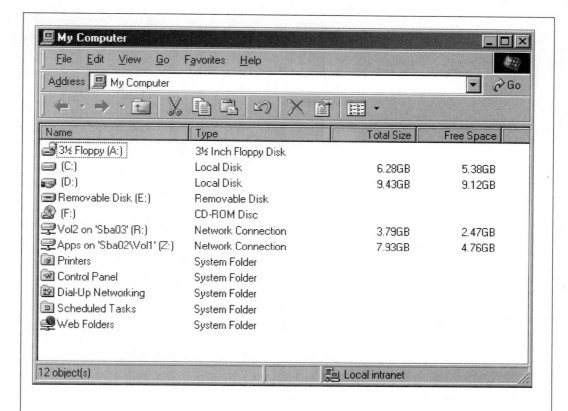

Dear Professor,

Please find above the contents of My Computer (displayed in the Classic style) as it exists on my computer system. As you can see, I have one floppy drive, labeled drive A, and two hard drives, labeled C and D. There are 5.38Gb free on drive C and 9.12Gb free on drive D. I still have a lot of free space left. I have a high-capacity removable disk drive (drive E) and a CD-ROM drive (drive F). In addition to my local drives, I have access to two network drives, drives R and Z.

I enjoyed reading the chapter and I look forward to learning more about the Active Desktop and Internet Explorer.

Sincerely,

Eric Simon

FIGURE 13   My Computer (Exercise 1)

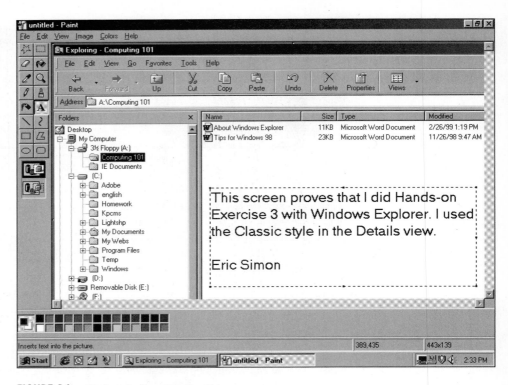

FIGURE 14 Windows Explorer (Exercise 2)

3. Companion Web Sites: Each book in the *Exploring Microsoft® Office 2000* series is accompanied by an online study guide or Companion Web site as shown in Figure 15. Start Internet Explorer and go to the Exploring Windows home page at <u>www.prenhall.com/grauer</u>. Click the book to Office 2000, click the Companion Web site link at the top of the screen, then choose the appropriate text (e.g., *Exploring Microsoft Office Professional Volume I*) and chapter within the text (e.g., *Essentials of Windows 95/98*).

Each study guide contains a series of short-answer exercises (multiple-choice, true/false, and matching) to review the material in the chapter. You can take practice quizzes by yourself and/or e-mail the results to your instructor. You can try the essay questions for additional practice and engage in online chat sessions. We hope you will find the online guide to be a valuable resource.

4. Organize Your Work: A folder may contain documents, programs, or other folders. The My Classes folder in Figure 16, for example, contains five folders, one folder for each class you are taking this semester, and in similar fashion, the Correspondence folder contains two additional folders according to the type of correspondence. We use folders in this fashion to organize our work, and we suggest you do likewise. The best way to practice with folders is on a floppy disk, as was done in Figure 16. Accordingly:

a. Format a floppy disk or alternatively, use the floppy disk you have been using throughout the chapter.

b. Create a Correspondence folder. Create a Business and Personal folder within the Correspondence folder as shown in Figure 16.

c. Create a My Courses folder. Create a separate folder for each course you are taking within the My Courses folder as shown in Figure 16.

d. Use the technique described in problem 2 to capture the screen shown in Figure 16. Add your name to the captured screen, and then submit it to your instructor as proof that you have done the exercise.

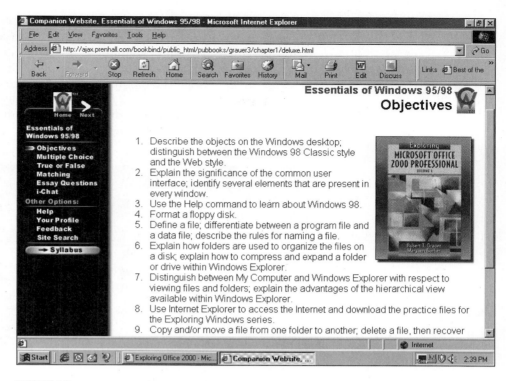

FIGURE 15   Companion Web Sites (Exercise 3)

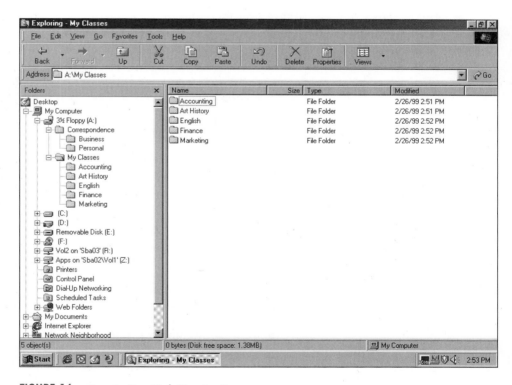

FIGURE 16   Organize Your Work (Exercise 4)

5. View Folders as a Web Page: Windows 98 enables you to view a folder as a Web page, as shown in Figure 17. Start Windows Explorer, collapse all of the drives on your system, select the My Computer icon, then pull down the View menu and click the As Web Page command. Click the Views button to cycle through the different views until your screen matches ours. Use the Folder Options command in the Views menu to experiment with additional ways to view the folders on your system. Summarize your option of this feature in a brief note to your instructor.

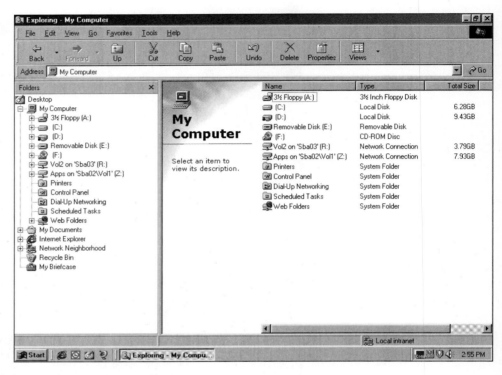

FIGURE 17   View Folders as a Web Page (Exercise 5)

6. Discover Windows 98: This exercise requires the Windows 98 CD. The opening screen in Windows 98 displays a Welcome window that invites you to take a discovery tour of Windows 98. (If you do not see the Welcome window, click the Start button, click Run, enter C:\windows\welcome in the Open text box, and press enter.) Click the option to discover Windows 98, which in turn displays the screen in Figure 18. Take a tour of Windows 98, then summarize the highlights in a short note to your instructor.

7. Implement a Screen Saver: A screen saver is a program that protects your monitor by producing a constantly changing pattern after a designated period of inactivity. This is not something you can do in a laboratory setting, but it is well worth doing on your own machine.

    Point to a blank area of the desktop, click the right mouse button to display a context-sensitive menu, then click the Properties command to open the Display Properties dialog box in Figure 19. Click the Screen Saver tab, click the down arrow in the Screen Saver list box and select Scrolling Marquee. Click the Settings command button, enter the text and other options for your message, then click OK to close the Options dialog box. Click OK a second time to close the Display Properties dialog box.

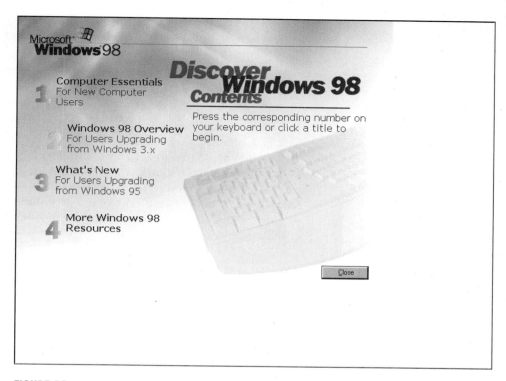

FIGURE 18   Discover Windows 98 (Exercise 6)

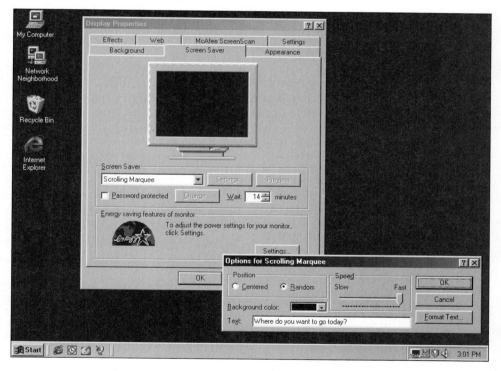

FIGURE 19   Implement a Screen Saver (Exercise 7)

Planning for Disaster

Do you have a backup strategy? Do you even know what a backup strategy is? You had better learn, because sooner or later you will wish you had one. You will erase a file, be unable to read from a floppy disk, or worse yet suffer a hardware failure in which you are unable to access the hard drive. The problem always seems to occur the night before an assignment is due. The ultimate disaster is the disappearance of your computer, by theft or natural disaster. Describe, in 250 words or less, the backup strategy you plan to implement in conjunction with your work in this class.

The Boot Disk

We don't want to give you undue cause for concern, but there is a real possibility that the hard drive on your machine will fail some time in the future and hence you will be unable to start your system. Should that occur, you will want to have a boot (startup) disk at your disposal to start the system from the floppy drive in order to access your hard drive. Use the Help command to learn how to create a startup disk, then follow the instructions if you haven't yet created one. Put the disk in a safe place. We hope you never have to use it, but you should be prepared.

File Compression

You've learned your lesson and have come to appreciate the importance of backing up all of your data files. The problem is that you work with large documents that exceed the 1.44MB capacity of a floppy disk. Accordingly, you might want to consider the acquisition of a file compression program to facilitate copying large documents to a floppy disk in order to transport your documents to and from school, home, or work. You can download an evaluation copy of the popular WinZip program at www.winzip.com. Investigate the subject of file compression, then submit a summary of your findings to your instructor.

The Threat of Virus Infection

A computer virus is an actively infectious program that attaches itself to other programs and alters the way a computer works. Some viruses do nothing more than display an annoying message at an inopportune time. Most, however, are more harmful, and in the worst case, erase all files on the disk. When is a computer subject to infection by a virus? What precautions does your school or university take against the threat of virus infection in its computer lab? What precautions, if any, do you take at home? What is the difference between the scan function in an antivirus program versus leaving the antivirus program active in memory? Can you feel confident that your machine will not be infected if you faithfully use a state-of-the-art antivirus program that was purchased in January 1997?

INDEX